PRINCIPLES OF REAL ESTATE PRACTICE IN NEW YORK

1ST EDITION

PERFORMANCE PROGRAMS COMPANY

STEPHEN METTLING
DAVID CUSIC
RYAN METTLING

Material in this book is not intended to represent legal advice and should not be so construed. Readers should consult legal counsel for advice regarding points of law.

© 2024 by Performance Programs Company
6810 190th Street East, Bradenton, FL 34211
info@performanceprogramscompany.com
www.performanceprogramscompany.com

ISBN: 978-1955919999

Table of Contents

1   License Law And Regulations   6
Introduction To License Law   6
License Categories   8
And Responsibilities   8
Requirements For Licensure   15
Maintaining A License   19
License Renewal   20
Promulgated Regulations   21
Place Of Business Requirements   22
Advertising Guidelines   22
License Law Violations   24
Unlicensed Assistants   27
Property Condition   28
Disclosure Act   28
Gas Well Disclosure   29

2   Law Of Agency And Disclosure   38
The Agency Relationship   38
Fiduciary Duties   41
Misrepresentation   49
Terminating an Agency Relationship   50
Forms of Real Estate Agency and
       Alternatives   51
Antitrust Laws   56
Types of Listings   59
Listing Agreement Requirements   61
Listing Agreement Termination   63
New York Agency Disclosure Requirements   64
Seller/Landlord Disclosures   66

3   Estates And Interests   78
Interests and Estates In Land   86
Freehold Estates   89
Leasehold Estates   93
Forms of Ownership   95
Trusts   98
Ownership By Business Entities   100

4   Liens And Easements   108
Liens   108
Deed Restrictions   113
Easements   114
Encroachments   119

5   Deeds And Conveyances   124
Title To Real Estate   124
Deeds   126
Conveyance After Death   131

6   Title Closing And Costs   138
Title Closing   138
Title Records   159

7   Contract of Sale and Leases   166
Leases   166
Sales Contracts   174
Classifications of Contracts   181
Option-To-Buy   188

8   Real Estate Finance   195
Mortgage Transaction   195

Mortgage Clauses   201
Loan Qualification   203
Mortgage Laws   209
Mortgage Market   212
Types of Mortgage Loans   217
Predatory Lending   226
Foreclosure   227
Sale of Mortgaged Property   230
Recording And Satisfaction   232

9   Land Use Regulation   241
Land Use Definitions   241
Land Use Planning   242
Public Land Use Controls   246
Private Land Use Controls   253

**10   Construction And Environmental
Issues   260**
Construction   260
Construction Regulation   264
Site Requirements   266
Environmental Issues   269
Cercla   281
Environmental Laws   282

**11   Valuation Process and Pricing
Properties   289**
Concepts and Principles Of Value   289
Market Value Requirements   294
Sales Comparison Approach   295
Cost Approach   299
Income Capitalization Approach   303
Preparing a Comparative   308
Market Analysis   308
Salesperson's Role   310

12   Human Rights and Fair Housing   316
Federal Fair Housing Laws   316
New York Human Rights Law   327
Implications For Licensees   329
Fair Housing and Protected Classes   331
Bias and Discrimination   332
Implicit Bias In Real Estate   332
Battling Biases   334

13   Municipal Agencies   343
Municipal Bodies   343

14   Property Insurance   357
Purpose of Insurance   357
Property Insurance   357
Provider Entities   357
Types of Coverage   359
Types of Policies   360
Agent's Role   362
Obtaining Insurance   362
Insurance Policy Deductibles   363
Commercial and Umbrella Policies   363

15   Licensee Safety   369
Precautions   369

16   Taxes And Assessments   **375**
        General Tax and Special   375
        Assessments   375
        Taxation Process   376
        Grievance and Contesting   382
        Assessments   382
        Exemptions   383
        Tax Lien Enforcement   386
        Tax Lien Enforcement   389

17   Condominiums And Cooperatives   **392**
        Condominiums   392
        Housing Cooperatives   398

18   Commercial And Investment Properties
                                                           406
        Investment Foundations   406
        Types of Investments   408
        Real Estate as an Investment   409
        Real Estate Investment Entities   411
        Real Estate Investment Property Types   412
        Investment Property Analysis   416
        Commercial Property Space Measurement   424
        Commercial Property Concepts   426

19   Income Tax Issues In Real Estate
        Transactions   **436**
        Tax Reform Act Of 2018   436
        Like-Kind Exchanges   445
        Low-Income Housing Tax Incentives   446

20   Mortgage Brokerage   **450**
        Mortgage Broker Defined   450
        Mortgage Broker Requirements   450
        Mortgage Broker Responsibilities   451
        Mortgage Broker Vs Mortgage Banker   451
        Role Of Mortgage Broker In A   452
        Real Estate Transaction   452

21   Property Management   **456**
        Property Manager Defined   456
        The Management Agreement   456
        Management Functions   461
        Leasing Considerations   468

22   Real Estate Mathematics   **477**
        Basic Math   477
        Leases   483
        Contracts for The Sale of Real Estate   483
        Finance   486
        Investment   490
        Commissions   494
        Closing Costs, Prorations   495
        Insurance Coverage   497

Section Tests Answer Key   **499**

New York Practice Exam   **505**

Practice Examination Answer Key   **515**

Glossary Of General Real Estate Terms   **517**

Index   **528**

PREFACE

About the text

Principles of Real Estate Practice in New York is a modern learning tool for the student preparing to enter the real estate business in New York as a licensed professional. It contains the essentials of real estate law, principles, and practices taught in New York real estate schools and colleges, including all those fundamentals that real estate educators, practicing professionals, testing services, and licensing officials agree are necessary for basic competence. **Principles of Real Estate Practice in New York** covers the prelicense requirements mandated by New York license law.

Principles of Real Estate Practice is tailored to the needs of the prelicense student. It is designed to

- make it easy for students to learn the material
- prepare students for numerous career applications
- stress practical, rather than theoretical, skills and knowledge.

Inside the cover

Each section begins with an overview of the main heads covered in the section. As each of these heads is expanded, the subheads are displayed in the margin. Key terms are printed in bold type the first time they are used and defined. The sections conclude with a study aid called the "Snapshot Review," which compresses the main points of the section into one or two pages. After the last section are tests for all the sections. The answer key following the tests refers to the page in the text that explains the correct answer. The book is also provided with a special section on real estate math, a practice exam reflecting the content of the New York licensing examination, and two glossaries of real estate terminology.

About the authors

For over forty years, Stephen Mettling and David Cusic have operated one of the nation's most successful custom training organizations specializing in real estate program development. Mr. Mettling has also served as vice president and author for a major real estate training and publishing organization. Under various capacities, he has managed the acquisition, development, and sale of national real estate textbooks and publications, as well as directed the country's largest affiliated group of real estate schools.

Mr. Cusic, an author and educator with international real estate training experience, has been engaged in vocation-oriented education since 1966. Specializing in real estate training since 1983, he has developed numerous real estate training programs for corporate and institutional clients around the country.

Ryan Mettling, partner and publisher of Performance Programs, is an experienced online curriculum designer, author, and course developer.

1 License Law and Regulations

Introduction to License Law
License Categories and Responsibilities
Requirements for Licensure
Maintaining A License
License Renewal
Promulgated Regulations
Place of Business Requirements
Branch Office Requirements
Advertising Guidelines
License Law Violations
Unlicensed Assistants
Property Condition Disclosure Act
Gas Well Disclosure

INTRODUCTION TO LICENSE LAW

Purpose
State Board of Real Estate
Activities requiring licensure
Licensure exemptions

Purpose

The primary purpose of real estate license law is to protect the general public.

To protect consumers from misrepresentation and fraud, real estate license laws have been enacted to regulate the practices of real estate professionals. New York enacted its own laws in 1922 to regulate the industry and to protect the health, welfare, and safety of the general public. The laws protect consumers from financial loss as a result of dishonest and incompetent practices by real estate professionals in exchange for a fee or other compensation. These New York laws are covered in the following statutes:

▸ Real Property Law, License Law and Regulations Article 12-A

▸ Real Property Law, Conveyances & Mortgages Article 8

▸ Real Property Law, Recording Instruments Affecting Real Property Article 9

▸ Real Property Law, Property Condition Disclosure in The Sale of Residential Real Property Article 14

▸ Executive Law, Human Rights Law Article 15

- United States Code, Section 42 USCA 3604
- Rules and Regulations Title 19 NYCRR, Real Estate Brokers and Salespersons, Subchapter D
- N.Y. Comp. Codes Rules & Regulations Title 19 § 175.25 - Advertising

State Board of Real Estate

Real estate regulatory duties are shared between the state's **Division of Licensing Services** and the **New York State Board of Real Estate**. The Board was established in 1996 and consists of 15 members, including the Secretary of State serving as chairperson and the Superintendent of Financial Services. The other 13 members consist of at least 5 licensed real estate brokers who have been engaged in real estate for at least 10 years prior to appointment to the Board and members of the public who are not real estate licensees.

Seven of the 13 members are appointed by the Governor, with 3 of those members being licensed brokers and 4 being members of the public. Two of the 13 are appointed by the temporary President of the Senate, with 1 being a licensed broker and the other being a member of the public. Two more of the 13 are appointed by the Speaker of the Assembly, with 1 being a licensed broker and the other being a member of the public. The remaining 2 members are appointed as follows: 1 licensed broker or member of the public by the Minority Leader of the Senate and 1 licensed broker or member of the public by the Minority Leader of the Assembly.

Members of the Board serve 2-year terms and may be reappointed for a total of 10 years. They are not paid for their regulatory services.

The Board has the following powers and duties:

- Promulgate rules or regulations affecting real estate licensees which fall under the auspices of the Secretary of State;
- Prescribe content for prelicensing courses and administer the license examination;
- Approve real estate schools;
- Study the operation of laws and regulations regarding rights, responsibilities, and liabilities of licensees related to the transfer of real property and make recommendations on related legislation;
- Enforce programs and activities related to enforcement of real estate laws;
- Submit annual reports to the appropriate legislative committees regarding complaints

Activities requiring licensure

A person who performs any real estate activity, as listed in the following sections, for another and for compensation or valuable consideration or in anticipation of compensation or consideration must hold a current real estate license. Exemptions from this requirement are as follows.

Licensure exemptions

The following individuals are not required to hold a New York real estate license:

- persons appointed by or acting under the judgment or order of any court (referees, receivers, administrators, executors, guardians)

- public officers while performing their official duties

- attorneys at law

- resident managers of single-owner properties employed to manage, maintain, lease, and collect rent

- tenant organizations and not-for-profit corporations authorized to enforce New York City's housing code

---

LICENSE CATEGORIES AND RESPONSIBILITIES

Real estate broker
Real estate associate broker
Real estate salesperson
Out of state licenses
Other licenses or registrations

Real estate broker

A real estate broker is any appropriately licensed person, firm, limited liability company or corporation who

- lists real property for sale,

- sells (at auction or otherwise), exchanges, buys or rents, or

- offers or attempts to negotiate a sale (at auction or otherwise), exchange, purchase or rental of an estate or interest in real estate, or

- collects, offers, or attempts to collect rent for the use of real estate, or

- negotiates, offers, or attempts to negotiate, a loan secured or to be secured by a mortgage, other than a residential mortgage loan (as defined in §590 of the Banking Law), or other incumbrance upon or transfer of real estate, or

- is engaged in the business of a tenant relocator, or

- who, notwithstanding any other provision of law, performs any of the above stated functions with respect to the resale of condominium property originally sold pursuant to the provisions of the General Business Law governing real estate syndication offerings

for another and for a fee, commission, or other valuable consideration or the expectation of a fee, commission, or other valuable consideration.

Activities requiring licensure. Anyone engaging in any of the above activities must hold a real estate broker's license unless otherwise exempt from licensure.

Responsibilities to public. Brokers have the following responsibilities to the public:

- ▶ Undertaking fair and honest dealings using professional techniques and training so as never to defraud members of the public

- ▶ Accountability for all funds that belong to others and that have been placed in the broker's possession

- ▶ Limited and minimum disclosure of material facts or defects related to the subject property that would impact

  - ○ the property's value -- disclosure to a buyer is necessary when such facts or defects are known to the seller's agent

  - ○ the buyer's financial ability to purchase the property -- disclosure to a seller is necessary when such facts or defects are known to the buyer's agent

Responsibilities to licensees. Brokers have the following responsibilities to associated licensees:

- ▶ Supervision of the associated licensees in their performance of real estate activities

- ▶ Provision of guidance, training, and oversight to associated licensees

- ▶ Holding licenses

- ▶ Collecting commissions and paying salespersons and associate brokers

- ▶ Providing office space, documents, supplies, and administrative support

Dual licensure. Dual licensure occurs when a licensed broker holds two or more licenses.

Real estate associate broker

A real estate associate broker is any individual who holds a broker's license but chooses to work as a salesperson under the name and supervision of another licensed Real Estate Broker or another broker who is licensed under a partnership, trade name, limited liability company or corporation. An associate broker must meet the qualifications for broker licensure but must be sponsored by a licensed broker and must perform real estate activities under the laws and provisions that govern real estate salespersons.

An associate broker may retain a separate broker's license under an individual, partnership, trade name, limited liability company, or corporation.

As an associate broker, the licensee may

- ▶ facilitate the purchase and sale of property on behalf of customers,
- ▶ obtain lists of property for sale with employing broker,
- ▶ assist buyers (customers) of real estate to locate and purchase property (listed with employing brokers or another broker),
- ▶ list and negotiate the sale, lease, or rental of real property for others for compensation.

Activities requiring licensure. Anyone engaging in any of the above activities as an associate broker must hold a real estate broker's license with a designated sponsoring broker.

Responsibilities to the sponsoring broker. Associate brokers have the following responsibilities to sponsoring brokers:

- ▶ Conduct all real estate activities in the name of the sponsoring broker
- ▶ Conduct all activities in compliance with their licenses and related real estate laws, rules, and regulations

Responsibilities to the public. Associate brokers have the same responsibilities to the public as brokers have:

- ▶ Fair and honest dealings
- ▶ Accountability
- ▶ Disclosures

Real estate salesperson

A real estate salesperson is any appropriately licensed person who, under the association and supervision of a licensed Real Estate Broker,

- ▶ handles the sale, lease, or rental of real property for others for compensation;
- ▶ lists for sale, sells or offers for sale, at auction or otherwise,
- ▶ buys or offers to buy or negotiates the purchase, sale, or exchange of real estate,
- ▶ obtains lists of property for sale with employing broker and assists buyers (customers) of real estate to locate and purchase such properties listed with employing broker or another broker,

- ▸ negotiates a loan on real estate other than a mortgage loan as defined in section 590 of the banking law,

- ▸ leases or rents or offers to lease, rent, or place for rent any real estate,

- ▸ collects or offers or attempts to collect rent for the use of real estate for or in behalf of such real estate broker, or

- ▸ notwithstanding any other provision of law, performs any of the above stated functions with respect to the resale of a condominium property originally sold pursuant to the provisions of the general business law governing real estate syndication offerings.

A salesperson cannot operate independently and is responsible for understanding the Real Estate License Law. A salesperson acts as the sponsoring broker's agent with all listings to be accepted by the broker, even if the listing is negotiated by the salesperson.

Activities requiring licensure. Anyone engaging in any of the above activities must hold a real estate salesperson's license unless otherwise exempt from licensure.

Responsibilities to the sponsoring broker. Salespersons have the following responsibilities to sponsoring brokers:

- ▸ Conduct all real estate activities in the name of the sponsoring broker

- ▸ Conduct all activities in compliance with their licenses and related real estate laws, rules, and regulations

Responsibilities to the public. Salespersons have the same responsibilities to the public as brokers have:

- ▸ Fair and honest dealings

- ▸ Accountability

- ▸ Disclosures

Dual licensure. Dual licensure occurs when a licensed salesperson holds two or more licenses to work under the sponsorship and supervision of two or more brokers. The salesperson must hold a separate license for each sponsoring broker.

Out of state licenses

Nonresident licensees

A nonresident of New York who is a licensed broker or salesperson in another state may obtain a New York real estate license by meeting the New York licensure requirements. A nonresident broker who practices real estate in New York does not need to maintain a place of business in New York as long as the broker is licensed and maintains a place of business in the other state. However, the other state must offer the same nonresident license opportunity to New York licensees. If the other state prohibits nonresident licensure to New York licensees, then New York will prohibit nonresident licensure to the other state's resident licensees.

Every nonresident license applicant is required to file an *irrevocable consent* which places the licensee under the jurisdiction of New York courts. It also designates the New York Secretary of State as the licensee's agent to be served with any summons, subpoena or other process against the licensee. Service on the Secretary is considered the same as service on the licensee personally.

Reciprocal license

A nonresident licensee may practice real estate in New York if the licensee's resident state has a reciprocity agreement with New York. Reciprocity agreements allow a licensee in one state to become licensed in another state without meeting the other state's education and examination requirements. States with these agreements recognize each other's real estate laws and licensure requirements. States with reciprocity agreements with New York must also issue reciprocal licenses to New York resident licensees.

Nonresidents seeking a New York reciprocal license must live and work in their resident state and must submit a New York application, the appropriate fee, and an irrevocable consent form. A nonresident salesperson's home state broker must also have a New York broker's license and sponsor the salesperson's reciprocity application.

Currently, New York has reciprocity agreements with nine states with the following restrictions:

> ▸ **Arkansas** – only brokers with 2 years of Arkansas licensure
>
> ▸ **Colorado** – only brokers and associate brokers; associate brokers to submit a salesperson application and fee
>
> ▸ **Connecticut** – brokers and salespersons
>
> ▸ **Georgia** – brokers and salespersons who passed Georgia license exam
>
> ▸ **Massachusetts** – only brokers with 2 years of Massachusetts licensure
>
> ▸ **Mississippi** – only brokers with 2 years of Mississippi licensure
>
> ▸ **Oklahoma** – brokers and salespersons, each with 2 years of Oklahoma licensure
>
> ▸ **Pennsylvania** – brokers and salespersons
>
> ▸ **West Virginia** – brokers and salespersons

Members of Armed Forces households

An individual who is a part of the household of a member of the United States armed forces, National Guard, or Reserves may also obtain a New York license.

The individual must have been part of the household prior to the member relocating to New York. The individual must also meet certain licensure, certification, or registration requirements and must submit a New York licensure application. While licensed and living in New York, the individual is required to complete 11 of the 22 ½ hours of continuing education within the first year. The 11 hours must include 3 hours of New York License Law and regulations.

Mutual recognition

For a nonresident licensee to practice real estate in New York when there is no reciprocity agreement or nonresident license, the licensee's home state would need a mutual recognition agreement with New York. In mutual recognition, both states agree to recognize and apply the education and experience of a licensee from one state to those required in the second state. The nonresident licensee may then practice real estate in the other state without obtaining a license in that state.

Other licenses or registrations

Corporation, partnership, limited liability company

Any corporation, partnership, or limited liability company (LLC) wishing to conduct real estate activities must have at least one designated officer, partner, or LLC member or manager who is licensed as a broker, having met all broker licensing requirements. No officer, partner, or LLC member or manager may be licensed as a salesperson, and no employee of the entity may be licensed and operate as a broker for the entity.

Office manager

An individual who works as an office manager under the name and supervision of a broker must be licensed as an associate broker and have been an active associate broker for at least two of the four years prior to becoming the office manager. The individual is required to maintain the broker license and perform supervision duties over salespersons and other associate brokers.

Mortgage banking companies

Mortgage banking companies provide real estate loans that can then be sold to investors. If the company continues to service the loan once it is sold, the company will receive a fee for the service. Unlike thrift institutions, savings and loan associations, and savings banks, mortgage banking companies do not provide checking or savings accounts. However, they do provide a great percentage of all mortgage loans. Although they operate under fewer regulations than thrift institutions, they are required to file a $50,000 surety bond or establish a $50,000 trust fund to reimburse customers for improper fees.

Mortgage broker

A real estate license is required for anyone in New York who negotiates or attempts to negotiate a mortgage loan for non-residential property. A licensed broker or a licensed salesperson who is associated with a licensed broker may negotiate such mortgage loans. The licensee must also be registered with the State Banking Department.

Mortgage brokers are typically paid by the borrower to find an appropriate lender for the sought-after loan. The mortgage broker may be required to obtain a surety bond or set up a $25,000 trust fund.

However, negotiating a mortgage loan on one-to-four residential unit(s) requires registration with the Department of Financial Services.

Home inspector

Home inspectors in New York must be licensed as such, having completed the required coursework or earned the required supervised experience, passed the exam, and paid the license fee. License terms are for two years and require completion of continuing education prior to license renewal. Prior to recommending a home inspector to a home buyer, real estate licensees should confirm the inspector holds a current license.

Real estate appraiser

Appraisers are licensed or certified to analyze and form a professional opinion as to the quality and value of real property. Education and experience requirements are based on the category of licensure or certification. Applicants must also pass the examination and pay the appropriate exam and license fees. License/certification terms are for 2 years and require completion of continuing education prior to renewal.

Apartment information vendor

Any person who engages in the business of providing information on the location and availability of residential rental property for a fee paid by the customer is called an apartment information vendor. The vendor sets up meetings between the customer and the owner of the rental property or between the customer and the current occupant who wishes to share the housing. The license term begins on November 1 and ends on October 31 each year.

To qualify for licensure, the vendor must be at least 18 years old, trustworthy, and able to maintain a special interest-bearing account within a national or state chartered bank located within New York State with $5,000 for the main office and $2,500 for each branch office. The vendor needs written consent from the Secretary of State to withdraw funds from the account, followed by a 6-month waiting period after the request to withdraw funds.

Coursework, examinations, and fees are not required for licensure. Vendors are required to provide potential tenants with a contract or receipt that includes the services they offer, with the same services displayed on signage in their offices. If they do not find acceptable housing, they must refund a percentage of the fee paid by the customer.

Apartment sharing agent

An apartment sharing agent is paid a fee to find potential roommates for current owners or occupants of housing. Licensure is valid for one year from November 1 to October 31 of the next year. As with apartment information vendors, coursework, examinations, and fees are not required for licensure. Agents must maintain a special interest-bearing account within a national or state-chartered bank located within New York State with at least $2,500 for the main office and $1,200 for each branch office and must obtain written consent from the Secretary of State and then wait 6 months to withdraw funds from the account

---

REQUIREMENTS FOR LICENSURE

Broker
Associate broker
Salesperson
Department of State denial of license

Broker   **General requirements**

▸   20 years of age

▸   Licensees cannot have a criminal, sex offense, or sexual violence conviction unless the Secretary does not bar licensure based on such conviction

▸   Must have proof of honesty and trustworthiness

▸   Must have proficient knowledge of the English language (State examinations are available in English only to confirm the applicant's competency in the English language.)

▸   Must be a citizen or lawful permanent resident of the United States

▸   Must have experience as a licensed salesperson for at least 2 years, or experience in general real estate field for at least 3 years, or a combination of both

▸   Must have minimum points for experience type, e.g., buying and selling own property, managing employer's property, etc.

▸   Must have current NYS photo driver's license or photo non-driver ID card

Application, education, and examination requirements

License applicants must:

- complete and submit the 13-page application found online at **dos-0036-f-a-real-estate-broker-application_02.2023.pdf (ny.gov)** and the application fee to the Department of State [current fees are listed online at **Real Estate Broker | Department of State (ny.gov)**].

- submit all proposed business names in writing to the Division of Licensing Services for approval, then file appropriate document for use of the chosen approved name with either the County Clerk's office or the NYS Department of State, Division of Corporations.

- satisfactorily complete 152 hours of approved education to include

  o the 45-hour salesperson course,

  o the 30-hour salesperson remedial,

  o a 2-hour Fair Housing and/or implicit bias training continuing education course, and

  o the 75-hour broker course.

  Education requirements may be satisfied by attending the approved classroom-instructed course for at least 90% of the instruction time or by completing the required hours through online distance learning. Online courses must be completed within 12 months. Satisfying coursework includes passing the school's final exam.

  These courses are valid for 8 years following the course completion date. If they are not used within the 8 years, they will expire and must be retaken.

  A Bachelor's Degree earned in the United States with a concentration in real estate may qualify for a salesperson or broker course waiver. An official transcript must be submitted. (Rules and Regulations, Title 19 NYCRR §176.15)

- Pass the State examination

  o exams are multiple choice based on the 152-hour pre-licensing course(s) and must be completed within 2 ½ hours

  o exams are pass/fail with no numeric score provided

  o exam results are available for 2 years

  o passed exams allow submission of the licensure application and fee.

  o failed exams can be rescheduled

  Exam sites throughout the State can be found online at Real Estate Salesperson Exam Sites | Department of State (ny.gov).

▶ Pay the license fee

The DOS will issue the broker's license after the applicant has demonstrated competency and trustworthiness and met all licensure requirements. The license will include the broker's name and principal business address.

Licenses are issued for 2-year terms.

Associate broker

All requirements for associate broker licensure are the same as for broker licensure, except the associate broker applicant must obtain a sponsoring broker prior to obtaining the license.

Salesperson

General requirements

▶ 18 years of age

▶ Proof of honesty and trustworthiness

▶ No criminal, sex offense, or sexual violence conviction unless the Secretary does not bar licensure based on such conviction

▶ Obtain a sponsoring broker who must authorize the application after which the DOS will review it for completeness and qualifications for the real estate salesperson license.

▶ Have legal right to work in the United States

▶ Have an appropriate understanding of the English language (State examinations are available in English only to confirm the applicant's competency in the English language.)

▶ Current NYS photo driver's license or photo non-driver ID card

Application, education, and examination requirements

▶ Complete and submit the 7-page application found online at dos-0022-f-a-real-estate-salesperson-application_02.2023.pdf (ny.gov) and the application fee to the Department of State [current fees are listed online at Real Estate Salesperson | Department of State (ny.gov)].

Individuals applying based on attorney status, requesting an additional salesperson license, or having been previously licensed should submit a paper application by regular mail. Individuals who completed education outside of New York State and have received an education waiver must pass the state examination and submit an application to the State Licensing office for processing.

▶ Satisfactorily complete 77 hours of approved education to include

o the 45-hour salesperson qualifying course,

- the 30-hour salesperson remedial, and
- a 2-hour Fair Housing and/or implicit bias training continuing education course.

- ▸ Complete a school administered proctored examination
- ▸ Pass the State examination
- ▸ Pay the license fee

Education requirements may be satisfied by attending the approved classroom-instructed course for at least 90% of the instruction time or by completing the required hours through online distance learning. Online courses must be completed within 12 months. Satisfying coursework includes passing the school's final exam.

A Bachelor's Degree earned in the United States with a concentration in real estate may qualify for a salesperson or broker course waiver. An official transcript must be submitted. (Rules and Regulations, Title 19 NYCRR §176.15)

The DOS will issue the salesperson's license after the applicant has demonstrated competency and trustworthiness and met all licensure requirements. The license will include the salesperson's name and business address along with the sponsoring broker's name and principal business address.

Licenses are issued for 2-year terms.

Department of State denial of license

Before denying a license, the DOS will notify the applicant in writing of the reasons for the denial. The notification is served personally or sent by certified mail. The DOS is also to notify the proposed sponsoring broker. The applicant then has 30 days to request the chance to be heard in person or by council. If the request is not received within 30 days, the denial becomes final.

Licenses may be denied for any of the following reasons:

- ▸ Failure to disclose pending criminal charges or convictions
- ▸ Conviction of a felony or misdemeanor related to the qualifications, functions, and duties of a real estate licensee
- ▸ Administrative action taken against the business or license of the real estate agency
- ▸ Determination that the facts of a particular case warrant denial

MAINTAINING A LICENSE

Who holds the license
Pocket cards
License changes

Who holds the license

Licenses are issued by the Department of State with the licensee's name and photo obtained from the Department of Motor Vehicles. A salesperson's license is held by the sponsoring broker.

Pocket cards

In addition to the applicant's license, the DOS will issue a pocket card to the new licensee. The card will include the broker licensee's photo, name, and business address. For a salesperson licensee, the card will include the licensee's photo, name, and the sponsoring broker's name and business address. The card for all licensees will also include certification that the card holder is a licensed real estate broker or salesperson. If the card is ever lost or damaged, the licensee may provide proof of the loss or damage, pay a $10 fee, and request a replacement card from the Secretary of State. Pocket cards are held by the licensee and must be shown whenever asked.

License changes

Changes of association or termination

If a salesperson or associate broker stops working for the supervising broker or is terminated, the broker is to file a termination notice on the appropriate online form. The licensee will be terminated by the Department of State within 5 days from the date the licensee leaves the broker's association. The broker is required to terminate a salesperson or associate broker prior to the change of association being completed by the new sponsoring broker. The salesperson's license may be endorsed to a new sponsoring broker when the new record of association is filed with the DOS and the appropriate fee is paid.

For a licensee with an expired license who wishes to change broker association and renew the license under a different broker, the new broker must change the licensee's association prior to the license's renewal. With an expired license, the licensee does not need the former broker to submit a termination notice to the State.

All association changes must be approved by the Department of State who will mail a new license to the licensee's business address.

Changes in broker name/status/location

If the broker's name, status, or address changes, the broker must notify the DOS of the change. [Change form can be found online at DOS-1473 (ny.gov).] The broker's own name and the names of each associated salesperson and associate broker must be included along with a $10 filing fee for each named licensee. Failure to notify the DOS of such changes will result in license suspension.

Changing the real estate company's name requires submission of a new broker application.

Death of broker

If a sole proprietor broker dies, the broker's license can be used by the duly appointed administrator or executor to complete any transactions unfinished at the time of the broker's death. This applies to transactions by the broker or any associated salespersons and provides up to 120 days from the date of the broker's death for the transactions to be completed. Upon submission of an application to the Secretary of State, the time period may be extended another 120 days for good cause. If the license expires during either the initial 120 days or the extension, it will automatically be renewed until the applicable time period expires. No renewal fee is charged in this case.

The broker's license must be modified to include "deceased" after the broker's name, the date of the death, and the name of the administrator or executor

Felony conviction

If a broker or salesperson is convicted of a felony, regardless of the state where the felony occurred, the licensee must submit a certified copy of the conviction judgment to the DOS.

LICENSE RENEWAL

Renewal requirements
Continuing education requirements
Sponsoring broker requirements

Renewal requirements

Licenses are good for 2 years and must be renewed prior to the expiration date printed on the license. Three months prior to the expiration date, renewal reminders will be sent to the licensee with instructions on how to renew the license online at http://www.dos.ny.gov/licensing/eaccessny.html.

Continuing education requirements

Licensees are required to complete 22.5 hours of continuing education (CE) within the 2 years prior to license renewal. The CE must include 3 hours in Fair Housing and/or discrimination in the sale or rental of real property and at least 1 hour in Law of Agency. Salespersons renewing for the first time must also include 2 hours of Agency in addition to all other designated hours.

A new law effective in September 2022 mandates both brokers and salespersons CE to include at least 2 hours of instruction in "implicit bias awareness," which concerns the attitudes or stereotypes affecting an individual's understanding, actions, and decisions in ways the person may not be aware of. The new law also mandates at least 2 hours of cultural competency training, which is understanding cultural norms, preferences, and challenges within U.S. diverse communities.

Classroom courses require licensees to maintain a 90% attendance record to pass the course. CE requirements may be met through attending in-person classroom instruction, computer-based distance learning programs that record the student's interaction and inactivity times, or a combination of classroom and distance learning to equal the required hours and coursework.

CE exemptions

As of July 1, 2021, the CE exemption for brokers practicing real estate for 15 or more years was removed. All brokers, regardless of their tenure of licensure, are now required to complete CE.

Those exempt from licensure, such as attorneys, executors, public officers, etc., are also exempt from continuing education.

Renewal extension

If a licensee has a bona fide hardship precluding CE completion prior to the license renewal date, the licensee must file the renewal application, proof of the hardship, and a waiver request to the DOS for approval.

Renewing expired licenses

If a licensee fails to complete the required CE and renew the license by the expiration date, the licensee will be required to retake and pass the state written examination. The licensee is not permitted to work while the license is expired.

Licenses that are expired for more than 2 years cannot be renewed without retaking and passing the licensing examination and then reapplying for the license. No qualifying education is required as long as the DOS has a record of the education previously being completed and the license previously being issued. No CE is required for this renewal since the applicant is starting over.

Sponsoring broker requirements

Sponsoring brokers are responsible to assure associated salespersons and associate brokers are properly and currently licensed. They are also responsible for maintaining an online account for each associated licensee and to assure licensees are completing CE requirements and license renewals in a timely manner as required.

PROMULGATED REGULATIONS

Rules and regulations regarding the rights, licensing, responsibilities, and liabilities of real estate licensees as well as the marketing, sale, and rental of real property are promulgated by several national and state government agencies. For example, the Department of Law issues regulations related to cooperative interests in real estate, such as cooperatives and condominiums. The New York State Board of Real Estate establishes regulations that affect real estate licensure and related education. The Secretary of State adopts rules and regulations related to licensees handling clients' funds and property, complaints and violation investigations, license applicants' business practice and methods investigations, and approval, denial, suspension, or revocation of licenses.

PLACE OF BUSINESS REQUIREMENTS

Broker's place of business
Branch offices
Display of license

Broker's place of business

New York real estate brokers are required to maintain a place of business within the state. The business name must be approved by the DOS and then posted conspicuously on the exterior of the building. The signage must be large enough to be read from the sidewalk and must include the broker's name and the words *Licensed Real Estate Broker*. If the real estate office is located inside an office building, hotel, or apartment building, the broker's name and *Licensed Real Estate Broker* must be posted in the list of other businesses within the building. A residence that is properly licensed by the DOS may also be used as an office.

Branch offices

In addition to the principal place of business, brokers may maintain multiple branch offices. Each branch office must be separately licensed by the principal broker and under the direct supervision of the same broker. Corporations, partnerships, or LLCs may appoint a representative broker or office manager to supervise the branch office.

Display of license

The principal broker's license is to be conspicuously displayed in the principal place of business at all times. Branch office licenses must also be displayed in the licensed branch office at all times. The principal broker may choose to display the licenses of associated salespersons and associate brokers within the appropriate office. No expired license may be displayed in any office at any time.

ADVERTISING GUIDELINES

Guidelines
E-mail and internet advertising
For Sale signs
Teams

Guidelines

Title 19 § 175.25 of the New York Codes, Rules, and Regulations defines *advertising* as "promotion and solicitation related to licensed real estate activity, including but not limited to, advertising via mail telephone, websites, e-mail, electronic bulletin boards, business cards, signs, billboards, and flyers. Advertising and advertisement shall not include commentary made by a duly licensed real estate salesperson, real estate associate broker or real estate broker that is not related to promoting licensed real estate activity."

Advertising is one of the most effective tools licensees can use to serve their clients. As such, all advertising must be accurate and honest so as to avoid misleading or harming the public.

Advertisements for the sale or lease of property must be placed only by a licensed broker and must include the broker's name, the fact the advertiser is a real estate broker, and the broker's address or phone number. The ads may include the names of associate brokers and/or salespersons within the same brokerage and must include the type of license held by each. The ads must also include a true description of the property being sold or leased. Ads that do not include the broker's name and identify the broker as a real estate broker are *blind ads* and are illegal.

No broker may advertise another broker's exclusively listed property without obtaining the consent of the listing broker. The advertising broker must then clearly and conspicuously include the listing broker's name and identify that broker as the listing broker.

E-mail and internet advertising

Internet advertising by associate brokers, salespersons, and teams is allowed but must be authorized and supervised by the sponsoring broker. Each page of a website must include the broker's name and other information required for all ads. The homepage of the site created by the associated licensees must also include a link to the sponsoring broker's website.

Brokers who use programs that generate leads, such as Zillow, StreetEasy, Trulia, etc., must clearly disclose the listing agent in any advertisements and must ensure the listed buyer's broker includes the word "advertisement" in the ad. Current regulations require that this information is also visible to the public on Thumbnail views on Zillow or the broker's webpage.

The first e-mail sent to a client or potential client must include the same identifying information required for all advertisements: the broker's name, address or phone, the fact the e-mail sender is a real estate broker, and the type of license held by the sender. This information is not required in subsequent e-mails sent to the same recipient.

For Sale signs

For sale signs are another means of advertising property for sale or lease. These signs must identify the advertising broker and may be placed on the associated property only with the property owner's consent.

Teams

The regulations also define *teams* as an associate broker or salesperson who operates together with another licensee from the same brokerage as a team. The team name must include each team members' full licensed name, or, otherwise, the team name must be followed by the words "at/of" followed by the full name of the broker/brokerage. For example, "Team Blue of the John Smith Real Estate Brokerage."

Team names must include the word "team" and cannot use other terms such as associate, realty, or group. Names of unlicensed individuals may not be included in the team name. Team advertisements that include unlicensed members' names must conspicuously indicate which members are licensed and which are not.

LICENSE LAW VIOLATIONS

Common violations
Compensation-related violations
Referral fees
Kickbacks
Penalties
Appeals

Common violations

Common violations of New York License Law by brokers and other licensees include the following:

> ▶ Misleading or misrepresenting material facts regarding a property or transaction

> ▶ Practicing law without a law license

> ▶ Breaching fiduciary duty to clients

> ▶ Practicing real estate without a license

> ▶ Fraudulently obtaining a real estate license

> ▶ Failing to provide required disclosures

> ▶ Offering a listing agreement that does not include the appropriate explanations of exclusive-right-to-sell and exclusive-agency listings

> ▶ Engaging in fraud or fraudulent practices

> ▶ Demonstrating untrustworthiness or incompetency

> ▶ Discriminating against anyone in violation of the Americans with Disabilities Act or Fair Housing Laws

> ▶ Failing to account for monies belonging to others being held by the licensee

- ▶ Attempting to do business with the client of another real estate broker

- ▶ Listing a property for sale or lease or placing a sign on a property without the property owner's approval

- ▶ Failing to maintain a current license during the process of initiating and completing a real estate transaction that requires licensure

Compensation-related violations

The following actions violate New York License Law:

- ▶ Real estate brokers paying a commission or other compensation to an unlicensed, unassociated individual for performing any real estate activity that requires licensure, e.g., buying, selling, exchanging, leasing, etc. real property

- ▶ Unlicensed individuals accepting a commission or other compensation for performing any real estate activity that requires licensure, e.g., buying, selling, exchanging, leasing, etc. real property

- ▶ Salespersons or associate brokers accepting a commission from anyone other than the current sponsoring broker, unless the commission is paid by a former sponsoring broker for activities performed during that broker's supervision

- ▶ Brokers receiving compensation from more than one party to a real estate transaction without the knowledge and consent of all parties to the same transaction

- ▶ Brokers sharing a commission with anyone other than associated salespersons and associate brokers or other licensed brokers for assisting with a real estate transaction

- ▶ Brokers paying a commission or other compensation to any party to the transaction for which the broker was paid

  - o Rebate exception: brokers paying part of the commission as a *rebate* to a seller, buyer, landlord, or tenant as an incentive and not as payment for performing any real estate activity that requires licensure; rebates must be disclosed to the broker's client in the same transaction

Referral fees

Referral fees are often paid by one professional to another for referring a client or customer to the paying professional. This occurs when one licensee refers a customer to another licensee when the referring licensee cannot assist the customer. Referrals also occur when a licensee refers a client to a particular mortgage company or to a specific insurance carrier or even to a specific appraiser or inspector.

Referral fees are legal when the referral is disclosed and agreed to by the involved parties and the involved parties give consent for the broker to receive the fee.

Referral fees are illegal in the following situations:

- A real estate broker pays a referral fee to an unlicensed person for referring customers to the broker

- The fee is not disclosed to or consented to by the involved parties

- A broker pays or receives an after-the-fact referral fee, that is,

  o a fee for finding a seller after a listing agreement has been signed,

  o a fee for finding a buyer after a purchase offer has been accepted, or

  o a fee for finding a property after a buyer's agency agreement has been signed

Kickbacks

Kickbacks typically involve unethically recommending another business or service and include illegal commission splitting, illegal referral fees, and undisclosed profits. They are sometimes referred to as a type of bribery because they are intended as compensation for preferential treatment or improper services. Kickbacks may be in the form of money, credit, gifts, or anything of value.

One example of a kickback would be a broker accepting a referral fee from a property inspector without disclosing the fee to the buyer.

Kickbacks are illegal under the Real Estate Settlement and Procedures Act (RESPA) of 1974 and can result in a $10,000 fine and up to 1 year prison.

Penalties

Complaints of violations of the New York License Law are investigated and, if evidence is found to indicate the complaint is valid, can result in a hearing conducted by the DOS. If the licensee is found guilty of the violation, the DOS may impose any of the following penalties or combined penalties:

- License revocation or suspension

  o If a broker's license is revoked, all licensees under the broker's supervision will automatically be suspended until they find a new sponsoring broker and have their licenses reissued.

  o If the revoked broker is reinstated, the associated licensees may have their licenses reissued under that broker's sponsorship.

- Broker or licensee reprimand

- Fine up to $150 for first violation; $500 for second violation, and up to $1,000 for each subsequent violation

- ▸ Attorney General prosecution of criminal actions with potential prison sentence

- ▸ Financial liability to the aggrieved person of one to four times the monetary amount received as commission, compensation, or profit during the performance of the violation

Appeals
A guilty finding by the DOS that results in one of the above penalties may be appealed to the Secretary of State. Criminal convictions may be appealed through the New York Supreme Court.

UNLICENSED ASSISTANTS

Allowed activities
Prohibited activities

Unlicensed assistants are supervised by the employing licensed broker who is responsible for controlling their activities performed under the real estate business's name. The broker is responsible for providing training.

Unlicensed assistants should be paid on an hourly basis, per activity, or salary basis by either the broker or salesperson. Compensation for completed transactions requires the assistant hold a salesperson license and be compensated directly by the employing broker.

Allowed activities
To assist brokers, associate brokers, and salespersons in the real estate business, employees, secretaries, or assistants without real estate licenses may generally perform what are called *ministerial activities*, as exemplified by the following:

- ▸ answer the phone, forward calls, and take messages,

- ▸ arrange appointments, by telephone, for the licensee,

- ▸ follow up on loan commitments after a contract has been negotiated and generally secure status reports on loan progress,

- ▸ assemble documents for closing,

- ▸ write ads for approval of broker and place approved classified advertising,

- ▸ type contract forms for approval by broker,

- ▸ compute commission checks,

- ▸ place or remove signs from property,

- ▸ order items of repair as directed by the broker,

- ▸ prepare flyers and promotional information for approval by broker,

- ▸ schedule appointments for licensees to show listed property,

- ▸ gather information for a comparative market analysis,

- gather information for an appraisal,

- monitor licenses and personnel files, and

- perform secretarial and clerical duties such as typing of letters and filing.

Prohibited activities

Unlicensed assistants and personnel may not engage in any office activity that is specified in Section 440 of Article 12A of the New York State Real Property Law. In other words, they may not perform any activity that requires a real estate license.

PROPERTY CONDITION DISCLOSURE ACT

Requirements
Exemptions

Requirements

As mandated by Article 14, known as the Property Condition Disclosure Act, New York sellers of residential property are required to provide the purchaser with a Property Condition Disclosure Statement. The statement must be completed and provided to the purchaser *prior to signing a contract with the seller*. When the statement is signed by both the buyer and seller, it must be attached to the purchase contract.

The disclosure requirements apply whether the transaction involves a purchase contract, lease with option to purchase, or an installment sale agreement.

The disclosure statement may be found online at dos-1614-f-property-condition-disclosure-statement_06.2023.pdf (ny.gov).

The seller's real estate agent is required to inform the seller of the obligation to provide the disclosure statement. The buyer is to be informed of the buyer's rights and obligations by either the buyer's agent or the seller's agent if no buyer's agent is involved.

Even with a property condition statement, buyers should still have a property inspection completed. The buyer and seller are not prohibited from agreeing to transfer the property 'as is,' or from entering into any other agreement regarding the property's physical condition.

If the seller discovers facts that render the statement materially inaccurate, the seller must provide the buyer with a revised statement as soon as possible. If the seller fails to provide the statement within the time frame required, the buyer may be credited $500 at closing. If the seller fails to disclose property defects, the seller can be held liable for the buyer's actual damages resulting from the failed disclosure.

Exemptions

The following residential real property transfers are the essential exemptions from requiring a property condition disclosure:

- ▸ transfer by **deed in lieu of foreclosure**

- ▸ transfer pursuant to a **foreclosure sale**

- ▸ transfer by a mortgagee who has acquired the property pursuant to a **deed in lieu of foreclosure** or at a foreclosure sale.

- ▸ **transfer** by a fiduciary in the course of the administration **of the decedent's estate.**

- ▸ **transfer from one co-owner** to one or more other co-owners.

- ▸ **transfer to a spouse** or children.

- ▸ transfer pursuant to **a divorce**.

GAS WELL DISCLOSURE

New York State Real Property Law (RPP 8- 242.3) states that a seller with knowledge of the existence of an unplugged gas well must disclose this information to the purchaser prior to the property sale. The disclosure form can be found online at Uncapped_Gas_Well_Disclosure.pdf (nystatemls.com).

1 License Law and Regulations Snapshot Review

INTRODUCTION TO LICENSE LAW

Purpose
- protect general public
- protect property consumers from misrepresentation and fraud
- protect consumers from financial loss

State Board of Real Estate
- 15 members, including Secretary of State
- at least 5 licensed brokers with 10 years experience
- remaining members unlicensed public
- serve 2-year terms
- powers include setting rules & regulations, setting licensure course content, approving schools, enforce programs and activities, submit annual reports to legislative committees

Licensure exemptions
- persons acting under court order
- public officers in line of duty
- attorneys at law
- resident managers employed by single-owner property owners
- tenant organizations and not-for-profit corporations authorized by NY housing code

LICENSURE CATEGORIES AND RESPONSIBILITES

Real estate broker
- appropriately licensed person, firm, LLC, or corporation who, for consideration,
  - lists, sells, exchanges, buys, rents, or offers to negotiate any of these actions
  - collects or offers to collect rent
  - negotiates mortgage loans
  - relocates tenants
- all above activities require licensure
- **responsibilities to public** – fair and honest dealings, accountability for funds belonging to others, appropriate disclosure of material facts related to subject property
- **responsibilities to licensees** – supervision, guidance, training, holding licenses, paying licensees, providing office space and supplies
- **dual licensure** – licensed broker holds 2 or more licenses

Associate broker
- holds broker license but works as salesperson under supervision of sponsoring broker
  - facilitates sale and purchase of property for buyers and sellers
  - lists, negotiates, leases, or rents property for compensation
- above activities require broker's license with sponsoring broker
- **responsibilities to public** – fair and honest dealings, accountability, disclosures
- **responsibilities to sponsoring broker** – conduct activities in broker's name, conduct activities in compliance with licensure and related laws

Salesperson
- holds salesperson license to perform real estate activities under supervision of sponsoring broker and for compensation; cannot operate independent of sponsoring broker
  - handles sale, purchase, lease, rental, exchange, listings, negotiations of property for others
  - negotiates real estate loans other than mortgage loans

- collects rent
- all above activities require licensure
- **responsibilities to public** – fair and honest dealings, accountability, disclosures
- **responsibilities to sponsoring broker** – conduct activities in broker's name, conduct activities in compliance with licensure and related laws
- **dual licensure** – licensed salesperson holds two or more licenses to work under two or more sponsoring brokers

Out of state licenses

- **nonresident license** – resident of another state meets NY licensure requirements to obtain NY license to practice real estate in NY without place of business in NY; other state must offer same opportunity to NY licensees; must file irrevocable consent
- **reciprocal license** – NY nonresident licensee may practice in NY if home state has reciprocity agreement with NY to recognize each other's laws and requirements; NY has agreements with nine states with some restrictions
- **members of armed forces households** – members of an armed forces member's household may obtain NY license if part of household prior to relocating to NY, if meet certain licensure requirements, submit an application, and complete 11 of 22 ½ CE hours
- **mutual recognition** – agreement between two states to recognize education and experience from each other's state to allow nonresident licensee to practice without obtaining license in nonresident state

Other licenses or registrations

- **corporation, partnership, LLC** – must have one designated officer, partner, or member licensed as broker
- **office manager** – must hold associate broker license for 2 of prior 4 years; supervises salespersons and other associate brokers
- **mortgage banking companies** – provide mortgage loans to be sold to investors; do not provide checking or savings accounts, but do provide large percentage of mortgage loans; must file surety bond and establish trust fund
- **mortgage broker** – NY real estate license required to negotiate mortgage loan for nonresidential property; license to be registered with State Banking Department; typically paid by borrower to find lender; and may be required to obtain surety bond and establish trust fund.
- **home inspector** – must be licensed with 2-year terms and CE requirements
- **real estate appraiser** – licensed or certified to form opinion on property value; education requirements based on category of licensure; 2-year terms require CE
- **apartment information vendor** – paid by customer to provide information on availability and location of rental property; 1-year license term with age and financial requirements
- **apartment sharing agent** – paid to find roommates for residential owners or occupants; 1-year license term with financial requirements

REQUIREMENTS FOR LICENSURE

Broker

- **general requirements** – 20 years old, no criminal convictions, honest and trustworthy, speaks English language, citizen or lawful resident of U.S., 2 years salesperson experience or 3 years real estate experience or combination, minimum points for experience type, current NY photo ID
- **application, education, exam** – submit application and fee with proposed business name, complete required pre-license education in classroom or online, pass state exam, pay license fee

Associate broker

- general and education requirements – same as broker plus obtain sponsoring broker

Salesperson	• **general requirements** – 18 years old, no criminal convictions, honest and trustworthy, speaks English language, legal right to work in U.S., current NY photo ID, obtain sponsoring broker
	• **application, education, exam** – submit application and fee, complete required pre-license education in classroom or online, complete school proctored exam, pass state exam, pay license fee
DOS denial of license	• DOS to notify applicant and sponsoring broker of reason; applicant can appeal within 30 days
	• reasons for denial include criminal conviction related to real estate law, failure to disclose charges or conviction, administrative action taken against real estate agency, other facts warranting denial

MAINTAINING A LICENSE

Who holds the license	• salesperson and associate broker licenses held by sponsoring broker
Pocket cards	• includes licensee's photo, name, business address, salesperson's sponsoring broker, certification that cardholder is licensed real estate broker or salesperson; card held by licensee
License changes	• changes of association or termination – **broker to file termination notice;** DOS then terminates licensee within 5 days; broker to terminate licensee prior to change to new broker; association changes to be approved by DOS who issues new license
	• **broker name/status/location** – broker to notify DOS and include associated licensees; failure to notify DOS results in license suspension
	• **death of broker** – deceased broker's license used for 120 days to complete current transactions; automatic renewal if expires during the 120 days
	• **felony conviction** – licensee to submit certified copy of conviction judgment to DOS

LICENSE RENEWAL

Renewal requirements	• license to be renewed prior to expiration of 2-year term
Continuing education requirements	• licensees to complete 22 ½ hours of CE prior to renewal, to include
	▪ 3 hours of Fair Housing
	▪ 1 hour of Agency Law
	▪ 2 hours of implicit bias awareness
	▪ 2 hours of cultural competency
	▪ also, 2 hours of Agency for salesperson's first renewal
	• 90% attendance required for classroom courses or
	• online program that records student's interaction and inactivity times
	• **CE exemptions** – no exemption for brokers practicing real estate for 15 years; if exempt from licensure, then exempt from CE
	• **renewal extension** – extension provided for hardship that prevents CE completion; must file renewal application, proof of hardship, waiver request to DOS
	• **expired license** – renewal and CE not completed by license expiration date, licensee to retake state exam and stop work while expired; licensees expired 2 or more years must retake exam and reapply for license, with no CE required
Sponsoring broker requirements	• sponsoring broker responsible for licensees' current licensure, CE completion, and renewals; must also maintain online account for each associated licensee

PROMULGATED REGULATIONS

• rules and regulations related to real estate promulgated by Department of Law, NYS Board of Real Estate, Secretary of State

PLACE OF BUSINESS REQUIREMENTS

Broker's place of business
- brokers required to maintain NY place of business with name approved by DOS
- business name to be posted on exterior of building, large enough to be read from sidewalk; must include broker's name and "Licensed Real Estate Broker

Branch offices
- each branch office to be separately licensed and supervised by principal broker
- corporations, partnerships, LLCs may appoint office manager or representative broker to supervise the branch office

Display of license
- principal broker's license to be displayed in principal office
- branch office licenses to be displayed in branch office
- expired licenses not to be displayed

ADVERTISING GUIDELINES

Guidelines
- not to include licensee commentary unrelated to promoting real estate activity
- must be accurate and honest
- placed only by broker, include broker's name, address or phone, and fact advertiser is licensed broker; blind ads do not include broker information and are illegal
- must also include property description and may include sales persons and associate brokers within same agency
- need listing broker's consent to advertise exclusively listed property and must include listing broker's information

E-mail and internet advertising
- must be authorized and supervised by the sponsoring broker and include broker' name and information on each page
- homepage created by licensees must include link to sponsoring broker's website
- Internet programs that generate leads must disclose listing agent in all ads
- first e-mail to include broker identifying information as in all advertising; not required in subsequent e-mails

For Sale signs
- placed on property on with owner's consent
- must identify advertising broker

Teams
- pairs or groups of licensees from same brokerage
- team name to include all members' names or team name to be followed by "at/of" and then the full name of the broker or brokerage; name must include "team"
- no unlicensed individuals to be included in team name
- ads must indicate which members are licensed and which are not

LICENSE LAW VIOLATIONS

Common violations
- misrepresentation, fraud, untrustworthiness, incompetency, practicing real estate without license, practicing law without license, fraudulent real estate license, violating ADA or Fair Housing laws
- breaching fiduciary duties, failing to provide disclosures, failing to account for monies belonging to others, failing to maintain current license while performing real estate transaction
- listing agreements without explanation of types of listings, listing property for sale or lease without owner's consent, placing sign on property without owner's consent; attempting to do business with another broker's client

Compensation – related violations
- paying unlicensed or unassociated individual for real estate services that require licensure, unlicensed individuals accepting payment for real estate services that require licensure, licensee accepting commission from anyone other than current sponsoring broker
- brokers receiving compensation from more than one party to transaction without consent of all parties, broker sharing commission with anyone not affiliated with broker, broker paying commission to any party to a transaction except as rebate

paid as incentive and not payment for services that require licensure, not disclosing rebates to client

Referral fees	• paid for referring client to another professional, legal if disclosed and agreed upon by involved parties
	• illegal when paid to unlicensed person for referring customers to broker, when not disclosed or consented to by involved parties, when paid as after-the-fact fee
Kickbacks	• unethically recommending another business with illegal commission splitting, illegal referral fees, or undisclosed profits; referred to as bribery
	• illegal under RESPA and can result in fine and prison
Penalties	• license revocation or suspension, reprimand, fines, prosecution for criminal actions, financial liability to aggrieved person
Appeals	• noncriminal guilty findings may be appealed to Secretary of State
	• criminal convictions may be appealed to NY Supreme Court

UNLICENSED ASSISTANTS

Allowed activities	• paid on hourly or salary basis; payment on transaction basis requires license
	• secretarial duties such as answering phone, arranging appointments, assembling documents, typing contracts, scheduling property showings, gathering information for market analyses and appraisals; other duties such as checking loan commitments, computing commission checks, monitoring licenses and personnel files
Prohibited activities	• any activity requiring a real estate license

PROPERTY CONDITION DISCLOSURE ACT

Requirements	• sellers of residential property to provide disclosure to buyers prior to signing sales contract
	• seller's agent required to inform seller of disclosure requirement; buyer to be informed of disclosure rights
	• seller's failure to provide disclosure in required timeframe results in $500 credit to buyer at closing; seller's failure to disclose defects can result in seller's liability for buyer's damages
Exemptions	• transfers by deed in lieu of foreclosure, transfer pursuant to foreclosure sale
	• transfer by mortgagee who acquired property pursuant to deed in lieu or at foreclosure sale
	• transfer by fiduciary while administering a decedent's estate
	• transfer between co-owners, to spouse or children, or pursuant to divorce

GAS WELL DISCLOSURE

	• unplugged gas wells on the property must be disclosed to buyer prior to the sale

CHAPTER ONE: LICENSE LAW AND REGULATIONS

Section Quiz

1.1. Why does New York State have real estate laws?

    a. To gather statistics on real property sales
    b. To obtain funds to monitor real estate licensees' business practices
    c. To protect the general public
    d. To teach license applicants how to be successful in practicing real estate

1.2. Which of the following is exempt from real estate licensure?

    a. Property managers
    b. Individuals employed to collect rent for multiple clients
    c. Tenant relocators
    d. Attorneys at law

1.3. Real estate brokers have the following responsibilities to the public EXCEPT

    a. honest dealings.
    b. accounting for funds belonging to others.
    c. use of professional techniques to avoid fraud.
    d. maintaining confidentiality of all material facts related to the property.

1.4. Which of the following is a salesperson prohibited from doing?

    a. Collecting rent
    b. Operating independently
    c. Negotiating non-mortgage loans
    d. Negotiating the sale of a condominium

1.5. When may a nonresident of New York practice real estate in New York if there is no corresponding exchange of privileges between New York and the nonresident's home state?

    a. Under a mutual agreement
    b. Under reciprocal licensure
    c. Under nonresident licensure
    d. None of the given circumstances would enable the party to legally practice real estate in New York.

1.6. Who may work as a real estate office manager?

    a. The office's broker or a qualified associate broker
    b. Only the practice's broker
    c. The broker, any affiliated associate broker, or any affiliated salesperson
    d. Anyone except a salesperson

1.7. Which of the following is a requirement for a salesperson license?

    a. The party must be at least 20 years old
    b. The party must complete 77 hours of approved education
    c. One must complete 5 hours of Fair Housing education
    d. One must be a citizen of the United States

1.8. If a salesperson with an expired license wishes to change his or her broker association,

    a. the salesperson must renew the license prior to the new broker changing the licensee's association.
    b. the former broker must submit a termination of association notice prior to the salesperson renewing the license.
    c. the new broker must change the licensee's association prior to the licensee renewing the license.
    d. a salesperson with an expired license is not allowed to change broker association.

1.9. If a broker or salesperson is convicted of a felony,

    a. the license will be suspended.
    b. the license will be revoked.
    c. the licensee must submit proof of penalty satisfaction to the DOS.
    d. the licensee must submit a certified copy of the conviction judgment to the DOS.

1.10. Prior to renewing a license, a licensee must complete _____ hours of continuing education.

   a. 15
   b. 17 ½
   c. 20
   d. 22 ½

1.11. Which of the following statements is true?

   a. Licenses that are not renewed within 1 year of expiration cannot be renewed.
   b. Licenses that are expired for more than 2 years require starting over by retaking the education courses and the state examination.
   c. Licenses that are expired for more than 2 years require retaking and passing the examination and then reapplying for the license.
   d. Licenses that are expired for more than 1 year require retaking the state examination and completing CE requirements before the license can be renewed.

1.12. Who adopts regulations related to licensees handling funds belonging to clients?

   a. Secretary of State
   b. Department of Law
   c. NY State Board of Real Estate
   d. Superintendent of Financial Services

1.13. Which of the following must be on any real estate place of business signage?

   a. Names of all licensees
   b. Name of office manager
   c. The words *Licensed Real Estate Broker*
   d. The words *Real Estate Brokerage*

1.14. Which of the following is the operating rule for placing real estate ads to sell listings?

   a. The ad must identify the broker's name as the listing broker.
   b. The ad must identify the listing licensee.
   c. The ad must include the property's legal description.
   d. Any party may place the ad provided it is honest and reliable.

1.15. Which of the following statements is false?

   a. Teams can include unlicensed individuals.
   b. Team names can include the word *group* or *associate*.
   c. Team names may not include the names of unlicensed individuals.
   d. Team advertisements that include members' names must indicate which members are licensed and which are not.

1.16. Which of the following is not an after-the-fact referral fee?

   a. A fee for finding a seller after a listing agreement has been signed
   b. A fee for finding a buyer after a purchase offer has been accepted
   c. A fee for finding a buyer after a listing agreement has been signed
   d. A fee for finding a property after a buyer's agency agreement has been signed

1.17. Kickbacks are illegal and can result in

   a. a 2-year license suspension.
   b. license revocation.
   c. a $ 20,000 fine for each kickback.
   d. a $10,000 fine and up to 1 year prison.

1.18. Unlicensed assistants are prohibited from

   a. placing signs on property.
   b. following up on loan commitments.
   c. gathering information for a comparative market analysis.
   d. collecting rent.

1.19. If a property seller fails to disclose known property defects to a buyer, the seller

   a. and the agent can be fined up to $5,000.
   b. the seller can be charged $500 at closing.
   c. the seller can be held liable for the buyer's actual damages caused by the nondisclosed defects.
   d. the buyer may cancel the contract up to 30 days after the defect is discovered.

1.20. Sellers with existing unplugged gas wells on their property

    a. must disclose the well to the buyer prior to signing a purchase contract.

    b. must disclose the well to the seller's agent at time of signing a listing agreement.

    c. must disclose the well to the buyer's agent within 5 days after closing the purchase transaction.

    d. need not disclose an unplugged gas well.

1.21. Which of the following activities is an unlicensed assistant prohibited from doing?

    a. Arrange an appointment for a licensee

    b. Design new promotional materials for a licensee

    c. Negotiate sales transactions on a licensee's behalf

    d. Gather data for a comparative market analysis

1.22. Which of the following is true regarding brokerage branch offices?

    a. The principal broker must license each branch office separately.

    b. Office managers may not serve as supervisors for branch offices.

    c. Brokerages are limited to three branch offices.

    d. Principal brokers may designate a senior salesperson to supervise a branch office.

1.23. Margaret failed to finish her required CE and renew her license by the expiration date. Assuming she still wants to work in the industry, what must she do now to renew or reinstate her license?

    a. She must retake a prelicense course and then retake the exam.

    b. She will be required to retake and pass the state written examination.

    c. She is required to take the required CE and reapply for a license.

    d. She must apply for an extension.

1.24. Since 2022, New York licensees must take at least 2 hours instruction in _____ as part of their continuing education (CE) requirement.

    a. Risk management

    b. Personal safety

    c. Legal updates

    d. Implicit bias awareness

1.25. A broker who operates a brokerage as a sole proprietor dies. Which of the following is true?

    a. All in-process transactions terminate.

    b. An appointed licensee in the office may take over any work in process for 30 days.

    c. The broker's license is automatically suspended.

    d. The duly appointed administrator may use the license to complete any unfinished business within 120 days.

2 Law of Agency and Disclosure

The Agency Relationship
Fiduciary Duties
Termination of Agency
Misrepresentation
Terminating an Agency Relationship
Forms of Real Estate Agency and Alternatives
Antitrust Laws
Dual Agency
Types of Listings
Listing Agreement Requirements
Listing Agreement Termination
New York Agency Disclosure Requirements
Seller/Landlord Disclosures

THE AGENCY RELATIONSHIP

Basic roles
Types of agency
Creating an agency relationship

The most primary of relationships in real estate brokerage is that between broker and client, the relationship known in law as the **agency relationship**. In every state, a body of law, generally called the **law of agency,** defines and regulates the legal roles of this relationship. The parties to the relationship are the **principal** (a client), the **agent** (a broker), and the **customer** (a third party, or consumer).

The laws of agency are distinct from laws of contracts, although the two groups of laws interact with each other. For example, the listing agreement -- a contract -establishes an agency relationship. Thus, the relationship is subject to contract law. However, agency law dictates how the relationship will achieve its purposes, regardless of what the listing contract states.

The essence of the agency relationship is *trust, confidence, and mutual good faith*. The principal trusts the agent to exercise the utmost skill and care in fulfilling the authorized activity, and to promote the principal's best interests. The agent undertakes to strive in good faith to achieve the desired objective, and to fulfill the fiduciary duties.

It is important to understand that the agency relationship does *not* require compensation or any form of consideration. compensation also does not define an agency relationship: a party other than the principal may compensate the agent without having an agency relationship with the agent.

Basic roles

In an agency relationship, a principal hires an agent as a *fiduciary* to perform a desired service on the principal's behalf. As a fiduciary, the agent has a legal obligation to fulfill specific *fiduciary duties* throughout the term of the relationship.

The **principal,** or **client**, is the party who hires the agent. The agent works *for* the client. The principal may be a seller, a buyer, a landlord, or a tenant.

The **agent** is hired to perform the authorized work for the client and bound to fulfill fiduciary duties to the client. In real estate brokerage, the agent *must* be a licensed broker.

The **fiduciary** is the legal term for the agent's role within the agency relationship. The agency agreement or contract determines the agent's responsibilities and powers for transacting real estate business for the client.

The **customer** or **prospect** is a third party in the transaction whom the agent does not represent. The agent works *with* a customer in fulfilling the client's objectives. A seller, buyer, landlord, or tenant may be a customer. A third party who is a potential customer is a **prospect**. The agent does not have a contracted fiduciary relationship with either a customer or prospect.

Types of agency

The level of authority delegated to the agent determines the type of agency: *universal, general, special, or agency coupled with an interest.*

Universal agency. In a universal agency relationship, the principal empowers the agent to perform any and all actions that may be legally delegated to an agency representative. The instrument of authorization is the power of attorney. New York State's General Obligations law not only requires the power of attorney but also requires that it be notarized. The agent holding the power of attorney is referred to as an attorney-in-fact but does not need to be an actual attorney at law.

General agency. In a general agency, the principal delegates to the agent ongoing tasks and duties within a particular business or enterprise. Such delegation may include the authority to enter into contracts. These duties are determined and limited by the agency contract and do not require a power of attorney.

Special, or **limited, agency.** Under a special agency agreement, the principal delegates authority to conduct a specific activity with specific directions, after which the agency relationship terminates. In most cases, the special agent *may not* bind the principal to a contract.

In most instances, real estate brokerage is based on a special agency. The principal hires a licensed broker to procure a ready, willing, and able buyer or seller. When the objective is achieved, the relationship terminates, although certain fiduciary duties survive the relationship.

Agency coupled with an interest. When an agent has an interest in the property being sold, the principal may not cancel or rescind the agency relationship, and the relationship may also not be terminated if the principal dies.

Creating an agency relationship

An agency relationship may arise from an express oral or written agreement between the principal and the agent or from the actions of the parties that imply a relationship.

Expressed written or oral agreements. The most common way of creating an agency relationship is by an agreement with expressed words, either in writing or orally. The most common agreement used to create an agency relationship between an agent and a property seller is a listing agreement. The agreement sets forth the various authorizations and duties, as well as requirements for compensation. A listing agreement establishes an agency for a specified transaction and has a stated expiration.

Agency relationships are also created between an agent and a property buyer or tenant. An agreement used for this relationship is called a buyer or tenant broker agreement, an agreement to procure, a buyer or tenant agency agreement, or a buyer or tenant representation agreement. These agreements set forth the tasks and duties for the agent to fulfill in procuring a property for the principal.

While some oral agreements are permissible, having a written agreement is the most effective means of assuring all involved parties understand and agree to the relationship and its terms and is the most effective means of meeting statutory requirements. In New York, the Statute of Frauds mandates listing agreements for more than a year must be in writing to be enforceable. New York's License Law indirectly mandates that exclusive listing agreements be in writing so as to include the required text explaining the terms "exclusive right to sell" and "exclusive agency."

Implied agency. An agency relationship also can be implied in that the relationship is formed when the parties act *as if* there is an agreement. Whether intentionally or unintentionally, their conduct, assumptions, and even common law practices take the place of a spoken or written agreement. Implied agencies occur by default when parties have dealings without explicitly stating their terms.

For example, if an agent promises a buyer to do everything possible to find a property at the lowest possible price and the buyer accepts the proposition, there may be an implied agency relationship even though there is no specific agreement. Even if the agent does not wish to establish an agency relationship, the agent's actions may be construed to imply a relationship.

Similar implications can be made, intentionally or unintentionally, if an agent gives a seller advice on an asking price and shows the property to potential buyers. If the seller takes the advice and allows the agent to show the house, then the actions of both seller and agent have implied that they have an agency relationship:

▸ **Agency by ratification.** Implied agency can be created through ratification wherein one party performs an act on behalf of the another party without prior agreement or approval. The receiving party's eventual approval can be done implicitly through the party's conduct that indicates acceptance of the act. In other words, someone without authority acts on behalf of someone else and then the acts of the first person are eventually approved by the second person (for example, an agent acting on behalf of a seller without an agency agreement). Once the actions have been approved, the agency relationship is ratified.

▸ **Agency by estoppel.** An agency by estoppel is created when one party knowingly allows another party to believe that certain statements or actions are true, and the second party believes the statements or actions to that party's detriment. It also occurs when one party knowingly accepts the benefits from an unauthorized person's acts or services and allows the acts to continue on the first person's behalf.

When the agency is implied and not expressly specified, the seller's agent may step outside the boundaries of the relationship and offer advice to or assist a potential buyer or customer and, thus, create an illegal undisclosed dual agency. (See upcoming section on dual agency for more information.)

Whether intended or accidental, the creation of implied agency obligates the agent to fiduciary duties and professional standards of care. If these are not fulfilled, the agent may be held liable.

FIDUCIARY DUTIES

Duties to client
Duties to customer
Principal's duties
Breach of duty

A fiduciary is a person who transacts business or handles money or property on behalf of or for the benefit of someone else. Being a fiduciary means one person is bound both legally and ethically to act in the other person's best interests in a relationship of trust. Putting the other person's interests first is an obligation called a fiduciary duty.

The agency relationship imposes fiduciary duties on the client and agent, but particularly on the agent. An agent must also observe certain standards of conduct in dealing with customers and other outside parties.

Duties to client

Skill, care, and diligence. The agent is hired to do a job and is therefore expected to do it with diligence and reasonable competence. Competence is generally defined as a level of real estate marketing skills and knowledge comparable to those of other practitioners in the area. Competence and skill are gained through the agent's education (both pre-license and continuing education) and experience while practicing real estate. Consequently, the client relies on the agent to have the skills and be diligent in using those skills.

A broker should be competent in the following skills:

▶ Identifying and understanding the client's needs

▶ Knowing when to recommend the client seek other professional help, such as legal or accounting

▶ Determining the appropriate listing or purchase price based on the value of the property

▶ Seeking and disclosing information about the property, its neighborhood, and all parties involved in the transaction

▶ Explaining listing agreements, buyer agency agreements, offers, and sales contracts to the client.

▶ Completing contract forms with the client without crossing the line into practicing law without a license

▶ Effectively marketing the seller's property

▶ Using diligence and skill in finding or selling a property

▶ Assisting the client in negotiating offers and counteroffers

▶ Assisting the client in understanding varying financing options offered by lenders

▶ Exercising effective communication skills

The notion of care extends to observing the limited scope of authority granted to the agent. A conventional listing agreement does not authorize an agent to obligate the client to contracts, and it does not allow the agent to conceal offers, to buy, sell, or lease coming from a customer or another agent. Further, since a client relies on a broker's representations, a broker must exercise care not to offer advice outside of his or her field of expertise. Violations of this standard may expose the agent to liability for the unlicensed practice of a profession such as law, engineering, or accounting.

Exhibit 2.1 Agent's Fiduciary Duties to Client

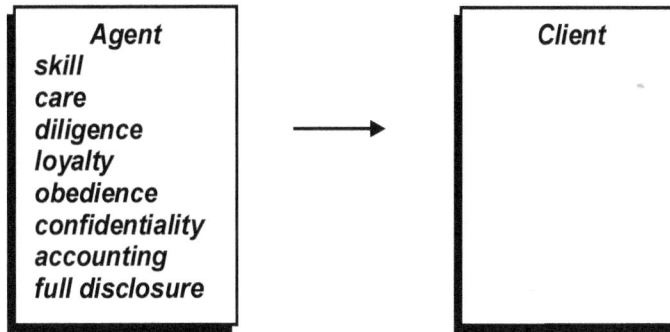

Agent	Client
skill care diligence loyalty obedience confidentiality accounting full disclosure	

In addition to skill, care, and diligence, the agent owes the duties of loyalty, obedience, confidentiality, accounting, and full disclosure to the client.

Loyalty. The duty of loyalty is based on trust and requires the agent to place the interests of the client above those of all others, particularly the agent's own. This standard is especially relevant whenever an agent discusses transaction terms with a prospect.

Fulfilling the duty of undivided loyalty becomes impossible within a dual agency relationship where the agent is transacting business with both the seller and the buyer. While the agent must consider each client's best interest, the relationship itself makes the agent legally incapable of putting one client's interests above the other's. Consequently, both clients must be aware that they will not be provided undivided loyalty.

Obedience. An agent has a duty to discover a client's needs and follow the client's directions and instructions in meeting those needs. This is the duty of obedience. Just as there is a circumstance when the agent cannot fulfill the duty of loyalty, so is there one when the agent cannot fulfill the duty of obedience. If the client's directions or instructions are illegal, the agent cannot and must not obey. If a client provides illegal directions, the agent must refuse and most likely withdraw from the agency relationship. Even if the directions are legal but the agent is unable to obey for whatever reason, then the agent should discuss the reasons with the client and then most likely withdraw from the relationship.

Confidentiality. An agent must hold in confidence any personal or business information received from the client during the term of the agency relationship. An agent may not disclose any information that would harm the client's interests or bargaining position or anything else the client wishes to keep private. For example, the seller's agent may not disclose why the client wishes to sell the property or that the seller may take a lower offer price. At the same time, a buyer's agent may not disclose that the buyer may make an offer higher than the asking price or why the buyer is interested in the subject property.

However, an agent must exercise care in fulfilling this duty; that is, if confidentiality conflicts with the agent's legal requirements to disclose material facts, the agent must inform the client of this obligation and make the required disclosures. An agent must comply with any law that requires certain information to be disclosed, but the agent may also disclose anything that is public information or anything about which the client waives confidentiality.

The confidentiality standard is one of the duties that extends *beyond the termination of the agency relationship*; at *no time* in the future may the agent disclose confidential information.

Accounting. An agent must safeguard and account for all monies, documents, and other property received from a client or customer. Brokers must be willing and able to report on any funds being held in relation to a transaction in which the broker is involved. Brokers are also required to immediately deposit such monies into a trust or escrow account that is labeled as such. The money is to stay in the account until the related transaction is completed, either through fulfillment or termination. The trust or escrow account may not also be used for the broker's own business or personal funds, referred to as comingling.

Full disclosure. The traditional notion of *caveat emptor* (let the buyer beware) which puts the onus on the buyer to discover material facts and defects in the property, no longer applies unequivocally to real estate transactions in every state. New York still recognizes the principle of caveat emptor (let the buyer beware) but limits the buyer's responsibility by mandating the seller to disclose material facts about the property. New York Property Condition Disclosure Act requires a seller to make a written disclosure about a property's condition to a prospective buyer in a timely manner.

New York's laws mandate that an agent has the duty to disclose all material facts and reports that might affect a party's interests in the property transaction. Material facts are considered to be any supportable information about a property that could potentially affect a buyer's *decision to purchase* the property or the price to be paid for the property. A material fact could change the value of the property. This could be anything from known defects in the structure itself, prior water damage, the property being located in a flood zone, termites or asbestos contained in the structure, or the property containing lead paint or other environmental hazards. It could also be a fact about the property itself, such as the ability of either party to complete the transaction, restrictions on the use of the property, toxic substances being spilled on the property, homeowners' association rules, and other details.

Sellers are also required to disclose known **latent defects,** which are hidden defects that are typically not discovered during a property inspection. They are often only discovered after the closing of the sale and after the buyer has taken possession of the property. Examples could include mold hidden inside a wall, faulty electrical wiring, tree root problems, hazardous chemical use or drug manufacturing, contaminated soil, etc.

New York state law Section 462 requires agents and sellers to disclose items that a practicing agent knows or *should have known at the time of closing*. This includes known latent defects.

The most obvious example of a "should have known" disclosure is a property defect, such as an inoperative central air conditioner, that the agent failed to notice. If the air conditioner becomes a problem, the agent may be held liable for failing to disclose a material fact if a court rules that the typical agent in that area would detect and recognize a faulty air conditioner.

There is no obligation for a broker to verify the seller's disclosures or statements. However, if the agent knows the seller's disclosures are not true or do not disclose pertinent material facts, it is then the agent's duty to disclose those facts.

There is also no obligation for the agent to obtain or disclose information related to a customer's race, creed, color, religion, sex or national origin. Anti-discrimination laws hold such information to be immaterial to the transaction. Disclosing or even discussing this information could result in the agent and possibly the client being held liable for discrimination.

Stigmatized properties. A stigmatized property is a dwelling where an emotionally upsetting event has become associate with a given property. Such an association may cause buyers to find the house undesirable – even though there is nothing physically wrong with the structure itself.

Events that can stigmatize properties include the following:

> ▸ Murder, suicide, or other death within the home

> ▸ The property became a crime scene where a serious felony occurred

> ▸ Previous residents were afflicted with HIV, AIDS, or other disease not transmitted by occupying the same dwelling

New York State Real Property Law, Section 443-A states that stigmatized properties do not constitute material facts and, therefore, are not required to be disclosed by the seller or the agent. The law also states the buyer may ask in writing for information regarding these events. However, the seller may choose not to respond to the inquiry, and there will be no liability on the seller's agent or the seller's part.

Haunted house disclosure. While the law does not manifestly require that haunted houses must be disclosed as such, the New York Supreme Appellate Division has ruled that the seller was liable for failing to disclose the haunted-house stigma. The agent, however, was not held liable. When in doubt, it is perhaps favorable to go ahead and disclose what facts are known.

Registered sex offenders. Another fact not considered to be material and, therefore, not subject to required disclosure is the presence of registered sex offenders in the neighborhood. Under Megan's Law, federal legislation that requires convicted offenders to register with the state of residence, New York does not require agents to search state records for registered offenders and their addresses. While buyers' agents are also not obligated to disclose sex offenders in the neighborhood, they can and should provide their clients information about the registry's public records.

Exhibit 2.2 Disclosure of Material Facts

Critical material facts for disclosure include:

- the agent's opinion of the property's condition

- information about the buyer's financial qualifications

- discussions between agent and buyer regarding the possibility of the agent's representing the buyer in another transaction

- any relationship between the agent and another party to the transaction

- if the agent for the seller or the buyer has a personal interest in the property

- fee sharing or commission split arrangements with another broker

- adverse material facts, including property condition, title defects, environmental hazards, and property defects

Duties to customer Agents have certain obligations to customers even though they do not represent them. In general, they owe a third party:

- honesty and fair dealing
- reasonable care and skill
- proper disclosure

Exhibit 2.3 Agent's Fiduciary Duties to Customers

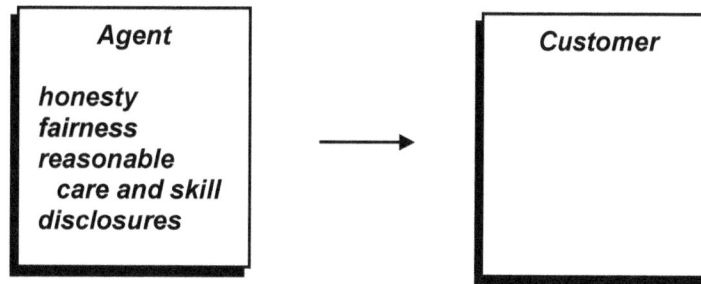

```
┌─────────────────┐              ┌─────────────────┐
│  Agent          │              │  Customer       │
│                 │              │                 │
│  honesty        │              │                 │
│  fairness       │    ──────▶   │                 │
│  reasonable     │              │                 │
│    care and skill│             │                 │
│  disclosures    │              │                 │
└─────────────────┘              └─────────────────┘
```

Honesty and Fairness. An agent has a duty to deal fairly and honestly with a customer. Thus, an agent may not deceive, defraud, or otherwise take advantage of a customer.

Reasonable skill and care. Reasonable care and skill means that an agent will be held to the standards of knowledge, expertise, and ethics that are commonly maintained by other agents in the area.

Disclosures. Proper disclosure primarily concerns disclosure of agency, property condition, environmental hazards, and material facts all of which the agent knows or should know and that may not be easily discovered by the customer.

An agent who fails to live up to prevailing standards may be held liable for negligence, fraud, or violation of state real estate license laws and regulations. Agents should be particularly careful about misrepresenting and offering inappropriate expert advice when working with customers.

Principal's duties   The obligations of a principal in an agency relationship concern *availability, information, and compensation.*

Exhibit 2.4 Principal's Duties to Agent

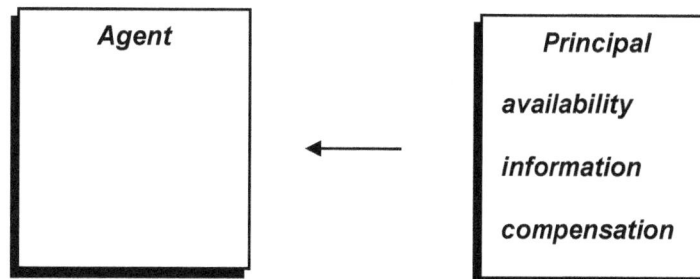

```
┌─────────────────┐              ┌─────────────────┐
│  Agent          │              │  Principal      │
│                 │              │                 │
│                 │              │  availability   │
│                 │    ◀──────   │                 │
│                 │              │  information    │
│                 │              │                 │
│                 │              │  compensation   │
└─────────────────┘              └─────────────────┘
```

Availability. In a special agency, the power and decision-making authority of the agent are limited. Therefore, the principal must be available for consultation, direction, and decision-making. Otherwise, the agent cannot complete the job.

Information. The principal must provide the agent with a sufficient amount of information to complete the desired activity. This may include property data, financial data, and the client's timing requirements.

Compensation. The terms of an agency relationship are outlined in the agency agreement. While listing terms are being negotiated between the agent and the principal, the agent's compensation must also be determined.

Keep in mind an agency relationship does not necessarily result in compensation to the agent. An agency can actually be created and exist even when no compensation, fee, or commission is involved.

Traditionally, the listing agreement provides the terms for how the agent is to be paid. The agent's compensation is typically based on a percentage of funds related to the transaction. For example, a commission paid to a seller's broker is typically approximately 6% of the property sale price. Often times, that commission is split with a cooperating broker, such as the buyer's broker. Brokers may only split their commission with a licensed real estate professional.

However, compensation can also be paid as a flat fee or, as in the case of net listings (illegal in New York), as the difference between the seller's asking price and the actual purchase price.

Before an agent is compensated *by more than one party* to the same transaction, all parties must consent in writing.

To qualify for compensation, the agent must have been a licensed broker throughout the term of the agency agreement, must have an agreement with the client, and must have been the ***procuring cause*** of the sale, i.e., the agent whose actions brought about the final sale as indicated by the sales contract.

If the agent and the client have an agreement that includes compensation and the agent performs in accordance with the agreement, the client is obligated to compensate the agent, regardless of how the compensation is computed.

Also keep in mind that an associate broker or a salesperson may not create the agency agreement/relationship and may not be compensated directly by anyone other than the supervising broker. The supervising broker and the salesperson will have an agreement regarding how the salesperson is to be compensated. Typically, the salesperson who handled the transaction will be paid a percentage of the broker's commission. The exception to this law is if a former supervising broker owes the salesperson compensation for transactions the salesperson handled while associated with the former broker.

Breach of duty

Agents owe fiduciary duties to clients and customers. When they fail to uphold those duties, they have breached their duties. A breach of duty can occur when agents act on their own benefit to the detriment of their clients or customers, when agents fail to disclose material facts and conflicts of interest, when agents hides information, or even gains their own advantage in a transaction.

Following are common examples of an agent's breach of fiduciary duty:

- ▸ receiving compensation without disclosing it to the client

- ▸ failing to inform a seller of every offer

- ▸ not advising a buyer of known material facts regarding the subject property

- ▸ entering into a dual agency relationship without informing and obtaining approval from all parties involved

- ▸ accepting or declining offers without the client's approval

- ▸ violating confidentiality by sharing a client's personal information with a third party

An agent is liable for a breach of duty to client or customer. Since clients and customers rely on the expertise and actions of agents performing within the scope of their authority, a breach of fiduciary duty can result in damage to the client and/or legal action against the agent. Consequently, regulatory agencies and courts aggressively enforce agency laws, standards, and regulations.

A breach of duty may result in:

- ▸ rescission of the listing agreement (causing a loss of a potential commission)

- ▸ forfeiture of any compensation that may have already been earned

- ▸ disciplinary action by state license law authorities, including license suspension or revocation

- ▸ civil suit for damages in court

MISREPRESENTATION

Opinions
Intentional misrepresentation
Negligent misrepresentation
Misrepresentation of expertise

Opinions

Misrepresentation comes from statements that simply are not true, whether they are clear-cut lies or exaggerations. To avoid misrepresenting the facts, agents must be careful not only in what they say, but in how they say it. Presenting indisputable facts about a property or transaction is one thing, but expressing an opinion can be another. For example, an agent may state that the property is located on the banks of a particular river. This is a provable fact. If the agent states the property is located on the banks of the most beautiful river in the country, that is an opinion. If the agent talks about how gorgeous the property's view of the river is, how clean and clear the water is, and how great the river is for swimming, then the agent may be exaggerating. If that same river is publicly known to be dirty with raw sewage and toxic chemicals, the agent is not only exaggerating, but could be found guilty of *misrepresentation*. Consequently, it may be best if an agent expresses facts and not opinions because intentionally leading a buyer to believe something that may not be true is fraud.

Intentional misrepresentation

An agent may intentionally or unintentionally defraud a buyer by misrepresenting or concealing facts. While it is acceptable to promote the features of a property to a buyer or the virtues of a buyer to a seller, it is a fine line that divides promotion from misrepresentation. Silent misrepresentation, which is intentionally failing to reveal a material fact, is just as fraudulent as a false statement. Such an omission is called negligent misrepresentation.

Negligent misrepresentation

An agent can be held liable for failure to disclose facts the agent was not aware of if it can be demonstrated that the agent *should have known* such facts. For example, if it is a common standard that agents inspect property, then an agent can be held liable for failing to disclose a leaky roof that was not inspected.

Misrepresentation of expertise

An agent should not act or speak outside his or her area of expertise. A customer may rely on anything an agent says, and the agent will be held accountable. For example, an agent represents that a property value will appreciate. The buyer interprets this as expert investment advice. Subsequently, if the property does not appreciate, the buyer may hold the agent liable.

TERMINATING AN AGENCY RELATIONSHIP

Full performance of all obligations by the parties terminates an agency relationship. In addition, the parties may terminate the relationship at any time by *mutual agreement*. Thirdly, the agency relationship automatically terminates on the *expiration* date, whether the obligations were performed or not.

Involuntary termination. An agency relationship may terminate contrary to the wishes of the parties for any of the following reasons:

- ▸ death or incapacity of either party

- ▸ condemnation or destruction of the property

- ▸ renunciation by the agent (the agent cancels without the principal agreeing)

- ▸ revocation by the principal (the principal cancels without the agent agreeing; allowed at any time in New York if the principal acts in good faith)

- ▸ breach of the agreement or fiduciary duties

- ▸ bankruptcy of either party

- ▸ revocation of the agent's license

Involuntary termination of the relationship may create legal and financial liability for a party who defaults or cancels. For example, a client may renounce an agreement but then be held liable for the agent's expenses or commission.

FORMS OF REAL ESTATE AGENCY AND ALTERNATIVES

Single Agency
Dual Agency
Cooperative Sales
Subagency
No Agency
No Subagency

The primary forms of agency relationship between brokers and principals are: *single agency and dual agency. Cooperative sales, subagency, no agency, and no subagency* are agency alternatives without written agency agreements.

Exhibit 2.5 Forms of Agency and No Agency in Real Estate Brokerage

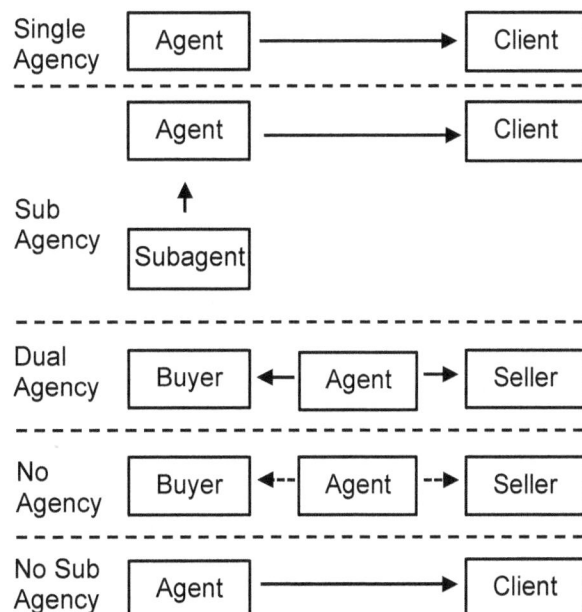

Single agency   In a single agency, the agent represents only one party in a transaction. The client may be either the seller or the buyer. It may also be either the landlord or the tenant.

Seller agency. In the traditional situation, a seller or landlord is the agent's client. A buyer or tenant is the customer. The seller agent's job is to secure a buyer for the seller's property at a price and terms that are acceptable to the seller, all while providing fiduciary duties required of the agent to the client and to the buyer.

Buyer agency. In a buyer agency, the agent represents a buyer or tenant. In this relationship, the property buyer or tenant is the client, and the property owner is the customer. The buyer agent's job is to find an acceptable property for the buyer, negotiate the purchase at a price and terms that are acceptable to the buyer, all while providing fiduciary duties required of the agent to the client and to the seller as the customer.

In real estate terminology, an agent of the seller or owner is called the *listing broker*. An agent who works for the listing broker and who obtained the listing is the *listing agent*. A broker who represents a buyer is the *buyer's broker*. A broker or salesperson who represents tenants is a *tenant representative*.

A broker may choose to practice single agency either as just a seller agency or as just a buyer agency or may choose not to limit the practice to one or the other. However, in a single agency, the broker may only represent one or the other in the same transaction. The broker owes the client fiduciary duties, and the client can be held liable for the agent's actions as related to the transaction.

Dual Agency   Dual agency means representing both principal parties to a transaction. The agent represents both buyer and seller or tenant and owner. For instance, if a salesperson completes a buyer agency agreement with a party on behalf of a broker, and the party then becomes interested in a property listed by the same broker, the broker becomes a dual agent representing the seller in an already existing listing agreement and now the buyer in the new buyer agency agreement. Situations like this are referred to as *in-house sales* because both clients are represented by the same broker within the same brokerage "house." In-house sales such as this create dual agencies. With in-house sales, the broker does not have to split the commission with another broker.

Conflict of Interest. Dual agency is a relationship that is illegal in many states because of its inherent conflict of interest given that many of the agent's fiduciary duties are for the benefit of one client and impossible to render equally to both clients. Take loyalty as an example. It simply is not possible to give both clients undivided loyalty. It's also not possible to place one client's best interests first when there are two clients whose best interests the agent is responsible for.

Dual agency is legal in New York with the caveat that brokers are prohibited from collecting commission or other compensation from both parties in the same transaction unless both parties are informed and provide advanced written consent to the dual relationship and compensation. The dual agency disclosure must be provided to the prospective client prior to entering into a listing agreement or a buyer's agreement. The disclosure must then be provided to the second prospective client at the first substantive contact with that individual.

Both clients are to sign an acknowledgement that they have be given the disclosure form to sign giving consent to the dual agency relationship. The agent is to provide a copy of the signed acknowledgement to each client and is to maintain a copy in the agent's records for at least 3 years. If either party refuses to sign the acknowledgement, the agent is to make a written declaration under oath of the facts regarding the refusal and maintain a copy of the declaration for at least 3 years.

Prior to signing the disclosure form, both clients must be informed of the limitations on the agent's fiduciary duties to each of them.

Without the advanced written disclosure from the agent and consent from both parties, the dual agency is illegal. The agency relationship disclosure form is set forth in Article 12-A of New York Real Property Law, §443. (https://dos.ny.gov/system/files/documents/2023/07/real-estate-license-law_06.2023_0.pdf)

Duties. If both parties accept the dual agency and sign the disclosure form, the agent owes all the fiduciary duties to both parties except full disclosure, undivided loyalty, and exclusive representation of one principal's interests. The duty of confidentiality of each client's information remains intact.

Designated Agent. When a broker enters into a dual agency relationship with a seller and a buyer (or landlord and tenant), it is possible for the broker to designate two agents within the brokerage to represent the two clients, one for the seller and the other for the buyer. These agents are then referred to as designated agents acting as single agents who owe full fiduciary duties to their respective clients. The advance disclosure rules still apply requiring the procurement of written consent from both parties for the designated agency relationship within a dual agency. The same form is used for disclosing dual agency with designated agents as is used for disclosing dual agency.

Undisclosed dual agency. If a broker or agent acts in any way that leads a customer to believe that the agent is representing the customer, a dual agency has potentially been created. For example, a buyer makes confidential disclosures to the agent who works for the seller and exhorts the agent to keep them confidential. The buyer wants the house but knows he is going to lose his job in a month and probably will not qualify for financing. If the agent agrees to keep the information confidential, the agent has not only created an agency relationship with the buyer but has now entered into a dual agency situation. Moreover, if the agent fails to disclose the buyer's confidence to the seller, the agent has violated fiduciary duty to the seller.

Whether the dual agency was intentional, implied, or accidental, the penalties for nondisclosure are the same: potential disiplinary action such as loss of license, loss of compensation, recission of the sale, and/or liability for damages by either party.

Company Dual Agency Policy. A broker's company policy should include discussing in-house sales with salespersons, associate brokers, and clients. The broker should explain how in-house sales can result in dual agencies and what that entails as far as disclosures and consent form are concerned. Then the broker can show how designated agents are one way to handle dual agencies, just as allowing one agent to handle both clients is another way. Preparing salespeople and clients helps in the transition from single agency to dual agency should the situation occur.

Cooperative Sales

When a broker sells a property that has its own listing broker, the two brokers need to establish who has an agency relationship with whom. Is the selling broker acting as the buyer's agent, as the seller's subagent, or as a broker with no agency relationship with any of the parties to the transaction.

It is common practice for brokers and salespersons to cooperate with a listing broker in finding buyers or tenants. A listing broker, in return, agrees to share the commission with a cooperating broker. Multiple listing services (MLS) are a common avenue for brokers to find properties for buyers and then cooperate with the listing agent in bringing the transaction to fruition. It is cooperating brokers who form multiple listing services to facilitate the process of bringing together buyers and sellers. However, it must be determined if the cooperating broker is the seller's subagent or the buyer's agent.

Subagency

In a subagency, a broker is the client's agent – either a seller's agent or a buyer's agent. Any salesperson or associate broker who works as an agent for the broker in the same transaction becomes a subagent of the client. For example, all of a listing broker's salespeople who have agreed to work for the broker to find a buyer are subagents of the listing broker.

Additionally, a cooperating licensed broker and that broker's licensed salespeople may all become subagents of the client when they agree to work for the original broker on behalf of the client.

In effect, a subagent is an agent of the broker who is agent of the client. As such, the subagent owes the same fiduciary duties to the broker/agent as the agent owes to the client. By extension, a subagent owes all the fiduciary duties to the client. The client is also liable for the subagent's actions related to the transaction.

No Agency

In recent years, the brokerage industry has striven to clear up the question of who works for whom, and who owes fiduciary duties to whom. One solution allows a broker to represent *no one* in a transaction. That is, the broker acts as a **transaction broker**, or **facilitator**, and is not an agent of either the buyer or seller. In this relationship, the facilitator does not advocate the interests of either party.

Duties of the transaction broker, or facilitator. In the role of transaction broker, the broker's duties and standards of conduct are to

- account for all money and property received or handled

- exercise reasonable skill and care

- provide honesty and fair dealing

- present all offers in a timely fashion

> ▸ assist the parties in closing the transaction

> ▸ keep the parties fully informed

> ▸ advise the parties to obtain expert advice or counsel

> ▸ disclose to both parties in residential sale transactions all material facts affecting the property's value

> ▸ protect the confidences of both parties in matters that would materially disadvantage one party over the other.

Duties not imposed on the transaction broker. Since there are no fiduciary duties binding the transaction broker, the broker is held to standards for dealing with customers as opposed to clients. These include honesty, fair dealing, and reasonable care. The transaction broker is under no obligation to inspect the property for the benefit of a party or verify the accuracy of statements made by a party.

Currently, transaction brokers are not legal in all states, including New York.

No Subagency

As discussed earlier, agents often look on MLS for properties that meet their clients' needs. When the agent finds an appropriate property and the buyer shows interest in that property, the listing broker and the buyer's broker cooperate to close the transaction. During the process, it is necessary to determine the roles of the agents involved. The listing agent will remain as such. The buyer's agent could remain as such or could become a subagent of the listing agent and seller.

However, there are times when the property is listed on MLS but no subagency is offered. In those cases, if another agent provides a buyer for the property, the listing agent would split the commission with that agent with no subagency established. That second, cooperating agent could operate as the listing agent's agent but not the seller's subagent or could operate as the buyer's agent.

When operating as the listing agent's agent but not the seller's subagent, the agent would be referred to as a ***broker's agent***. A broker's agent is engaged by a listing agent or a buyer's agent but does not work for the same brokerage as either of these two agents. The broker's agent does not have a direct relationship with the client and does not take directions directly from the client. Therefore, the client is not held liable for the broker agent's actions unless the agent was acting on specific directions from the client. However, the broker's agent does take instructions directly from the agent being assisted, thus making that agent liable for the actions of the broker's agent.

ANTITRUST LAWS

Sherman Antitrust Act
Clayton Antitrust Act
Federal Trade Commission Act
Violations
Penalties

Antitrust laws are a collection of federal and state laws that regulate the conduct and organization of businesses. These laws encourage fair competition and benefit consumers by upholding a free market.

Brokerage companies, like other businesses, are subject to the following antitrust laws designed to prevent monopolies and unfair trade practices.

Sherman Antitrust Act

The Sherman Act was the first antitrust law passed in 1890 to prohibit monopolistic business practices. The Act makes it illegal for contracts, agreements, certain forms of mergers, and conspiracies among competitors to unfairly restrict interstate trade by fixing prices, rigging bids, or any other way. An unlawful monopoly is created when one company becomes the only supplier of a product or service by getting rid of competition via secret agreements with other companies. The Sherman Act empowers the federal government to proceed against antitrust violators.

Unfortunately, the Sherman Antitrust Act was nonspecific in its language, leaving much open to interpretation and, thus, allowing businesses to find loopholes that helped them violate the law and engage in unethical practices.

Clayton Antitrust Act

The Clayton Act was enacted in 1914 to strengthen the Sherman Act and give power back to consumers. This law explicitly lists business practices such as acquisitions and mergers that compromise free competition and increase prices to consumers, practices that are deemed as violations of both the Sherman Act and the Clayton Act.

Federal Trade Commission Act

Also created in 1914, the Federal Trade Commission Act (FTC) was established to enforce the Clayton Act and support principles like fair housing. The FTC was given authority to oversee business practices, label certain trade practices as unfair, and enforce business practice compliance with the Sherman Antitrust Act and the Clayton Antitrust Act. While the FTC prohibits unfair competition in interstate commerce, it establishes no criminal penalties.

Violations

The effect of antitrust legislation is to prohibit trade practice and trade restraints that unfairly disadvantage open competition. Business practices and behaviors which violate antitrust laws include collusion and boycotting, price fixing, market allocation, bid rigging, restricting market entry, exclusive dealing, and predatory pricing.

Collusion. Collusion is the illegal practice of two or more businesses joining forces or making joint decisions which have the effect of putting another business at a competitive disadvantage. Businesses may not collude to fix prices, allocate markets, create monopolies, or otherwise interfere with free market operations.

Group boycotting. When two or more brokers agree not to deal with another company, that is a violation of antitrust laws called boycotting. The intent would be to drive the other company out of business to eliminate the competition.

Price fixing. Brokers may legally set their own fee schedule and charge different clients different fees. However, antitrust laws forbid brokers to band together to set a standard price for their services in listing and selling property regardless of market conditions or competitors. In essence, such pricing avoids and disturbs the dynamics of a free, open market. Even being overheard discussing commission rates or being present at such a conversation can lead to charges of price fixing.

For example, the two largest brokerages in a market jointly decide to cut commission rates by 50% in order to draw clients away from competitors. The cut-rate pricing could destroy smaller agencies that lack the staying power of the large companies.

Market allocation. Market allocation is the practice of colluding to restrict competitive activity in portions of a market in exchange for a reciprocal restriction from a competitor: "we won't compete against you here if you won't compete against us there."

For example, Broker A agrees to trade only in single family re-sales, provided that Broker B agrees to focus exclusively on apartment rentals and condominium sales. The net effect is an illegally restricted market where collusion and monopoly supplant market forces.

Tie-in Agreement. A tie-in agreement is when a seller refuses to sell unless the buyer purchases another product or service tied into the transaction. Tie-in agreements manipulate consumers into buying a tied product or service they may not necessarily want.

A tie-in agreement is illegal under the following conditions:

> ▸ If the individual or firm selling the tied products has sufficient economic power in the product

> ▸ If the tie-in sale has actual or probable adverse effects on the competition

> ▸ If the buyer has no choice but to purchase the tied product to acquire the first product

However, not every tie-in arrangement is against the law. If a seller offers a tied product but has no market power over the product, then the seller has not violated federal antitrust law. It's also important to note that bundling products is a perfectly legal business practice. Bundling is when a broker offers the sale of two products together but allows consumers the option to purchase them separately.

The general rule is that tying products raises antitrust questions when it restricts competition without providing benefits to consumers.

The Supreme Court seems to take tie-in agreement violations more seriously than lower courts who are more flexible when it comes to tie-in agreements. Lower courts typically apply the "rule of reason" to each case. Rule of reason is a doctrine created to interpret the Sherman Act and determine the negative effects of the tied sale before ruling.

Penalties

Violations of fair trade and anti-trust laws may be treated as felonies, and penalties can be substantial. They may include the following:

▶ fines for individuals and corporations

▶ possible imprisonment

▶ liability for three times the damages incurred by private parties, plus court costs and attorney fees

Loss of one's license is also a possibility.

The government does not prosecute all agreements between companies but only those that will raise prices for the public or deny the public new and better products. The law does recognize that some cooperative arrangements between firms, such as joint development projects, may help consumers by allowing these firms to compete more effectively against each other.

Enforcement. Federal antitrust laws are enforced in three main ways:

▶ the Antitrust Division of the Department of Justice (DOJ) brings criminal and civil enforcement actions

▶ the FTC brings civil enforcement actions

▶ private parties bring lawsuits claiming damages

To collect evidence, Department of Justice lawyers often work with the Federal Bureau of Investigation (FBI) on court-authorized searches of a business, monitoring phone calls and employing informants equipped with secret listening devices.

State attorneys general may sue under the Clayton Act on behalf of injured consumers in their states, and groups of consumers often bring lawsuits on their own.

Anyone associated with an organization found guilty of an antitrust violation and determined to have had knowledge of that violation may also suffer legal consequences.

TYPES OF LISTINGS

Exclusive right-to-sell
Exclusive right-to-lease
Exclusive agency
Open agency
Net listings
Multiple listing service
Buyer and tenant agency agreements

A broker may represent any principal party of a transaction: seller, landlord, buyer, tenant. An owner listing authorizes a broker to represent an owner or landlord. There are three main types of owner listing agreement: *exclusive right-to-sell (or lease)*; *exclusive agency*; and *open listing*. Another type of listing, rarely used today and illegal in many states, is a *net listing*. The first three forms differ in their statement of conditions under which the broker will be paid. The net listing is a variation on how much the broker will be paid.

General license requirements

The exclusive right-to-sell is the most widely used owner agreement and the one that offers the broker the greatest protection related to collecting a compensation for the broker's marketing efforts. Under the terms of this listing, a seller contracts exclusively with a single broker to procure a buyer or effect a sale transaction. If a buyer is procured during the listing period, the broker is entitled to a commission, *regardless of who is procuring cause*. Thus, if anyone – the owner, another broker – sells the property, the owner must pay the listing broker the contracted commission. This contract must be in writing.

The exclusive right-to-lease is an equivalent contract for a leasing transaction. Under the terms of this listing, the owner or landlord must pay the listing broker a commission regardless of who procures a tenant for the named premises.

Exclusive right-to-lease

The most commonly used leasing contract between a property owner and a broker is an *exclusive right-to-lease* agreement, the equivalent of an exclusive right-to-sell. In this agreement, the property owner contracts with one broker to become the owner's exclusive leasing agent. As with the exclusive right-to-sell agreement, regardless of who procures the tenant, the listing broker is paid the commission.

Exclusive agency

An exclusive agency listing authorizes a single broker to sell the property and earn a commission. However, this listing leaves the owner the right to sell the property without the broker's assistance and without owing the broker a commission for the sale. If the contracted broker or anyone other than the owner is the procuring cause in a completed sale of the property, the commission is owed to the contracted broker. This type of listing may lead to dual marketing efforts for the property's sale in that the broker and the owner may both market the property. This contract must be in writing.

This arrangement may also be used in a leasing transaction: if any party other than the owner procures the tenant, the owner must compensate the listing broker.

Open agency

An open agency listing, or, simply, open, is a *non-exclusive* authorization to sell or lease a property. The owner may allow any number of brokers to market the property with the opportunity to procure a buyer and earn a commission. With an open listing, the broker who is the first to perform under the terms of the listing is the sole party entitled to a commission. If the owner sells the property with no help from any broker, no commission is owed to any of the brokers.

An open listing may seem advantageous to the property seller in that it opens the door for multiple brokers to market and sell the property, but it is not necessarily favorable to the brokers. Open listings offer no assurance of compensation to individual brokers for their marketing efforts. They also open the door for commission disputes.

Open listings may be oral or written and are commonly created by the listing agreement failing to include specific wording to indicate either an exclusive agency or exclusive-right-to-sell agreement.

Net listings

A net listing is one in which an owner sets a minimum acceptable amount to be received from the sale of the property. The owner then allows the broker to sell the property for any price over the minimum amount set. Once the property is sold, the broker keeps the amount received in excess of the owner's required minimum. The amount the broker keeps is considered the commission.

For example, let's say a property seller and broker enter into a net listing agreement. The seller sets a minimum sale price at $350,000. Now let's say the broker sells the property for $380,000. The difference between the seller's minimum price and the actual sale price is $30,000, the amount the broker is allowed to keep as commission.

This may sound like a good deal for brokers, but it is illegal in most states, including New York, for several reasons. First, it creates a conflict of interest for the broker who has a fiduciary duty to put the client's interests above the broker's interests. It also leads to fraud in encouraging the broker to convince the seller to set a lower minimum price, possibly even lower than current market value, so the broker can acquire a larger commission.

Multiple listing service

A multiple listing service (MLS) is an organization of member brokers who agree to cooperate in the sale of properties listed by other brokers in exchange for a share of the broker's resulting commission. The service includes properties and members within a designated geographic area.

The members of the area service agree to post and share information on listed properties in a timely manner so that other members in the organization can participate in the sale of the property as subagents. Rules and obligations for members of an MLS may vary to some extent from local to local, but for the most part, listing brokers are obligated to add their listings to the MLS within a specified time frame. How commission is shared is between listing and selling brokers is also varied by pre-arrangement among member brokers.

A multiple listing service is just that – a service among broker members. It is not a type of listing or a listing contract.

Buyer and tenant agency agreements
A **buyer agency** or **tenant representation agreement** authorizes a broker to represent a buyer or tenant and creates a fiduciary relationship with the buyer or tenant just as seller listings create a fiduciary relationship with the seller. Generally, buyer and tenant representation agreements are subject to the same laws and regulations as those applying to owner listings. A representation agreement may be an exclusive, exclusive agency, or open listing. As with owner listings, the most widely used agreement is the exclusive. In this arrangement, the buyer agrees to only work with the buyer representative in procuring a property.

LISTING AGREEMENT REQUIREMENTS

For exclusive listing agreements, the contract requirements include the following:

- Type of listing (in title), e.g., exclusive right-to-sell

- Names of all legal owners of the property

- Physical address and/or legal description of the property

- Listing price

- Listing execution and expiration dates

- Name and address of listing broker

- Commission rate and terms, as well as conditions under which the listing broker may offer or share the commission with another broker

- Listing authority, i.e., what the broker is allowed to do

- Broker's duties and responsibilities

- List of real property, personal property, and fixtures included in the listing

- Listing termination terms and date

- Extension or protection clause stating that, after the listing expires, the owner is liable for paying the commission to the listing broker if the property sells to a party that the broker procured, unless the seller has since listed the property with another broker.

- ▶ Seller's consent for use of multiple listing service

- ▶ Cooperation with other agents clause, which requires the seller to agree or refuse to cooperate with subagents or buyer agents in selling the property, under what terms, and whether the seller agrees to compensate these parties.

- ▶ Seller's agreement to refer all inquiries to the listing agent and have offers submitted by the listing agent or the selling agent from another brokerage.

- ▶ Fair housing and anti-discrimination affirmation stating the agent and the seller will conduct all affairs in compliance with state and federal fair housing and anti-discrimination laws.

- ▶ Seller's consent or refusal to allow a dual agency in the sale of the property

- ▶ Required broker disclosures, such as the agency disclosure, the broker's personal interest in the property, special compensation being paid to the broker from other parties, etc.

- ▶ Seller's consent or refusal to allow the broker to place a for sale sign on the property

- ▶ Seller's property condition disclosure

- ▶ Provision that seller will deliver a good and marketable title, title insurance, and will convey the property using a general warranty deed to the buyer.

- ▶ Seller's disclosure of required flood insurance

- ▶ Explanation of listing types and the seller's acknowledgement of having received the explanations

- ▶ Signatures by all owners and broker or sales agent.

New York specific requirements:

- ▶ Broker must print the following statements on the back of the listing agreement or attach them to the agreement for a one- to three-family dwelling:

  An exclusive right-to-sell listing means that if you, the property owner, find a buyer for your house or if another broker finds a buyer, you must pay the agreed-upon commission to the present broker.

An exclusive agency listing means that if you, the property owner, find a buyer, you will not have to pay a commission to the broker. However, if another broker finds a buyer, you will owe a commission to both the selling broker and your present broker.

▶ If the broker with an exclusive listing agreement is a member of an MLS, the agreement is to provide the seller with the choice of whether the listing broker or the selling broker submits negotiated offers to purchase to the seller with the buyer's broker in attendance.

LISTING AGREEMENT TERMINATION

A listing agreement may terminate on grounds of any of the following:

▶ *performance*: all parties perform and reach the intended outcome

▶ *infeasibility*: it is not possible to perform under the terms of the agreement

▶ *mutual agreement*: both parties agree to cancel the listing

▶ *revocation*: either party cancels the listing, with or without the right to do so

▶ *abandonment*: the broker does not attempt to perform

▶ *breach*: the terms of the listing are violated

▶ *lapse of time*: the listing expires

▶ *invalidity of contract*: the listing does not meet the criteria for validity

▶ *incapacitation or death of either party*

▶ *involuntary title transfer*: condemnation, bankruptcy, foreclosure

▶ *destruction of the property*

▶ *property use change:* zoning or other changes by outside forces

Listing expiration regulations. The listing generally must specify a termination date and may not have an automatic renewal mechanism. In New York, automatic renewal or extension clauses in exclusive listings are illegal. Extensions or renewals are to be arranged prior to the listing expiration date.

NEW YORK AGENCY DISCLOSURE REQUIREMENTS

Section 443 Disclosure
Signatures Required
Maintaining Records

When brokers and sales associates interact with customers, it is important that the customer knows whose interest the agent is serving. Consequently, agents need to know what disclosures they must make, to whom, and when in the encounter they must make the disclosure.

Section 443
Disclosure

In most states, including New York, real estate license laws require brokers and their licensees to disclose what role they will be taking in a particular transaction and for whom they will be working. New York's Department of State (DOS) Regulation175.7 mandates the following:

A real estate broker shall make it clear for which party he is acting, and he shall not receive compensation from more than one party except with the full knowledge and consent of the broker's client.

Further, New York's Real Property Law Section 443 states that a listing agent must provide the disclosure form set forth in the law to a seller or landlord prior to entering into a listing agreement with either and obtain a signed acknowledgement from the seller or landlord confirming the disclosure was provided.

Additionally, the listing agent must then provide the disclosure form to a buyer, buyer's agent, tenant or tenant's agent at the time of the first substantive contact with the buyer or tenant to ensure the customer knows the agent is in an agency relationship with the seller or landlord. Again, the agent is to obtain the customer's signed acknowledgement of receiving the disclosure. Each agent involved in the transaction must provide an agency disclosure form to customers and prospective clients. Each disclosure form must be signed by the customer to confirm the form was provided.

The disclosure form includes sections for the client to give advance consent, or not, to a dual agency and/or designated sales agent representation. Even though the seller and the customer (buyer, tenant) receive and sign the agency relationship disclosure form giving advanced consent to dual agency, if and when a dual agency is created, both parties in the transaction must sign a dual agency consent form. It is the agent's fiduciary duty to provide the disclosure and consent forms.

The form also includes explanations for each type of agency relationship. The current disclosure form can be found online at Microsoft Word - 1736.doc (ny.gov).

.

Signatures required

In the course of real estate transactions and agency relationships, the law requires the involved parties to sign several disclosures and documents.

> ▸ A **seller** must receive and sign an **agency relationship disclosure** provided by the listing agent.
> ▸ A **buyer** must receive and sign an agency relationship disclosure provided by the buyer's agent.

Both of these disclosures are to be signed when the seller and buyer are entering into agency relationships with the perspective agents.

> ▸ A seller's agent must provide an agency relationship disclosure to any prospective buyer or the buyer's agent and have the individuals sign the form in acknowledgement of receiving the disclosure. This must be done at the first substantive contact with any of these individuals.
> ▸ A buyer's agent must provide an agency relationship disclosure to any seller and seller's agent and receive their signatures in acknowledgement of receiving the disclosure. This must be done at the first substantive contact with the seller or seller's agent.

These disclosures and signatures serve to ensure the recipient of the disclosure form understands that the agent is already in an agency relationship. Failing to provide the disclosure to customers could potentially lead to an unauthorized dual agency should the agent and customer discuss the subject property and exchange confidential information.

The associated law also states the broker is not to receive compensation from more than one party without the full knowledge and consent of the broker's client. Such compensation includes not only commission but any other form of compensation, commission, fees, or payments the broker might receive from any party or act related to the subject transaction.

Maintaining records

Under New York Codes, Rules, and Regulations, Title 19 § 175.23a, licensed real estate brokers are mandated to maintain all paper and electronic records of each real estate transaction in which the broker is involved. These records are to include the seller and buyer's names, the subject property's purchase contract, the amount of the broker's commission, and the listing agreement. The records are to be maintained for at least 3 years.

If the seller, buyer, landlord, tenant, or any associated agent refuses to sign an acknowledgement that the disclosure was provided, the agent who provided the disclosure must document the refusal under oath or affirmation and in writing. The document should include details and reasons for the refusal. The broker is required to maintain a copy of the written declaration for at least 3 years.

SELLER/LANDLORD DISCLOSURES

Property Condition Disclosure Statement
Lead paint
Window guards
Carbon monoxide and smoke detectors
Truth-in-heating law
Bedbug disclosure

Property Condition Disclosure Statement

New York's Real Property Law Section 462 mandates that every seller of residential property who has a valid purchase contract must complete a property condition disclosure statement. The statement must then be delivered to the buyer or the buyer's agent prior to the buyer signing the sales contract. After the disclosure statement has been signed by both seller and buyer, it is to be attached to the purchase contract and maintained with other transaction records.

The law allows the parties to the transaction to enter into their own agreements in regard to the physical condition of the property. One such agreement may be for the property to be sold "as is."

The disclosure requirement applies to residential real property, defined as a one- to four-family dwelling that is used as a home or residence by one or more people or is intended to be used as a home or residence. It does not apply to condominiums, cooperatives, vacant land, or property in an HOA that is not owned by the seller.

Failure of the seller to provide the disclosure prior to the buyer signing the sales contract will result in the buyer receiving a $500 discount on the sale price.

To quote directly from the form itself:
"In the event a seller fails to perform the duty prescribed in this article to deliver a Disclosure Statement prior to the signing by the buyer of a binding contract of sale, the buyer shall receive upon the transfer of title a credit of $500 against the agreed upon purchase price of the residential real property."

The Property Condition Disclosure Statement can be found online at dos-1614-f-property-condition-disclosure-statement_06.2023.pdf (ny.gov).

Exceptions. A property condition disclosure statement is not required when the following residential property transfers occur:

▶ A court ordered property transfer to include in accordance with a will, a writ of execution, by a trustee in bankruptcy, through eminent domain

▶ A transfer by deed in lieu of foreclosure

▶ A transfer to a beneficiary of a deed of trust

- ▸ A foreclosure

- ▸ From one co-owner to another co-owner

- ▸ To a spouse, ex-spouse, or family member

- ▸ To a government entity

- ▸ A transfer by the sheriff

- ▸ A transfer due to a partition action

Lead paint

Lead is typically contained in paint found in homes built before 1978. It can be present in the air, drinking water, food, contaminated soil, deteriorating paint, and dust from the paint. Children are particularly susceptible because young children are known to eat chips of the paint, allowing the lead to enter their bloodstreams.

Consequently, potential buyers and tenants of these homes must be warned of the presence of lead in the paint or other lead-related hazards. The hazard must be disclosed both at the time of the property listing and before the purchase closing or rental lease signing. Home owners and landlords must give buyers and renters the EPA-HUD-US Consumer Product Safety Commission's booklet, "Protect Your Family from Lead in Your Home." A lead-based paint disclosure form must be attached to the tenant's lease. The form can be found online at Free Lead-Based Paint Disclosure Forms | For Sellers & Landlords - PDF – eForms.

New York City landlords must annually inspect the residence for lead hazards and must attach a special form to the lease indicating children under 6 years old are in residence.

Failure to disclose lead-based paint hazards can result in a civil penalty up to $10,000 per violation. [42 U.S. Code § 3545 (f) (2)]

Disclosure of Information on Lead-Based Paint and/or Lead-Based Paint Hazards

Lead Warning Statement

Housing built before 1978 may contain lead-based paint. Lead from paint, paint chips, and dust can pose health hazards if not managed properly. Lead exposure is especially harmful to young children and pregnant women. Before renting pre-1978 housing, lessors must disclose the presence of known lead-based paint and/or lead-based paint hazards in the dwelling. Lessees must also receive a federally approved pamphlet on lead poisoning prevention.

Lessor's Disclosure

(a) Presence of lead-based paint and/or lead-based paint hazards (check (i) or (ii) below):

   (i) ☐ Known lead-based paint and/or lead-based paint hazards are present in the housing (explain).

_____

   (ii) ☐ Lessor has no knowledge of lead-based paint and/or lead-based paint hazards in the housing.

(b) Records and reports available to the lessor (check (i) or (ii) below):

   (i) ☐ Lessor has provided the lessee with all available records and reports pertaining to lead-based paint and/or lead-based paint hazards in the housing (list documents below).

_____

   (ii) ☐ Lessor has no reports or records pertaining to lead-based paint and/or lead-based paint hazards in the housing.

Lessee's Acknowledgment (initial)

(c) _____ Lessee has received copies of all information listed above.

(d) _____ Lessee has received the pamphlet *Protect Your Family from Lead in Your Home.*

Agent's Acknowledgment (initial)

(e) _____ Agent has informed the lessor of the lessor's obligations under 42 U.S.C. 4852d and is aware of his/her responsibility to ensure compliance.

Certification of Accuracy

The following parties have reviewed the information above and certify, to the best of their knowledge, that the information they have provided is true and accurate.

Lessor	Date	Lessor	Date
Lessee	Date	Lessee	Date
Agent	Date	Agent	Date

Window guards   New York City also requires landlords to install window guards on apartments where children under 11 years old reside or when tenants without children request them.

Carbon monoxide and smoke detectors   Sellers of one- to two-family homes, condominiums, and cooperative units are required in New York State to install working carbon monoxide and smoke detectors.

Truth-in-heating law   New York State sellers of one- to two-family homes are required to provide heating and cooling bills for the past 2 years when requested in writing by any prospective buyer. Sellers must also provide information on the amount and type of insulation installed in the home both by the current owner and by previous owners.

Bedbug disclosure   Bed bugs are small insects that feed primarily on human blood. The bugs can enter homes on used furniture, luggage, and clothing and by traveling along connecting pipes and wiring. Bed bug infestations in New York City have become more and more common. If not treated in a timely and thorough manner, bed bugs can spread quickly.

New York City lists bedbugs as a Class B violation, meaning they are considered hazardous. The landlord has 30 days to get rid of the infestation and keep the affected units from getting infested again.

New York State law requires property owners to have bed bug infestations treated promptly and only by pest control professionals licensed by the **New York State Department of Environmental Conservation (DEC)**. Once the property has been treated, the owner needs to make follow-up visits to ensure the bugs have not re-infested.

NYC Housing Maintenance Code requires an owner or managing agent of residential rental property to provide each new tenant a written history of the building's bedbug infestation for the past year.

Owners of residential rental properties are also required to file a Bed Bug Annual Report and then provide the report's filing receipt to each tenant when signing a new lease and at each lease renewal. In lieu of providing the receipt to each tenant, the owner may post the receipt in a prominent location in the building.

Additionally, the property owner must provide each tenant with the official *Preventing and Getting Rid of Bedbugs Safely* guide either by posting it in the building along with the filing receipt or by distributing it directly to each tenant.

2 Law of Agency and Disclosure
Snapshot Review

THE AGENCY RELATIONSHIP

Basic roles	• principal, or client, hires agent (broker) to find a ready, willing, and able customer (buyer, seller, tenant); client-agent fiduciary foundations: trust, confidence, good faith
Types of agency	• universal: represent in business and personal matters; can contract for principal
	• general: represent in business matters; agent can contract for principal
	• special: represent in single business transaction; normally agent cannot contract for principal; the brokerage relationship is usually special agency
Creating an agency relationship	• created by express written or oral agreement or as an implied agreement by actions of either party

FIDUCIARY DUTIES

Duties to client	• skill, care, diligence; loyalty; obedience; confidentiality; disclosure; accounting
Duties to customer	• honesty and fair dealing; exercise of reasonable care and skill; proper disclosures; danger areas: misrepresentation; advising beyond expertise
Principal's duties	• availability; provide information; compensation
Breach of duty	• liabilities: loss of listing, compensation, license; suit for damages

MISREPRESENTATION

Opinions	• statements that may or may not be true; exaggerations
Intentional misrepresentation	• failing to reveal material fact
Negligent misrepresentation	• failing to disclose facts agent should have known
Misrepresentation of expertise	• speaking outside agent's area of expertise

TERMINATING AN AGENCY RELATIONSHIP

	• causes: fulfillment; expiration; mutual agreement; incapacity; abandonment; or destruction of property; renunciation; breach; bankruptcy; revocation of license

FORMS OF REAL ESTATE AGENCY AND ALTERNATIVES

Single agency	• one agent, one party represented: buyer or seller agent
Dual agency	• one agent represents both seller and buyer; potential conflict of interest; illegal in NY unless clients sign disclosure

Cooperative sales	• selling broker cooperates with listing broker
Subagency	• salesperson associated with listing broker are subagents of the broker
No agency	• broker acts as transaction broker and is not agent to either buyer or seller
No subagency	• buyer's agent cooperates with listing agent without becoming subagent
ANTITRUST LAWS	• Sherman Act and Clayton Act pioneered antitrust laws to prohibit unfair trade practices, trade restraints, and monopolies; FTC enforces Clayton Act, oversees business practices, and prohibits unfair competition in interstate commerce with no penalties
Violations	• include collusion and boycotting, price fixing, market allocation, bid rigging, restricting market entry, exclusive dealing, and predatory pricing.
Penalties	• include fines, imprisonment, liability, court costs and fees, loss of license
DUAL AGENCY	• one agent represents both seller and buyer in same transaction; requires signed disclosure; legal in NY
TYPES OF LISTINGS	
Exclusive right-to-sell	• seller contracts with one agent who is paid commission regardless of who sells the property
Exclusive right-to-lease	• same as exclusive right-to-sell except for leasing
Exclusive agency	• contract with one broker who receives commission regardless of who sells, except if owner sells, no commission is owed
Open agency	• non-exclusive allowing any agent to sell and receive commission, except if owner sells, no commission is owed
Net listings	• owner sets minimum sale price; agent sells at any price above minimum and keeps the difference as commission; creates conflict of interest; illegal in NY
Multiple listing service	• organization of brokers cooperating in selling properties
Buyer and tenant agency agreements	• agreements with buyers or tenants to procure property
LISTING AGREEMENT REQUIREMENTS	• type of agreement, names of property owners, address, listing price, expiration date, listing broker name and address, commission rate and terms, broker's duties, appropriate clauses, anti-discrimination statement, parties' signatures, NY requirements, MLS use agreement
LISTING AGREEMENT TERMINATION	• grounds include performance, infeasibility, mutual agreement, revocation, abandonment, breach, lapse of time, contract invalidity, incapacitation or death or either party, involuntary title transfer, property destruction, zoning change
NEW YORK AGENCY DISCLOSURE REQUIREMENTS	• agent's role in transaction; dual agency consent, agency relationships explanation
SELLER/LANDLORD DISCLOSURES	• property condition disclosure; lead disclosure; window guards required; smoke and carbon monoxide detectors required, heating and cooling bills; bedbug disclosure

CHAPTER TWO: LAW OF AGENCY AND DISCLOSURE

Section Quiz

2.1. In an agency relationship, the principal is required to

    a. promote the agent's best interests.
    b. accept the advice of the agent.
    c. provide sufficient information for the agent to complete the agent's tasks.
    d. maintain confidentiality.

2.2. In an agency relationship, the principal is the

    a. customer.
    b. client.
    c. broker.
    d. salesperson.

2.3. The fiduciary in an agency relationship is the

    a. mortgage lender.
    b. agency agreement.
    c. agent's role.
    d. principal.

2.4. A property seller empowers an agent to market and sell a property on his behalf. This is an example of

    a. general agency.
    b. special agency.
    c. universal agency.
    d. no agency.

2.5. A principal empowers an agent to conduct the ongoing activities of one of her business enterprises. This is an example of

    a. limited agency.
    b. general agency.
    c. universal agency.
    d. special agency.

2.6. In which type of agency may the principal not cancel or rescind the relationship?

    a. Special agency
    b. Universal agency
    c. Limited agency
    d. Agency coupled with an interest

2.7. What is the most common agreement used to create an agency relationship between an agent and a property seller?

    a. Listing agreement
    b. Limited agency agreement
    c. Offer
    d. Broker agreement

2.8. Implied agency arises when

    a. an agent accepts an oral listing.
    b. a principal accepts an oral listing.
    c. a party creates an agency relationship outside of an express agreement.
    d. a principal agrees to all terms of a written listing agreement, whether express or implied.

2.9. Within an implied agency, if the seller's agent assists a potential buyer, the agent has created

    a. an unlimited agency relationship.
    b. an undisclosed dual agency.
    c. a universal agency.
    d. a broker's agreement.

2.10. Which of the agent's fiduciary duties remains after the agency relationship has terminated?

    a. Confidentiality
    b. Loyalty
    c. Full disclosure
    d. Obedience

2.11. A principal discloses that she would sell a property for $375,000. During the listing period, the house is marketed for $425,000. No offers come in, and the listing expires. Two weeks later, the agent grumbles to a customer that the seller would have sold for less than the listed price. Which of the following is true?

a. The agent has violated the duty of confidentiality.
b. The agent has fulfilled all fiduciary duties since the listing had expired.
c. The agent is violating the duties owed this customer.
d. The agent has created a dual agency situation with the customer.

2.12. A material fact is

a. information regarding products used in constructing a house.
b. information regarding a potential buyer's finances.
c. information regarding a property that might affect the buyer's decision to purchase the property.
d. information about the agent's role in the transaction.

2.13. Which of the following acts by an agent is illegal?

a. Disclosing a property's latent defects to a potential buyer
b. Disclosing material facts to a potential buyer
c. Disclosing a potential buyer's national origin to the property seller
d. Disclosing the agent/seller relationship to the potential buyer

2.14. A principal instructs an agent to market a property only to families with children. The agent refuses to comply. In this case,

a. the agent has violated fiduciary duty.
b. the agent has not violated fiduciary duty.
c. the agent is liable for breaching the listing terms.
d. the agent should obey the instruction to salvage the listing.

2.15. An agent owes customers several duties. These may be best described as

a. fairness, care, and honesty.
b. obedience, confidentiality, and accounting.
c. diligence, care, and loyalty.
d. honesty, diligence, and skill.

2.16. Which of the following is a material fact which an agent must disclose to a potential buyer?

a. Suicide on the subject property
b. Previous resident with HIV
c. Previous flooding in the basement
d. Presence of registered sex offenders in the neighborhood

2.17. Which of the following is a duty owed to an agent by the principal?

a. Loyalty
b. Confidentiality
c. Obedience
d. Availability

2.18. Which of the following methods of compensating an agent is illegal in New York State?

a. A percentage of funds related to the transaction
b. The difference between the seller's asking price and the actual purchase price
c. Splitting the commission with another licensed real estate broker
d. As a line item on the seller's closing costs

2.19. Silent misrepresentation is a type of

a. opinion.
b. intentional misrepresentation.
c. negligent misrepresentation.
d. misrepresentation of expertise.

2.20. An agency relationship may be involuntarily terminated for which of the following reasons?

a. Death or incapacity of the agent
b. Mutual consent
c. Full performance
d. Renewal of the agent's license

2.21. Which of the following involves a written agency agreement?

a. Subagency
b. No agency
c. Cooperative sales
d. Dual agency

2.22. Under what circumstances are dual agencies illegal in New York State?

a. When one broker represents both parties in the transaction
b. When there is consent from only one party in the transaction
c. When both parties consent but one refuses to sign the disclosure
d. All dual agencies are illegal in New York State.

2.23. When a broker chooses one affiliated agent to represent the seller and a second agent to represent the buyer in the same transaction, these agents are referred to as

a. single agents.
b. dual agents.
c. designated agents.
d. subagents.

2.24. Which of the following are illegal in New York State?

a. Subagency
b. Cooperative sales
c. Tenant representative
d. Transaction broker

2.25. A licensee risks violating antitrust law by

a. being present at a conversation where the setting of commission rates is discussed.
b. being present at a discussion of antitrust laws.
c. charging a commission rate that happens to be the same as that charged by another firm.
d. cooperating with another firm to do market research.

2.26. Two or more businesses who join together to make decisions that result in putting another business at a competitive disadvantage are guilty of

a. collusion.
b. group boycotting.
c. price fixing.
d. market allocation.

2.27. To be valid, a listing agreement

a. must be in writing.
b. may be oral or written.
c. must be an express agreement.
d. must be enforceable.

2.28. The type of listing that assures a broker of compensation for procuring a customer, regardless of the procuring party, is a(n)

a. exclusive right-to sell agreement.
b. exclusive agency agreement.
c. open listing.
d. net listing.

2.29. An owner agrees to pay a broker for procuring a buyer unless it is the owner who finds the buyer. This is an example of a(n)

a. exclusive right-to sell agreement.
b. exclusive agency agreement.
c. open listing.
d. net listing.

2.30. A landlord promises to compensate a broker for procuring a tenant, provided the broker is the procuring cause. This is an example of a(n)

a. exclusive right-to sell agreement.
b. exclusive agency agreement.
c. open listing.
d. net listing.

2.31. A property owner agrees to pay a broker a commission, provided the owner receives a minimum amount of proceeds from the sale at closing. This is an example of a(n)

a. exclusive right-to sell agreement.
b. exclusive agency agreement.
c. open listing.
d. net listing.

2.32. Which listing agreement must be in writing?

   a. Open agency
   b. Exclusive right-to-sell listing
   c. Net listing
   d. All listings must be in writing to be enforceable.

2.33. A "protection period" clause in an exclusive listing provides that

   a. the owner is protected from all liabilities arising from the agent's actions performed within the agent's scope of duties.
   b. the agent has a claim to a commission if the owner sells or leases to a party within a certain time following the listing's expiration.
   c. agents are entitled to extend a listing agreement's term if a transaction is imminent.
   d. an owner is not liable for a commission if a prospective customer delays in completing an acceptable offer.

2.34. Listing agreement requirements exclusive to New York State include

   a. the agreement termination only by mutual consent.
   b. all listing agreements must have an automatic renewal clause.
   c. printing an explanation of exclusive right-to-sell and exclusive agency listings on the back of the listing agreement for a one- to three-family dwelling.
   d. prohibiting brokers from listing properties on MLS sites.

2.35. One of the parties to an agency relationship defaults, and the agreement terminates. Which of the following is true?

   a. All obligations are extinguished.
   b. Both parties must continue to perform all other obligations of the agreement.
   c. The defaulting party may have a financial consequence.
   d. The damaged party has no claim against the defaulting party.

2.36. Among the fiduciary duties imposed on a real estate agent is the requirement to

   a. refuse offers the agent knows will be unacceptable to the principal.
   b. present all offers to the principal regardless of their amount.
   c. advise the principal against accepting an offer that is below full price.
   d. advise a prospect that the principal will not accept the prospect's offer in order to elicit a better offer.

2.37. A subagent is the agent of

   a. the seller.
   b. the buyer.
   c. a broker who has an agency relationship with a client.
   d. the client's and the customer's agents.

2.38. Which of the following is a dual agency situation?

   a. Two agents share the exclusive right to represent the same client on all transactions.
   b. One agent represents both sides in a transaction.
   c. A selling agent from one brokerage works with a listing agent from another brokerage to complete a transaction.
   d. One agent represents two sellers at the same time.

2.39. In which of the following contact situations would a seller's agent be expected to disclose his agency relationships?

   a. The agent is showing the client's property to a prospective buyer.
   b. The agent tells an acquaintance at a party about the client's property.
   c. The agent answers questions about the client's property for a telephone caller responding to a newspaper ad.
   d. The agent is showing a potential buyer houses in a certain price range in the multiple listing book.

2.40. The essential foundation of the agency relationship consists of

   a. mutual respect, compensation, and confidentiality.
   b. diligence, results, and compensation.
   c. service, marketing, and respect.
   d. good faith, trust and confidence.

2.41. From an agent's point of view, the most desirable form of listing agreement is a(n)

a. exclusive agency.
b. exclusive right-to-sell.
c. open listing.
d. net listing.

2.42. What is a multiple listing?

a. A listing shared by a listing agent and a selling agent.
b. A listing that a listing agent delegates to a subagent.
c. A listing that is entered in a multiple listing service to enable cooperation with member brokers.
d. A listing that authorizes a listing agent to market more than one property for a seller.

2.43. Broker Bob and Broker John decided to conduct business in a way they believe will benefit both of them. Bob will work only with clients looking to sell single-family homes while John will narrow his clients down to only those looking to sell condominiums. What have Bob and John actually agreed to?

a. A savvy business deal
b. A situation where they will need to send potential clients to each other
c. An illegal market allocation
d. A tie-in agreement

2.44. Who is responsible for enforcing antitrust laws?

a. Local law enforcement where the violation occurred
b. The Central Intelligence Agency (CIA)
c. The US Supreme Court
d. The Department of Justice

2.45. Which type of agency relationship allows the property owner to engage any number of brokers to market and sell the property, with the procuring broker being the only one who is paid commission?

a. Open agency listing
b. Net listing
c. Exclusive agency
d. Exclusive right-to-sell

2.46. What is a Section 443 Disclosure?

a. A property condition disclosure
b. A lead-based paint disclosure
c. An agency relationship disclosure
d. Bedbug disclosure

2.47. Real estate brokers are required to keep all transaction records for

a. 1 year.
b. not more than 2 years.
c. at least 3 years.
d. 5 years.

2.48. When must a property condition disclosure statement be signed by the buyer?

a. Prior to the buyer submitting an offer
b. Prior to the buyer signing the sales contract
c. Prior to the seller accepting the offer
d. Prior to the seller showing the property

2.49. Which property type requires a property condition disclosure statement?

a. A 4-family dwelling
b. A grocery store
c. An office building
d. A clothing store

2.50. When must the presence of lead-based paint be disclosed?

a. Only when remodeling the dwelling
b. Prior to a rental lease being signed
c. Only when the property is being sold
d. Only when a family with children will be residing in the dwelling

2.51. What is the potential penalty for failing to disclose lead-based paint hazards?

a. Forfeiture of the property
b. Loss of real estate licensure
c. Civil fine up to $10,000
d. Receipt of a disclosure violation letter

2.52. When are window guards required on apartments in New York City?

  a. When remodeling work is taking place inside the apartment
  b. When an adult with a disability resides in the apartment
  c. When a disabled person with a service dog resides in the apartment
  d. When children under 11 years old reside in the apartment

2.53. What is required under the New York State Truth-in-Heating Law?

  a. Smoke detectors must be installed in every condominium being sold.
  b. Heating and cooling bills for the past 2 years are to be provided when requested by prospective buyers of one- to two-family homes.
  c. Co-op purchasers are required to request and pay for heating system installations within the co-op.
  d. Heat provided by heating systems is to be restricted to no higher than 75 degrees Fahrenheit.

2.54. In New York City, landlords are given _____ to rid a residential dwelling of a bedbug infestation.

  a. 10 days
  b. 20 days
  c. 30 days
  d. 45 days

2.55. NYC Housing Maintenance Code requires an owner or managing agent of residential rental property to provide each new tenant a written history of the building's bedbug infestation for the past

  a. 30 days.
  b. 60 days.
  c. 6 months.
  d. year.

3 Estates and Interests

Rights
Freehold Estates
Leasehold Estates
Forms of Ownership
Trusts
Ownership by Business Entities

RIGHTS

Land, real estate, real property
Real vs personal property
Property characteristics
Bundle of rights
Real property rights
Littoral rights
Riparian rights
Dower, curtsey

**Land, real estate,
real property**

A simple definition of real estate is that it is air, water, land, and everything affixed to the land. Real estate in the United States may be owned privately by individuals and private entities or publicly by government entities. Private ownership rights in this country are not absolute. The government can impose taxes and restrictions on private ownership rights, and it can take private property away altogether. In addition, other private parties can exert their rights and interests on one's real property. A bank, for example, can take a property if the owner fails to pay the mortgage. A neighbor can claim the right to walk across one's property whether the owner likes it or not, provided he or she has done so for a certain number of years.

In attempting to define real estate, it is essential to understand *what rights and interests' parties have in a parcel of real estate*. And to understand real estate rights and interests, one must first recognize the distinctions between:

> ▸ land and real estate

> ▸ real estate and property

> ▸ real property and personal property

Land. The legal concept of land encompasses

- the surface area of the earth,

- everything beneath the surface of the earth extending downward to its center,

- all *natural* things permanently attached to the earth,

- the air above the surface of the earth extending outward to infinity.

Land, therefore, includes minerals beneath the earth's surface, water on or below the earth's surface, and the air above the surface. In addition, land includes all plants attached to the ground or in the ground, such as trees and grass. A **parcel**, or **tract**, of land is a portion of land delineated by boundaries.

Land is also used as a term to describe more than the surface of the earth. It is used (along with the term *fee*) to indicate the ownership and rights to the land. The term *estate* is used to indicate the level and type of interest someone owns in the land.

Real estate. Real estate can be defined as the land and any structures attached to the land, whether the structures are natural or man-made. Keep in mind that, since the definition includes land, real estate includes the land's surface and everything below the surface down to the center of the earth as well as above the surface up into space.

Real estate includes, in addition to land, such things as fences, streets, buildings, wells, sewers, sidewalks and piers. Such man-made structures attached to the land are called **improvements**. The phrase "permanently attached" refers primarily to one's intention in attaching the item. Obviously, very few if any manmade structures can be permanently attached to the land in the literal sense. But if a person constructs a house with the intention of creating a permanent dwelling, the house is considered real estate. By contrast, if a camper affixes a tent to the land with the intention of moving it to another camp in a week, the tent would not be considered real estate.

Real property. In addition to all that is included in real estate, real property includes the ownership rights.

Exhibit 3.1 The Legal Concept of Land and Real Estate

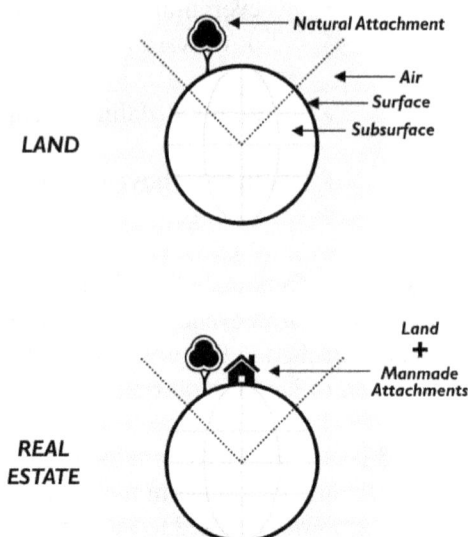

Real vs personal property

Our legal system recognizes two classifications of property: *real property* and *personal property*. The primary criterion for distinguishing real from personal property is whether the item is permanently attached to the land or to structures attached to the land.

Real property is ownership of real estate, and the bundle of rights associated with owning the real estate. This includes the land, and items attached to it, such as buildings, sidewalks, driveways, in-ground pools, trees, and other immovable items.

Note: since all real estate in the United States is owned by some person, private organization, or government entity, all real estate in the country *is* real property.

Real property can become personal property if it is unattached from the land, such as digging up a tree and potting it.

Personal property is ownership of anything which is not real estate. It is also the rights associated with owning the personal property item. Items of personal property are also called **chattels** or **personalty**. Personal property includes items such as clothing, jewelry, appliances, vehicles, boats, furniture, tools, technology devices, stocks, bonds, money, and anything else that is movable.

Just as real property can become personal property, so can personal property become real property by attaching it to the land, such as taking a potted plant, digging a hole, and putting the plant into the hole, thereby attaching it to the land.

Fixtures. A personal property item that has been converted to real property by attachment to real estate is called a fixture. Typical examples are chandeliers, toilets, water pumps, septic tanks, and window shutters.

The owner of real property inherently owns all fixtures belonging to the real property. When the owner sells the real property, the buyer acquires rights to all fixtures. Fixtures not included in the sale must be itemized and excluded in the sale contract.

Trade fixtures, or **chattel fixtures,** are items of a tenant's *personal property* that the tenant has temporarily affixed to a landlord's real property in order to conduct business. Trade fixtures may be detached and removed before or upon surrender of the leased premises. Should the tenant fail to remove a trade fixture, it may become the property of the landlord through *accession*. Thereafter, the fixture is considered real property.

Examples of trade fixtures include a grocer's food freezers, a merchant's clothes racks, a tavern owner's bar, a dairy's milking machines, and a printer's printing press.

Emblements. Growing plants, including agricultural crops, may be either real property or personal property. Plants and crops that grow naturally without requiring anyone's labor or machinery are considered real property.

Plants and crops requiring human intervention and labor are called **emblements**. Emblements, despite their attachment to land, are considered personal property. If an emblement is owned by a tenant farmer, the tenant has the right to the harvested crop whether the tenant's lease is active or expired. If the tenant grew the crop, it is his or her personal property, and the landlord cannot take it.

Factory-built housing consists of dwelling units constructed off-site and transported to and assembled on a building site. The category also includes readily moveable housing of the type that can be relocated from place to place, once known by the term **mobile home.** The National Manufactured Housing Construction and Safety Standards Act of 1976 defined the types of factory-built housing and retired the mobile home designation. **Manufactured housing** is factory-built housing that conforms to HUD standards. Factory-built housing may be considered real property or personal property, depending on whether it is permanently affixed to the ground, and according to state law. Real estate practitioners should understand the local laws before selling any kind of factory-built housing.

Conversion. The classification of an item of property as real or personal is not necessarily fixed. The classification may be changed by the process of conversion. **Severance** is the conversion of real property to personal property by detaching it from the real estate, such as by cutting down a tree, detaching a door from a shed, or removing an antenna from a roof. **Affixing**, or attachment, is the act of converting personal property to real property by attaching it to the real estate, such as by assembling a pile of bricks into a barbecue pit or constructing a boat dock from wood planks.

Property characteristics

Land has three unique physical characteristics: *immobility, indestructibility, and heterogeneity.*

Land is immobile, since a parcel of land cannot be moved from one site to another. In other words, the geographical location of a tract of land is fixed and cannot be changed. One can transport portions of the land such as mined coal, dirt, or cut plants. However, as soon as such elements are detached from the land, they are no longer considered land.

Land is indestructible in the sense that one would have to remove a segment of the planet all the way to the core in order to destroy it. Even then, the portion extending upward to infinity would remain. For the same reason, land is considered to be permanent.

Land is non-homogeneous, since no two parcels of land are exactly the same. Admittedly, two adjacent parcels may be very similar and have the same economic value. However, they are inherently different because each parcel has a unique location.

Bundle of rights

In common understanding, property is something that is owned by someone. From a more technical standpoint, property is not only the item that is owned but also a *set of rights to the item enjoyed by the owner*. These rights are commonly known as the "bundle of rights."

In owning property, one has the right to possess and use it as the law allows. The owner has the right to

- possess the item,

- use the item in a legal manner,

- transfer ownership of the item (sell, rent, donate, assign, or bequeath),

- encumber the item by mortgaging it as collateral for debt, and

- exclude others from use of the item

For example, a car is the property of Bill Brown if Bill Brown owns the car. When Bill Brown bought the car, the car became his property: he owned the car itself. At the same time, he also acquired the legal rights to transfer, trade, use, license, encumber, exclude, and possess the car.

Real property rights

Real property rights consist of the bundle of rights associated with owning a parcel of real estate. Foremost of these rights is the right of possession.

The *right to use* a property refers to the right to use it in certain ways, such as mining, cultivating, landscaping, razing, and building on the property. The right is subject to the limitations of local zoning and the legality of the use. One's right to use may not infringe on the rights of others to use and enjoy their property. For example, an owner may be restricted from constructing a large pond on her property if in fact the pond would pose flooding and drainage hazards to the next-door neighbor.

The *right to transfer* interests in the property includes the right to sell, bequeath, lease, donate, or assign ownership interests. An owner may transfer certain individual rights to the property without transferring total ownership. Also, one may transfer ownership while retaining individual interests. For example, a person may sell mineral rights without selling the right of possession. On the other hand, the owner may convey all rights to the property except the mineral rights.

While all rights are transferrable, the owner can only transfer what the owner in fact possesses. A property seller, for example, cannot sell water rights if there are no water rights attached to the property.

The *right to encumber* the property essentially means the right to mortgage the property as collateral for debt. There may be restrictions to this right, such as a spouse's right to limit the degree to which a homestead may be mortgaged.

The *right to exclude* gives the property owner the legal right to keep others off the property and to prosecute trespassers.

The bundle of real property rights also applies separately to the individual components of real estate: the air, the surface, and the subsurface. An owner can, for example, transfer subsurface rights without transferring air rights. Similarly, an owner can rent air space without encumbering surface or subsurface rights. This might occur in a city where adjoining building owners want to construct a walkway over a third owner's lot. Such owners would have to acquire the air rights for the walkway. If the city wants to construct a subway through the owner's subsurface, the city has to obtain the subsurface rights to do so.

An ordinary lease is a common example of the transfer of a portion of one's bundle of rights. The owner relinquishes the right to possess portions of the surface, perhaps a building, in return for rent. The tenant enjoys the rights to possess and use the building over the term of the lease, after which these rights revert to the landlord. During the lease term, the tenant has no rights to the property's subsurface or airspace other than what the building occupies. Further, the tenant does not enjoy any of the other rights in the bundle of rights: he cannot encumber the property or transfer it. To a limited degree, the tenant may exclude persons from the property, but he may not exclude the legal owner.

Surface rights. Surface rights apply to the real estate contained within the surface boundaries of the parcel. This includes the ground, all natural things affixed to the ground, and all improvements. Surface rights also include water rights.

Air rights. Air rights apply to the space above the surface boundaries of the parcel, as delineated by imaginary vertical lines extended to infinity. Since the advent of aviation, air rights have been curtailed to allow aircraft to fly over one's property, provided the overflights do not interfere with the owner's use and enjoyment of the property. The issue of violation of air rights for the benefit of air transportation is an ongoing battle between airlines, airports, and nearby property owners.

Subsurface rights. Subsurface rights apply to land beneath the surface of the real estate parcel extending from its surface boundaries downward to the center of the earth. Notable subsurface rights are the rights to extract mineral and gas deposits and subsurface water from the water table.

Littoral rights

Littoral rights concern properties abutting bodies of water that are not moving, such as lakes and seas. Owners of properties abutting a navigable, non-moving body of water enjoy the littoral right of use, but do not own the water nor the land beneath the water. Ownership extends to the high-water mark of the body of water.

Exhibit 3.2 Littoral Rights

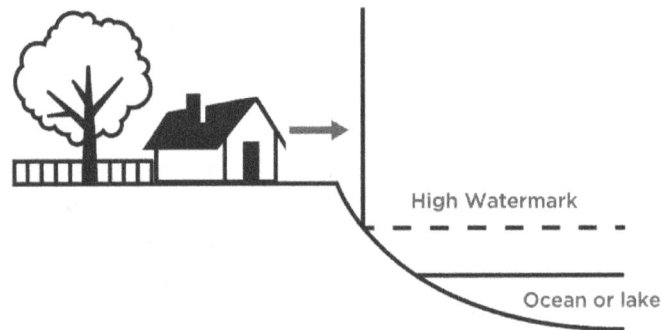

High Watermark

Ocean or lake

Oceans, Seas and Lakes

The legal premise underlying the definition of littoral rights is that a lake or sea is a *navigable body of water, therefore, public property* owned by the state. By contrast, a body of water entirely contained within the boundaries of an owner's property is not navigable. In such a case, the owner would own the water as well as unrestricted rights of usage.

Littoral rights attach to the property. When the property is sold, the littoral rights transfer with the property to the new owner.

Riparian rights

Riparian rights concern properties abutting moving water such as streams and rivers. If a property abuts a stream or river, the owner's riparian rights are determined by whether the water *is navigable or not navigable.* If the property abuts a non-navigable stream, the owner enjoys unrestricted use of the water and *owns the land beneath the stream to the stream's midpoint.* If the waterway in question is navigable, the waterway is considered to be a public easement. In such a case, the owner's property extends *to the water's edge* as opposed to the midpoint of the waterway. The state owns the land beneath the water.

Exhibit 3.3 Riparian Rights

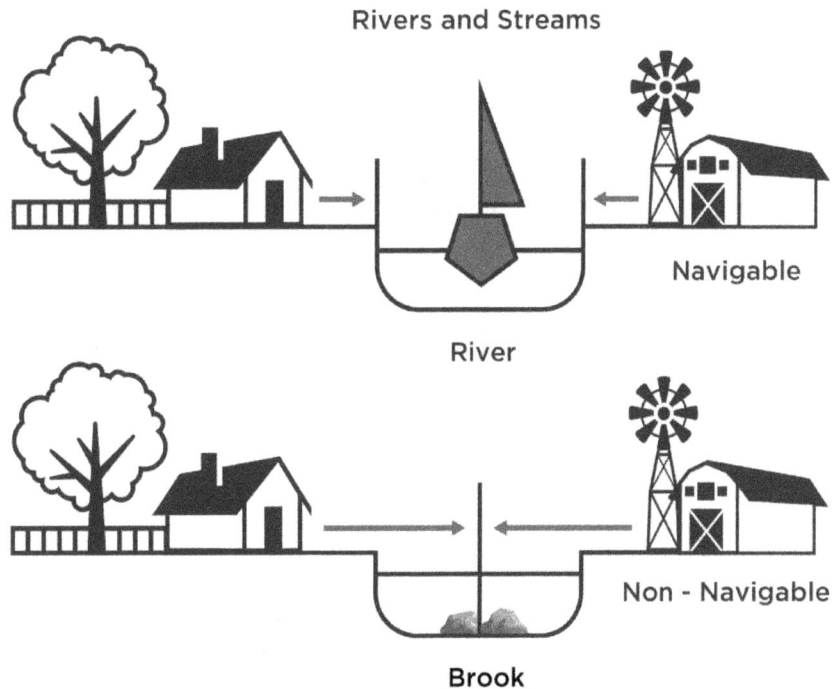

Rivers and Streams

Navigable

River

Non - Navigable

Brook

One's riparian rights to use flowing water are subject to the conditions that:

▶ the usage is reasonable and does not infringe on the riparian rights of other owners downstream

▶ the usage does not pollute the water

▶ the usage does not impede or alter the course of the water flow.

Like littoral rights, riparian rights attach to the property.

Dower, curtsey, community property, and homestead

Dower is a wife's life estate interest in the husband's property. When the husband dies, the wife can make a claim to portions of the decedent's property. Curtesy is the identical right enjoyed by the husband in a deceased wife's property. Property acquired under dower laws is owned by the surviving spouse for the duration of his or her lifetime.

To transfer property within dower and curtesy states, the husband (or wife) must obtain a release of the dower interest from the other spouse in order to convey clear title to another party. If both parties sign the conveyance, the dower right is automatically extinguished.

Dower and curtesy laws have been supplanted in some states by community property laws. Under community property laws, any property obtained during the marriage, except inheritances and gifts, belongs equally to both the husband and the wife.

A homestead estate provides the owner with special rights when the property is used as the family home or primary residence.

New York does not recognize dower, curtesy, or community property. New York recognizes a homestead only as the term used for a home used as the primary residence by the owner occupant. The state does not recognize any special rights of homesteads.

INTERESTS AND ESTATES IN LAND

Interests
Estates in land

Interests

An interest in real estate is *ownership of any combination of the bundle of rights* to real property, including the rights to

- possess
- use
- transfer
- encumber
- exclude

Undivided interest. An undivided interest is an owner's interest in a property in which two or more parties share ownership. The terms "undivided" and "indivisible" signify that the owner's interest is in a fractional part of the entire estate, not in a physical portion of the real property itself. If two co-owners have an undivided equal interest, one owner may not lay claim to the northern half of the property for his or her exclusive use.

Examples of interests include:

- an owner who enjoys the complete bundle of rights

- a tenant who temporarily enjoys the right to use and exclude

- a lender who enjoys the right to encumber the property over the life of a mortgage loan

- ▸ a repairman who encumbers the property when the owner fails to pay for services

- ▸ a buyer who prevents an owner from selling the property to another party under the terms of the sale contract

- ▸ a mining company which temporarily owns the right to extract minerals from the property's subsurface

- ▸ a local municipality which has the right to control how an owner uses the property

- ▸ a utility company which claims access to the property in accordance with an easement

Interests differ according to

- ▸ how long a person may enjoy the interest

- ▸ what portion of the land, air, or subsurface the interest applies to

- ▸ whether the interest is public or private

- ▸ whether the interest includes legal ownership of the property

. Exhibit 3.4 Interests in Real Estate

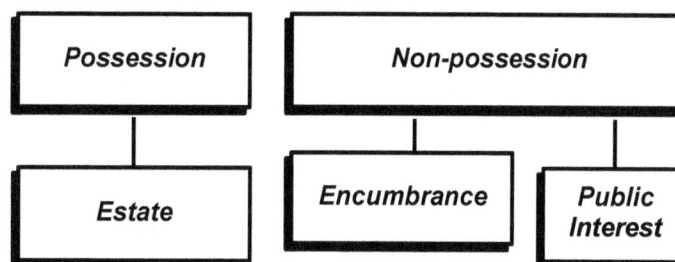

```
┌──────────────┐    ┌──────────────────────────────┐
│  Possession  │    │        Non-possession        │
└──────┬───────┘    └───────┬──────────────┬────────┘
       │                    │              │
┌──────┴───────┐    ┌───────┴──────┐  ┌────┴─────┐
│    Estate    │    │  Encumbrance │  │  Public  │
│              │    │              │  │ Interest │
└──────────────┘    └──────────────┘  └──────────┘
```

Interests are principally distinguished by whether they include possession. If the interest-holder enjoys the right of possession, the party is considered to have an **estate in land**, or, familiarly an estate. If a private interest-holder does not have the right to possess, the interest is an **encumbrance.** If the interest-holder is not private, such as a government entity, and does not have the right to possess, the interest is some form of *public interest.*

An encumbrance enables a non-owning party to restrict the owner's bundle of rights. Tax liens, mortgages, easements, and encroachments are examples.

Public entities may own or lease real estate, in which case they enjoy an estate in land. However, government entities also have non-possessory interests in real estate which act to control land use for the public good within the entity's jurisdiction. The prime example of public interest is **police power**, or the right of the local or county government to **zone**. Another example of public interest is the right to acquire ownership through the power of eminent domain.

Estates in land

An estate in land is an interest that includes the right of possession. Depending on the length of time one may enjoy the right to possess the estate, the relationships of the parties owning the estate, and specific interests held in the estate, decides whether an estate is a freehold or a leasehold estate.

Exhibit 3.5 Estates in Land

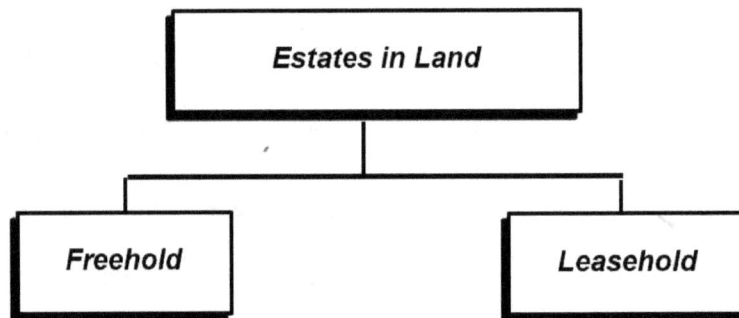

```
          ┌─────────────────────┐
          │   Estates in Land   │
          └──────────┬──────────┘
              ┌───────┴───────┐
    ┌─────────┴──────┐  ┌──────┴─────────┐
    │    Freehold    │  │    Leasehold   │
    └────────────────┘  └────────────────┘
```

In a **freehold estate**, the duration of the owner's rights cannot be determined: the rights may endure for a lifetime, for less than a lifetime, or for generations beyond the owner's lifetime.

A **leasehold estate** is distinguished by its specific duration, as represented by the lease term.

Ownership of a freehold estate is commonly equated with ownership of the property, whereas ownership of a leasehold estate is not so considered because the leaseholder's rights are temporary.

Both leasehold and freehold estates are referred to as **tenancies**. The owner of the freehold estate is the **freehold tenant**, and the renter, or lessee, is the **leasehold tenant**.

FREEHOLD ESTATES

Fee simple estate
Life estate
Conventional life estate
Legal life estate

Freehold estates differ primarily according to the duration of the estate and what happens to the estate when the owner dies. A freehold estate of potentially unlimited duration is a fee simple estate: an estate limited to the life of the owner is a life estate.

Exhibit 3.6 Freehold Estates

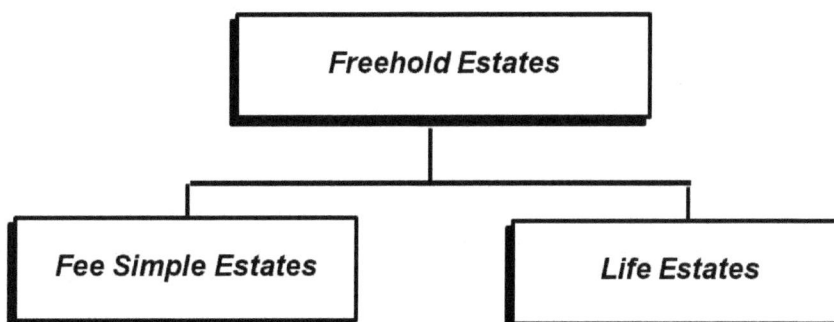

```
          ┌─────────────────────────┐
          │    Freehold Estates     │
          └─────────────────────────┘
                       │
        ┌──────────────┴──────────────┐
┌───────────────────┐        ┌───────────────────┐
│ Fee Simple Estates │        │    Life Estates   │
└───────────────────┘        └───────────────────┘
```

Fee simple estate

The **fee simple** freehold estate is the *highest form of ownership interest* one can acquire in real estate. It includes the complete bundle of rights, and the tenancy is unlimited, with certain exceptions indicated below. The fee simple interest is also called the "fee interest," or simply, the "fee." The owner of the fee simple interest is called the **fee tenant**.

Fee simple estates, like all estates, remain subject to government restrictions and private interests.

There are two forms of fee simple estate: **absolute** and **defeasible**.

Exhibit 3.7 Fee Simple Estates

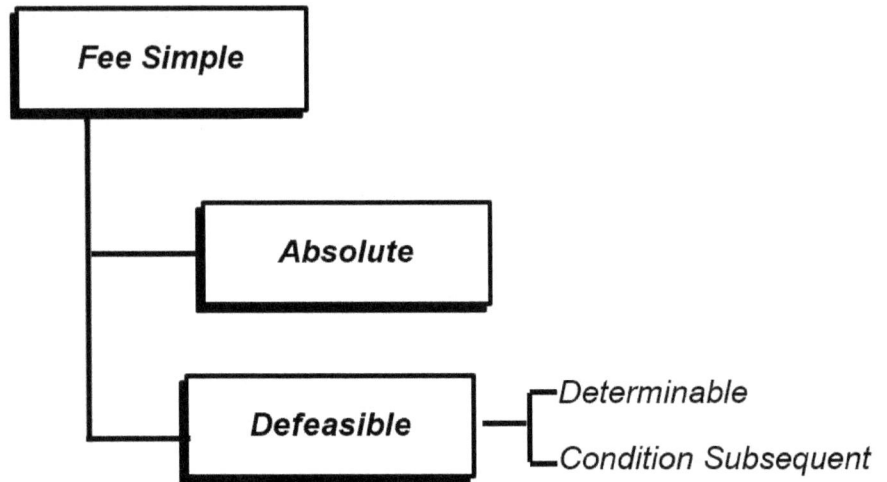

```
┌─────────────────┐
│  Fee Simple     │
└─────────────────┘
        │
        │        ┌─────────────────┐
        ├────────│   Absolute      │
        │        └─────────────────┘
        │
        │        ┌─────────────────┐   ┌─Determinable
        └────────│   Defeasible    │───┤
                 └─────────────────┘   └─Condition Subsequent
```

Fee Simple Absolute. The fee simple absolute estate is a perpetual estate that is *not conditioned by stipulated or restricted uses.* It may also be freely passed on to heirs. For these reasons, the fee simple absolute estate is the most desirable estate that can be obtained in residential real estate. It is also the most common.

Fee Simple Defeasible. The defeasible fee estate is perpetual, provided the usage *conforms to stated conditions.* Essential characteristics are:

▸ the property must be used for a certain purpose or under certain conditions

▸ if the use changes or if prohibited conditions are present, the estate reverts to the previous grantor of the estate.

The two types of fee simple defeasible are **determinable** and **condition subsequent**.

Determinable. The deed to the determinable estate states usage limitations. If the restrictions are violated, the estate automatically reverts to the grantor or heirs.

Condition subsequent. If any condition is violated, the previous owner may repossess the property. However, reversion of the estate is not automatic: the grantor must re-take physical possession within a certain time frame.

Life estate

A life estate is a freehold estate that is limited in duration to the life of the owner or other named person. Upon the death of the owner or other named individual, *the estate passes to the original owner or another named party.* The holder of a life estate is called the **life tenant**.

The distinguishing characteristics of the life estate are:

> ▸ the owner enjoys full ownership rights during the estate period
>
> ▸ holders of the future interest own either a reversionary or a remainder interest
>
> ▸ the estate may be created by agreement between private parties, or it may be created by law under prescribed circumstances.

Remainder. If a life estate names a third party to receive title to the property upon termination of the life estate, the party enjoys a future interest called a remainder interest or a remainder estate. The holder of a remainder interest is called a **remainderman**.

Reversion. If no remainder estate is established, the estate reverts to the original owner or the owner's heirs. In this situation, the original owner retains a reversionary interest or estate.

The two types of life estates are the **conventional** and the **legal** life estate.

Exhibit 3.8 Life Estates

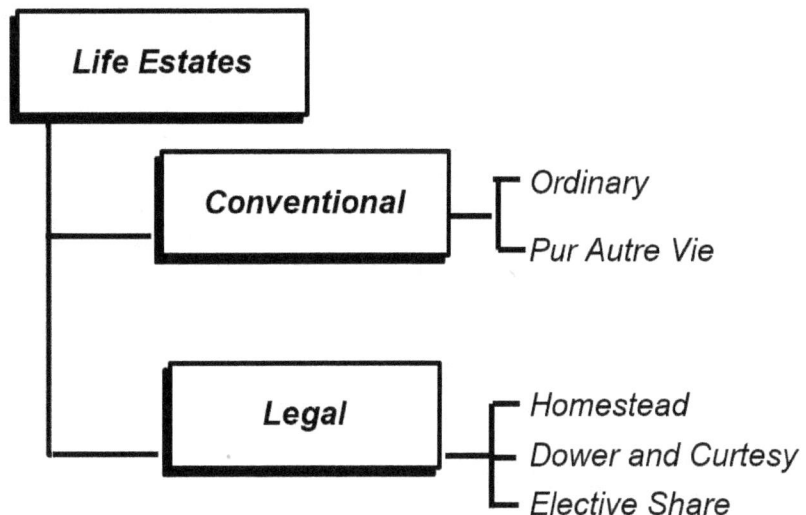

**Conventional
life estate**

A conventional life estate is created by grant from a fee simple property owner to the grantee, the life tenant. Following the termination of the estate, rights pass to a remainderman or revert to the previous owner.

During the life estate period, the owner enjoys all ownership rights, provided he or she does not infringe on the rights of the remainder or reversion interest holders, such as by damaging the property or jeopardizing its value. Should such actions occur, holders of the future interest may take legal action against the property owners.

The two types of conventional life estate are the **ordinary** and the **pur autre vie** life estate.

Exhibit 3.9 Conventional Life Estates

	Ordinary Life Estate	Pur Autre Vie
With reversion	duration: owner's life reverts to grantor	duration: another's life reverts to grantor
With remainder	duration: owner's life reverts to another	duration: another's life reverts to another

Ordinary life estate. An ordinary life estate *ends with the death of the life estate owner* and may pass back to the original owners or their heirs (reversion) or to a named third party (remainder).

For example, John King grants a life estate in a property to Mary Brown, to endure over Mary's lifetime. John establishes that when Mary dies, the property will revert to himself.

Pur autre vie. A pur autre vie life estate endures over the lifetime of a third person, after which the property passes from the tenant holder to the original grantor (reversion) or a third party (remainderman).

For example, Yvonne grants a life estate to Ryan, to endure over the lifetime of Yvonne's husband Steve. Upon Steve's death, Yvonne establishes that her mother, Rose, will receive the property.

Legal life estate

A legal life estate is *created by state law* as opposed to being created by a property owner's agreement. Provisions vary from state to state. The focus of a legal life estate is defining and protecting the property rights of surviving family members upon the death of the husband or wife.

The major forms of legal life estate are the **homestead, dower and curtesy,** and **elective share.**

Homestead. A homestead is one's principal residence. Homestead laws protect family members against losing their homes to general creditors attempting to collect on debts.

Homestead laws generally provide that:

▸ all or portions of one's homestead *are exempt* from a forced sale executed for the collection of general debts (judgment liens). The various states place different limits on this exemption.

▸ tax debts, seller financing debt, debts for home improvement, and mortgage debt are *not exempt*

▸ the family *must occupy* the homestead

▸ the homestead interest *cannot be conveyed by one spouse*; both spouses must sign the deed conveying homestead property

▸ the homestead exemption and restrictions *endure over the life* of the head of the household and pass on to children under legal age. State laws define specifically how the interest transfers upon the death of the household head

▸ homestead interests in a property *are extinguished* if the property is sold or abandoned

▸ in some states the exemption is automatic; in others, homeowners must file for the exemption

LEASEHOLD ESTATES

Estate for years
Estate from period-to-period
Estate at will
Estate at sufferance

A leasehold estate, or **leasehold**, arises from the execution of a lease by a fee owner- the **lessor,** or **landlord**-- to a **lessee,** or **tenant.** Since tenants do not own the fee interest, a leasehold estate is technically an item of personal property for the tenant.

Leasehold tenants are entitled to possess and use the leased premises during the lease term in the manner prescribed in the lease. They also have restricted rights to exclusion.

Estate for years

The estate for years is a leasehold estate for a definite period of time, with a beginning date and an ending date. The estate for years may endure for any length of term. At the end of the term, the estate automatically terminates, without any requirement of notice.

For example, a landlord grants a tenant a three-year lease. After the three years, the leasehold terminates, and the landlord may re-possess the premises, renew the lease, or lease to someone else.

Estate from period-to-period

In an estate from period-to-period, also called a **periodic tenancy**, the tenancy period automatically renews for an indefinite period of time, subject to timely payment of rent. At the end of a tenancy period, if the landlord accepts another regular payment of rent, the leasehold is considered to be renewed for another period.

For example, a two-year lease expires, and the landlord grants a six-month lease that is automatically renewable, provided the monthly rent is received on time. At the end of the six months, the tenant pays, and the landlord accepts another monthly rent payment. The acceptance of the rent automatically extends the leasehold for another six months.

The most common form of periodic tenancy is the month-to-month lease, which may exist without any written agreement.

Either party may terminate a periodic tenancy by giving proper notice to the other party. Proper notice is defined by state law.

Estate at will

The estate at will, also called a **tenancy at will**, has no definite expiration date and hence no "renewal" cycle. The landlord and tenant agree that the tenancy will have no specified termination date, provided rent is paid on time and other lease conditions are met.

For example, a son leases a house to his father and mother "forever," or until they want to move.

The estate at will is terminated by proper notice, or by the death of either party.

Estate at sufferance

In an estate at sufferance, a tenant occupies the premises without consent of the landlord or other legal agreement with the landlord. Usually such an estate involves a tenant who fails to vacate at the expiration of the lease, continuing occupancy without any right to do so.

For example, a tenant violates the provisions of a lease and is evicted. The tenant protests and refuses to leave despite the eviction order.

FORMS OF OWNERSHIP

Tenancy in severalty
Tenancy in common
Joint tenancy
Termination
Tenancy by the entireties

There are numerous ways of holding ownership of a freehold estate according to how many parties share the ownership and how they share it. The primary distinction is between ownership by a single party, and ownership by multiple parties. If more than one person, or a legal entity such as a corporation, owns an estate in land, the estate is held in some form of co-ownership. Co-owners are also called **cotenants**. Various trust structures enable an owner to employ a trustee to hold and manage an estate.

When referring to a property's ownership, the term tenant or tenancy is used to indicate the owner, not someone who is renting or leasing the property.

Tenancy in severalty   If *a single party owns* the fee or life estate, the ownership is a **tenancy in severalty**. This type of ownership is also referred to as **sole ownership**, **ownership in severalty**, or **estate in severalty**. When the property owner dies, the estate of the tenant in severalty passes to heirs as indicated in the owner's will.

When the would-be sole owner is a husband or wife, state laws may require homestead, dower, curtesy, or elective share rights to be released to allow ownership free and clear of any marriage-related claims. However, as discussed earlier, New York does not recognize homestead, dower, curtesy, or elective share rights in property ownership.

Tenancy in common   The tenancy in common, also known as the **estate in common,** is the most common form of co-ownership when the owners are not married. The defining characteristics are:

- two or more owners

- identical rights

- interests individually owned

- electable ownership shares

- no survivorship

- no unity of time

Two or more owners. Any number of people may be co-tenants in a single property.

Identical rights. Co-tenants share an indivisible interest in the estate, i.e., all have equal rights to possess and use the property subject to the rights of the other cotenants. No co-tenant may claim to own any physical portion of the property exclusively. They share what is called undivided possession or unity of possession.

Interests individually owned. All tenants in common have distinct and separable ownership of their respective interests. Co-tenants may sell, encumber, or transfer their interests without obstruction or consent from the other owners. (A co-tenant may not, however, encumber the entire property.)

Electable ownership shares. The share of the estate that each tenant in common will own may be stated in the deed. In the absence of stated ownership shares, each will have a share equal to that of the others.

No survivorship. A deceased co-tenant's estate passes by probate to the decedent's heirs and devisees rather than to the other tenants in common. Any number of heirs can share in the ownership of the willed tenancy.

No unity of time. It is not necessary for tenants in common to acquire their interests at the same time. A new co-tenant may enter into a pre-existing tenancy in common.

Joint tenancy

In a joint tenancy, two or more persons collectively own a property as if they were a single person. Rights and interests are indivisible and equal: each has a shared interest in the whole property which cannot be divided up. Joint tenants may only convey their interests to outside parties as tenant-in-common interests. One cannot convey a joint tenant interest.

The defining characteristics and requirements of joint tenancy are:

- ▶ unity of ownership
- ▶ equal ownership
- ▶ transfer of interest
- ▶ survivorship

Unity of ownership. Whereas tenants in common hold separate titles to their individual interests, joint tenants together hold a single title to the property.

Equal ownership. Joint tenants own equal shares in the property, without exception. If there are four co-tenants, each owns 25% of the property. If there are ten co-tenants, each owns 10%.

Transfer of interest. A joint tenant may transfer his or her interest in the property to an outside party but only as a tenancy in common interest. Whoever acquires the interest co-owns the property as a tenant in common with the other joint tenants. The remaining joint tenants continue to own an undivided interest in the property, less the new cotenant's share.

Survivorship. In New York, joint tenants enjoy rights of survivorship: if a joint tenant dies, all interests and rights pass to the surviving joint tenants free from any claims of creditors or heirs. When only one joint tenant survives, the survivor's interest becomes an estate in severalty, and the joint tenancy is terminated. The estate will be then probated upon the severalty owner's death.

If the property's owners are not married to each other and right of survivorship is not mentioned in the property title documents, the arrangement is assumed to be a tenancy in common with the deceased person's interest passing to their heirs or other persons mentioned in the deceased person's will.

The survivorship feature of joint tenancy presents an advantage to tenancy in common, in that interests pass without probate proceedings. On the other hand, joint tenants relinquish any ability to will their interest to parties outside of the tenancy.

Creation of joint tenancy. To create a joint tenancy, all owners must acquire the property at the same time, use the same deed, acquire equal interests, and share in equal rights of possession. These are referred to as the **four unities**.

1. **Unity of time** – all parties must acquire the joint interest at the same time

2. **Unity of title** – all parties must acquire the property in the same deed of conveyance

3. **Unity of interest** – all parties must receive equal undivided interests

4. **Unity of possession** – all parties must receive the same rights of possession

Termination

Termination of joint tenancies. An owner within a joint tenancy may sell or transfer that owner's shares to someone outside the joint tenancy. The individual obtaining the shares does not become a joint tenant with the other owners. Instead, the individual becomes a tenant in common with the other joint tenants. Thus, the joint tenancy between the existing joint tenants and the new tenant in common has been terminated.

If any of the existing joint tenants dies, those shares are divided equally among the remaining joint tenants. The new tenant in common does not receive any of those shares. If, on the other hand, the new tenant in common dies, those shares are passed on to the tenant in common's heirs.

Termination by partition suit. A partition suit can terminate a joint tenancy or a tenancy in common. Foreclosure and bankruptcy can also terminate these estates. A partition suit is a legal avenue for an owner who wants to dispose of his or her interest against the wishes of other co-owners. The suit petitions the court to divide, or **partition**, the property physically, according to the owner's respective rights and interests. If this is not reasonably feasible, the court may order the property sold, whereupon the interests are liquidated and distributed proportionately.

Tenancy by the entireties

Tenancy by the entireties is a form of ownership reserved for married couples. It features survivorship, equal interests, and limited exposure to foreclosure. Unless the couple specifies differently, the tenancy is automatically created by default when the married couple purchases real estate.

Survivorship. The right of survivorship exists for property held as tenants by the entirety. Thus, on the death of one spouse, the decedent's interest passes automatically to the other spouse.

Equal, undivided interest. Each spouse owns the estate as if there were only one owner. Fractional interests cannot be transferred to outside parties. The entire interest may be conveyed but only with the consent and signatures of both parties.

No foreclosure for individual debts. The estate is subject to foreclosure only for jointly incurred debts.

Termination. The estate may be terminated by divorce, death, mutual agreement, and judgments for joint debt.

TRUSTS

Living trust
Land trust

In an estate in trust, a fee owner-- the **grantor** or **trustor**-- transfers legal title to a fiduciary-- the **trustee**-- who holds and manages the estate for the benefit of another party, the **beneficiary**. The trust may be created by a deed, will, or trust agreement.

The trustee has fiduciary duties to the trustor and the beneficiary to maintain the condition and value of the property. The specific responsibilities and authorities are set forth in the trust agreement.

Living trust

A living trust allows the trustor, during his or her lifetime, to convey title to a trustee for the benefit of a third party. The trustor charges the trustee with all necessary responsibilities for managing the property, protecting its value, and securing whatever income it may produce. The trustee may also be ordered to sell the property at a given point. The beneficiary receives all income and sales proceeds, net of the trustee's fees.

Testamentary trust. A testamentary trust is structurally and mechanically the same as a living trust, except that it takes effect only when the trustor dies. Provisions of the decedents will establish the trust.

Living and testamentary trusts may involve personal property as well as real property.

Land trust

A land trust allows the trustor to convey the fee estate to the trustee and *to name himself or herself the beneficiary*. The land trust applies only to real property, not to personal property. The agreement, or **deed in trust**, grants the beneficiary the rights to possess and use the property, and to exercise control over the actions of the trustee.

Conventional trust structure. The trustee holds legal title and has conventional fiduciary duties. The trustor must be a living person, but the beneficiary may be a corporation.

The distinguishing features of the land trust are:

> ▶ **beneficiary controls property** – includes occupancy and control of rents and sale proceeds

> ▶ **beneficiary controls trustee** – the trustee is empowered to sell or encumber the property, but generally only with the beneficiary's approval

> ▶ **beneficiary identity not on record** – public records do not identify the beneficiary; the beneficiary owns and enjoys the property in secrecy

> ▶ **limited term** – the term of the land trust is limited and must be renewed or else the trustee is obligated to sell the property and distribute the proceeds

Beneficial interest. The beneficiary's interest in a land trust is *personal property*, not real property. This distinction offers certain advantages in transferring, encumbering, and probating the beneficiary's interest:

> ▸ **transferring** – the beneficiary may transfer the interest by assignment instead of by deed

> ▸ **encumbering** – the beneficiary may pledge the property as security for debt by collateral assignment rather than by recorded mortgage

> ▸ **probating** – the property interests are probated in the state where the beneficiary resided at the time of death rather than the state where the property is located

---

OWNERSHIP BY BUSINESS ENTITIES

Corporation
Tenancy in partnership
Limited lability company

Corporation

A corporation is a legal entity owned by stockholders. An elected board of directors oversees the business. Officers and managers conduct day-to-day activities. Officers and directors may be held fully liable for the corporation's actions, while shareholders are liable only to the extent of the value of their shares. Corporations, like individuals, may own real estate in severalty or as tenants in common.

Tenancy in partnership

Tenancy in partnership is a form of ownership held by business partners, as provided by the **Uniform Partnership Act**. The partnership tenancy grants equal rights to all partners, but the property must be used in connection with the partnership's business. Individual rights are not assignable.

In a partnership, two or more persons agree to work together and share profits. A general partnership is not a distinct legal entity like a corporation. All the partners bear full liability for debts and obligations. A limited partnership has two or more partners, one or more being general partners and the others limited partners. The general partners run the business and are liable for debts and obligations. The limited partners are liable only to the extent of their investment in the partnership. Both general and limited partnerships may own real estate.

Limited liability company

A limited liability company (LLC) combines features of the corporation and the limited partnership. The LLC offers its members limited liability like a corporation, but income is passed directly to the members and is taxed to them as individual income. The management structure is flexible. Like a corporation or a partnership, an LLC may own real estate.

3 Estates and Interests
Snapshot Review

RIGHTS

Land, Real Estate, Real Property

- *Land:* surface, all **natural things** attached to it, subsurface, and air above the surface.
- *Real estate:* land + **manmade** permanent attachments
- *Real property* real estate + bundle of rights

Real vs personal property

- *Real property*: land, fixtures, attachments
- *Personal property:* chattels, trade fixtures, emblements
- *Difference criteria*: based on why and how item is attached to real estate
- *Fixtures:* attached to real estate
- *Difference criteria*: based on why and how item is attached to real estate
- *Personal property:* chattels, trade fixtures, emblements
- *Difference criteria*: based on why and how item is attached to real estate

Property characteristics

- *immobility:* land cannot be moved from one site to another
- *indestructibility:* land is permanent and cannot be destroyed
- *non-homogeneity:* no two parcels are exactly alike; each has a unique location

Bundle of rights

- set of rights to the property enjoyed by the owner
- owner has right to possess the item, use the item in a legal manner; transfer ownership; encumber; and exclude others from using the item

Real property rights

- includes bundle of rights
- surface rights of real estate; air rights of the space above the surface; subsurface rights of the land beneath the surface of real estate parcel

Littoral rights

- rights pertaining to use of properties abutting non-moving bodies of water
- property owner does not own the water or the land beneath the water; ownership extends to high-water mark of the body of water
- littoral rights transfer with property when it is sold

Riparian rights

- rights pertaining to use of properties abutting moving bodies of water
- if water is non-navigable, owner has unrestricted use of water and owns the land beneath the water to the stream's midpoint
- if water is navigable, property ownership extends to the water's edge; state owns land beneath the water

Dower, curtsey, community property, and homestead

- dower and curtesy allows spouse to claim portions of deceased spouse's property
- community property means any property obtained during the marriage belongs to both spouses
- homestead estate provides owner with special rights when property is family's primary residence
- New York does not recognize dower, curtesy, or community property; does not recognize special rights of homestead

INTERESTS AND ESTATES IN LAND

Interests
- ownership of any combination of the bundle of rights to real property
- *undivided interest:* owner's interest in property shared by two or more owners; fraction of entire estate, not physical portion of the real estate
- interests based on how long the interest may be enjoyed, what portion of the estate the interest applies to; whether the interest is public or private, whether the interest includes legal ownership of the property

Estates in land
- includes right of possession
- *freehold estate* allows rights to endure for indeterminable length of time; equated with ownership of property
- *leasehold estate* allows rights to endure for specific duration determined by the lease term; leaseholder's rights are temporary, so no ownership is considered

FREEHOLD ESTATES

Fee simple estate
- freehold estate of potentially unlimited duration
- highest form of real estate ownership interest
- *fee simple absolute:* not conditioned by stipulated or restricted uses; can be freely passed to heirs; most desirable real estate interest
- *fee simple defeasible:* perpetual with stated conditions
- *determinable fee simple:* states usage limitations
- *condition subsequent fee simple:* previous owner may repossess the property within certain time frame if any condition is violated

Life estate
- freehold estate limited in duration to life of owner or other named person; when owner dies, estate passes to original owner or another named party
- full ownership rights during estate period; future interest holders own reversionary or remainder interest
- *remainder:* third party receives title to property when life estate terminates and enjoys future interest
- *reversion:* with no remainder estate established, estate reverts to original owner

Conventional life estate
- *limited* to lifetime of life tenant/ named party
- *ordinary*: estate passes to remainderman or previous owner when life tenant dies
- *pur autre vie*: limited to lifetime of another, passes to remainderman or previous owner

Legal life estate
- created by operation of state law as opposed to a property owner's agreement
- designed to protect family survivors
- *Homestead*: rights to one's *principal residence*
  - laws protect homestead from creditors
  - family must occupy the homestead
  - cannot be conveyed by one spouse
  - endures over life of head of household
  - interests extinguished if property destroyed

LEASEHOLD ESTATES

Estate for years
- specific, *stated duration*, per lease; expires at end of term

Estate from period-to-period
- lease term *renews automatically* upon acceptance of rent; renews indefinitely if landlord accepts rent

Estate at will
- specific, *stated duration*, per lease; expires at end of term

Estate at sufferance
- tenancy *against landlord's will* and without an agreement

FORMS OF OWNERSHIP

Tenancy in severalty
- *sole* ownership of a freehold estate; passes to heirs

Tenancy in common
- co-tenants individually own undivided interests
- *any ownership share possible*
- no survivorship
- can convey to outside parties

Joint tenancy
- equal undivided interest jointly owned
- survivorship (may require express provision)
- requires *four unities* to create: time, title, interest, possession

Termination
- owner in joint tenancy may sell or transfer shares; receiver of shares becomes tenant in common, not joint tenant
- *termination by partition suit:* suit petitions court to physically divide the property; used when an owner wants to dispose of interest against wishes of other owners; court can also order property to be sold with interests distributed proportionately
- NY Insurance law requires deductible disclosure

Tenancy by the entireties
- spouses own undivided equal interest
- *survivorship:* deceased spouse's interest passes automatically to other spouse
- *equal, undivided interest:* each spouse owns estate as though there is only one owner
- *no foreclosure for individual debts:* foreclosure only for jointly incurred debts
- *termination* by divorce, death, mutual agreement, and judgments for joint debt

TRUSTS
- *trustor* gives title, deed, trust agreement to trustee
- *trustee* renders fiduciary duties to trustor and beneficiary
- *beneficiary* receives ownership benefits

Living trust
- conveyance of real, personal property during one's lifetime

Land trust
- grantor and beneficiary are same party; beneficiary uses, controls property but does not appear on public records

OWNERSHIP BY BUSINESS ENTITIES

Corporation
- legal entity owned by stockholders with elected board of directors
- may own real estate in severalty or as tenants in common

Tenancy in partnership
- ownership held by business partners with equal rights to all partners and property to be used only related to business
- not a distinct legal entity
- partners bear liability for debts and obligations and share profits

Limited liability company
- offers limited liability to members like a corporation but passes income directly to members and taxes income to members as individual income
- may own real estate

CHAPTER THREE: ESTATES & INTERESTS

Section Quiz

3.1. What guarantees the right of private ownership of real estate in the United States?

    a. Common law
    b. Local statutes
    c. The Napoleonic Code
    d. The Constitution

3.2. Which of the following is the best definition of real estate?

    a. Land and personal property
    b. Unimproved land
    c. Land and everything permanently attached to it
    d. An ownership interest in land and improvements

3.3. Which of the following is included in the legal concept of land?

    a. The surface of the earth and all natural things permanently attached to the earth
    b. Only the surface of the earth that is delineated by boundaries
    c. The surface of the earth except for lakes and streams
    d. Everything above, on and below the surface of the earth

3.4. What are the three unique physical characteristics of land?

    a. Fixed, unchangeable, homogeneous
    b. Immobile, indestructible, heterogeneous
    c. Three-dimensional, buildable, marketable
    d. Natural, measurable, inorganic

3.5. The primary distinction between the legal concepts of land and real estate is that

    a. real estate includes air above the surface and minerals below the surface.
    b. real estate is indestructible.
    c. land has no defined boundaries.
    d. land does not include man-made structures.

3.6. The primary distinction between the legal concepts of real estate and real property is that

    a. real property includes ownership of a bundle of rights.
    b. real property includes improvements.
    c. real property is physical, not abstract.
    d. real estate can be owned.

3.7. Which of the following is included in the bundle of rights inherent in ownership?

    a. To inherit
    b. To tax
    c. To transfer
    d. To vote

3.8. Which of the following is an example of intangible property?

    a. Real estate
    b. Personal property
    c. Artwork
    d. Stock

3.9. The right to use real property is limited by

    a. the right of others to use and enjoy their property.
    b. the police.
    c. taxation and subordination.
    d. Title 12 of the U.S. Civil Code.

3.10. Surface rights, air rights, and subsurface rights are

    a. inviolable.
    b. unrelated.
    c. separable.
    d. not transferrable.

3.11. Which of the following terms refers to the rights of a property owner whose property abuts a stream or river?

    a. Allodial
    b. Alluvial
    c. Littoral
    d. Riparian

3.12. What part of a non-navigable waterway does the owner of an abutting property own?

   a. To the low-water mark
   b. To the middle of the waterway
   c. To the high-water mark
   d. None

3.13. Which of the following are recognized in New York State?

   a. Homestead for a primary residence
   b. Dower
   c. Curtesy
   d. Community property

3.14. Which of the following is considered real property?

   a. A tree growing on a parcel of land
   b. A tree that has been cut down and is lying on a parcel of land
   c. A tractor used to mow grass on a parcel of land
   d. A prefabricated shed not yet assembled on a parcel of land

3.15. The overriding test of whether an item is a fixture or personal property is

   a. how long it has been attached to the real property.
   b. its definition as one or the other in a sale or lease contract.
   c. how essential it is to the functioning of the property.
   d. how it was treated in previous transactions.

3.16. What is an emblement?

   a. A piece of equipment affixed to the earth
   b. A limited right to use personal property
   c. A sign indicating a property boundary
   d. A plant or crop that is considered personal property

3.17. An item can be converted from real to personal property and vice versa by means of which processes?

   a. Assemblage and plottage
   b. Application and dissolution
   c. Affixing and severance
   d. Personalty and severalty

3.18. What is an undivided interest in a property?

   a. The physical section of land owned by one party.
   b. The entire plot of land owned by one party
   c. The fractional part of the entire estate owned by one of the property's owners.
   d. The entire property owned by two or more parties who do not divide ownership.

3.19. What is a freehold tenant?

   a. A tenant who pays no rent
   b. The owner of a leasehold estate
   c. The owner of a freehold estate
   d. A tenant in a leasehold estate

3.20. Which of the following estates are the two freehold estates?

   a. Fee simple and defeasible
   b. Absolute and defeasible
   c. Life and absolute
   d. Life and fee simple

3.21. What are the two types of life estates?

   a. Conventional and legal
   b. Legal and homestead
   c. Dower and curtesy
   d. Ordinary and pur autre vie

3.22. A leasehold estate for a definite period of time with a beginning and ending date is an

   a. estate from period-to-period.
   b. estate for years.
   c. estate at will.
   d. estate at sufferance.

3.23. Which is the most common form of co-ownership when the owners are not married?

   a. Tenancy in severalty
   b. Tenancy in common
   c. Joint tenancy
   d. Tenancy by the entireties

3.24. Which of the following is a distinguishing feature of a land trust?

   a. The trustee controls beneficiary.
   b. The beneficiary's identity is part of the public records.
   c. The beneficiary controls the property.
   d. The term of the land trust is unlimited with no renewals necessary.

3.25. Which type of business is owned by stockholders?

    a. Corporation
    b. Partnership
    c. Tenancy in Partnership
    d. Proprietorship

4 Liens and Easements

Liens
Deed Restrictions
Easements
Encroachments

LIENS

Lien defined
Features
Lien types
Lien priority
Superior liens
Junior liens

Lien defined

A lien is a creditor's **claim** against personal or real property as security for a debt of the property owner. If the owner defaults, the lien gives the creditor the right to force the sale of the property to satisfy the debt.

For example, a homeowner borrows $5,000 to pay for a new roof. The lender funds the loan in exchange for the borrower's promissory note to repay the loan. At the same time, the lender places a lien on the property for $5,000 as security for the debt. If the borrower defaults, the lien allows the lender to force the sale of the house to satisfy the debt.

The example illustrates that a lien is an encumbrance that restricts free and clear ownership by securing the liened property as **collateral** for a debt. If the owner sells the property, the lienholder is entitled to that portion of the sales proceeds needed to pay off the debt. In addition, a defaulting owner may lose ownership altogether if the creditor forecloses.

In addition to restricting the owner's bundle of rights, a recorded lien effectively reduces the owner's equity in the property to the extent of the lien amount.

The creditor who places a lien on a property is called the **lienor**, and the debtor who owns the property is the **lienee**.

Features

Liens have the following legal features:

> ▶   **A lien does not convey ownership, with one exception**

A lienor generally has an equitable interest in the property, but not legal ownership. The exception is a **mortgage lien** on a property in a title-theory state. In these states, the mortgage transaction conveys legal title to the lender, who holds it until the mortgage obligations are satisfied. During the mortgage loan period, the borrower has equitable title to the property. Since New York is a lien theory state, this exception does not apply.

▸ **A lien attaches to the property**

If the property is transferred, the *new owner acquires the lien securing the payment of the debt.* In addition, the creditor may take foreclosure action against the new owner for satisfaction of the debt.

▸ **A property may be subject to multiple liens**

There may be numerous liens against a particular property. The more liens there are recorded against property, the less secure the collateral is for a creditor, since the total value of all liens may approach or exceed the total value of the property.

▸ **A lien terminates on payment of the debt and recording of documents**

Payment of the debt and recording of the appropriate satisfaction documents ordinarily terminate a lien. If a default occurs, a suit for judgment or foreclosure enforces the lien. These actions force the sale of the property

Lien types

Liens may be voluntary or involuntary, general or specific, and superior or inferior.

Voluntary and involuntary. A property owner may create a **voluntary** lien to borrow money or some other asset secured by a mortgage. An **involuntary** lien is one that a legal process places against a property regardless of the owner's desires.

If statutory law imposes an involuntary lien, the lien is a **statutory lien**. A real estate tax lien is a common example. If court action imposes an involuntary lien, the lien is an **equitable lien**. An example is a judgment lien placed on a property as security for a money judgment.

General and specific. A **general** lien is one *placed against any and all real and personal property* owned by a particular debtor. An example is an inheritance tax lien placed against all property owned by the heir. **A specific** lien *attaches to a single item* of real or personal property and does not affect other property owned by the debtor. A conventional mortgage lien is an example, where the property is the only asset attached by the lien.

Superior and inferior lien. The category of superior, or **senior**, liens ranks above the category of inferior, or **junior**, liens, meaning that superior liens receive first payment from the proceeds of a foreclosure. The superior category includes liens for real estate tax, special assessments, and inheritance tax. Other liens, including income tax liens, are inferior.

Lien priority

Within the superior and inferior categories, a ranking of lien priority determines the order of the liens' claims on the security underlying the debt. The highest ranking lien is first to receive proceeds from the foreclosed and liquidated security. The lien with lowest priority is last in line. The owner receives any sale proceeds that remain after all lienors receive their due.

Lien priority is of paramount concern to the creditor, since it establishes the level of risk in recovering loaned assets in the event of default.

Establishment of priority. Two factors primarily determine lien priority:

▸ the lien's categorization as superior or junior

▸ the date of recordation of the lien

Exhibit 4.1 Priority of Real Estate Liens

Superior liens in rank order
1. Real estate tax liens 2. Special assessment liens 3. Federal estate tax liens 4. State inheritance tax liens

Junior liens: priority by date of recording
Federal income tax liens State corporate income tax liens State intangible tax liens Judgment liens Mortgage liens Vendor's liens Mechanic's liens (priority by date work was performed)

All superior liens take precedence over all junior liens regardless of recording date, since they are considered to be matters of public record not requiring further constructive notice. Thus, a real estate tax lien (senior) recorded on June 15 has priority over an income tax lien (junior) recorded on June 1.

A junior lien is automatically inferior, or **subordinate**, to a superior lien. Among junior liens, date of recording determines priority. The rule is: *the earlier the recording date of the lien, the higher its priority*. For example, if a judgment lien is recorded against a property on Friday, and a mortgage lien is recorded on the following Tuesday, the judgment lien has priority and must be satisfied in a foreclosure ahead of the mortgage lien.

The mechanic's lien is an exception to the recording rule. Its priority dates from the point in time when the work commenced or ended, as state law determines, rather than from when it was recorded.

The following example illustrates how lien priority works in paying off secured debts. A homeowner is foreclosed on a second mortgage taken out in 2018 for $25,000. The first mortgage, taken in 2016, has a balance of $150,000. Unpaid real estate taxes for the current year are $1,000. There is a $3,000 mechanic's lien on the property for work performed in 2017. The home sells for $183,000.

The proceeds are distributed in the following order:

1. $1,000 real estate taxes
2. $150,000 first mortgage
3. $3,000 mechanic's lien
4. $25,000 second mortgage
5. $4,000 balance to the homeowner

Note the risky position of the second mortgage holder: the property had to sell for at least $179,000 for the lender to recover the $25,000.

Subordination. A lienor can change the priority of a junior lien by voluntarily agreeing to subordinate, or lower, the lien's position in the hierarchy. This change is often necessary when working with a mortgage lender who will not originate a mortgage loan unless it is senior to all other junior liens on the property. The lender may require the borrower to obtain agreements from other lien holders to subordinate their liens to the new mortgage.

For example, interest rates fall from 8% to 6.5% on first mortgages for principal residences. A homeowner wants to refinance her mortgage, but she also has a separate home-equity loan on the house. Since the first-mortgage lender will not accept a lien priority inferior to a home equity loan, the homeowner must persuade the home equity lender to subordinate the home equity lien to the new first-mortgage lien.

Superior liens

Real estate tax lien. The local legal taxing authority annually places a real estate tax lien, also called an **ad valorem tax lien**, against properties as security for payment of the annual property tax. The amount of a particular lien is based on the taxed property's assessed value and the local tax rate.

Special assessment lien. Local government entities place assessment liens against certain properties to ensure payment for local improvement projects such as new roads, schools, sewers, or libraries. An assessment lien applies only to properties that are expected to benefit from the municipal improvement.

Federal and state inheritance tax liens. Inheritance tax liens arise from taxes owed by a decedent's estate. The lien amount is determined through probate and attaches to both real and personal property.

Junior liens

Tax liens. All tax liens other than those for ad valorem, assessment, and estate tax are junior liens. They include the following:

▸   **Federal income tax lien**

placed on a taxpayer's real and personal property for failure to pay income taxes

▸   **State corporate income tax lien**

filed against corporate property for failure to pay taxes

▸   **State intangible tax lien**

filed for non-payment of taxes on intangible property

▸   **State corporation franchise tax lien**

filed to ensure collection of fees to do business within a state

Judgment lien. A judgment lien attaches to real and personal property as a result of a money judgment issued by a court in favor of a creditor. The creditor may obtain a **writ of execution** to force the sale of attached property and collect the debt. After paying the debt from the sale proceeds, the debtor may obtain a **satisfaction of judgment** to clear the title records on other real property that remains unsold.

During the course of a lawsuit, the plaintiff creditor may secure a **writ of attachment** to prevent the debtor from selling or concealing property. In such a case, there must be a clear likelihood that the debt is valid, and that the defendant has made attempts to sell or hide property.

Certain properties are exempt from judgment liens, such as homestead property and joint tenancy estates.

Mortgage and trust deed lien. In lien-theory states, mortgages and trust deeds secure loans made on real property. In these states, the lender records a lien as soon as possible after disbursing the funds in order to establish lien priority.

Vendor's lien. A vendor's lien, also called a **seller's lien**, secures a purchase money mortgage, a seller's loan to a buyer to finance the sale of a property.

Municipal utility lien. A municipality may place a utility lien against a resident's real property for failure to pay utility bills.

Mechanic's lien. A mechanic's lien secures the costs of labor, materials, and supplies incurred in the repair or construction of real property improvements. If a property owner fails to pay for work performed or materials supplied, a worker or supplier can file a lien to force the sale of the property and collect the debt.

Any individual who performs approved work may place a mechanic's lien on the property to the extent of the direct costs incurred. Note that unpaid subcontractors may record mechanic's liens *whether the general contractor has been paid or not*. Thus it is possible for an owner to have to double-pay a bill in order to eliminate the mechanic's lien if the general contractor neglects to pay the subcontractors. The mechanic's lienor must enforce the lien within a certain time period, or the lien expires.

In contrast to other junior liens, the priority of a mechanic's lien *dates from the time when the work was begun or completed*. For example, a carpenter finishes a job on May 15. The owner refuses to pay the carpenter in spite of the carpenter's two-month collection effort. Finally, on August 1, the carpenter places a mechanic's lien on the property. The effective date of the lien for purposes of lien priority is May 15, not August 1.

DEED RESTRICTIONS

A deed restriction is a limitation imposed on a buyer's use of a property by stipulation in the deed of conveyance or recorded subdivision plat.

A deed restriction may apply to a single property or to an entire subdivision. A developer may place restrictions on all properties within a recorded **subdivision plat**. Subsequent re-sales of properties within the subdivision are thereby subject to the plat's covenants and conditions.

A private party who wants to control the quality and standards of a property can establish a deed restriction. Deed restrictions take precedence over zoning ordinances if they are more restrictive.

Deed restrictions typically apply to:

- the land use

- the size and type of structures that may be placed on the property

- minimum costs of structures

- engineering, architectural, and aesthetic standards, such as setbacks or specific standards of construction

Deed restrictions in a subdivision, for example, might include a minimum size for the residential structure, setback requirements for the home, and prohibitions against secondary structures such as sheds or cottages.

Deed restrictions are either covenants or conditions. A **condition** can only be created within a transfer of ownership. If a condition is later violated, a suit can force the owner to forfeit ownership to the previous owner. A **covenant** can be created by mutual agreement. If a covenant is breached, an injunction can force compliance or payment of compensatory damages.

EASEMENTS

Easement appurtenant
Easement by necessity
Easement by implication
Easement by prescription
Easement in gross
Easement creation
Easement termination

An **easement** is an interest in real property that gives the holder the right to use portions of the legal owner's real property in a defined way. Easement rights may apply to a property's surface, subsurface, or airspace, but the affected area must be defined.

The receiver of the easement right is the **benefited party**; the giver of the easement right is the **burdened party**.

Essential characteristics of easements include the following:

> ▸ An easement must involve the owner of the land over which the easement runs, and another, non-owning party. *One cannot own an easement over one's own property.*

> ▸ an easement pertains to a specified physical area within the property boundaries

> ▸ an easement may be **affirmative**, allowing a use, such as a right-of-way, or **negative**, *prohibiting a use*, such as an airspace easement that prohibits one property owner from obstructing another's ocean view

The two basic types of easements are appurtenant and gross

Easement appurtenant

An easement appurtenant gives a property owner a right of usage to portions of an *adjoining property* owned by another party. The property enjoying the usage right is called the **dominant tenement**, or **dominant estate**. The property containing the physical easement itself is the **servient tenement**, since it must serve the easement use.

The term appurtenant means "attaching to." An easement appurtenant attaches to the estate and transfers with it unless specifically stated otherwise in the transaction documents. More specifically, the easement attaches as a beneficial interest to the dominant estate, and as an encumbrance to the servient estate. The easement appurtenant then becomes part of the dominant estate's bundle of rights and the servient estate's obligation, or encumbrance.

Transfer. Easement appurtenant rights and obligations automatically transfer with the property upon transfer of either the dominant or servient estate, whether mentioned in the deed or not. For example, John grants Mary the right to share his driveway at any time over a five-year period, and the grant is duly recorded. If Mary sells her property in two years, the easement right transfers to the buyer as part of the estate.

Exhibit 4.2 Easements Appurtenant

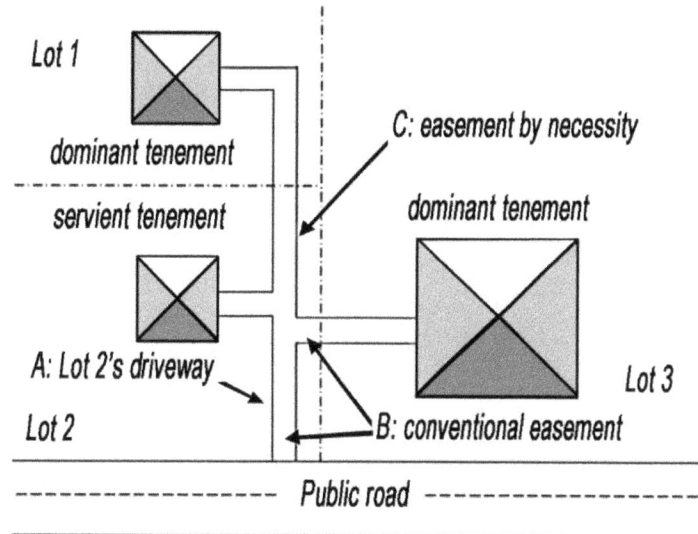

Non-exclusive use. The servient tenement, as well as the dominant tenement, may use the easement area, provided the use does not unreasonably obstruct the dominant use.

The exhibit below shows a conventional easement appurtenant. The driveway marked A belongs to lot #2. An easement appurtenant, marked B, allows lot #3 to use #2's driveway. Lot #3 is the dominant tenement, and #2 is the servient tenement.

Easement by necessity

An easement by necessity is an easement appurtenant granted by a court of law to a property owner because of a circumstance of necessity, most commonly the need for access to a property. Since property cannot be legally **landlocked**, or *without legal access to a public thoroughfare*, a court will grant an owner of a landlocked property an easement by necessity over an adjoining property that has access to a thoroughfare. The landlocked party becomes the dominant tenement, and the property containing the easement is the servient tenement.

In the exhibit above, lot #1, which is landlocked, owns an easement by necessity, marked C, across lot #2.

Easement by implication

Unlike an easement by necessity, an easement by implication arises when the easement or access is reasonably necessary. The easement is not an express statement between the property owners but is understood between the parties based on the circumstances that make it appear as though the parties must have intended the easement. For example, if one individual continually walks on his neighbor's road for many years, or if he begins digging sewer lines on his neighbor's property and the property owner doesn't stop him, that may constitute an implied easement.

Easement by prescription

An easement by prescription arises when someone uses another's property as an easement without permission for a statutory period of time and under certain conditions. In New York, the party using the easement must do so openly (with the landowner's knowledge) for 10 continuous and uninterrupted years.

For a prescriptive easement order to be granted, the following circumstances must be true:

▶ **Adverse and hostile use**

the use has been occurring without permission or license

▶ **Open and notorious use**

the owner knows or is presumed to have known of the use

▶ **Continuous use**

the use has been generally uninterrupted over the statutory prescriptive period

▶ **Physical use**

the user must physically be on the land

For example, a subdivision owns an access road, which is also used by other neighborhoods to access a grocery store. One day, the subdivision blocks off the road, claiming it has never granted the neighbors permission to use the road. If the neighbors have been physically using the road for the prescribed period, they may obtain a court order for an easement by prescription, since the subdivision owners can be assumed to have known of the usage.

Easement in gross

An easement in gross is a *personal right* that one party grants to another to use the grantor's real property. The right *does not attach* to the grantor's estate. It involves only one property, and, consequently, does not benefit any property owned by the easement owner. *There are no dominant or servient estates in an easement in gross.* An easement in gross may be personal or commercial.

Exhibit 4.3 Easements in Gross

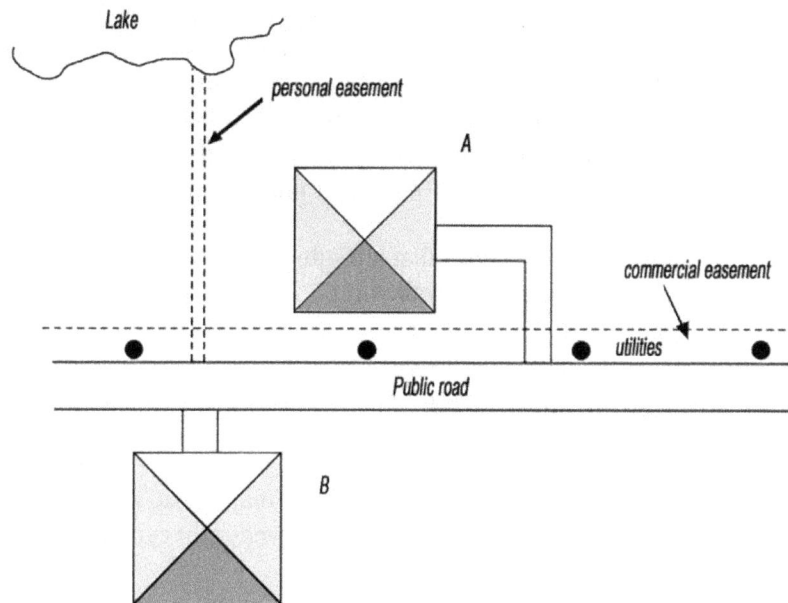

Personal. A personal easement in gross is granted for the grantee's lifetime. The right is irrevocable during this period, but terminates on the grantee's death. It may not be sold, assigned, transferred, or willed. A personal gross easement differs from a license in that the grantor of a license may revoke the usage right.

The exhibit shows that a beachfront property owner (A) has granted a neighbor (B) across the street the right to cross A's property to reach the beach.

Commercial. A commercial easement in gross is granted to a business entity rather than a private party. The duration of the commercial easement is not tied to anyone's lifetime. The right may by assigned, transferred, or willed.

Examples of commercial gross easements include:

▶ a marina's right-of-way to a boat ramp

▶ a utility company's right-of-way across a lot owners' property to install and maintain telephone lines (as illustrated in the exhibit).

A party wall is a common wall shared by two separate structures along a property boundary.

Party wall agreements generally provide for severalty ownership of half of the wall by each owner, or at least some fraction of the width of the wall. In addition, the agreement grants a *negative* easement appurtenant to each owner in the other's wall. This is to prevent unlimited use of the wall, in particular a destructive use that would jeopardize the adjacent property owner's building. The agreement also establishes responsibilities and obligations for maintenance and repair of the wall.

For example, Helen and Troy are adjacent neighbors in an urban housing complex having party walls on property lines. They both agree that they separately own the portion of the party wall on their property. They also grant each other an easement appurtenant in their owned portion of the wall. The easement restricts any use of the wall that would impair its condition. They also agree to split any repairs or maintenance evenly.

Other structures that are subject to party agreements are common fences, driveways, and walkways.

Easement creation

An easement may be created by *voluntary action, by necessary or prescriptive operation of law,* and *by government power of eminent domain.*

Voluntary. A property owner may create a voluntary easement by express grant in a sale contract, or as a reserved right expressed in a deed.

Necessity. A court decree creates an easement by necessity to provide access to a landlocked property.

Easement by prescription. If the easement user meets the descriptive criteria, a court order may give the user the easement right by **prescription**, *regardless of the owner's desires.*

Eminent domain. Government entities can create easements through the exercise of eminent domain, wherein they condemn a portion of a property and cause it to be sold "for the greater good." A typical example is a town's condemnation of private land to create a new municipal sewer system.

Easement termination

Easements terminate by any of the following:

▸ *express release of the right* by the easement holder

▸ *merger*, as when a dominant tenement acquires the servient property, or vice versa

▸ *purposeful abandonment* by the dominant tenement

▸ *condemnation* through eminent domain

▸ *change or cessation of the purpose* for the easement

▸ *destruction* of an easement structure, such as a party fence

▸ *non-use* of an easement by prescription

ENCROACHMENTS

An encroachment is the unauthorized, physical intrusion of one owner's real property into that of another.

Examples of encroachments in most areas include the following:

> ▸ a structure built in such a way that it overlaps the property line between two separately owned properties

> ▸ a driveway extending beyond the lot line onto the neighbor's land

> ▸ a fence built beyond the property line

New York's legislature has added a provision to the law to exclude "de minimus non-structural encroachments," such as fences, hedges, shrubbery, sheds, tree branches, from being adverse. In other words, simply installing a fence or planting bushes on a neighbor's land is not enough to claim title to the land.

Encroachments cause infringements on the rights of the trespassed owner and may diminish the property's value, particularly when the property is to be sold.

Encroachments often do not appear on a property's title records. A survey may be required to detect or demonstrate the existence of an encroachment.

An owner may sue for removal of an encroachment or for compensation for damages. If an encroached owner takes no remedial action over a period of 10 years, the encroachment may become an easement by prescription or even give the land ownership to the encroacher through **adverse possession**.

In New York, legislature requires trespassers to have reasonable belief that they have legal title to the property in question. This requirement makes establishing adverse possession in New York more difficult than any other jurisdiction.

To claim title through adverse possession, or a **claim of right**, New York laws require the following criteria:

> ▸ the possession and use of the property must be adverse

> ▸ the use of the land must be under claim of right, or reasonable belief the property belongs to the trespasser

> ▸ open and notorious use of the property

> ▸ continuous use for 10 years, per New York Real Property Actions Section 511

> ▸ exclusive possession of the trespasser

▶   actual possession or control of the property by the trespasser

By meeting these requirements for a claim of right, a trespasser cannot occupy someone else's land with the intention of gaining ownership after the 10 years.

4 Liens and Easements
Snapshot Review

LIENS

Definition
- creditor's claim against personal or real property as security for the property owner's debt

Features
- only conveys ownership if it is a mortgage lien; attaches to the property; property may have multiple liens; terminates on payment of debt

Lien types
- voluntary and involuntary; general and specific; superior and junior

Lien priority
- rank ordering of claims established by lien classification and date of recording; determines who gets paid first if lienee defaults

Superior liens
- rank over junior liens; not ranked by recording date; real estate tax and assessment liens and inheritance taxes

Junior liens
- rank by recording date: judgment; mortgage, vendor's, utility, mechanic's, other tax liens; mechanic's lien priority "dates back" to when work or sale transpired

DEED RESTRICTIONS
- conditions and covenants imposed on a property by deed or subdivision plat

EASEMENTS
- a right to use portions of another's property

Easement appurtenant
- dominant tenement's right to use or restrict adjacent servient tenement; attaches to the real estate
- easement by necessity: granted by necessity, e.g. to landlocked owners
- party wall: negative easement in a shared structure

Easement in gross
- a right to use property that does not attach to the real estate
- personal: not revocable or transferrable; ends upon death of easement holder
- commercial: granted to businesses; transferrable

Easement creation
- voluntary grant, court decree by necessity or prescription, eminent domain
- by prescription: obtainable through continuous, open, adverse use over a period

Easement termination
- release; merger; abandonment; condemnation; change of purpose; destruction; non-use

ENCROACHMENTS
- intrusions of real estate into adjoining property; can become easements

CHAPTER FOUR: LIENS AND EASEMENTS

Section Quiz

4.1. Which of the following cannot be accomplished by a lien?

   a. A forced sale of the liened property
   b. An automatic default on the mortgage loan
   c. A reduction in the property owner's equity in the property
   d. Restricting the owner's bundle of rights.

4.2. When does a lien terminate?

   a. After 60 days
   b. When a second lien is placed against the property
   c. When the debt is paid in full and recorded
   d. When the amount of the lien exceeds the value of the property.

4.3. Which of the following is a legal feature of liens?

   a. A lien attaches to the property.
   b. In New York, mortgage liens provide the lender with legal title to the property.
   c. A property may be subject to only one lien at a time.
   d. A lien conveys ownership.

4.4. If court action imposes an involuntary lien, the lien is a(n)

   a. statutory lien.
   b. general lien.
   c. junior lien.
   d. equitable lien.

4.5. A lien placed against all real and personal property owned by a specific debtor is a(n).

   a. general lien.
   b. statutory lien.
   c. inferior lien.
   d. equitable lien.

4.6. Which type of real estate lien has first priority?

   a. Special assessment lien
   b. Real estate tax lien
   c. Federal estate tax lien
   d. State inheritance tax lien

4.7. The two factors that determine lien priority are whether a lien is superior or junior and

   a. when the lien was recorded, with exceptions.
   b. the type of property on which the lien was placed.
   c. the balance amount of the debt resulting in the lien.
   d. the type of lien.

4.8. What determines the priority of junior liens?

   a. Whether or not the lien is a matter of public record
   b. When the debt was incurred
   c. When the lien was recorded
   d. When the borrower defaulted

4.9. What is an ad valorem tax lien?

   a. A lien placed because the property owner did not pay property taxes
   b. A lien placed against a property as security for annual property tax payment
   c. A lien placed against a property to ensure payment for local improvement projects
   d. A lien placed against a decedent's estate for unpaid taxes

4.10. Which of the following is a junior lien?

   a. Mechanic's lien
   b. Federal estate tax lien
   c. Real estate tax lien
   d. State inheritance tax lien

4.11. What is the purpose of a writ of attachment?

   a. To attach personal property to a real property lien
   b. To attach the lien to the debtor and not the property
   c. To attach all of the debtor's debts to the same lien
   d. To prevent the debtor from selling or hiding the property

4.12. Dan had some remodeling work done at his single-family home. When the work was completed, he paid the general contractor in full. However, the general contractor failed to pay the subcontractors for the work they performed on Dan's house. Because Dan paid the general contractor, Dan is in the clear, right?

a. Absolutely, he paid for the work in full.
b. Maybe, but the contractor could tell the subcontractors that Dan never paid.
c. No, when the subcontractors sue the general contractor for their payment, they could name Dan as an accomplice.
d. No, the subcontractors can place a mechanic's lien on Dan, causing him to pay twice for the work.

4.13. When may a deed restriction take precedence over zoning ordinances?

a. Deed restrictions never take precedence over zoning ordinances.
b. Deed restrictions can take precedence over zoning ordinances if the deed restrictions are more restrictive.
c. Zoning ordinances always take precedence.
d. Deed restrictions always take precedence over zoning ordinances.

4.14. What can happen if a deed restriction condition is breached by a new owner?

a. An injunction can be obtained to force compliance with the condition.
b. An injunction can be obtained for compensatory damages.
c. A lawsuit can force the new owner to forfeit ownership to the previous owner.
d. The new owner can be evicted from the property.

4.15. Essential characteristics of all easements include

a. involving the land owner and a second, non-owning party.
b. allowing the land owner to own an easement over the owner's own property.
c. affirmative use, that is, allowing the land owner to use a section of the easement owner's land in return.
d. negative use, wherein one party owns the easement but is still not allowed to use any of the land owner's land.

4.16. Which type of easement attaches to the estate and transfers with it unless specifically stated otherwise in the transaction documents?

a. Affirmative easement
b. Easement by Necessity
c. Easement by Implication
d. Easement Appurtenant

4.17. Which of the following is an encroachment?

a. A fence built along the property line
b. A shed that overlaps onto the neighbor's property
c. A driveway from the public roadway up to the land owner's house
d. A child's swing set located in the corner of the land owner's lot.

4.18. A town's government created an easement by purchasing a section of a land owner's lot in order to place various electrical system boxes on the land? What type of easement is this?

a. Eminent domain
b. Voluntary
c. Necessity
d. Prescription

4.19. What type of easement is created when someone uses another's property as an easement for 10 continuous years without permission but with the land owner's knowledge?

a. Easement by Implication
b. Easement in Gross.
c. Party Wall Easement
d. Easement by Prescription

4.20. Which of these is a superior lien?

a. Federal income tax lien
b. Mortgage lien
c. Judgment lien
d. Federal estate tax lien

5 Deeds and Conveyances

Title
Deeds
Conveyance after Death

TITLE TO REAL ESTATE

Legal and equitable title
Notice of title
Transfer of title (Alienation)

Legal and equitable title

Owning title to real property commonly connotes owning the complete bundle of rights that attach to the property, including the right to possession. More accurately, someone who possesses all ownership interests owns **legal title** to the property. Legal title is distinct from **equitable title**, which is the interest or *right to obtain legal title* to a property in accordance with a sale or mortgage contract between the legal owner and a buyer or creditor. During the contractual period of time when ownership of legal title is contingent upon the contract, the buyer or lender owns equitable title to the property.

For example, a buyer enters into a contract for deed to purchase a house. The seller lends the bulk of the purchase price to the buyer for a term of three years. The buyer takes possession of the property and makes payments on the loan. During this period, the seller retains legal title, and the buyer owns equitable title. If the buyer fulfills the terms of the agreement over the three-year period, the buyer has an enforceable contract to obtain legal title.

Another common example is a mortgage loan transaction that gives the lender the right to execute a strict foreclosure, which transfers legal title to the lender in the event of a default. With this contractual right, the lender has equitable title to the property.

In practice, the terms "title" and "legal title" are often used interchangeably.

Notice of title

In any legal system that permits private ownership of real property, there will always be disputes as to who truly owns a particular parcel of real estate. For example, an owner might "sell" his property to three unrelated parties. The first party buys the property at the earliest date, the second party pays the highest price, and the third party receives the best deed, a warranty deed. Who owns legal title to the property?

Ownership of legal title is a function of evidence. A court will generally rule that the person who has the preponderance of evidence of ownership is the owner of the property. In the example, if the first two buyers did not receive a deed while the third party did, the third party may have the best evidence and be ruled the legal title-holder. However, what if the first buyer had moved into the house and occupied it for six months before the original owner sold the property to the second and third buyers? And what if the second buyer, after searching title records, reports that the seller never really owned the property and therefore could not legally sell it to anyone! Now who owns the property?

The illustration underscores the difficulty of proving title to real estate: there is no absolute and irrefutable proof that a party holds legal title. Our legal system has developed two forms of title evidence-- actual notice and constructive notice-- to assist in the determination.

Actual notice. The term "notice" is synonymous with "knowledge." A person who has received *actual* notice has *actual knowledge* of something. Receiving actual notice means learning of something through direct experience or communication. In proving real estate ownership, a person provides actual notice by producing direct evidence, such as by showing a valid will. Another party receives actual notice by seeing direct evidence, such as by reviewing the deed, reading title records, or physically visiting the property to see who is in possession.

Thus if Mary Pierce drives to a property and sees directly that John Doe is in possession of the home, Mary then has received actual notice of John Doe's claim of ownership. Her knowledge is obtained through direct experience.

Constructive notice. Constructive notice, or **legal notice**, is knowledge of a fact that a person *could have or should have obtained*. The foremost method of imparting constructive notice is by recordation of ownership documents in public records, specifically, *title records*. Since public records are open to everyone, the law generally presumes that when evidence of ownership is recorded, the public at large *has received constructive notice* of ownership. By the same token, the law presumes that the owner of record is in fact the legal owner.

Thus, if John Doe records the deed of conveyance, he has imparted, and Mary Pierce has received, constructive notice of ownership. Possession of the property can also be construed as constructive notice, since a court may rule that Mary *should have visited the property* to ascertain whether it was occupied.

A combination of actual and constructive notice generally provides the most indisputable evidence of real property ownership.

Transfer of title (Alienation)

Transfer of title to real estate, also called **alienation**, occurs voluntarily and involuntarily. When the transfer uses a written instrument, the transfer is called a **conveyance.**

Exhibit 5.1 Transferring Title to Real Estate

Voluntary	Involuntary
public grant deed will dedication	descent escheat foreclosure eminent domain adverse possession estoppel

Voluntary alienation. Voluntary alienation is an unforced transfer of title by sale or gift from an owner to another party.

If the transferor is a government entity and the recipient is a private party, the conveyance is a **public grant** through the use of a land patent.

If the transferor is a private party, the conveyance is a **private grant**. A living owner makes a private grant by means of a **deed of conveyance**, or **deed**. A private grant that occurs when the owner dies is a **transfer by will**.

If the transferor is a developer who transfers roads, sidewalks, and/or other public areas within a newly constructed subdivision, the conveyance is **dedication** or **dedication by deed**. Dedication transfers any of these areas to a municipality to lessen or alleviate the subdivision's expenses related to maintaining these areas.

Involuntary alienation. Involuntary alienation is a transfer of title to real property without the owner's consent. Involuntary alienation occurs primarily by the processes of descent and distribution, escheat, foreclosure, eminent domain, adverse possession, and estoppel.

DEEDS

Purpose
Elements
Types of deeds

Purpose

A deed is a written and signed legal instrument used by a property owner, the **grantor**, to transfer title to real estate voluntarily to another party, the **grantee**.

Elements   New York Property Law § 258 provides examples of short form deeds and includes required elements for each deed. To be valid, the deed must meet the following criteria:

▶   It must be in writing.

▶   It must state on its face that it is a deed, using specific words such as "This Deed..." or "executed as a deed."

▶   It must indicate that the instrument itself conveys an interest in real property to someone, and who that someone is (grantee).

▶   It must include the names and addresses of both the grantor and the grantee.

▶   It must adequately describe the real property for which the interest is being transferred.

▶   The grantor must be of sound mind and legal age (18) to grant the interest, and the grantee must have the legal capacity to receive it. Deeds signed by incompetent or underage grantors can be voided by the courts.

▶   It must include a consideration clause that acknowledges that the grantor received valuable consideration for the transfer of the property. The clause does not need to include the actual amount given for the transfer of ownership, or the purchase price.

▶   It must include a granting clause stating the property is being transferred intentionally by the grantor to the grantee.

▶   It must include a habendum clause which describes the type of estate being conveyed. The type of estate sought by the transfer will determine exactly how this clause is worded. For example, if there are multiple grantees, the granting clause must indicate the rights and portion of the property granted to each grantee and which type of tenancy will be created.

▶   When appropriate, it must contain a reddendum or reserving clause which includes restrictions and limitations to the estate being transferred, such as deed restrictions, liens, easements, etc.

▶   Also when appropriate, it must contain a tenendum clause which identifies any property being conveyed in addition to the land.

▶   It must be signed by the grantor(s) and acknowledged by a New York notary public. No witnesses are required in New York.

▶   It must be delivered to (delivery) and accepted by the grantee (acceptance).

▸   It must be recorded in the county where the property is located.

Since New York uses the Torrens system, title passes only when the *deed has been registered on the certificate of title and a transfer certificate has been issued to the new owner.*

Once accepted, the title passes to the grantee. The deed has fulfilled its legal purpose, and it cannot be used again to transfer the property.

Types of deeds

In New York, there are several different types of deeds, depending on what rights are being transferred and who is transferring the rights. The most common types of deeds include deed with full covenants, bargain and sale deed with covenant, bargain and sale deed, executor's deed, quitclaim deed

Full covenant and warranty deed. This deed provides the most protection for the grantee in that the grantor makes the following promises and warranties:

▸   **Warrant of seisin**

assures that the grantor owns the estate to be conveyed, and has the right to do so

▸   **Warrant of quiet enjoyment**

assures that the grantee will not be disturbed by third party title disputes

▸   **Warrant of further assurance**

assures that the grantor will assist in clearing any title problems discovered later

▸   **Warranty forever; warranty of title**

assures that the grantee will receive good title, and that grantor will assist in defending any claims to the contrary

▸   **Warrant of encumbrances**

assures that there are no encumbrances on the property except those expressly named

▸   **Warranty against grantor's acts**

states the assurance of a trustee, acting as grantor on behalf of the owner, that nothing has been done to impair title during the fiduciary period

This deed is most often used in upstate New York counties, when transfers are between family members or when transfers by the grantor are to a trust or other entity for no consideration.

Bargain and sale deed with covenant. This deed is also called a special or limited warranty deed wherein the grantor warrants that the grantor has title to the property and has not done anything to encumber the property during the grantor's ownership, except what is stated in the deed. Although this deed offers the second most protection for the grantee, it does not protect the grantee against claims that predate the grantor's period of ownership.

Special warranty deeds are often used by trustees and grantors who acquired the property through a tax sale. This deed is typically used in the New York City area.

Bargain and sale deed without covenant. While this deed implies the grantor has title to the property, it provides no covenants and very little protection for the grantee. The grantor provides no promises or warranties. The grantee is acquiring real property without knowing if there are encumbrances on it unless any are stated in the deed.

If it turns out that the grantor indeed does not have a valid title to the property, the grantee has no legal recourse and cannot sue the grantor. For this reason, the use of a bargain and sale deed without covenant is often combined with the purchase of a title insurance policy which does warrant good title.

This form of deed is most commonly used in real estate transactions in downstate New York (New York City, surrounding suburbs, and Long Island).

Executor's deed or Administrator's deed. Both of these deeds offer the same protection as a bargain and sale deed with covenants. They are both used to transfer property in a deceased person's estate to either the beneficiaries of the estate or to a third party in a sale.

The deed provides details about the estate and the fiduciary's appointment. It also typically provides a covenant that nothing has been done to encumber the property during the fiduciary's ownership unless stated otherwise in the deed.

The executor's deed is used when the decedent died with a will. The administrator's deed is used when the decedent died without a will.

Quitclaim deed. This deed provides the grantee with the least protection because it contains no promises or warranties. A quitclaim deed is basically saying that the grantor might have an interest in the property and is transferring that interest to the grantee without necessarily defining what that interest might be. The grantor might be the legal owner, or the grantor might never have formally been identified on a deed describing the property.

This type of deed is generally used between family members or in a divorce situation.

General warranty deed. This is the most commonly used deed. and contains the fullest possible assurances of good title and protection for the grantee. These warranty deeds contain three main guarantees:

(1) the grantor has not sold the property to anyone else;

(2) the property is not burdened by any encumbrances apart from those the seller has already told the buyer about; and

(3) the grantor will warrant and defend title against the claims of all persons.

This means the grantor is guaranteeing there are no defects that may affect the title to the real property being transferred, even if the defect was caused by a prior owner.

Although warranty deeds can be used anywhere in New York State, they are typically used in upstate New York real estate transactions.

Tax deed. When property taxes are unpaid (the numbers of delinquent years vary from state to state), and the property is sold for the payment of back taxes, typically a tax deed is used to convey title to the buyer.

Deed-in-lieu of foreclosure. Sellers who are behind in payments to the lender will sometimes negotiate with a lender to accept a deed-in-lieu of foreclosure, which means the seller has deeded the property to the lender to avoid foreclosure.

Special purpose deeds. A special purpose deed is one tailored to the requirements of specific parties, properties, and purposes.

> ▶ **Guardian's deed**
>
>   used by a court-appointed guardian to transfer property of minors or mentally incompetent persons

> ▶ **Sheriff's deed**
>
>   used to convey foreclosed property sold at public auction

> ▶ **Deed *of* trust**
>
>   used to convey property to a third party trustee as collateral for a loan; on satisfaction of the loan terms, the trustee uses a **reconveyance deed** to convey the property back to the borrower

> ▶ **Deed *in* trust**
>
>   used to convey property to the trustee of a land trust. not to be confused with deed *of* trust

▶ **Master deed**

used to convey land to a condominium developer; accompanied by the condominium declaration when recorded

▶ **Partition deed**

used to convey co-owned property in compliance with a court order resulting from a partition suit; a partition suit terminates an estate when one or more co-owners want to dissolve their relationship and are unable to do so without the assistance of a court.

▶ **Patent deed**
used to transfer government property to private parties

CONVEYANCE AFTER DEATH

Wills
Types of wills
Validity
Probate

Wills

A will, or more properly, a **last will and testament**, is a legal instrument for the voluntary transfer of real and personal property *after the owner's death*. It describes how the maker of the will, called the **testator** or **devisor,** wants the property distributed. A beneficiary of a will is called an **heir** or **devisee**. The property transferred by the will is the **devise**.

A will takes effect only after the testator's death. It is an **amendatory** instrument, meaning that it can be changed at any time during the maker's lifetime.

Commonly, the testator names an **executor**, or **personal representative**, to oversee the settlement of the estate. If a minor is involved, the testator may identify a **guardian** to handle legal affairs on behalf of the minor.

The actual transfer of the property occurs either by operation of law or by an executor's deed. Transfer by operation of law is determined by how the property was held, such as being held by a joint tenancy with the right of survivorship. In that case, the deceased owner's rights to the property cannot be transferred to a beneficiary in a will but are automatically transferred to the surviving joint tenant(s). Transfer by executor's deed happens when there is a will that names beneficiaries and provides details about the estate itself and the fiduciary's appointment.

If a property owner dies without a will, it is called dying **intestate**. Without a will to determine how the decedent's estate is to be distributed, the property will be distributed through a court process called estate administration which is governed by New York's laws of intestacy (EPTL 4-1.1). The law takes into account the decedent's surviving spouse and other legal relatives and distributes the assets according to the relationship of the survivors to the decedent.

If there is no will and no natural heirs, the decedent's estate will transfer to the state of New York through **escheat**, a process where the state is deemed the last surviving heir by default.

Types of wills

Wills in New York generally take one of the following forms:

> ▸ **Simple will** – this is the most common type of will and the one people are most familiar with. It allows the testator to decide who inherits the assets and who will be the guardian of any minor children.

> ▸ **Pour-over-will** – this type of will is used when the estate plan includes a living trust. It specifies the distribution of assets and transfers any unplaced assets to the trust after the testator dies. The trustee then distributes the property to beneficiaries as indicated in the trust.

> ▸ **Reciprocal/joint wills** – this type is created by two testators, typically spouses or business partners, each leaving their assets to the other. Reciprocal wills are two separate documents. Joint wills accomplish the same distribution goals but do so in a single document created by the two people.

> ▸ **Holographic will** – this type of will is hand written by the testator and typically does not go to probate because its authenticity is difficult to prove. However, if the holographic will is created during a military armed conflict and is signed by another member of the military, an accompanying civilian, or a Maritimer at sea, it will be deemed valid.

> ▸ **Nuncupative** – this type of will is not typically valid and would not go to probate because it is not written. It is an oral will spoken in front of at least two witnesses. However, like a holographic will, if a nuncupative will is created by a member of the military or a mariner at sea, it will be deemed valid.

Validity

Because a will provides instructions for distributing a deceased person's assets, the will needs to be created in a way that it is legally binding. Under New York estate laws, a will must meet the following requirements:

> ▸ The creator of the will (the testator) must be at least 18 years old and have the mental capacity to understand the nature and consequences of his or her actions.

> ▸ The testator must not have been subjected to undue influence or coercion when creating the will.

- ▶ The will must be in writing; in some rare situations, an oral will may be accepted.

- ▶ The testator must sign the will in front of two uninterested witnesses who must also sign the will within 30 days of the testator's signing.

New York does not require the will to be notarized, but it can include an attestation clause at the end of the will. With an attestation clause, the witnesses would sign the clause, stating they witnessed the testator signing the will and they believe the testator was of sound mind at the time of signing.

The testator may also include a self-proving affidavit which allows the will to be admitted to probate without the witnesses needed to testify in court for the probate process. The affidavit is to be signed by the testator and the witnesses in front of a notary public.

If the creator of the will fails to meet these requirements, the will could be contested and deemed invalid.

Probate

A court proceeding called **probate** generally settles a decedent's estate, whether the person has died **testate** (having left a valid will) or **intestate** (having failed to do so). Real property may be exempted from probate if it is held in a land trust. Probate of real property occurs *under jurisdiction of courts in the state where the property is located, regardless of where the deceased resided.*

The probate court's objectives are to:

- ▶ validate an existing will

- ▶ identify and settle all claims and outstanding debts against the estate

- ▶ distribute the remainder of the estate to the rightful heirs

If the will does not name an executor, the court will appoint an **administrator** to fulfill the role of distributing the estate to the heirs.

5 Deeds and Conveyances
Snapshot Review

TITLE

Legal and equitable title	• how ownership is evidenced to the public
	• actual notice: knowledge acquired or imparted directly through demonstrable evidence, e.g., presenting or inspecting a deed, visiting a party in possession
Notice of title	• how ownership is evidenced to the public
	• actual notice: knowledge acquired or imparted directly through demonstrable evidence, e.g., presenting or inspecting a deed, visiting a party in possession
	• constructive notice: knowledge one could or should have obtained, as presumed by law; imparted by recording in public records "for all to see"
Transfer of title	• voluntary by grant, deed, or will
	• involuntary by descent, escheat, eminent domain, foreclosure, adverse possession, estoppel

DEEDS

Purpose	• instruments of voluntary conveyance by grantor to grantee
Elements	• in writing; state it is a deed; conveys interest in property; name grantee and grantor; describe property; grantor sound mind and legal age; consideration clause; granting clause; habendum clause, reserving clause; tenendum clause, signed and notarized delivered and accepted by grantee; recorded in county where property is located
Statutory deeds	• bargain and sale: "I own but won't defend"
	• general warranty: "I own and will defend"
	• special warranty: "I own and warrant myself only"
	• quitclaim: "I may or may not own, and won't defend"
Special Purpose Deeds	• used for different purposes, to convey certain interests, or by certain parties

CONVEYANCE AFTER DEATH

Wills	• last will and testament: voluntary transfer to heirs after death
	• maker: devisor or testator; heir: devisee; estate: devise
Types of will	• witnessed; holographic; approved; nuncupative
Validity	• adult; competent; indicates "last will and testament"; signed; witnessed; voluntary
Probate	• if testate, estate passes to heirs; if intestate, to successors by descent; if intestate with no heirs, estate escheats to state or county
	• process: validate will; validate, settle claims and pay taxes; transfer balance of estate to heirs

SECTION FIVE: Real Estate Brokerage Activities & Procedures

Section Quiz

5.1. Transfer of title to real estate is also called:

a. an encumbrance.
b. subrogation.
c. a sale.
d. alienation.

5.2. Suppose two people each claim they have legal title to a property. In court, how will ownership be determined?

a. The person who filed an ownership claim first is the rightful owner.
b. The person who paid the most for the property is the rightful owner.
c. The person who has the preponderance of evidence of ownership is the rightful owner.
d. The person who first occupied the property is the rightful owner.

5.3. A _____ is a written and signed legal instrument a property owner uses to transfer title to real estate voluntarily to another party.

a. deed
b. contract
c. lease
d. mortgage

5.4. In New York, there are several different types of deeds, depending on what rights are being transferred and who is transferring the rights. Which type of deed expresses that the grantor might have an interest in the property and is transferring that interest to the grantee without necessarily defining what that interest might be?

a. General warranty deed
b. Tax deed
c. Quitclaim deed
d. Deed of trust

5.5. Which of the following is an example of involuntary transfer of title?

a. Public grant
b. Estoppel
c. Dedication
d. Deed

5.6. Under New York estate laws, a will must meet certain requirements, including

a. the testator must be at least 18 years old.
b. the will must be notarized.
c. the will may be in writing or oral, whichever the testator prefers.
d. the testator must sign the will in front of one disinterested witness.

5.7. What happens when a person dies intestate in New York?

a. The property will automatically transfer to the deceased's closest living relative according to New York's probate laws.
b. The property will be distributed through a court process called estate administration per New York's laws of intestacy.
c. The property will be auctioned off, and the proceeds will go to the state's general fund.
d. The state will take ownership of the property through escheat.

5.8. A person who possesses all ownership interests in a property owns

a. equitable title.
b. legal title.
c. common title.
d. actual title.

5.9. When might real property be exempted from probate?

a. The decedent died testate.
b. It is zoned for commercial use.
c. The decedent died intestate.
d. It is held in a land trust.

5.10. John is in the process of purchasing a house from Mary via seller financing. He has signed a sales contract and has arranged for a three-year payment plan with Mary. John moves into the house and begins making monthly payments to Mary. Fast forward one year. Which of the following is true about this scenario at the current point in time?

a. Mary holds legal title to the property, and John holds equitable title.
b. John holds legal title to the property, and Mary holds equitable title.
c. Mary holds beneficial title to the property, and John holds equitable title.
d. Mary holds legal title to the property, and John holds contingent title.

5.11. A _____ will is not typically valid and would not go to probate because it is an oral will that is spoken in front of two or more witnesses.

a. holographic
b. reciprocal
c. simple
d. nuncupative

5.12. What does the warrant of seisin assure?

a. The grantee will not be disturbed by third party title disputes.
b. The grantee will receive good title, and that grantor will assist in defending any claims to the contrary.
c. The grantor owns the estate to be conveyed and has the right to do so.
d. There are no encumbrances on the property except those expressly named.

5.13. What happens to property owned in joint tenancy with right of survivorship when one of the owners dies testate?

a. The decedent's portion of the property is transferred by executor's deed to the beneficiary named in the owner's will.
b. The decedent's portion of the property will automatically be transferred to the remaining joint tenants.
c. The decedent's jointly held property will transfer to the state of New York through escheat.
d. The specifics of the will and its property distributions, including the jointly held property, will be decided during probate.

5.14. Armand records the deed to the property he purchased. What kind of evidence does this give to others that he has title to the property?

a. Actual notice
b. Recordation evidence
c. Title evidence
d. Constructive notice

5.15. Which deed provides the most protection for the grantee because the grantor makes a number of promises and warranties to the grantee?

a. Bargain and sale deed with covenant
b. Full covenant and warranty deed
c. Executor's deed
d. General warranty deed

5.16. An owner transfers title to a property to a buyer in exchange for a consideration. This is an example of

a. voluntary alienation.
b. escheat.
c. hypothecation.
d. estoppel.

5.17. Constructive notice of ownership of a parcel of real estate is primarily demonstrated through

a. direct inspection to see who is in possession.
b. title insurance.
c. title records.
d. a construction permit.

5.18. A deed in which the grantor warrants that the grantor has title to the property and has not done anything to encumber the property during the grantor's ownership is called a

a. bargain and sale deed with covenant.
b. sheriff's deed.
c. partition deed.
d. general warranty deed

5.19. A _____, a required element in a deed, describes the type of estate being conveyed from the grantor to the grantee.

a. reddendum or reserving clause
b. tenendum clause
c. granting clause
d. habendum clause

5.20. What does a warrant of quiet enjoyment in a deed assure for the grantee?

a. The grantor owns the estate to be conveyed and has the right to do so.
b. The grantor will assist in clearing any title problems discovered later.
c. The grantee will not be disturbed by third party title disputes.
d. The grantee will receive good title, and that grantor will assist in defending any claims to the contrary.

6 Title Closing and Costs

Title Closing
Computing Prorations
Title records

TITLE CLOSING

The setting
Closing process
Broker's role in closing
RESPA
TRID/TILA
The H-25 Closing Disclosure form
Settlement process
Closing costs
Computing prorations

The setting

The closing event is the culmination of the real estate transaction. During this event, the buyer pays the purchase price and receives title to the purchased real estate. At the same time, the buyer completes financing arrangements, and buyer and seller pay all required taxes, fees, and charges.

Time. The sale contract sets the date of the closing, usually within 60 days of signing. The time period between signing and closing is expected to be sufficient for the removal of any contingencies, such as the buyer's obtaining of financing, the performance of inspections, and the correction of identified physical defects. Failure of either buyer or seller to perform pre-closing actions specified in the contract can delay or terminate the transaction. If the contract includes a statement that "time is of the essence," all parties agree to meet the time limitations exactly as stated. If both parties consent, however, they can re-schedule the closing date.

Location. Closings occur at various locations, such as the office of the title company, the lender, the escrow agent, one of the attorneys, the broker, or the county recorder. The sale contract specifies the location.

Parties at closing. The primary parties at the closing are normally the buyer, seller, and a closing agent or escrow officer. Other parties who might be present include the title officer, attorneys, brokers or agents, and the lender's representative. It is not actually necessary for any of these parties to attend the meeting. The closing agent can complete the transaction, provided all documents have been duly executed in advance.

Closing process   Although agents are not involved in the actual closing of the real estate transaction, they do need to be educated on the process so they can assist their clients in preparing for the closing. The agent should be able to explain expenses and what each party will pay and receive at closing. The agent should also assist the client in understanding mortgage terms and becoming familiar with New York's property records. The property records provide a history of transactions related to the property such as liens and potential legal issues tied to the property. Resolving any issues prior to closing is critical to avoid potential disputes.

The closing process also involves hiring an attorney. New York State is unique in that it requires the involvement of an attorney in the real estate closing process. Although the attorney is not required to attend the actual closing event, the attorney is instrumental in navigating contractual complexities, negotiating terms, and ensuring all legal requirements are met prior to and during closing to protect both parties' interests.

The closing process consists of the buyer and the seller verifying that each has fulfilled the terms of the sale contract. Terms the seller is responsible for include delivering a good and marketable title to the property, the deed, proof of lien and encumbrance removal, and the property in the promised condition. Terms the buyer is responsible for include obtaining appropriate financing and delivering the funds for the property purchase.

If both parties have fulfilled their terms, then the mortgage loan, if any, is closed, all expenses are apportioned and paid, the consideration is exchanged for the title, final documents are signed, and arrangements are made to record the transaction according to local laws.

Exhibit 6.1 The Closing Process

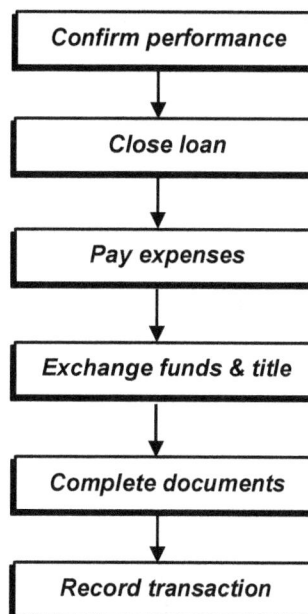

```
┌─────────────────────┐
│ Confirm performance │
└─────────────────────┘
          │
          ▼
┌─────────────────────┐
│     Close loan      │
└─────────────────────┘
          │
          ▼
┌─────────────────────┐
│    Pay expenses     │
└─────────────────────┘
          │
          ▼
┌─────────────────────┐
│ Exchange funds & title │
└─────────────────────┘
          │
          ▼
┌─────────────────────┐
│ Complete documents  │
└─────────────────────┘
          │
          ▼
┌─────────────────────┐
│ Record transaction  │
└─────────────────────┘
```

Transfer of title. The seller must produce evidence of marketable title, such as a commitment for title insurance by a title insurer. Before making a title commitment, a title company performs a title search to discover any liens, encumbrances, restrictions, conditions, or easements attaching to the title.

If there are any encumbrances or liens that damage the title, the seller is expected to remove these prior to the date specified in the contract. The most common title cloud is an unpaid lien.

The seller may also be asked to execute an affidavit of title stating that, since the date of the original title search, the seller has incurred no new liens, judgments, unpaid bills for repairs or improvements, no unrecorded deeds or contracts, no bankruptcies or divorces that would affect title, or any other defects the seller is aware of.

The purchaser, purchaser's lender, or title company may require a survey to verify the location and size of the property. The survey also identifies any easements, encroachments, or flood plain hazard.

The buyer should inspect the property to make certain that the property is in the condition in which the seller states that it is, and that any repairs or other required actions have been performed. A final inspection, called a **buyer's walk-through**, should be conducted as close to the closing date as possible.

If the seller's mortgage lien(s) are to be satisfied at closing, the lender will provide a **payoff statement**, also called an **offset statement**, specifying the amount of unpaid principal and any interest due as of the closing date, plus fees that will be due the lender and any credits or penalties that may apply. The holder of a note secured by a trust deed will provide a similar statement, called a **beneficiary statement**, to show any unpaid balance. Even if the buyer is assuming the seller's mortgage loan, the buyer will want to know the exact amount of the unpaid balance as of the closing date.

Finally, the seller produces and/or deposits with the escrow agent the deed that conveys the property to the buyer.

Transfer of purchase funds. The buyer usually produces and/or deposits with the escrow agent the following:

▶ earnest money
▶ loan funds and documents
▶ any other cash needed to complete the purchase

Escrow procedures. If the closing occurs "in escrow" rather than face-to-face, the principal parties deposit funds and documents with the appointed escrow agent, and the escrow agent disburses funds and releases documents to the appropriate parties when all the conditions of the escrow have been met. If for any reason the transaction cannot be completed, for instance if the buyer refuses the title as it is offered, or the buyer fails to produce the necessary cash, the escrow instructions usually provide a mechanism for reconveying title to the seller and funds to the buyer. In such a case, both parties return to their original status as if no sale had occurred.

Lender closing requirements. A lender is concerned about the quality of the collateral a borrower is providing in return for the mortgage loan. The collateral would be endangered by defects in the title, by liens that would take precedence over the mortgage lien, such as a tax lien, and by physical damage to the property which is not repaired. Consequently, the lender typically requires a survey; a property inspection; hazard insurance; a title insurance policy; a reserve account for taxes and insurance; and possibly, private mortgage insurance. In some cases the lender may also require a *certificate of occupancy* verifying that any new construction performed complies with local building codes.

Broker's role in closing

A broker usually continues to provide service between the signing of the sale contract and the closing by helping to make arrangements for pre-closing activities such as inspections, surveys, appraisals and repairs and generally taking steps to ensure that the closing can proceed as scheduled. These steps may include arranging the buyer's final walk-through of the property to assure it is in the promised condition.

A broker may conduct proceedings at the closing meeting, or may have no further role in the transaction after the sale contract is signed, depending on local practices and the transaction in question. The broker may have been given the responsibility for accuracy and timely delivery of the closing documents to the principal parties. A broker may also have the responsibility for reporting the transaction to the Internal Revenue Service.

Finally, if the seller of the property is a non-resident alien, United States law may require the broker to withhold and transmit to the Internal Revenue Service a portion of the sale proceeds to cover the alien seller's income tax liability. There are also special reporting requirements when the transaction involves a non-resident alien.

RESPA

The **Real Estate Settlement Procedures Act** (RESPA) is a consumer protection statute enacted in 1974. Its purpose is to clarify settlement costs and to eliminate kickbacks and fees that increase settlement costs. RESPA specifies certain closing procedures when a purchase:

▶ involves a residential property, including one- to four-family residences, cooperatives and condominiums;

▶ involves a first or second mortgage lien; and

▶ is being financed by a "federally-related" mortgage loan, which includes loans made by a federally-insured lender; loans insured or guaranteed by the VA or FHA, loans administered by HUD, and loans intended to be sold to FNMA, FHLMC, or GNMA.

RESPA regulations do not apply to transactions being otherwise financed except in the case of an assumption in which the terms of the assumed loan are modified or the lender's charges for the assumption are greater than $50.

RESPA is directed at lenders and settlement companies, but licensees should be familiar with requirements and changes implemented as of January, 2014. The Dodd-Frank Act of 2010 granted rule-making authority under RESPA to the Consumer Financial Protection Bureau (CFPB) and generally granted the CFPB authority to supervise and enforce compliance with RESPA and its implementing regulations.

In 2013, the CFPB made substantive and technical changes to the existing regulations. Substantive changes included modifying the servicing transfer notice requirements and implementing new procedures and notice requirements related to borrowers' error resolution requests and information requests. The amendments also included provisions related to escrow payments and limited the amounts lenders car require borrowers to place in escrow for purposes of paying taxes, hazard insurance, and other property-related expenses. The amendments further addressed force-placed insurance, general servicing policies, procedures, and requirements, early intervention, continuity of contact, loss mitigation and the relation of RESPA's servicing provisions to State law. These RESPA amendments went into effect on January 10, 2014.

TRID/TILA

Effective October 3, 2015, a TILA/RESPA Integrated Disclosure Rule (TRID) integrated the disclosure requirements of RESPA and Truth-in-Lending, replacing the old Good Faith Estimate form and HUD-1 Uniform Settlement Statement with a new Loan Estimate form and Closing Disclosure form, respectively.

TRID changes introduced new mandatory forms and procedures to replace the old ones:

- **Consumer booklet**. Lenders must give the consumer a copy of the **booklet**, "Your Home Loan Toolkit" **within 3 days** of loan application. This booklet describes loans, closing costs, and the Closing Disclosure form.

- **Loan estimate**. Lenders must deliver or mail the **Loan Estimate** (Form H-24) to the consumer **no later than the third business day** after receiving a loan application. (A "business day" in this context is any day on which the lender's offices are open for business. An "application" exists when the consumer has given the lender or mortgage broker six pieces of information: name; income; Social Security number; property address; estimated value of property; loan amount sought).

- **Closing Disclosure**. Lenders must provide the **Closing Disclosure** (Form H-25) to the consumer **at least 3 business days** before consummation of the loan. (A "business day" in this context is any calendar day except a Sunday or the day on which a legal public holiday is observed. "Consummation" refers to the day on which the borrower becomes indebted to the creditor; this may or may not correspond to the day of closing the transaction.)

The Closing Disclosure shows the financial settlement of a transaction. At closing, the closing agent also generally provides a statement to the buyer and/or seller detailing receipts and disbursements from relevant escrow accounts to which the buyer and seller have contributed funds as part of the transaction.

Good faith. Creditors are responsible for ensuring that the figures stated in the Loan Estimate are made in good faith and consistent with the best information reasonably available to the creditor at the time they are disclosed.

Good faith is measured by calculating the difference between the estimated charges originally provided in the Loan Estimate and the actual charges paid by or imposed on the consumer in the Closing Disclosure.

Generally, if the charge paid by or imposed on the consumer exceeds the amount originally disclosed on the Loan Estimate it is not in good faith, regardless of whether the creditor later discovers a technical error, miscalculation, or underestimation of a charge, although there are exceptions.

Types of charges. For certain costs or terms, creditors are permitted to charge consumers more than the amount disclosed on the Loan Estimate without any tolerance limitation.

These charges are as follows:

▶ prepaid interest; property insurance premiums; amounts placed into an escrow, impound, reserve or similar account

▶ charges for services required by the creditor if the creditor permits the consumer to shop and the consumer selects a third-party service provider not on the creditor's written list of service providers

▶ charges paid to third-party service providers for services not required by the creditor (may be paid to affiliates of the creditor)

However, creditors may only charge consumers more than the amount disclosed when the original estimated charge, or lack of an estimated charge for a particular service, was based on the best information reasonably available to the creditor at the time the disclosure was provided.

Charges for third-party services and recording fees paid by or imposed on the consumer are grouped together and subject to a 10% cumulative tolerance ("10% tolerance" charges). This means the creditor may charge the consumer more than the amount disclosed on the Loan Estimate for any of these charges so long as the total sum of the charges added together does not exceed the sum of all such charges disclosed on the Loan Estimate by more than 10%.

For all other charges ("zero tolerance" charges), creditors are not permitted to charge consumers more than the amount disclosed on the Loan Estimate under any circumstances other than changed circumstances that permit a revised Loan Estimate.

If the amounts paid by the consumer at closing exceed the amounts disclosed on the Loan Estimate beyond the applicable tolerance threshold, the creditor must refund the excess to the consumer no later than 60 calendar days after consummation.

Applicable transactions. The Integrated Disclosures rule applies to most closed-end consumer mortgages. It does not apply to the following:

- home equity lines of credit (HELOCs)
- reverse mortgages
- mortgages secured by a mobile home or by a dwelling that is not attached to real property (i.e., land)
- loans made by persons who are not considered "creditors" by virtue of the fact they make five or fewer mortgages in a year.

However, certain types of loans that used to be subject to TILA but not RESPA are now subject to the TILA-RESPA rule's integrated disclosure requirements, including:

- construction-only loans
- loans secured by vacant land or by 25 or more acres
- credit extended to certain trusts for tax or estate planning

Guides, detailed information about the current TILA-RESPA rule, and applicable forms can be found on the Consumer Financial Protection Bureau (CFPB) website at https://www.consumerfinance.gov/policy-compliance/guidance/tila-respa-disclosure-rule/.

The H-25 Closing Disclosure form

The H-25 Closing Disclosure form consists of five pages. Pages 1, 4, and 5 vary, depending on the loan type. To illustrate the form, we use a sample disclosure for a *30-year fixed rate* loan that is presented on the CFPB website.

Page 1 has four sections: general information, Loan Terms, Projected Payments, and Costs at Closing.

General information. This section has three columns:

- Closing information –issue date, closing date, disbursement date, settlement agent, file number, property address, and sale price
- Transaction information – names and addresses for borrower, seller and lender
- Loan information – loan term, loan purpose, product type, loan type and loan ID number

Loan Terms. This section states the loan amount, interest rate, and monthly principal and interest payment, and indicates whether any of those amounts can increase after closing. It also gives specifics of any prepayment penalty or balloon payment.

Projected Payment. This section displays the borrower's payment for principal and interest and mortgage insurance, an estimated escrow payment, and the total estimated monthly mortgage payment for years 1-7 and 8-30 of the loan term. It also provides an estimate of monthly tax, insurance, and assessment payments and indicates whether the payments will be held in escrow.

Costs at Closing. The last section of page 1 on the H-25 shows the borrowers' total closing costs (brought forward from page 2) and the total amount of cash the buyer needs to close (brought forward from page 3).

Page 2 details the closing costs. There are two sections divided into four columns:

- ▶ Description of the costs—loan costs and other costs
- ▶ Costs paid by the borrower – "at closing" or "before closing"
- ▶ Costs paid by the seller – "at closing" or "before closing"
- ▶ Costs paid by others (in the example, someone other than buyer or seller pays for the appraisal)

Loan Costs. The first section deals with the loan costs:

A. Origination charges, such as points, application fee, and underwriting fee

B. Charges for services the borrower did not shop for - items the lender requires, such as appraisals and credit reports

C. Services the borrower did shop for - items the borrower orders on his own, such as pest inspections, survey fees, and title insurance

D. The total of A, B, and C above

Other Costs. The second section deals with additional transaction-related costs:

E. Taxes and other government fees, such as recording fees and transfer taxes

F. Prepaid items, such as homeowner's insurance, mortgage insurance, prepaid interest, and property taxes to be paid before the first scheduled loan payment

G. Initial escrow payment at closing – an amount the borrower will pay the lender each month to be held in escrow until due, typically for insurance premiums and tax instalments

H. Other costs not covered elsewhere on the disclosure, such as items as association fees, home warranty fees, home inspection fees, real estate commission, and prorated items

I. The total of the costs of E, F, G, and H above

J. The total borrower-paid closing costs from D + I above. This total is carried to the bottom of page 1 as "Costs at Closing – Closing Costs."

Page 3 has two sections, one for calculating cash to close, the other for summarizing the transactions of borrower and seller.

Calculating Cash to Close. The first section compares the final costs of the loan with the lender's original Loan Estimate. This calculation considers costs paid before closing, down payment, deposits, seller credits, adjustments, and other credits. The last line of the calculation is "Cash to close," the amount the borrower needs to produce at closing.

When an amount has changed, the creditor must indicate where the consumer can find the amounts that have changed on the Loan Estimate. For example, if the Seller Credit amount changed, the creditor can indicate that the consumer should "See Seller Credits in Section L." When the increase in Total Closing Costs exceeds the legal limits, the creditor must disclose this fact and the dollar amount of the excess in the "Did this change?" column. A statement directing the consumer to the Lender Credit on page 2 must also be included if the creditor owes a credit to the consumer at closing for the excess amount.

Summaries of Transactions. The second section of page 3 is divided into two columns (or subsections), one to summarize the borrower's transaction and the other for the seller's transaction. The borrower's column includes:

K. amounts due from the borrower at closing, including the sale price and adjustments for items paid by the seller in advance.

L. amounts already paid by or on behalf of the borrower at closing, such as deposit, loan amount, loan assumptions, seller credits, other credits, and adjustments for items unpaid by the seller, such as taxes and assessments.

The calculation at the bottom of the left column subtracts the totals already paid by the borrower (line L) from the total due from the borrower (line K) to derive the Cash to Close due from the borrower at closing. This figure is the same as that at the bottom of page 1 under "Costs at Closing – Cash to Close."

The seller's column of the Summaries section includes:

M. amounts due to the seller at closing, including the sale price of the property and adjustments for items paid by the seller in advance.

N. amounts due from the seller at closing, such as closing costs the seller will pay, payoff of first or second mortgages, seller credit, and adjustments for items unpaid by the seller, such as taxes and assessments.

Page 4 provides additional Loan Disclosures:

▶ Assumption –whether the lender will allow a loan assumption on a future transfer

▶ Demand feature –whether the lender can require early repayment

▶ Late payment – the fee the lender will charge for a late payment

- ▸ Negative amortization –whether the loan is negatively amortized, which increases the loan amount and diminishes the borrower's equity over the loan term

- ▸ Partial payments –whether the lender accepts partial payments and applies them to the loan

- ▸ Security interest –identifies the property securing the loan

- ▸ Escrow account – itemizes what is included in the escrow account and states the monthly escrow payment

Page 5 provides additional calculations, disclosures, and contact information:

- ▸ Loan Calculations –the total amount of all payments on the loan, the dollar amount of the finance charges over the life of the loan, the amount financed, the annual percentage rate (APR), and the total interest percentage (TIP)

- ▸ Other Disclosures –other important information for the borrower, including the right to a copy of the appraisal report and an indication of whether the borrower is protected against liability for the unpaid balance in the event of a foreclosure

- ▸ Contact Information –names, addresses, license numbers, contact names, email addresses, and phone numbers for persons involved in the transaction.

- ▸ Confirm Receipt –the borrowers' signatures confirming receipt of the Closing Disclosure document. **Signing the document does not indicate acceptance of the loan.**

Exhibit 6.2 Sample H-25 Closing Disclosure, Page 1

Closing Disclosure

This form is a statement of final loan terms and closing costs. Compare this document with your Loan Estimate.

Closing Information		Transaction Information		Loan Information	
Date Issued	4/15/2013	Borrower	Michael Jones and Mary Stone	Loan Term	30 years
Closing Date	4/15/2013		123 Anywhere Street	Purpose	Purchase
Disbursement Date	4/15/2013		Anytown, ST 12345	Product	Fixed Rate
Settlement Agent	Epsilon Title Co.	Seller	Steve Cole and Amy Doe		
File #	12-3456		321 Somewhere Drive	Loan Type	☒ Conventional ☐ FHA
Property	456 Somewhere Ave		Anytown, ST 12345		☐ VA ☐ _____
	Anytown, ST 12345	Lender	Ficus Bank	Loan ID #	123456789
Sale Price	$180,000			MIC #	000654321

Loan Terms

		Can this amount increase after closing?
Loan Amount	$162,000	NO
Interest Rate	3.875%	NO
Monthly Principal & Interest *See Projected Payments below for your Estimated Total Monthly Payment*	$761.78	NO
		Does the loan have these features?
Prepayment Penalty		YES • As high as $3,240 if you pay off the loan during the first 2 years
Balloon Payment		NO

Projected Payments

Payment Calculation		Years 1-7		Years 8-30
Principal & Interest		$761.78		$761.78
Mortgage Insurance	+	82.35	+	—
Estimated Escrow *Amount can increase over time*	+	206.13	+	206.13
Estimated Total Monthly Payment		**$1,050.26**		**$967.91**

Estimated Taxes, Insurance & Assessments *Amount can increase over time* *See page 4 for details*	$356.13 a month	This estimate includes ☒ Property Taxes ☒ Homeowner's Insurance ☒ Other: Homeowner's Association Dues *See Escrow Account on page 4 for details. You must pay for other property costs separately.*	In escrow? YES YES NO

Costs at Closing

Closing Costs	$9,712.10	Includes $4,694.05 in Loan Costs + $5,018.05 in Other Costs – $0 in Lender Credits. *See page 2 for details.*
Cash to Close	$14,147.26	Includes Closing Costs. *See Calculating Cash to Close on page 3 for details.*

Exhibit 6.3 Sample H-25 Closing Disclosure, Page 2

Closing Cost Details

Loan Costs		Borrower-Paid		Seller-Paid		Paid by Others
		At Closing	Before Closing	At Closing	Before Closing	
A. Origination Charges		**$1,802.00**				
01 0.25 % of Loan Amount (Points)		$405.00				
02 Application Fee		$300.00				
03 Underwriting Fee		$1,097.00				
04						
05						
06						
07						
08						
B. Services Borrower Did Not Shop For		**$236.55**				
01 Appraisal Fee	to John Smith Appraisers Inc.					$405.00
02 Credit Report Fee	to Information Inc.		$29.80			
03 Flood Determination Fee	to Info Co.	$20.00				
04 Flood Monitoring Fee	to Info Co.	$31.75				
05 Tax Monitoring Fee	to Info Co.	$75.00				
06 Tax Status Research Fee	to Info Co.	$80.00				
07						
08						
09						
10						
C. Services Borrower Did Shop For		**$2,655.50**				
01 Pest Inspection Fee	to Pests Co.	$120.50				
02 Survey Fee	to Surveys Co.	$85.00				
03 Title – Insurance Binder	to Epsilon Title Co.	$650.00				
04 Title – Lender's Title Insurance	to Epsilon Title Co.	$500.00				
05 Title – Settlement Agent Fee	to Epsilon Title Co.	$500.00				
06 Title – Title Search	to Epsilon Title Co.	$800.00				
07						
08						
D. TOTAL LOAN COSTS (Borrower-Paid)		**$4,694.05**				
Loan Costs Subtotals (A + B + C)		$4,664.25	$29.80			

Other Costs						
E. Taxes and Other Government Fees		**$85.00**				
01 Recording Fees	Deed: $40.00 Mortgage: $45.00	$85.00				
02 Transfer Tax	to Any State			$950.00		
F. Prepaids		**$2,120.80**				
01 Homeowner's Insurance Premium (12 mo.) to Insurance Co.		$1,209.96				
02 Mortgage Insurance Premium (mo.)						
03 Prepaid Interest ($17.44 per day from 4/15/13 to 5/1/13)		$279.04				
04 Property Taxes (6 mo.) to Any County USA		$631.80				
05						
G. Initial Escrow Payment at Closing		**$412.25**				
01 Homeowner's Insurance $100.83 per month for 2 mo.		$201.66				
02 Mortgage Insurance per month for mo.						
03 Property Taxes $105.30 per month for 2 mo.		$210.60				
04						
05						
06						
07						
08 Aggregate Adjustment		− 0.01				
H. Other		**$2,400.00**				
01 HOA Capital Contribution	to HOA Acre Inc.	$500.00				
02 HOA Processing Fee	to HOA Acre Inc.	$150.00				
03 Home Inspection Fee	to Engineers Inc.	$750.00			$750.00	
04 Home Warranty Fee	to XYZ Warranty Inc.			$450.00		
05 Real Estate Commission	to Alpha Real Estate Broker			$5,700.00		
06 Real Estate Commission	to Omega Real Estate Broker			$5,700.00		
07 Title – Owner's Title Insurance (optional) to Epsilon Title Co.		$1,000.00				
08						
I. TOTAL OTHER COSTS (Borrower-Paid)		**$5,018.05**				
Other Costs Subtotals (E + F + G + H)		$5,018.05				

J. TOTAL CLOSING COSTS (Borrower-Paid)		**$9,712.10**				
Closing Costs Subtotals (D + I)		$9,682.30	$29.80	$12,800.00	$750.00	$405.00
Lender Credits						

CLOSING DISCLOSURE

Exhibit 6.4 Sample H-25 Closing Disclosure, Page 3

Calculating Cash to Close
Use this table to see what has changed from your Loan Estimate.

	Loan Estimate	Final	Did this change?
Total Closing Costs (J)	$8,054.00	$9,712.10	YES •See Total Loan Costs (D) and Total Other Costs (I)
Closing Costs Paid Before Closing	$0	– $29.80	YES •You paid these Closing Costs before closing
Closing Costs Financed (Paid from your Loan Amount)	$0	$0	NO
Down Payment/Funds from Borrower	$18,000.00	$18,000.00	NO
Deposit	– $10,000.00	– $10,000.00	NO
Funds for Borrower	$0	$0	NO
Seller Credits	$0	– $2,500.00	YES •See Seller Credits in Section L
Adjustments and Other Credits	$0	– $1,035.04	YES •See details in Sections K and L
Cash to Close	$16,054.00	$14,147.26	

Summaries of Transactions
Use this table to see a summary of your transaction.

BORROWER'S TRANSACTION

K. Due from Borrower at Closing	$189,762.30
01 Sale Price of Property	$180,000.00
02 Sale Price of Any Personal Property Included in Sale	
03 Closing Costs Paid at Closing (J)	$9,682.30
04	
Adjustments	
05	
06	
07	

Adjustments for Items Paid by Seller in Advance	
08 City/Town Taxes to	
09 County Taxes to	
10 Assessments to	
11 HOA Dues 4/15/13 to 4/30/13	$80.00
12	
13	
14	
15	

L. Paid Already by or on Behalf of Borrower at Closing	$175,615.04
01 Deposit	$10,000.00
02 Loan Amount	$162,000.00
03 Existing Loan(s) Assumed or Taken Subject to	
04	
05 Seller Credit	$2,500.00
Other Credits	
06 Rebate from Epsilon Title Co.	$750.00
07	
Adjustments	
08	
09	
10	
11	

Adjustments for Items Unpaid by Seller	
12 City/Town Taxes 1/1/13 to 4/14/13	$365.04
13 County Taxes to	
14 Assessments to	
15	
16	
17	

CALCULATION	
Total Due from Borrower at Closing (K)	$189,762.30
Total Paid Already by or on Behalf of Borrower at Closing (L)	– $175,615.04
Cash to Close ☒ From ☐ To Borrower	**$14,147.26**

SELLER'S TRANSACTION

M. Due to Seller at Closing	$180,080.00
01 Sale Price of Property	$180,000.00
02 Sale Price of Any Personal Property Included in Sale	
03	
04	
05	
06	
07	
08	

Adjustments for Items Paid by Seller in Advance	
09 City/Town Taxes to	
10 County Taxes to	
11 Assessments to	
12 HOA Dues 4/15/13 to 4/30/13	$80.00
13	
14	
15	
16	

N. Due from Seller at Closing	$115,665.04
01 Excess Deposit	
02 Closing Costs Paid at Closing (J)	$12,800.00
03 Existing Loan(s) Assumed or Taken Subject to	
04 Payoff of First Mortgage Loan	$100,000.00
05 Payoff of Second Mortgage Loan	
06	
07	
08 Seller Credit	$2,500.00
09	
10	
11	
12	
13	

Adjustments for Items Unpaid by Seller	
14 City/Town Taxes 1/1/13 to 4/14/13	$365.04
15 County Taxes to	
16 Assessments to	
17	
18	
19	

CALCULATION	
Total Due to Seller at Closing (M)	$180,080.00
Total Due from Seller at Closing (N)	– $115,665.04
Cash ☐ From ☒ To Seller	**$64,414.96**

CLOSING DISCLOSURE

Exhibit 6.5 Sample H-25 Closing Disclosure, Page 4

Additional Information About This Loan

Loan Disclosures

Assumption

If you sell or transfer this property to another person, your lender

☐ will allow, under certain conditions, this person to assume this loan on the original terms.

☒ will not allow assumption of this loan on the original terms.

Demand Feature

Your loan

☐ has a demand feature, which permits your lender to require early repayment of the loan. You should review your note for details.

☒ does not have a demand feature.

Late Payment

If your payment is more than 15 days late, your lender will charge a late fee of 5% of the monthly principal and interest payment.

Negative Amortization (Increase in Loan Amount)

Under your loan terms, you

☐ are scheduled to make monthly payments that do not pay all of the interest due that month. As a result, your loan amount will increase (negatively amortize), and your loan amount will likely become larger than your original loan amount. Increases in your loan amount lower the equity you have in this property.

☐ may have monthly payments that do not pay all of the interest due that month. If you do, your loan amount will increase (negatively amortize), and, as a result, your loan amount may become larger than your original loan amount. Increases in your loan amount lower the equity you have in this property.

☒ do not have a negative amortization feature.

Partial Payments

Your lender

☒ may accept payments that are less than the full amount due (partial payments) and apply them to your loan.

☐ may hold them in a separate account until you pay the rest of the payment, and then apply the full payment to your loan.

☐ does not accept any partial payments.

If this loan is sold, your new lender may have a different policy.

Security Interest

You are granting a security interest in

456 Somewhere Ave., Anytown, ST 12345

You may lose this property if you do not make your payments or satisfy other obligations for this loan.

Escrow Account

For now, your loan

☒ will have an escrow account (also called an "impound" or "trust" account) to pay the property costs listed below. Without an escrow account, you would pay them directly, possibly in one or two large payments a year. Your lender may be liable for penalties and interest for failing to make a payment.

Escrow		
Escrowed Property Costs over Year 1	$2,473.56	Estimated total amount over year 1 for your escrowed property costs: *Homeowner's Insurance Property Taxes*
Non-Escrowed Property Costs over Year 1	$1,800.00	Estimated total amount over year 1 for your non-escrowed property costs: *Homeowner's Association Dues* You may have other property costs.
Initial Escrow Payment	$412.25	A cushion for the escrow account you pay at closing. See Section G on page 2.
Monthly Escrow Payment	$206.13	The amount included in your total monthly payment.

☐ will not have an escrow account because ☐ you declined it ☐ your lender does not offer one. You must directly pay your property costs, such as taxes and homeowner's insurance. Contact your lender to ask if your loan can have an escrow account.

No Escrow		
Estimated Property Costs over Year 1		Estimated total amount over year 1. You must pay these costs directly, possibly in one or two large payments a year.
Escrow Waiver Fee		

In the future,

Your property costs may change and, as a result, your escrow payment may change. You may be able to cancel your escrow account, but if you do, you must pay your property costs directly. If you fail to pay your property taxes, your state or local government may (1) impose fines and penalties or (2) place a tax lien on this property. If you fail to pay any of your property costs, your lender may (1) add the amounts to your loan balance, (2) add an escrow account to your loan, or (3) require you to pay for property insurance that the lender buys on your behalf, which likely would cost more and provide fewer benefits than what you could buy on your own.

Loan Calculations

Total of Payments. Total you will have paid after you make all payments of principal, interest, mortgage insurance, and loan costs, as scheduled.	$285,803.36
Finance Charge. The dollar amount the loan will cost you.	$118,830.27
Amount Financed. The loan amount available after paying your upfront finance charge.	$162,000.00
Annual Percentage Rate (APR). Your costs over the loan term expressed as a rate. This is not your interest rate.	4.174%
Total Interest Percentage (TIP). The total amount of interest that you will pay over the loan term as a percentage of your loan amount.	69.46%

Questions? If you have questions about the loan terms or costs on this form, use the contact information below. To get more information or make a complaint, contact the Consumer Financial Protection Bureau at **www.consumerfinance.gov/mortgage-closing**

Other Disclosures

Appraisal
If the property was appraised for your loan, your lender is required to give you a copy at no additional cost at least 3 days before closing. If you have not yet received it, please contact your lender at the information listed below.

Contract Details
See your note and security instrument for information about
- what happens if you fail to make your payments,
- what is a default on the loan,
- situations in which your lender can require early repayment of the loan, and
- the rules for making payments before they are due.

Liability after Foreclosure
If your lender forecloses on this property and the foreclosure does not cover the amount of unpaid balance on this loan,

☒ state law may protect you from liability for the unpaid balance. If you refinance or take on any additional debt on this property, you may lose this protection and have to pay any debt remaining even after foreclosure. You may want to consult a lawyer for more information.

☐ state law does not protect you from liability for the unpaid balance.

Refinance
Refinancing this loan will depend on your future financial situation, the property value, and market conditions. You may not be able to refinance this loan.

Tax Deductions
If you borrow more than this property is worth, the interest on the loan amount above this property's fair market value is not deductible from your federal income taxes. You should consult a tax advisor for more information.

Contact Information

	Lender	Mortgage Broker	Real Estate Broker (B)	Real Estate Broker (S)	Settlement Agent
Name	Ficus Bank		Omega Real Estate Broker Inc.	Alpha Real Estate Broker Co.	Epsilon Title Co.
Address	4321 Random Blvd. Somecity, ST 12340		789 Local Lane Sometown, ST 12345	987 Suburb Ct. Someplace, ST 12340	123 Commerce Pl. Somecity, ST 12344
NMLS ID					
ST License ID			Z765416	Z61456	Z61616
Contact	Joe Smith		Samuel Green	Joseph Cain	Sarah Arnold
Contact NMLS ID	12345				
Contact ST License ID			P16415	P51461	PT1234
Email	joesmith@ ficusbank.com		sam@omegare.biz	joe@alphare.biz	sarah@ epsilontitle.com
Phone	123-456-7890		123-555-1717	321-555-7171	987-555-4321

Confirm Receipt

By signing, you are only confirming that you have received this form. You do not have to accept this loan because you have signed or received this form.

_____   _____   _____   _____
Applicant Signature   Date   Co-Applicant Signature   Date

CLOSING DISCLOSURE   PAGE 5 OF 5 • LOAN ID # 123456789

Settlement process   The process of settlement consists of five basic steps:

    1.   Identify selling terms and closing costs.
    2.   Determine non-prorated debits and credits.
    3.   Determine prorated debits and credits.
    4.   Complete the closing statement.
    5.   Disburse funds.

Closing costs   **Selling terms and closing costs.** Selling terms are the price of the property, the buyer's deposit and downpayment, and the terms and amounts of the buyer's financing arrangements. Closing costs are final expenses that buyer or seller must pay at closing to complete the transaction. The sale contract identifies all selling terms and who pays which costs. The apportionment of expenses is subject to negotiation, and in the absence of a specific agreement, is determined by custom.

Closing costs include such items as brokerage fees, mortgage-related fees, title-related expenses, and real estate taxes (transfer tax, state mortgage tax, property tax).

Debits and credits. The closing statement accounts for the debits and credits of the buyer and seller to settle and complete the transaction. A debit is an amount that one party must pay at closing or has already paid prior to closing. A credit is an amount that a party must receive at closing or that has already been received prior to closing.

Exhibit 6.7 Debit and Credit

The excess of the buyer's debits over the buyer's credits is the amount the buyer must bring to the closing. The excess of the seller's credits over the seller's debits is the amount the seller will receive at closing.

An individual expense item that one party owes to a party unrelated to the transaction, such as an attorney or the state, is treated as *a debit to that party only*. An income or expense item that affects both parties is apportioned, or **prorated**, to each party to reflect the proper amount that each owes or should receive. A prorated item is treated as *a debit to one party and a credit to the other party for the same amount*.

Buyer's debits and credits. To determine how much money the buyer owes at closing, the buyer's debits are totaled and compared with the total of the buyer's credits. The excess of debits over credits is the amount the buyer must bring to the closing, usually in the form of a cashier's check or certified check. The items typically debited and credited to the buyer are illustrated in the following exhibit.

Exhibit 6.8 Buyer's Credits and Debits

Buyer's Credits

earnest money
loan amount (borrowed or assumed)
seller's share of prorated items the buyer will pay

Buyer's Debits

purchase price
expenses (per agreement or custom)
buyer's share of prorated items prepaid by seller

Seller's credits and debits. To determine how much the seller will receive at closing, the same procedure is followed for the seller's debits and credits. The excess of credits over debits is what the seller will receive. The items typically debited and credited to the seller are illustrated in the following exhibit.

Exhibit 6.9 Seller's Debits and Credits

Seller's Debits

expenses (per agreement or custom)
seller's share of prorated items the buyer will pay
loan balance or other lien to be paid off

Seller's Credits

purchase price
buyer's share of prorated items prepaid by seller

Non-prorated items. Non-prorated items are costs *incurred by one party only.* Items not prorated include those listed in the next exhibit.

Exhibit 6.10 Non-Prorated Items

Buyer usually pays	Seller usually pays
Mortgage recording fees Documentary stamp tax Intangible tax on mortgage Mortgage-related fees: appraisal, credit, survey, loan Impound reserves: insurance, taxes Attorney fees	Stamp tax on deed Title insurance Brokerage fee Inspection fees Title-related expenses Attorney fees

Prorated items. Many of the items to be settled at the closing are partly the responsibility of the buyer and partly of the seller. Some are expense items that the seller has *paid in advance*, where the buyer owes the seller part of the expense. Some are income items that the seller received in advance, and the seller owes the buyer a part of the income. Others are items the buyer will have to pay *in arrears*, and the seller owes the buyer part of the expense. The method of dividing financial responsibility for such items is **proration**. With a prorated item, there is always a debit to one party and a corresponding credit for the same amount to the other party.

Items paid in advance. At the time of closing, the seller has paid some items in advance that cover a period of time that goes beyond the closing date. In effect, the seller has prepaid some of the buyer's expenses, and the buyer must reimburse the seller. Heating oil and natural gas are typical items. By the same token, the seller of a rental property may have received rent or rental deposits in advance, and must reimburse the buyer for the part that belongs to the buyer.

For an expense the seller paid in advance, *the buyer receives a debit, and the seller receives a credit.*

For income the seller received in advance, *the buyer receives a credit, and the seller receives a debit.*

Items paid in arrears. At the time of closing, the seller has incurred certain expenses that have not been billed or paid at the time of closing and that the buyer will have to pay later. A typical item is real estate taxes.

For an item the buyer will pay in arrears, *the buyer receives a credit, and the seller receives a debit.*

Exhibit 6.11   Items Paid in Arrears and Advance

	arrears	advance
real estate taxes	x	
mortgage interest	x	
rents received by seller		x
utilities	x	

Charging shares. If the seller has paid the buyer's share of an item, *charge the buyer for the buyer's share of the period.* If the buyer will pay the seller's share of an item, *charge the seller for the seller's share of the period.* If the seller has received the buyer's share of an income item, *charge the seller for the buyer's share of the period.*

Exhibit 6.12   Who Gets Charged

Seller paid for the year: charge buyer for buyer's share

Annual expense – closing August 7											
Jan	Feb	Mar	Apr	May	Jun	Jul	Aug	Sep	Oct	Nov	Dec
							7 8				
Seller's share							Buyer's share				

Buyer will pay for the month: charge seller for seller's share

Monthly expense – closing August 7							
August							
1	2	3	4	5	6	7	8-31
Seller's share							Buyer's share

Computing prorations

The primary methods of calculating prorations are the 360/30-day method, which computes prorations on the basis of a 360-day year and 30-day month, and the 365-day method, which computes prorations on the basis of a 365-day year. In New York, the 360/30-day method is commonly used for prorating mortgage interest, taxes, utility bills, and other similar expenses.

In New York, the practice is typically that the buyer owns the property starting on and including the closing date.

360/30-day method. The 360/30-day method determines an average daily rate of payment for an item to be prorated *based on a 30-day month and a 360-day year*. The method consists of the following steps for annual and monthly items.

Annual items

1. Identify the total amount to be prorated.
2. Divide this amount by 12 to obtain an average monthly rate.
3. Divide the monthly rate by 30 to obtain an average daily rate.
4. Multiply the monthly amount times the seller's number of months of ownership in the year of the sale up to the month of closing. For the month of closing, multiply the seller's number of days of ownership times the daily amount and add the result to the previous result. The final result is the seller's pro rata share of this item.
5. The buyer's pro rata share of an item is the total amount less the seller's pro rata share.

Monthly items

1. Identify the total amount to be prorated.
2. Divide this amount by 30 to obtain the average daily amount.
3. Multiply the daily amount times the seller's number of days of ownership. The result is the seller's pro rata share of this item.
4. The buyer's pro rata share of an item is the total amount less the seller's pro rata share.

Exhibit 6.13 Prorating Annual Item: Real Estate Tax 12-month/30-day Method

A sale transaction on a single-family house closes on March 2. County taxes for the previous year, to be paid in arrears, amount to $1,730. The seller owns the house through the day of closing. What are the seller's and buyer's prorated shares of this item?

Total amount due:		=	$	1,730.00
Monthly amount:	1,730 ÷ 12	=	$	144.17
Daily amount:	144.17 ÷ 30	=	$	4.81
Seller's share:	144.17 x 2 mo.	=	$	288.34
	4.81 x 2 days	=	$	9.62
	288.34 + 9.62	=	$	297.96
Buyer's share	1,730 - 297.96	=	$	1,432.04

Closing statement entries. The seller will be charged for the seller's share of the proration; an amount of $297.96 will be entered as a debit to the seller and a credit to the buyer because the buyer will have to pay the seller's share when the tax bill is received.

Exhibit 6.14 Prorating Monthly Item: Rent Received 12-month/30-day Method

The house in the previous example has been rented during the listing and selling period at a rate of $1800 per month. Rent for the month of March was paid to the seller on March 1. What is the buyer's prorated share of this rent? The day of closing, March 2, belongs to the seller.

Total received:		=	$ 1,800.00
Daily amount:	$1800 \div 30$	=	$ 60.00
Seller's share:	60.00 x 2 days	=	$ 120.00
Buyer's share	1800.00 – 120.00	=	$ 1,680.00

Closing statement entries. The seller will be charged for the buyer's share of the proration; an amount of $1,680.00 will be debited to the seller's account and credited to the buyer's account because the seller has received rent that belongs to the new owner after closing.

365-day method. The 365-day method uses the actual number of days in the calendar. The steps in the calculation are the same for annual and monthly prorations. The steps are:

1. Identify the total annual or monthly amount to be prorated.
2. For an annual proration, divide the total amount by 365 to obtain a daily amount (366 in a Leap Year). For a monthly proration, divide the total amount by the actual number of days in the month to obtain the daily amount.
3. Multiply the daily amount times the seller's number of days of ownership. The result is the seller's pro rata share of the item.

The buyer's pro rata share of an item is the total amount less the seller's pro rata share.

Exhibit 6.15 Prorating an Annual Tax Bill, 365-day Method

The seller in the previous example has a $1,730 tax bill, paid annually in arrears on December 31. Closing is on March 2, and the seller owns the day of closing. What is the seller's prorated share of this item?

Total amount due:		=	$	1.730.00
Daily amount:	1730 ÷ 365	=	$	4.74
Seller's share:	61 days x 4.75 =		$	289.14
Buyer's share:	1730 - 289.14 =		$	1,440.86

Closing statement entries. The seller will be charged for the seller's share of the proration; an amount of $289.14 will be debited to the seller's account and credited to the buyer's account because the buyer will have paid the seller's share of the tax bill in arrears.

TITLE RECORDS

Chain of title
Recording system
Title evidence

New York requires the recording of all documents that affect rights and interests in real estate in the public real estate records of the county where the property is located. These public records, or **title records**, contain a history of every parcel of real estate in the county, including names of previous owners, liens, easements, and other encumbrances that have been recorded.

Title records serve a number of purposes, not the least of which is to avoid ownership disputes. Other important purposes include the following:

▶   **Public notice**

Title records protect the public by giving all concerned parties **constructive notice** of the condition of a property's legal title: who owns the property, who maintains claims and encumbrances against the property.

> ▸ **Buyer protection**
>
> Title records protect the buyer by revealing whether a property has **marketable title**, one free of undesirable encumbrances. The buyer is legally responsible for knowing the condition of title, since it is a matter of public record. Recording a transaction also protects a buyer by replacing the deed as evidence of ownership.

> ▸ **Lienholder protection**
>
> Title records protect the lienholder by putting the public on notice that the lien exists, and that it may be the basis for a foreclosure action. Recording also establishes the lien's priority.

Chain of title

Chain of title refers to the succession of property owners *of record* dating back to the original grant of title from the state to a private party. New York chains of title can date back in time to a grant from the King of England. Typically, New York title searches reach back 30-60 years. If there is a missing link in the chronology of owners, or if there was a defective conveyance, the chain is said to be broken, resulting in a **clouded title** to the property. To remove the cloud, an owner may need to initiate a **suit to quiet title**, which clears the title record of any unrecorded claims.

Abstract of Title. An abstract of title is a written, chronological summary of the property's title records and other public records affecting rights and interests in the property. It includes the property's chain of title and all current recorded liens and encumbrances, by date of filing. A title abstractor or title company analyst conducts the search of public records, called a **title search**, needed to produce an abstract. Insurers and lenders generally require the search to identify title defects and ascertain the current status of encumbrances.

A **title plant** is a duplicate set of records of a property copied from public records and maintained by a private company, such as a title company.

Recording system

There are no federal recording standards. Each state prescribes procedures and requirements for recording in public title records: forms, proper execution, acknowledgment, and witnessing.

To be recorded in New York, documents must show proof of transfer tax and mortgage tax payments where appropriate. Further, most counties require a deed must have a property transfer report attached. In New York City, the deed must have a multiple dwelling registration statement or the following affidavits: one that shows no registration statement is due, one stating there is a smoke alarm on property, and a New York City Real Property Transfer Tax form. The City has an additional requirement that all transfer forms must be prepared online through their designated automated system, Automated City Register Information System (ACRIS). Other areas have similar requirements with their own systems.

The Torrens system. Certain states, including New York, and counties use the Torrens system of recording. The Torrens system differs from other title recording systems in that *title passes only when the conveyance has been duly* *registered on the title certificate itself.* Encumbrances likewise have no legal effect until they are recorded. In effect, the Torrens title record is the title itself. It is not necessary to search public records to ascertain the status of title; it is all reflected on the title certificate.

To enter a property in the Torrens system, a court action must first clear title by giving notice to all potential interest holders that they must express their claims. At the end of the proceeding, the court decrees that the title is accepted into Torrens registration. The Torrens registry retains the original registration documents and provides copies to the recorder or other appropriate office. All subsequent transactions affecting title must follow the proper Torrens recording procedures and requirements.

Title evidence

Marketable title. Since the value of a property is only as good as the marketability of its title, the evidence supporting the status of title is a significant issue. To demonstrate marketable title to a buyer, a seller must show that the title is free of

- ▸ doubts about the identity of the current owner
- ▸ defects, such as an erroneous legal description
- ▸ claims that could affect value
- ▸ undisclosed or unacceptable encumbrances

The four principal forms of evidence the owner can use to support these assurances are:

- ▸ a Torrens certificate
- ▸ a title insurance policy
- ▸ an attorney's opinion of the title abstract
- ▸ a title certificate

Torrens certificate. If available, the Torrens certificate is the best evidence, for the reasons given earlier-- it is not merely a record, but is the title itself.

Title insurance. In the absence of Torrens registration, a title insurance policy is commonly accepted as the best evidence of marketable title. A title insurance policy indemnifies the policy holder against losses arising from defects in the insured title.

The common policy types are the lender's policy and the owner's policy, which protect the respective policy holders' interests in the property. Thus, a lender who holds an $80,000 mortgage on a property will obtain protection worth $80,000 against the possibility that the lender's lien cannot be enforced. The owner's policy will insure against defective title to the extent of the property's initial or appreciated value.

An owner's policy may have *standard coverage* or *extended coverage.* Standard coverage protects against title defects such as incompetent grantors, invalid deeds, fraudulent transaction documents, and defects in the chain of title. Extended coverage protects against liabilities that may not be of public record, including fraud, unrecorded ownership claims, unintentional recording errors, and unrecorded liens. Extended coverage may also protect against adverse possessors, boundary disputes, and prescriptive easements. Neither standard nor extended coverage insures against defects expressly excluded by the policy or defects that the owner might have been aware of but did not disclose.

Before issuing a title insurance policy, a title company conducts a *title search* to uncover defects in title or unrecorded breaks in the chain of title. If the search fails to discover any uninsurable defects, the company issues a **binder**, or commitment to insure. The binder recapitulates the property description, interest to be insured, names of insured parties, and exceptions to coverage.

Attorney's opinion of abstract. An attorney's opinion of abstract states that the attorney has examined a title abstract and gives the attorney's opinion of the condition and marketability of the title. Generally, an opinion is not a proof or guarantee of clear title. Further, it offers no protection in the event title turns out to be defective.

Title certificate. A title certificate is a summary of the condition of title as of the date of the certificate, based on a search of public records by an abstractor or title analyst. The certificate does not guarantee clear title against defects, unrecorded encumbrances or encroachments.

6 Title Closing and Costs
Snapshot Review

TITLE CLOSING

The setting
- sale contract sets date, location, and who participates

Closing process
- verify contract fulfillment; exchange consideration and title; pay expenses; sign final documents; arrange for recording the transaction

Broker's role in closing
- broker's role ranges from nil to conducting the proceedings to reporting the transaction

RESPA
- for residential property, first or second mortgage, federally-related mortgage, assumption modifying loan terms, lender charging over $50 for assumption
- lender must provide borrower with CFPB booklet, "Your Home Loan Toolkit"
- lender must provide CFPB's H-24 Loan Estimate of settlement costs
- lender must use CFPB's H-25 Closing disclosure
- lender must disclose who will be servicing loan
- places ceiling on amounts lenders may compel borrowers to place in escrow
- RESPA prohibits payment of referral fees and kickbacks; business relationships between firms involved in the transaction must be disclosed

TRID/TILA
- includes bundle of rights
- surface rights of real estate; air rights of the space above the surface; subsurface rights of the land beneath the surface of real estate parcel

H-25 Closing Disclosure
- new form replaces older confusing forms

Settlement process
- identify closing costs; determine who pays what; do prorations; assign debits and credits; complete closing statement; disburse funds water

Closing costs
- price, deposits, downpayment, financing, final expenses to be paid at closing; apportionment of expenses determined by sale contract or custom
- excess of buyer's debits over credits is amount buyer must produce at closing; excess of seller's credits over debits is amount seller must receive
- Non-prorated items incurred by one party only; not shared
- Prorated items incurred by buyer or seller in advance or arrears; shared by buyer and seller; typical: real estate taxes, insurance premiums, mortgage interest, rents

Computing prorations
- sale contract or local custom establishes methods of proration to be used for particular items
- 12-month/30-day method determines average daily amount based on 12-month year and 30-day month
- 365-day method determines an amount using the actual number of calendar days

TITLE RECORDS
- all instruments affecting title must be recorded
- give public notice; protect owners; protect lienholders' claims

Chain of title
- successive property owners from original grant to present owner
- abstract of title: chronology of recorded owners, transfers, encumbrance

Recording system
- local property recording system governed by state law
- Torrens registry: requires court action initially: legal title does not pass until recordation occurs

Title evidence
- needed to prove marketable title as well as who owns
- forms of evidence: Torrens; title insurance; attorney's opinion of abstract; title certificate

CHAPTER SIX: TITLE CLOSING AND COSTS

Snapshot Review

6.1. What is the primary purpose of the Closing Disclosure in a real estate transaction?

   a. To serve as a preliminary estimate of the loan terms and costs before final approval
   b. To provide a detailed account of the final loan terms and closing costs to the borrower
   c. To offer a summary of the property inspection results and necessary repairs
   d. To detail the buyer's and seller's responsibilities for property maintenance post-closing

6.2. Which of these is usually a non-prorated item that a seller pays at closing?

   a. Mortgage recording fees
   b. Impound reserves
   c. Title insurance
   d. Appraisal

6.3. The excess of _____ is the amount the buyer must bring to the closing, usually in the form of a cashier's check or certified check.

   a. buyer debits over buyer credits
   b. seller debits over buyer credits
   c. seller debits over seller credits
   d. buyer credits over buyer debits

6.4. Lenders must deliver or mail the Loan Estimate (Form H-24) to the consumer no later than

   a. seven days before closing.
   b. the third business day after receiving a loan application.
   c. two weeks after receiving the loan application.
   d. five days after signing a contract to purchase.

6.5. Title records protect the _____ by putting the public on notice that a lien exists, and that it may be the basis for a foreclosure action.

   a. seller
   b. buyer
   c. lienholder
   d. insurance company

6.6. Which of the following laws primarily serves the purpose of clarifying settlement costs and eliminating kickbacks that increase settlement costs?

   a. TILA
   b. RESPA
   c. HOEPA
   d. ECOA

6.7. In New York, which method for computing prorations is commonly used for prorating mortgage interest, taxes, and utility bills?

   a. 12-month
   b. 6-month half year
   c. 365-day year
   d. 360/30-day

6.8. Which of the following would be considered a buyer's credit at closing?

   a. Purchase price
   b. Earnest money
   c. Seller's prepaids
   d. Down payment

6.9. How does the Torrens system, which is used in New York, differ from other title recording systems?

   a. Title is passed based on the oldest recorded deed in the county records.
   b. Title transfers automatically with a signed agreement, without the need for registration.
   c. Title is verified through a private title insurance company rather than public records.
   d. Title passes only when the conveyance has been duly registered on the title certificate itself.

6.10. A(n) _____ is a summary of the condition of title as of a certain date, based on a search of public records by an abstractor or analyst.

   a. attorney's opinion of abstract
   b. Torrens certificate
   c. title certificate
   d. title insurance policy

6.11. To be marketable, title must be

a. registered in Torrens.
b. free of undisclosed defects and encumbrances.
c. abstracted by an attorney.
d. guaranteed by a title certificate.

6.12. The Real Estate Settlement Procedures Act prescribes closing procedures that must be followed whenever

a. a first, second, or third mortgage lien is involved.
b. the loan is intended to be sold to FNMA.
c. the buyer pays all cash for the property.
d. the property is a residential complex in excess of four units.

6.13. Assume a seller at closing must pay transfer taxes at the rate of $1.00 for every $500 of purchase price, or fraction thereof. If the sale price is $345,600, how much tax must the seller pay?

a. $69.12
b. $70.00
c. $691
d. $692

6.14. The Integrated Disclosures rule applies to certain loans, including

a. HELOCs.
b. refinances.
c. reverse mortgages.
d. mobile home loans.

6.15. Which of the following items are typically paid in arrears?

a. Taxes and insurance
b. Rents and interest
c. Taxes and mortgage interest
d. Rents and insurance

7 Contract of Sale and Leases

Leases
Sales Contracts

LEASES

Definition
Types of leasehold estates
Requirements for validity
Standard provisions
Leasehold rights and obligations

Definition

A **lease** is an agreement between the owner of real property (**lessor**) and a tenant (**lessee**) to allow the tenant to possess, use, and occupy the property. The lease is both a conveyance and a contract between the two parties to identify and uphold certain covenants and obligations. The lease indicates the length of time the agreement will be in effect, the amount and timing of the rent the tenant will pay, and the covenants and obligations of both parties. As a conveyance, a lease conveys an interest, called the leasehold estate, but does not convey legal title to the property. For this reason, a leasehold is also called a **nonfreehold estate** or **less-than-freehold** estate.

The New York State Statute of Frauds allows leases for less than 1 year to be oral and not written. However, the statute mandates that any lease in effect for longer than 1 year must be in writing just as any agreement that conveys partial or total interest in real property must be in writing. A lease for longer than 1 year that is not in writing is simply not enforceable. Further, as standard practice, both the property owner and the tenant should sign the lease.

Types of leasehold estates

There are four principal types of leasehold estate, and all are recognized in New York:

▸   **estate for years**: has a specific lease term

▸   **estate from period-to-period**: the lease term automatically renews

▸   **estate at will**: has no specified lease term

▸   **estate at sufferance**: a tenancy without consent

The legal essence of a valid lease is that *it conveys an exclusive right to use and occupy a property for a limited period of time in exchange for rent and the return of the property after the lease term is over.* Leasehold estates are distinguished from freeholds by their temporary nature. Every leasehold has a limited duration, whether the term is 99 years or not stated at all, as in an estate at will.

Estate for years. This type of leasehold estate is for a period of time with a defined start and end date. It could be for days, weeks, months, or years. The lease may terminate when the end date arrives, when either of the parties has breached the lease, or when both parties mutually agree to terminate.

Estate from period-to-period. This estate is also referred to as a **periodic lease** and may not contain a specific termination date. Instead, the lease may continue indefinitely on a month-to-month, year-to-year, or even week-to-week basis with the renewal being automatic when the time frame is up. The automatic renewals continue with each rent payment until either or both of the parties terminates. To legally terminate, the acting party must give proper notice. Month-to-month leases require a one-month notice in New York State or 30 days' notice in New York City.

Tenants in New York who remain in the leased property after the lease expiration or at the end of the lease termination notice date are referred to as *holdover tenants.* If the tenant attempts to pay rent at this time and the landlord accepts the rent, then a month-to-month tenancy goes into effect.

Estate at will. Also called a tenancy at will, this estate allows the tenant to possess the property with no period of time indicated. Typically, the estate is indefinite but allows termination with proper notice. The death of either party automatically terminates the estate.

Estate at sufferance. This estate is one that occurs when a tenant remains in possession of the property against the landlord's wishes. If the tenant had a lease that expired but refuses to leave the property, the tenant has created an estate at sufferance or a tenancy at sufferance.

Requirements for validity

The requirements for a valid lease in New York include the following:

▸ **Parties.** The principal parties must be legally competent to enter into the agreement, i.e., meet certain age, sanity, and other requirements.

▸ **Lease form.** A lease for less than 1 year may be written or oral, but a lease for more than 1 year must be in writing. Residential leases in New York must also be in plain English.

▸ **Demising clause.** The landlord must agree to lease the property, and the tenant must agree to take possession of the property.

▸ **Property description.** The lease must identify the property by its legal description or other locally accepted reference.

▸ **Lease term.** The duration of the lease must be included.

▸ **Consideration.** The amount of rent, method of payment, and when it is due is required. New York tenants are expected to pay rent in arrears (at the end of the indicated time period) and not in advance. Rent of commercial spaces is listed in an annual amount split into monthly payments. If the lease simply lists monthly payments, it could be interpreted as a month-to-month lease.

▸ **Signatures.** The landlord must sign the lease to convey the leasehold interest. To enforce the terms of the lease, the tenant should also sign. Multiple tenants who sign a single lease are jointly and severally responsible for fulfilling lease obligations. Thus, if one renter abandons an apartment, the other renters remain liable for rent.

▸ **Delivery.** The landlord must make duplicate original leases, keep one for the landlord's own records, and deliver the other one to the tenant.

Standard provisions

Leases typically include clauses that further define the contractual possession of the premises by the tenant and the responsibilities of the landlord.

Rent and security deposit. A rent clause stipulates the time, place, manner and amount of rent payment. It defines any grace period that is allowed, and states the penalties for delinquency.

The lease may also call for a security deposit to protect the landlord against losses from property damage or the tenant's default. State law regulates the handling of the security deposit: where it is deposited and whether the tenant receives interest on the deposit.

New York General Obligations Law requires landlords to hold security deposits in trust where they are not commingled with the landlord's own monies or accounts. Landlords of residential buildings with six or more dwelling units are required to hold security deposits in a New York interest-bearing account and provide written notice to tenants as to where the funds are being held. Landlords are also required to give 99% of the earned interest to the tenants. The remaining 1% is considered an administrative charge to cover the bank account servicing fee. Tenants have the option of receiving the interest annually or in full when the lease terminates but may not be required to waive this provision. The same holds true for mobile home parks.

If the property owner sells the rental property, the security deposits must be transferred to the new owner within 5 days of delivery of the deed to the new owner. The original owner is required to notify the tenants by registered or certified mail of the new ownership and address. The notice must also include the fact that the tenants' deposits were transferred to the new owner who will then be responsible to return any deposits received from the original owner upon the tenant's lease termination. For buildings with six or more dwelling units, the new owner will be responsible for the eventual return of all security deposits whether or not they were transferred from the original owner. Consequently, purchasers of rental property should review all tenant and financial records thoroughly to ensure all deposits are accounted for and transferred.

Lease term. The lease needs to state the start and end dates of the lease term and include the actual lease period, i.e., the length of the total term. A statement similar to the following covers this requirement: *"This lease begins on January 1, 2023, and ends on December 31, 2025, for a period of 3 years."*

If the lease is to include options to extend or renew the lease period past the stated date, that too must be stated in the lease. A provisional option to renew included in the lease should state a deadline by which the tenant is to notify the landlord of the tenant's intention to renew.

If there is no term end date included, the lease is a periodic lease, or estate from period-to-period, that automatically renews with each rent payment.

While leases under rent control or rent stabilization automatically provide residential tenants with an option to renew for 1 or 2 more years, commercial leases do not guarantee renewal. It is the landlord's decision whether or not to offer a lease extension or renewal after the stated lease period.

Subletting. New York Real Property Law Section 226-B provides legal guidelines for subletting and assignment of rental property in the state.

Subletting (subleasing) is the transfer by a tenant, the **sublessor**, of a *portion* of the leasehold interest to another party, the **sublessee**, through the execution of a **sublease**. The sublease spells out all of the rights and obligations of the sublessor and sublessee, including the payment of rent to the sublessor. The sublessor remains *primarily liable* for the original lease with the landlord. The subtenant is *liable* only to the sublessor.

For example, John is a tenant renting a space from Terry, his landlord. John decides to sublease a portion of his occupied rental space to Clara for part of John's lease term. In this case, Clara will pay rent to John under the sublease. John will then pay his total rent to Terry under the terms of his original lease.

New York tenants may sublet only if the original lease allows it or if they obtain written consent from the landlord. Even with the consent, landlords are allowed to screen potential sublessees and deny them for reasons that are legally acceptable.

Leases typically have one of the following clauses regarding subleasing.

1.   A clause strictly prohibiting a sublease

New York leases that prohibits a tenant's right to sublease are considered void as a matter of public policy.

2.   A clause requiring the landlord's written consent to sublease

This clause allows the tenant to sublease if the landlord consents in writing, but the landlord is not required to consent.

3.   A clause allowing a tenant to sublease with no need for the landlord's additional written permission

With this clause, the tenant may sublease without landlord approval and without even notifying the landlord if the lease already provides the consent.

4.   No clause or other language consenting to sublease

The tenant is prohibited from subleasing without first obtaining the landlord's consent. However, the landlord is not required to give consent.

In New York, a landlord can prohibit a tenant from subleasing but only for reasonable grounds. If the landlord of a residential building with four or more units unreasonably refuses to allow a sublet, the tenant may still sublet.

A tenant's request to the landlord to sublet must include the following:

▸   The sublease term

▸   The sublessee's name and permanent home address

▸   The reason the sublease is being requested

▸   The current tenant's address during the sublease

▸   Written consent from any co-tenant or guarantor of the lease

Once the request to sublet has been received, the landlord has 10 days to request addition information. If the landlord fails to respond within 30 days, then the request is deemed approved.

The landlord may deny the request to sublet if the landlord believes the sublessee would not be able to pay the rent or if the sublessee is not reputable.

Once approved, the sublessee has the same rights and responsibilities as the original tenant in regards to privacy, health and safety standards, and due process for an eviction. If a tenant fails to obtain landlord consent and subleases the unit anyway, the tenant has breached the lease. Such a breach will result in the original tenant and the subtenant to be given a 10-day notice of eviction. The landlord may also sue the original tenant for any damages. Additionally, the sublessee may also have grounds to take legal action against the original tenant.

Subletting residential rent-stabilized apartments is allowed with the landlord's permission but only for half of a 4-year period. During the sublease, the original tenant must maintain the apartment as a primary residence and may not have a second primary residence. Landlords may terminate the tenancy of a tenant who has a second primary residence. If the apartment is sublet furnished, the original tenant may charge the sublessee 10% more than the original rent, and the original landlord may charge the original tenant 5% more than the original rent. Increases greater than these are illegal and can result in the original tenant losing rights to the dwelling and/or receiving a charge of rent gouging.

Assignment. Just as with subletting, a tenant may not assign the lease without obtaining written consent from the owner/landlord.

An assignment of the lease is a transfer of the *entire leasehold interest* by a tenant, the **assignor**, to a third party, the **assignee**. There is no second lease, and the assignor retains no residual rights of occupancy or other leasehold rights unless expressly stated in the assignment agreement. The assignee becomes primarily liable for the lease and rent, and the assignor, the original tenant, remains secondarily liable. The assignee pays rent directly to the landlord.

The original tenant's obligation to make rent payments can be waived by the landlord through a *novation agreement* which can substitute the new tenant for the original tenant or can substitute a new lease for the original tenant's lease.

If the landlord refuses to allow assignment without cause or with unreasonable cause, the tenant may then terminate the original lease with a 30-day notice. However, if the landlord reasonably refuses to allow an assignment, the tenant may not assign and will not be released from the original lease.

Use of premises. A **use of premises clause** is a provision that outlines the **permitted or lawful use** of the rented property by the tenant or landlord. The clause will outline how the tenant may use the property and what activities and uses are restricted or prohibited. In a residential lease, the clause may include the provision that the property is used only for residential purposes. If the lease is with a disabled tenant, the clause may state that the tenant may make reasonable alterations to accommodate the disability but must do so at the tenant's own expense. The clause may also state that the tenant will be required to restore the residence back to its original state when the disabled tenant terminates the lease.

A commercial lease will have specific uses that are permitted or prohibited to accommodate the business and associated activities. The clause may, for example, require the space be used only for one type of business as opposed to leaving it open ended for several. This restriction of use would be particularly relevant in a situation where the tenant intends to sublet or assign the space. While the original lease may provide the right to sublet, it may restrict the type of use which would in turn restrict who the sublessee could be. The commercial lease's clause may include detailed uses and restrictions such as limiting operating hours, signage, and the sale of alcohol.

Use provisions may impose specific rules and regulations for the property that are aimed at protecting the property's condition as well as the rights of other tenants.

Improvements and alterations. Tenants may not make alterations or improvements to the rental premises without landlord approval. A landlord typically wants to prevent a tenant from making alterations that later tenants may not desire. However, if the landlord allows the improvements, it opens the door for determining if the improvement is a fixture that becomes the landlord's property at the termination of the lease. It could also be determined that the improvement is a trade fixture that the tenant can remove prior to terminating the lease and then restoring the premises to its original state.

However, an improvements and alterations clause identifies necessary permissions and procedures as well as who owns improvements. Customarily, tenant improvements become the property of the landlord in the absence of an express agreement to the contrary.

Repairs and maintenance. Repairs and maintenance provisions define the landlord's and tenant's respective responsibilities for property repairs and maintenance. In New York, residential leases contain an implied warranty of habitability wherein the landlord guarantees the premises is fit for human habitation. The tenant is not to be exposed to any condition or situation that would endanger life, health, or safety and has the right of quiet enjoyment so as not to be disturbed by others.

Generally, the tenant is responsible for routine upkeep of the premises and for returning the premises in the same condition as when the tenant's lease began, with an allowance for ordinary wear and tear.

The landlord is responsible for maintaining the premises in a habitable condition and making general repairs to common elements, such as hallways, stairs, and other public spaces.

Leasehold rights and obligations

Tenant's rights and obligations. A lease conveys a **leasehold interest** or **estate** that grants the tenant the following rights during the lease term:

▶   exclusive possession and occupancy

▶   exclusive use

▶   quiet enjoyment

▶   profits from use

Tenants in New York State have the right to join a tenants' organization without a landlord's retaliation. Landlords are also prohibited from evicting a tenant strictly based on retaliation. If a lease stipulates that the landlord is to provide heat for the premises and the landlord fails to do so, New York allows the tenants to pay the utility company directly to obtain heat. The tenant may then deduct the payment amount from the next rent payment. New York City allows residential tenants to join together to initiate a special court proceeding that allows them to use their rent money to resolve conditions that are hazardous to life, health, or safety. This action requires at least one-third of the tenants in a multiple-dwelling building to participate.

A tenant has the sole right to occupy and use the premises without interference from outside parties, including the landlord. The landlord may enter the premises for specified purposes such as inspections, but the interference must be reasonable and limited. In addition, the landlord can do nothing outside of the lease's express provisions that would impair a commercial tenant's enjoyment of income deriving from use of the premises. For example, the landlord cannot place a kiosk in front of a retail tenant's entry in such a way as to prevent customers from entering the store.

The lease defines the tenant's obligations, which principally are to:

- pay the rent on time

- maintain the property's condition

- comply with the rules and regulations of the building

Landlord's rights and obligations. In conveying the leasehold estate, the landlord acquires a **leased fee estate,** which entails the rights to:

- receive rent

- re-possess the property following the lease term

- monitor the tenant's obligations to maintain the premises

The lease defines the landlord's obligations, which principally are to:

- provide the necessary building support and services

- maintain the condition of the property

Death of tenant or landlord. A valid lease creates obligations that survive the death of the landlord or tenant, with certain exceptions. A tenant's estate *remains liable for payment of rent if the tenant dies;* the landlord's estate *remains bound to provide occupancy despite the landlord's death.*

Conveyance of leased property. The landlord may sell, assign, or mortgage the leased fee interest. However, transferring and encumbering the leased property do not extinguish the obligations and covenants of a lease. Buyers and creditors, therefore, must take their respective interests subject to the terms of the lease.

SALES CONTRACTS

General contract law
Sales contracts
Contract for deed
Option-to-buy contract

General contract law

A **contract** is an agreement between two or more parties who, in a "meeting of the minds," have pledged to perform or refrain from performing some act. A *valid* contract is one that is *legally enforceable* by virtue of meeting certain requirements of contract law. If a contract does not meet the requirements, it is not valid and the parties to it cannot resort to a court of law to enforce its provisions.

Note that a contract is not a legal form or a prescribed set of words in a document, but rather the intangible agreement that was made in "the meeting of the minds" of the parties to the contract.

In terms of validity and enforceability, a court may construe the legal status of a contract in one of four ways:

> ▸ valid

> ▸ valid but unenforceable

> ▸ void

> ▸ voidable

Valid. A valid contract is one which meets the legal requirements for validity. These requirements are explained in the next section.

A valid contract that is in writing is enforceable within a statutory time period. A valid contract that is made orally is also generally enforceable within a statutory period, with the exceptions noted below.

Valid but unenforceable. State laws declare that some contracts are enforceable only if they are in writing. These laws apply in particular to the transfer of interests in real estate. Thus, while an oral contract may meet the tests for validity, if it falls under the laws requiring a written contract, the parties will not have legal recourse to enforce performance. An oral long-term lease and an oral real estate sales contract are examples of contracts that may be valid but not enforceable.

Note that such contracts, if valid, remain so even though not enforceable. This means that if the parties fully execute and perform the contract, the outcome may not be altered.

Void. A void contract is an agreement that does not meet the tests for validity and, therefore, is no contract at all. If a contract is void, neither party can enforce it.

For example, a contract that does not include consideration is void. Likewise, a contract to extort money from a business is void. Void contracts and instruments are also described as "null and void."

Voidable. A voidable contract is one which initially appears to be valid, but is subject to rescission by a party to the contract who is deemed to have acted under some kind of disability. Only the party who claims the disability may rescind the legal effect of the contract.

For example, a party who was the victim of duress, coercion, or fraud in creation of a contract, and can prove it, may disaffirm the contract. However, the disaffirmation must occur within a legal time frame for the act of rescission to be valid. Similarly, if the party who has cause to disaffirm the contract elects instead to perform it, the contract is no longer voidable but valid.

A voidable contract differs from a void contract in that the latter does not require an act of disaffirmation to render it unenforceable.

Criteria for validity

A contract is valid only if it meets all of the following criteria.

Exhibit 7.1 Contract Validity Requirements

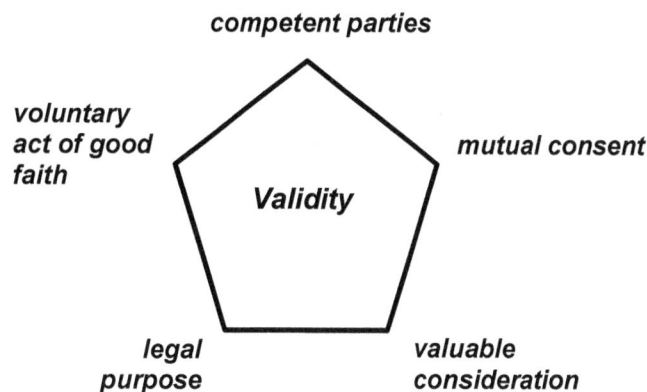

competent parties

voluntary
act of good
faith

mutual consent

Validity

legal
purpose

valuable
consideration

Competent parties. The parties to a contract must have the capacity to contract, and there must be at least two such parties. Thus, the owner of a tenancy for life cannot deed his interest to himself in the form of a fee simple, as this would involve only one party. Capacity to contract is determined by three factors:

> ▸ legal age

> ▸ mental competency

> ▸ legitimate authority

Depending on state law, a contract involving a minor as a party may be either void or voidable. If the law allows a minor to contract, the contract will generally be voidable and the minor can disaffirm the contract.

To be mentally competent, a party must have sufficient understanding of the import and consequences of a contract. Competency in this context is separate and distinct from sanity. Incompetent parties, or parties of "unsound mind," may not enter into enforceable contracts. The incompetency of a party may be ruled by a court of law or by other means. In some areas, convicted felons may be deemed incompetent, depending on the nature of the crime.

During the period of one's incompetency, a court may appoint a guardian who may act on the incompetent party's behalf with court approval.

If the contracting party is representing another person or business entity, the representative must have the *legal authority* to contract. If representing another person, the party must have a bona fide power of attorney. If the contracting party is representing a corporation, the person must have the appropriate power and approval to act, such as would be conferred in a duly executed resolution of the Board of Directors. If the contracting entity is a general partnership, any partner may validly contract for the partnership. In a limited partnership, only general partners may be parties to a contract.

Mutual consent. Mutual consent, also known as *offer and acceptance* and *meeting of the minds,* requires that a contract involve a clear and definite offer and an intentional, unqualified acceptance of the offer. In effect, the parties must agree to the terms without equivocation. A court may nullify a contract where the acceptance of terms by either party was partial, accidental, or vague.

Valuable consideration. A contract must contain a two-way exchange of valuable consideration as compensation for performance by the other party. The exchange of considerations must be two-way. The contract is not valid or enforceable if just one party provides consideration.

Exhibit 7.2 Consideration

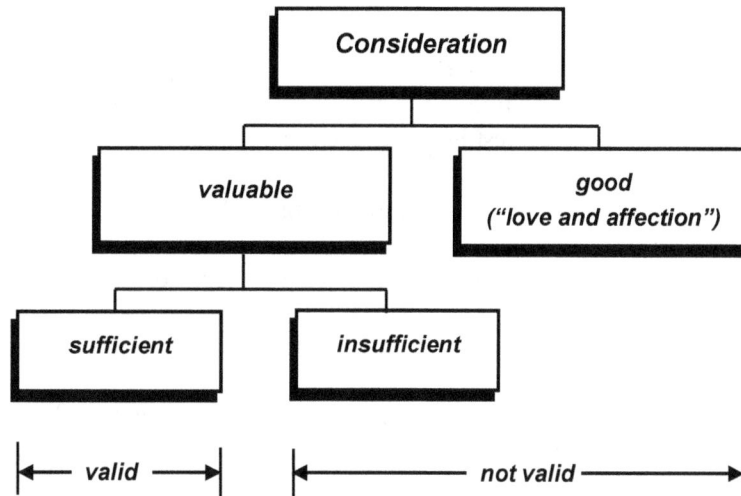

```
                    ┌─────────────────┐
                    │  Consideration  │
                    └────────┬────────┘
                ┌────────────┴────────────┐
        ┌───────┴───────┐        ┌────────┴────────┐
        │   valuable    │        │      good       │
        │               │        │("love and affection")│
        └───────┬───────┘        └─────────────────┘
        ┌───────┴───────┐
  ┌─────┴─────┐   ┌─────┴──────┐
  │ sufficient│   │insufficient│
  └───────────┘   └────────────┘

  ├── valid ──┤   ├──── not valid ────┤
```

Valuable consideration can be something of tangible value, such as money or something a party promises to do or not do. For example, a home builder may promise to build a house for a party as consideration for receiving money from the home buyer. Or, a landowner may agree not to sell a property as consideration for a developer's option money. Also, valuable consideration can be something intangible that a party must give up, such as a homeowner's occupancy of the house in exchange for rent. In effect, consideration is the price one party must pay to obtain performance from the other party.

Valuable consideration may be contrasted with good consideration, or "love and affection," which does not qualify as consideration in a valid contract. Good consideration is something of questionable value, such as a child's love for her mother. Good consideration disqualifies a contract because, while one's love or affection is certainly valuable to the other party, it is not something that is specifically offered in exchange for something else. Good consideration can, however, serve as a nominal consideration in transferring a real property interest as a gift.

In some cases, what is promised as valuable consideration must also be deemed to be *sufficient* consideration. Grossly insufficient consideration, such as $50,000 for a $2 million property, may invalidate a contract on the grounds that the agreement is a gift rather than a contract. In other cases where there is an extreme imbalance in the considerations exchanged, a contract may be invalidated as a violation of good faith bargaining.

Legal purpose. The content, promise, or intent of a contract must be lawful. A contract that proposes an illegal act is void.

Voluntary good faith act. The parties must create the contract in good faith as a free and voluntary act. A contract is thus voidable if one party acted under duress, coercion, fraud, or misrepresentation.

For example, if a property seller induces a buyer to purchase a house based on assurances that the roof is new, the buyer may rescind the agreement if the roof turns out to be twenty years old and leaky.

Validity of a conveyance contract

In addition to satisfying the foregoing requirements, a contract that conveys an interest in real estate must:

> ▶ be in writing, with edits initialed or signed by interested parties

> ▶ contain a legal description of the property

> ▶ be signed by one or more of the parties

A lease contract that has a term of one year or less is an exception. Such leases do not have to be in writing to be enforceable.

Enforcement limitations

Certain contracts that fail to meet the validity requirements are voidable if a damaged party takes appropriate action. The enforcement of voidable contracts, however, is limited by statutes of limitation. Certain other contracts which are valid may not be enforceable due to the statute of frauds.

Statute of limitations. The statute of limitations restricts the time period for which an injured party in a contract has the right to rescind or disaffirm the contract. A party to a voidable contract must act within the statutory period.

New York Civil Practice Law and Rules section 213(2) limits the time period for taking legal action to enforce the party's rights or to seek damages for breach of contract. For written contracts, legal action must commence within 6 years of the breach unless the contract specifies a shorter time period. For oral contracts, the time period is also 6 years. However, there are some oral contracts, e.g., contracts for the sale of goods, for which the time limit is 4 years. The time limit starts on the date the cause of action took place. However, under the *discovery rule*, if the breach is not immediately apparent, the time period for taking legal action would begin on the date the breach is discovered or should have been discovered.

Statute of frauds. New York Consolidated Laws, GOB Section 5-703 provides requirements under the statute of frauds. The statute requires that certain contracts *must be in writing* to be enforceable. Real estate contracts that convey an interest in real property fall in this category, with the exception that a lease duration of 1 year or less may be oral. All other contracts to buy, sell, exchange, or lease interests in real property must be in writing to be enforceable. This includes *listing agreements*.

The statute of frauds concerns the enforceability of a contract, not its validity. Once the parties to a valid oral contract have executed and performed it, even if the contract was unenforceable, a party cannot use the Statute of Frauds to rescind the contract.

For example, a broker and a seller have an oral agreement. Following the terms of the agreement, the broker finds a buyer, and the seller pays the commission. They have now executed the contract, and the seller cannot later force the broker to return the commission based on the statute of frauds.

Electronic contracting

Contracting electronically through email and fax greatly facilitates the completion of transactions. Clients, lenders, title agents, inspectors, brokers, and other participants in a transaction can quickly share documentation and information. Electronic contracting is made possible by the Uniform Electronic Transactions Act (UETA) and the Electronic Signatures in Global and National Commerce Act (E-Sign), which are federal laws. UETA, which has been accepted in most states, provides that electronic records and signatures are legal and must be accepted. E-Sign makes contracts, records, and signatures legally enforceable, regardless of medium, even where UETA is not accepted.

Offer and acceptance

The mutual consent required for a valid contract is reached through the process of offer and acceptance: The **offeror** proposes contract terms in an **offer** to the **offeree**. If the offeree accepts all terms without amendment, the offer becomes a contract. The exact point at which the offer becomes a contract is when the offeree gives the offeror notice of the acceptance.

Exhibit 7.3 Offer, Counteroffer and Acceptance

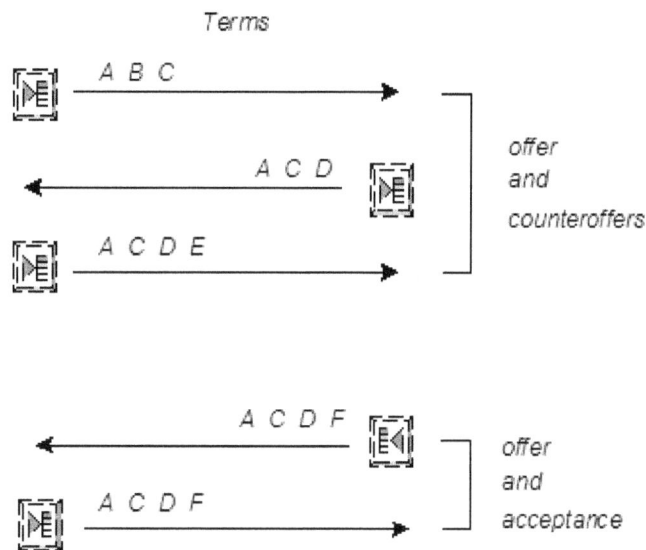

Offer. An offer expresses the offeror's intention to enter into a contract with an offeree to perform the terms of the agreement in exchange for the offeree's performance. In a real estate sale or lease contract, the offer must clearly contain all intended terms of the contract in writing and be communicated to the offeree.

If an offer contains an expiration date and the phrase "time is of the essence," the offer expires at exactly the time specified. In the absence of a stated time period, the offeree has a "reasonable" time to accept an offer.

Acceptance. An offer gives the offeree the power of accepting. For an acceptance to be valid, the offeree must manifestly and unequivocally accept all terms of the offer without change, and so indicate by signing the offer, preferably with a date of signing. The acceptance must then be communicated to the offeror. If the communication of acceptance is by mail, the offer is considered to be communicated as soon as it is placed in the mail.

Counteroffer

By changing any of the terms of an offer, the offeree creates a counteroffer, and the original offer is void. At this point, the offeree becomes the offeror, and the new offeree gains the right of acceptance. If the counteroffer is accepted, it becomes a valid contract provided all other requirements are met.

For example, a seller changes the expiration date of a buyer's offer by one day, signs the offer and returns it to the buyer. The single amendment extinguishes the buyer's offer, and the buyer is no longer bound by any agreement. The seller's amended offer is a counteroffer which now gives the buyer the right of acceptance. If the buyer accepts the counteroffer, the counteroffer becomes a binding contract.

Revocation of an offer

An offer may be revoked, or withdrawn, at any time before the offeree has communicated acceptance. The revocation extinguishes the offer and the offeree's right to accept it.

For example, a buyer has offered to purchase a house for the listed price. Three hours later, a family death radically changes the buyer's plans. She immediately calls the seller and revokes the offer, stating she is no longer interested in the house. Since the seller had not communicated acceptance of the offer to the buyer, the offer is legally cancelled.

If the offeree has paid consideration to the offeror to leave an offer open, and the offeror accepts, an option has been created which cancels the offeror's right to revoke the offer over the period of the option.

Termination of an offer

Any of the following actions or circumstances can terminate an offer:

▸ acceptance: the offeree accepts the offer, converting it to a contract

▸ rejection: the offeree rejects the offer

▸ revocation: the offeror withdraws the offer before acceptance

▸ lapse of time: the offer expires

▸ counteroffer: the offeree changes the offer

▸ death or insanity of either party

Assignment and novation of a contract

A real estate contract that is not a personal contract for services can be assigned to another party unless the terms of the agreement specifically prohibit assignment. When a contract is assigned, all of one party's rights are transferred to a third party. Novation involves substituting a new contract for the existing one and/or substituting a new party for one existing party to the contract.

Listing agreements, for example, are not assignable, since they are personal service agreements between agent and principal. Sales contracts, however, are assignable because they involve the purchase of real property rather than a personal service.

For an assignment or novation to be performed, the original contract must include a clause that allows either act. If the contract does not have such a clause or has a clause prohibiting the act, then no assignment or novation may occur.

Contract preparation

State laws define the extent to which real estate brokers and agents may legally prepare real estate contracts. Such laws, referred to as "broker-lawyer accords," also define what types of contracts brokers and agents may prepare. In some states, brokers and agents may not draft contracts, but they may use standard promulgated forms and complete the blanks in the form.

The New York Department of State prohibits brokers from actually drafting contracts or other legal documents as that would constitute an unauthorized practice of law. However, brokers are permitted to complete already drafted contracts. They may not add their own provisions to the document without obtaining approval of the addition from attorneys for both parties to the contract.

As a rule, a broker or agent who completes real estate contracts is engaging in the unauthorized practice of law unless the broker is a party to the agreement, such as a in a listing agreement or sales contract. Brokers and agents may not complete leases, mortgages, contracts for deed, or promissory notes to which they are not a party.

Agents must be fully aware of what they are legally allowed to do and not do in preparing and interpreting contracts for clients. In addition to practicing law without a license, agents expose themselves to lawsuits from clients who relied on a contract as being legally acceptable.

CLASSIFICATIONS OF CONTRACTS

Oral vs. written

A contract may be in writing or it may be an oral, or **parol**, contract. Certain oral contracts are valid and enforceable, others are not enforceable, even if valid. For example, most states require listing agreements, sales contracts, and leases exceeding one year to be in writing to be enforceable.

Express vs. implied

An **express contract** is one in which all the terms and covenants of the agreement have been manifestly stated and agreed to by all parties, whether verbally or in writing.

An **implied contract** is an unstated or unintentional agreement that may be deemed to exist when the *actions of any of the parties* suggest the existence of an agreement.

A common example of an implied contract is an implied agency agreement. In implied agency, an agent who does not have a contract with a buyer performs acts on the buyer's behalf, such as negotiating a price that is less than the listing price. In so doing, the agent has possibly created an implied contract with the buyer, albeit unintended. If the buyer compensates the agent for the negotiating efforts, the existence of an implied agency agreement becomes even less disputable.

Bilateral vs. unilateral

A **bilateral contract** is one in which both parties promise to perform their respective parts of an agreement in exchange for performance by the other party.

An example of a bilateral contract is an exclusive listing: the broker promises to exercise due diligence in the efforts to sell a property, and the seller promises to compensate the broker when and if the property sells.

In a **unilateral contract**, only one party promises to do something, provided the other party does something. The latter party is not obligated to perform any act, but the promising party must fulfill the promise if the other party chooses to perform.

An option is an example of a unilateral contract: in an option-to-buy, the party offering the option (optionor) promises to sell a property if the optionee decides to exercise the option. While the potential buyer does not have to buy, the owner must sell if the option is exercised.

Executed vs. executory

An **executed contract** is one that has been fully performed and fulfilled: neither party bears any further obligation. A completed and expired lease contract is an executed contract: the landlord may re-possess the premises, and the tenant has no further obligation to pay rent.

An **executory contract** is one in which performance is yet to be completed. A sales contract prior to closing is executory: while the parties have agreed to buy and sell, the buyer has yet to pay the seller, and the seller has yet to deed the property to the buyer.

Forms of contract termination

Termination of a contract, also called **cancellation** and **discharge**, may occur for any of the following causes.

Performance. A contract terminates when fully performed by the parties. It may also terminate for:

> ▸ partial performance, if the parties agree

> ▸ sufficient performance, if a court determines a party has sufficiently performed the contract, even though not to the full extent of every provision

Infeasibility. An otherwise valid contract can be canceled if it is not possible to perform. Certain personal services contracts, for example, depend on the unique capabilities of one person which cannot be substituted by someone else. If such a person dies or is sufficiently disabled, the contract is cancelable.

Mutual agreement. Parties to a contract can agree to terminate, or renounce, the contract. If the parties wish to create a new contract to replace the cancelled contract, they must comply with the validity requirements for the new contract. Such substitution is called **novation**.

Cooling-period rescission. Rescission is the act of nullifying a contract. In many states, parties to certain contracts are allowed a statutory amount of time after entering into a contract, or "cooling period", to rescind the contract without cause. No reason need be stated for the cancellation, and the cancelling party incurs no liability for performance.

For example, consider the unsuspecting buyer of a lot in a new resort development. Such buyers are often the targets of hard-sell tactics which lead to a completed sales contract and a deposit. The statutory cooling period gives the buyer an opportunity to reconsider the investment in the absence of the persistent salesperson.

Revocation. Revocation is cancellation of the contract by one party without the consent of the other. For example, a seller may revoke a listing to take the property off the market. While all parties have the *power* to revoke, they may not have a defensible *right*. In the absence of justifiable grounds, a revocation may not relieve the revoking party of contract obligations.

For example, a seller who revokes a listing without grounds may be required to pay a commission if the broker found a buyer, or reimburse the broker's marketing expenses if no buyer was found.

Abandonment. Abandonment occurs when parties fail to perform contract obligations. This situation may allow the parties to cancel the contract.

Lapse of time. If a contract contains an expiration provision and date, the contract automatically expires on the deadline.

Invalidity of contract. If a contract is void, it terminates without the need for disaffirmation. A voidable contract can be cancelled by operation of law or by rescission.

Breach of contract

A breach of contract is a failure to perform according to the terms of the agreement. Also called **default**, a breach of contract gives the damaged party the right to take legal action within the time period provided for in the Statute of Limitations.

The damaged party may elect the following legal remedies:

- ▸ rescission
- ▸ forfeiture
- ▸ suit for damages
- ▸ suit for specific performance

Rescission. A damaged party may rescind the contract. This cancels the contract and returns the parties to their pre-contract condition, including the refunding of any monies already transferred.

Forfeiture. A forfeiture requires the breaching party to give up something, according to the terms of the contract. For example, a buyer who defaults on a sales contract may have to forfeit the earnest money deposit.

Suit for damages. A damaged party may sue for money damages in civil court. The suit must be initiated within the time period allowed by the statute of limitations. When a contract states the total amount due to a damaged party in the event of a breach, the compensation is known as **liquidated damages**. If the contract does not specify the amount, the damaged party may sue in court for **unliquidated damages**.

Suit for specific performance. A suit for specific performance is an attempt to force the defaulting party to comply with the terms of the contract. Specific performance suits occur when it is difficult to identify damages because of the unique circumstances of the real property in question. The most common instance is a defaulted sale or lease contract where the buyer or seller wants the court to compel the defaulting party to go through with the transaction, even when the defaulter would prefer to pay a damage award.

Sales contracts

Real estate contracts are the legal agreements that underlie the transfer and financing of real estate, as well as the real estate brokerage business. Sale and lease contracts and option agreements are used to transfer real estate interests from one party to another. The contract includes the details of the buyer's offer and serves to initiate the negotiation process between the buyer and the seller. Mortgage contracts and promissory agreements are part of financing real estate. Listing and representation contracts establish client relationships and provide for compensation.

New York does not have any one specific sales contract form that must be used. Remember any form being used as a contract must be drafted by an attorney with the broker being allowed to fill in the blanks. The most common forms used are Standard Form Contract For Purchase and Sale of Real Estate, the New York Real Estate Purchase & Sale Agreement, which was revised in 2024, the Residential Contract for Sale, and Form 8041 Residential Contract of Sale. These contract forms include spaces for the following information:

- contract date

- seller and buyer names* and signatures*

- identification of the property*

- identification of items included and excluded in the sale

- mortgage contingency clause

- other contingencies and provisions

- purchase (offer) price (consideration)*

- terms and method of payment

- information related to the title, survey, deed, taxes, inspection

- closing date, time, and location

- buyer's earnest money deposit

- offer expiration date and time

- broker's name and compensation

- property condition

- names of attorneys for seller and buyer

Note that the essentials of a valid contract in New York are included in the contract and identified by an asterisk in the above list. Two additional essentials of validity are also met by the contract being in writing and the agreement to buy and sell being confirmed by the signatures of the buyer and seller.

Should the seller not fully agree with the buyer's offer price and contingencies, the seller may modify the contract and provide the buyer with a counteroffer. The buyer may then agree with the seller's changes and sign the contract. If the buyer does not fully agree with the changes, the buyer may also modify the changes and provide the seller with a counteroffer. At any point where both parties agree to the conditions of the offer or counteroffer, both may sign the offer and create the legally binding commitment to transfer the property.

The contract may be rescinded at any time before the seller accepts the offer.

Contract for deed

A contract for deed is also called a *land contract*, an *installment sale*, a *conditional sales contract,* and an *agreement for deed*. It is a bilateral agreement between a seller, the **vendor,** and a buyer, the **vendee**, in which the vendor defers receipt of some or all of the purchase price of a property over a specified period of time. During the period, the *vendor retains legal title* and the vendee acquires equitable title. The vendee takes possession of the property, makes stipulated payments of principal and interest to the vendor, and otherwise fulfills obligations as the contract requires. At the end of the period, the buyer pays the vendor the full purchase price and the vendor deeds legal title to the vendee.

Like an option, a contract for deed offers a means for more marginally qualified buyers to acquire property. In essence, the seller acts as lender, allowing the buyer to take possession and pay off the purchase price over time. A buyer may thus avoid conventional down payment and income requirements imposed by institutional lenders. During the contract period, the buyer can work to raise the necessary cash to complete the purchase or to qualify for a conventional mortgage.

A contract for deed serves two primary purposes for a seller. First, it facilitates a sale that might otherwise be impossible. Second, it may give the seller certain tax benefits. Since the seller is not liable for capital gains tax until the purchase price is received, the installment sale lowers the seller's tax liability in the year of the sale

Interests and rights

Vendor's rights and obligations. During the contract period, the seller may:

> ▸ mortgage the property
>
> ▸ sell or assign whatever interests he or she owns in the property to another party
>
> ▸ incur judgment liens against the property

The vendor, however, is bound to the obligations imposed by the contract for deed. In particular, the vendor may not breach the obligation to convey legal title to the vendee upon receipt of the total purchase price. In addition, the vendor remains liable for underlying mortgage loans.

Vendee's rights and obligations. During the contract period, the buyer may occupy, use, enjoy, and profit from the property, subject to the provisions of the written agreement. The vendee must make periodic payments of principal and interest and maintain the property. In addition, a vendee may have to pay property taxes and hazard insurance.

Legal form

Like other conveyance contracts, a contract for deed instrument identifies:

- ▶ the principal parties
- ▶ the property's legal description
- ▶ consideration: specifically, what the parties promise to do
- ▶ the terms of the sale
- ▶ obligations for property maintenance
- ▶ default and remedies
- ▶ signatures and acknowledgment

The contract specifies the vendee's payments, payment deadlines, when the balance of the purchase price is due, and how the property may be used.

Default and recourse

Seller default. If the seller defaults, such as by failing to deliver the deed, the buyer may sue for specific performance, or for cancellation of the agreement and damages.

Buyer default. States differ in the remedies they prescribe for the seller in case of buyer default. Some states consider the default a breach of contract that may be remedied by cancellation, retention of monies received, and eviction. Others provide foreclosure proceedings as a remedy

Usage guidelines

Many areas have no standardized contract for deed, or any form sanctioned by associations and agencies. Therefore, this kind of conveyance presents certain pitfalls for buyer and seller.

In some states, a breach of the contract for deed is remedied under *local contract law* rather than foreclosure law. The buyer may not have the protections of a redemption period or other buyer-protection laws which accompany formal foreclosure proceedings. The vendor might sue the vendee for breach of contract for the slightest infraction of the contract terms.

A second danger for the vendee is that the vendor has the power and the right to encumber the property in ways that may not be desirable for the buyer. For example, the seller could place a home equity loan on the property, then fail to make periodic payments. The bank could then foreclose on the vendor, thus jeopardizing the vendee's eventual purchase.

For the seller, the principal danger is that the buyer acquires possession in exchange for a minimal down payment. A buyer might damage or even vacate the property, leaving the seller to make repairs and retake possession. Further, since the contract is recorded, the seller must also bear the time and expense of clearing the title.

To minimize risk, principal parties in a contract for deed should observe the following guidelines:

▶ use an attorney to draft the agreement

▶ adopt the standard forms, if available

▶ become familiar with how the contract will be enforced

▶ utilize professional escrow and title services

▶ record the transaction properly

▶ be prepared for the possible effect on existing financing

Option-to-buy contract

An option-to-buy is an enforceable contract in which a potential seller, the **optionor**, grants a potential buyer, the **optionee**, the right to purchase a property before a stated time for a stated price and terms. In exchange for the right of option, the optionee pays the optionor valuable consideration.

For example, a buyer wants to purchase a property for $150,000, but needs to sell a boat to raise the down payment. The boat will take two or three months to sell. To accommodate the buyer, the seller offers the buyer an option to purchase the property at any time before midnight on the day that is ninety days from the date of signing the option. The buyer pays the seller $1,000 for the option. If buyer exercises the option, the seller will apply the $1,000 toward the earnest money deposit and subsequent down payment. If the optionee lets the option expire, the seller keeps the $1,000. Both parties agree to the arrangement by completing a sale contract as an addendum to the option, then executing the option agreement itself.

An option-to-buy places the optionee *under no obligation* to purchase the property. However, the seller must perform under the terms of the contract if the buyer exercises the option. An option is thus a *unilateral* agreement. Exercise of the option creates a bilateral sale contract where both parties are bound to perform. An unused option terminates at the expiration date.

An optionee can use an option to prevent the sale of a property to another party while seeking to raise funds for the purchase. A renter with a **lease option-to-buy** can accumulate down payment funds while paying rent to the landlord. For example, an owner may lease a condominium to a tenant with an option to buy. If the tenant takes the option, the landlord agrees to apply $100 of the monthly rent paid prior to the option date toward the purchase price. The tenant pays the landlord the nominal sum of $200 for the option.

Options can also facilitate commercial property acquisition. The option period gives a buyer time to investigate zoning, space planning, building permits, environmental impacts, and other feasibility issues prior to the purchase without losing the property to another party in the meantime

Contract requirements

Beyond the required elements, it is common for an option to include provisions covering:

> ▶ include actual, non-refundable consideration
>
> The option must require the optionee to pay a specific consideration *that is separate from the purchase price*. The consideration cannot be refunded if the option is not exercised. If the option is exercised, the consideration may be applied to the purchase price. If the option is a lease option, portions of the rent may qualify as separate consideration.

> ▶ include price and terms of the sale
>
> The price and terms of the potential transaction must be clearly expressed and cannot change over the option period. It is customary practice for the parties to complete and attach a sale contract to the option as satisfaction of this requirement.

> ▶ have an expiration date
>
> The option must automatically expire at the end of a specific period.

> ▶ be in writing
>
> Since a potential transfer of real estate is involved, most state statutes of fraud require an option to be in writing.

> ▶ include a legal description

> ▶ meet general contract validity requirements
>
> The basics include competent parties, the optionor's promise to perform, and the optionor's signature. Note that it is not necessary for the optionee to sign the option.

Common provisions

Beyond the required elements, it is common for an option to include provisions covering:

> ▶ how to deliver notice of election
>
> A clause clarifies how to make the option election, exactly when the election must be completed, and any additional terms required such as an earnest money deposit.

> ▶ forfeiture terms
>
> A clause provides that the optionor is entitled to the consideration if the option term expires.

▸ property and title condition warranties

The optionor warrants that the property will be maintained in a certain condition, and that title will be marketable and insurable.

▸ how option consideration will be credited

A clause states how the optionor will apply the option consideration toward the purchase price.

Legal aspects

Equitable interest. The optionee enjoys an equitable interest in the property because the option creates the right to obtain legal title. However, the option does not in itself convey an interest in real property, only a right to do something governed by contract law.

Recording. An option should be recorded, because the equitable interest it creates can affect the marketability of the title.

Assignment. An option-to-buy is assignable unless the contract expressly prohibits assignment.

7 Contract of Sale Leases
Snapshot Review

LEASES

Definition
- an agreement between the owner of real property (**lessor**) and a tenant (**lessee**) to allow the tenant to possess, use, and occupy the property

Types of leasehold estates
- estate for years; estate from period-to-period; estate at will; estate at sufferance

Requirements for validity
- parties; legal description; exclusive possession; legal use; lease term; consideration; offer and acceptance; signatures; written if over one year in term

Standard provisions
- parties; legal description; exclusive possession; legal use; lease term; consideration; offer and acceptance; signatures; written if over one year in term

Leasehold rights and obligations
- tenant rights: exclusive use and possession; quiet enjoyment; profits
- tenant obligations: pay rent; maintain premises; follow rules
- landlord rights: receive rent; repossess; monitor property condition
- landlord obligations: support and services; maintenance
- leasehold rights survive death and conveyance or encumbrance

SALES CONTRACT
- legal agreements that underlie the transfer and financing of real estate
- essentials for NY contract include parties' names and signatures, property identification, offer price, contract in writing, related dates, terms and conditions, commission and method of payment

CONTRACT FOR DEED
- purchase price is paid over time in installments; seller retains title; buyer takes possession; at end of period, buyer pays balance of price, gets legal title

Interests and rights
- seller may encumber or assign interest; remains liable for underlying mortgage
- buyer may use, possess, profit; must make periodic payments, maintain the property, and purchase at end of term

Default and recourse
- if seller defaults, buyer may sue for cancellation and damages or specific performance; seller's default remedies vary by area; may sue for specific performance or damages, or may need to foreclose

THE OPTION-TO-BUY CONTRACT
- optionor gives option to optionee; unilateral contract: seller must perform; buyer need not; if option exercised, option becomes bilateral sale contract

Contract requirements
- must include non-refundable consideration for the option right; price and terms of the sale; option period expiration date; legal description; must be in writing and meet contract validity requirements

Common clause provisions
- special provisions: how to exercise option; terms of option money forfeiture; how option money will be applied to purchase price

Legal aspects
- creates equitable interest; is assignable; should be recorded

CHAPTER SEVEN: CONTRACT OF SALE AND LEASES

Section Quiz

7.1. Which of the following would be considered a valid but unenforceable contract in New York?

    a. Oral real estate sales contract
    b. Contract that omits consideration
    c. One party to the contract is not of legal age
    d. Written long-term lease

7.2. Which type of leasehold estate is for a period of time with a defined start and end date?

    a. Estate from period-to-period
    b. Estate for years
    c. Estate at will
    d. Easte at sufferance

7.3. A(n) _____ contract is one in which performance is yet to be completed.

    a. executed
    b. express
    c. bilateral
    d. executory

7.4. A lease conveys a leasehold interest or estate that grants the tenant certain rights during the lease term. These rights do NOT include:

    a. exclusive possession and occupancy
    b. profits from use
    c. full disposition
    d. exclusive use

7.5. What form of contract termination occurs when parties fail to perform contract obligations in a timely manner?

    a. Invalidity of contract
    b. Revocation
    c. Abandonment
    d. Infeasibility

7.6. A bilateral agreement between a seller and a buyer in which the seller defers receipt of some or all of the purchase price of a property over a specified period of time is called a

    a. contract for deed.
    b. option contract.
    c. vendor contract.
    d. lease option contract.

7.7. A leasehold is also called a _____ estate.

    a. freehold
    b. landed
    c. vendee
    d. nonfreehold

7.8. To be considered valid, a conveyance contract must

    a. be either oral and witnessed, or in writing.
    b. contain a legal description of the property.
    c. be notarized.
    d. be signed by both parties.

7.9. Which of the following is true about New York's General Obligations Law requirements for tenant security deposits?

    a. Landlords are required to give 99% of interest earned on the trust account to tenants.
    b. Landlords must hold security deposits in trust in their general operating accounts.
    c. Landlords may choose to hold security deposits in either interest-bearing or non-interest-bearing accounts.
    d. Landlords are required to hold security deposits in a New York interest-bearing account.

7.10. Which of the following is a legal remedy that the damaged party in a breach of contract may pursue?

    a. Suit for reinstatement
    b. Suit for specific performance
    c. Lien administration
    d. Mediation

7.11. Several buyers are competing for the last available home in a desirable new subdivision. One buyer calls the owner-developer directly on the phone and offers $10,000 over and above the listed price. The developer accepts the offer. At this point

a. the parties have a valid, enforceable sale contract on the home.
b. the parties have completed an oral, executory contract.
c. the parties may not cancel their contract.
d. the developer could not entertain other offers on the property.

7.12. Which of the following best characterizes a conventional sale contract?

a. Voluntary, unilateral, and executory
b. Involuntary, bilateral, and contingent
c. Voluntary, bilateral, and executory
d. Involuntary, unilateral, and executory

7.13. An important legal characteristic of an option-to-buy agreement is that

a. the potential buyer, the optionee, is obligated to buy the property once the option agreement is completed.
b. the optionor must perform if the optionee takes the option, but the optionee is under no obligation to do so.
c. the contract can be executed at no cost to the optionee.
d. it is a bilateral agreement.

7.14. A potential danger involved in a contract for deed is that

a. the vendor may rightfully sell legal title to another party during the contract period.
b. the vendor's rights to encumber the property may not be beneficial to the vendee.
c. the vendee has a generous right of redemption that may be onerous to the vendor.
d. the vendee must make an inordinately high down payment, which can be lost.

7.15. Which of the following statements regarding contract preparation in New York is true?

a. Real estate brokers are permitted to draft real estate contracts, but salespersons are not.
b. A broker or agent who completes real estate contracts is engaging in the unauthorized practice of law.
c. Brokers may add their own provisions to attorney-drafted contracts.
d. Brokers and agents may complete standard promulgated forms as long as the broker is a party to the agreement.

7.16. Termination by _____ is when the offeror withdraws the offer before the offeree accepts it.

a. revocation
b. lapse of time
c. rejection
d. novation

7.17. A buyer made a written and signed offer to a seller. The seller accepted the offer and signed the contract. These actions meet the requirements of contract law's criterion of validity known as

a. competent parties.
b. legal purpose
c. mutual consent.
d. valuable consideration.

7.18. A tenant whose lease has expired still remains in possession of the leased property and refuses to move out. The landlord wants to lease the property to another person. What type of estate does the tenant in possession of the property have?

a. Estate at will
b. Estate at sufferance
c. Estate from period to period
d. No estate at all

7.19. With an option contract, the optionee has _____ interest in the property.

a. equitable
b. legal
c. lienor
d. contract

7.20. What type of real estate contract can be assigned to another party unless the terms of the agreement specifically prohibit assignment?

    a. Any real estate-related contract that includes a clause permitting assignment or novation
    b. One that is not a personal contract for services
    c. One that involves a personal contract for services instead of a real property purchase
    d. A lease contract only

7.21. New York's statute of frauds requires that certain contracts must be in writing to be

    a. valid.
    b. voidable.
    c. legal.
    d. enforceable.

7.22. New York residential leases contain an implied warranty of habitability wherein

    a. the landlord guarantees the premises is fit for human habitation.
    b. the tenant may improve and alter the leased property as they desire.
    c. the tenant is responsible for routine upkeep of the premises.
    d. the landlord is responsible for general repairs to common areas and routine upkeep of leased premises.

7.23. What happens when an offeree decides to change the terms of an offer?

    a. The offeree creates a counteroffer, and the original offer is voidable.
    b. The offeree rejects the offer, and the offeror has to submit a new offer.
    c. The offeree creates a new offer through the process of novation.
    d. The offeree creates a counteroffer, and the original offer is void.

7.24. In the event of a buyer's default, a provision for liquidated damages in a sale contract enables a seller to

    a. sue the buyer for the anticipated down payment.
    b. force the buyer to quitclaim equitable title.
    c. sue the buyer for all liquid assets lost as a result of the default.
    d. claim the deposit as relief for the buyer's failure to perform.

7.25. How can a lease option-to-buy agreement benefit a renter?

    a. It allows the renter to live rent-free until they decide to purchase the property.
    b. It enables the renter to accumulate down payment funds while paying rent.
    c. It guarantees the renter a discount on the purchase price of the property.
    d. It allows the renter to sublease the property to another tenant.

8 Real Estate Finance

Mortgage Transaction
Mortgage Clauses
Loan Qualification
Mortgage Laws
Mortgage Market
Types of Mortgages
Predatory Lending
Foreclosure
Sale of Mortgaged Property
Recording and Satisfaction

MORTGAGE TRANSACTION

Mechanics of a loan transaction
Financial components of a loan
Promissory note
Mortgage document and trust deed

Mechanics of a loan transaction

It is common to use borrowed money to purchase real estate. When a borrower gives a note promising to repay the borrowed money and executes a mortgage on the real estate for which the money is being borrowed as security, the financing method is called mortgage financing. The term "mortgage financing" also applies to real estate loans secured by a deed of trust. The process of securing a loan by pledging a property without giving up ownership of the property is called **hypothecation**.

States differ in their interpretation of who owns mortgaged property. Those that regard the mortgage as a lien held by the mortgagee (lender) against the property owned by the mortgagor (borrower) are called **lien-theory** states. Those that regard the mortgage document as a conveyance of ownership from the mortgagor to the mortgagee are called **title-theory** states. Some states interpret ownership of mortgaged property from a point of view that combines aspects of both title and lien theory. New York is a lien theory state where the borrower retains legal ownership of the property and the lender retains equitable title.

A valid mortgage or trust deed financing arrangement requires the following:

> ▶ a *note* as evidence of the debt

> ▶ the *mortgage or trust deed* as evidence of the collateral pledge

Note. In addition to executing a mortgage or trust deed, the borrower signs a promissory note for the amount borrowed. The amount of the loan is typically the difference between the purchase price and the down payment. A promissory note creates a personal liability for the borrower to repay the loan.

Mortgage. A mortgage is a legal document stating the pledge of the borrower (the **mortgagor**) to the lender (the **mortgagee**). The mortgage document pledges the borrower's ownership interest in the real estate in question as collateral against performance of the debt obligation.

The flow of funds and obligations in a mortgage transaction is shown in this illustration:

Exhibit 8.1 Flow of a Mortgage Transaction

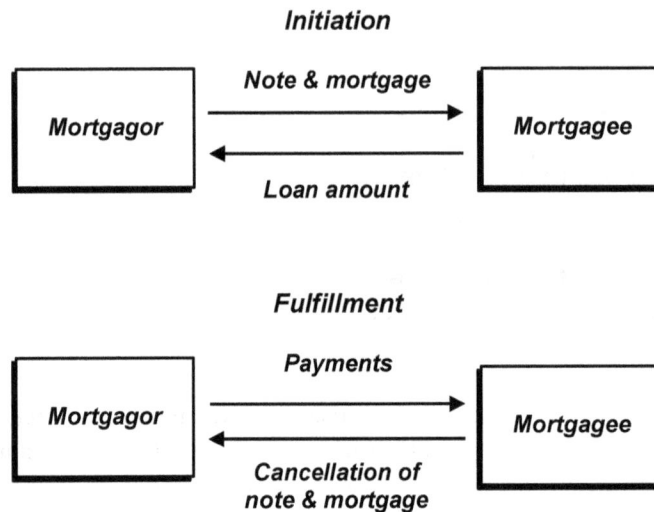

Initiation

| Mortgagor | Note & mortgage →
 ← Loan amount | Mortgagee |

Fulfillment

| Mortgagor | Payments →
 ← Cancellation of note & mortgage | Mortgagee |

The deed of trust. A deed of trust conveys title to the property in question from the borrower (**trustor**) to a **trustee** as security for the loan. The trustee is a third-party fiduciary to the trust. While the loan is in place, the trustee holds the title on behalf of the lender, who is the **beneficiary** of the trust. On repayment of the loan, the borrower receives the title from the trustee in the form of a deed of reconveyance.

The flow of funds and obligations in a trust deed transaction is shown in this illustration:

Exhibit 8.2 Flow of a Trust Deed Transaction

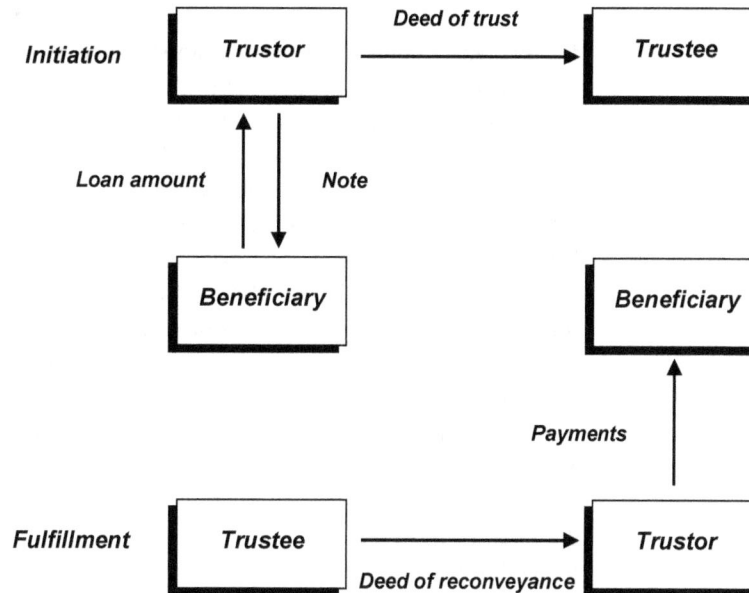

Financial components of a loan

The financial components of a mortgage loan include the following:

▸ principal
▸ interest and interest rate
▸ points
▸ term
▸ payments

Principal. The capital amount borrowed, on which interest payments are calculated, is the original loan **principal**. In an amortizing loan, part of the principal is repaid periodically along with interest, so that the principal balance decreases over the life of the loan. At any point during the life of a mortgage loan, the remaining unpaid principal is called the **loan balance**, or **remaining balance**.

Interest and interest rate. Interest is a charge for the use of the lender's money. Interest may be paid in *advance* at the beginning of the payment period, or in *arrears* at the end of the payment period, according to the terms of the note. Mortgage interest is most commonly paid in arrears. The **interest rate** is a percentage applied to the principal to determine the amount of interest due. The rate may be *fixed* for the term of the loan, or it may be *variable*, according to the terms of the note. A loan with a fixed interest rate is called a fixed-rate loan; a loan with a variable interest rate is commonly called an adjustable rate loan.

Because the interest rate on a mortgage loan does not reflect the full cost of the loan to the borrower, federal law requires a lender on a residential property to compute and disclose an **Annual Percentage Rate (APR)** that includes other finance charges in addition to the basic interest rate in the calculation.

Usury. Many states have laws against usury, which is the charging of excessive interest rates on loans. Such states have a maximum rate that is either a flat rate or a variable rate tied to an index such as the prime lending rate. Lenders are required to charge interest on loans, but state usury laws protect borrowers from excessively high interest rates. New York's General Obligations Law Section 5-501 prohibits usury and sets the maximum interest rate at 16% per annum. Interest rates below that can vary, but 16% is the maximum allowed. Lenders charging more than that can be held liable for civil usury. Charging interest higher than 25% constitutes criminal usury.

In New York, loans under $250,000 to individuals are required to comply with both civil and criminal usury rates. However, loans for $250,000 up to $2,500,000 need only comply with the criminal usury rate. While this is the law for individual borrowers, loans to corporations and LLCs for less than $2,500,000 are exempt from the civil 16% limit but must comply with the 25% criminal usury limit. Additionally, regardless of who the borrower is, all loans for more than $2,500,000 are exempt from both civil and criminal usury laws.

Borrowers who are victims of usury can bring a lawsuit against the lender to recover moneys paid above the maximum allowable interest rates.

Points. From the point of view of a lender or investor, the amount loaned in a mortgage loan is the lender's capital investment, and the interest paid by the borrower is the return earned by the invested capital. It is often the case that a lender needs to earn a greater return than the interest rate alone provides. For example, a lender may require additional yield on a low-interest VA loan which has an interest rate maximum. In such a case, the lender charges up-front **discount points** to make up the difference between the interest rate on the loan and the required return. This effectively raises the yield of the loan to the lender.

A discount point is *one percent of the loan amount*. Thus, one point on a $100,000 loan equals $1,000. The lender charges this as *pre-paid interest* at closing by funding only the face amount of the loan minus the discount points. The borrower, however, must repay the full loan amount, along with interest calculated on the full amount.

The value of one discount point to a lender is usually estimated to be equivalent to raising the interest rate on the loan by 1/8%. Thus, a lender has to charge eight points to raise the yield by 1%. If a lender needs to earn 7% on a loan offered at 6.5%, the number of points necessary would be figured as follows:

$$7.0\% - 6.5\% = .5\%$$
$$.5\% \times 8 \text{ (points per } 1\%) = 4 \text{ points}$$

On a loan of $100,000, the 4 points would cost the borrower:

$$100,000 \times .04 = \$4,000.$$

The borrower would effectively receive from the lender $96,000, and owe principal and interest based on $100,000. For tax reasons, it is usually advisable for the borrower to receive the full loan amount from the lender and pay the points in a check which is separate from that used for other closing costs. As pre-paid interest, points paid in this way may be deductible on the borrower's income tax return for the year of the purchase. The borrower should seek the advice of a tax consultant concerning this matter.

Term. The loan term is the period of time over which the loan must be repaid. A "30-year loan" is a loan whose balance must be fully paid off at the end of thirty years. A "five-year balloon loan" is a loan whose balance must be paid off at the end of five years, although its payments may be calculated on a term of another length, such as fifteen or thirty years. Such a loan is also sometimes described as a 30-year loan with a five-year "call."

Payments. The loan term, loan amount, and interest rate combine to determine the periodic payment amount. When these three quantities are known, it is possible to identify the periodic payment from a mortgage table or with a financial calculator. Mortgage payments are usually made on a monthly basis. On an amortizing loan, a portion of the payment goes to repay the loan balance in advance, and a portion goes to payment of interest in arrears.

For example, Mary and Jerry King borrow $400,000 to finance the purchase of a home. The loan has a term of thirty years at an interest rate of 5% and is amortizing. The monthly payment for this loan will be $2,147. For the first payment at the end of the month, the Kings owe interest on $400,000 for the monthly period. At 5%, this amounts to $1,666.67. Since their payment is $2,147 and the interest charge is $1,666.67, the difference, which is $480.33, is applied to an advance payment of principal. The following month, the Kings will pay interest on the new, smaller loan balance of $399,519.67 ($400,000.00 − 480.33).

If a borrower pays more than the scheduled payment amount, the excess is credited to repayment of the principal, which is reduced by the amount of the excess payment. The required minimum payment amount remains constant for the life of the loan, but the loan term can be reduced by this means, thereby also reducing the total amount of interest paid over the life of the loan.

Promissory note

A borrower who executes a promissory note is the **maker** or **payer** of the note. The lender is the **payee**. To be properly executed, all parties who have an interest in the property should sign the note. The note sets forth these terms of the loan:

> ▶ the loan amount

> ▶ the term of the loan

> ▶ the method and timing of repayment

> ▶ the interest rate to be paid

> ▶ the borrower's promise to pay

The note may also state that it is payable to the bearer, if used with a deed of trust, or to the mortgagee, if used with a mortgage. Other items in the mortgage document or deed of trust may be repeated in the promissory note, especially the following:

> ▶ the right to prepay the loan balance

> ▶ charges for late payment

> ▶ conditions for default

> ▶ notifications and cures for default

> ▶ other charges

A promissory note is a **negotiable instrument**, which means the payee may *assign* it to a third party. The assignee would then have the right to receive the borrower's periodic payments.

Mortgage document and trust deed

A borrower who executes a mortgage is a **mortgagor**. The lender named in the mortgage is the **mortgagee**. In a trust deed, the borrower is the **trustor** and the lender is **beneficiary**. The mortgage or trust document identifies the property being given as security, giving both its legal description and mailing address. The document contains much of the same information as the note, including these items:

> ▶ the debt amount

> ▶ the term of the loan

> ▶ method and timing of payments

The document does not usually provide details about the payment amount, interest rate, or charges

MORTGAGE CLAUSES

A typical mortgage usually includes the following major clauses:

Payment of Principal and Interest: Prepayment and Late Charges. The borrower must make timely payments according to the terms of the note.

Funds for Taxes and Insurance. Unless waived by the lender or prohibited by law, the borrower must make monthly payments to cover taxes and hazard insurance. If applicable, the borrower must also pay flood insurance and mortgage insurance installments.

Periodic payments of taxes and insurance are held in a reserve fund called the **escrow account**. The Real Estate Settlement Procedures Act (RESPA) limits the amount of funds that the lender can require and hold for this purpose.

The borrower's monthly payment to the lender for principal and interest is called the **P&I** payment (principal and interest). The amount which also includes the escrow payment is called **PITI** (principal, interest, taxes, insurance).

Application of Payments. The amount of each payment is applied to various items in order of priority. Unless local law provides otherwise, this order is: 1) prepayment charges; 2) escrow; 3) interest; 4) principal; 5) late charges.

Charges and Liens. The borrower is liable for paying any charges, liens, or other expenses that may have priority over the mortgage or trust instrument.

Hazard or Property Insurance. The borrower must keep the property insured as the lender requires. Insurance proceeds, in case of a claim, are applied first to restoring the property, or, if that is not feasible, to payment of the debt.

Occupancy, Preservation, Maintenance and Protection of the Property. The borrower must take and maintain occupancy of the property as the borrower's principal residence according to the lender's requirements. The borrower must not use or neglect the property in such a way as to impair the lender's lien on the property. This could include using the property for illegal purposes, creating hazardous waste on the property, or destroying the improvements.

Protection of Lender's Rights in the Property. The lender may take actions it believes are necessary to protect its rights in the property if the borrower's actions threaten them. The costs of these actions would be charged to the borrower and become part of the monthly payment.

Mortgage Insurance. The lender may require the borrower to obtain *private mortgage insurance, or PMI*. Mortgage insurance protects the lender against loss of a portion of the loan (typically 20-25%) in case of borrower default. Private mortgage insurance generally applies to loans that are not backed by the Federal

Housing Administration (FHA) or Veterans Administration (VA) and that have a down payment of less than 20% of the property value.

Inspection. With proper notice, the lender may inspect the property if there is reasonable cause to fear damage to its lien.

Condemnation. If the property is condemned or taken by eminent domain, the lender declares a claim on any resulting proceeds.

Borrower Not Released; Forbearance by Lender Not a Waiver. The lender reserves the right to take future action against the borrower for default, even if the lender decides not to take immediate action. If the lender agrees to change the terms of the loan, it does not release the borrower from the original liability.

Transfer of the Property or a Beneficial Interest in Borrower. If the borrower sells or transfers its interest in the property without the lender's approval, the lender may demand immediate and full repayment of the loan balance. This is an **alienation** clause, also known as a **due-on-sale** clause and a **call** clause. It allows the lender to prevent the assumption of the mortgage by a buyer if the borrower sells the property. The requirement to repay the loan before the scheduled date is called **acceleration**.

Borrower's Right to Reinstate. If the lender holds the borrower in default under the terms of the mortgage and proceeds to enforce its rights under the document, such as by foreclosing, the borrower has the right to reinstate his or her interest by performing certain actions. This usually means paying overdue mortgage payments and any other expenses the lender may have incurred in protecting its rights. The clause, also known as a **redemption** clause, gives the borrower a period of time to satisfy obligations and prevent the lender from forcing a sale of the property.

Release. The lender agrees to release the mortgage or trust document to the borrower when the borrower has paid off the loan and all other sums secured by the document. The release clause, also known as a **defeasance** clause, may specify that the mortgagee will execute a **satisfaction of mortgage** (also known as **release of mortgage** and **mortgage discharge**) to the mortgagor. In the case of a deed of trust, the lender as beneficiary requests the trustee to execute a **release deed** or **deed of reconveyance** to the borrower as trustor. The release deed or satisfaction should be recorded as necessary in county records to show that the mortgagee/trustee has extinguished all liens against the property

LOAN QUALIFICATION

Equal Credit Opportunity Act
Income qualification
Cash qualification
Net worth
Credit evaluation
Loan commitment

To qualify for a mortgage loan, a borrower must meet the lender's qualifications in terms of *income, debt, cash, and net worth*. In addition, a borrower must demonstrate sufficient *creditworthiness* to be an acceptable risk.

Equal Credit Opportunity Act

The Equal Credit Opportunity Act (ECOA) requires a lender to evaluate a loan applicant on the basis of that applicant's own income and credit rating, unless the applicant requests the inclusion of another's income and credit rating in the application. In addition, ECOA has prohibited a number of practices in mortgage loan underwriting, such as the following:

▶ Discount or disregard income from part-time work, a spouse, child support, alimony, or separate maintenance. Further, the loan officer may not ask whether any of the applicant's income is derived from these sources.

▶ Assume that income for a certain type of person will be reduced because of an employment interruption due to child-bearing or child-raising. The loan officer may not ask about the applicant's plans or behavior concerning child-bearing or birth control.

▶ Refuse a loan solely on the basis that the security is located in a certain geographical area.

▶ Ask applicants any question about their age, sex, religion, race or national origin, except as the law may require.

▶ Require a spouse to sign any document unless the spouse's income is to be included in the qualifying income, or unless the spouse agrees to become contractually obligated, or the state requires the signature for some purpose such as clearing clouded title.

If a lender denies a request for a loan, or offers a loan under different terms than those requested by an applicant, the lender must give the applicant written notice providing specific reasons for the action.

Qualifying the borrower. The lender must rely on eight types of information to determine that the borrower has the ability to repay the loan:

1. current income or assets (excluding the value of the mortgaged property)

2. current employment status

3. credit history

4. monthly payment for the mortgage

5. monthly payments being made on other loans on the same property

6. monthly payments for other mortgage-related expenses

7. other debts

8. monthly debt payments compared to monthly income (debt-to-income ratio)

The lender cannot use a temporarily low rate (introductory or "teaser" rate) to determine qualification. For an adjustable rate mortgage (ARM), the highest rate the borrower might have to pay is generally to be used.

The "ability to repay" requirements are relaxed in certain circumstances where the borrower is attempting to refinance from a riskier loan (such as an interest-only loan) to a less risky one (such as a fixed-rate mortgage loan.

Qualified Mortgage. A Qualified Mortgage is one that meets the "ability-to-repay" requirements, has certain required features, and is not allowed to have others. There are exceptions to these rules for certain kinds of small lenders. Issuing a Qualified Mortgage gives the lender certain legal protections in case the borrower fails to repay the loan.

Generally not allowed:

▸ an "interest-only" period – when interest, but not principal, is being repaid

▸ negative amortization – when principal increases over time

▸ balloon payment – larger than normal payment at the end of the loan term

▸ loan term longer than 30 years

▸ excessive upfront fees and points

Generally required:

- ▸ monthly debt no more than 43 % of monthly pre-tax income

- ▸ limits on points

Qualified Mortgages include loans that can be bought by Fannie Mae or Freddie Mac or insured by certain government agencies, such as the Department of Agriculture, even if the debt ratio is higher than 43 percent. Also, loans that are insured or guaranteed by the Department of Housing and Urban Development, including through the Federal Housing Administration, are qualified mortgages under rules issued by that agency.

Valuations. Before issuing a first mortgage loan, a lender must perform the following actions:

- ▸ Notify the borrower within three days of the loan application that a copy of any appraisal will be promptly provided

- ▸ Provide the borrower with a free copy of any valuation used, including appraisal reports, automated valuation model reports, and broker's price opinions, promptly when completed and no later than three days before closing

- ▸ Provide these copies even if the loan does not close

The lender may ask for the deadline to be waived so that the copies may be delivered at closing, and may charge a reasonable fee for obtaining the valuation.

Discovery and disclosure requirements. Creditors are required to provide applicants with free copies of all appraisals and other written valuations developed in connection with an application for a loan to be secured by a first lien on a dwelling and must notify applicants in writing that copies of appraisals will be provided to them promptly.

High cost loans. When the annual percentage rate (APR) or points and fees on a home loan, home equity loan, or home equity line of credit (HELOC) exceed certain limits, special consumer protections apply. The lender must provide information in advance that explains the costs, terms, and associated fees, and get a housing counselor to certify that the borrower has received counseling about the high-cost mortgage.

With high-cost mortgages, lenders are not allowed to add many kinds of fees and charges to the loan amount, namely the following:

- ▸ prepayment penalties for early loan payoff

- ▸ balloon payments

- late fees larger than 4 percent of the regular payment

- fees for payoff statements (statements of loan balance)

- loan modification fees

Income qualification

Lenders want to be assured that the borrower has adequate means to make all necessary periodic payments on the loan in addition to other housing expenses and debts such as credit card payments and car payments. Most lenders use two ratios to estimate an applicant's ability to fulfill a loan obligation: an *income ratio,* or *housing ratio*, and a *debt ratio*, or *housing plus debt ratio*. They also consider the stability of an applicant's income. Please note that the income and debt ratios in the discussion below do not necessarily reflect the latest ratios used by FHA, VA, or other lenders. Check for updates on the websites of those agencies.

Income ratio. The income ratio, or housing expense ratio, establishes borrowing capacity by limiting the percent of gross income a borrower may spend on housing costs. Housing costs include principal, interest, taxes, and homeowner's insurance, and may include monthly assessments, mortgage insurance, and utilities. The income ratio formula looks like this:

Income Ratio

$$\frac{monthly\ housing\ expense}{monthly\ GROSS\ income} = income\ ratio$$

To identify the maximum monthly housing expense an income ratio allows, modify the formula as follows:

monthly gross income x income ratio = monthly housing expense

Most conventional lenders require that this ratio be *no greater than 25-28%*. In other words, a borrower's total housing expenses cannot exceed 28% of gross income. For an FHA-backed loan, the ratio is 31%. VA-guaranteed loans do not use this qualifying ratio.

For example, if a couple has combined monthly gross income of $12,000, and a lender's maximum income ratio is 28%, the couple's monthly housing expense cannot exceed $3,360:

$$\$12,000 \times 28\% = \$3,360$$

Debt ratio. The debt ratio considers all of the monthly obligations of the income ratio *plus any additional monthly payments the applicant must make for other debts*. The lender will look specifically at minimum monthly payments due on revolving credit debts and other consumer loans. Following is the debt ratio formula:

Debt Ratio

$$\frac{monthly\ housing\ expense + monthly\ debt\ obligations}{monthly\ GROSS\ income} = debt\ ratio$$

To identify the housing expenses plus debt that a debt ratio allows, modify the formula as follows:

monthly gross income x debt ratio = monthly housing expense + monthly debt obligations

Most conventional lenders require that this debt ratio be *no greater than 36%.* For an FHA-backed loan, the debt ratio may not exceed 43%. The VA uses 41% and a variable "residual income" calculation. The FHA and VA include in the debt figure any obligation costing more than $100 per month and any debt with a remaining term exceeding six months.

Using the 36% debt ratio, the couple whose monthly income is $12,000 will be allowed to have monthly housing and debt obligations of $4,320:

$12,000 gross income x 36% = $4,320 expenses and debt

VA-guaranteed loans also require a borrower to meet certain qualifications based on net income after paying federal, state, and social security taxes, housing maintenance and utilities expenses. Such **residual income requirements** vary by family size, loan amount, and geographical region.

Income stability. A lender looks at factors beyond income and debt ratios to assess an applicant's income stability:

> ▶ How long the applicant has been employed at the present job

> ▶ How frequently and for what reasons the applicant has changed jobs in the past

> ▶ How likely secondary income such as bonuses and overtime is to continue on a regular basis

> ▶ How educational level, training and skills, age, and type of occupation may affect the continuation of the present income level in the future.

Cash qualification   Since a lender lends only part of the purchase price of a property according to the lender's loan-to-value ratio, a lender will verify that a borrower has the cash resources to make the required down payment. If some of a borrower's cash for the down payment comes as a gift from a relative or friend, a lender may require a gift letter from the donor stating the amount of the gift and lack of any requirement to repay the gift. On the other hand, if someone is lending an applicant a portion of the down payment with a provision for repayment, a lender will consider this another debt obligation and adjust the debt ratio accordingly. This can lower the amount a lender is willing to lend.

Net worth

An applicant's net worth shows a lender the depth of the applicant's cash reserves, the value and liquidity of assets, and the extent to which assets exceed liabilities. These facts are important to a lender as an indication of the applicant's ability to sustain debt payment in the event of loss of employment.

Credit evaluation

Credit report and credit score. A lender must obtain a written credit report on any applicant who submits a completed loan application. The credit report will contain the applicant's history regarding the following items:

▶ Outstanding debts

▶ Payment behavior (timeliness, collection problems)

▶ Legal information of public record (lawsuits, judgments, bankruptcies, divorces, foreclosures, garnishments, repossessions, defaults)

Problems with payment behavior and legal actions are likely to cause a lender to deny the application, unless the applicant can provide an acceptable explanation of mitigating and temporary circumstances that caused the problem.

If a lender denies a loan on the basis of a credit report, the lender must disclose in writing that the applicant is entitled to a statement of reason from any creditor responsible for the negative report.

Since 1995, the Federal Home Loan Mortgage Corporation and the Federal National Mortgage Association have been encouraging lenders to use *credit scoring* to evaluate loan applicants. **Credit scoring** is a computer-based method of assigning a numerical value to an applicant's credit. The credit score is a statistical prediction of a borrower's likelihood of defaulting on a loan.

Loan commitment

When a lender's underwriter has qualified an applicant and the lender has decided to offer the loan, the lender gives the applicant a written notice of the agreement to lend under specific terms. This written promise is the **loan commitment**. The commitment may take a number of common forms, including *a firm commitment, a lock-in commitment, a conditional commitment, and a take-out commitment.*

A **firm commitment** is a straightforward offer to make a specific loan at a specific interest rate for a specific term. This kind of commitment is the one most commonly offered to home buyers.

A **"lock-in" commitment** is an offer to lend a specific amount for a specific term at a specific interest rate, *but the interest rate is subject to an expiration date,* for instance, sixty days. This guarantees that the lender will not raise the interest rate during the application and closing periods. The borrower may have to pay points or some other charge for the lock-in.

A **conditional commitment** offers to make a loan if certain provisions are met. This kind of commitment generally applies to construction loans. A typical condition for funding the loan is completion of a development phase.

A **take-out commitment** offers to make a loan that will "take out" another lender's loan, i.e., pay it off and replace it. The take-out loan is most often used to retire a construction loan. The take-out lender agrees to pay off the short-term construction loan by issuing a long-term permanent loan

---

MORTGAGE LAWS

Truth-in-Lending and Regulation Z
Equal Credit Opportunity Act
Real Estate Settlement Procedures Act
National Flood Insurance Act

**Truth-in-Lending
and Regulation Z**

The Consumer Credit Protection Act, enacted in 1969 and since amended by the Truth-in-Lending Simplification and Reform Act, is implemented by the Federal Reserve's **Regulation Z**. Regulation Z applies to all loans secured by a residence. It does not apply to commercial loans or to agricultural loans over $25,000. Its provisions cover *the disclosure of costs, the right to rescind the credit transaction, advertising credit offers, and penalties for non-compliance with the act.*

The Dodd-Frank Wall Street Reform and Consumer Protection Act of 2010 (Dodd-Frank Act) established the Consumer Financial Protection Bureau (CFPB.) to protect consumers by carrying out federal consumer financial laws. The CFPB consolidates most Federal consumer financial protection authority in one place, including enforcement of RESPA, ECOA, and Truth in Lending.

Disclosure of costs. Under Regulation Z, a lender must disclose all finance charges as well as the true Annualized Percentage Rate (APR) in advance of closing. A lender does not have to show the total interest payable over the loan term or include in finance charges such settlement costs as fees for appraisal, title, credit report, survey, or legal work. Disclosure must be distinctly presented in writing.

Rescission. A borrower has a limited right to cancel the credit transaction, usually within three days of completion of the transaction. The right of rescission does not apply to "residential mortgage transactions," that is, to mortgage loans used to finance the purchase or construction of the borrower's primary residence. However, state law may require a rescission period and notice on these transactions as well.

Advertising. Any type of advertising to offer credit is subject to requirements of full disclosure if it includes any of the following items:

▸ A down payment percentage or amount

▸ An installment payment amount

▸ A specific amount for a finance charge

▸ A specific number of payments

▸ A specific repayment period

▸ A statement that there is no charge for credit

If any of these items appears in the advertising, the lender must disclose the down payment amount or percentage, repayment terms, the APR, and whether the rate can be increased after consummation of the loan.

Noncompliance. Willful violation of Regulation Z is punishable by imprisonment of up to a year and/or a fine of up to $5,000. Other violations may be punished by requiring payment of court costs, attorneys' fees, damages, and a fine of up to $1,000.

Equal Credit Opportunity Act

ECOA prohibits discrimination in extending credit based on race, color, religion, national origin, sex, marital status, age, or dependency upon public assistance. A creditor may not make any statements to discourage an applicant on the basis of such discrimination or ask any questions of an applicant concerning these discriminatory items. A real estate licensee who assists a seller in qualifying a potential buyer may fall within the reach of this prohibition. A lender must also inform a rejected applicant in writing of reasons for denial within 30 days. A creditor who fails to comply is liable for punitive and actual damages.

Real Estate Settlement Procedures Act

RESPA is a federal law which aims to *standardize settlement practices and ensure that buyers understand settlement costs*. RESPA applies to purchases of residential real estate (one- to four-family homes) to be financed by "federally related" first mortgage loans. Federally related loans include the following:

▸ VA- and FHA-backed loans

▸ Other government-backed or -assisted loans

▸ Loans that are intended to be sold to FNMA, FHLMC, GNMA, or other government-controlled secondary market institutions

▸ Loans made by lenders who originate more than one million dollars per year in residential loans.

▸ Reverse mortgages

RESPA does not apply to the following types of loans:

- ▶ Loans on properties larger than 25 acres.
- ▶ Agricultural loans
- ▶ Construction loans and temporary financing
- ▶ Commercial or business loans
- ▶ Vacant land
- ▶ Assumed loans
- ▶ Secondary market transactions
- ▶ Home equity line of credit
- ▶ Chattel dwelling loans (mobile homes)

In addition to imposing settlement procedures, RESPA provisions prohibit lenders from paying kickbacks and unearned fees to parties who may have helped the lender obtain the borrower's business. This would include, for example, a fee paid to a real estate agent for referring a borrower to the lender.

To assist in informing and educating borrowers, RESPA requires that lenders provide a loan applicant with a **loan information booklet** and a **loan estimate**. The booklet, produced by the Consumer Financial Protection Bureau, explains RESPA provisions, general settlement costs, and the required **Closing Disclosure** form. The lender must provide the estimate of closing costs within 3 days following the borrower's application.

Disclosures. The Consumer Financial Protection Bureau (CFPB) requires lenders to use two specific forms to disclose settlement costs to the buyer. A lender must provide a Loan Estimate (H-24) within three days of receiving the loan application and allow the buyer to see the Closing Disclosure (H-25) three days before loan consummation. A lender must also provide a buyer with a copy of the information booklet, "Your Home Loan Toolkit," concerning mortgage loan, closing costs, and closing procedures. The disclosures specify the following items:

- ▶ settlement charges
- ▶ title charges
- ▶ recording and transfer fees
- ▶ reserve deposits required
- ▶ tax and insurance escrow deposits required
- ▶ any other fees or charges
- ▶ total closing costs

The disclosure forms vary, depending on loan type. The costs in the Closing Disclosure must match those in the Loan Estimate within certain standards. A sample of the H-25 Closing Disclosure is provided in Chapter 6.

National Flood Insurance Act

Federal law requires that borrowers seeking to finance real estate through federally related loans obtain flood insurance if the property is located in a designated flood-hazard area. The Department of Housing and Urban Development administers a program to subsidize flood insurance for borrowers in communities that have entered the program and complied with its construction standards. The Army Corps of Engineers has prepared flood-zone maps for the entire country.

MORTGAGE MARKET

Supply and demand for money
The primary mortgage market
The secondary mortgage market
Role of SONYMA, FNMA, GNMA, and FHLMC

Money for mortgages primarily comes from cash savings of individuals, government, and businesses. This money may become available through the process of **intermediation**, in which funds on deposit with financial institutions are loaned out to borrowers, or **disintermediation**, in which the owners of the savings invest their money directly by making loans or other investments. Government actions and investor activities affect the supply of money for mortgage loans and encourage or discourage the market for mortgage loans as an investment

Supply and demand for money

Money is a limited commodity subject to the effects of supply and demand. The federal government's monetary policy *controls the supply of money* in order to achieve the country's economic goals. An excessive supply of money usually causes interest rates to fall and consumer prices to rise. Conversely, an excessive demand for money, such as for mortgage loans, causes interest rates to rise and prices to fall. Regulation of the money supply addresses these fluctuations with the aim to control and limit wide swings in the supply and demand cycle. These efforts, in turn, help to buffer the economy from severe inflationary or recessionary trends.

Regulating the money supply. The Federal Reserve System regulates the money supply by means of three methods:

> ▸ *Selling or re-purchasing government securities*, primarily Treasury bills

> ▸ Changing the *reserve requirement* for member banks. The reserve is a percentage of depositors' funds that banks and other regulated financial institutions may not lend out.

> ▸ Changing the interest rate, or *discount rate,* the system charges member institutions for borrowing funds from the Federal Reserve System central banks

When the Federal Reserve sells Treasury bills, the money paid for the securities is removed from the economy's money supply. Conversely, when it repurchases Treasury bills, the cash paid out to investors puts money back into the economy.

The second control, regulating reserve requirements, effectively restricts how much money banks can put into the economy through the disbursement of loans. When the Federal Reserve *raises* reserve requirements, banks have less money to lend, decreasing the money supply. When the Fed *lowers* reserve requirements, banks have more money to lend, increasing the money supply.

The third control, and perhaps the most effective, is regulation of the discount rate which member banks must pay to borrow money. If the discount rate goes up, it becomes more cost-prohibitive to borrow. Therefore, the money supply tightens. If the discount rate is lowered, banks have an incentive to borrow more money to lend to customers.

The primary mortgage market

The **primary mortgage market** consists of lenders who originate mortgage loans directly to borrowers. Primary mortgage market lenders include the following:

> ▸ savings and loans

> ▸ commercial banks

> ▸ mutual savings banks

> ▸ life insurance companies

> ▸ mortgage bankers

> ▸ credit unions

Mortgage brokers are also part of the primary mortgage market, even though they do not lend to customers directly. Rather, they are instrumental in procuring borrowers for primary mortgage lenders.

The primary lender assumes the initial risk of the long-term investment in the mortgage loan. Primary lenders sometimes also **service** the loan until it is paid off. Servicing loans entails collecting the borrower's periodic payments, maintaining and disbursing funds in escrow accounts for taxes and insurance, supervising the borrower's performance, and releasing the mortgage on repayment. In many cases, primary lenders employ mortgage servicing companies, which service loans for a fee.

Portfolio lenders. A primary mortgage market lender may or may not sell its loans into the secondary market. Many lenders originate loans for the purpose of retaining the investments in their own loan *portfolio.* These loans are referred to as *portfolio loans*, and lenders originating loans for their own portfolio are called *portfolio lenders*. Portfolio lenders are less restricted by the standards and forms imposed on other lenders by secondary market organizations. In retaining their portfolio loans, portfolio lenders may vary underwriting criteria and hold independent standards for down payment requirements and the condition of the collateral.

The secondary mortgage market

Lenders, investors and government agencies that buy loans already originated by someone else, or originate loans indirectly through someone else, constitute the **secondary mortgage market**.

Secondary mortgage market organizations include the following:

> ▸ Federal National Mortgage Association (FNMA, or Fannie Mae)
> ▸ Federal Home Loan Mortgage Corporation (FHLMC, or Freddie Mac)
> ▸ Government National Mortgage Association (GNMA, or Ginnie Mae)
> ▸ investment firms that assemble loans into packages and sell securities based on the pooled mortgages
> ▸ life insurance companies
> ▸ pension funds
> ▸ primary market institutions who also invest as secondary lenders

Secondary mortgage market organizations buy pools of mortgages from primary lenders and sell securities backed by these pooled mortgages to investors. By selling securities, the secondary market brings investor money into the mortgage market. By purchasing loans from primary lenders, the secondary market returns funds to the primary lenders, thereby enabling the primary lender to originate more mortgage loans.

Exhibit 8.3 The Mortgage Money Flow

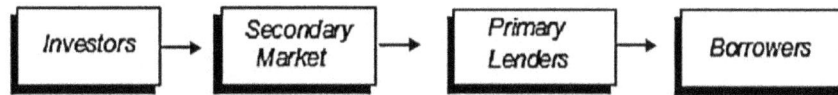

Primary lenders make a profit on the sale of loans to the secondary market. The secondary market acquires a profitable long-term investment without having to underwrite, originate, and service the loans. Secondary market organizations customarily hire primary lenders or loan servicing companies to service mortgage pools.

Secondary market loan requirements. The secondary market only buys loans that meet established requirements for quality of collateral, borrower and documentation. Since many primary lenders intend to sell their loans to the secondary market, the qualification standards of the secondary market limit and effectively regulate the kind of loans the primary lender will originate.

Role of SONYMA, FNMA, GNMA, and FHLMC

The State of New York Mortgage Agency (SONYMA). Sonny Mae is set up to help qualified buyers purchase their first home or their first home withing the previous 3 or more years by offering low-interest mortgage loans and programs. Applicants should have the following qualifications:

▸ 2 years of consistent and verifiable income

▸ A good credit history

▸ Adequate income to cover home-related expenses as well as other financial obligations

▸ Sufficient savings to cover a down payment and closing costs

Sonny Mae has multiple programs to assist homebuyers with down payments and other grants and subsidies. Although the loans are made with government funds, the agency works with mortgage lenders to assist low and moderate income buyers in obtaining 30-year, fixed-rate mortgages on single-family homes, homes with two to four dwellings, co-ops, and condominiums. Information and application procedures can be found online at State of New York Mortgage Agency (SONYMA) | Homes and Community Renewal.

Federal National Mortgage Association, or Fannie Mae. As a major player in the secondary mortgage market, Fannie Mae is a government-sponsored enterprise that became a private corporation in 1968, relying on investors in the real estate market. After widespread economic troubles in the late 2000s, Fannie

Mae has been under the Federal Housing Finance Agency conservatorship since 2008.

Farrie Mae purchases conventional mortgage loans from smaller lenders who qualify the applicant and close the loan. Fannie Mae then purchases the loan and guarantees it to investors who carry the loan for low to median income borrowers. As a secondary market player, it offers the following services:

- Buys conventional, FHA-backed and VA-backed loans

- Gives banks mortgage-backed securities in exchange for blocks of mortgages

- Offers lenders firm loan purchase commitments, provided they conform to Fannie Mae's lending standards

- Sells bonds and mortgage-backed securities

- Guarantees payment of interest and principal on mortgage-backed securities

When assessing an applicant for loan approval, Fannie Mae looks at the applicant's credit score, debt-to-income ratio, savings adequate for the down payment, and reserves to cover expenses in case of income loss.

Government National Mortgage Association, or Ginnie Mae. Ginnie Mae is a division of the Department of Housing and Urban Development (HUD). Its purpose is to administer special assistance programs and to help Fannie Mae in its secondary market activities. Specifically, GNMA guarantees the following:

- Payment on FNMA high-risk, low-yield mortgages and absorbs the difference in yield between the mortgages and market rates

- Privately generated securities backed by pools of VA-and FHA-guaranteed loans

- Mortgages designed to offer homeownership to more people, including those with less than great credit histories.

Ginnie Mae does not actually offer mortgage loans. Instead, it buys loans from mortgage originators who qualify the applicant and close the loan, at which point Ginnie Mae buys the loan to allow the lender to make additional loans.

Federal Home Loan Mortgage Corporation, or Freddie Mac. Freddie Mac is a government-sponsored enterprise, originally chartered as a corporation in 1970. As a secondary market player, FHLMC buys mortgages and pools them, selling bonds backed by the mortgages in the open market. Freddie Mac guarantees performance on FHLMC mortgages.

Along with Fannie Mae, Freddie Mac was placed under a federal conservator, the Federal Housing Finance Authority (FHFA), in 2008.

Conforming loans. Conventional loans that meet the FHFA standards for purchase by Fannie Mae and Freddie Mac are referred to as conforming loans. These loans may have fixed or adjustable rates and varying term lengths.

Non-conforming loans. Fannie Mae and Freddie Mac have set standards for the loans they will purchase. If a mortgage does not meet those standards, it is known as a non-conforming loan. The loan may be classified as non-conforming if it doesn't meet the standards set by the Federal Housing Finance Agency (FHFA), the conservator of Fannie Mae and Freddie Mac. The loan might also be considered non-conforming if it is too large to meet the standards. Non-conforming loans include the following:

▶ VA loans
▶ USDA loans for rural residents
▶ FHA loans
▶ Jumbo loans for high value properties
▶ Personalized solutions for those with credit or other issues

Non-conforming loans are not resold as conventional mortgage loans are.

TYPES OF MORTGAGE LOANS

Conventional loans
FHA-insured loans
VA-guaranteed loans
USDA loans
New York Section 502 Direct Loan Program
Common loan structures
Seller financing
Special-purpose loans

Conventional loans   A **conventional mortgage** loan is a permanent long-term loan that is not FHA-insured or VA-guaranteed. Market rates usually determine the interest rate on the loan. Because of the lack of insurance or guarantee by a government agency, the risk to a lender is greater for a conventional loan than for a non-conventional loan. This risk is usually reflected in higher interest rates and stricter requirements for the down payment and the borrower's income qualification. At the same time, conventional loans allow greater flexibility in fees, rates, and terms than do insured and guaranteed loans.

In contrast to nonconventional government-backed mortgage loans, conventional loans typically require higher down payments. The norm is 20%, allowing the loan to be for no more than 80% of the purchase price, thereby protecting funds deposited by other banking customers. Therefore, New York requires loans for more than 80% to be supported by private mortgage insurance (PMI) which protects lenders from loss in situations where the borrower fails to make loan payments, and the property ends up in foreclosure. The purchase of PMI often allows borrowers to purchase a home with less than 20% down payment.

In 1998, the Homeowners Protection Act was enacted as 12 U.S. Code Chapter 49, which was then amended in 2000. The Act is also known as the PMI Cancellation Act because it addresses the difficulties homeowners have when canceling PMI coverage once it is deemed no longer necessary. The Act provides provisions for canceling and terminating PMI, sets disclosure and notification requirements, and mandates unearned premiums be returned to the homeowner. The Act is supervised and enforced by the Consumer Financial Protection Bureau.

PMI is not intended to stay in effect for the entire length of the mortgage loan. If a borrower who obtained the loan after July 29, 1999, requests the coverage be dropped, the federal government mandates the lender to do so when accumulated equity reaches 20%. The government then mandates PMI be automatically dropped when the equity reaches 22%.

In addition to the federal government's mandates, New York State law mandates PMI coverage be dropped when the loan balance reaches 75% of the value of the home at the time of the original loan.

The primary sources of conventional loans are banks and savings and loan associations. Other conventional lenders include credit unions, life insurance companies, pension funds, mortgage bankers, and private individuals. Various types of lenders specialize in mortgage lending for specific purposes and type of borrower, such as commercial, construction, or single-family residential loans.

FHA-insured loans

The Federal Housing Administration (FHA) is an agency of the Department of Housing and Urban Development (HUD). It does not lend money, but *insures* permanent long-term loans made by others. The lender must be approved by the FHA, and the borrower must meet certain FHA qualifications. In addition, the property used to secure the loan must meet FHA standards. The FHA ensures that the lender will not suffer significant loss in the case of borrower default. To provide this security, FHA provides insurance and charges the borrower an insurance premium. FHA loans typically have a higher loan-to-value ratio than conventional loans, enabling a borrower to make a smaller down payment.

The basic FHA-insured loan program is the **Title II, Section 203(b)** program for loans on one- to four-family residential properties. Borrowers are required to occupy the property as the primary residence. Among the features of this program are the following.

FHA mortgage insurance. The FHA determines how much mortgage insurance must be provided and charges the borrower an appropriate mortgage insurance premium (MIP). The initial premium is payable at closing or is added to the borrower's loan balance and financed. Further annual premiums are charged monthly. The amount of the premium varies according to the loan term and the applicable loan-to-value ratio.

Borrower default. The FHA reimburses the lender for losses due to default by the borrower, including costs of foreclosure.

Appraisal. The property must be appraised by an FHA-approved appraiser. The property must also meet the FHA's standards for type and quality of construction, neighborhood quality, and other features.

Maximum loan amount. The FHA has set maximum loan amounts which vary throughout New York State, with higher limits set for New York City and its surrounding areas. Borrowers within a specific area are limited to the loan ceiling amount in effect for the region. In addition, the maximum loan amount is restricted by the loan-to-value ratios in effect. The maximum FHA-backed loan a borrower can obtain will be the lesser of the regional ceiling amount or the amount dictated by the loan-to-value standard. Calculations are based on the lesser of sale price or appraised value. FHA does increase the limits over time.

Down payment requirement. The minimum down payment for an FHA-backed loan is based on the lower of the appraised value or the sales price. The present requirement for single-family residential loans is 3.5%.

Maximum loan term. 30 years is the maximum length of the repayment period.

Prepayment privilege. The borrower has the right to pay off the loan at any time without penalty, provided the lender is given prior notice. The lender may charge up to 30 days' interest if the borrower provides less than 30 days' notice.

Assumability. FHA-backed loans on owner-occupied properties are assumable if the buyer is qualified. Lenders and borrowers should check with FHA for current requirements.

Interest rate. The lender and borrower negotiate the interest rate on an FHA-backed loan without any involvement by FHA.

Points, fees and costs. The lender may charge discount points, a loan origination fee, and other such charges. These may be paid by buyer or seller. However, if the seller pays more than a specified percentage of the costs normally paid by a buyer, the FHA may regard these as sales concessions and lower the sales price on which the loan insurance amount is based.

In addition to Section 203(b) loan programs, FHA offers insurance coverage for other loan products to include the following:

> ▸ home improvement loans

> ▸ subsidized loans for low- and middle-income families

- ▶ loans for condominiums

- ▶ loans for multi-family projects

- ▶ graduated-payment loans

- ▶ adjustable-rate loans

VA-guaranteed loans

The Veterans Administration (Department of Veterans Affairs) offers *loan guarantees to qualified veterans* who are required to occupy the premises. The VA, like the FHA, does not lend money except in certain areas where other financing is not generally available. Instead, the VA partially guarantees permanent long-term loans originated by VA-approved lenders on properties that meet VA standards. The VA's guarantee enables lenders to issue loans with higher loan-to-value ratios than would otherwise be possible. The interest rate on a VA-guaranteed loan is usually lower than one on a conventional loan. The borrower does not pay any premium for the loan guarantee but does pay a VA funding fee at closing.

Borrower default. The VA reimburses the lender for losses up to the guaranteed amount if foreclosure sale proceeds fail to cover the loan balance.

Appraisal. The property must be appraised by a VA-approved appraiser. The VA issues a *Certificate of Reasonable Value* which creates a maximum value on which the VA-guaranteed portion of the loan will be based. The property must meet certain VA specifications.

Down payment requirement. The VA usually requires no down payment, although the lender may require one.

Maximum loan amount. The VA does not cap the loan amount, but it does limit the liability it can assume, which usually influences the amount an institution will lend. The amount a qualified veteran with full entitlement can borrow without making a downpayment determines the practical loan limits. This amount varies by county. The basic entitlement available to each eligible veteran is $36,000. Lenders will generally lend a maximum of four times that amount without a down payment if the veteran is fully qualified and the property appraises for the asking price.

Eligibility. A veteran must apply for a *Certificate of Eligibility* to find out how much the VA will guarantee in a particular situation. Eligibility for a VA loan includes the following:

- ▶ currently on active duty and have served 90 continuous days

- ▶ meet 90 days in wartime and 181 days in peacetime general length-of-service requirements

- ▸ 90 days of active duty service or 6 creditable years in the Selected Reserve or National Guard

- ▸ are the surviving spouse of a veteran who died while in service or from a service-related disability and have not remarried

- ▸ are the surviving spouse of a veteran who died while in service or from a service-related disability and have remarried after the age of 57 or after December 16, 2003

- ▸ are the surviving spouse of a service member who is missing in action or a prisoner of war

Maximum loan term. The maximum loan term for one- to four-family residences is 30 years. For loans secured by farms, the maximum loan term is 40 years.

Prepayment privilege. The loan may be paid off early without penalty.

Assumability. VA loans are assumable with lender approval. Usually, the person assuming the loan must have VA eligibility, and the assumption may have to be approved by the VA.

Interest rate. Lender and borrower negotiate the interest rate for all VA-insured loans.

Points, fees and costs. The lender may charge discount points, origination fees, and other reasonable costs. These may be paid by seller (with some limits) or buyer but may not be financed. The VA funding fee, however, may be included in the loan amount. The funding fee is a percentage of the loan amount which varies based on the type of loan, military category, whether the loan is a first-time loan, and whether there is a down payment.

Other VA programs. In addition to insuring loans to veterans, the VA may insure loans for lenders who set up a special account with the VA. The VA may also actually lend money directly when an eligible veteran cannot find other mortgage money locally.

USDA loans

With a mission of improving the quality of life in rural areas, the United States Department of Agriculture (USDA) offers qualified borrowers home loans to purchase, refinance, or renovate homes in certain towns and rural areas. To meet the rural eligibility requirements, the town or area must be outside a major urban or metropolitan area and have a population of no more than 20,000 residents. The property must be non-income producing and must be a single-family home that is owner occupied as the primary residence. There are also property condition requirements.

As for the loan itself, there is no down payment or PMI requirement. The loans are issued by partner lenders but can be issued directly by the Department to certain borrowers based on their income. The USDA Rural Development Guaranteed Housing Loan Program guarantees the loans with interest rates lower than with conventional loans. For example, on January 1, 2024, the interest rate for USDA loans was set at 5.125% while the rate for 30-year conventional loans on that same day was approximately 6.3%.

Borrower eligibility requirements include the following:

> ▸ consistent employment with steady income for at least 2 years

> ▸ low to median, not large, income relative to the area

> ▸ appropriate debt-to-income ratio

> ▸ no minimum credit score required but questionable scores must show a history of improvement

USDA Section 502 Direct Loan Program

The USDA Rural Development's Section 502 Direct Loan Program is also known as the **Single Family Housing Direct Home Loans in New York** program. The program is set up to help low- and very-low-income applicants purchase decent and safe housing in eligible rural areas in New York. The program provides payment assistance for a designated time period so the homebuyer can afford the mortgage payments. It also provides low fixed interest loans with no down payment and loan terms up to 33 years and 38 years for those who cannot afford the 33-year loan term.

The goal of the program is to promote prosperity by providing "a path to homeownership for low- and very-low-income families living in rural areas, and families who truly have no other way to make affordable homeownership a reality." In turn, the success of the program helps rural communities thrive.

Common loan structures

Variations in the structure of interest rate, term, payments, and principal payback produce a number of commonly recognized loan types. Among these are the following.

Term loan. With a term loan, the borrower receives a lump sum of money and repays the lender over a set time period. The interest rate and repayment term typically depends on the market conditions at the time of the loan. Interest rates are usually low and are somewhat negotiable.

Amortizing loan. Amortization provides for gradual repayment of principal and payment of interest over the term of the loan. The borrower's periodic payments to the lender include a portion for interest and a portion for principal. In a fully amortizing mortgage, the principal balance is zero at the end of the term. In a partially amortizing loan, the payments are not sufficient to retire the debt. At the end of the loan term, there is still a principal balance to be paid off.

Negatively amortized loan. Negative amortization causes the loan balance to increase over the term. This occurs if the borrower's periodic payment is insufficient to cover the interest owed for the period. The lender adds the amount of unpaid interest to the borrower's loan balance. Temporary negative amortization occurs on graduated payment loans and may occur on an adjustable rate mortgage.

Adjustable and fixed rate loans. Loans may have fixed or variable rates of interest over the loan term. *Fixed rate loans* have interest rates that remains the same throughout the life of the loan, regardless of the term length. The borrower then always knows the consistent payment amount. The interest rate and payment amount does not change regardless of any market fluctuations.

Adjustable rate mortgages (ARMs) allow the lender to change the interest rate at specified intervals and by a specified amount based on market conditions.

With ARMs, not only does the interest rate change, but so does the loan payment amount. Consequently, the borrower does not always have the predictability of payment amounts as does the borrower of a fixed interest loan.

ARMs have two periods: the fixed period is a time frame during which the interest rate does not change. The fixed period typically occurs during the first few years of the loan's life. The adjustable period is the time frame during which the interest rate starts changing based on fluctuations in market conditions. Federal regulations place limits on incremental interest rate increases and on the total amount by which the rate may be increased over the loan term.

Senior and junior loans. When there are multiple loans on a single property, there is an order of priority in the liens which the mortgages create. The first, or senior, loan generally has priority over any subsequent loans. Second loans are riskier than first loans because the senior lender will be satisfied first in case of default. Therefore, interest rates on second mortgages are generally higher than on first mortgages.

Fixed and graduated payment loans. Loans may have variable payment amounts over the term of the loan, or a single fixed payment amount. With a graduated payment mortgage (GPM), the payments at the beginning of the loan term are low and not sufficient to amortize the loan fully, and unpaid interest is added to the principal balance. Payments are gradually increased every year to a level that will fully amortize the loan's increased balance over the remaining loan term.

GPMs are available only for FHA mortgage loans. The initial lower payment schedule allows home buyers to qualify for a loan when they might not qualify for a loan with higher payments. The GPMs tend to be most beneficial to young or first-time homebuyers with the idea their incomes will rise over time, just as the payment amounts will increase.

Interest-only loan. In an interest-only loan, payments over the first 7 to 10 years of the loan term apply only to interest owed, not to principal. Then one of two things happen:

1. From that point on to the end of the term, payments go toward paying down both the principal and the interest; or

2. At the end of the term, the full balance must be paid off in a lump-sum, "balloon" payment.

Since these loans have no periodic principal payback, their monthly payments are smaller than amortizing loans for the same amount at the same rate of interest.

Buydown loan. A buydown loan entails a prepayment of interest on a loan. The prepayment effectively lowers the interest rate and the periodic payments for the borrower. Buydowns typically occur in a circumstance where a builder wants to market a new development to a buyer who cannot quite qualify for the necessary loan at market rates. By "buying down" a borrower's mortgage, a builder enables the borrower to obtain the loan. The builder may then pass the costs of the buydown through to the buyer in the form of a higher purchase price.

Seller financing

The seller may provide some or all of the financing for the buyer's purchase. Some of the most common methods of seller financing are purchase money mortgages, including the wraparound, and the contract for deed.

Purchase money mortgage. With a purchase money mortgage, the borrower gives a mortgage and note to the seller to finance some or all of the purchase price of the property. The seller in this case is said to "take back" a note, or to "carry paper," on the property. Purchase money mortgages may be either senior or junior liens.

Wraparound. In a wraparound loan arrangement, the seller receives a junior mortgage from the buyer and uses the buyer's payments to make the payments on the original first mortgage. A wraparound enables the buyer to obtain financing with a minimum cash investment. It also potentially enables the seller to profit from any difference between a lower interest rate on the senior loan and a higher rate on the wraparound loan. A wraparound is possible only if the senior mortgagee allows it.

Contract for deed. Under a contract for deed arrangement, the seller retains title and the buyer receives possession and equitable title while making payments under the terms of the contract. The seller conveys title when the contract has been fully performed.

Special-purpose loans

Home equity loan. The ostensible purpose of this type of loan is to obtain funds for home improvement. Structurally, the home equity loan is a junior mortgage secured by the homeowner's equity. For some lenders, the maximum home equity loan amount is based on the difference between the property's appraised value and the maximum loan-to-value ratio the lender allows on the property, inclusive of all existing mortgage loans. Thus if a home is appraised at $500,000 and the lender's maximum LTV is 80%, the lender will lend a total of $400,000. If the owner's existing mortgage balance is $325,000, the owner would qualify for a $75,000 home equity loan.

Reverse equity mortgage loan. The reverse equity loan is available to homeowners at least 62 years old who have substantial equity in their home. The mortgage pays the existing mortgage in full and then allows the homeowner to choose one of the following options:

- ▸ Receive a single lump sum payment, or

- ▸ Receive scheduled monthly payments, or

- ▸ Establish a line of credit, or

- ▸ Bland any of these options.

With this loan, senior homeowners can access the equity they have in their homes and not make monthly mortgage payments. However, the homeowner is still responsible for property taxes, insurance, and maintenance expenses. The loan is only repaid when the homeowner either passes away, sells the home, or moves to another home.

Package loan. A package loan finances the purchase of real estate and personal property. For example, a package loan might finance a furnished condominium, complete with all fixtures and decor.

Open-end mortgage. When home buyers apply for a mortgage loan, they typically qualify for a maximum dollar amount for the loan. If the home being purchased costs less than that maximum, open-end mortgage loans allow borrowers to take out the maximum loan amount they qualify for to buy the house and then use the remaining amount borrowed to perform home improvements. This remaining amount can only be used for home improvements, and borrowers do not pay interest on that amount until they actually use it.

Construction loan. A construction loan finances construction of improvements. This type of loan is paid out by the lender in installments linked to stages of the construction process. The loan is usually interest-only, and the borrower makes periodic payments based on the amount disbursed so far. As short-term, high-risk financing, the interest rates are usually higher than those for long-term financing. The borrower is expected to find permanent ("take out") financing elsewhere to pay off the temporary loan when construction is complete.

Bridge loan. A bridge, or gap, loan is used to cover a gap in financing between short-term construction financing and long-term permanent financing. For instance, a developer may have difficulty finding a long-term lender to take out the construction lender. However, as the construction loan is expensive and must be paid off as soon as possible, the developer may find an interim lender who will pay off the construction loan but not agree to a long-term loan.

Participation loan. In a participation loan, the lender participates in the income and/or equity of the property, in return for giving the borrower more favorable loan terms than would otherwise be justified. For instance, the borrower makes smaller periodic payments than the interest rate and loan amount require, and the lender makes up the difference by receiving some of the property's income. This type of loan usually involves an income property.

Permanent (take-out) loan. A permanent loan is a long-term loan that "takes out" a construction or short-term lender. The long-term lender pays off the balance on the construction loan when the project is completed, leaving the borrower with a long-term loan under more favorable terms than the construction loan offered.

Reverse annuity. In a reverse annuity mortgage, a homeowner pledges the equity in the home as security for a loan which is paid out in regular monthly amounts over the term of the loan. The homeowner, in effect, is able to convert the equity to cash without losing ownership and possession.

Blanket. A blanket mortgage is one loan secured by more than one property, such as multiple parcels of real estate in a development. These loans are used primarily by developers who subdivide the purchased land. Blanket mortgages come with release clauses that allow individual parcels of the property to be sold without needing to sell all of the property at once. When one parcel is sold, the developer makes a payment to the lender so that parcel can be released from the total mortgage. The developer may also use funds from the sale to purchase other property without paying off the original loan.

PREDATORY LENDING

Subprime mortgage

The term *predatory lending* refers to **unfair practices** that benefit lenders while making it **difficult for borrowers to repay their debt.** These practices may include high interest rates, excessive or hidden fees, penalties for loan prepayment, large balloon payments, packing other services or products into the loan terms, and loan flipping. Predatory lenders tend to target people with poor credit ratings and low income that prevent them from qualifying for conventional loans and reasonable interest rates. These lenders rely on borrowers' inexperience and lack of understanding financial transactions when they offer loans without requiring the borrower to qualify or show the ability to repay. Then, when borrowers fail to meet the required payments on a mortgage with excessive rates attached to it, the home is lost through foreclosure.

In New York, a loan is considered predatory when it should never have been granted based on the requirements for home mortgages as outlined in Part 226 Truth in Lending (Regulation Z). The law prohibits extending credit without regard to the borrower's ability to repay or to the borrower's current and expected income, obligations, and employments. In addition to federal laws such as RESPA and TILA, New York Banking Law requires "due diligence" by lenders when looking at a borrower's income and ability to pay the loan.

A subprime mortgage is one offered to a home loan borrower with a limited credit history or less than prime credit. To qualify for a prime conventional mortgage loan, borrowers need a credit score of at least 620. However, to qualify for a subprime loan, the borrower's credit score would be between 580 and 619. Subprime loans have higher interest rates than prime loans and are geared toward borrowers who are less likely to maintain their mortgage payments and, thus, likely to end up in foreclosure.

Prior to 2007, subprime lending was prevalent and led to the country's financial crisis. Subprime loans accounted for approximately 30% of all mortgages in 2006. In 2020, the COVID-19 pandemic led to borrowers decreased income and affected their ability to make mortgage payments. To assist those borrowers, the CARES ACT was created to provide struggling borrowers a 180-day forbearance, further impacting the state of the country's finances. As a result, subprime mortgages are now subject to more oversight. They are now regulated by the Consumer Financial Protection Bureau (CFPB) which was created as part of the Dodd-Frank Act.

Borrowers classified as 'subprime' are borrowers who have a history of at least two late payments in the last year. They also may have a judgment or foreclosure on their record and have possibly filed for bankruptcy within the previous 5 years. Under the CFPB's rules, subprime borrowers are required to undergo homebuyer counseling through HUD. Lenders are required to follow Dodd-Frank standards when underwriting subprime mortgages. One such standard is the requirement for the lender to assess if the borrower is financially capable of repaying the loan. Lenders who do not comply with this rule are subject to regulatory enforcement, resulting in subprime loans being offered more carefully.

FORECLOSURE

Mortgage lien foreclosure
Judicial foreclosure
Non-judicial foreclosure
Strict foreclosure
Deed in lieu of foreclosure

All liens can be enforced by the sale or other transfer of title of the secured property, whether by court action, operation of law, or through powers granted in the original loan agreement. The enforcement proceedings are referred to as foreclosure.

State law governs the foreclosure process. Broadly, a statutory or court-ordered sale enforces a general lien, including a judgment lien. A lawsuit or loan provision authorizing the sale or direct transfer of the attached property enforces a specific lien, such as a mortgage. Real estate tax liens are enforced through **tax foreclosure sales**, or **tax sales**.

Mortgage lien foreclosure

Three types of foreclosure process enforce mortgage liens:

- ▸ judicial foreclosure
- ▸ non-judicial foreclosure
- ▸ strict foreclosure

Exhibit 8.4 Foreclosure Processes

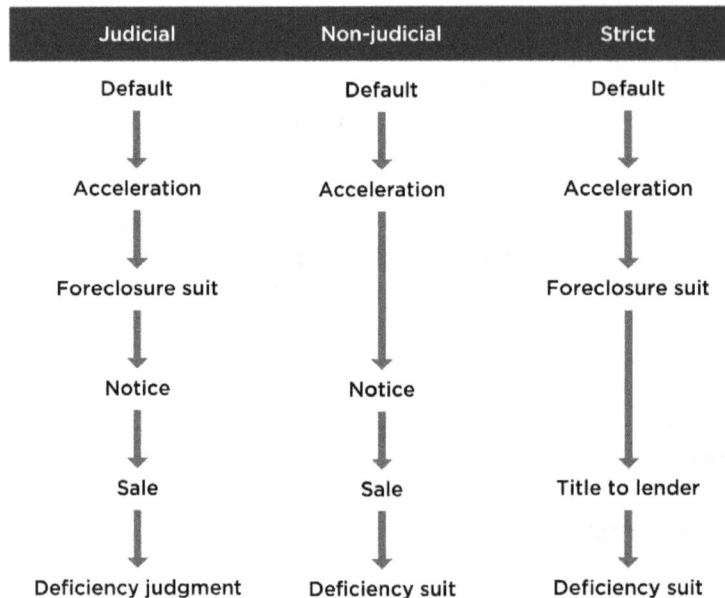

Judicial	Non-judicial	Strict
Default	Default	Default
↓	↓	↓
Acceleration	Acceleration	Acceleration
↓	↓	↓
Foreclosure suit		Foreclosure suit
↓	↓	↓
Notice	Notice	
↓	↓	↓
Sale	Sale	Title to lender
↓	↓	↓
Deficiency judgment	Deficiency suit	Deficiency suit

Judicial foreclosure   Judicial foreclosure occurs in states that use a two-party mortgage document (borrower and lender) that does not contain a "power of sale" provision. Lacking this provision, a lender must file a **foreclosure suit** and undertake a court proceeding to enforce the lien.

Acceleration and filing. If a borrower has failed to meet loan obligations in spite of proper notice and applicable grace periods, the lender can **accelerate** the loan or declare that the loan balance and all other sums due on the loan are payable immediately.

If the borrower does not pay off the loan in full, the lender then files a foreclosure suit, naming the borrower as defendant. The suit asks the court to:

- ▸ terminate the defendant's interests in the property
- ▸ order the property sold publicly to the highest bidder
- ▸ order the proceeds applied to the debt

Lis Pendens. In the foreclosure suit, a **lis pendens** gives public notice that the mortgaged property may soon have a judgment issued against it. This notice enables other lienholders to join in the suit against the defendant.

Writ of execution. If the defendant fails to meet the demands of the suit during a prescribed period, the court orders the termination of interests of any and all parties in the property and orders the property to be sold. The court's **writ of execution** authorizes an official, such as the county sheriff, to seize and sell the foreclosed property.

Public sale and sale proceeds. After public notice of the sale, the property is auctioned to the highest bidder. The new owner receives title free and clear of all previous liens, whether the lienholders have been paid or not. Proceeds of the sale are applied to payment of liens according to priority. After payment of real estate taxes, lienholders' claims and costs of the sale, any remaining funds go to the mortgagor (borrower).

Deficiency judgment. If the sale does not yield sufficient funds to cover the amounts owed, the mortgagee may ask the court for a deficiency judgment. This enables the lender to attach and foreclose a judgment lien on other real or personal property the borrower owns.

Right of redemption. The borrower's right of redemption, also called equity of redemption, is the right to *reclaim a property* that has been foreclosed by paying off amounts owed to creditors, including interest and costs. Redemption is possible within a **redemption period**. Some states allow redemption during the foreclosure proceeding at any time "until the gavel drops" at the sale. Other states have statutory periods of up to a year following the sale for the owner of a foreclosed property to redeem the estate.

Non-judicial foreclosure

When there is a "power of sale" provision in the mortgage or trust deed document, a non-judicial foreclosure can force the sale of the liened property *without a foreclosure suit*. The "power of sale" clause in effect enables the mortgagee to order a public sale without court decree.

Foreclosure process. On default, the foreclosing mortgagee records and delivers notice to the borrower and other lienholders. After the proper period, a "notice of sale" is published, the sale is conducted, and all liens are extinguished. The highest bidder then receives unencumbered title to the property.

Deficiency suit. The lender does not obtain a deficiency judgment or lien in a non-judicial foreclosure action. The lender instead must file a new deficiency suit against the borrower.

Re-instatement and redemption. During the notice of default and notice of sale periods, the borrower may pay the lender and terminate the proceedings. Exact re-instatement periods vary from state to state. There is no redemption right in non-judicial foreclosure.

Strict foreclosure

Strict foreclosure is a court proceeding that gives the lender title directly, by court order, instead of giving cash proceeds from a public sale.

On default, the lender gives the borrower official notice. After a prescribed period, the lender files suit in court, whereupon the court establishes a period within which the defaulting party must repay the amounts owed. If the defaulter does not repay the funds, the court orders transfer of full, legal title to the lender.

Deed in lieu of foreclosure

A defaulting borrower who faces foreclosure may avoid court actions and costs by voluntarily deeding the property to the mortgagee. This is accomplished with a deed in lieu of foreclosure , which transfers legal title to the lienholder. The transfer, however, does not terminate any existing liens on the property.

SALE OF MORTGAGED PROPERTY

Selling a home that still carries a mortgage is a common practice. Homeowners with mortgages who wish to sell the home typically use the proceeds from the sale to pay off the mortgage balance. To do that, the home must have positive equity. In other words, the market value or sale price of the home must be higher than the balance owed on the mortgage.

For example, Terri owns a home with a market value of $350,000. Her mortgage has a balance of $160,000. Thus, the equity in the home is $190,000. If she sells her home for the market value, she can pay the balance of her mortgage and still have the equity (minus sale expenses such as closing costs) as profit.

A problem would arise, however, if the mortgage balance is higher than the market value or sale price of the home. If the market falls, leaving the home's value at an amount lower than the mortgage balance, then the sale of the home at market value would not provide a profit, or even enough funds to pay off the mortgage balance. When this situation arises, the home is considered *underwater* which means the home is worth less than the amount owed on its mortgage.

A seller whose home is underwater has three options:

▸ Sell the home in a short sale

In short sales, the lender must agree to the sale and approve any purchase offer. If the lender agrees to accept a lower payoff of the mortgage, the lender will be taking a loss. However, the lender could agree to the short sale and a lower purchase price but not to taking a loss. After the short sale, the lender could take action to collect the difference in the sale price and the mortgage balance from the original homeowner.
Short sales negatively impact the homeowner's credit score.

▶ Pay the difference out of pocket

The seller could pay out of pocket to cover the difference between the sale price and the balance of the mortgage. This way, the mortgage is paid in full and the seller's credit score will not be damaged. Unfortunately, this will have a critical impact on the seller's finances.

▶ Reconsider selling the home

The seller could wait until a later time to sell the home. During the wait, more payments will be made to lower the mortgage balance; the seller can possibly save up more money towards a final payoff of the mortgage, or the real estate market could change resulting in an increase of the home's value.

Another option when selling a home with a mortgage is to have the buyer take over the seller's mortgage. There are two ways to handle this: 1. The buyer may take the home *subject to the mortgage*. 2. The buyer may *assume the mortgage*.

Subject to the mortgage. In this arrangement, the buyer agrees to take over the seller's mortgage payments. In return, the buyer is given the deed to the property. Over time, the buyer would pay the mortgage in full. The amount of the mortgage that the buyer pays is deemed part of the purchase price. There are several risks to this arrangement:

▶ The loan remains in the seller's name, so the buyer is not held responsible for the loan balance. If the buyer fails to make payments, the seller will be held financially responsible.

▶ Often, mortgages contain a *due-on-sale clause* wherein the lender can demand the mortgage balance to immediately be paid in full if ownership of the home is transferred.

▶ Market changes could result in the home's value decreasing, resulting in a loss if the buyer decides to sell.

▶ Since the mortgage remains in the seller's name, the buyer has little or no control over terms of the mortgage or potential changes.

▶ Even though the buyer is paying the seller, the seller could stop making the mortgage payments to the lender, causing the home to go into foreclosure.

Assume the mortgage. When the mortgage is assumed, the current loan balance, interest rate, loan term, payment schedule, and other terms of the seller's loan are transferred to the buyer. Only certain types of loans are assumable and must be approved by the lender. If the loan is assumed without lender approval and the lender discovers the assumption, the lender can demand immediate payment in full. Most lenders include *alienation or due-on-sale clauses* in the loan contract just for this purpose. There are advantages and disadvantages to assuming a mortgage:

- Interest rates at the time of the assumption may be lower than they were at the time of the original loan, thereby saving the buyer money and making the sale easier to accomplish for the seller.

- Both the buyer and seller will have fewer closing costs.

- On the negative side, the buyer will need a substantial amount of money or a second mortgage to pay the seller the difference between the mortgage balance and the market value of the home.

Not all mortgages are assumable in New York State. Only federally guaranteed or insured mortgages are assumable, that is, FHA, VA, and USDA loans. Conventional loans are not assumable.

RECORDING AND SATISFACTION

Recording a mortgage
Mortgage lien satisfaction

Recording a mortgage

Mortgages are to be recorded in the Office of the County Clerk of the county where the mortgaged property is located. The lender is responsible for ensuring the mortgage document meets the legal recording requirements. New York requires that mortgages being recorded must have original signatures and acknowledgements. Mortgage recording tax must also be paid when recording a mortgage in New York State. The location of the mortgaged property determines the tax rate. Additional local mortgage taxes are imposed in some counties, such as New York City and Yonkers. Tax rates are based on 25 to 50 cents per $100 of mortgage debt and on the type of tax: basic tax, special additional taxes, and city or county mortgage tax. Taxes are due at the time the mortgage is recorded.

Mortgage lien satisfaction

Whenever the full amount of principal and interest on a mortgage is paid, the lender who holds the mortgage is required to give a certificate of discharge of mortgager to the borrower. The certificate serves to release or satisfy the mortgage of record and show that the mortgage is no longer a lien on the property. The recording information for the mortgage record must appear on the satisfaction certificate. The recording officer is to mark the word "discharged" on the mortgage record, specifying the mortgage has been paid and is discharged.

The satisfaction certificate must be in writing, signed, and recorded within 30 days in the same county where the mortgage is recorded. If the lender fails to record a satisfaction within set time limits, the lender may be responsible for damages for failing to timely cancel the lien. The lender can be held liable to the borrower for $500 if the certificate is not provided within 30 days, $1,000 if it is not provided within 60 days, and $1,500 if it is not provided within 90 days..

8 Real Estate Finance
Snapshot Review

MORTGAGE TRANSACTION

Mechanics of a loan transaction

- mortgage financing: using borrowed money secured by a mortgage to finance the purchase of real estate
- Instruments: note and mortgage or trust deed
- mortgage mechanics: borrower gives lender note and mortgage; lender gives borrower funds and records a lien
- trust deed mechanics: trust deed conveys title from the borrower/trustor to a third-party trustee who holds title on behalf of the lender/beneficiary until the debt is repaid

Financial components of a loan

- original principal: capital amount borrowed on which interest payments are calculated
- loan balance: remaining unpaid principal at any point in the life of the loan
- interest: charge for the use of money; rate fixed or variable
- Annual Percentage Rate (APR) includes interest and all other finance charges; lender must disclose on residential properties
- point: one percent of the loan amount, charged by lender at origination to obtain required return
- term: period of time for repayment of interest and principal
- payment: the periodic payment of interest and/or principal

Promissory note

- legal instrument executed by borrower stating debt amount, loan term, method and timing of repayment, interest rate, promise to pay; may repeat other provisions from mortgage document or deed of trust; negotiable instrument assignable to a third party

Mortgage document and trust deed

- the legal documents which pledge the property as collateral for the loan
- may include clauses covering payment of principal and interest, prepayment, late charges, escrow for taxes and insurance, liens, insurance requirements, occupancy and maintenance, lender's rights, private mortgage insurance, inspection, and other conditions of performance

MORTGAGE CLAUSES

Payment of principal And interest: prepayment And late charges

- borrower must make timely payments according to the terms of the note
- late payments or early payoffs may trigger penalties

Funds for taxes and insurance

- borrower must make monthly payments to cover taxes and hazard insurance
- borrower may also have to pay flood insurance and mortgage insurance premiums
- **escrow account:** reserve account for periodic payments of taxes and insurance.
- Real Estate Settlement Procedures Act (RESPA) limits funds the lender can require for this purpose.

PITI	• borrower's monthly payment for principal and interest is called the p&i payment (principal and interest)
	• the amount which includes the escrow payment is called PITI (principal, interest, taxes, insurance).
Charges and liens	• borrower is liable for paying any charges, liens, or other expenses that may have priority over the mortgage or trust instrument
Hazard or property insurance	• borrower must keep property insured as the lender requires
Occupancy, preservation, maintenance and protection of the property	• borrower must take and maintain occupancy as the borrower's principal residence according to requirements
	• borrower must not abuse or neglect the including use for illegal purposes, creating hazardous waste on the property, or destroying the improvements
Protection of lender's rights in the property	• lender may take actions to protect its rights in the property if the borrower jeopardizes the property value. The costs of these actions would be charged to the borrower
Mortgage insurance	• Lender may require private mortgage insurance, or PMI which protects the lender against loss from borrower default
	• applies to loans that are not backed by the Federal Housing Administration (FHA) or Veterans Administration (VA) and that have a down payment of less than 20% of the property value
Inspection	• lender may inspect the property with reasonable cause to fear damage to the collateral
Condemnation	• if the property is condemned or taken by eminent domain, lender reserves a claim on any resulting proceeds
Transfer of the property or a beneficial interest in borrower	• if borrower sells the property without the lender's approval, the lender may demand immediate repayment of the loan balance. this alienation clause, aka a due-on-sale clause, allows lender to prevent unapproved loan assumptions
	• the requirement to repay the loan before the scheduled due date is called **acceleration**.
Borrower's right to reinstate	• if lender holds borrower in default, borrower has the right to reinstatement by performing certain actions, usually paying overdue payments plus expenses the lender
	• clause is called a redemption clause
	• gives the borrower time to satisfy obligations and prevent a forced sale
Funds for taxes and insurance	• agreement to release the lien obligation when borrower has paid off the loan
	• release clause, may require lender to execute a **satisfaction of mortgage**, aka **release of mortgage**
	• if deed of trust, lender directs trustee to execute a **release deed** or **deed of reconveyance** to the borrower as trustor.

	• release deed or satisfaction should be recorded as necessary
Escalation clause	• allows lender to increase the loan's interest rate

LOAN QUALIFICATION

Equal Credit Opportunity Act	• lender must evaluate applicant according to applicant's own income and credit information
Income qualification	• income ratio and debt ratio qualify borrower's income; income ratio applied to gross income determines housing expense maximum; debt ratio takes revolving debt into account
Cash qualification	• lender verifies applicant's sources of cash for down payment; extra cash enhances income qualification evaluation
Net worth	• extent to which applicant's assets exceed liabilities as a further source of reserves
Credit evaluation	• lender obtains credit reports to evaluate applicant's payment behavior
Loan commitment	• written pledge by lender to grant loan under specific terms; firm, lock-in, conditional, take-out

MORTGAGE LAWS

Truth-in-Lending and Regulation Z	• Reg Z implements Truth-in-Lending Simplification and Reform Act and Consumer Credit Protection Act • provisions: lender must disclose finance charges and APR prior to closing; borrower has limited right of rescission; lender must follow disclosure requirements in advertising
Equal Credit Opportunity Act	• ECOA prohibits discrimination in lending
Real Estate Settlements and Procedures Act	• RESPA standardizes settlement practices • provisions: lender must provide CFPB booklet explaining loans, settlement costs and procedures; lender must provide CFPB Loan Estimate of settlement costs within three days of application; lender must provide CFPB Closing Disclosure three days before loan consummation
National Flood Insurance Act	• borrowers of "federally-related loans" must obtain flood insurance if property is in designated flood-hazard area

MORTGAGE MARKET

Supply and demand for money	• relationship between money supply and demand affects interest rates, consumer prices, availability of mortgage money • Federal Reserve controls: T-bills; reserve requirement, discount rate
The Primary mortgage market	• originates mortgage loans directly to borrowers; savings and loans, commercial banks, mutual savings banks, life insurance companies, mortgage bankers, credit unions

The Secondary mortgage market	• buys existing loans to provide liquidity to primary lenders; Fannie Mae, Ginnie Mae, Freddie Mac, investment firms, life insurance companies, pension funds
Role of FNMA, GNMA, and FHLMC	• FNMA buys conventional, FHA- and VA-backed loans and pooled mortgages; guarantees payment on mortgage-backed securities; GNMA guarantees payment on certain types of loans; FHLMC buys and pools mortgages; sells mortgage-backed securities

TYPES OF MORTGAGES

Conventional loans	• permanent, long-term loans not insured by FHA or guaranteed by VA
FHA-insured loans	• insured loans granted by FHA-approved lenders to borrowers who meet FHA qualifications
VA-guaranteed loans	• guaranteed loans granted by VA-approved lenders to qualified veterans
USDA	• offers loans to purchase, refinance, or renovate non-income homes in rural areas
New York Section 502 Direct Loan Program	• New York single family housing direct home loans for low- and very-low-income applicants in rural areas with payment assistance
Common loan structures	• amortizing, negative amortizing, interest only, fixed rate, adjustable rate, senior, junior, fixed or graduated payment, balloon, buydown
Seller financing	• purchase money mortgages: loans by the seller to the property buyer for all or part of the purchase price; contract for deed: installment sale where seller finances buyer and retains title until contract terms are met
Special- purpose loans	• home equity, package, construction, bridge, equity participation, take-out, reverse annuity, and blanket
PREDATORY LENDING	• unfair loan practices that benefit lenders and fall outside requirements for mortgages pursuant to Truth in Lending
Subprime mortgage	• for borrowers with limited credit history or less than prime credit
FORECLOSURE	• enforcement of liens through liquidation or transfer of encumbered property
Mortgage lien foreclosure	• liquidation or transfer of collateral property by judicial, non-judicial, or strict foreclosure
Judicial foreclosure	• lawsuit and court-ordered public sale; deficiency judgments, redemption rights
Non-judicial foreclosure	• "power of sale" granted to lender; no suit; no deficiency judgment; no redemption period after sale
Strict foreclosure	• court orders legal transfer of title directly to lender without public sale
Deed in lieu of foreclosure	• defaulted borrower deeds property to lender to avoid foreclosure
SALE OF MORTGAGED PROPERTY	• proceeds from sale of home used to pay off mortgage
RECORDING AND SATISFACTION	• mortgages with original signatures to be recorded in county where property is located
	• lender to give certificate of mortgage discharge to borrower when mortgage is paid in full

CHAPTER EIGHT: REAL ESTATE FINANCE

Section Quiz

8.1. A _____ conveys title to the property from the borrower to a third-party fiduciary.

    a. mortgage
    b. trust deed
    c. deed of trust
    d. note

8.2. The Equal Credit Opportunity Act prohibits a number of practices in mortgage loan underwriting, such as

    a. counting income from part-time work.
    b. asking about an applicant's plans for childbearing.
    c. requesting information about current income.
    d. permitting a spouse to sign any document.

8.3. A _____ is a negotiable instrument, which means the payee may assign it to a third party.

    a. promissory note
    b. loan
    c. deed of trust
    d. mortgage

8.4. In a valid mortgage or trust deed financing arrangement, the _____ serves as evidence of the collateral pledge.

    a. note
    b. mortgage or trust deed
    c. promissory memorandum
    d. commitment

8.5. The qualification criterion that establishes a borrower's borrowing capacity by limiting the percent of gross income a borrower may spend on housing costs is called the

    a. income ratio.
    b. income stability factor.
    c. debt ratio.
    d. loan commitment.

8.6. Conventional loans that meet the FHFA standards for purchase by Fannie Mae and Freddie Mac are referred to as

    a. non-conforming loans.
    b. guaranteed loans.
    c. common loans.
    d. conforming loans.

8.7. Which mortgage clause permits the lender to demand immediate and full repayment on the loan balance if the borrower sells or otherwise conveys its interest in the property without the lender's approval?

    a. Borrower Not Released; Forbearance by Lender Not a Waiver
    b. Transfer of the Property or a Beneficial Interest in Borrower
    c. Borrower's Right to Reinstate
    d. Protection of Lender's Rights in the Property

8.8. Which of these entities is active on the primary mortgage market?

    a. Federal National Mortgage Association
    b. Savings and loans
    c. Government National Mortgage Association
    d. Federal Home Loan Mortgage Corporation

8.9. A charge for the use of the lender's money is

    a. principal.
    b. mortgage insurance.
    c. interest.
    d. term.

8.10. Which of the following is generally NOT allowed with a qualified mortgage?

    a. Amortization
    b. Limits on points
    c. Loan term longer than 15 years
    d. Balloon payment

8.11 A homeowner borrows money from a lender and gives the lender a mortgage on the property as collateral for the loan. The homeowner retains title to the property. This is an example of

a. intermediation.
b. forfeiture.
c. hypothecation.
d. subordination.

8.12 A mortgage that contains a due-on-sale clause means

a. the loan remains in the seller's name, so the buyer is not held responsible for the loan balance.
b. the lender can demand the mortgage balance be immediately paid in full if ownership is transferred.
c. the buyer is free to assume the seller's loan and take over payments.
d. the lender waives the right to foreclose on the property if the buyer defaults on the loan.

8.13 What happens in a deed of trust transaction?

a. The beneficiary conveys title to a trustee in exchange for loan funds.
b. The trustee conveys title to a beneficiary in exchange for loan funds.
c. The trustor conveys title to a trustee to hold on behalf of the beneficiary.
d. The trustee conveys title to a trustor to hold on behalf of the beneficiary.

8.14 In a _____, a lender lends money to a homeowner and takes legal title to the property as collateral during the payoff period.

a. lien-theory state.
b. land trust state.
c. title-theory state.
d. mortgage-theory state.

8.15 A lien is an encumbrance that restricts free and clear ownership by securing the liened property as _____ for a debt.

a. collateral
b. promissory
c. conveyance
d. title

8.16 A New York lender who charges a rate of interest in excess of 16% per annum is guilty of

a. fraud.
b. criminal usury.
c. redlining.
d. civil usury.

8.17 The Equal Credit Opportunity Act (ECOA) requires lenders to

a. offer equal credit terms to all prospective borrowers.
b. specialize lending activity by geographical area for enhanced credit opportunities.
c. consider a spouse's income when evaluating a family's creditworthiness.
d. evaluate a loan applicant on the basis of that applicant's own income and credit rating.

8.18 What is the purpose of using the debt ratio in the buyer qualification process?

a. Determine the borrower's total monthly debt obligations
b. Identify the appropriate loan term for the borrower
c. Find the highest possible interest rate that the borrower can afford
d. Assess an applicant's income stability

8.19 A lender's offer to lend a specific amount for a specific term at a specific interest rate that is subject to an expiration date is called a

a. conditional loan commitment.
b. lock-in loan commitment.
c. firm loan commitment.
d. take-out loan commitment.

8.20 One of FNMA's principal roles is to _____ conventional, FHA-backed, and VA-backed loans.

a. guarantee
b. insure
c. purchase
d. originate

8.21 In a wraparound loan arrangement

    a. the seller retains title and the buyer receives possession and equitable title while making payments under the terms of the contract.
    b. the seller receives a junior mortgage from the buyer and uses the buyer's payments to make the payments on the original first mortgage.
    c. the loan is used to obtain funds for home improvements.
    d. the borrower gives a mortgage and note to the seller to finance some or all of the purchase price of the property.

8.22 Which of the following is true of a loan with negative amortization?

    a. The loan requires a prepayment of interest.
    b. The loan has a variable interest rate.
    c. The loan is a graduated payment mortgage.
    d. The loan balance increases over the term of the loan.

8.23 Which of the following is a type of seller financing?

    a. Purchase money mortgage
    b. Buydown loan
    c. Graduated payment loan
    d. Amortizing mortgage

8.24 A borrower's housing expense ratio is calculated by

    a. dividing the total debt by the monthly debt payments.
    b. dividing the gross income by total assets.
    c. dividing the gross income by total debts.
    d. dividing the monthly housing expense by monthly gross income.

8.25 The process of enforcing a lien by forcing sale of the secured property is called

    a. execution.
    b. attachment.
    c. foreclosure.
    d. subordination.

8.26 What is meant by the term "short sale"?

    a. The transaction closes before the end of the contingency period.
    b. Buyer and seller finalize a sale without the assistance of a licensed agent.
    c. The seller agrees to accept less than the listing price.
    d. The proceeds of the sale do not cover the seller's outstanding mortgage loan balance.

8.27 Which of the following is a primary purpose of the secondary mortgage market?

    a. Purchase loans from primary lenders so primary lenders can make more mortgage loans
    b. Issue second mortgages and sell them in the home equity market
    c. Lend funds to banks so they can make more loans
    d. Pay off defaulted loans made by primary mortgage lenders

8.28 When the borrowers pays the full amount of principal and interest on a mortgage, the lender who holds the mortgage is required to

    a. give a certificate of discharge of mortgager to the borrower.
    b. send the borrower the original note to be shredded.
    c. record a new mortgage in the borrower's name.
    d. update the mortgage terms to reflect a zero balance.

8.29 A defaulting borrower who faces foreclosure may avoid court actions and costs by voluntarily executing

    a. a wraparound mortgage.
    b. a lis pendens.
    c. a deed in lieu of foreclosure.
    d. a waiver of redemption.

8.30 What is one difference between a judicial foreclosure and a non-judicial foreclosure?

a. The lender may not obtain a deficiency judgment or lien in a non-judicial foreclosure action.
b. There is no right of redemption in a judicial foreclosure.
c. A non-judicial foreclosure does not publish a notice of sale.
d. A power of sale clause kicks off a judicial foreclosure.

9 Land Use Regulation

Land Use Definitions
Land Use Planning
Public Land Use Controls
Private Land Use Controls

LAND USE DEFINITIONS

Accessory building – A structure on the same property as the main residential dwelling that is not used for the same purpose as the main dwelling, e.g., a garage, workshop, storage shed.

Accessory use – A use of a building or portion of a lot that is typically incidental or subordinate to the principal use of the main building, e.g., a daycare center in a church or dormitories on school grounds.

Building code – A standard of construction of an improved property established by local government officials

Certificate of occupancy – A document confirming that a newly constructed or renovated property has fully complied with all building codes and is ready for occupancy

Concurrency – A planning policy that requires developers to correct foreseen negative impacts of a development during the construction period of the project itself rather than afterward

Condemnation – 1. A decree that a parcel of private property is to be taken for public use under the power of eminent domain. 2. A government order that a is no longer fit for use and must be demolished.

Deed restriction – A provision in a deed that limits or places rules on how the deeded property may be used or improved

Eminent domain – A power of a government entity to force the sale of private property for subsequent public use

Land use control – Regulation of how individual owners use property in a municipality or planning district. Control patterns are in accordance with a master plan

Master plan – An amalgamated land use plan for a municipality, county, or region which incorporates community opinion, the results of intensive research, and the various land use guidelines and regulations of the state. Acts as a blueprint for subsequent zoning ordinances and rulings

Non-conforming use – A legal or illegal land use that is not consistent with the current zoning ordinance

Police power – A government's legal authority to create, regulate, tax, and condemn real property in the interest of the public's health, safety, and welfare

Restriction – A limitation on the use of a property imposed by deed, zoning, state statute, or public regulation

Special exception – A land use in conflict with current zoning that is authorized because of its perceived benefit to the public welfare

Variance – A land use that conflicts with current zoning but is authorized for certain reasons, including undue hardship to comply and minimal negative impact to leave it alone

Zoning ordinance – A municipal land use regulation.

LAND USE PLANNING

Goals of land use control
The master plan
Planning objectives
Plan development
Planning management

While the Constitution guarantees the right of individual ownership of real estate, it does not guarantee the uncontrolled sale, use, and development of real estate. As American history demonstrates, unregulated use of real estate has significant potential for eventual damage to property values as well as to the environment. Moreover, with the explosive urban growth in this century, it has become clear that regulation of land use is necessary to preserve the interests, safety, and welfare of the community.

Without a central authority to exert control, land use tends to be chaotic. For example, rapid growth can outpace the support capabilities of basic municipal services such as sewers, power, water, schools, roads and communications. On an aesthetic level, communities need controls to keep certain commercial and industrial land uses away from residential areas to avoid the undermining of property values by pollution, noise, and traffic congestion.

With community growth comes increasing demands on our limited natural resources, making it necessary for cities, towns, and villages to develop and even increase their limitations on the private use of land. There are now controls over noise, air, water pollution, and even population density. Regulations governing the use of privately owned land include planning, zoning, subdivision regulations, building codes, public safety and health. Regulations even include environmental protection legislation.

Goals of land use control

Over time, public and private control of land use has come to focus on certain core purposes as follows:

- preservation of property values

- promotion of the highest and best use of property

- balance between individual property rights and the public good, i.e., its health, safety and welfare

- control of growth to remain within infrastructure capabilities

- incorporation of community consensus into regulatory and planning activities

The optimum management of real property usage must take into account both the interests of the individual and the interests of the surrounding community. While maintaining the value of an individual estate is important, the owner of an estate must realize that unregulated use and development can jeopardize the value not only of the owner's estate but of neighboring properties. Similarly, the community must keep in mind the effect of government actions on individual property values, since local government is largely supported by taxes based on the value of property.

Exhibit 9.1 Public Land Use Control

MASTERPLAN
- goals
- objectives

PLANNING COMMISSION

ZONES
CODES
PERMITS

Develepmont   Administration   Implementation

A community achieves its land usage goals through a three-phase process, as the exhibit illustrates:

> ▶ *development of a master plan* for the jurisdiction

> ▶ *administration of the plan* by a municipal, county, or regional planning commission

> ▶ *implementation of the plan* through public control of zoning, building codes, permits, and other measures

Municipal, county, and regional authorities develop comprehensive land use plans for a particular community with the input of property owners. A planning commission manages the master plan and enforces it by exercising its power to establish zones, control building permits, and create building codes.

In addition to public land use planning and control, some private entities, such as subdivision associations, can impose additional standards of land use on owners within the private entity's legal jurisdiction. Private controls are primarily implemented by deed restrictions (as discussed in Chapter 4).

The master plan

Public land use planning incorporates long-term usage strategies and growth policies in a **land use plan**, or **master plan**. In many states, the process of land use planning begins when the state legislature enacts laws *requiring all counties and municipalities to adopt a land use plan*. The land use plan must not only reflect the needs of the local area, but also conform to state and federal environmental laws and the plans of regional and state planning agencies. The state enforces its planning mandates by giving state agencies the power to approve county and local plans.

The master plan, therefore, fuses state and regional land use laws with local land use objectives that correspond to the municipality's social and economic conditions. The completed plan becomes the overall guideline for creating and enforcing zones, building codes, and development requirements.

Planning objectives

The primary objectives of a master plan are generally to control and accommodate social and economic growth.

Amount of growth. A master plan *sets specific guidelines on how much growth the jurisdiction will allow*. While all communities desire a certain degree of growth, too much growth can overwhelm services and infrastructure. If the community begins to see too much growth, a *moratorium* can be put into effect to stop or slow construction.

To formulate a growth strategy, a plan initially forecasts growth trends, then estimates how well the municipality can keep pace with the growth forecast. The outcome is a policy position that limits building permits and development projects to desired growth parameters.

A growth plan includes these considerations:

- ▶ nature, location and extent of permitted uses

- ▶ availability of sanitation facilities

- ▶ adequacy of drainage, waste collection, and potable water systems

- ▶ adequacy of utilities companies

- ▶ adequacy and patterns of thoroughfares

- ▶ housing availability

- ▶ conservation of natural resources

- ▶ adequacy of recreational facilities

- ▶ ability and willingness of the community to absorb new taxes, bond issues, and assessments

Growth patterns. In addition to the quantity of growth, a master plan also *defines what type of growth will occur, and where* and includes these major considerations:

- ▶ the type of enterprises and developments to allow

- ▶ residential density and commercial intensity

- ▶ effects of industrial and commercial land uses on residential and public sectors, i.e., where to allow such uses

- ▶ effect of new developments on traffic patterns and thoroughfares

- ▶ effects on the environment and environmental quality (air, water, soil, noise, visual aspects)

- ▶ effect on natural resources that support the community

- ▶ code specifications for specific construction projects

Accommodating demand. As the master plan sets forth guidelines for how much growth will be allowed, it must also *make plans for accommodating expanding or contracting demand for services and infrastructure*. The plan must identify specific requirements:

- ▶ facilities requirements for local government

- ▶ new construction requirements for streets, schools, and social services facilities such as libraries, civic centers, etc.

> ▸ new construction required to provide power, water and sewer services

Plan development

In response to land use objectives, community attitudes, and conclusions drawn from research, the planning personnel formulate their plan. In the course of planning, they analyze

- ▸ population and demographic trends
- ▸ economic trends
- ▸ existing land use
- ▸ existing support facilities
- ▸ traffic patterns

Planning management

Public land use management takes place within county and municipal **planning departments**. These departments are responsible for:

- ▸ long-term implementation of the master plan

- ▸ creating rules and restrictions that support plans and policies

- ▸ enforcing and administering land use regulation on an everyday basis

The planning commission. In most jurisdictions, a planning commission or board comprised of officials appointed by the government's legislative entity handles the planning function.

The commission oversees the operations of the department's professional planning staff and support personnel. In addition, the commission makes recommendations to elected officials concerning land use policy and policy administration.

The planning commission is responsible for:

- ▸ approving site plans and subdivision plans

- ▸ approving building permits

- ▸ ruling on zoning issues

PUBLIC LAND USE CONTROLS

Zoning
Zoning Board of Appeals
Subdivision regulation
Building codes

At the state level, the legislature enacts laws that control and restrict land use, particularly from the environmental perspective. At the local level, county and city governments control land use through the authority known as **police power**. The most common expressions of police power are county and municipal **zoning**. Other examples of public land use control include the following:

▸ subdivision regulations

▸ building codes

▸ eminent domain

▸ environmental restrictions

▸ development requirements

Governments also have the right to **own** real property for public use and welfare. In exercising its ownership rights, a municipality may **annex** property adjacent to its existing property or purchase other tracts of land through conventional transfers. Where necessary, it may force property owners to sell their property through the power of **eminent domain**.

Zoning

Zoning is the primary tool by which cities and counties regulate land use and implement their respective master plans. The Constitution grants the states the legal authority to regulate, and the states delegate the authority to counties and municipalities through legislation called **enabling acts**.

The zoning ordinance. The vehicle for zoning a city or county is the zoning ordinance, a regulation enacted by the local government. The intent of zoning ordinances is to specify land usage for every parcel within the jurisdiction. In some areas, state laws permit zoning ordinances to apply to areas immediately beyond the legal boundaries of the city or county.

Zoning ordinances implement the master plan by regulating three main components.

▸ **Use.** Zoning regulates how the land in each district is allowed to be used. For example, one area of the district may be zoned for residential while another area is zoned for commercial or light industrial. Some areas may even be zoned for a combination of uses.

▸ **Density.** Zoning may regulate or restrict the number of housing units in a residential zone and may set minimum and/or maximum lot sizes.

▸ **Siting.** Through setbacks, height limitations, and limitations on building in certain areas, such as in floodplains or on steep slopes, zoning regulates where primary and accessory structures can be built on a parcel of land.

Ordinance validity. Local planners do not have unlimited authority to do whatever they want. Their zoning ordinances must be clear in import, apply to all parties equally, and promote the health, safety, and welfare of the community in a reasonable manner.

New York does not have state level zoning regulations. Instead, municipal governments regulate zoning by establishing zoning ordinances for their own municipality, granting zoning variations as appropriate, conducting planning meetings, and hearing zoning appeals.

Building permits. Local governments enforce zoning ordinances by issuing building permits to those who want to improve, repair, or refurbish a property. To receive a permit, the project must comply with all relevant ordinances and codes. Further zoning enforcement is achieved through periodic inspections.

Types of zones. One of the primary applications of zoning power is the separation of residential properties from commercial and industrial uses. Proper design of land use in this manner preserves the aesthetics and value of neighborhoods and promotes the success of commercial enterprises through intelligently located zones.

There are six common types of zones:

> ▶   residential
>
> ▶   commercial
>
> ▶   industrial
>
> ▶   agricultural
>
> ▶   public
>
> ▶   planned unit development (PUD)

Residential. Residential zoning restricts land use to private, non-commercial dwellings. Sub-zones in this category further stipulate the types of residences allowed, whether single-family, multi-unit complexes, condominiums, publicly subsidized housing, or other forms of housing.

Residential zoning regulates:

> ▶   *density by limiting the number and size of dwelling units and lots in an area*
>
> ▶   *values and aesthetics by limiting the type of residences allowed. Some areas adopt **buffer zones** to separate residential areas from commercial and industrial zones.*

Commercial. Commercial zoning regulates the location of office and retail land usage. Some commercial zones allow combinations of office and retail uses on a single site. Sub-zones in this category may limit the type of retail or office activity permitted, for example, a department store versus a strip center.

Commercial zoning regulates:

▶ intensity of usage by limiting the area of store or office per site area. Intensity regulation is further achieved by minimum parking requirements, setbacks, and building height restrictions.

Industrial. Industrial zoning regulates:

▶ intensity of usage

▶ type of industrial activity

▶ environmental consequences

A municipality may not allow some industrial zones, such as heavy industrial, at all.

Agricultural. Agricultural zoning restricts land use to farming, ranching, and other agricultural enterprises.

Public. Public zoning restricts land use to public services and recreation. Parks, post offices, government buildings, schools, and libraries are examples of uses allowed in a public zone.

Planned Unit Development (PUD). Planned unit development zoning restricts use to development of whole tracts that are designed to use space efficiently and maximize open space. A PUD zone may be for residential, commercial, or industrial uses, or combinations thereof.

New York additional zoning classifications. In addition to the above types of zones, many communities in New York also include cluster zoning and multiple use zoning. Cluster zoning allows housing to be right next to or have a common boundary with other housing to allow more open space within the community. Multiple use zoning allows unusual PUDs.

New York has determined that single-family homes should be occupied by individuals related by blood, marriage, or adoption. They also include unrelated individuals who are living together in a group of three or fewer. This criteria has been applied to group homes and other unconventional family units.

Building permits. Property owners must obtain a building permit prior to building on their land, and the proposed building must adhere to the zoning for that parcel of land. The permits assist in enforcing zoning laws and provide critical property information to the taxing authorities for potential value reassessment for taxing purposes.

**Zoning Board
of Appeals**

In New York, any municipality with zoning ordinances is required to have a zoning board of appeals. The zoning board of appeals has the authority to vary the provisions of zoning laws and to prevent the zoning restrictions from becoming overly rigid.

The board exists primarily for its appellate functions, in which it rules on interpretations of zoning ordinances as they apply to specific land use cases presented by property owners based on decisions of the zoning enforcement officer and the State Supreme Court. In effect, the zoning board is a court of appeals for owners and developers who desire to use land in a manner that is not entirely consistent with existing ordinances.

The board interprets zoning regulations and reviews applications for land use and area variances. It then conducts hearings of specific cases and renders official decisions regarding the land use based on evidence presented.

A zoning board generally deals with such issues and appeals as:

- ▶ nonconforming use

- ▶ variance

- ▶ special exception or conditional use permit

- ▶ zoning amendment

If the board rejects an appeal, the party may appeal the ruling further in a court of law.

Exhibit 9.2 Zoning Appeals

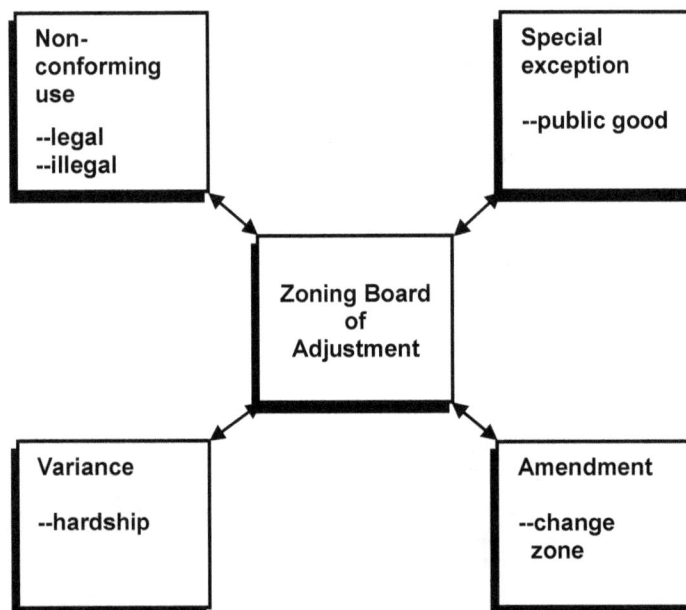

Nonconforming use. A nonconforming use is one *that clearly differs from current zoning.* Usually, nonconforming uses result when a zoning change leaves existing properties in violation of the new ordinance. This type of use is a **legal** nonconforming use. A board usually treats this kind of situation by allowing it to continue for one of the following time frames:

- indefinitely
- until the structures are torn down
- only while the same use continues, or
- until the property is sold

For instance, a motel is situated in a residential area that no longer allows commercial activity. The zoning board rules that the motel may continue to operate until it is sold, destroyed, or used for any other commercial purpose.

An **illegal nonconforming use** is one that conflicts with ordinances that were in place before the use commenced. For instance, if the motel in the previous example is sold and the new owner continues to operate the property as a motel, the motel is now an illegal, nonconforming use.

One type of nonconforming use that is illegal in New York is **spot zoning**, which singles out a small parcel of land for a use that benefits the land owner but that is different from the allowed land use for that area. Further, the use is detrimental to other owners in the area. When reviewing the spot zoning permit, the zoning board of appeals would consider whether or not the zoning change for the permit was part of a well considered and comprehensive plan developed for the general welfare of the affected community. Spot zoning that benefits only the one land owner and not the entire area is illegal in New York.

Variance. A zoning variance allows a use that differs from the applicable ordinance for a variety of *justifiable* reasons, including the following:

- compliance will cause unreasonable hardship

- the use will not change the essential character of the area

- the use does not conflict with the general intent of the ordinance

For example, an owner mistakenly violates a setback requirement by two feet. His house is already constructed, and complying with the full setback now would be extremely expensive, if not impossible. The zoning board grants a variance on the grounds that compliance would cause an unreasonable hardship.

A grant of a zoning variance may be unconditional, or it may require conditions to be fulfilled, such as removing the violation after a certain time.

Special exception. A special exception grant authorizes a use that is not consistent with the zoning ordinance in a literal sense, yet is clearly *beneficial* *or essential to the public welfare* and does not materially impair other uses in the zone.

A possible example is an old house in a residential zone adjacent to a retail zone. The zoning board might grant a special exception to a local group that proposes to renovate the house and convert it to a local museum, which is a retail use, since the community stands to benefit from the museum.

Amendment. A current or potential property owner may petition the zoning board for an outright change in the zoning of a particular property. For example, a property zoned for agricultural use has been idle for years. A major employer desires to develop the property for a local distribution facility, which would create numerous jobs, and petitions for an amendment. The board changes the zoning from agricultural to light industrial to permit the development. Since a change in zoning can have significant economic and social impact, an appeal for an amendment is a difficult process that often involves public hearings.

Subdivision regulation

In addition to complying with zoning ordinances, a developer of multiple properties in a subdivision must meet Article 9-A of the New York Real Property Law requirements for subdivisions. Prior to subdividing the land or building on the land, developers must meet requirements set by the Interstate Land Sales Full Disclosure Act and the New York State Environmental Quality Review Act to consider environmental factors early during the planning process.

Subdivision plat approval. The developer submits a plat of subdivision containing surveyed plat maps and comprehensive building specifications. The plat, as a minimum, shows that the plan complies with local zoning and building ordinances. The project can commence only after the relevant authority has approved the plat.

Subdivision requirements typically regulate the following:

- location, grading, alignment, surfacing, street width, highways
- sewers and water mains
- lot and block dimensions
- building and setback lines
- public use dedications
- utility easements
- ground percolation
- environmental impact report
- zoned density

Concurrency. Many states have adopted policies that require developers, especially of subdivisions, to take responsibility for the impact of their projects on the local infrastructure by taking corrective action. Concurrency is a policy that requires the developer to make accommodations *concurrently* with the development of the project itself, not afterwards. For example, if a project will create a traffic overload in an area, the developer may have to widen the road while constructing the project.

FHA requirements. In addition to local regulation, subdivisions must meet FHA (Federal Housing Authority) requirements to qualify for FHA financing insurance. The FHA sets standards similar to local ordinances to ensure an adequate level of construction quality, aesthetics, and infrastructure services.

Building codes

Building codes allow the county and municipality to protect the public against the hazards of unregulated construction. Building codes establish standards for virtually every aspect of a construction project, including offsite improvements such as streets, curbs, gutters, drainage systems, and onsite improvements such as the building itself.

Building codes typically address the following:

  ▸ architectural and engineering standards

  ▸ construction materials standards

  ▸ building support systems such as life safety, electrical, mechanical, and utility systems

Certificate of occupancy. Building inspectors inspect a new development or improvement for code compliance. If the work complies, the municipality or county issues a **certificate of occupancy** which officially clears the property for occupation and use.

PRIVATE LAND USE CONTROLS

Deed restriction
Declaration restriction
Deed condition
Eminent domain

Deed restriction. A restriction expressed in a conveyance (deed or lease) of a residential, commercial, or industrial property places limits on the use of the property. Such restrictions are also referred to as "covenants, conditions, and restrictions," or CCRs.

Property owners in the private sector can regulate land use to some extent through deed restrictions and deed conditions. Subdivision developers may set restrictions on land use with restrictive covenants in a deed or a declaration. To be considered valid, the restrictions must be reasonable and beneficial for neighboring property owners. Once the restrictions are set, they remain in effect for all owners, current and future. The restrictions are typically placed on the type of building that may be constructed on the land, the allowable use of the land, and details of the building's construction, i.e., height, square footage, setbacks, and cost.

Typical restrictions concern:

- required minimum area of a residence
- setback
- prohibition against construction of sheds or secondary buildings
- prohibition against conducting certain commercial activities

Deed restrictions may not be discriminatory by restricting ownership or use on the basis of race, religion, marital status, or gender. A quitclaim deed can terminate a private deed restriction.
Restrictions on commercial property use may not violate fair trade and anti-trust laws.

Declaration restriction

The declaration of a subdivision, Planned Unit Development, condominium, and commercial or industrial park contains private use restrictions. These have the same legal effect as a deed restriction, as the declaration attaches to the rights in the property. A private party cannot, however, extinguish a declaration restriction by agreement or quitclaim deed.

The kinds of restrictions found in declarations are much the same as those found in deeds: construction restraints, aesthetics standards, etc.

The underlying purpose of restrictions is to preserve the value and quality of the neighborhood, commercial center, or industrial park.

Injunction. A private usage restriction can be enforced by filing for a court injunction. A court can order the violator to cease and desist, or to correct the infraction. If, however, owners in a subdivision or park allow a violation to continue for a sufficient length of time, they can lose their right to legal recourse.

Deed condition. A deed condition may restrict certain uses of a property, much like a deed restriction. However, violation of a deed condition gives the grantor the right to re- take possession of the property and file suit for legal title.

Eminent domain. If efforts to regulate privately owned property are inadequate or impractical in a particular situation, or if there is a compelling public need, a county or local government may acquire property by means of direct purchase. A government body might acquire land because of the public need for any of the following:

- thoroughfares and public rights-of-way
- recreational facilities
- schools

- ▸ essential public facilities
- ▸ urban renewal or redevelopment

In many cases, public acquisition of property is a voluntary transaction between the government entity and the private owner. However, if the private party is unwilling to sell, the government may purchase the property anyway. The power to do this is called **eminent domain**.

Eminent domain. Eminent domain allows a government entity to purchase a fee, leasehold, or easement interest in privately owned real property for the **public good** and for **public use**, regardless of the owner's desire to sell or otherwise transfer any interest. In exchange for the interest, the government must pay the owner "just compensation."

To acquire a property, the public entity initiates a condemnation suit. Transfer of title extinguishes all existing leases, liens, and other encumbrances on the property. Tenants affected by the condemnation sale may or may not receive compensation, depending on the terms of their agreement with the landlord. Public entities that have the power of eminent domain include:

- ▸ all levels of government
- ▸ public districts (schools, etc.)
- ▸ public utilities
- ▸ public service corporations (power companies, etc.)
- ▸ public housing and redevelopment agencies
- ▸ other government agencies

To acquire a property, the public entity must first adopt a formal resolution to acquire the property, variously called a "resolution of necessity." The resolution must be adopted at a formal hearing where the owner may voice an opinion. Once adopted, the government agency may commence a condemnation suit in court. Subsequently, the property is purchased and the title is transferred in exchange for just compensation. Transfer of title extinguishes all existing leases, liens, and other encumbrances on the property. Tenants affected by the condemnation sale may or may not receive compensation, depending on the terms of their agreement with the landlord.
In order to proceed with condemnation, the government agency must demonstrate that the project is necessary, the property is necessary for the project, and that the location offers the greatest public benefit with the least detriment.

As an eminent domain proceeding is generally an involuntary acquisition, the condemnation proceeding must accord with due process of law to ensure that it does not violate individual property rights. Further, the public entity must justify its use of eminent domain in court by demonstrating the validity of the intended public use and the resulting "public good" or "public purpose" ultimately served.

The issue of eminent domain versus individual property rights has recently come under scrutiny in light of a 2005 Supreme Court ruling that affirmed the rights of state and local governments to use the power of eminent domain for urban re-development and revitalization. The ruling allowed that private parties could undertake a project for profit without any public guarantee that the project would be satisfactorily completed. The ruling brought the issue of "public use" into question, as the use of the re-development could well be private and even a private for-profit enterprise. The winning argument was that the "public purpose" is served when redevelopment creates much needed jobs in a depressed urban area. As a result of this decision, many see the power of eminent domain and the definition of public good as being in conflict with the constitutional rights of private property ownership. New and different interpretations of the public's right to pre-empt private property ownership by eminent domain may be expected.

9 Land Use Regulation
Snapshot Review

REAL ESTATE PLANNING

Goals of land use control
- preserve property values; promote highest and best use; safeguard public health, safety and welfare; control growth; incorporate community consensus
- process: develop plan; create administration; authorize controls

The master plan
- long term growth and usage strategies; often required by state law
- local plans fuse municipal goals and needs with state and regional laws

Planning objectives
- control growth rates: how much growth will occur and at what rate
- control growth patterns: type of growth desired, where it should be located
- accommodate demand for services and infrastructure

Plan development
- research trends and conditions; blend local and state objectives into master plan

Planning management
- commission makes rules, approves permits, codes, and development plans

PUBLIC LAND USE CONTROL
- state laws; local regulations, zones, codes; public ownership; private restrictions

Zoning
- "police power" granted by state-level enabling acts; zoning ordinance: creates zones, usage restrictions, regulations, requirements

Zoning administration
- Zoning Board of Adjustment oversees rule administration and appeals
- nonconforming use: legal if use prior to zone creation; variance: exception based on hardship; special exception: based on public interest; amendment: change of zones; rezoning

Subdivision regulation
- plat of subdivision and relevant requirements must be met and approved; must meet FHA requirements for insured financing

Building codes
- comprehensive onsite and offsite construction and materials standards; must be met to receive certificate of occupancy

Public acquisition and ownership
- eminent domain: public power to acquire property for public use

PRIVATE LAND USE CONTROL

Deed restriction
- single-property use restriction as stipulated in a deed; may not be discriminatory

Declaration restriction
- use restriction in multiple-property declarations; enforced by court injunction

Deed condition
- usage restriction that can trigger repossession by a previous owner if violated

CHAPTER NINE: LAND USE REGULATION

Section Quiz

9.1. _____ allow the county and municipality to protect the public against the hazards of unregulated construction.

    a. FHA requirements
    b. Zoning laws
    c. Building codes
    d. Subdivision regulations

9.2. Which of these is a regulation enacted by the local government to specify land usage for every parcel within the jurisdiction?

    a. Zoning ordinance
    b. Property annex
    c. Enabling act
    d. Building code

9.3. What type of zoning may be legal in other jurisdictions but is illegal in New York?

    a. Zoning variance
    b. Spot zoning
    c. Nonconforming use
    d. Special exception

9.4. _____ allows a government entity to purchase a fee, leasehold, or easement interest in privately owned real property for the public good and for public use, whether the owner wants to transfer interest or not.

    a. Injunction
    b. Annexation
    c. Concurrency
    d. Eminent domain

9.5. Public land use planning incorporates long-term usage strategies and growth policies in a(n):

    a. land use plan.
    b. municipal plat.
    c. eminent domain strategy.
    d. control pattern.

9.6. County and municipal planning departments are responsible for

    a. approving site plans and subdivision plans.
    b. approving building permits.
    c. enforcing and administering land use regulation on an everyday basis.
    d. ruling on zoning issues.

9.7. A private usage restriction that, when violated, gives the grantor the right to repossess the property and file site for legal title is a

    a. deed prohibition.
    b. deed condition.
    c. declaration restriction.
    d. injunction

9.8. The primary objectives of a master plan are generally to control and accommodate social and economic growth. Which of the following would NOT be considered a primary objective?

    a. Methods of growing tourism revenue
    b. How much growth the jurisdiction will allow
    c. What type of growth will occur
    d. Plans for accommodating demand for services and infrastructure

9.9. One additional zoning classification recognized in some New York communities, which allows housing to be right next to or have a common boundary with other housing, is called

    a. multiple use zoning.
    b. public zoning.
    c. density zoning.
    d. cluster zoning.

9.10. Public and private control of land use focuses on certain core purposes, including

    a. slowing real property sales in the jurisdiction.
    b. promoting the highest and best use of property.
    c. exercising rights of eminent domain.
    d. applying their powers of enabling acts.

9.11. What is a main reason that local governments issue building permits to those who want to improve, repair, or refurbish a property?

a. Restrict the number of new development projects
b. Establish the basis for an inspection
c. Issue certificates of occupancy
d. Ensure that improvements comply with ordinances and codes

9.12. To obtain approval to develop multiple properties in a subdivision, the developer must submit a

a. covenant of restriction.
b. plat of subdivision.
c. court order.
d. developer's pro forma.

9.13. A county or municipal authority usually grants a certificate of occupancy for new construction only after

a. all contractors have been paid for services.
b. all work has been completed for at least 30 days.
c. the tax assessor has valued the improvement.
d. the construction complies with building codes.

9.14. Counties and municipalities have the legal right to regulate land use and implement their master plans via

a. state legislation called enabling acts.
b. the doctrine of appropriation.
c. local referendums.
d. the power of eminent domain.

9.15. Zoning, building codes, and environmental restrictions are forms of local land use control known as

a. police power.
b. force majeure.
c. pre-emption.
d. concurrency.

9.16. A non-profit organization wants to erect a much-needed daycare center in a residential zone. To which local authority will the organization apply for permission to do so?

a. Planning commission
b. Zoning board of appeals
c. Building code department
d. Planned Unit Development

9.17. A deed restriction or declaration of restriction may be enforced by a

a. sheriff's warrant.
b. zoning commission order.
c. foreclosure action.
d. court injunction.

9.18. One situation in which a zoning board might permit a variance is when

a. compliance with zoning ordinances would cause the property owner unreasonable hardship
b. the property owner is the one who brings the variance to the attention of the zoning board.
c. the variance was caused by a contractor rather than by the property owner.
d. the property is in conflict with no more than one zoning ordinance.

9.19. The optimum management of real property usage must

a. take into account both the interests of the individual and the interests of the surrounding community.
b. develop an accord between property owners and tenants.
c. impede development by for-profit developers and construction contractors.
d. subordinate private interests of property owners to the interests of the public.

9.20. An area that was once residential has slowly changed to commercial over the years, and the zoning board recently changed the zoning to commercial. One property is still used as a residence. That property is considered to be a(n)

a. special exception.
b. variance.
c. legal nonconforming use.
d. anomaly.

10 Construction and Environmental Issues

Construction
Construction Regulation
Site Requirements
Construction Components
Environmental Issues
CERCLA
Environmental Laws

CONSTRUCTION

Styles of homes
Foundations
Exterior construction
Interior construction

In its broadest sense, the real estate industry is the largest single industry in the American economy. Within it, one might include the construction industry, which is often considered our country's largest business. That industry may be said to include the creation, management, and demolition of every residence and business facility in the nation: houses, apartments, condominiums, offices, warehouses, factories, stores, and special purpose buildings such as hospitals and government facilities.

Creation and improvement. In addition to the financial aspects of property development, creating real properties from raw land involves construction contracting and regulatory approvals. The key parties involved in this aspect of the business are generally the developer, the landowner, and the governing bodies with their regulatory practices. Also involved are financial experts, architects, engineers, space planners, construction subcontractors, and inspectors.

Demolition. Demolition experts, in conjunction with excavation and debris removal experts, serve to remove properties that are no longer sustainable or economically viable.

Styles of homes

Construction regulations and standards dictate how homes are to be built, what safety measures are required during the construction process, zoning restrictions for the size and placement of the building, environmental issues to be considered, and so on. However, while meeting those requirements, home builders have a considerable variety of architectural styles to use for homes in New York, including but not limited to the following styles....

Row houses. These homes are built in rows and are attached to neighboring homes with a shared wall. They typically consist of two to six stories, are quite narrow in structure, and have front stoops that raise their doorways above street level. Row houses were originally built for working-class families due to their affordability. They are mostly found in neighborhoods within a city environment.

Brownstones. This style of home was originally built for function rather than popular style. Because they are built with two or more stories, they afford the homeowner more square footage of living space without taking up an abundance of ground space. Because of the vertical structure of these homes, they are mostly found in metropolitan areas of larger cities where they are typically connected to one another, taking up an entire street block. They are known for their brick and stone exteriors with large front stoops. Brownstones are a type of row house.

Victorian houses. There are several types of Victorian houses, including Italianate homes that have low sloping or flat roofs that overhang the exterior walls of the house. Italianate homes have ornate trim and often have cupolas. Queen Anne is another type of Victorian house that have high, pitched roofs, wrap-around porches, and ornate trim. Other types of Victorian homes include stick-style, shingle-style, second empire, and folk Victorian.

Tudor houses. These houses have steeply pitched roofs, chimneys, and brick or stucco exterior walls with wood framing. Often, these houses have leaded glass windows and arched doorways. They are said to look like "storybook" houses because they have a combined medieval and Gothic architect appearance.

Colonial houses. A popular feature of Colonial houses is a central doorway with windows on both sides. They also have pitched roofs, dormer windows, and a chimney in the center of the roof. They are usually brick, stone, or wood and painted white. This style home often has living and dining rooms on the main floor and bedrooms on the second floor. These houses are found in older neighborhoods, typically in villages and towns.

Contemporary houses. These houses have clean lines with a simple design that features open spaces and natural light. They are typically made of concrete, metal, and glass and emphasize a modern lifestyle that has become more popular in recent times.

Ranch houses. This style of home is also known as rambler homes and are typically found in suburban areas with significant outdoor space surrounding the home. They are single-story homes with low profiles and simple designs. Ranch houses are often made of brick or stone with large picture windows.

Modern buildings. The appearance of these buildings differs from other buildings and homes in their clean lines, geometric shapes, and large expanses of glass. Their emphasis is on functionality, simplicity, and glass and metal materials. They may include flat roofs and solar panels on the exterior with high ceilings, open spaces, and minimalistic furnishings on the interior. Most new construction in cities such as New York City is done in this modern style.

High-rise apartment buildings. These are residential buildings with multiple dwelling units and 10 or more floors. They have steel and/or concrete exteriors with glass facades. Unlike other architectural styles that feature ornate trim, these buildings have sleek lines and a modern style. They typically have balconies or terraces, large windows, and common amenities such as pools and gyms.

Co-op buildings. Co-ops are set up for residents to own shares in a corporation that owns the entire building. The residents own the shares and not their individual unit. Co-ops are usually located in heavily populated areas of cities and are built or remodeled in a variety of housing styles including apartment buildings, townhouses, and single-family homes or various architectural styles.

Foundations

Home foundations provide the structural support for the building. Types of foundations include **concrete slab** with concrete footings and steel rod reinforcement, **pier and beam** with concrete piers driven into the ground to support the beams of the home, **crawl spaces** with short walls and footings connecting to the walls of the home, and **full basements** with tall concrete walls under the walls of the home.

Exterior construction

Exterior construction of the home consists of the first level flooring, framing for the exterior and interior bearing walls using studs spaced in compliance with construction codes, and headers for doorways and window openings.

Framing using wood is done using one of three methods:

> ▸ **platform frame construction** where one floor of the home is built first to serve as the platform for the second floor using wall studs and plates

> ▸ **balloon frame construction** where studs extend from the sole plate (bottom floor) to the rafter plate (roof)

> ▸ **post-and-beam frame construction** where vertical posts and horizontal beams create a framework that allows for expansive flooring and flexible wall structuring

Insulation. Construction of the home's exterior includes adding insulation to the exterior walls and ceiling below the roof. If the house has an attic, the insulation goes between the upstairs ceiling and the attic flooring. New York building code should be followed regarding insulation requirements in different parts of the State. The original building plan must include the type and R-value of the insulation to be used and must be certified by a licensed engineer or architect. The energy code to be used will vary based on the area where the home is being built.

Windows and doors. Additional exterior construction involves installing windows and doors. The available types of windows include those with side hinges, those with vertical hinges, and those that slide up and down without hinges. Doors come in various materials, thicknesses, and designs, including various types of wood doors, glass doors, screen doors, metal or steel doors.

Roof. There are various types and styles of roofs including flat, gabled, hip, shed, saltbox, A-frame, dormer, and several others. The pitch or slant of a roof allows rain and snow to slide off the roof, preventing the damage that may occur on a flat roof after snow has sat on it for an extended time. Slanted roofs also have eaves which is the edge of the roof that overhangs the exterior walls of the house. The layers of roof coverings and the material used must all meet building code requirements.

Interior construction

Electrical. The part of an electrical system that is actually an exterior component of a building is the power line that runs from the power source to a transformer and meter and then through the external wall of the home. The continuation of that power line into a circuit breaker or fuse box transforms the electricity into an interior component of the building. The component is expanded throughout the house into circuits and electrical sockets from which appliances, lighting fixtures, heating and cooling systems, and other devices draw power to operate.

Electrical installations and parts of existing electrical systems must be inspected by the building official pursuant to the 2020 Residential Code of New York State.

Plumbing. If a house is to obtain its water from a private well, standards set by the New York State Department of Health must be met regarding location and installation of the well so as to avoid water contamination.

Septic systems for the house fall under the jurisdiction of the New York State Department of Environmental Conservation and must meet their standards for installation and maintenance.

Additional plumbing installations must be conducted in compliance with local building codes with plumbing pipes and other materials and parts meeting the legislative standards with the use of lead pipes or solder limited to prevent lead from contaminating water.

Interior finishing. The interior finishing of the home consists of ceilings and walls which are created by wood studs covered with drywall, plaster, or wood; ceiling and wall texture and paint; trim around doorways, windows, sometimes around the edge of the ceiling, and baseboards around the edge of floors; cabinets for kitchens and bathrooms; and floor coverings such as wood, carpet, vinyl, ceramic tile, and brick.

CONSTRUCTION REGULATION

New York statues   All development is to some degree regulated by government. The principal areas of regulation are usage, construction, safety, and environmental concerns. Professional regulatory functions include public planners, zoning administrators, building inspectors, assessors, and administrators of specific municipality, county, state, and federal statutes, such as building codes.

Codes, rules, and regulations that govern construction, demolition and asbestos abatement operations in New York State and City include but are not limited to the following:

- ▸ Energy Conservation Construction Code of New York State
- ▸ State Uniform Fire Prevention and Building Code (Uniform Code)
- ▸ Administrative Code of the City of New York
- ▸ New York City Energy Conservation Code
- ▸ New York City Fire Code
- ▸ New York City Construction Codes
- ▸ Department of Buildings rules
- ▸ New York City Air Code
- ▸ DEP Asbestos Rules and Regulations

Solid waste management. The New York State Department of Environmental Conservation develops solid waste management initiatives for the purpose of increasing waste material recovery, reducing solid waste disposal needs, and limiting the impacts that waste management has on the environment.

The Solid Waste Management Facility Permitting Policy spells out the Department's permitting requirements, procedures, and responsibilities for new facility construction, expansion of existing facilities, and rate increase acceptance. Article 27, Section 27 of the New York Environmental Conservation Law is the presiding statute regarding solid waste management and waste management facility permits. The goals of the statute are the following:

1. to reduce the amount of waste generated

2. to reuse or recycle materials

3. to use environmentally acceptable methods to recover energy from solid waste that cannot be reused or recycled

4. to dispose of solid waste that cannot be reused, recycled, or processed for energy recovery and to do so through land burial or other approved methods

Water supply wells. Individual water supply wells (IWS wells) fall under the regulatory auspices of the New York State Residential Code. To reduce contamination risk and maintain a long-term water supply, they must be located and constructed in accordance with the New York State Department of Health standards. The Department requires wells to be installed by certified and registered water well driller and to have groundwater as the water source. Code Enforcement Officials review the location and construction plans prior to issuing the construction permit. Individual counties may also have their own approval requirements for the IWS wells.

New York State Energy Code. New York has adopted the 2020 Uniform Code of New York State and the 2020 Energy Conservation Construction Code of New York State. The Code applies to the entire State. Consequently, every city, town, village, and county is required to administer and enforce both the Energy Code and the Uniform Code within its individual municipality. Changes to either code are made only by the State Fire Prevention and Building Code Council, known as the Code Council. Code enforcement is performed by the Department of State. Municipalities are permitted to adopt even stricter energy conservation codes.

The Energy Code requires *"economically reasonable energy conservation techniques be used in the design and construction of all public and private buildings in the state."* The goal of the Code is to reduce the usage of energy, boost building performance, and lessen the impact on the environment.

The Code regulates energy conservation requirements for both commercial and residential buildings and construction. It covers HVAC, lighting, water heating, and electrical systems for buildings and appliances as well as insulation and renewable energy such as solar panels. The Energy Code can be found in its entirety with additional information online at 2020-ecccnys-november-2019.pdf.

Smoke and carbon monoxide detectors required. New York requires every one- or two-family house, condo, or co-op to have a smoke detector and a carbon monoxide detector.

New home warranty requirements. Buyers of newly constructed homes must be provided with a 1-year warranty against defective materials and faulty workmanship, a 2-year warranty for plumbing, electrical, heating, cooling, and ventilation systems, and a 6-year warranty against structural defects.

Fire sprinklers. In compliance with the New York City Building Code, sprinkler systems must be installed in office buildings that are 100 feet or higher. As of 2019, the City also requires all residential buildings 40 feet tall or higher to have commercial sprinkler systems.

SITE REQUIREMENTS

When a parcel of land is to be used as the location for a new building or other structure, the land must be prepared not only for the building to be constructed but for the actual construction work that will occur in the creation of the improvements. The land will be designated as the construction *site* and will need to comply with site and construction regulations. New York's construction site requirements focus on safety and protection of the site components, human workers and occupants, and the environment.

In addition to the project's plans, permits, and possible variances, there are several regulations and safety measures that property owners, contractors, and construction site managers must follow prior to and during construction:

▸ If the project will involve disturbing one or more acres of soil, a General Permit for Stormwater Discharges from Construction Activity (the Construction General Permit, or CGP) must be obtained.

▸ A Site Safety Plan that includes the building height, stories, footprint, and additional considerations for alteration and demolition must be submitted to and approved by the Department of Buildings.

▸ The project plan must comply with zoning ordinances regarding land use, setback requirements, land area use, building size and height, etc., or the appropriate variance must have been obtained.

▸ Licensed contractors involved with the project must carry General Liability Insurance for at least one million dollars for each occurrence, Workers Compensation Insurance to be proven at the time a permit is issued or renewed, and Disability Benefits Insurance which is required for issuance or renewal of a permit.

▸ No smoking or open fires are allowed on the construction site.

▸ Fire extinguishers are required on any floor where combustible liquids or materials are stored.

▸ Coal-fired heaters may only be used with a Fire Department variance.

▸ Contractors are required to notify and obtain approval from the Fire Department of New York any time sprinkler systems, standpipes, or fire protection systems are to be relocated or modified.

- Sprinklers and standpipe lines must meet Building Code requirements and be protected from freezing.

- When appropriate, installation of wells and/or on-site septic systems must meet Department of Health standards.

- Installation of heating, cooling, and electrical systems must meet New York State Energy Code standards.

- A Tenant Protection Plan that covers safety measures for the safety of building occupants during construction is required.

- A certified Site Safety Manager is to be on site, especially for buildings that are 15 stories or higher.

- Daily inspections are to be performed to ensure safety and code compliance

CONSTRUCTION COMPONENTS

GENERAL STRUCTURE

balloon frame A house framing method in which studs extend from foundation to roof. Floor joists are hung on the studs. Generally replaced by platform framing after 1945.

basement An area below grade level, generally accessible from inside the house, with sufficient clearance that a person can stand up in it. A full basement covers the area of the entire first floor.

bay A portion of a building that projects beyond the face of the building.

beam A horizontal structural member. May be solid timber, laminated wood, or metal.

bearing wall A wall that supports part of the load above it.

blueboard A type of rough gypsum board used for sheathing interior walls.

bridging Diagonal bracing between floor joists to spread load.

building paper An asphalt-saturated paper used as a covering over wall sheathing, roof decking, or a subfloor.

casing Finish trim around a framed wall opening.

crawl space The area between first floor joists and ground in a house without a basement. Often filled with gravel. Clearance is not sufficient to allow a person to stand up.

deck A horizontal wooden surface attached to the exterior of a house.

dormer A windowed structure with its own roof that projects from the main roof of a building.

downspout An externally mounted vertical tube that carries rain water from gutter to ground or drain tile.

drain tile An underground tube that carries water away from the foundation footing or from the top of the foundation wall at the downspout.

drywall A type of smooth gypsum board used as an interior wall covering. Also called sheetrock and plasterboard.

masonry Construction using brick, stone, or concrete block.

partition A dividing wall, usually not a bearing wall.

plaster A mixture of gypsum, sand and lime applied by trowel over lath, plasterboard, or other plaster layer.

plate The top or bottom horizontal element of a stud wall.

platform frame A house framing method in which each floor is built up individually and serves as the foundation for stud walls. Also called western framing.

post A vertical structural member that supports a beam or girder.

rafter One of the parallel supporting members that holds the roof decking. Usually 2 x 6 or 2 x 8 solid timber (2 x 4 in some older houses).

rise The number of vertical inches per horizontal foot (run) of a sloped roof; the height of a flight of stairs; the height of one step.

riser The vertical board that covers the front of a stair.

run The horizontal dimension of a roof or stairway.

sheathing The rough covering of the shell of a structure, fastened to studs, rafters or joists as a support for a finish covering; typically composition board, plywood, or solid lumber (in older houses).

sheetrock Drywall.

shoe Sole plate; finish trim around edges of a finished floor.

sill Bottom horizontal member of a door or window frame; horizontal framing member bolted to a slab or foundation wall.

soffit The horizontal under-surface covering the area between the exterior wall and the end of rafters; the boxed-in area between

eave The part of a roof that hangs beyond the external supporting wall.

facad The front face of a building.

fascia A board that covers the ends of the roof rafters.

flashing Metal sheets or strips installed as waterproofing at roof edges and around junctures of roof surfaces and other wall and roof locations where leakage must be prevented.

girder A horizontal beam that supports other beams.

greenboard A water-resistant type of gypsum board.

gutter A trough at the roof eave or other low point that collects rain water from the roof and carries it to a downspout.

gypsum board A wall paneling material composed of a core of gypsum between outer layers of heavy paper.

half-timber A type of timber framing in which the timbers and filled space between timbers are left exposed on the exterior surface.

joist One of the parallel, horizontal beams that supports a floor or ceiling.

knee wall A short wall from floor to rafter in a room with a sloped ceiling, such as an attic.

lath A wood or metal support for a semi-liquid wall covering material such as plaster or stucco.

lintel A horizontal supporting member across the top of a door or window opening.

FOUNDATION TYPES AND PARTS

brick A foundation of brick laid on a concrete footing, found in some older houses.

cement block A foundation of cast blocks laid on a concrete footing.

footing The base on which the foundation walls sit. Usually poured concrete, twice the thickness of the walls.

poured concrete A foundation in which the walls consist of concrete poured into forms.

slab A horizontal concrete section used as a foundation.

stone A foundation of field stone.

ELECTRICAL

240 volt service The type of electrical supply required by such household appliances as air conditioners, washers and dryers. Usually separate from the normal household supply of 120 volts.

amperage A measure of the overall capability of the household supply. 100 amp service is the modern minimum standard.

bus bar A solid metal bar in a service entrance panel or subpanel. A hot bus bar is connected to the main power source. A neutral bus bar provides a terminal for all neutral wires and is part of the grounding connection.

BX A flexible, metal-armored type of self-contained wiring that is installed without conduit. Also called AC (armored cable).

circuit breaker A resettable device that interrupts a circuit when there is an overload or fault on the line.

conduit Metal piping used to carry flexible wiring.

fuse A device that interrupts a circuit when there is an overload or fault. The fuse must be replaced after it has performed the interruption.

ground fault circuit interrupter A device that monitors the current entering and leaving a receptacle or circuit. When incoming and outgoing currents are unequal, the device instantly opens the circuit. Used particularly in bathroom, garage and outdoor receptacles.

junction box A box that contains wire splices or cable connections, but devices.

outlet box A box that protects wire connections and holds a device such as a switch or receptacle.

rheostat A dimmer switch that allows gradient control of current.

Romex A type of nonmetallic, sheathed, multi-conductor cable.

service entrance panel The main control box for a household electrical system, containing the connection to the power supply, the main disconnect, circuit breakers, and the grounding connection.

subpanel A panel containing hot and neutral bus bars to distribute power coming from the service entrance panel.

EXTERIOR COVERINGS

beveled siding Siding consisting of horizontally overlapped boards that are thinner on the upper edge than on the lower.

board and batten Siding that is applied in vertical panels or boards with the vertical joints covered by narrow strips.

brick Outside structural wall or veneer consisting of brick and mortar. In residences, generally regarded as low-maintenance, fireproof and decorative.

clapboard A type of smooth beveled siding, generally narrow, that is common in older frame houses.

redwood siding Siding, usually beveled, made of cedar or redwood. Noted for resistance to weather, it may be installed with rough or smooth side out, and may be stained, painted, or only sealed.

shingle A type of thick, wooden shingle, also called a shake, which can be applied vertically as siding.

shiplap A type of wooden siding milled on both edges so that the edge of one board overlaps the edge of the next board.

siding Exterior finish or "skin" of a wall; typical types are vinyl, aluminum, beveled wood, shingle, and board and batten.

stucco A cement-based material applied in semi-liquid form over metal lath. A kind of false stucco is sometimes applied to plywood panels.

tongue and groove A type of wooden siding milled with a groove on one edge and a protruding "tongue" on the other so that the edge of one board fits into the edge of the next board.

switch A device installed on a hot wire to break the connection between the hot bus bar and a device connected beyond the switch.	

ENVIRONMENTAL ISSUES

Hazards: responsibilities and liabilities
Water
Waste disposal
Septic
Sewers
Termites
Asbestos
Carbon monoxide
Formaldehyde
Lead, lead disclosure
Radon
Mold
Underground tanks
Polychlorinated biphenyls
Chlorofluorocarbons
Illegal drug manufacturing

Hazards:
responsibilities
and liabilities   Environmental hazards, conditions and issues exist within real estate structures, on real estate parcels, and surrounding any specific parcel of real estate in any particular development zone. They may occur naturally or as a result of human activity. Constructing, selling, buying, and occupying are all impacted by environmental issues. The value of real property is often determined by the range and intensity of local environmental hazards.

Environmental laws regulate some, but not all, of the hazards that affect real estate. The *Environmental Protection Agency* (EPA) was established on December 2, 1970 to bring together federal research, monitoring, standard-setting, and enforcement activities into one agency dedicated to environmental protection. The EPA, working with state, local, and tribal governments, enforces such environmental laws as the Clean Air and Clean Water Acts along with other environmental legislation.

Disclosure obligations and liabilities. Real estate developers, agents, owners, and sellers have various responsibilities for detecting, disclosing, and remediating regulated hazards. Licensees are expected to be aware of environmental issues and to know where to look for professional help. They are not expected to have expert knowledge of environmental law nor of physical conditions in a property. Rather, *they must treat potential environmental hazards in the same way they treat other material facts about a property -- through disclosure*.

Most states require disclosure of known material facts regarding residential properties of one to four units. If a licensee knows the result of an inspection, this is a material fact to be disclosed. Disclosure of environmental issues on commercial and industrial properties is often not mandated. Where disclosure is not required, real estate licensees should suggest the use of a professional environmental audit.

In dealing with environmental issues and hazards, licensees should be careful to:

> ▸ be aware of potential hazards

> ▸ disclose known material facts

> ▸ distribute the HUD booklet (below)

> ▸ know where to seek professional help.

Home inspections should include looking for common environmental issues that can affect the property and the residents of the property. Environmental hazards can have a significant impact on the sale of a property. An environmental site assessment (ESA) may be conducted to identify environmental impairments and protect parties against becoming involved in contamination issues.

Sale of a contaminated property. Selling a property with an environmental problem does not avoid liability for the seller, although seller and buyer may agree to share or transfer some liability. If there is a concern, a Phase I audit or Environmental Site Assessment (ESA) should be conducted before proceeding with the transaction. A Phase I audit identifies prior uses and the presence of hazardous materials.

The Phase I ESA reviews environmental documents; conducts a title search for environmental liens and restrictions; and includes a visual inspection of the site and surrounding properties. There is no sampling or testing. Fannie Mae, Freddie Mac, and HUD require special Phase I ESAs on certain properties.

A Phase II audit (ESA) is conducted if a site is considered contaminated. This is a more detailed investigation using chemical analysis to uncover hazardous substances and/or petroleum hydrocarbons in samples of soil, groundwater or building materials.

A Phase III audit (ESA) involves remediation. Intensive testing, sampling, monitoring, and modeling are applied to design plans for remediation, cleanup, and follow-up monitoring. Remediation may use a variety of techniques and technologies, such as excavation and removal, dredging, chemical treatment, pumping, and solidification. Major remediation efforts usually require extensive consultation with the surrounding community.

Environmental impact statements. When a construction project is federally funded, the responsible parties must provide an environmental impact statement (EIS) detailing how the project will affect the environment. Privately funded projects are also often required to prepare an EIS before any permits are issued. An EIS is expected to address air and water quality issues, noise, health and safety, wildlife, vegetation, water and sewer requirements, traffic, population density, and other issues as appropriate.

Water

Water quality. Soil, groundwater, and drinking water supplies are easily contaminated by leaking landfills, improper waste disposal, poorly maintained septic systems, agricultural runoff, industrial dumping in waterways, landfills, pesticides, animal waste, highway and rail spills, industrial emissions, internal combustion emissions, underground tanks leaking fuels and chemicals, and more. Hydraulic fracturing (fracking) in oil and gas production poses one of the greatest current threats to groundwater.

Many people who rely on ground water for drinking must be aware that contaminated water can cause problems from mild indigestion to cancer and death. The EPA sets standards for protecting ground water from contamination. It also offers advice and resources to facilitate the rehabilitation of contaminated ground water sources.

Underground water sources also contain a threat to health and safety when it is contaminated by leakage of underground storage tanks and waste disposal sites. To protect the public from this hazard, the EPA recommends that private well users have the well water tested at least once a year.

In Westchester County, New York, the Private Well Water Testing Law was passed in 2007 to protect property buyers from purchasing property in Westchester County with contaminated well water. The law requires new wells be tested prior to first use and private wells not in use for 5 years also be tested. The test results must be provided to the property's seller and buyer as well as any tenants. The test results are also provided to the county health department.

In addition to the Westchester County law, the New York State Residential Code includes requirements for reviewing the location and construction of residential wells prior to Code Enforcement issuing building permits and certificates of occupancy. The wells must meet the State's Department of Health standards for contamination risk reduction.

The Clean Water Act, officially known as the Federal Water Pollution Control Act Amendments of 1972, together with revisions contained in the Clean Water Act of 1977 and the Water Quality Act of 1987, is the primary federal law governing water pollution. It applies to all waters connected with navigable waters, but the interpretation of exactly which waters are covered remains open to dispute. The Clean Water Act does not directly deal with groundwater contamination, which is addressed in the Safe Drinking Water Act, Resource Conservation and Recovery Act, and the Superfund act.

Safe Drinking Water Act. Congress passed the Safe Drinking Water Act (SDWA) in 1974 (amended 1986 and 1996) to regulate and protect the public supply of drinking water. The act authorizes the setting of standards, protection of water sources, training of operators, funding of improvements, and dissemination of information.

Property sellers generally must disclose the source of drinking water for the property and the presence, type, and location of any septic system on the property. A water supply other than a municipal one and any septic system other than a standard one should be tested.

Waste disposal   **Solid waste.** At home, work and school, New Yorkers generate a lot of trash - over 4.5 pounds per person per day in New York State. This trash needs to be disposed of without contaminating water sources. One disposal solution is to separate actual trash from recyclable, reusable, and compostable items, such as cans, bottles, paper, glass, aluminum, metals as well as the peels from potatoes, bananas, and carrots.

Currently, New York has approximately 30 landfills that accept an estimated 6 million tons of waste a year from across the entire state. Additionally, a few million tons of trash are sent to waste-to-energy (WTE) facilities with several more million tons being sent to neighboring states.

There are various types of solid waste landfills in the state:

> ▸ *municipal solid waste landfills for residential, commercial, and institutional wastes*

> ▸ *construction and demolition debris landfills limited to waste from construction, remodeling, repair, and demolition of structures, buildings, and roads*

> ▸ *industrial waste landfills for waste from industrial operations, such as sludge from paper mills*

> ▸ *land clearing debris landfills for tree debris, uncontaminated soil and rock from land clearings, utility line maintenance, storm-related cleanups, uncontaminated concrete, asphalt pavement, brick, glass, soil, and rock*

To create the landfills, large holes are excavated into the ground and then lined with a clay and/or polyethylene to prevent contaminants from leaking into the soil below the landfill. The sites are located, designed, operated, and monitored to ensure compliance with federal, state, and local regulations, such as the Resource Conservation and Recovery Act. They are prohibited from being built in environmentally sensitive areas and have on-site environmental monitoring systems which check for any sign of groundwater contamination and for landfill gas. Soil, water, and wells near landfills are consistently tested for potential contamination.

The New York State Legislature established the *State Solid Waste Management Policy* within the Solid Waste Management Act of 1988. Following are the solid waste management priorities in New York State according to the New York State Environmental Conservation Law 27-0106(1):

1. reduce the amount of solid waste generated;

2. reuse material as it was originally intended to be used or recycle material that cannot be reused;

3. recover, in an environmentally safe manner, energy from solid waste that cannot be economically and technically reused or recycled; and

4. bury or otherwise dispose of solid waste that is not being reused, recycled, or used to recover energy by approved methods approved.

Hazardous waste. According to the EPA, some household products that are flammable or explosive under the right circumstances, that are corrosive, or that are toxic are deemed household hazardous waste. This includes such products as paints, cleaners, batteries, pesticides, and other products that contain hazardous ingredients. Care must be taken when disposing of any of these products to prevent water and soil contamination and threats to human health. Disposal of hazardous waste is regulated by Subtitle C of the Resource Conservation and Recovery Act (RCRA) and by state and local laws.

Septic systems

When homes are built in areas with no municipal sewage system, each home will need to handle its sewage waste with its own sewage disposal system, typically referred to as a septic system. Each septic system includes a pipe for waste to leave the home, a large underground tank usually made of concrete or fiberglass where wastewater is partially cleaned by bacteria living in the tank, and a leach field with a series of perforated pipes that filter and distribute the waste water into the surrounding soil. The solid waste remains inside the tank and must be pumped out on a schedule based on the number of occupants and sources (toilets, washing machines, sinks, etc.) contributing to the waste.

The private septic system should be inspected periodically to prevent potential contamination from a faulty system. Since the water is released into the soil, making sure the water is adequately treated before release is critical to protect groundwater, local streams, other bodies of water, and nearby wells.

Potential buyers and septic system users should have the county health department conduct an inspection of the system.

Termites

Termites are small insects that resemble ants. They live in colonies that grow often times into the thousands if left untreated. Termites feed on wood, plants, and paper products. They swarm in the spring and summer and can be found within the wood structure of a building or in the soil at the base of a building. To prevent termite infestation, treated wood should be used in construction, and there should be a barrier between wood and the ground. Additionally, the soil around the base of the home can be treated with termiticides. Any chemical treatment used must follow the label directions to prevent contamination to nearby water sources and to protect human health and safety.

Once termites infest a structure, they usually do considerable damage before they are discovered. Signs that termites have moved into a structure include discarded wings, sawdust at the base of wood structures, wood that sounds hollow when tapped, wood that has become soft and easily penetrable with a knife or screwdriver, and mud tubes on the home's foundation.

Homes in areas where termites are prevalent should be inspected on a regular basis. Home buyers should have the home inspected for termites prior to closing the sale. If termites are found or any signs of current or past infestation are found, pest control professionals should be contracted to perform a thorough extermination; and the damaged wood must be repaired or replaced. In New York, the extermination must be performed by a professional licensed by the New York State Department of Environmental Conservation (DEC).

If the signs of the insects and their damage have been discovered early enough, a specialized pesticide spray may be enough to end the infestation. However, when the insects have taken up residence throughout the structure and are causing extensive damage, the professional may recommend "tenting" the home. For this treatment, the occupants of the home must remove any living being or plant from the home, place food in protective containers, and leave the premises for 2 to 3 days. While the residents are gone, the home is covered in specialized sheeting and a fumigant gas is pumped into the home. After approximately 24 hours, the tenting is removed, and the home is ventilated and then tested to ensure the air is clear for the humans to re-occupy. If humans return to the home before the air is clear, they may experience nausea, dizziness, headaches, and lung or eye irritation.

Air

Air quality, both indoor and outdoor, has been a matter of concern since the 1960's. With today's construction methods creating airtight, energy-efficient structures, attention to sources of indoor air pollution is more important than ever. Off-gassing from synthetic materials and lack of ventilation can lead to such consequences as Sick Building Syndrome (SBS) and Building-Related Illness (BRI) as well as other health problems.

Sick building syndrome is a somewhat mysterious situation wherein occupants of a building have health complaints such as headache, dizziness, nausea, eye and throat irritation, fatigue, dry cough, and/or itchy skin, etc. The mystery is that no specific cause of the symptoms has been identified, but the symptoms only occur when the time is spent inside the building. The following are suspected contributing factors to SBS: inadequate ventilation, chemical contaminants in the interior air, and biological contaminants such as molds and bacteria.

Building-related illness involves symptoms of diagnosable illnesses that are exacerbated by airborne contaminants within the building. The health complaints related to BRI include cough, fever, muscle aches, and chills. These complaints are not relieved by leaving the building and typically require medical treatment.

The quality of air in a home or any building can be adversely impacted by the presence of carbon monoxide, radon, deteriorating asbestos and lead-based paint, methamphetamine production, formaldehyde, and other toxic chemicals. Homes can and should be tested for many of these contaminants prior to purchase.

Asbestos

Asbestos is a mineral fiber formerly used in buildings to aid in insulation and fire resistance. The powdery material has been used as a fireproof insulating material around pipes, in floor tiles and linoleum, in siding and roofing, in wallboard, joint compound, and many other applications. Homes built prior to 1980 often contain high levels of asbestos. Asbestos is also readily found in military facilities and ships and in public schools.

Asbestos is basically harmless if left undisturbed. Its danger to human health and life occurs when the product disintegrates through normal wear and tear or is disturbed and becomes airborne dust. Inhaling the dust causes lung diseases and cancer and is the primary cause of mesothelioma cancer.

While asbestos has been banned in many countries, its use is still legal in the United States, although highly restricted.

People who suspect their homes may contain asbestos should have the home inspected by a licensed professional asbestos inspector who will test any asbestos containing materials (ACM) and suggest action to be taken. Unless the material has been damaged, it is usually best to leave it alone. However, if the ACM is in poor condition, it must be removed to protect the occupants of the home.

Signs of poor maintenance or problems with the ACM include cracks, holes, visible wear and tear, and so on. Since the dangers are so great, handling and removing asbestos must be performed by an asbestos abatement professional licensed by the New York State Department of Labor.

Carbon monoxide

Carbon monoxide is a colorless, odorless, toxic gas that can kill a person before its presence is known. It can be a result of unvented kerosene and gas space heaters, leaking chimneys, back-drafting from furnaces, gas water heaters, gas and wood stoves and fireplaces, gasoline powered equipment, vehicle exhaust in garages, and tobacco smoke.

Carbon monoxide can be detected in a structure by a unit similar to a smoke alarm which should be included in every home, especially those with gas equipment and fireplaces or furnaces.

Formaldehyde

Formaldehyde is a chemical used in building materials such as pressed wood products and in other items such as fabrics and carpeting. Plastic furniture, new carpeting, and other vinyl materials also emit formaldehyde gases during the first few months after installation.

Formaldehyde gives off a colorless, pungent gas that causes health issues in some people, i.e., watery, burning eyes and throat, nausea, difficulty breathing, and asthma attacks. Tests have shown it to cause cancer in animals and possibly in humans.

This type of hazard is found in foam thermal insulation in homes built before 1980. The formaldehyde gas emissions from the insulation decrease over time, so most homes with the insulation no longer pose a threat. Its use is currently regulated by federal and state laws and agencies, such as the EPA and the FDA. New York regulates its use in certain types of products, such as clothing and children's toys. The Toxic Substances Control Act (TSCA) gives the EPA authority to mandate reporting, recordkeeping and testing requirements, and restrictions relating to chemical substances and/or mixtures (formaldehyde emissions). The Act also regulates significant new uses of formaldehyde.

Professional testing can identify levels and, in some cases, sources of formaldehyde gas and other volatile organic compounds. Using air conditioning and dehumidifiers, reducing formaldehyde products in the home, and overall increasing ventilation all work towards cleaner air in the home and less chance of health issues related to formaldehyde's emissions.

Lead

Lead is an element that occurs naturally and can be found in the earth's crust. From there, it can be released and found in the air, soil, water, and inside homes and other buildings. Lead and lead compounds have been used in many products such as paint, ceramics, pipes and plumbing materials, solders, gasoline, batteries, ammunition, and cosmetics.

Although lead does have some benefits, it can be toxic to humans and animals. Its toxicity is a serious health threat, particularly to children, as it occurs in airborne paint particles, paint chips, and soil and groundwater polluted by various external sources of emission. In children, it can cause behavior and learning problems, slowed growth, anemia, and in some cases, seizures and potential death. In adults, it can increase blood pressure and lead to heart disease. It also can affect kidney function and the reproductive system in both men and women.

Because lead is yet another contaminant found in drinking water as a result of corrosion of lead water supply pipes, faucets, and fixtures, the Safe Drinking Water Act has reduced the maximum allowable lead content in plumbing fixtures that are considered to be lead free. Under the act, water suppliers must report health risks to the EPA within 24 hours of discovery. Hydraulic fracturing (fracking) oil and gas production poses one of the greatest current threats to groundwater.

Lead's toxicity has mainly been addressed in relation to its use in paint. This hazard cannot be absorbed through the skin, but it becomes dangerous when it is ingested or inhaled. It can be found in most homes built before 1978 and can be present in the air, drinking water, food, contaminated soil, deteriorating paint, and dust from the paint. Children are particularly susceptible because young children are known to eat chips of the paint, allowing the lead to enter their bloodstreams. Consequently, lead has been banned in paint since 1978 and in new plumbing since 1988. However, because so many residences still contain the paint and because of the danger of lead to children, Congress passed the Residential Lead-Based Paint Hazard Reduction Act of 1992.

Lead disclosure. The Residential Lead-Based Paint Hazard Reduction Act mandates buyers and tenants of homes built before 1978 be informed of the dangers of lead and lead-based paint. Sellers and landlords and their agents must disclose any known lead-based paint to the buyer or tenant and must also provide copies of any available reports. Sales contracts and leasing agreements must also include certain notification and disclosure language. The Act also mandates that homebuyers and renters be given the EPA-HUD-US Consumer Product Safety Commission's booklet, "Protect Your Family from Lead in Your Home" [lead-in-your-home-portrait-color-2020-508.pdf (epa.gov)] and must be informed if lead-based paint is present in the home. Real estate agents are required to add language or attach to the contract a "Lead Warning Statement" and confirmation that all notification requirements have been met. (NYStateMLS_Lead_Paint_Disclosure_Seller.pdf)

New York City also provides a pamphlet online for landlords and tenants called "Lead Paint Hazards in the Home." lead-in-home-bro.pdf (nyc.gov)

The seller is not required to test for lead or repair any exposed areas but must allow the buyer a 10-day period for lead inspection. However, New York City requires landlords to test for lead dust and repair chipping paint if their tenants include children under 7 years old. Only a licensed lead professional is permitted to deal with testing, removal, or encapsulation. It is the real estate practitioner's responsibility to ensure compliance.

If inspection or testing reveals lead in the home, it can be addressed by covering the area with a solid substance such as drywall, paneling, or other similar material. The lead can also be removed by licensed professionals following regulated guidelines for removal and disposal. However, if the lead is not exposed or causing a risk to the home's occupants, it can simply be left alone. In that case, though, the homeowners should keep an eye out for future deterioration or exposure and be prepared to have it professionally removed at that time.

Lead is regulated by several federal and New York State laws, including but not limited to the following:

- ▶ Toxic Substances Control Act (TSCA)
- ▶ Residential Lead-Based Paint Hazard Reduction Act of 1992 (Title X)
- ▶ Clean Air Act (CAA)
- ▶ Clean Water Act (CWA)
- ▶ Safe Drinking Water Act (SDWA)
- ▶ Resource Conservation and Recovery Act (RCRA)
- ▶ Comprehensive Environmental Response, Compensation, and Liability Act (CERCLA)

- ▶ Rules and Regulations of the State of New York (NYCRR) Title 10 and Title 18

- ▶ New York State Public Health Law and Regulations

- ▶ New York City's **Local Law 31 of 2020**

Lead-based paint testing, recordkeeping, and audits are now mandated by changes to the following New York City local laws:

- ▶ Local Law 122 of 2023 – owners are to provide annual notice and investigation records for dwellings with lead-based paint

- ▶ Local Law 111 of 2023 – owners are to have XRF testing conducted of common areas

- ▶ Local Law 123 of 2023 – if a child under 6 years old resides in the dwelling, owners are to abate the lead-based paint on door and window friction surfaces, and remediate lead paint hazards, including making all floors smooth and cleanable

New York State's Department of Health website provides extensive information on lead exposure and lead poisoning under the heading *About Us/Health Topics A to Z* [New York State Department of Health (ny.gov)].

Radon

Radon is a colorless, odorless, radioactive gas that occurs naturally in the soil from decaying uranium in soil, rock, and water. It can enter the home through any cracks, gaps, or cavities, including crawl spaces and openings around pipes. It cannot be seen or smelled, which often leaves the gas undetected. The amount of radon that enters the home depends on the weather, the soil, and the suction within the home. Both local geology and home construction features can affect radon levels in a home. The levels can vary greatly between houses in the same neighborhood and can change over time, so one home's test result or a previous owner's test result are not good indicators of the current radon levels in a particular home.

There are no completely safe levels of radon, but the EPA notes that levels of 4 picocuries (pCi/L) are detrimental to human health and need immediate action. The EPA estimates that radon has become the leading cause of lung cancer among non-smokers. Signs and symptoms of the disease include persistent cough, shortness of breath, chest pain, frequent bouts of bronchitis and pneumonia, loss of appetite, and fatigue. Unfortunately, the symptoms of lung cancer are typically the signs of elevated levels of radon in the home.

Tests for radon can be performed using a kit from the hardware store or by a professional. If testing reveals high levels of radon in the home, mitigation is necessary. The first step in mitigation is to open all windows and use fans to circulate the air. Since this is a temporary fix, having a mitigation system installed by a professional to cleanse the air is recommended. To remove or lower the levels of radon in drinking water, the installation of a specialized filtration system is recommended.

Mold

Mold is a fungus that grows in the presence of moisture and oxygen on virtually any kind of organic surface. It often destroys the material it grows on and emits toxic irritants into the air. Tightly sealed structures with inadequate ventilation are most susceptible. Roof leaks, improper venting of appliances, runoff from gutters and downspouts, and flood damage are common contributors. Mold is often found in basements with water seepage and moisture problems and in buildings with insufficient ventilation.

While mold is not as toxic a hazard as lead-based paint, its growth can destroy the substance on which it is growing and can cause health problems such as allergic reactions, asthma attacks, and other respiratory complaints. It is important to point out, however, that most mold is not harmful to one's health. For example, the mold commonly seen on shower tiles is not harmful.

The New York landlord-tenant laws state that, regarding buildings with three or more apartments or buildings of any size where a tenant has asthma, the landlord is required to keep the units free of mold. To be compliant, landlords must have water leaks safely repaired and persistently high humidity levels corrected.

The EPA has published guidelines for mold remediation and cleanup. Extensive information can be found on the EPA website at https://www.epa.gov/mold.

Underground tanks (USTs)

USTs have at least 10 percent of their volume underground and are used to store fuel oil, gasoline, and other toxic fluids. Tanks made of steel can corrode over time and leak their contents into the surrounding soil, contaminating groundwater. A leaking UST can present other health and environmental risks, including a potential for fire and explosion. Tank removal is expensive, so that's not typically an option.

USTs have been regulated since 1984 when the U.S. Congress added Subtitle I to the Resource Conservation and Recovery Act. That addition mandated that the EPA is to regulate USTs with goals to prevent and find leaks, to correct problems caused by leaks, to ensure owners could pay for any spill cleanup, and to develop a State regulatory program for USTs. In 1988 and 2015, the EPA passed additional regulations for monitoring and upgrading USTs throughout the United States. New York based its petroleum bulk storage regulations on these federal regulations, with the addition of including aboveground storage tanks.

Polychlorinated biphenyls

Polychlorinated Biphenyl (PCB) is a substance formerly widely used as an electrical insulation. PCBs belong to a broad family of man-made organic chemicals known as chlorinated hydrocarbons. PCBs were manufactured from 1929 until 1979 when manufacturing was banned by the Toxic Substances Control Act (TSCA). They have a range of toxicity and vary in consistency from thin, light-colored liquids to yellow or black waxy solids. PCBs have been used in electrical and hydraulic equipment, oil-based paints, adhesives, caulking, thermal insulation material such as fiberglass, and carbonless copy paper.

When the products containing PCBs leak or are disposed of, the chemical is released into the air, water, and soil, depending on the location and type of product. Once released, PCBs do not break down very quickly and can cycle between air, water, and soil for long periods of time. Because they can be transferred long distances, they can end up in areas far from where they were released, further spreading their contamination.

PCBs are one of the most widely studied environmental contaminants and have been found to cause a variety of adverse health effects. Most significantly, they have been found to cause cancer in animals.

Title 40 of the Code of Federal Regulations in part 761 outlines disposal and storage regulations for PCB. In accordance with this law, the EPA has approved close to 100 storage and disposal facilities throughout the United States, several of which are located in New York State.

Chlorofluorocarbons   In the 1920s, ammonia, sulfur dioxide, and chloromethane were used as refrigerants in refrigerators. Unfortunately, these toxic gases were involved in a series of fatal accidents, resulting in the 1930s development of a non-toxic, non-flammable alternative called Freon [the brand name given to Chlorofluorocarbons (CFCs)]. Since the CFCs were mostly non-toxic, they became the popular coolant in air conditioners. They were also designated by city public health codes as the only gases allowed as refrigerants in public buildings.

However, in 1974, it was discovered that CFCs were causing a significant depletion in the Earth's ozone layer. This discovery initiated an effort to protect the ozone layer and resulted in the 1987 enactment of the Montreal Protocol, an international treaty for the purpose of protecting the ozone layer. The goal of the Protocol is to reduce and eventually eliminate the use of substances that harm the ozone layer.

The commercial manufacturing and use of CFCs and aerosol propellants were banned by the Toxic Substance Control Act in 1976. In 1990, the Clean Air Act was amended to address depletion of the ozone layer. The Act prohibited intentional venting of CFC refrigerants during servicing and disposing of air conditioners and refrigeration equipment. In support of the Montreal Protocol, the United States set a schedule for the ban on production, import, and use of CFCs with a goal of complete ban on any CFC for any reason by 2030.

In addition to the damage to the ozone layer, a human's overexposure to CFCs causes dizziness, loss of concentration, depression of the central nervous system, and cardiac arrhythmia, as well as asphyxiation in confined spaces:

Illegal drug manufacturing

Manufacturing illegal drugs such as methamphetamine produces highly toxic fumes that last a long time. Continued exposure to the fumes can cause fatal burns to the lungs, can damage the liver and spleen, and can lead to learning disabilities. Any property suspected as having been a place for drug manufacturing should be investigated prior to being sold or leased, and the possible health hazards must be disclosed to the potential buyer or renter.

CERCLA

The United States has literally thousands of manufacturing facilities, processing plants, landfills, and mining sites that have become contaminated from the dumping of hazardous waste. When the dangers of dump sites came to the public's attention in the 1970s, the Comprehensive Environmental Response, Compensation, and Liability Act (CERCLA) was established to allow EPA to clean up the contaminated sites. The Act created a tax on chemical and petroleum industries that resulted in $1.6 billion being collected over the next 5 years. The money was placed in a trust fund (Superfund) to be used to clean up abandoned or uncontrolled hazardous waste sites. CERCLA also holds those responsible for the contamination liable for either cleaning up the sites or reimbursing the government for the cost of the cleanups. Consequently, current landowners as well as previous owners of a property may be held liable for the entire cost of remediating soil, groundwater, or indoor air contamination. Sellers often carry the greatest exposure, and real estate licensees may be held liable for improper disclosure. However, when no responsible party is identified, the EPA uses money from the Superfund to clean up the contaminated site.

The Superfund Amendments and Reauthorization Act (SARA) was enacted in 1986 as an amendment to CERCLA to reauthorize the cleanup authority, provide new enforcement authorities, and increase the Superfund to $8.5 billion, among other provisions. The amendment also provided for the *innocent landowner defense* when determining who is liable for the cost of cleanup. If the landowner made appropriate and thorough research prior to purchasing the property and did not know the property was contaminated, then that owner would not be held liable for the cleanup.

Additional information can be found online on the EPA's website at www.epa.gov/superfund.

ENVIRONMENTAL LAWS

Major legislation
Environmental control legislation

Over time, federal and state legislatures have enacted laws to conserve and protect the environment against the hazards of growth and development, particularly in terms of air, water, and soil quality.

Major legislation

National Environmental Policy Act (1969). This act created the Environmental Protection Agency (EPA) and the Council for Environmental Quality, giving them a mandate to establish environmental standards for land use planning. The act also required environmental impact surveys on large development projects.

Clean Air Amendment (1970). This act authorized the EPA to establish air quality standards for industrial land uses as well as for automobile and airplane emissions.

Water Quality Improvement Act (1970), the Water Pollution Control Act amendment (1972), the Clean Water Act Amendment (1977). These acts addressed standards to control water pollution and industrial wastes from the standpoints of future prevention as well as remediation of existing pollution.

Resource Recovery Act (1970), the Resource Conservation and Recovery Act (1976), the Comprehensive Environmental Response, Compensation and Liability Act (Superfund) (1980), the Superfund Amendment and Reauthorization Act (1986). These acts addressed disposal of solid and toxic wastes and measures for managing waste. In addition, the Superfund act provided money for hazardous waste disposal and the authority to charge cleanup costs to responsible parties.

Lead-based paint ban (1978) and Residential Lead-based Paint Hazard Reduction Act (1992, 1996). These regulations banned lead in the manufacture of paint and established disclosure requirements and guidelines for testing and remediation.

Environmental control legislation

Exhibit 10.4 Landmarks in Environmental Control Legislation

Legislation	Date	Regulated
Solid Waste Disposal Act (later part of RCRA)	1965 (1976, 1999, 2002)	landfills
Air Quality Act, Clean Air Act	1967 (1970)	air quality standards
National Environmental Policy Act (NEPA)	1969 (1970)	created EPA
Flood Control Act	amended 1969	building in flood zones; flood insurance
Resource Recovery Act	1970	solid waste disposal
Water Quality Improvement Act	1970	dumping in navigable waters; wetlands
Water Pollution Control Act amendment	1972	dumping in navigable waters; wetlands
Clean Water Act	1972 (1977)	dumping in navigable waters; wetlands
Lead-based paint ban (US Consumer Product Safety Commission rule)	1978	lead-based paint in residences
PCB ban (EPA rule)	1979	polychlorinated biphenyls
RCRA amendment	1984	underground storage tanks
Comprehensive Environmental Response, Compensation and Liability Act (CERCLA)	1980	hazardous waste disposal
Superfund Amendment and Reauthorization Act	1986	hazardous waste cleanup costs
Asbestos ban (EPA rule)	1989	asbestos in building materials
Residential Lead-based Paint Hazard Reduction Act (EPA and HUD rule)	1992 (1996)	lead-based paint disclosure and treatment
Flood Insurance Reform Act	1994	flood insurance in flood zones
Brownfields legislation	2002	industrial site cleanup

Energy Policy Act	2005	increase types of energy production
Clean Energy Act	2007	increase production of clean renewable fuels
Frank R. Lautenberg Chemical Safety for the 21st Century Act	2016	new chemicals; amends Toxic Substances Control Act (1976)

The following additional laws help to protect human health and the environment. They are administered fully or in part by the EPA.

- American Innovation and Manufacturing Act (AIM)
- Atomic Energy Act (AEA)
- Beaches Environmental Assessment and Coastal Health (BEACH) Act
- Chemical Safety Information, Site Security and Fuels Regulatory Relief Act
- Emergency Planning and Community Right-to-Know Act (EPCRA)
- Endangered Species Act (ESA)
- Energy Independence and Security Act (EISA)
- EO 12898: Federal Actions to Address Environmental Justice in Minority Populations and Low-Income Populations
- EO 13045: Protection of Children From Environmental Health Risks and Safety Risks
- EO 13211: Actions Concerning Regulations That Significantly Affect Energy Supply, Distribution, or Use
- EO 14096: Revitalizing our Nation's Commitment to Environmental Justice for All
- EO 12898: Federal Actions to Address Environmental Justice in Minority Populations and Low-Income Populations
- Federal Food, Drug, and Cosmetic Act (FFDCA)
- Federal Insecticide, Fungicide, and Rodenticide Act (FIFRA)
- Food Quality Protection Act (FQPA) - See also FFDCA and FIFRA
- National Technology Transfer and Advancement Act (NTTAA)
- Nuclear Waste Policy Act (NWPA)
- Occupational Safety and Health (OSHA)
- Ocean Dumping Act - See Marine Protection, Research, and Sanctuaries Act
- Oil Pollution Act (OPA)
- Pesticide Registration Improvement Act (PRIA) - See FIFRA
- Pollution Prevention Act (PPA)
- Shore Protection Act (SPA)

10 Construction and Environmental Issues
Snapshot Review

CONSTRUCTION

Styles of homes	• include row houses, brownstones, Victorian, Tudor, colonial, contemporary, ranch, modern, high-rise apartments, co-op buildings
Foundations	• includes concrete slab, pier and beam, crawl spaces, full basements
Exterior construction	• platform frame, balloon frame, post-and-beam; insulation; windows and doors; roof
Interior construction	• electrical, plumbing, ceilings, walls, flooring, cabinets

CONSTRUCTION REGULATION

New York statutes	• govern construction, demolition, and asbestos abatement; include solid waste management; water supply wells; NYS Energy Code; smoke and carbon monoxide detectors; new home warranties; fire sprinklers
SITE REQUIREMENTS	• includes appropriate permits; safety and project plans; insurance policies; fire safety and approvals; Department of Health standards; Energy Code standards; Building Code requirements; tenant protection plan; site safety manager and daily inspections

ENVIRONMENTAL ISSUES

Responsibilities & liabilities	• disclosure and information for practitioners; remediation for owners; lead disclosure; CERCLA/Superfund exposure; Phase I, II, III Environmental Site Assessments to detect and mitigate contamination
Areas of concern	• air, waste disposal, water quality; septic systems, termites, asbestos, carbon monoxide, formaldehyde, lead, radon, mold, underground storage tanks, polychlorinated biphenyls, chlorofluorocarbons, illegal drug manufacturing
Major legislation	• limits damage to environment; standards for air, land, water, materials use
CERCLA	• established to allow EPA to clean up contaminated waste dump sites; created a tax on chemical and petroleum industries; money placed in Superfund
ENVIRONMENTAL LAWS	• to conserve and protect the environment against the hazards of growth and development, particularly in terms of air, water, and soil quality

CHAPTER TEN: CONSTRUCTION AND ENVIRONMENTAL ISSUES

Section Quiz

10.1. What does the Solid Waste Management Facility Permitting Policy in New York State include?

a. Guidelines for recycling program advertising
b. Procedures for new facility construction, expansion, and rate increase acceptance
c. Standards for residential composting practices
d. Requirements for the disposal of hazardous waste materials

10.2. What are real estate developers, agents, owners, and sellers responsible for in terms of regulated hazards?

a. Ignoring potential environmental issues unless explicitly asked
b. Detecting, disclosing, and remediating regulated hazards
c. Providing free remediation services to buyers
d. Having expert knowledge of environmental law

10.3. The 2020 Energy Conservation Construction Code of New York State requirements address all of the following EXCEPT

a. HVAC systems.
b. solar panels.
c. insulation.
d. individual water supply wells.

10.4. What measures are taken to ensure landfills comply with regulations and do not contaminate the environment?

a. Building landfills in environmentally sensitive areas
b. Ignoring groundwater contamination to save costs
c. Utilizing on-site environmental monitoring systems
d. Allowing unrestricted landfill gas emissions

10.5. Besides the financial side of property development, key parties involved in creating real properties from raw land include

a. Mortgage lenders and insurance agents
b. Developers, landowners, and governing bodies
c. Real estate agents and property managers
d. Buyers and tenants

10.6. Since 2019, which of the following is a requirement for 40-foot-tall and higher residential buildings in New York City?

a. Commercial fire sprinkler systems
b. Smoke and carbon monoxide detectors on every floor
c. Solar panels for energy cost savings
d. Hurricane resistant construction

10.7. What standards must residential septic systems meet in New York?

a. They must follow the guidelines set by the local homeowners' association.
b. They need to be inspected, approved, and installed by the New York State Health Department.
c. They must meet the state Department of Environmental Conservation standards for installation and maintenance.
d. They are required to comply with federal EPA regulations exclusively.

10.8. The _____ develops solid waste management initiatives for the purpose of increasing waste material recovery, reduce solid waste disposal needs, and limit the impacts waste management has on the environment.

a. New York State Department of Health
b. New York State Department of Environmental Conservation
c. New York City Energy Conservation Code
d. New York State Residential Code

10.9. What does the construction of a home's exterior include regarding insulation, and what must be considered according to New York building code?

    a. Adding insulation only to the roof and basement walls

    b. Installing insulation without any specific requirements for type or R-value

    c. Adding insulation to exterior walls and the ceiling below the roof

    d. Using only recycled materials for insulation regardless of building code

10.10. What do construction regulations and standards dictate within the process of building homes?

    a. Financing options available for homebuyers

    b. Materials suppliers must use

    c. Safety measures during construction

    d. Marketing strategies for selling new homes

10.11. What are some health results of poor indoor air quality due to off-gassing from synthetic materials and lack of ventilation?

    a. Sick Building Syndrome (SBS) and Building-Related Illness (BRI)

    b. Increased physical fitness and well-being

    c. Reduced energy consumption and lower utility bills

    d. Enhanced cognitive function and productivity

10.12. What factors affect the amount of radon that enters a home?

    a. The number of occupants in the home

    b. The amount of sunlight the home receives

    c. The weather, the soil, and the suction within the home

    d. The age of the home's appliances

10.13. Which of these is a foundation that provides structural support for a home?

    a. Asphalt slab with metal reinforcements

    b. Concrete slab

    c. Wooden beams with gravel footings

    d. Steel frame with no additional support

10.14. What are some examples of household products deemed hazardous waste by the EPA?

    a. Food scraps and paper products

    b. Paints, cleaners, batteries, and pesticides

    c. Clothing and textiles

    d. Glass and plastic containers

10.15. What measures can be taken to prevent termite infestation in a building?

    a. Use untreated wood and maintain direct wood-to-ground contact

    b. Use treated wood, create a barrier between wood and the ground, and treat the soil with termiticides

    c. Keep the building well-ventilated and free of moisture

    d. Only inspect the building annually for termites

10.16. Which of the following is a mineral fiber formerly used in buildings to aid in insulation and fire resistance?

    a. Asbestos

    b. Radon

    c. Synthetic insulation

    d. Formaldehyde

10.17. The _____ authorized the EPA to establish air quality standards for industrial land uses as well as for automobile and airplane emissions.

    a. Clean Air Amendment

    b. National Environmental Policy Act

    c. Comprehensive Environmental Response, Compensation, and Liability Act

    d. Clean Water Act Amendment

10.18. What is a major health and environmental concern that can occur with USTs?

    a. Lead contamination

    b. Improper waste disposal on the site

    c. Disturbed asbestos that becomes airborne dust

    d. Corrosion that results in leaks

10.19. When a construction project is federally funded, the responsible parties must provide a(n)

a. report of test results of well water quality to prove no contamination exists.
b. plan of the associated landfill detailing location, design, operations, and monitoring system.
c. disclosure of potential environmental hazards and a plan for remediation.
d. environmental impact statement (EIS) detailing how the project will affect the environment.

10.20. New York's warranty requirements for newly constructed homes include providing buyers with

a. a property disclosure that serves as a home warranty.
b. a 5-year warranty against any kind of defect.
c. a 1-year warranty for all systems.
d. a 6-year warranty against structural defects.

10.21. The New York State Department of Health requires that IWS wells utilize _____ as their water source.

a. groundwater
b. municipally treated water
c. public water supplies
d. water drawn from local waterways and treated

10.22. What type of hazard can be found in foam thermal insulation in homes built before 1980?

a. Formaldehyde
b. Lead
c. Asbestos
d. Radon

10.23. A Phase I ESA includes

a. chemical analysis to uncover hazardous substances.
b. environmental documents review, a title search, and a visual site inspection.
c. intensive testing, sampling, monitoring, and modeling for remediation plans.
d. excavation and removal, dredging, chemical treatment, pumping, and solidification.

10.24. The federal regulation that enables the EPA to clean up the sites contaminated by hazardous waste dumping is

a. SARA
b. National Environmental Policy Act
c. Residential Lead-based Paint Hazard Reduction Act
d. CERCLA

10.25. With this type of wood framing, studs extend from the sole plate (bottom floor) to the rafter plate (roof).

a. Platform frame
b. Balloon frame
c. Post-and-beam frame
d. Timber frame

11 Valuation Process and Pricing Properties

Concepts and Principles of Value
Market Value Requirements
Sales Comparison Approach
Cost Approach
Income Capitalization Approach
Preparing a Comparative Market Analysis
Salesperson's Role

CONCEPTS AND PRINCIPLES OF VALUE

Foundations of real estate value
Real estate supply and demand
Economic principles underlying value
Types of value

Foundations of real estate value

The valuation of real property is one of the most fundamental activities in the real estate business. Its role is particularly critical in the transfer of real property, since the value of a parcel establishes the general price range for the principal parties to negotiate.

Real estate value in general is *the present monetary worth of benefits arising from the ownership of real estate*. The following are the primary benefits that contribute to real estate value:

▸ income

▸ appreciation

▸ use

▸ tax benefits

Income. Ownership of real estate produces income when there are leases on the land, the improvements, or on air, surface, or subsurface rights. Such income is part of real estate value because an investor will pay money to buy the income stream generated by ownership of the property.

Appreciation. Appreciation is an increase in the market value of a parcel of land over time, usually resulting from a general rise in sale prices of real estate throughout a market area. Such an increase, whether actual or projected, is another investment benefit that contributes to real estate value.

Use. The way a property is used -- whether residential, commercial, agricultural, recreational, etc. -- in large part determines the property's value. Each kind of use has its own benefits.

Tax benefits. Depending on current tax law, tax benefits from ownership of a property may take the form of preferred treatment of capital gain, tax losses, depreciation, and deferrals of tax liability. These tax benefits contribute to the income and potential sale price of a property.

Real estate supply and demand

Supply. In real estate, supply is the *amount of property available* for sale or lease at any given time. Note that supply is generally not the number of properties available, except in the case of residential real estate. The units of supply used to quantify the amount of property available differ for different categories of property. These supply units, by property type, are:

> ▸ residential: dwelling units
> ▸ commercial and industrial: square feet
> ▸ agricultural: acreage

Factors influencing supply. In addition to the influences of demand and the underlying determinants of value, real estate supply responds to

> ▸ development costs, particularly labor
> ▸ availability of financing
> ▸ investment returns
> ▸ a community's master plan
> ▸ government police powers and regulation

Demand. Real estate demand is the amount of property buyers and tenants wish to acquire by purchase, lease, or trade at any given time. The availability of certain properties interacts with the strength of the demand for those properties to establish value and price.

> ▸ When demand for properties exceeds supply, a condition of scarcity exists, and real estate values rise.

> ▸ When supply exceeds demand, a condition of surplus exists, and real estate values decline.

> ▸ When supply and demand are generally equivalent, the market is considered to be in balance, and real estate values stabilize.

These relationships reflect simple common sense: if a certain type of property becomes increasingly scarce, its value and price go up as consumers compete for the limited supply. If there is an overabundance of a certain type of property, the value and price fall, as demand is largely met. On the other side, if demand for a certain type of property increases in relation to supply, prices will go up as consumers compete for the property. If demand diminishes, the price decreases and value drops with it.

Economic principles underlying value

In addition to supply and demand, a number of other economic forces interact in the marketplace to contribute to real estate value. Among the most recognized of these principles are those listed below.

Exhibit 11.1 Economic Principles Underlying Real Estate Value

utility	highest and best use
transferability	conformity
anticipation	progression and regression
substitution	assemblage
contribution	subdivision
change	

Utility. The fact that a property has a use in a certain marketplace contributes to the demand for it. Use is not the same as function. For instance, a swampy area may have an ecological function as a wetland, but it may have no economic utility if it cannot be put to some use that people in the marketplace are willing to pay for.

Transferability. How readily or easily title or rights to real estate can be transferred affects the property's value. Property that is encumbered has a value impairment since buyers do not want unmarketable title. Similarly, property that cannot be transferred due to disputes among owners may cause the value to decline, because the investment is wholly illiquid until the disputes are resolved.

Anticipation. The benefits a buyer *expects to derive from a property over a holding period* influence what the buyer is willing to pay for it. For example, if an investor anticipates an annual rental income from a leased property to be one million dollars, this expected sum has a direct bearing on what the investor will pay for the property.

Substitution. According to the principle of substitution, a buyer will *pay no more for a property than the buyer would have to pay for an equally desirable and available substitute property*. For example, if three houses for sale are essentially similar in size, quality and location, a potential buyer is unlikely to choose the one that is priced significantly higher than the other two.

Contribution. The principal of contribution focuses on the degree to which a particular improvement affects market value of the overall property. In essence, the contribution of the improvement is *equal to the change in market value that the addition of the improvement causes*. For example, adding a bathroom to a house may contribute an additional $15,000 to the appraised value. Thus the contribution of the bathroom is $15,000. Note that an improvement's contribution to value has little to do with the improvement's cost. The foregoing bathroom may have cost $5,000 or $20,000. Contribution is what the market recognizes as the change in value, not what an item cost. If continuous improvements are added to a property, it is possible that, at some point, the cost of adding improvements to a property no longer contributes a corresponding increase in the value of the property. When this occurs, the property suffers from *diminishing marginal return,* where the costs to improve exceed contribution.

Change. Market conditions are in a state of flux over time, just as the condition of a property itself changes. These fluctuations and changes will affect the benefits that can arise from the property, and should be reflected in an estimate of the property's value. For example, the construction of a neighborhood shopping center in the vicinity of a certain house may increase the desirability of the house's location, and hence, its value.

Highest and best use. This principle holds that there is, theoretically, a single use for a property that produces the greatest income and return. A property achieves its maximum value when it is put to this use. If the actual use is not the highest and best use, the value of the property is correspondingly less than optimal. Technically, highest and best use must be legally permissible, physically possible, financially feasible, and maximally productive.

For example, a property with an old house on it may not be in its highest and best use if it is surrounded by retail properties. If zoning permits the property to be converted to a retail use, its highest and best use may well be retail rather than residential.

Conformity. This principle holds that a property's maximal value is attained when its form and use are in tune with surrounding properties and uses. For example, a two-bedroom, one-bathroom house surrounded by four-bedroom, three-bathroom homes may derive maximal value from a room addition.

Progression and regression. The value of a property influences, and is influenced by, the values of neighboring properties. If a property is surrounded by properties with higher values, its value will tend to rise (progression); if it is surrounded by properties with lower values, its value will tend to fall (regression).

Assemblage. Assemblage, or the conjoining of adjacent properties, sometimes creates a combined value that is greater than the values of the unassembled properties. The excess value created by assemblage is called **plottage value.**

Subdivision. The division of a single property into smaller properties can also result in a higher total value. For instance, a one-acre suburban site appraised at $50,000 may be subdivided into four quarter-acre lots worth $30,000 each. This principle contributes significantly to the financial feasibility of subdivision development.

Types of Value

The purpose of a property appraisal influences an estimate of the value of a parcel of real estate. This is because there are different types of value related to different appraisal purposes. Some of the possibilities are listed below.

Exhibit 11.2 Types of Real Estate Value

market	reversionary
reproduction	appraised
replacement	rental
salvage	leasehold
plottage	insured
assessed	book
condemned	mortgage
depreciated	

Market value. Market value is an estimate of the price at which a property will sell at a particular time. This type of value is the one generally sought in appraisals and used in brokers' estimates of value.

Reproduction value. Reproduction value is the value based on the cost of constructing a precise duplicate of the subject property's improvements, assuming current construction costs.

Replacement value. Replacement value is the value based on the cost of constructing a functional equivalent of the subject property's improvements, assuming current construction costs.

Salvage value. Salvage value refers to the nominal value of a property that has reached the end of its economic life. Salvage value is also an estimate of the price at which a structure will sell if it is dismantled and moved.

Plottage value. Plottage value is an estimate of the value that the process of assemblage adds to the combined values of the assembled properties.

Assessed value. Assessed value is the value of a property as estimated by a taxing authority as the basis for ad valorem taxation.

Condemned value. Condemned value is the value set by a county or municipal authority for a property which may be taken by eminent domain.

Depreciated value. Depreciated value is a value established by subtracting accumulated depreciation from the purchase price of a property.

Reversionary value. Reversionary value is the estimated selling price of a property at some time in the future. This value is used most commonly in a proforma investment analysis where, at the end of a holding period, the property is sold, and the investor's capital reverts to the investor.

Appraised value. Appraised value is an appraiser's opinion of a property's value.

Rental value. Rental value is an estimate of the rental rate a property can command for a specific period of time.

Leasehold value. Leasehold value is an estimate of the market value of a lessee's interest in a property.

Insured value. Insured value is the face amount a casualty or hazard insurance policy will pay in case a property is rendered unusable.

Book value. Book value is the value of the property as carried on the accounts of the owner. The value is generally equal to the acquisition price plus capital improvements minus accumulated depreciation.

Mortgage value. Mortgage value is the value of the property as collateral for a loan.

Investment value. Investment value is the value of an income property as indicated by the capitalized value of the cash flow the property generates.

MARKET VALUE REQUIREMENTS

Market value is an opinion of the price that a willing seller and willing buyer would probably agree on for a property at a given time if the following requirements are met:

 ▶ The transaction is a cash transaction.

 ▶ The property is exposed on the open market for a reasonable period.

 ▶ Buyer and seller have full information about market conditions and about potential uses.

 ▶ There is no abnormal pressure on either party to complete the transaction.

 ▶ Buyer and seller are not related (it is an "arm's length" transaction).

 ▶ Title is marketable and conveyable by the seller.

 ▶ The price is a "normal consideration," that is, it does not include hidden influences such as special financing deals, concessions, terms, services, fees, credits, costs, or other types of consideration.

Another way of describing market value is that it is the highest price that a buyer would pay and the lowest price that the seller would accept for the property.

The market price, as opposed to market value, is what a property actually sells for. Market price should theoretically be the same as market value if all the conditions essential for market value were present. Market price, however, may not reflect the analysis of comparables and of investment value that an estimate of market value includes.

SALES COMPARISON APPROACH

Steps in the approach
Identifying comparables
Adjusting comparables
Weighting comparables

The sales comparison approach, also known as the *market data approach*, is used for almost all properties. It also serves as the basis for a broker's opinion of value. It is based on the principle of substitution-- that a buyer will pay no more for the subject property than would be sufficient to purchase a comparable property. In addition, the value principle of contribution -- that specific characteristics add value to a property – also plays into the derivation of the final value estimate in one's sales comparison analysis.

The sales comparison approach is widely used because it takes into account the subject property's specific amenities in relation to competing properties. In addition, because of the currency of its data, the approach incorporates present market realities.

The sales comparison approach is limited in that every property is unique. As a result, may be difficult to find good comparables, especially for special-purpose properties. In addition, the market must be active; otherwise, sale prices lack currency and reliability.

Steps in the approach

The sales comparison approach consists of comparing sale prices of recently sold properties that are comparable with the subject, then making dollar adjustments to the value estimate of each comparable to account for competitive differences with the subject. After identifying the adjusted value of each comparable, the appraiser weights the reliability of each comparable and the factors underlying how the adjustments were made. The weighting yields a final value range based on the most reliable factors in the analysis.

Exhibit 11.3 Steps in the Sales Comparison Approach

> 1. Identify comparable sales.
> 2. Compare comparables to the subject and make adjustments to comparables.
> 3. Weight values indicated by adjusted comparables for the final value estimate of the subject.

Identifying comparables

To qualify as a comparable, a property must:

- resemble the subject in size, shape, design, utility and location
- have sold recently, generally within six months of the appraisal
- have sold in an arm's-length transaction

An appraiser considers three to six comparables, and usually includes at least three in the appraisal report.

Appraisers have specific guidelines within the foregoing criteria for selecting comparables, many of which are set by secondary market organizations such as FNMA. For example, to qualify as a comparable for a mortgage loan appraisal, a property might have to be located within one mile of the subject. Or perhaps the size of the comparable must be within a certain percentage of improved area in relation to the subject.

The time-of-sale criterion is important because transactions that occurred too far in the past will not reflect appreciation or recent changes in market conditions.

An arm's length sale involves objective, disinterested parties who are presumed to have negotiated a market price for the property. If the sale of a house occurred between a father and a daughter, for example, one might assume that the transaction did not reflect market value.

Principal sources of data for generating the sales comparison are tax records, title records, and the local multiple listing service.

Adjusting comparables

The appraiser adjusts the sale prices of the comparables to account for competitive differences with the subject property. Note that the sale prices of the comparables are known, while the value and price of the subject are not. Therefore, adjustments can be made *only to the comparables' prices, not to the subject's*. Adjustments are made to the comparables in the form of a value deduction or a value addition.

Adding vs. deducting value. If the comparable is *better* than the subject in some characteristic, an amount is *deducted* from the sale price of the comparable. This neutralizes the comparable's competitive advantage in an adjustment category.

For example, a comparable has a swimming pool and the subject does not. To equalize the difference, the appraiser deducts an amount, say $10,000, from the sale price of the comparable. Note that the adjustment reflects the contribution of the swimming pool to market value. The adjustment amount is not the cost of the pool or its depreciated value.

If the comparable is *inferior* to the subject in some characteristic, an amount is *added* to the price of the comparable. This adjustment equalizes the subject's competitive advantage in this area.

Adjustment criteria. The principal factors for comparison and adjustment are *time of sale, location, physical characteristics, and transaction characteristics.*

    ▶   **time of sale**

        An adjustment may be made if market conditions, market prices, or financing availability have changed significantly since the date of the comparable's sale. Most often, this adjustment is to account for appreciation.

    ▶   **location**

        An adjustment may be made if there are differences between the comparable's location and the subject's, including neighborhood desirability and appearance, zoning restrictions, and general price levels.

    ▶   **physical characteristics**

        Adjustments may be made for marketable differences between the comparable's and subject's lot size, square feet of livable area (or other appropriate measure for the property type), number of rooms, layout, age, condition, construction type and quality, landscaping, and special amenities.

    ▶   **transaction characteristics**

        An adjustment may be made for such differences as mortgage loan terms, mortgage assumability, and owner financing.

Weighting comparables

Adding and subtracting the appropriate adjustments to the sale price of each comparable results in an adjusted price for the comparables that indicates the value of the subject. The last step in the approach is to perform a weighted analysis of the indicated values of each comparable. The appraiser, in other words, must identify which comparable values are more indicative of the subject and which are less indicative.

An appraiser primarily relies on experience and judgment to weight comparables. There is no formula for selecting a value from within the range of all comparables analyzed. However, there are three quantitative guidelines: the total number of adjustments; the amount of a single adjustment; and the net value change of all adjustments.

As a rule, *the fewer the total number of adjustments, the smaller the adjustment amounts, and the less the total adjustment amount, the more reliable the comparable.*

Number of adjustments. In terms of total adjustments, the comparable with the fewest adjustments tends to be most similar to the subject, hence the best indicator of value. If a comparable requires excessive adjustments, it is increasingly less reliable as an indicator of value. The underlying rationale is that there is a margin of error involved in making any adjustment. Whenever a number of adjustments must be made, the margin of error compounds. By the time six or seven adjustments are made, the margin becomes significant, and the reliability of the final value estimate is greatly reduced.

Single adjustment amounts. The dollar amount of an adjustment represents the variance between the subject and the comparable for a given item. If a large adjustment is called for, the comparable becomes less of an indicator of value. The smaller the adjustment, the better the comparable is as an indicator of value. If an appraisal is performed for mortgage qualification, the appraiser may be restricted from making adjustments in excess of a certain amount, for example, anything in excess of 10-15% of the sale price of the comparable. If such an adjustment would be necessary, the property is no longer considered comparable.

Total net adjustment amount. The third reliability factor in weighting comparables is the total net value change of all adjustments added together. If a comparable's total adjustments alter the indicated value only slightly, the comparable is a good indicator of value. If total adjustments create a large dollar amount between the sale price and the adjusted value, the comparable is a poorer indicator of value. Fannie Mae, for instance, will not accept the use of a comparable where total net adjustments are in excess of 15% of the sale price.

For example, an appraiser is considering a property that sold for $100,000 as a comparable. After all adjustments are made, the indicated value of the comparable is $121,000, a 21% difference in the comparable's sale price. This property, if allowed at all, would be a weak indicator of value.

COST APPROACH

**Types of cost appraised
Depreciation
Steps in the approach**

The cost approach is most often used for recently built properties where the actual costs of development and construction are known. It is also used for special-purpose buildings which cannot be valued by the other methods because of the lack of comparable sales or income data.

The strengths of the cost approach are that it:

▸ provides an upper limit for the subject's value based on the undepreciated cost of reproducing the improvements

▸ is very accurate for a property with new improvements which are the highest and best use of the property.

The limitations of the cost approach are that:

▸ the cost to create improvements is not necessarily the same as market value

▸ depreciation is difficult to measure, especially for older buildings

Types of cost appraised

The cost approach generally aims to estimate either the *reproduction cost* or the *replacement cost* of the subject property.

Reproduction cost is the cost of constructing, at current prices, a *precise duplicate* of the subject improvements. **Replacement cost** is the cost of constructing, at current prices and using current materials and methods, a *functional equivalent* of the subject improvements.

Replacement cost is used primarily for appraising older structures, since it is impractical to consider reproducing outmoded features and materials. However, reproduction cost is preferable whenever possible because it facilitates the calculation of depreciation on a structure.

Depreciation

A cornerstone of the cost approach is the concept of depreciation. Depreciation is the *loss of value in an improvement over time*. Since land is assumed to retain its value indefinitely, *depreciation only applies to the improved portion of real property*. The loss of an improvement's value can come from any cause, such as deterioration, obsolescence, or changes in the neighborhood. The sum of depreciation from all causes is referred to as accrued depreciation.

An appraiser considers depreciation as having three causes: physical deterioration, functional obsolescence, and economic obsolescence.

Physical deterioration. Physical deterioration is wear and tear from use, decay, and structural deterioration. Such deterioration may be either *curable or incurable.*

Curable deterioration occurs when the costs of repair of the item are less than or equal to the resulting increase in the property's value. For example, if a paint job costs $6,000, and the resulting value increase is $8,000, the deterioration is considered curable.

Incurable deterioration is the opposite: the repair will cost more than can be recovered by its contribution to the value of the building. For example, if the foregoing paint job cost $10,000, the deterioration would be considered incurable.

Functional obsolescence. Functional obsolescence occurs when a property has outmoded physical or design features which are no longer desirable to current users. If the obsolescence is curable, the cost of replacing or redesigning the outmoded feature would be offset by the contribution to overall value, for example, a lack of central air conditioning. If the functional obsolescence is incurable, the cost of the cure would exceed the contribution to overall value, for example, a floor layout with a bad traffic pattern that would cost three times as much as the ending contribution to value.

Economic obsolescence. Economic (or **external**) obsolescence occurs when the property owner can no longer obtain a fair rate of return on the ownership and operation of the property. This type of obsolescence is the loss of value due to adverse changes in the surroundings of the subject property that make the subject less desirable. Since such changes are usually beyond the control of the property owner, economic obsolescence is considered *an incurable value loss*. Examples of economic obsolescence include a deteriorating neighborhood, a rezoning of adjacent properties, or the bankruptcy of a large employer.

Steps in the Approach

The cost approach consists of estimating the value of the land "as if vacant;" estimating the cost of improvements; estimating and deducting accrued depreciation; and adding the estimated land value to the estimated depreciated cost of the improvements.

Exhibit 11.4 Steps in the Cost Approach

1. Estimate land value.
2. Estimate reproduction or replacement cost of improvements.
3. Estimate accrued depreciation.
4. Subtract accrued depreciation from reproduction or replacement cost.
5. Add land value to depreciated reproduction or replacement cost.

Estimate land value. To estimate land value, the appraiser uses the sales comparison method: find properties which are comparable to the subject property in terms of land and adjust the sale prices of the comparables to account for competitive differences with the subject property. Common adjustments concern location, physical characteristics, and time of sale. The indicated values of the comparable properties are used to estimate the land value of the subject. The implicit assumption is that the subject land is vacant (unimproved) and available for the highest and best use.

Estimate reproduction or replacement cost of improvements. There are several methods for estimating the reproduction or replacement cost of improvements. These are as follows.

▸ **Unit comparison method (square-foot method)**

The appraiser examines one or more new structures that are similar to the subject's improvements, determines a cost per unit for the benchmark structures, and multiplies this cost per unit times the number of units in the subject. The unit of measurement is most commonly denominated in square feet.

▸ **Unit-in-place method**

The appraiser uses materials cost manuals and estimates of labor costs, overhead, and builder's profit to estimate the cost of constructing separate components of the subject. The overall cost estimate is the sum of the estimated costs of individual components.

▸ **Quantity survey method**

The appraiser considers in detail all materials, labor, supplies, overhead and profit to get an accurate estimate of the actual cost to build the improvement. More thorough than the unit-in-place method, this method is used less by appraisers than it is by engineers and architects.

▸ **Cost indexing method**

The original cost of constructing the improvement is updated by applying a percentage increase factor to account for increases in nominal costs over time.

Estimate accrued depreciation. Accrued depreciation is often estimated by the **straight-line** method, also called the **economic age-life method**. This method assumes that depreciation occurs at a steady rate over the economic life of the structure. Therefore, a property suffers the same incremental loss of value each year.

The **economic life** is the period during which the structure is expected to remain useful in its original use. The cost of the structure is divided by the number of years of economic life to determine an annual amount for depreciation. The straight-line method is primarily relevant to depreciation from physical deterioration.

Subtract accrued depreciation from reproduction or replacement cost. The sum of accrued depreciation from all sources is subtracted from the estimated cost of reproducing or replacing the structure. This produces an estimate of the current value of the improvements.

Add land value to depreciated reproduction or replacement cost. To complete the cost approach, the estimated value of the land "as if vacant" is added to the estimated value of the depreciated reproduction or replacement cost of the improvements. This yields the final value estimate for the property by the cost approach.

Exhibit 11.5 Cost Approach Illustration

I. LAND VALUE

Land value, by direct sales comparison	80,000

II. IMPROVEMENTS COST

Main building (by one or more of the four methods)	260,000
Plus: other structures	16,000
Total cost new	276,000

III. ACCRUED DEPRECIATION

Physical depreciation	
Curable	10,000
Incurable	14,000
Functional obsolescence	6,000
External obsolescence	
Total depreciation	30,000

IV. IMPROVEMENTS COST MINUS DEPRECIATION

Total cost new	276,000
Less: total depreciation	30,000
Depreciated value of improvements	246,000

V. OVERALL ESTIMATED VALUE

Total land value	80,000
Depreciated value of improvements	246,000
Indicated value by cost approach	326,000

INCOME CAPITALIZATION APPROACH

Steps in the approach
Gross rent and gross income multiplier approach

The income capitalization approach, or income approach, is used for income properties and sometimes for other properties in a rental market where the appraiser can find rental data. The approach is based on the principle of anticipation: the expected future income stream of a property underlies what an investor will pay for the property. It is also based on the principle of substitution: that an investor will pay no more for a subject property with a certain income stream than the investor would have to pay for another property with a similar income stream.

The strength of the income approach is that it is used by investors themselves to determine how much they should pay for a property. Thus, in the right circumstances, it provides a good basis for estimating market value.

The income capitalization approach is limited in two ways. First, it is difficult to determine an appropriate capitalization rate. This is often a matter of judgment and experience on the part of the appraiser. Secondly, the income approach relies on market information about income and expenses, and it can be difficult to find such information.

Steps in the approach   The income capitalization method consists of estimating annual net operating income from the subject property, then applying a capitalization rate to the income. This produces a principal amount that the investor would pay for the property.

Exhibit 11.6 Steps in the Income Capitalization Approach

1.	Estimate potential gross income.
2.	Estimate effective gross income.
3.	Estimate net operating income.
4.	Select a capitalization rate.
5.	Apply the capitalization rate.

Estimate potential gross income. Potential gross income is the scheduled rent of the subject plus income from miscellaneous sources such as vending machines and telephones. Scheduled rent is the total rent a property will produce if fully leased at the established rental rates.

```
         Scheduled rent
  +      Other income
         --------------------
         Potential gross income
```

An appraiser may estimate potential gross rental income using current market rental rates (market rent), the rent specified by leases in effect on the property (contract rent), or a combination of both. Market rent is determined by market studies in a process similar to the sales comparison method. Contract rent is used primarily if the existing leases are not due to expire in the short term and the tenants are unlikely to fail or leave the lease.

Estimate effective gross income. Effective gross income is potential gross income minus an allowance for vacancy and credit losses.

```
         Potential gross income
       - Vacancy & credit losses
         --------------------
         Effective gross income
```

Vacancy loss refers to an amount of potential income lost because of unrented space. Credit loss refers to an amount lost because of tenants' failure to pay rent for any reason. Both are estimated on the basis of the subject property's history, comparable properties in the market, and assuming typical management quality. The allowance for vacancy and credit loss is usually estimated as a percentage of potential gross income.

Estimate net operating income. Net operating income is effective gross income minus total operating expenses.

```
         Effective gross income
       - Total operating expenses
         --------------------
         Net operating income
```

Operating expenses include fixed expenses and variable expenses. Fixed expenses are those that are incurred whether the property is occupied or vacant, for example, real estate taxes and hazard insurance. Variable expenses are those that relate to actual operation of the building, for example, utilities, janitorial service, management, and repairs.

Operating expenses typically include an annual reserve fund for replacement of equipment and other items that wear out periodically, such as carpets and heating systems. Operating expenses do not include debt service, expenditures for capital improvements, or expenses not related to the operation of the property.

Select a capitalization rate. The capitalization rate is an estimate of the *rate of return* an investor will demand on the investment of capital in a property such as the subject. The judgment and market knowledge of the appraiser play an essential role in the selection of an appropriate rate for the subject property. In most cases, the appraiser will research capitalization rates used on similar properties in the market.

Apply the capitalization rate. An appraiser now obtains an indication of value from the income capitalization method by dividing the estimated net operating income for the subject by the selected capitalization rate.

$$\frac{NOI}{capitalization\ rate} = value$$

Using traditional symbols for income (I), rate (R) and value (V), the formula for value is

$$\frac{I}{R} = V$$

Exhibit 11.7 Income Capitalization Method Illustration

I. ESTIMATE POTENTIAL GROSS INCOME

Potential gross rental income	192,000
Plus: other income	2,000
Potential gross income	194,000

II. ESTIMATE EFFECTIVE GROSS INCOME

Less: vacancy and collection losses	9,600
Effective gross income	184,400

III. ESTIMATE NET OPERATING INCOME

Operating expenses	
Real estate taxes	32,000
Insurance	4,400
Utilities	12,000
Repairs	4,000
Maintenance	16,000
Management	12,000
Reserves	1,600
Legal and accounting	2,000
Total expenses	84,000

Effective gross income	184,400
Less: total expenses	84,000
Net operating income	100,400

IV. SELECT CAPITALIZATION RATE

$$\frac{NOI}{capitalization\ rate} = value$$

Capitalization rate: 7%

V. APPLY CAPITALIZATION RATE

$$\frac{I}{R} = V = \frac{100,400}{.07} = 1,434,300 \text{ (rounded)}$$

Indicated value by income approach: 1,434,300

Gross rent and gross income multiplier approach

The gross rent multiplier (GRM) and gross income multiplier (GIM) approaches are simplified income-based methods used primarily for properties that produce or might produce income but are not primarily income properties. Examples are single-family homes and duplexes.

The methods consist of applying a multiplier to the estimated gross income or gross rent of the subject. The multiplier is derived from market data on sale prices and gross income or gross rent.

The advantage of the income multiplier is that it offers a relatively quick indication of value using an informal methodology. However, the approach leaves many variables out of consideration such as vacancies, credit losses, and operating expenses. In addition, the appraiser must have market rental data to establish multipliers.

Steps in the gross rent multiplier approach. There are two steps in the gross rent multiplier approach.

First, select a gross rent multiplier by examining the sale prices and monthly rents of comparable properties which have sold recently. The appraiser's judgment and market knowledge are critical in determining an appropriate gross rent multiplier for the subject. The gross rent multiplier for a property is:

$$\frac{Price}{Monthly\ rent} = GRM$$

Second, estimate the value of the subject by multiplying the selected GRM by the subject's monthly income.

GRM x Subject monthly rent = estimated value

Exhibit 11.8 Gross Rent Multiplier Illustration

Property	Sale price	Monthly rent	GRM
Comparable A	500,000	1660	151
Comparable B	248,000	1500	165
Comparable C	324,000	2,200	147
Comparable D	304,000	1,800	169
Subject	320,000	2,000	160

In the illustration, the indicated GRM for the subject is 160, based on the appraiser's research and judgment. Applying the GRM to a rental rate of $2,000, the indicated value for the subject is $320,000.

Steps in the gross income multiplier approach. The GIM approach is identical to the GRM approach, except that a different denominator is used in the formula. Step one is to select a gross income multiplier by examining the sale prices and gross annual incomes of comparable properties which have sold recently. The gross income multiplier for a property is:

$$\frac{Price}{Gross\ annual\ income} = GIM$$

Step two is to estimate the value of the subject by multiplying the selected GIM by the subject's gross annual income:

GIM x Subject gross annual income = estimated value

Exhibit 11.9 Gross Income Multiplier Illustration

Property	Sale price	Gross income	GIM
Comparable A	250,000	19,920	12.55
Comparable B	248,000	18,000	13.78
Comparable C	324,000	26,400	12.27
Comparable D	304,000	21,600	14.07
Subject	324,000	24,000	13.50

In the illustration, the indicated GIM for the subject is 13.5 , based on the appraiser's research and judgment. Applying the GIM to the property's gross annual income gives an indicated value for the subject of $324,000.

PREPARING A COMPARATIVE MARKET ANALYSIS

Broker's comparative market analysis

Broker's comparative market analysis

The gross rent multiplier (GRM) and gross income multiplier (GIM) approaches are simplified income-based methods used primarily for properties that produce or might produce income but are not primarily income properties. Examples are single-family homes and duplexes.

The following exhibit illustrates the sales comparison approach. An appraiser is estimating market value for a certain house. Four comparables are adjusted to find an indicated value for the subject. The grid which follows the property and market data shows the appraiser's adjustments for the differences between the four comparables and the subject.

Exhibit 11.10 Sales Comparison Approach Illustration

Data

Subject property:

8 rooms-- 3 bedrooms, two baths, kitchen, living room, family room; 2,000 square feet of gross living area; 2-car attached garage; landscaping is good. Construction is frame with aluminum siding.

Comparable A:

Sold for 1,000,000 within previous month; conventional financing at current rates; located in subject's neighborhood with similar locational advantages; house approximately same age as subject; lot size smaller than subject; view similar to subject; design less appealing than subject's; construction similar to subject; condition similar to subject; 7 rooms-- two bedrooms, one bath; 1,900 square feet of gross living area; 2-car attached garage; landscaping similar to subject.

Comparable B:

Sold for 1,200,000 within previous month; conventional financing at current rates; located in subject's neighborhood with similar locational advantages; house six years newer than subject; lot size smaller than subject; view is better than the subject's; design is more appealing than subject's; construction (brick and frame) better than subject's; better condition than subject; 10 rooms-four bedrooms, three baths; 2,300 square feet of gross living area; 2-car attached garage; landscaping similar to subject.

Comparable C:

Sold for 1,150,000 within previous month; conventional financing at current rates; located in subject's neighborhood with similar locational advantages; house five years older than subject; lot size larger than subject; view similar to subject; design and appeal similar to subject's; construction similar to subject; condition similar to subject; 8 rooms-- three bedrooms, two baths; 2,000 square feet of gross living area; 2-car attached garage; landscaping similar to subject.

Comparable D: Sold for 1,090,000 within previous month; conventional financing at current rates; located in a neighborhood close to subject's, but more desirable than subject's; house approximately same age as subject; lot size same as subject; view similar to subject; design less appealing than subject's; construction (frame) poorer than subject's; poorer condition than subject; 7 rooms-- two bedrooms, one and one half baths; 1,900 square feet of gross living area; 2-car attached garage; landscaping similar to subject.

Exhibit 11.10, cont. Sales Comparison Approach Illustration

Adjustments

	Subject	A	B	C	D
Sale price		1,000,000	1,200,000	1,150,000	1,090,000
Financing terms		standard	standard	standard	standard
Sale date	NOW	equal	equal	equal	equal
Location		equal	equal	equal	-20,000
Age		equal	-12,000	+10,000	equal
Lot size		+10,000	+10,000	-10,000	equal
Site/view		equal	-10,000	equal	equal
Design/appeal		+10,000	-12,000	equal	+5,000
Construction quality	good	equal	-30,000	equal	+10,000
Condition	good	equal	-50,000	equal	+20,000
No. of rooms	8				
No. of bedrooms	3	+5,000	-5,000	equal	+5,000
No. of baths	2	+10,000	-15,000	equal	+5,000
Gross living area	2,000	+10,000	-20,000	equal	+10,000
Other space					
Garage	2 car/attd.	equal	equal	equal	equal
Other improvements					
Landscaping	good	equal	equal	equal	equal
Net adjustments		+45,000	-144,000	0	+35,000
Indicated value	1,120,000	1,045,000	1,056,000	1,150,000	1,125,000

For comparable A, the appraiser has made additions to the lot value, design, number of bedrooms and baths, and for gross living area. This accounts for the comparable's *deficiencies* in these areas relative to the subject. A total of five adjustments amount to $45,000, or 4.5% of the purchase price.

For comparable B, the appraiser has deducted values for age, site, design, construction quality, condition, bedrooms, baths, and living area. This accounts for the comparable's superior qualities relative to the subject. The only addition is the lot size, since the subject's is larger. A total of nine adjustments amount to $144,000, or 12% of the sale price.

For comparable C, the appraiser has added value for the age and deducted value for the lot size. The two adjustments offset one another for a net adjustment of zero.

For comparable D, one deduction has been made for the comparable's superior location. This is offset by six additions reflecting the various areas where the comparable is inferior to the subject. A total of seven adjustments amount to $35,000, or 3.2% of the sale price.

In view of all adjusted comparables, the appraiser developed a final indication of value of $1,120,000 for the subject. Underlying this conclusion is the fact that Comparable C, since it only has two minor adjustments which offset each other, it is by far the best indicator of value. Comparable D might be the second best indicator, since the net adjustments are very close to the sale price. Comparable A might be the third best indicator, since it has the second fewest number of total adjustments. Comparable B is the least reliable indicator, since there are numerous adjustments, three of which are of a significant amount. In addition, Comparable B is questionable altogether as a comparable, since total adjustments alter the sale price by 12%.

SALESPERSON'S ROLE

One of the roles of the real estate agent is to recommend an appropriate listing price for the client's property by determining the property's market value. To do this, the broker or salesperson develops the Comparative Market Analysis but must be careful when presenting it to the property owner so as not to lead the owner to think the CMA holds the same weight as an actual appraisal.

The agent should also cooperate with a professional licensed appraiser and provide the appraiser with all information the agent has gathered on the property and answer any questions the appraiser may have. If the agent completed the CMA prior to the appraisal, providing the appraiser with a copy of the CMA and its supporting materials would be beneficial to the appraiser.

The agent should provide the property owner with a copy of the CMA and ensure the owner also receives a copy of the appraisal (if completed). The agent should also keep a copy of the CMA and related documents.

The agent's role also includes explaining to the property owner how the property's value was determined and how the owner can utilize that information.

11 Valuation Process and Pricing Properties
Snapshot Review

CONCEPTS AND PRINCIPLES OF VALUE

Foundations of real estate value
- present monetary worth of benefits arising from ownership, including income, appreciation, use, tax benefits

Real estate supply and demand
- supply is the *amount of property available* for sale or lease at any given time.
- demand is the amount of property buyers and tenants wish to acquire by purchase, lease, or trade at any given time.

Economic principles underlying value
- anticipation, substitution, contribution, change, highest and best use, conformity, supply, demand, progression, regression, assemblage, subdivision, utility, transferability

Types of value
- market, reproduction, replacement, salvage, plottage, assessed, condemned, depreciated, reversionary, appraised, rental, leasehold, insured, book, mortgage

MARKET VALUE REQUIREMENTS

Market value
- price willing buyer and seller would agree on given: cash transaction, exposure, information, no pressure, arm's length, marketable title, no hidden influences

SALES COMPARISON APPROACH
- most commonly used; relies on principles of substitution and contribution

Steps in the approach
- compare sale prices, adjust comparables to account for differences with subject

Identifying comparables
- must be physically similar, in subject's vicinity, recently sold in arm's length sale

Adjusting comparables
- deduct from comp if better than subject; add to comp if worse than subject

Weighting adjustments
- best indicator has fewest and smallest adjustments, least net adjustment from the sale price

COST APPROACH
- most often used for recently built properties and special-purpose buildings

Types of cost appraised
- reproduction: precise duplicate; replacement: functional equivalent

Depreciation
- loss of value from deterioration, or functional or economic obsolescence

Steps in the approach
- land value plus depreciated reproduction or replacement cost of improvements

INCOME CAPITALIZATION APPROACH
- used for income properties and in a rental market with available rental data

Steps in the approach
- value = NOI divided by the capitalization rate

GRM AND GIM APPROACH
- GRM: price divided by monthly rent; value: GRM times monthly rent; GIM: price divided by gross annual income; value: GIM times annual income

BROKER'S COMPARATIVE MARKET ANALYSIS

- abridged sales comparison approach by brokers and agents to find a price range

SALESPERSON'S ROLE

- to recommend appropriate listing price for the client's property by determining the property's market value

- also includes explaining to the property owner how the property's value was determined and how the owner can utilize that information

Legal aspects

- creates equitable interest; is assignable; should be recorded

CHAPTER ELEVEN: VALUATION PROCESS AND PRICING PROPERTIES

Section Quiz

11.1. Select the economic principle of real estate value the following statement describes: how readily title to real estate can be sold to another party.

    a. Utility
    b. Transferability
    c. Substitution
    d. Contribution

11.2. The sales comparison approach to valuation relies on

    a. the concept of depreciation.
    b. good comparable properties.
    c. a capitalization rate.
    d. the gross rent multiplier.

11.3. _____ value is the estimated selling price of a property at some time in the future.

    a. Appraised
    b. Assessed
    c. Reversionary
    d. Market

11.4. Which valuation approach is the most widely used in residential brokerage?

    a. Replacement
    b. Income capitalization
    c. Cost
    d. Sales comparison

11.5. _____ is what a property actually sells for.

    a. Market price
    b. Marketable value
    c. Market value
    d. Appraised price

11.6. As a component of real estate value, the principle of substitution suggests that

    a. if two similar properties are for sale, a buyer will purchase the cheaper of the two.
    b. if one of two adjacent homes is more valuable, the price of the other home will tend to rise.
    c. if too many properties are built in a market, the prices will tend to go down.
    d. people will readily move to another home if it is of equal value.

11.7. The concept of market value can be described as

    a. the face amount a casualty or hazard insurance policy will pay in case a property is rendered unusable.
    b. the value of the property as carried on the accounts of the owner.
    c. the value of the property as collateral for a loan.
    d. the highest price that a buyer would pay and the lowest price that the seller would accept for the property.

11.8. Why is a broker's opinion of value less reliable than an appraisal?

    a. The appraiser tends to use all three approaches to value in each appraisal.
    b. The broker does not usually consider the full range of data about market conditions.
    c. The broker is subject to government regulation in generating the opinion.
    d. The appraiser uses less current market data.

11.9. The cost of constructing a functional equivalent of a subject property is known as

    a. reproduction cost.
    b. replacement cost.
    c. restitution cost.
    d. reconstruction cost.

11.10. A home for sale has suffered a loss in value because other homeowners on the block have failed to maintain their properties. This is an example of

    a. curable external obsolescence.
    b. economic obsolescence.
    c. functional obsolescence.
    d. physical deterioration

11.11. What are the basic steps in the market data approach?

  a. Choose nearby comparables, adjust the subject for differences, estimate the subject's value
  b. Gather relevant price data, apply the data to the subject, estimate the subject's value
  c. Select comparable properties, adjust the comparables, estimate the subject's value
  d. Identify previous price paid, apply an appreciation rate, estimate the subject's value

11.12. One weakness of the cost approach for appraising market value is that

  a. builders may not pay market value for materials or labor.
  b. market value is not always the same as what the property cost to build.
  c. new properties have inestimable costs and rates of depreciation.
  d. comparables used may not have similar quality of construction.

11.13. Which of the following is a primary shortcoming of the gross rent multiplier approach to estimating value?

  a. Numerous expenses are not taken into account.
  b. The multiplier does not relate to the market.
  c. It is too complex and cumbersome.
  d. It only applies to residential properties.

11.14. Net operating income is equal to

  a. gross income minus potential income minus expenses.
  b. effective gross income minus total operating expenses.
  c. potential gross income minus vacancy and credit loss minus expenses.
  d. effective gross income minus vacancy and credit loss.

11.15. An office building for sale lacks sufficient cooling capability to accommodate modern computer equipment. This type of depreciation is called

  a. physical deterioration.
  b. economic obsolescence.
  c. incurable depreciation.
  d. functional obsolescence.

11.16. The income capitalization approach to appraising value is most applicable for which of the following property types?

  a. Single family homes
  b. Apartment buildings
  c. Undeveloped land
  d. Places of worship

11.17. Which of the following best describes the steps in the income capitalization approach?

  a. Estimate gross income, multiply the gross income multiplier
  b. Estimate effective income, subtract tax, apply a capitalization rate.
  c. Estimate net operating income and apply a capitalization rate to it
  d. Estimate potential gross income and apply a capitalization rate to it

11.18. Which of the following is the last step in the sales comparison approach just before finding a final value estimate for the subject?

  a. Averages the adjustments
  b. Weight the comparables
  c. Discard all comparables having a lower value
  d. Identify the subject's value as that of the nearest comparable

11.19. In appraisal, loss of value in a property from any cause is referred to as

  a. deterioration.
  b. obsolescence.
  c. depreciation.
  d. deflation.

11.20. The sales comparison approach to value is limited because

    a. it is based on the principle of anticipation.
    b. every property is unique
    c. it is not based on the principle of substitution.
    d. the approach is only accurate with unique, special purpose properties

12 Human Rights and Fair Housing

Federal Fair Housing Laws
New York Human Rights Law
Implications for Licensees
Fair Housing and Protected Classes
Discrimination and Bias
Implicit Bias in Real Estate
Battling Bias

FEDERAL FAIR HOUSING LAWS

Fair housing
Exemptions to Federal Fair Housing Act
Americans with Disabilities Act
Fair financing laws
Jones v. Mayer
Types of housing covered
Protected classes
Forms of discrimination
Advertising guidelines

Fair housing   Federal and state governments have enacted laws prohibiting discrimination in the national housing market. The aim of these **fair housing laws,** or **equal opportunity housing laws,** is to give all people in the country an equal opportunity to live wherever they wish, provided they can afford to do so, without impediments of discrimination in the purchase, sale, rental, or financing of property. Housing discrimination also includes the refusal to make reasonable accommodations or modifications for people with disabilities, or failure to build certain multi-family housing so that it is accessible to people with disabilities.

Federal Fair Housing Laws. The Civil Rights Division of the United States Department of Justice is the federal agency that is responsible for enforcing federal anti-discrimination laws.

> ► **Civil Rights Act of 1866,** the original fair housing statute, prohibits discrimination in housing *based on race.* The prohibition relates to selling, renting, inheriting, and conveying real estate.

> ► **Executive Order 11063** was issued in 1962 by President John Kennedy to strengthen the Civil Rights Act of 1866 and to *prevent discrimination in residential properties financed by FHA and VA*

loans. The order facilitated enforcement of fair housing where federal funding was involved.

▶ **Civil Rights Act of 1964** prohibited discrimination based on race, religious belief, national origin, and sex as protected classes.

▶ **Title VIII** of the Civil Rights Act of 1968, known today as the **Fair Housing Act**, prohibits discrimination in housing *based on race, color, sex, religion, national origin, familial status, and disability. The Act also prohibits steering and blockbusting.* Under the Disparate impact theory, landlords are prohibited from refusing to rent based on someone's criminal record except when convicted of the manufacture and distribution of a controlled substance. Also under the Disparate impact theory, discrimination in any way based on the individuals Limited English Proficiency is also prohibited.

The 1988 amendments to the Fair Housing Act prohibit discrimination against families with children. The Act allows for an exemption related to familial status and age discrimination by allowing housing for "older person" aged 55 years or older. The Fair Housing Act is enforced by the United States Department of Housing and Urban Development (HUD), a federal agency that enforces compliance, administers fair housing programs, and educates consumers.

▶ **Rehabilitation Act of 1973, Age Discrimination in Employment Act of 1975, Pregnancy Discrimination Act of 1978, Immigration Reform and Control Act of 1986, Americans with Disabilities Act of 1990** each added characteristics to the protected classes to include age, pregnancy, citizenship, and disability.

Who must comply with Fair Housing laws? Any person or entity involved in activities related to housing falls under the requirements of Fair Housing laws. The Fair Housing Act prohibits discriminatory actions by the following:

▶ Landlords

▶ Property owners and managers

▶ Developers

▶ Real estate agents

▶ Mortgage lenders and brokers

▶ Homeowner associations

▶ Insurance providers

▶ Anyone else who impacts housing opportunities

Activities unlawful under Fair Housing laws. Fair housing laws cover selling and renting housing accommodations as well as mortgage lending. When a real estate licensee is involved in any housing transaction, the licensee is also required to comply with federal, state, and local fair housing laws. The following are some but not all activities that are unlawful under fair housing laws:

▶ Refusal to sell, rent, or negotiate for housing or loans

▶ Discriminating in services, provisions, conditions of contracts and/or transactions

▶ Discriminating within printed advertisements or promotions

▶ Falsifying the availability of housing

▶ Refusing to accommodate the needs of a disabled person

▶ Denying brokerage services based on a protected class

▶ Harassing, threatening, intimidating, coercing, sexual harassment

▶ Discriminating in financing conditions

▶ Refusing insurance coverage or charging different rates based on a protected class

▶ Refusing to make reasonable accommodations for a resident's disability

▶ Refusing to make or allow reasonable modifications to a dwelling or common area for a resident's disability

Exemptions to Federal Fair Housing Act

Although the Fair Housing Act covers most housing situations, there are some exemptions:

▶ Buildings with one to four units where the owner lives in one of the units are exempt.

▶ Single-family houses being sold or rented by the owner without the use of a real estate licensee are exempt when the owner does not own more than three homes at one time. This exemption is not recognized under New York State and New York City fair housing and civil rights laws.

▶ Housing for older people are exempt from age discrimination when at least 80 percent of the units are each occupied by at least one resident over 55 years old or older or when 100 percent of the units are occupied by people 62 years old or older.

▶ Housing provided by religious organizations may give preference to members of the same religion as long as there is no membership discrimination based on any other protected class.

▸ Private clubs that are not open to the public may provide housing to its members as long as there is no membership discrimination.

Americans with Disabilities Act

Purpose. The Americans with Disabilities Act (ADA), which became law in 1990, is a civil rights law that prohibits discrimination against individuals with disabilities in all areas of public life. Although people with disabilities is one of the classes protected by civil rights and fair housing laws, the ADA guarantees equal opportunities in public accommodations and locations, employment, transportation, government services, and telecommunications for people with disabilities. The ADA has been amended several times to change the definition of disability, to update accessibility standards, and to require closed captioning in theaters.

The Americans with Disabilities Act Amendments Act (ADAAA) became effective on January 1, 2009. Among other things, the ADAAA clarified that a disability is "a physical or mental impairment that substantially limits one or more major life activities." This definition applies to all titles of the ADA and covers private employers with 15 or more employees to include real estate agents working as independent contractors, state and local governments, employment agencies, labor unions, agents of the employer, joint management labor committees, and private entities considered places of public accommodation. Examples of the latter include hotels, restaurants, retail stores, doctor's offices, golf courses, private schools, day care centers, health clubs, sports stadiums, and movie theaters.

In 2010, Titles II and III were revised to clarify several issues that had arisen over the past several years, one such issue being the use of service animals. The definition of a service animal was revised to include only dogs who are trained to work for or perform tasks for individuals with disabilities. Exceptions are made for miniature horses that meet size and training requirements. All entities covered under Titles II and III are required to allow service dogs to accompany their handlers in all areas where members of the public are allowed to go. However, dogs who only provide comfort or emotional support are not included in the definition of service dogs under the ADA, even though emotional support animals are recognized under fair housing laws.

ADA components. The ADA itself consists of five parts, each labelled as titles.

▸ **Title I (Employment)** gives people with disabilities equal employment opportunities as those without disabilities. It requires employers to provide reasonable accommodations or modifications to a work environment to enable the disabled employee to perform assigned job functions. Title I defines disability and the direct threat of a risk of harm to the employee with a disability. It is enforced by the U.S. Equal Employment Opportunity Commission.

▸ **Title II (State and Local government)** applies to state and local governments in prohibiting discrimination in programs and services of public entities. It also includes standards of operation for public transportation systems, requirements for reasonable modifications, and effective communication with people who have hearing, vision, or speech disabilities. It is enforced by the U.S. Department of Justice.

> **Title III (Public Accommodations)** covers public accommodations by requiring minimum standards of accessibility and removal of barriers, as well as requiring businesses to modify their usual ways of serving people to accommodate individuals with disabilities It is enforced by the U.S. Department of Justice.

> **Title IV (Telecommunications)** concerns accommodations in telecommunications and public service messaging. It requires telephone and Internet companies to provide systems that allow people with hearing and speech disabilities to communicate over the telephone. It is enforced by the Federal Communications Commission.

> **Title V (Miscellaneous)** concerns a variety of general situations including how the ADA affects other laws, insurance providers, and lawyers. It includes prohibition against retaliation, and the ADA's impact on insurance providers. This section also covers certain conditions that are not considered disabilities.

Real estate practitioners are most likely to encounter Titles I and III and should acquire familiarity with these. In advising clients, licensees are well advised to seek qualified legal counsel.

Requirements. The Act requires landlords in certain circumstances to modify housing and facilities so that disabled persons can access them without hindrance.

The ADA also requires that disabled employees and members of the public be provided access that is equivalent to that provided to those who are not disabled.

> Employers with at least fifteen employees must follow nondiscriminatory employment and hiring practices.

> Reasonable accommodations must be made to enable disabled employees to perform essential functions of their jobs.

> Modifications to the physical components of a building may be necessary to provide the required access to tenants and their customers, such as widening doorways, changing door hardware, changing how doors open, installing ramps, lowering wall-mounted telephones and keypads, supplying Braille signage, and providing auditory signals.

> Existing barriers must be removed when the removal is "readily achievable," that is, when cost is not prohibitive. New construction and remodeling must meet a higher standard.

> If a building or facility does not meet requirements, the landlord must determine whether restructuring or retrofitting or some other kind of accommodation is most practical.

Penalties. Violations of ADA requirements can result in citations, business license restrictions, fines, and injunctions requiring remediation of the offending conditions. Business owners may also be held liable for personal injury damages to an injured plaintiff.

Fair Financing laws

Parallel anti-discrimination and consumer protection laws have been enacted in the mortgage financing field to promote equal opportunity in housing.

Equal Credit Opportunity Act (ECOA). Enacted in 1974, the Equal Credit Opportunity Act requires lenders to be fair and impartial in determining who qualifies for a loan. A lender may not discriminate on the basis of race, color, religion, national origin, sex, marital status, or age. The act also requires lenders to inform prospective borrowers who are being denied credit of the reasons for the denial.

Home Mortgage Disclosure Act. This statute requires lenders involved with federally guaranteed or insured loans to exercise impartiality and non-discrimination in the geographical distribution of their loan portfolio. In other words, the act is designed to prohibit redlining. It is enforced in part by requiring lenders to report to authorities where they have placed their loans.

Jones v. Mayer

In 1968, the Supreme Court ruled in *Jones v. Mayer* that all discrimination in selling or renting residential property based on race is prohibited under the provisions of the Civil Rights Act of 1866. Thus, while the Federal Fair Housing Act exempts certain kinds of discrimination, there are no exemptions related to race in the private or public sale and rental of property. Thus, anyone who feels victimized by discrimination *based on race* may seek legal recourse under the 1866 law.

Types of housing covered

The federal Fair Housing Act applies to housing-based discrimination and covers apartments, mobile home parks, condominiums, dormitories, single family homes, public housing, homeless shelters, nursing homes, building lots, and housing sold or rented by real estate agents, leasing agents, rental managers, financial institutions, contractors, developers, or individuals.

Protected classes

The term "protected class" is used for groups of people who are legally protected from practices and policies that discriminate against them or treat them unfavorably due to a shared characteristic (e.g., race, gender, etc.) with which people identify. They are the features or social markers that categorize people. The Fair Housing Act was enacted with the understanding that some social markers are stigmatized and prevent qualified groups of people from accessing the housing of their choice. These groups are protected by several federal, state, and local anti-discrimination laws.

The Fair Housing Act prohibits discrimination in housing related activities because of race, color, national origin, religion, sex (including gender identity and sexual orientation), familial status (including families with minor children, pregnant women, and adults in the process of obtaining custody of a minor child), and disability. Because the Fair Housing Act is a federal law, this means that every state has at least these seven protected classes. In essence, anyone who attempts to rent, buy, or sell a home, take out a mortgage, or obtain housing assistance, is protected. The protected classes include the following:

1. **Race**

   Race was the first discriminatory characteristic prohibited in the Civil Rights Act of 1866. Race encompasses more than a person's skin color. It includes characteristics that are commonly associated with a particular ethnic group. The characteristics can be physical or genetic, such as facial features or hair texture. Discrimination based on any characteristic associated to race is strictly a violation of the Fair Housing Act, as well as several other federal, state, and local anti-discrimination laws.

2. **Color**

   Race and color are closely related but not the same. Color relates to the pigmentation or skin tone and can vary among people of different races or within the same racial group. The Fair Housing Act prohibits discrimination based on the lightness or darkness of a person's skin and reinforces the idea that everyone should have the same opportunities regardless of their skin color.

3. **Religion**

   Another practice prohibited by the Fair Housing Act is discrimination against someone based on the person's religious beliefs or lack of religious beliefs. The goal of this prohibition is to hopefully foster an environment where diverse religious backgrounds and beliefs are respected and upheld.

4. **National origin**

   A person's place of birth or ancestry is protected from discrimination under the Fair Housing Act. The goal of the protection provided is to prevent people from different countries and cultural backgrounds from being treated disparagingly in activities related to housing.

5. **Gender**

   The Fair Housing Act prohibits gender-based discrimination that interferes with equal housing opportunities based on the gender a person identifies with, i.e., male, female, transgender, or non-binary. The prohibitions provide protection against gender-based sexual harassment and stereotyping.

6. **Familial status**

   The Fair Housing Act designates familial status to mean families with children under 18 years old, pregnant persons, any person in the process of obtaining legal custody of a minor child, and persons with written permission of the parent or legal guardian. Discrimination via different rental terms, denying housing, or limiting housing availability options is a violation of the terms of the Act.

7.   **Disability**

While the ADA prohibits discrimination based on disability in public accommodations, employment, and state and local government, the Fair Housing Act prohibits disability-related discrimination specifically in housing. It also includes mandates for providing reasonable accommodations so disabled persons have equal access to housing opportunities. The Act defines disability broadly to include both physical and mental impairments that limit major life activities.

The New York State Human Rights Law covers all the same classes as the federal Fair Housing Law, but also protects against discrimination based on creed, age, sexual orientation, gender identity or expression, marital status, military status, or lawful source of income (public or housing assistance, social security, supplemental security income, pension, child support, alimony, foster care subsidies, annuities or unemployment benefits).

Many local governments have additional protections. For example, the **New York City Human Rights Law** also covers gender, citizenship status, partnership status, or lawful occupation.

Forms of discrimination

The Fair Housing Act specifically prohibits such activities in residential brokerage and financing as the following.

Discriminatory misrepresentation. An agent may not conceal available properties, represent that they are not for sale or rent, or change the sale terms for the purpose of discriminating. For example, an agent may not inform a minority buyer that the seller has recently decided not to carry back second mortgage financing when in fact the owner has made no such decision.

Discriminatory advertising. An agent may not advertise residential properties in such a way as to restrict their availability to any prospective buyer or tenant.

Providing unequal services. An agent may not alter the nature or quality of brokerage services to any party based on race, color, sex, national origin, or religion. For example, if it is customary for an agent to show a customer the latest MLS publication, the agent may not refuse to show it to any party. Similarly, if it is customary to show qualified buyers prospective properties immediately, an agent may not alter that practice for purposes of discrimination.

Restricting MLS participation. It is discriminatory to restrict participation in any multiple listing service based on one's race, religion, national origin, color, or sex.

Steering. Steering is the practice of directly or indirectly channeling customers toward or away from homes and neighborhoods. Broadly interpreted, steering occurs if an agent describes an area in a subjective way for the purpose of encouraging or discouraging a buyer about the suitability of the area. The agent deliberately steers prospective homebuyers away from certain areas or towards other areas based on the buyer's race, national origin, familial status, religion, gender, sexual orientation, or other legally protected classification. Historically, guiding Black people away from white neighborhoods has been the most prevalent form of steering.

For example, an agent tells Buyer A that a neighborhood is extremely attractive and that desirable families are moving in every week. The next day, the agent tells Buyer B that the same neighborhood is deteriorating and that values are starting to fall. The agent has blatantly steered Buyer B *away* from the area and Buyer A *into* it.

Blockbusting. Blockbusting is the practice of inducing owners in an area to sell or rent to avoid an impending change in the ethnic or social makeup of the neighborhood. **Blockbusting** occurs when a real estate agent tries to convince homeowners that their neighborhood is undergoing a significant change in demographics – typically portrayed as negative, in that it will cause home values to go down – so the homeowners will sell or rent their homes at lower-than-market-value prices.

For example, Agent Smith tells neighborhood owners that several minority families are moving in and that they will be bringing their relatives next year, causing home values to decline. Smith informs homeowners that, in anticipation of the value decline, several families have already made plans to move.

Redlining. Redlining is the residential financing practice of refusing to make loans on properties in a certain neighborhood regardless of a mortgagor's qualifications. In effect, the lender denies all financing to applicants within particular area. Redlining was the name given to this discriminatory lending practice dating back to the 1930s when lenders would draw red lines on maps around neighborhoods that were predominantly Black as a way to deny a mortgage, claiming it was high risk.

Redlining began in the 1930s when the FHA issued a loan underwriting manual for lenders to use when assessing property value based on demographics and location. The manual was explicit in deterring lenders from loaning to minorities by stating that "a change in social or racial occupancy generally contributes to instability and a decline in values." Consequently, lenders began denying mortgage loans because of where an applicant lived rather than the applicant's creditworthiness and financial qualifications. In 1977, the Community Reinvestment Act was passed to end the discriminatory practice.

Advertising guidelines

State and federal laws regulate advertising, including the federal Fair Housing laws as they pertain to discriminatory advertising and providing of services. Advertising includes electronic communication, social media/networking, internet marketing, as well as printed and published materials. Usage must be consistent with company image and legal requirements. The license laws of most states list illegal advertising actions subject to discipline, such as the following:

- making any substantial and intentional misrepresentation

- making any promise that might cause a person to enter into a contract or agreement when the promise is one the licensee cannot or will not abide by

- making continued and blatant misrepresentations or false promises through affiliate brokers, other persons, or any advertising medium

- making misleading or untruthful statements in any advertising, including using the term "Realtor" when not authorized to do so and using any other trade name, insignia or membership in a real estate organization when the licensee is not a member.

The Fair Housing Act forbids real estate advertising for most housing, including private, public, and federally funded housing, that indicates a preference, limitation, or discrimination based on any of the protected classes. The prohibition applies to publishers, such as newspapers and directories, as well as to persons and entities who place real estate advertisements in newspapers and on websites. The prohibition applies to all advertisements even if the property being advertised is exempt from the provisions of the Act.

Examples of advertising that may violate the Act include phrases such as "no children," which indicates discrimination on the basis of familial status, or "no wheelchairs," which indicates disability discrimination.

Risk can be reduced by the use of street names or other non-biased geographical references when stating where the property is located and by describing the property rather than the type of persons who might live in or around it. Even if a home appears "ideal for a young family," it is best not to advertise it as such. Such advertising would exclude other groups such as singles, the elderly, and older families and could, thus, be considered discriminatory.

In advertising the sale or rental of housing covered by the Fair Housing Act, HUD recommends using the Fair Housing Logo or phrase "Equal Housing Opportunity.

Exhibit 12.1 Equal Opportunity in Housing Poster

U. S. Department of Housing and Urban Development

EQUAL HOUSING OPPORTUNITY

We Do Business in Accordance With the Federal Fair Housing Law

(The Fair Housing Amendments Act of 1988)

It is illegal to Discriminate Against Any Person Because of Race, Color, Religion, Sex, Handicap, Familial Status, or National Origin

- In the sale or rental of housing or residential lots
- In advertising the sale or rental of housing
- In the financing of housing
- In the provision of real estate brokerage services
- In the appraisal of housing
- Blockbusting is also illegal

Anyone who feels he or she has been discriminated against may file a complaint of housing discrimination:
1-800-669-9777 (Toll Free)
1-800-927-9275 (TTY)
www.hud.gov/fairhousing

U.S. Department of Housing and Urban Development
Assistant Secretary for Fair Housing and Equal Opportunity
Washington, D.C. 20410

Previous editions are obsolete

form HUD-928.1 (6-2011)

NEW YORK HUMAN RIGHTS LAW

New York Civil Rights Law
New York Real Property Law
New York Public Housing Law
New York State Anti-Discrimination Disclosure and notice requirements
Types of housing covered
Local regulations

While states have enacted fair housing laws that generally reflect the provisions of national law, each state may have slight modifications of national law. For that reason, it is incumbent upon real estate students to learn their state laws and, in particular, note where these laws differ from national fair housing laws. New York has enacted several laws that provide anti-discrimination and human rights mandates.

New York State Human Rights Law

The New York State Human Rights Law protects against discrimination when selling, renting, or leasing housing. The Law recognizes the following protected classes:

- Race
- Creed
- Color
- National origin
- Sex
- Familial status
- Age
- Sexual orientation
- Gender identity or expression
- Military status
- Marital status (single, married, separated, divorced, widowed, never been married, and unmarried couple living together)
- Status as a victim of domestic violence
- Lawful source of income
- Blindness
- Hearing impairment
- Other disability (including the use of a service dog as a reasonable accommodation to alleviate symptoms or effects of a disability).

In addition to protecting against discrimination based on these protected classes, New York's Human Rights Law also prohibits blockbusting and steering. The Law also prohibits asking for a credit report from recipients of public housing.

**New York Civil
Rights Law**

New York Civil Rights Law prohibits discrimination in publicly assisted housing based on race, religion, color, national origin, ancestry, disability, and the need for a service dog. The Law also prohibits discrimination based on creed and any questions related to a person's creed.

**New York Real
Property Law**

New York Real Property Law prohibits discrimination based on someone being a victim of domestic violence and **requires compliance with federal and state anti-discrimination and steering legislation. The Law also prohibits discrimination in renting to persons with children.**

**New York Public
Housing Law**

The law regarding public housing prohibits discrimination related to any public housing project based on race, creed, color, or national origin. The Law also prohibits discrimination based on the resident's need for a service dog.

**New York State
Anti-Discrimination
Disclosure and notice
requirements**

These requirements mandate that real estate licensees are to provide clients and customers at the first substantive contact a copy of the "Housing and Anti-Discrimination Disclosure Form."   Click 'Control" plus the following link to access this form: 2156.pdf (ny.gov)

**Types of housing
covered**

In New York State, anti-discrimination legislation applies to all types of housing with three or more units, to include apartment buildings, condominiums, cooperatives, public housing, assisted living projects, hospices, transitional housing, HOPE VI projects, single room occupancy units, and homeless shelters. The exceptions to these prohibitions include the following:

> ▶ Buildings that house one or two families where the owner occupies one of the units

> ▶ Room rentals in housing for persons of the same sex, such as school dormitories

> ▶ Room rentals in buildings with the owner in residence

> ▶ Housing specifically for people 55 years old and older or 62 years old or older

Buildings built after 1991 that have four or more units and an elevator must be accessible to individuals with disabilities. Accessibility includes doorways wide enough for wheelchairs, electrical outlets and light switches placed low enough on the walls so as to be reachable, grab bars installed in bathrooms, and so on. These requirements, along with additional Americans with Disabilities Act requirements, also apply to detached single family homes that are supported by any government funds.

Local regulations

The Fair Housing Act prohibits a broad range of practices that discriminate against individuals in a protected class. The Act does not pre-empt local zoning laws. However, the federal Act applies to municipalities and other local government entities and prohibits them from making zoning or land use decisions or implementing land use policies that exclude or otherwise discriminate against protected persons, including individuals with disabilities. In addition to the federal and State human rights laws, several counties, cities, and towns within the State have their own anti-discrimination laws and human rights commissions who promote the laws.

New York City Human Rights Law (Title 8 of the Administrative Code of the City of New York) prohibits discrimination in housing, employment, and public accommodations (restaurants, stores, hospitals, museums, theaters, etc.) within the City. In addition to the following protected classes, the City's law also prohibits discriminatory lending practices, retaliation, discriminatory harassment, and law enforcement bias-based profiling.

- Age
- Immigration or citizenship status
- National origin
- Color
- Disability
- Gender, gender identity, sexual orientation, sexual harassment
- Marital status and partnership status
- Pregnancy and lactation accommodations
- Race
- Religion/creed
- Height and weight
- Status as a veteran or active military service member
- Lawful occupation, lawful source of income
- Children
- Victim of domestic violence, stalking, and sex offenses

IMPLICATIONS FOR LICENSEES

In transactions related to housing, every person involved must comply with anti-discrimination laws, not only because it is the right thing to do but because compliance works to avoid recriminations. The risk of violating fair housing laws can be minimized through ongoing education that addresses both the content and the intent of the laws. Real estate professionals are held responsible for complying with the laws and ensuring the licensees who operate under the broker's name also comply. To prevent fair housing and human rights violations, brokers should adhere to the following guidelines:

- Ensure that each licensee associated with the broker provides available housing notices and the Housing and Anti-Discrimination

Disclosure Form to all prospective sellers, buyers, landlords, and tenants at the first substantive contact.

▸ Use the fair housing logo and/or slogan in all advertising.

▸ Prominently and conspicuously display a link to the Fair Housing notice on the homepage of all websites owned and operated by the broker or associated licensee.

▸ Do not indicate to anyone that a neighborhood has or will change based on potentially new residents being of any particular race.

▸ Avoid discriminating against someone based on criminal history or limited English proficiency. Furthermore, the broker should train licensees to avoid intentional or inadvertent discrimination.

▸ Seek an attorney's advice to determine if a landlord's behaviors or practices could potentially be discriminatory.

▸ Display the Fair Housing poster conspicuously at each office, model home, and wherever other properties are for sale or rent under the broker's contract.   fairhousingnotice.pdf (ny.gov)

▸ Ensure the availability of all housing that meets the client's requirements is presented equally to any member of a protected class.

▸ Offer services to potential clients with no denial based on any protected class.

▸ Educate licensees and employees on fair housing and anti-discrimination laws and establish practices and policies for them to follow.

▸ When faced with questions that might lead to a steering charge or other violation of fair housing laws, limit responses to features of the home and to the process of selling, buying, and listing properties.

▸ Ensure clients understand the licensee's requirement to adhere to anti-discrimination laws. Before entering into a listing agreement, obtain the potential client's acknowledgement and agreement.

▸ Reject a client's use of discriminatory language or actions and terminate the listing if the client refuses to comply.

▸ Treat all buyers and sellers equally, showing no preference for one over another.

▸ Ensure the requirements of the Equal Credit Opportunity Act are being followed and refuse to participate in any form of discriminatory lending.

> - Establish office policies regarding adherence to anti-discrimination laws and appropriate behavior and responses so as to prevent the appearance of discrimination.
>
> - Display the Division of Human Rights poster in a conspicuous place within each office and branch office. This poster can be found online at nysdhr-racial-discrimination-guide.pdf.

Although real estate professionals may learn the federal, state, and local fair housing laws and believe they are complying without fault, they must understand that people are sensitive about discrimination and may interpret another person's behavior or words differently than the person intended. Consequently, it remains critical that brokers and their licensees learn and avoid actions that could be interpreted as discriminatory.

FAIR HOUSING AND PROTECTED CLASSES

Fair Housing Legislation
Protected Classes

Fair Housing Legislation

Our discussion of bias in real estate begins with an overview of the federal Fair Housing Act and protected classes at the federal and New York State levels.

The history of fair housing legislation in the United States began with the passage of the Civil Rights Act of 1964. This legislation was meant to end discrimination based on race, color, religion, or national origin. However, it did little to curtail discrimination in housing or otherwise because it did not address enforcement or discrimination in housing.

The Civil Rights Act of 1968, signed into law by President Lyndon Johnson in the aftermath of the Martin Luther King assassination riots, included Titles VIII and IX. These titles are commonly known as the Fair Housing Act. They specifically prohibit housing discrimination based on race, religion, and national origin. Additional legislation through the years has expanded and strengthened the original Act, but all the legislation has at its core the intent to eliminate housing discrimination.

Protected Classes

Current federal legislation prohibits housing discrimination based on seven protected classes: race, color, national origin, religion, sex, disability, and familial status.

New York laws extend those protections by adding several other protected classes that must be included in the anti-discrimination legislation: age, citizenship, lawful job or income source, gender, gender identity, or gender expression, marriage or partnership status, current children or plans to have children, status as a victim of domestic violence, stalking, or sex offense, and military service.

While one would like to believe that these laws prevent discrimination and bias, anecdotal and statistical evidence suggest otherwise.

BIAS AND DISCRIMINATION

Explicit Bias
Implicit Bias
Discrimination

We will begin the discussion of bias and discrimination by providing three definitions.

Explicit Bias

Explicit bias is an overt, conscious preference for, or aversion to, an individual or group of individuals, generally based on their identity.

Implicit Bias

Implicit bias is a covert, unconscious, and unrecognized prejudice against an individual or group.

When unveiling its implicit bias training, the National Association of REALTORS® noted, "The human brain uses shortcuts that allow us to quickly make judgments and solve problems without conscious thought. These mental shortcuts, or heuristics, help our unconscious minds process around 11 million bits of information per second." They go on to identify how this relates to implicit bias because of our "brain's automatic, instant association of negative stereotypes with particular groups of people, often without our awareness."

Discrimination

Discrimination refers to the treatment of different individuals or groups based on various factors. Note that it is critical to distinguish between the *act of discriminating against someone*, versus the *underlying reason(s)* for the discriminatory behavior. The latter is irrelevant. Our focus is the discriminatory act itself.

Understanding implicit bias is crucial for promoting fair and equitable housing practices in New York. All individuals must have equal opportunities in the housing market. Thus, we must focus on implicit bias in the real estate industry and identify potential interventions that mitigate implicit bias and discriminatory behaviors.

IMPLICIT BIAS IN REAL ESTATE

Bias and Discrimination
Bias Types

Bias and Discrimination

Beyond legislation prohibiting housing discrimination, individual ethics and morals should guide licensees as they perform real estate transactions. Most individuals like to believe they have no biases. In reality, most people do have certain biases. The key is to identify those biases and avoid discriminating based on them.

Implicit bias can influence how licensees, landlords, and property managers interact with consumers and make decisions relative to renting or selling properties. Bias can also influence how sellers react to buyers from specific groups.

Bias does not always equate to discrimination, especially when individuals learn to recognize their biases and avoid allowing them to lead to discrimination.

Bias Types

To hear and see examples of bias, we need look no further than social media and even standard media sources, as well as everyday conversations. From seemingly simple (though misdirected) statements such as "people who drive (insert specific kind of vehicle here) are _____," to more damaging comments such as "those Section 8 renters will just tear your property up," stereotypes abound. Society seems intent on labeling individuals and groups in multiple ways, most of them inaccurate and not only hurtful but harmful, particularly when they result in discriminatory behavior.

Bias and discrimination impact fair housing in many ways. While many types of bias exist, we will focus on those most commonly seen in the real estate industry.

Discrimination based on **income bias** occurs when individuals are singled out because of their source of income. Many states and municipalities (including New York, (as previously mentioned) prohibit discrimination based on legal sources of income. Why? Some landlords (and their property managers) hesitate to accept housing vouchers, other government assistance and income sources, alimony, or child support as viable income when renting properties.

Discrimination based on **ethnicity, language, and culture** bias occurs when licensees, sellers, landlords/property managers, or lenders view and treat consumers differently based on how they look or speak. For example, a landlord may object to renting an apartment to individuals of a specific culture because "their food smells up the whole place" or "their music is annoying."

Disability bias results in discrimination when individuals treat those with disabilities differently based on an obvious or stated disability. Often, this discrimination related to this bias is well-intentioned. For example, licensees may unconsciously evaluate properties and steer consumers away from some because of perceived accessibility or other issues. It may also occur when landlords or property managers are fearful of or don't understand how disability laws impact their responsibilities and requirements when working with those who are disabled. A third growing concern is tenants with "emotional support" animals (ESA) because of the relative ease with which individuals can obtain a letter authorizing them to have an ESA. This may result in discrimination against those who truly need support.

Sexual orientation bias most often occurs when individuals are or are perceived to be anything but heterosexual. This bias may result in licensees, landlords, sellers, or lenders refusing to work with gay or transgender consumers, for example, or steering them toward communities where it is believed they will be more "accepted."

Gender bias occurs when individuals give preference to members of one gender over another. In some situations, this may be a conscious or unconscious attempt to "protect" consumers. For example, a licensee working with a young female client may evaluate properties that meet the client's criteria and reject any deemed to be in an unsafe neighborhood.

Religious or political affiliation discrimination based on implicit biases may occur on a more limited basis than in other instances because it is often not readily apparent what an individual's political or religious affiliation is. However, implicit bias may result in individuals assuming that consumers are of a certain political or religious affiliation based on where they are from, their surnames, and other factors. As with other biases, "discrimination" may be well-intentioned when licensees attempt to steer consumers to or away from communities where the licensee perceives the consumers may be more comfortable.

BATTLING BIASES

How do we identify and combat the biases we hold? Many real estate associations and training providers offer implicit bias training. These sessions help participants recognize their implicit biases and develop tools and strategies to assist in acting objectively and avoiding discrimination.
Implicit association tests are available to assist in identifying implicit biases. Perform an online search to find training sessions that include this type of test.

While perhaps uncomfortable, a thorough self-analysis can lead to light-bulb moments related to bias. Biases are formed through life experiences from childhood on. Reflect on how, where, and by whom you were raised, how and where you received your education, where you have worked and in what types of jobs, and other life experiences. How might these have impacted your worldview?

Review previous transactions with a focus on any actions taken that may have resulted from an implicit bias. Question assumptions. For example, a licensee working with a young female first-time homebuyer unconsciously steers her toward neighborhoods the licensee believes are safer. The licensee assumed that this was in the buyer's best interest. But was it?

Seek diverse perspectives. Participate in activities with groups of individuals you ordinarily have not associated with or that you know hold different views from yours. Learn about different cultures.

Set and follow objective criteria when working with consumers. Make a checklist of the tasks and activities to perform and questions to ask and use it with every consumer.

Hold yourself and others accountable. When you recognize a bias in yourself or a colleague that may lead to discriminatory behavior, call it out (tactfully, of course).

Commit to change. A bias recognized can be managed and even eliminated.

12 Human Rights and Fair Housing
Snapshot Review

FEDERAL FAIR HOUSING LAWS

Fair Housing
- to give all people equal opportunity to live wherever they wish, provided they can afford to do so, without impediments of discrimination in the purchase, sale, rental, or financing of property

Exemptions to Federal Fair Housing Act
- privately-owned single-family with no broker and no discriminatory advertising; 1-4 unit apartment building where owner is resident and no discriminatory advertising; private club facilities leased to members; religious organization-owned facilities for members and no discrimination

Americans with Disabilities Act
- no discrimination against those with disabilities; applies to employment, education, transportation, public facilities; equivalent access
- Titles I (employment) and III (public accommodation) most common for real estate agents

Fair Financing Laws
- Equal Credit Opportunity Act: no discrimination in housing finance based on race, color, religion, sex, marital status, age; Home Mortgage Disclosure Act: no redlining

Jones v. Mayer
- no race discrimination, without exception

Types of Housing Covered
- covers apartments, mobile home parks, condominiums, dormitories, single family homes, public housing, homeless shelters, nursing homes, building lots, and housing sold or rented by real estate agents, leasing agents, rental managers, financial institutions, contractors, developers, or individuals

Protected classes
- race, color, religion, national origin, gender, familial status, disability,

Forms of discrimination
- discriminatory misrepresentation, advertising, and financing; unequal services; steering; blockbusting; restricting access to market; redlining
- NY also covers creed, age, sexual orientation, gender identity or expression, marital status, military status, lawful source of income, gender, citizenship status, partnership status, and lawful occupation

Advertising guidelines
- no discrimination in electronic communication, social media/networking, internet marketing, printed and published materials

NEW YORK HUMAN RIGHTS LAW
- no discrimination in selling, renting, or leasing housing based on race, creed, color, national origin, sex, familial status, age, sexual orientation, gender identity or expression, military status, marital status (single, married, separated, divorced, widowed, never been married, and unmarried couple living together), status as a victim of domestic violence, lawful source of income, blindness, hearing impairment

New York Civil Rights Law • no discrimination in publicly assisted housing based on race, religion, color, national origin, ancestry, disability, and the need for a service dog

**New York
Real Property Law** • no discrimination based on victim of domestic violence or persons with children

**New York
Public Housing Law** • no discrimination in pubic housing project based on race, creed, color, national origin, or need for a service dog

**New York State
Anti-Discrimination
Disclosure and Notice** • real estate licensees to provide "Housing and Anti-Discrimination Disclosure Form" to clients and customers at first substantive contact

Types of Housing Covered • all types of housing with three or more units, to include apartment buildings, condominiums, cooperatives, public housing, assisted living projects, hospices, transitional housing, HOPE VI projects, single room occupancy units, and homeless shelters
• exceptions include one or two family dwellings where owner occupies one unit; room rentals for same sex persons; room rentals in buildings with owner in residence; housing for people 55 and/or 62 years or older

Local regulations • New York City Human Rights Law prohibits discrimination in housing, employment, and public accommodations within the City based on age, immigration or citizenship status, national origin, color, disability, gender, gender identity, sexual orientation, sexual harassment, marital status and partnership status, pregnancy and lactation accommodations, race, religion/creed, height and weight, status as a veteran or active military service member, lawful occupation, lawful source of income, children, victim of domestic violence, stalking, and sex offenses

**IMPLICATIONS FOR
LICENSEES** • comply with Fair Housing laws and practices; do not discriminate; seek attorney's advice when appropriate, display notices and posters; ensure available housing is presented, educate licensees; reject client's discriminatory actions; establish office policies

FAIR HOUSING LEGISLATION AND PROTECTED CLASSES

Fair Housing Legislation

• Civil Rights Act of 1964 – prohibited discrimination based on race, color, religion, or national origin; no "teeth" in the law
• Civil Rights Act of 1968 – expanded on previous legislation and included housing discrimination
• Titles VIII and IV of the Civil Rights Act of 1968 = Fair Housing Act

Protected Classes

• Federally protected classes: race, color, national origin, religion, sex, disability, familial status
• New York State protected classes: age, citizenship, lawful job or income source, gender, gender identity, gender expression, marriage or partnership status, current children or plans to have children, status as victim of domestic violence, stalking, or sex offense, and military service

BIAS AND DISCRIMINATION

- Explicit bias – overt, conscious
- Implicit bias – covert, unconscious
- Discrimination – an action based on some form of bias

IMPLICIT BIAS IN REAL ESTATE

Bias and Discrimination

- Ethics and morals should guide licensees
- Most individuals hold biases
- The key is to identify biases and avoid discriminating based on them
- Implicit bias influences how individuals interact with others and make decisions
- Bias does not result in discrimination if individuals recognize biases and avoid discriminating

Bias Types

- Income
- Ethnicity, language, and culture
- Disability
- Sexual orientation
- Gender bias
- Religious or political affiliation bias

BATTLING BIASES

- Training
- Self-analysis
- Question assumptions
- Seek diverse perspectives
- Set and follow objective criteria
- Hold yourself and others accountable
- Commit to change

CHAPTER TWELVE: HUMAN RIGHTS AND FAIR HOUSING

Section Quiz

12.1. Which of the following is a protected class per New York State Human Rights Law but is NOT protected at the federal level, either specifically or inferentially?

    a. Military status
    b. Children
    c. Pregnancy
    d. Religion/creed

12.2. Which of the following phrases is considered discriminatory and should NOT be used in real estate advertising?

    a. "Cozy bungalow with a large backyard"
    b. "Spacious condo in a quiet neighborhood"
    c. "Perfect for young families"
    d. "Newly renovated kitchen with modern appliances"

12.3. Which of the following does HUD recommend using in advertising for the sale or rental of housing?

    a. Neighborhood crime ratings
    b. Energy efficiency ratings
    c. Equal housing opportunity logo
    d. Preferred tenant age group

12.4. Real estate agent John tells a minority buyer that the seller is not considering offers from buyers using FHA or VA loans. However, John later tells a non-minority buyer that the same property is available, and that the seller is open to all types of financing. Which discriminatory practice is John engaging in?

    a. Discriminatory misrepresentation
    b. Redlining
    c. Providing unequal services
    d. Steering

12.5. What was the first protected class noted in federal law?

    a. Color
    b. Race
    c. Sex
    d. Disability

12.6. Which of the following is true about service dogs and/or emotional support animals?

    a. Service dogs are required to wear special vests that identify them as service dogs.
    b. Service dogs are not specially trained to work for or perform tasks for individuals with disabilities.
    c. Emotional support dogs are not considered service dogs under the ADA.
    d. Emotional support animals are not recognized under fair housing laws.

12.7. A leasing agent could not communicate clearly with a rental applicant who did not speak English. Frustrated after about 10 minutes, she told him no apartments were available when there actually were. Which statement is true about the leasing agent's actions?

    a. She discriminated against the applicant based on national origin.
    b. She did not discriminate but she was not fair, either.
    c. She made a reasonable business decision.
    d. She acted in the applicant's best interest.

12.8. Which law prohibits asking for a credit report from recipients of public housing?

    a. Fair Housing Act
    b. New York State Human Rights Law
    c. Rehabilitation Act of 1973
    d. Civil Rights Act of 1964

12.9. Which of the following describes the practice of blockbusting in real estate?

    a. Refusing to rent or sell housing to individuals based on their race, color, religion, sex, or national origin
    b. Encouraging homeowners to sell their properties by suggesting that the entry of a particular race or ethnic group into the neighborhood will lead to a decline in property values
    c. Guiding potential homebuyers towards or away from certain neighborhoods based on their race or ethnicity.
    d. Denying loans or insurance to people living in certain neighborhoods based on the racial or ethnic composition of those areas.

12.10. Which of these actions is legal under federal fair housing laws?

 a. Falsifying the availability of housing
 b. Refusing to make reasonable accommodations for a resident's disability
 c. Declining to fund loans for people who do not qualify
 d. Discriminating in advertisements or promotions

12.11. Which of the following would be exempt from familial status discrimination?

 a. Young at Heart Apartments requires all tenants to be 62 or older.
 b. Lake Crossing development is designed for active people "50 and better."
 c. L'Esprit Urbain seeks young, single professionals as tenants.
 d. Serenity Grove plans several monthly events for young children and their families.

12.12. Which act is designed to prohibit redlining?

 a. Equal Credit Opportunity Act
 b. Federal Home Financing Act
 c. Jones-Mayer Act
 d. Home Mortgage Disclosure Act

12.13. Which of the following is true related to advertising guidelines for residential real estate sales and rentals?

 a. Discriminatory language in social media marketing is considered protected free speech.
 b. Advertising may not include any substantial and intentional misrepresentation.
 c. Agents and property managers may make any oral statements or promises to obtain business.
 d. Multi-unit residential properties are prohibited from discrimination in advertising, but residential properties of four units or fewer are not.

12.14. Which of the following situations would be exempt from the federal Fair Housing Act's provisions in New York?

 a. William is selling his home by owner, and it is the only real property he owns.
 b. The Sterling Society, a private club, offers dormitory-style housing to its members only.
 c. Happy Days Apartments offers housing exclusively to families with children.
 d. Danielle owns an eight-unit apartment building and lives in one unit.

12.15. Many states have enacted fair housing laws that generally reflect the provisions of federal law. Which of the following is true of New York fair housing laws?

 a. They are the same as federal laws.
 b. They are less preventive than federal laws.
 c. They are more robust than federal laws.
 d. There are no fair housing laws in New York.

12.16. Agent Mary's new buyer client Beth expresses interest in a particular neighborhood. Mary, believing the neighborhood is not safe, tells Beth that there are no suitable properties available there even though there are. Instead, Mary shows Beth homes in different neighborhoods. Which illegal practice is Mary engaging in?

 a. Providing unequal services
 b. Steering
 c. Discriminatory advertising
 d. Redlining

12.17. Two mortgage loan applicants with good credit histories, Alex and Jamie, are seeking home loans from E-Z Lending. Alex is using employment income to qualify, and Jamie is using employment income and Social Security benefits. Despite having similar credit profiles, E-Z Lending offers Alex a lower interest rate compared to Jamie. What is true about this situation?

a. E-Z Lending has the right to offer different interest rates based on the type of income, as long as both applicants meet the credit requirements.
b. Jamie should accept the higher interest rate since Social Security benefits are considered a less stable source of income compared to employment income.
c. E-Z Lending's practice of offering a higher interest rate to Jamie may constitute unlawful source of income discrimination under New York law.
d. Jamie can only qualify for the same interest rate as Alex by reapplying for the loan solely using employment income.

12.18. Which of the following housing types is exempt, whether conditionally or unconditionally, from federal Fair Housing Act stipulations?

a. Public housing
b. Nursing homes
c. Senior housing
d. Homeless shelters

12.19. The Fair Housing Act forbids real estate advertising for most housing from indicating

a. a limitation on the number of pets allowed on the premises.
b. a range of available amenities or prices.
c. the area of town of neighborhood where the property is located.
d. a preference or discrimination based on a protected class.

12.20. A property manager created a marketing brochure that includes several photos, all of white singles, couples, and families. Could this be considered a discriminatory advertisement?

a. No, as long as she does not discriminate in renting the units.
b. Yes, if the brochure does not include the current rental rates.
c. No, because the photos depict different familial statuses.
d. Yes, the brochure might convey a preference for white tenants.

12.21. The principal theme of federal fair housing laws is to

a. ensure all Americans enjoy home ownership.
b. prohibit discrimination in housing transactions.
c. ensure that housing transactions are negotiated fairly.
d. prohibit agents from dealing unfairly with clients and customers.

12.22. Which of the following circumstances allows for older people to be exempt from adhering to the familial status protected class requirements?

a. At least 80 percent of the units are each occupied by at least one resident 55 years old or older.
b. All activities and events are geared toward senior citizens.
c. 100 percent of the units are occupied by people 60 years old or older.
d. Senior housing is not exempt from familial status protections.

12.23. What was the result of the Supreme Court's ruling on *Jones v. Mayer*?

    a. No state's fair housing laws may be more restrictive than the federal Fair Housing Act and its amendments or other federal laws related to legal protections based on protected class status.

    b. A disability is a "a physical or mental impairment that substantially limits one or more major life activities."

    c. Lenders are required to use fair and impartial determinations in their loan qualification process and standards.

    d. Although the federal Fair Housing Act allows exemptions for certain kinds of discrimination, no exemptions related to race in the private or public sale and rental of property are permitted.

12.24. Laura, a real estate agent who specializes in high-end property sales, arranges a listing appointment with her aunt's friend as a favor to her aunt. The area of town has lower property values and a different overall demographic than Laura is used to. As she told a friend later "It is very ethnic." She decides it would be a waste to use the extensive marketing materials she normally uses for her listings. Instead, she simply enters the home in the MLS and places a yard sign in the yard. What form of discrimination could Laura be exhibiting?

    a. Discriminatory advertising
    b. Steering
    c. Discriminatory misrepresentation
    d. Providing unequal services

12.25. Which of the following protected classes is specifically included in federal fair housing laws and the New York State Human Rights Law?

    a. Sex
    b. Lawful source of income
    c. Victim of domestic violence
    d. Marital status

12.26. Which of the following types of housing is an exception to New York State's anti-discrimination legislation pertaining to housing of three of more units?

    a. Assisted living projects
    b. Homeless shelters
    c. Single room occupancy units
    d. Room rentals in buildings with the owner in residence

12.27. Which of the following apartment complex rules violate the federal Fair Housing Act?

    a. Restricting the age limit on playground equipment to 10 and under
    b. Hosting an ethnic food party and inviting everyone
    c. Limiting a Spanish-speaking person's unit options to a floor where other Spanish speakers live
    d. Prohibiting bike riding and roller skating on sidewalks

12.28. Mortgage Lender Ted limits the number of loans he makes to homebuyers in a certain minority neighborhood because he believes they are more likely to default on the loans. Which unlawful practice has Ted engaged in?

    a. Pandering
    b. Streamlining
    c. Redlining
    d. Blockbusting

12.29. Which state law specifically prohibits discrimination in publicly assisted housing based on race, religion, color, national origin, ancestry, disability, and the need for a service dog?

    a. New York Real Property Law
    b. New York Civil Rights Law
    c. New York Public Housing Law
    d. New York State Human Rights Law

12.30. Familial status applies to all of the following EXCEPT

    a. pregnant women.
    b. anyone securing custody of a child under 18 years old.
    c. a couple whose 21-year-old son moved back in with them.
    d. a single mother who has a 16-year-old teenager.

12.31. How does implicit bias differ from discrimination?

    a. Implicit bias is conscious and deliberate, while discrimination is unconscious.
    b. Implicit bias is based on stereotypes, while discrimination is based on explicit prejudices.
    c. Implicit bias is an unconscious mental process, while discrimination is an action taken based on an implicit or explicit bias.
    d. Implicit bias results in overt actions, while discrimination results from explicit biases.

12.32. A landlord's reluctance to accept housing vouchers as income is an example of _____.

    a. Ethnicity bias
    b. Income bias
    c. Disability bias
    d. Gender bias

12.33. Which statement about sexual orientation and gender bias in real estate is most accurate?

    a. It often results in higher property prices.
    b. It results in preferential treatment for LGBTQ+ consumers.
    c. It is primarily influenced by legal regulations.
    d. It involves stereotyping based on lifestyle choices.

12.34. How does implicit bias training attempt to mitigate discriminatory behaviors?

    a. By enforcing strict legal regulations
    b. By identifying and addressing unconscious prejudices
    c. By increasing awareness of fair housing laws
    d. By promoting diverse marketing strategies

12.35. When evaluating the impact of implicit bias, what is the most important step in fostering objective decision-making?

    a. Avoiding interactions with diverse consumer groups
    b. Reviewing personal biases without external guidance
    c. Prioritizing emotional responses over factual data
    d. Setting and following objective criteria for all transactions

12.36. Which of the following is the best example of holding oneself accountable for avoiding discrimination?

    a. Providing additional services to preferred clients
    b. Encouraging colleagues to adopt similar biases
    c. Recognizing and challenging biased assumptions
    d. Focusing solely on profitability in transactions

13 Municipal Agencies

Municipal Bodies

MUNICIPAL BODIES

The government of New York State is comprised of many agencies, corporations, committees, and subcommittees. Cities, counties, towns, and villages within the State also have their own agencies and other entities that handle the business and concerns of the municipalities. City councils, town boards, village boards of trustees, school boards, commissions, legislative bodies, and committees and subcommittees consisting of members of those groups all work for the good of the people of New York.

One of the main concerns of these agencies is the growth and development of the counties, cities, and towns. Consequently, zoning and land use become critical issues to control population density and regulate the demands on natural resources. Unregulated use of land can adversely impact property values and related taxes that are needed to fund a municipality's services and functions. Having these agencies in place helps to assure successful social and economic growth.

Legislative body
A legislative body governs the city, town, or village where it is located. Cities have a city council; towns have a town board; and villages have a village board of trustees. One of legislative body's major roles is administering and enforcing zoning ordinances. In doing so, the legislative body is responsible for the following:

> ▶ Appointing members to boards and commissions who handle land use planning and zoning, to include the municipality's planning board, the town or village's zoning commission, and the zoning board of appeals along with the zoning enforcement officer

> ▶ Approving all laws and regulations that govern planning and zoning boards

> ▶ Approving procedures that are used to administer planning and zoning laws

> ▶ Enacting land use laws and procedures drafted by various other boards

> ▶ Enacting, performing, or delegating site plan reviews

> ▶ Performing or delegating special permit approvals

> ▸ Delegating zoning enforcement to the Zone Enforcement Officer

If the legislative body does delegate any of its powers or responsibilities, it cannot then override decisions made by the delegated individual or body.

New York City Council

The City of New York contains 51 council districts that are spread across the 5 boroughs of the city. Each district is represented by 1 elected council member with each member serving two consecutive 4-year terms. After serving 8 consecutive years, members may take a 4-year hiatus and then run for election again.

The Council was presided over by the Council president until 1993 when a vote changed the leader position to Public Advocate who became the presiding officer and a member of every committee. Then in 2002, a city charter revision made the Council Speaker the presiding officer and the Public Advocate a non-voting member of the Council. It is now the Speaker who sets the agenda and presides at meetings.

The New York City Council is the only entity with the full power to approve the City's budget. As a legislative body, it also has power over zoning and land use decisions, including approving any regulation changes. Additionally, the Council has the authority to create laws for the City.

Council members serve on at least three committees and use committee meetings and hearings to propose legislation, obtain updates from citywide agencies, and hear from residents of the City. Committees oversee the City's human services, infrastructure, and government affairs. Committees include but are not limited to the following:

> ▸ Committee on Aging
>
>   o Subcommittee on Senior Centers and Food Insecurity
>
> ▸ Civil and Human Rights
>
> ▸ Civil Service and Labor
>
> ▸ Criminal Justice
>
> ▸ Economic Development
>
> ▸ Education
>
> ▸ Environmental Protection
>
> ▸ Fire & Emergency Management
>
> ▸ Health
>
> ▸ Higher Education
>
> ▸ Housing and Buildings

- ▶ Land Use
  - ○ Subcommittee on Landmarks, Public Sitings, and Dispositions
  - ○ Subcommittee on Zoning and Franchises

- ▶ Housing and Buildings

- ▶ Public Housing

- ▶ Public Safety

- ▶ Sanitation and Solid Waste Management

- ▶ Transportation and Infrastructure

- ▶ Veterans

- ▶ Women and Gender Equity

- ▶ Taskforce to Combat Hate

Village Board of Trustees

Members of a Village Board of Trustees must be at least 18 years old, a resident of the village (with some exceptions for smaller villages), and a United States citizen. Trustees are elected for 2-year terms. Convicted felons are not eligible for election to the board.

Village boards of trustees consist of the mayor and four trustees. However, the law allows the board to change that number at election time. The board also has the power to add, eliminate, or consolidate village offices.

New York Law Section 4-412 gives the Village Board of Trustees the power to manage the village property and finances and to take any legal action necessary to protect the village's property and "the safety, health, comfort, and general welfare" of the village's residents. As the legislative body, the board is also granted the power to adopt laws and ordinances, such as zoning ordinances related to land use planning. Trustees may have steps taken to prevent damage to village property from floods or erosion and may acquire property to use for related improvements such as drains and dredge channels. They may also acquire property to be used as public waste disposal sites or disposal plants.

Town Board

Just as with the city council and village board of trustees, the town board is the governing body of the town. All legislative authority falls on the town board. The board adopts a budget for the town, hires and sets salaries for officers and employees of the town agencies, sees that flood control and drainage facilities are constructed, has towers built for monitoring forest fires, provides for some public health services and town improvements, and much more. The town board may also adopt laws as needed pursuant to the New York Municipal Home Rule Law.

Adoption of budget and tax rate

When adopting an annual budget, taxing jurisdictions (school districts, cities, towns, counties, etc.) decide what services they need to provide to their residents. They then determine their funding requirements to provide those services. The funding requirements are determined based on the upcoming fiscal year, which may be the same as a calendar year or any other 12-month timeframe. From these requirements, the jurisdiction formalizes its annual budget.

The county or district then examines its sources of revenue, such as sales taxes, business taxes, income taxes, state and federal grants, fees, and so forth, to determine how many of the services and other expenses this revenue can cover. Budgeted expenditures that cannot be funded from these income sources will be covered by the annual ad valorem tax levies.

Tax levies are calculated by applying the individual jurisdiction's tax rate to the assessed value of each property. To determine the jurisdiction's tax rate, the amount of funds needed to cover those expenses not covered by the other income sources is divided by the total assessed tax value of the real properties in the jurisdiction, known as the tax base. The resulting percentage is that jurisdiction's tax rate for the subject year.

Not only may different jurisdictions have different tax rates, but within each jurisdiction, homestead and non-homestead properties may have different tax rates. Homestead properties are residential dwellings consisting of four or fewer units, condominiums, separately assessed owner-occupied mobile homes, farms with residential dwellings, and some vacant land that qualifies as being fit for residential buildings. Non-homestead properties are those not used for residential, such as commercial and industrial properties. In New York, the tax rate for homestead properties is lower than the rate for non-homestead properties.

Planning board
Cities with fewer than one million residents may create a planning board. The mayor appoints five to seven members with a chairperson. The planning board's main concern is for the city's development and growth policies. To fulfill its duties, the planning board may participate in preparing a comprehensive plan for development. They may perform investigations, create maps and reports, and give advice related to local planning. Within its advisory role, the planning board makes recommendations to the city legislative body and other local boards for regulations pertaining to development planning and land use. Adoption of the recommended regulations is strictly up to the legislative body.

If the legislative body so chooses, it may grant authority to the planning board to review and approve special permits, site plans, and other land use concerns. When the legislative body delegates various powers to other agencies, the planning board is the only agency that can be given the power to approve subdivisions.

In New York City, the Planning & Land Use Division uses planning as the primary practice when considering land use. Planning involves recognizing the conditions and challenges of the city, identifying goals and principles, and using specific policies to achieve those goals.

The Master Plan
A municipality's master plan is a strategic vision for future development. It is typically applicable to a time period of 10 to 20 years. It is developed by a planning board or zoning commission with input from the area's stakeholders. The plan is set up as a blueprint for urban growth and takes population growth, infrastructure requirements, economic objectives, and environmental considerations into account. The plan is used to guide decisions related to land

use, infrastructure, transportation, and community services. It influences zoning decisions and how land is used within the municipality. A master plan involves the following:

▸ **Land Use & Zoning** – designates zoning districts and development standards for specific land uses, such as residential or commercial

▸ **Transportation & Infrastructure** – identifies transportation, public facilities, and utilities needs and the infrastructure development required to support those needs

▸ **Housing & Demography** – includes population demographics (age, cultural, economic status, etc.) and needs for residential needs and expansion

▸ **Economic Growth** – identifies needs and opportunities for commercial and industrial development

▸ **Environmental Protection** – utilizes a *Conservation Advisory Council* and *Wetlands Commission* to identify and monitor the use and protection of the local environmental resources pursuant to municipal ordinances

A master plan also includes strategies and priorities for meeting the goals that serve as the basis for the plan, such as zoning modifications and ordinances, sources of funding, and incentives for developers. Last but not least, the plan requires the involvement of the citizens of the municipality to ensure their needs will be addressed.

The Zoning Commission

New York State law mandates each legislative body to appoint a zoning commission to create the municipality's initial zoning law. The law allows the legislative body to designate the existing planning board as the zoning commission or to appoint a separate zoning commission. The purpose of the commission is solely to draft the zoning law, so the commission will be eliminated after the final report and zoning law draft are accepted by the legislative body.

Zoning ordinances

Master plans include principles and objectives for a municipality's growth and development. To realize those objectives, local laws are put into place to regulate land use in compliance with the master plan. These laws are zoning ordinances which establish how land can be used, such as for residential dwellings, commercial buildings, and industrial sites. The ordinances also include specific standards for building structures, such as heights, setbacks, parking requirements, and so forth. Developers must be diligent in complying with these ordinances so as to avoid penalties when enforcement action is taken.

Zoning ordinance enforcement is handled by a *zoning enforcement officer* who is appointed by the municipality's legislative body. The officer's major duties include preparing necessary forms for administering zoning ordinances, issuing zoning permits, conducting inspections, issuing zoning certificates of occupancy, maintaining related records, and enforcing the zoning ordinances.

The zoning enforcement officer has the power to enforce the existing laws but not to change or waive any part of the laws. Zoning ordinances may only be changed or amended by the legislative body, and this is something the legislative body may not delegate.

Cluster zoning approval

A cluster development is a subdivision plat that utilizes methods for the plat's layout, configuration and design of lots, buildings, roads, infrastructure, parks, and landscaping that differ from those methods allowed by existing zoning ordinances. The purpose of the cluster development is to encourage and allow for open space and scenic quality in conjunction with the subdivision.

To allow the cluster development, the relevant zoning ordinances are modified. Local law gives the town board the power to authorize the planning board to approve a cluster development if the board determines the town will benefit from the development. The cluster development is approved simultaneously with the subdivision plat approval.

Conservation Advisory Council

Throughout New York, local legislative bodies and planning and zoning boards rely on Conservation Advisory Councils to bring environmental concerns into local planning, land use proposals, and the development of master plans. The council is established by individual municipalities and include three to nine members who are appointed by the legislative body. Although knowledge and experience in the environmental sciences, planning, engineering, and law are not required, members with such qualifications would be considerably beneficial to the council's work. To contribute to community planning, members are required to maintain inventories and maps of local open spaces, to include forests, fields, and wetlands. Members are responsible for conducting site visits, analyzing resources, and documenting potential impacts on the environment. Council members also perform policy research, develop education programs, implement stewardship projects, and provide information to other town agencies, land-use applicants, and the general public.

Wetlands Commission

Wetlands are areas that are submerged in freshwater and include marshes, swamps, bogs, and flats that support aquatic or semi-aquatic vegetation. Wetlands are necessary resources for ground water protection, wildlife habitats, flood control, and open spaces as well as water resources. Wetlands are important considerations in planning and zoning decisions because human activities and community development can potentially destroy these areas. New York State's Freshwater Wetlands Act mandates the preservation and protection of wetlands. The State's **Freshwater Wetlands Regulatory Program** has the following purposes:

- prevent damage and destruction of freshwater wetlands;

- preserve, protect, and enhance the present and potential values of wetlands;

- protect the public health and welfare; and

- be consistent with the reasonable economic and social development of the State.

Tax assessor

In New York, municipalities have tax assessors who are responsible for assessing all real property to determine the amount of tax to be levied on each homeowner to meet the needs of the annual budget. The assessed home values are posted on a tentative assessment roll for property owners to review for accuracy. As a result of any owner's disagreement with the assessment, the tax assessor may perform a reassessment of the subject property. Then the assessor posts any modifications on the final assessment roll.

Board of Assessment Review

When tax assessments are listed on the assessment roll, homeowners may disagree with the assessment. In such cases, the owner may take the complaint to the Board of Assessment Review who may require a reassessment and/or make adjustments to the assessment. The day designated for complaints to be heard is referred to as Grievance Day.

The Board of Assessment Review consists of three to five members who are appointed by the legislative body of the municipality. The majority of the members must not be municipality officers and/or employees. Additionally, the tax assessor may not serve on the Board.

Receiver of Taxes

The responsibility for collecting town, city, county, and special district taxes falls on either a tax collector or a receiver of taxes and assessments, depending on the municipality's structure. Real property taxes are levied and collected based on the final assessment roll. Once the taxes are collected, they are turned over to the proper agencies for whom they were levied. School taxes are levied separately.

Historic Preservation/ Landmark Commission

In an effort to recognize, preserve, and revitalize New York's historic and archeological buildings, areas, and landmarks, programs and regulations are administered by the Historic Preservation/Landmark Commission. The programs are authorized by the National Historic Preservation Act of 1966 and the New York State Historic Preservation Act of 1980.

New York's State Historic Preservation Office assigns teams across the State to provide the various programs to raise awareness of historic preservation efforts and to give New Yorkers pride in their state's history. To support preservation efforts, regulations may restrict remodeling and alterations made to the exterior of designated historical buildings.

Properties may be recommended for listing on the National Register of Historic Places through nominations to the New York State Board for Historic Preservation

Planning department

A municipality's planning department works with the planning board to develop the comprehensive master plan to address land use and socioeconomic and physical growth.

The department is involved in administering zoning ordinances, subdivision regulations, and site plan reviews, among other responsibilities. The planning department provides advice and technical expertise to other agencies and boards to ensure site designs and practices are consistent with local, state, and federal laws as well as the municipality's long-term goals.

The Department of Planning for New York City performs the following functions:

- work with agencies and residents to develop strategies for growth that will meet community needs

- promote community economic development

- utilize State and local zoning ordinances and maps as the basis for land use and development

- advise agencies and the public with policy analysis, technical assistance, and relevant data for application to planning decisions

- provide technical support to the City Planning Commission for reviewing land use applications and approvals

Zoning Board of Appeals

Zoning controls how property can be used and the size and structure of buildings constructed on the land. Zoning actually provides protection from undesirable or harmful development. When this country's first zoning ordinance was enacted in New York City in 1916, there were doubts in how effectively it would be followed. Consequently, "safety valves" were included in the ordinance to utilize at times when the ordinance was considered too strict.

One such safety valve was the establishment of the board of appeals to stand between property owners and the court. The board would be used to interpret and ensure the legitimacy of the subject zone and was granted discretionary powers to examine situations of hardship or inappropriate classification. In doing so, the board hears complaints from property owners about how zoning ordinances are negatively affecting their specific properties.

A board of appeals is required in any municipality where zoning ordinances exist. By law, the boards consist of three or five members with three-member boards serving 3 years and five-members serving 5 years. The members are appointed by the mayor. Villages and towns are allowed to vary the number of members on their boards.

Zoning variances

Boards of appeal hear zoning appeals and have the power to grant variances, that is, grant special permits for the subject property to be used in a way that differs from what the zoning allows.

There are two types of appeals:

A **use appeal** is one requesting a land use variance from what the zoning ordinance allows. For a use variance to be granted based on unnecessary hardship, all of the following must be shown:

- If the subject land is used only as zoning permits, the property owner will suffer from a lack of an economic return;

- the circumstances causing the hardship are unique to that particular property owner and not to the common conditions of most of the neighborhood;

- the use variance will not impact the essential character of the neighborhood; and

- the alleged hardship was not self-created.

An **area variance** applies using the land differently than the physical and dimension requirements included in the zoning ordinance allow. When considering an area variance, the benefit the variance applicant will receive must be balanced against any potential detriment to the neighborhood's health, safety, and general welfare. For the area variance to be granted, all of the following must be shown:

- The variance will not create an undesirable change or detriment to the character of the neighborhood or nearby properties;

- the sought-after benefit cannot feasibly be achieved by a method other than the variance;

- the requested variance is not substantial;

- the variance will not adversely affect the physical or environmental conditions of the area; and

- even though a self-created difficulty would not necessarily prevent the variance from being granted, the actual difficulty was not self-created.

Architectural Review Board

The Architectural Review Board reviews applications related to construction or remodeling that affects the exterior appearance of a structure or building, especially for those visible from a public street. The Board considers the historical and architectural style and design, arrangement, texture, material, and color of the proposed components to be remodeled or erected to ensure compliance with the New York State Historic Preservation Act.

In addition to buildings and other structures, the board is also responsible for reviewing all commercial signage to ensure it complies with the municipality's guidelines. The goal of the board is to ensure that alterations and new construction keep with the look of the area and offer a pleasant addition to the neighborhood.

Any of the following alterations require approval from the Architectural Review Board:

- change the color of the building façade

- alter the structure of the façade

- change the size, color, or wording of an existing sign

- create a new sign

> ‣ add new doors or windows

Buildings department

Within each city, town, and village, the local buildings department's main goal is to ensure safety within the construction industry and for the general public. To achieve their goal, the departments must enforce the municipality's building code, electrical code, zoning resolutions, New York State Labor Law, and New York State Multiple Dwelling Law. The buildings department is considered the gatekeeper for construction. Building codes are generally created to set standards for construction and alteration projects. In New York, a statewide building code has been created to cover areas that may not be addressed in local municipality codes.

The department reviews building plans, issues building permits, licenses, issues certificates of occupancy, issues demolition permits, registers and disciplines specific construction trades, responds to structural emergencies, and inspects newly constructed as well as existing buildings. They also inspect existing and remodeled building facades.

All demolition, alterations, additions, or new construction requires a building permit that has been issued by the local buildings department. Obtaining a permit requires payment of the applicable fee based on the scope of the project as well as a review of the project plans. A State licensed engineer or architect must prepare the construction plans and submit them to the building department. If issues are found during the review of the plans, it is up to the engineer or architect to resolve them.

Any construction project taking place in a historic or preservation district requires approval by the historic preservation/landmark commission as well as other specific permits. If any planned construction project does not adhere to applicable zoning ordinances, a relevant variance is required prior to the start of the project. Based on the type of project to be initiated, permits and approvals may be required from other agencies and governing bodies.

When construction is completed, the property owner needs to obtain a certificate of occupancy for new buildings or a certificate of compliance for remodeled buildings.

City/Town/Village Engineer

Any time construction or infrastructure projects are undertaken in a city, town, or village, having the municipality's designated engineer involved is necessary to ensure the work meets safety and engineering standards. Engineers are utilized for consulting, planning, designing, surveying, and overseeing construction and remodeling projects involving roads, buildings, water and sewer systems, bridges, and much more.

County Health Department

Septic approval. A septic system, also called an onsite wastewater treatment system (OWTS), is made up of a house sewer drain, septic tank, distribution box, and soil absorption (leach) field. Anyone designing or installing a residential OWTS must comply with and meet the standards of the New York State Department of Health's (NYSDOH) Administrative Rules and Regulations, most specifically the New York Codes, Rules and Regulations, Appendix 75-A.

Public sewer systems are preferred for the collection and treatment of household wastewater. However, there are situations where public sewer facilities are not possible or available. Consequently, it may be necessary to use an OWTS but only where site conditions are suitable to support OWTSs. Further, summer camps, restaurants, motels, mobile home parks, recreation and tourist facilities in New York typically rely on OWTSs.

Because many illnesses are transmitted by water, food, insects, animals, and toys that have been contaminated by human waste, it is critical for OWTSs to be properly designed, constructed, and maintained to provide safe and sanitary means of handling wastewater and to restrict contamination.

Similar to zoning variances, the law allows for specific waivers to individuals due to hardships or circumstances that make it impractical to comply with OWTS design and installation standards.

The New York State Public Health Law grants county and local boards of health the authority to create ordinances to protect public health, many of which relate to the installation of OWTSs. Designers and installers must also comply with watershed regulations and receive approval from the county health department for septic system plans. Local municipal Code Enforcement Officers, watershed inspectors, County Health Department staff, and State Health Department District Office staff are all responsible for ensuring OWTS design and installations comply with related regulations.

13 Municipal Agencies Snapshot Review

MUNICIPAL BODIES

Legislative body
- governs city, town, or village; city council, town board, village board of trustees; enforces zoning ordinances

NY City Council
- full power to approve City budget, power over zoning and land use, creates City laws

Village Board of Trustees
- manages village property and finances; adopts laws

Town Board
- governing body, adopts town budget, manages flood control, adopts laws

Adoption of budget and tax rate
- taxing jurisdictions determine services and funds needed, creates annual budget, determines where needed funds will come from
- divide funds needed by total assessed tax value of jurisdiction's real property

Planning Board
- participates in creating comprehensive plan for city development

Master Plan
- vision for municipality's future development; used to guide decisions regarding land use

Zoning Commission
- creates municipality's initial zoning law and is then eliminated

Zoning Ordinances
- regulate land use and includes standards for building structures

Cluster zoning approval
- requires modification of zoning ordinances

Conservation Advisory Council
- brings environmental concerns into local planning and land use

Wetlands Commission
- preservation and protection of wetlands and public health and welfare

Tax assessor
- assesses real property's value for tax levies

Board of Assessment Review
- reviews homeowner complaints regarding property value assessment

Receiver of Taxes
- collects municipality's taxes and distributes them to appropriate agencies

Historic Preservation/ Landmark Commission
- administers programs and regulations for preserving and revitalizing historic and archeological buildings and areas

Planning department
- participates in creating master plan; administering zoning ordinances, subdivision regulations, site plan reviews; provides technical expertise to other agencies

Zoning Board of Appeals
- interprets legitimacy of specific zones; hears complaints from property owners; required where zoning ordinances exist

Zoning variances	• allows property owners to use property in a different way than zoning allows
	• use variance – allows different land use than zoning allows based on hardship
	• area variance – allows different physical and dimension land use than zoning allows based on benefits
Architectural Review Board	• reviews construction applications for building exteriors considering historical and architectural style as well as design, arrangement, texture, material, color of proposed components
Building department	• ensures safety by enforcing building codes, electrical code, zoning resolutions, NYS labor law and NYS multiple dwelling law; gatekeeper for construction
City/Town/Village Engineer	• ensures safety measures are utilized for construction and remodeling roads, buildings, water and sewer systems, bridges, and more
County Health Department	• regulates installation of septic systems; provides waivers based on hardships

CHAPTER THIRTEEN: MUNICIPAL AGENCIES

Section Quiz

13.1. Taylor owns a small piece of undeveloped property in a single-family residential zone located on the edge of a commercial district. Due to local economy changes and the property's location, Taylor has struggled to sell or develop the property as a single-family residence. Taylor believes that a small coffee shop would be more beneficial for the community and financially viable. What is a good option for Taylor?

   a. Contact the municipality's planning department to ask for a change to the master plan.
   b. Ask the zoning board of appeals for an area variance.
   c. File a use appeal to request a land use variance.
   d. Request a board of assessment review.

13.2. When tax assessments are listed on the assessment roll, homeowners may disagree with the assessment on a day designated for complaints to be heard, called

   a. Grievance Day
   b. Day of Complaints
   c. Assessment Roll Review
   d. Tax Relief Period

13.3. _____ controls how property can be used and the size and structure of buildings constructed on the land.

   a. Planning
   b. Zoning
   c. Budgeting
   d. Enforcing

13.4. Whenever construction or infrastructure projects are undertaken in a city, town, or village, what is necessary to ensure the work meets safety and engineering standards?

   a. Involving the municipality's designated engineer
   b. Securing the approval of the State Health Department
   c. Consulting the Architectural Review Board
   d. Seeking a zoning variance

13.5. How are zoning ordinances changed?

   a. By popular vote
   b. By the municipality's zoning enforcement officer
   c. By the municipal planning board
   d. By the local legislative body

13.6. Local buildings departments have several responsibilities in ensuring safety within the construction industry, such as:

   a. controlling how property can be used.
   b. reviewing all commercial signage.
   c. issuing certificates of occupancy.
   d. administering zoning ordinances.

13.7. Real property taxes in New York are levied and collected based on

   a. the final assessment roll.
   b. the homeowner's estimate of value.
   c. the initial property appraisal.
   d. the property's purchase price.

13.8. New York's _____ assigns teams across the state to provide the various programs to raise awareness and to give New Yorkers pride in their state's history.

   a. Freshwater Wetlands Regulatory Program
   b. Municipal Home Rule Law
   c. Planning & Land Use Division
   d. State Historic Preservation Office

13.9. Which of the following bring environmental concerns into local planning, land use proposals, and the development of master plans?

   a. Town boards
   b. Zoning commissions
   c. Conservation Advisory Councils
   d. Village Boards of Trustees

13.10. Which type of municipality is governed by a board of trustees?

   a. Town
   b. Village
   c. City
   d. State

14 Property Insurance

Purpose
Provider Entities
Types of Coverage
Types of Policies
Agent's Role
Obtaining Insurance
Insurance Policy Disclosure
Commercial and Umbrella Policies

PURPOSE OF INSURANCE

Purpose

The purpose of insurance is to protect an asset against possible loss, whether that loss be related to property, flood, auto, health, business, life or pets. Some types of insurance are required because of where one lives and what one owns. For example, most mortgage lenders require homeowner's insurance to protect a property that is collateral for the lender's loan. A lender may require flood insurance on a property located in a flood zone.

PROPERTY INSURANCE PROVIDER ENTITIES

Lender-placed
Owner-placed
Agents
Insurance companies
Insurance brokers

Property insurance covers the home itself, personal property or contents of the home, and liability for injury others may suffer on the insured property. Property insurance policies can be obtained by any of the following entities.

Lender-placed

Most lenders will place homeowner's insurance on a home if the owner has let the insurance lapse. Premiums for lender-placed, or forced-place, insurance are considerably higher than those for insurance an owner would buy. The coverage is also typically much less and limited to the structure itself. The lender will usually add the amount of the premium payment to the mortgage payments and require the homeowner to pay the higher amount. The lender will do this until the homeowner obtains a policy on his or her own.

Owner-placed

A property owner should consider the following when seeking homeowner's insurance coverage:

> ▶ the size and value of the property
>
> ▶ the potential for an increase or decrease in the property's value
>
> ▶ the value of the items contained in the home
>
> ▶ the age of the items in the home and how much depreciation will impact their coverage if they need replacing
>
> ▶ the area where the property is located and what weather conditions may threaten the home
>
> ▶ what type of structure is being insured
>
> ▶ whether the property is rented or owner occupied
>
> ▶ the lender's coverage requirements
>
> ▶ the cost and terms of the policy

Another factor to consider is where the insurance will be purchased. Insurance can be purchased from an agent, an insurance company, or a broker.

Agents

Agents can be independent and sell insurance for several different companies, or they can be employed by only one company and sell insurance for that company alone. Independent agents can offer a larger selection of price and terms and reduce or eliminate the need shop around for the best policy. On the other hand, some companies sell their policies only through their own agents. Consequently, a homeowner who prefers one company over others will have to go directly to an agent who works for that company. Either kind of agent can provide coverage and loss prevention advice and help with losses and claims.

Insurance companies

Insurance companies sell insurance through agents, sales representatives, and the Internet. Agents and sales representatives provide advice, while the Internet facilitates comparing similar coverage from different companies and often allows purchase of a policy online. Most major companies also have local offices that provide walk-in assistance.

Insurance brokers

Insurance brokers work for the client and not an insurance company. They perform the search for the best policy and terms for the client. They negotiate terms and prices, assist with claims, and provide risk management advice. Brokers may be authorized to issue a policy or to bind an insurance company to issue a policy. The client pays the broker, who then pays the company.

TYPES OF
COVERAGE

Dwelling coverage
Other structures coverage
Personal property
Loss of use
Liability
Medical payment
Exclusions
Endorsements
Conditions
The 80% Rule

Each policy contains certain types of coverage. The coverages can be basic or comprehensive, providing more extensive coverage. The main types of coverage and those most commonly included in homeowners' policies are as follows.

Dwelling coverage

Insurance on the dwelling covers damage to the home itself and any structures or fixtures attached to the home. Coverage would include attached garages, plumbing, electrical systems, HVAC systems, and so forth. This is the most basic and common coverage and typically includes fire, windstorm, hail, tornadoes, vandalism, smoke, etc. It may not cover hurricanes, earthquakes, or mold unless specifically added.

Other structures coverage

This insurance pays for damage to structures not attached to the home. These include unattached garages, fences, sheds, pool houses, or any other structure located on the property but not attached to the home.

Personal property coverage

Personal property insurance pays for the loss of personal belongings that are not considered to be part of the home itself. Examples include furniture, appliances, clothing, computers, televisions, home décor, books, and so forth. This coverage typically includes damage, loss, and theft of the personal property, whether or not it is actually on the property. For example, if the homeowner is traveling and loses a laptop computer during the trip, the personal property coverage on the owner's policy would pay for the laptop.

Loss of use coverage

Loss of use insurance pays some expenses to live elsewhere after one's home has been damaged or destroyed by a covered peril. Again, if the peril is not covered, the policy will not pay for loss of use. If there is no earthquake coverage under the policy and a home is damaged by an earthquake, the policy holder will not receive loss of use payment while the home is being repaired.

Liability coverage

Liability insurance pays if the homeowner is sued and found to be responsible for someone being injured on the owner's property. If the stairs leading up to a home are covered with ice and the homeowner has not cleared the stairs, the owner might be held responsible for a visitor's injuries from a fall on the stairs. Liability insurance would cover the financial penalty imposed by the injured visitor's lawsuit. Liability also covers damage to someone else's property caused by the policyholder's negligence.

Medical payment coverage

Medical payment insurance pays the medical bills if someone is hurt on the homeowner's property. When that same visitor slips on the icy stairs and is injured, the medical payment coverage would pay for the visitor's hospital and medical bills related to the fall. Also, if the homeowner owns a dog that injures someone, the medical payments coverage would pay for the resulting medical bills. However, some insurance companies exclude dogs altogether or exclude certain breeds of dogs that they deem to be dangerous breeds. In this case, if the policy excluded pit bulls and it was the homeowner's pit bull which bit someone, the policy would not pay for those medical bills.

Exclusions

It is worth mentioning again that numerous perils are typically excluded from any particular policy. These include hurricanes, earthquakes, and mold. However, for an increased premium, these perils can be added to the policy. Some types of coverage are always excluded from homeowners' policies, for example, flood insua. Separate flood policies are purchased through federal insurance programs.

Endorsements

An endorsement (or rider) provides coverage for property or perils not covered in the original policy. An example of an endorsement would be coverage for expensive jewelry.

Conditions

A condition is a specific requirement for coverage in a policy. For example, a car may be covered only when it is parked in the garage.

The 80% Rule

Homeowner policies should insure the home for at least 80% of the home's replacement cost. With this coverage, the insurance company will pay losses in full up to the face amount of the policy, minus the deductible. For example, if the total coverage amount is $300,000 and the deductible is $500, a total loss of the home would pay $299,500.

However, if the home is not insured for 80% of the replacement cost, the loss would be paid based on the actual cash value of the property. This coverage amount would be based on depreciation and the home's age. For example, the recovery from a total loss of the same $300,000 home may be considerably less than the cost to replace the home if the home is 10 years old. A 10-year depreciation amount would be figured into the loss, and the company would pay the loss based on that factor.

TYPES OF POLICIES

Insurance policies can be either monoline or package policies.

Monoline policy. These policies include only one kind of coverage. Examples include liability policies and homeowners' policies.

Package policy. These policies include more than one kind of coverage, such as homeowner's insurance and liability insurance in the same policy . Package policies typically cost less than separate policies for similar coverages.

Homeowners' policies

Homeowners' insurance policies are based on the Homeowners 2000 Program which made revisions to forms and endorsements in 2010. Under HO 2000, there are six major policies that cover homeowners, renters, and condominium or cooperative owners. Mobile homes or house trailers can only be covered by other insurance policies.

HO-1 is the basis for most homeowners' policies. It provides coverage for losses from the following perils:

- theft
- lightning, wind, and hail
- fire and smoke
- theft and vandalism
- explosion
- civil damage and riots
- war and terrorism
- damage from vehicles and aircraft
- glass breakage
- damage to property being removed in an emergency situation such as fire

In addition, the **HO-1** policy includes liability coverage for

- personal injury – resulting from negligence on the part of the insured
- medical payments – for injuries occurring to guests or resident employees of the insured
- physical damage – caused by the insured to the property of others

HO-2, also known as a peril policy, covers items in addition to those included in the HO-1 policy. These items include electric current, accidental discharge of water, weight of ice and snow, falling objects and building collapse. In a peril policy, if the item is not listed, it is not covered.

HO-3 is a more comprehensive all-risk policy that differs from the HO-2 in that it covers all perils unless they are listed in the policy.

HO-4 is a policy is for renters. This policy covers personal property and liability for damage to the property or injuries to other people in the rented unit.

HO-5 policies have the most comprehensive coverage of all the homeowners' policies. It includes coverage for structures, personal property and loss of use.

HO-6 policies are specific to condominiums and cooperatives. This policy type does not cover the structure itself but does cover semi-permanent structures such as cabinets, carpeting, wallpaper, etc. It also covers personal property. The condominium association or cooperative would carry coverage for the actual structure.

HO-7 policies provide an extended form of real and personal property coverage designed specifically for very expensive houses.

HO-8 policies are for older homes with replacement costs higher than the home's market value. This policy type pays to repair or replace damaged property with cheaper common construction materials and methods, referred to as functional replacement.

AGENT'S ROLE

Not all home buyers are aware that mortgage lenders require property insurance to be placed on the home and maintained at least until the mortgage loan is paid in full. While real estate agents are not required to disclose this requirement to buyer clients, not doing so could result in a delay in closing or a potential failure of the sale to close at all.

Consequently, an agent should consider informing a buyer of the need for property insurance coverage. In doing so, the agent will want to explain to the buyer why the lender requires the coverage, how much the coverage will cost, and where the buyer can obtain a property insurance policy. The agent may even want to contact an insurance broker to meet with the buyer so the buyer can obtain the coverage in advance of closing. To provide advice to the buyer on covering the cost of the policy, the agent can explain the process of having the insurance and even property taxes set up through escrow along with the mortgage.

If the buyer is paying cash for the home, there is no mortgage and, therefore, no lender requirement for property insurance coverage. However, the agent should explain the advisability for the coverage as protection for the new home owner.

OBTAINING INSURANCE

As discussed earlier, insurance policies may be obtained through insurance agents or brokers and directly from the insurance company. Most coverage is fairly easy to obtain, although often times quite expensive. However, there are situations where the coverage may be more difficult or almost impossible to obtain. For example, often times, once an impending hurricane or wind storm is declared, no insurance company will place a property insurance policy within 30 days of the storm's expected arrival.

Additionally, the very cost of insurance policies makes it more difficult to obtain coverage. The New York Property Insurance Underwriting Association is in place to assist property owners in obtaining coverage. Likewise, the National Flood Insurance Program is in place to make flood insurance obtainable for homeowners whose mortgage lenders require flood coverage based on the location of the home and the type of mortgage loan on the home. The Federal Emergency Management Agency (FEMA) is also in place to help people "before, during, and after disasters," and while FEMA is not an insurance program, it does fill in financially where insurance is lacking related to natural disasters

INSURANCE POLICY DEDUCTIBLES

People obtain insurance policies to cover the costs of repairing damages or replacing lost items. The policies have a limit on how much they will pay, based on dollar amounts set when the policy is purchased.

However, when an insured suffers a loss, before the policy pays up to its limit, the insured is required to pay a *deductible* amount toward the repair or replacement. The deductible amount is set when the policy is purchased and impacts the cost of the policy. The higher the deductible amount, the lower the cost of the policy. The deductible is then subtracted from the amount the policy will pay.

For example, assume a homeowner purchases a property insurance policy with a $2,500 deductible. If the insured's home then suffers $20,000 in damages due to a covered peril such as a fire, the insured homeowner will be required to pay the initial $2,500 deductible out of pocket. The policy will then pay the remaining $17,500.

New York's Insurance (ISC) Charter 28, Article 34 § 3445 imposes a windstorm insurance notice wherein a homeowner's insurance policy deductible disclosure requirement is established. The disclosure notice is to be provided by the insurer to the insured and is to explain in clear and plain language the deductible amount and under what circumstances the deductible applies.

COMMERCIAL AND UMBRELLA POLICIES

**Commercial
policies**
In New York, business or commercial insurance typically includes general liability insurance and property insurance. The general liability protects the commercial business from lawsuits for bodily injury and property damage claims. When a claim is made, the liability insurance covers medical expenses, legal fees, and financial settlements or judgments. In certain cases, the liability insurance will even cover personal injury claims such as slander and/or libel.

Commercial property insurance covers damage to the insured's building and contents when a claim is made for damages caused by any covered peril, such as weather, fire, theft, vandalism, etc.

Some business owners also obtain commercial insurance policies to cover the business-owned autos and trucks for property damage and liability claims where the vehicle is involved. Business owners with employees typically obtain workers' compensation insurance to cover medical expenses and lost wages caused by a work-related injury.

Umbrella policies   Umbrella insurance policies are typically referred to as excess liability insurance. They provide coverage for claims related to third-party property damages or personal injuries. Umbrella policies are also available for auto-related claims against the policyholder. They cover damages and injuries exceeding the limits of the insured's personal liability policy. Commercial umbrella policies cover similar events but only when business related.

14 Property Insurance
Snapshot Review

PURPOSE
- to protect asset against possible loss; may be required by mortgage lender

PROVIDER ENTITIES

Lender-placed
- mortgage lenders require insurance coverage
- will place insurance at higher cost if homeowner fails to do so
- adds insurance premium payments on to mortgage payments

Owner-placed
- owner searching for policy with several considerations, such as type and size of structure

Agents
- may work for one company or be independent and sell for different companies
- some companies limit sales only through their own agents

Insurance companies
- sell insurance through agents, sales representatives, and the Internet

Insurance brokers
- work for client, not company
- searches for best policy for client, negotiate terms, assist with claims, provide advice

TYPES OF COVERAGE

Dwelling
- covers damage to home itself and other structures attached to the home

Other structures
- covers damage to structures not attached to the home

Personal property
- covers damage, loss, theft of personal property not considered the home itself

Loss of use
- covers off site residence if home is damaged by covered peril

Liability
- covers lawsuits against property owner for injuries to visitors

Medical payment
- covers medical expenses for injuries occurring on the insured's property

Exclusions
- perils not covered in policy

Endorsements
- adds coverage for additional property or peril

Conditions
- specific requirement for coverage

The 80% Rule
- Homes should be insured for 80% of replacement cost minus deductible
- not insured for 80% of replacement cost, loss paid based on property actual cash value

TYPES OF POLICIES

Policy types
- *monoline* – include only one kind of coverage
- *package* – include a combination of coverages

Homeowners' policies
- HO-1 – covers several perils and liability for injury, medical payments, physical damage
- HO-2 – covers additional perils
- HO-3 – covers all perils, all risks
- HO-4 – covers personal property and liability for renters
- HO-5 – most comprehensive, covers structures, personal property, loss of use

- HO-6 – covers condos and coops, covers interiors but not structures
- HO-7 – extended coverage for real and personal property for expensive homes
- HO-8 – covers older homes with functional replacement

AGENT'S ROLE
- agent should inform home buyer of lender-required insurance
- failure to do so could delay closing

OBTAINING INSURANCE
- may be obtained through agent, broker, or company
- cost of insurance makes it sometimes difficult to obtain

DEDUCTIBLES
- amount insured is to pay before insurance pays
- NY Insurance law requires deductible disclosure

COMMERCIAL AND UMBRELLA POLICIES

Commercial
- *general liability* – coverage for lawsuits for bodily injury and property damage
- *property insurance* – coverage for damage to business property from covered perils

Umbrella
- *excess liability* – coverage for claims related to third-party damages or injuries

CHAPTER FOURTEEN: PROPERTY INSURANCE

Section Quiz

14.1. Alison lost her job and, facing financial strain, left her property insurance lapse on her house. She has 20 years remaining on her 30-year mortgage. Which of the following is likely to occur?

    a. The insurance company will renew the policy and raise her rates.
    b. Her lender will foreclose on the property.
    c. Her lender will place homeowner's insurance on the house.
    d. The state will place a government-issued policy on the property.

14.2. Which of the following would be a reason a homeowner would consider adding an endorsement to a homeowner's insurance coverage?

    a. To cover items or situations not included in the standard policy
    b. To pay the medical bills if someone is hurt on the homeowner's property
    c. To cover expenses to live elsewhere after the home has been damaged
    d. To pay for damage to structures not attached to the home

14.3. What is a monoline insurance policy?

    a. It covers only one property.
    b. It covers one type of damage only (e.g., fire).
    c. It covers 100% of the property's replacement cost.
    d. It includes only one kind of coverage.

14.4. What is a factor that a homeowner would likely NOT consider when seeking homeowner's insurance coverage?

    a. The potential for an increase or decrease in the home's value
    b. The lender's coverage requirements
    c. The architectural style of the home
    d. The value of the items contained in the home

14.5. What type of insurance do business owners with employees typically obtain to cover medical expenses and lost wages caused by a work-related injury?

    a. Liability coverage
    b. Loss of use coverage
    c. Medical payment coverage
    d. Workers' compensation insurance

14.6. Which of the following best describes the purpose of dwelling coverage?

    a. To increase the property's market value
    b. To protect the property from possible loss due to damage
    c. To ensure compliance with zoning laws
    d. To increase the property's assessed value for tax purposes

14.7. In New York, what entity can assist property owners in obtaining insurance coverage?

    a. Federal Emergency Management Agency
    b. New York Property Insurance Underwriting Association
    c. The National Association of REALTORS®
    d. Any local REALTOR® association

14.8. What is the 80% rule pertaining to property insurance?

    a. Homeowner's policies only cover 80% of the value of personal property within the home.
    b. Commercial insurance covers 80% property insurance and 20% general liability insurance.
    c. Homeowner's policies should insure the home for at least 80% of the home's replacement cost.
    d. Deductibles can only be 80% of the cost to repair or replace any damaged item that is covered.

14.9. Marcus wants to make sure that his homeowner's insurance covers his extensive collection of guitars. What coverage should he make sure he obtains?

a. Dwelling
b. Personal property
c. Liability
d. Other structures

14.10. Under HO 2000, which major policy is the foundation for most homeowner's policies?

a. HO-1
b. HO-3
c. HO-5
d. HO-7

15 Licensee Safety

Precautions

PRECAUTIONS

Protect yourself
At the office
Client protection
Technology applications

Safety precautions   A major concern for residential licensees is personal safety. Because no one can guarantee your personal safety, the best way to keep yourself safe is to employ safety measures as a matter of common sense and habit. One cannot be too cautious about personal safety or that of the client.

Protect yourself   As a real estate agent, you will often work outside of the office and away from your colleagues. You will find yourself in situations where you are in the company of one or more strangers at a property or inside an unoccupied structure. Consequently, for your own safety, get into the habit of taking the following steps:

> ▶ **Always meet a new client at your office.** On the first meeting, do not meet at a property. Before meeting outside the office or alone, get as much personal information as possible. A copy of the driver's license is a good start not only for safety but also for the client database.

> ▶ **Show properties before dark.** Evening showings can be dangerous. Inform home buyers that you only do viewings during the day. If you must show a property after dark, turn on all lights and do not lower any shades or draw curtains or blinds throughout the house.

> ▶ **Do not get lost.** Always know the exact address of where you are going. If you are relying on your GPS in an unfamiliar area, make mental notes of landmarks, points of interest, and intersections. This makes a quick exit easier.

> ▶ **Practice the buddy system.** Bring a colleague or buddy with you when you meet clients at a property. Having a second person often adds to the safety and comfort of the situation. The buddy can drive separately or wait in the car after you let him or her know you feel

comfortable enough to continue the showing alone. Don't allow a client to ride in your car unless you know them well.

▶ **Make your location known.** Always tell your office colleagues or broker where you are going, who you will be with, when you will return, and when you will next be in touch. Leave the name and phone number of the client you are meeting. Make sure the person you are meeting knows that you have given your office this information. Also, schedule a time for your office to call you to check in. Beforehand, establish a method of being able to relate an emergency situation to the office or a contact person. Have a secret word or phrase to notify the office you are in trouble, one that can be worked into any conversation for cases where you feel that you are in danger. For example: "Hi, this is Jennifer. I am with Mr. Henderson at the Elm Street listing. Could you email me the RED FILE?"

▶ **Park on the street.** If you park in the driveway, another car can block you in. You want to have a clean escape route if necessary. Park in a well-lit, visible location. Keep the keys to your vehicle and your cell phone with you at all times. Keep your handbag and other valuables locked in the trunk of your vehicle.

▶ **Take two seconds to pause and look around as you enter your destination.** Does anything seem out of place? Is anyone present who shouldn't be there or who is not expected? Are there potential hiding places? Have a plan for what to do if something or someone doesn't seem right.

▶ **Never turn your back to a client.** Always let the client enter a doorway and go upstairs first. Stay in the doorway of each room. Never let your client get between you and the exit. Make sure you have previewed the property and know all of the accessible exits and how to contact the closest neighbors. Leave the doors unlocked for easy exit and leave one door open at all times, if possible. Do not enter attics or crawl spaces. Allow the clients to do so if they wish, but you should remain outside.

▶ **Open house safety.** Do not hold an open house alone. Inform a neighbor that you will be hosting an open house, and ask if he or she would keep an eye and ear open for anything out of the ordinary. Be alert to visitors' comings and goings, especially groups near the end of showing hours. There have been reports of some group members distracting the agent while others go through the house and steal anything they can quickly take. Also, do not assume that everyone has left the premises at the end of an open house. Check all of the rooms and the backyard prior to locking the doors. If you find yourself to be the last one in an open house and your car is not in the immediate vicinity of the venue, then make a phone call as you walk. Assailants will be less willing to attack if you are in mid conversation with another person.

> ▸ **Prepare to defend yourself.** Never assume that you can talk your way out of a situation. Learn some self-defense skills. Also, while carrying pepper spray may seem extreme, it can save your life if you have it on hand. Know how to use it and any self-defense moves, and do not hesitate to use either if you are threatened or attacked.

> ▸ **Dress appropriately.** Wear practical clothing that makes it easy to escape a dangerous situation. This might mean swapping heels for sensible flats and wearing something with pockets to hold your keys and cell phone. Also, never wear expensive jewelry.

> ▸ **Limit the amount of personal information you share.** This means avoiding mention of where you live, whether you live alone, your after-work or vacation plans, and similar details.

> ▸ **Set up your cell phone.** Check in advance to be sure your phone is serviceable in the area in which you are showing the property and that the phone is fully charged. Always remain aware of your surroundings when utilizing electronic devices such as cellphones and iPods. To best prepare for an emergency, pre-program important numbers into your cell phone. These may include your office, your roadside assistance service or garage, and 911.

> ▸ **Be careful with cash.** If you must transport cash deposits, use the buddy system or arrange for a security service or police escort.

> ▸ **Do not invite criminals.** Do not advertise a property as vacant. Report suspicious activity, i.e., a person's conduct or action that does not fit the norm of the neighborhood. If you think or feel that something is wrong or suspicious, it probably is. Most agents who have been victims of crime said they felt something was off but did not do anything. If something feels out of place, do not hesitate to stop a showing or open house and leave immediately.

At the office

In addition to protecting oneself outside of the office, there are several steps to be taken inside the practice's office to offer additional protection.

> ▸ **Keep a file on each agent's vehicle.** Record each vehicle's make, year, model, color, and license number.

> ▸ **Keep daily schedules.** Keep a schedule of agents' outside appointments with times, locations, and client names.

> ▸ **Require guest registries.** Require that agents set up a guest registry for persons attending an open house or viewing a model home.

> ▸ **Do not include personal information on business cards.** No home addresses or telephone numbers on the agents' business cards.

▶ **Maintain a record of agents' health conditions.** Be prepared to alert emergency responders to any existing health conditions that may result in a sudden and dangerous situation.

▶ **Require a buddy system.** Not only should agents not show properties alone, but they should not be alone in the office after hours.

▶ **Protect from scams and theft of personal information.** Keep up to date on email scams and warn agents. Shred documents containing personal and financial information. Train agents on recognizing telephone scams, adware, and malware.

Client protection

In addition to precautions to protect the agent, following are steps that can be taken for client protection:

▶ **Require a buddy system.** Tell your clients not to show their home by themselves, not to talk to other agents or buyers, and to refer all inquiries to you. Tell sellers if someone they do not know walks up to the home asking for a showing, do not let them in.

▶ **Protect from theft of personal items.** Remind your clients that strangers will be walking through their home during showings or open houses. So, valuables and personal items should be stored out of sight. Do a walk-through with the client to make sure you have identified everything that needs to be removed or secured, such as medications, valuables, and personal information.

▶ **Protect from scams.** Remind the client not to give out personal information to strangers asking about or viewing the home.

Technology applications

There are several technology applications and devices on the market that provide safety for real estate agents by tracking the agent's location, sounding an alarm, sending a distress signal to a contact list, and more. Some are tiny, wearable devices connected to professional monitoring services and to smartphones. When a crisis or threat occurs, the agent would press the device, and the monitoring team will send emergency resources to the agent's location without requiring the agent to say a single word.

The National Association of Realtors® has information, tips, courses, training videos, and other resources on their website at https://www.nar.realtor/safety. The site also includes information on safety products, programs, and smartphone applications.

15 Licensee Safety
Snapshot Review

SAFETY PRECAUTIONS

Protect yourself

- Do not meet strangers alone after dark and away from the office

- Be aware of your location, exit routes, and anything that seems out of place

- Use extra safety during open houses

- Prepare for defending yourself by knowing self-defense, dressing appropriately, not sharing personal information, not carrying cash, and setting up your cell phone

At the office

- Maintain agent vehicle records, daily schedules, health conditions

- Require buddy system and guest registries for open houses and model homes

- Train on email and phone scams and ID theft

Client protection

- Tell client not to show home alone or without agent

- Perform walk-through to identify items to be removed or secured

Technology applications

- Use tracking devices, cell phone apps, monitoring services

- Check NAR's website for further information

CHAPTER FIFTEEN: LICENSEE SAFETY

Section Quiz

15.1. Which of the following statements is true?

    a. Female agents should keep their purses with them at all times when away from the office.
    b. Agents should have visitors enter doorways ahead of themselves.
    c. Agents should not let the person they are meeting know the office has been given the person's name and location of the meeting place.
    d. Agents should rely only on their GPS in unfamiliar areas.

15.2. The purpose of having a secret word or phrase when contacting the office is to

    a. let the broker know if the potential buyer has submitted an offer.
    b. let the office know the potential buyer did not arrive for the property showing.
    c. let the office know the agent is in trouble.
    d. let the office know the open house is over and the agent is leaving.

15.3. Why should the broker keep a record of agents' health conditions?

    a. To judge the agent's performance
    b. To determine the agent's workload
    c. To alert emergency responders
    d. To select appropriate health benefits

15.4. Which of the following items should clients secure in preparation for an open house?

    a. Photos
    b. Toys
    c. Large televisions
    d. Prescription medications

15.5. Which of the following would be a safety concern during an open house?

    a. A group of visitors near the end of the day
    b. A neighbor's interest in the event
    c. An agent finding the house completely empty prior leaving
    d. An agent talking on her cell phone when walking to her car

15.6 Which of the following would be a best practice related to agent safety?

    a. Holding an open house alone
    b. Going upstairs ahead of a client during a showing
    c. Sharing your living arrangements with consumers at an open house
    d. Making sure your cell phone is fully charged before showing property

15.7 Brokerage offices should take steps to help ensure agent safety, such as

    a. including personal information on business cards.
    b. requiring a buddy system after office hours.
    c. keeping documents containing personal and financial information.
    d. expecting agents to transport cash deposits alone.

16 Taxes and Assessments

General Tax and Special Assessments
Taxation Process
Grievance and Contesting Assessments
Exemptions
Tax Lien Enforcement

GENERAL TAX AND SPECIAL ASSESSMENTS

Ad Valorem tax
Special Assessment

Ad valorem tax

Real estate taxation refers to the taxation of real estate as property. Real estate taxes are known as ad valorem taxes, which is a Latin term meaning "according to the value." Thus, an ad valorem tax is one that is charged against a property's value.

Ad valorem property taxes are imposed by "taxing entities" or "taxing jurisdictions" at county and local levels of government. States may legally levy taxes on real property, but most delegate this power to counties, cities, townships, and local taxing jurisdictions that levy the taxes to raise funds for providing local services.

County and local governments establish **tax s** to collect funds for providing specific services. The boundaries of such jurisdictions typically do not coincide with municipal boundaries, which is why they are established separately from the municipal jurisdictions. The major tax district in most areas is the school district. Other important tax jurisdictions are those for fire protection, community colleges, and parks.

In addition to generally established tax jurisdictions, a local government authority may establish a **special tax district** to pay for the cost of a specific improvement or service that benefits that area. For instance, a special tax district might be created to fund extension of municipal water service to a newly incorporated area. Unlike a permanent tax district such as the school district, a special tax district is temporary, ceasing to exist once the costs of the specific project have been paid for.

There are *no federal taxes on real property*. The Constitution of the United States specifically prohibits such taxes. The federal government does, however, tax income derived from real property and gains realized on the sale of real property.

Special assessment   A special assessment is a tax levied against specific properties that will benefit from a public improvement. The improvement may be requested by property owners who see the need for the improvement or may be initiated by the local government. The area where the improvement will be completed is referred to as a special assessment district. Common examples of special assessments are those for sidewalks, water service, sewers, and even parks and recreation areas.

In New York City, special assessment districts are called Business Improvement Districts (BID). To establish a BID, the majority of residents in the impacted area must agree to the special assessment. Once the scope of the improvement has been defined and has resulted in the establishment of the BID, the properties within the BID that will benefit from the improvement will be charged a special ad valorem levy at the same time as their annual ad valorem taxes are charged. The amount of the levy will be based on the total cost of the improvement, the number of properties that will benefit from the improvement, and the variance of benefit different properties will receive. In other words, some properties may benefit more than others and, thus, will be levied a higher tax than others.

For example, a dredging project is approved to deepen the canals for a canal-front subdivision. The project cost is $200,000. Although there are 100 properties in the subdivision, only the 50 that are directly on the canal stand to benefit. Therefore, the other 50 properties will not be assessed because they will receive no benefit from the project. Then, assuming each canal-front lot receives equal benefit, the 50 properties are each assessed $4,000 as a special assessment tax. Note that once the work is completed and paid, the assessment is discontinued.

If a taxing entity initiates an assessment, the assessment creates an **involuntary tax lien**. If property owners initiate the assessment by requesting the local government to provide the improvement, the assessment creates a **voluntary tax lien.**

Special assessments are usually paid in installments over a number of years based on the total assessment. However, taxpayers generally have the option of paying the tax in one lump sum or otherwise accelerating payment.

TAXATION PROCESS

Assessment
How properties are assessed
Equalization
Assessment roll
Reassessments
Tax levy
Tax rates
Appropriation
Tax bill
Grievance and contesting assessments

Assessment   A property's assessment is based on the property's market value and is used to determine property taxes. A government assessor estimates the value of the property to determine the tax assessment. The assessor will use one of the three approaches to determine value: the sales approach, cost approach, or income approach (all discussed in detail in an earlier chapter.). In New York, the assessors are government employees who work within an assessing unit. An approved assessing unit is certified by the Commissioner and is granted the power to assess real property in accordance with the commissioner's rules and regulations.

There are several occurrences that could potentially impact the property's value and resulting assessment:

- undeclared home improvements (made without building permits)
- unrepaired damage to the home
- sales of comparable homes
- changes in the market
- special assessments for neighborhood improvements
- the failure to perform needed neighborhood improvements

Obtaining a building permit for home improvements triggers an inspection and/or assessment of the improvement and potentially the entire home.

How properties are assessed

Properties are assessed either at market value or at a set percentage of market value. For properties being assessed fully at market value, the assessment should be the same as the property's potential sale price.

For properties being assessed at a percentage of market value, the market values are found on an *assessment roll which lists every property in the municipality* along with the assessment and related information. The percentage rate is referred to as a ***set uniform percentage*** which varies by tax jurisdiction. The assessments set at a percentage of market value are calculated by multiplying the market value (MV) dollar amount by the jurisdiction's set uniform percentage (%).

For example:
$500,000 MV x 29% = $145,000 Assessment

New York State Legislative changes in 1982 mandated that properties in the State were to be assessed at a uniform percentage of market value each year. The assessed value of a property is determined by taking the property's market value and multiplying it by the set **uniform percentage** being used in the jurisdiction where the property is located. This uniform percentage is typically 80% to 90% of full market value. The resulting assessed value is then used to calculate the taxable value of the property. The percentage of market value at which properties are assessed is called the Level of Assessment (LOA). When the Level of Assessment is not at 100% of market value, the administration of the property tax becomes less transparent.

However, New York City and Nassau County were exempt from the 1982 mandate and were allowed to use four classes of property when assessing taxes.

Assessment Ratios:

Tax class 1   6%
Tax classes 2, 3, 4   45%

The class determines how much the assessed values can increase each year based on the tax class:

▶ Tax class 1 – 6% per year, no more than 20% over 5 years.

▶ Tax class 2a, 2b, 2c – 8% per year, no more than 30% over 5 years for a building with 10 or fewer units.

▶ Tax classes 2 and 4 – class 2 properties with more than 10 units and class 4 no more than 20% each year over 5 years; must use lower of actual assessed value and transitional assessed value each year

Equalization

Some taxing bodies recognize that local assessments can lead to unfairly high or low values for properties in certain areas. Therefore, the jurisdiction may establish *equalization factors* to level out the unevenness of valuations. For instance, if assessed values of properties in one county are consistently 10% below the average for other counties, an *equalization board* may multiply each assessed value in that county by a factor of 110% to raise them to the average level for the state.

The percentage a property is assessed at compared to 100% market value is called the property tax *equalization rate.* In New York, the equalization rate is the measure of a municipality's level of assessment as determined by the uniform percentage.

A municipality's equalization rate = total assessed value ÷ total market value

Examples:

Equalization rate = 100%

▶ property is being assessed at 100% of market value
▶ recent reassessment was performed
▶ property assessments should equal market value

Equalization rate < 100%

▶ all property is being assessed lower than market value
▶ no recent reassessment has been performed
▶ 43 equalization rate = property assessed at 43% of market value

Equalization rate > 100%

▶ property is being assessed higher than market value
▶ assessments were not adjusted to reflect decrease in property values since last reassessment

New York State has determined that equalization rates are necessary in the State for the following reasons:

   ▶ a high number of taxing jurisdictions and school districts do not share taxing boundaries with the cities and towns who assess properties;

   ▶ each municipality sets its own uniform percentage for its level of assessment.

There are more than 700 school districts spread across several municipalities with each school district having up to 15 or more municipal segments. Each municipality may have a different level of assessment. So the school and county taxes can be distributed among all of the municipalities, each municipality's level of assessment must be equalized to full market value.

A municipality's full market value = total assessed value ÷ equalization rate

If all municipalities consistently assessed property at 100% of market value, equalization rates would not be needed. Since they do not assess at 100%, equalization rates are used to measure the level of assessment for the municipality as a whole, not for individual properties. Assessments are more likely to be fair and correct when reassessments are routinely conducted when market values change.

Assessment roll

The assessment roll is an online list of all properties within a municipality. It is available so homeowners can review their property's market value and tax assessment. A tentative assessment roll is typically published on May 1 each year in most towns and municipalities. Property owners are encouraged to check their properties listed on the roll to ensure a fair assessment with appropriate exemptions. If the assessment or estimated market value of an owner's property is higher than the price for which the property could be sold, there may be an error in the assessment.

Reassessments

Property owners are advised to check the tentative assessment roll prior to *Grievance Day*, the fourth Tuesday in May. If the owner believes the assessment is too high, the owner should contact the assessor and request a review or reassessment.

Reassessments performed throughout the municipality are the most effective means of ensuring fair and accurate assessments. The reassessment should include reviewing the market values of all of the properties in the area and making any appropriate adjustments to those listed on the assessment roll. The reassessment may also include collecting property information from the owners and/or performing physical inspections of the interiors of the subject properties.

To maintain assessment values that coordinate with current market values, reassessments should be completed frequently. Otherwise, properties may be over-assessed or under-assessed due to the market increases and decreases in property values.

The sale of comparable homes typically initiates reassessments of other homes throughout the municipality, including the subject home. The assessor should thoroughly examine the tax base in effect the year the homes were sold, the difference in taxes between the year the homes were sold and the year of the subject home's assessment (known as the transition tax), and the current assessment of the subject home.

Evaluating these three factors will result in a transitional assessment. If that assessment is more than 20% higher that the previous year's assessment, New York City regulations say the homeowner cannot be charged an annual tax increase more than 20%. Consequently, the tax will need to be spread out over 5 years with the annual assessment value increasing each year by one-fifth of the original transition assessment.

Example:

> **$450,000 = subject home's assessment resulting from its sale**
- **$300,000 = sale year's tax assessment**
> **$150,000 = transition assessment to be spread over 5 years**

$150,000 ÷ 5 years = $30,000 annual assessment increase

When a reassessment is completed, the assessment and the assessment roll will be modified and notice of the new assessment will be sent to the affected property owners. Once modifications to the assessment roll have been made, the final assessment roll will be published on July 1.

Tax levy

After the assessments and reassessments are completed and posted online in the final assessment roll, taxing jurisdictions (school districts, cities, towns, and counties) must determine their funding requirements to provide services for the year. The funding requirement is formalized in the annual budget. Then the county or district looks at its sources of revenue, such as sales taxes, business taxes, income taxes, state and federal grants, fees, and so forth. The part of the budgeted expenditures that cannot be funded from other income sources *must come from real property taxes*. This budgetary shortfall becomes the ad valorem *tax levy* which will be collected from property owners in municipalities that fall within the boundaries of the various jurisdictions. The tax levy is derived every year since budget requirements and revenue tallies are performed on an annual cycle.

Tax rates

The *tax base* of a municipality is the total of the appraised or assessed values of all real property within the municipality's boundaries, excluding partially or totally exempt properties:

tax base = assessed values - exemptions

Taxing jurisdictions generate the annual revenues they require by levying taxes on the tax base. The *tax rate*, or *millage rate*, is a rate per one hundred dollars of assessed value expressed in dollars and cents. This rate is what determines how much of a tax levy the tax base will receive.

Each individual taxing jurisdiction has its own tax rate. The tax rate for each taxing jurisdiction is calculated by dividing the amount of revenue required by the assessed value from the specific jurisdiction (the tax base) and would equal the tax rate per $100 of assessed valuation.

tax rate = required revenue ÷ tax base

This rate is then applied to the taxable value of each individual real property to determine its tax levy.

Some states, counties, or other taxing jurisdictions place limitations or *caps* on the tax rate or the annual increase in millage for property taxes. In such situations, taxing jurisdictions are forced to limit their budget requirements, unless there has been a sufficient increase in tax base to produce the required funds without raising the millage rate. New York sets its property tax limit to the rate of inflation or at 2%, whichever is lower. The State does allow a local government to override the cap with a 60% vote of the government's board or the voters in the district.

Appropriation

After properties are assessed and the taxing jurisdictions determine their budgets and tax rates, the jurisdictions need to adopt ordinances or laws that mandate how the tax base is to be taxed. This process is referred to as *appropriation* of the taxes, or the allocation of the funds obtained through taxation. The tax levy is then charged to each property owner in the jurisdiction on the annual ad valorem tax bill.

Tax bill

The next step in the New York ad valorem taxing processes is to bill the property owners for their tax levies. Most New York taxpayers will receive two tax bills each year.

The type of bill and when it will be received depends on the schedule for the municipality in which the property is located. However, property owners typically will receive a school tax bill first in early September. The school tax bill may also include taxes for libraries. The municipality taxes are sent in a second bill which arrives in early January. This bill may also include other special district taxes. Property owners whose taxes are paid through escrow accounts will receive receipts on the same schedule as the tax bills are sent out.

In addition to showing the amount of money the taxpayer owes (the tax levy), tax bills also include the tax rate for the jurisdiction as well as information on how the taxes will be spent. The bill shows any applicable exemptions and how they are deducted from the total assessed value of the property. If an equalization factor was used to determine the levy, that too will appear on the bill. The bills show payment due dates, often allowing taxes to be paid in two or four payments. Penalty dates are shown on some bills with the late payment amount or percentage.

GRIEVANCE AND CONTESTING ASSESSMENTS

If a property owner does not agree with the property's market value and/or assessment listed on the tentative assessment role, the owner should contact the county assessor. At this point, a reassessment should be performed. Whether or not a reassessment is performed, if the property owner and assessor are unable to agree on the assessment, the owner may contest the assessment by following the grievance procedure and pursuing a formal review. Contesting the assessment must be initiated by Grievance Day. There is no charge to contest or grieve an assessment.

In New York, anyone who pays property taxes may file a grievance but only on the current tentative assessment roll. This includes property owners, purchasers of a property, and tenants who pay the taxes in compliance with their leases. The individual filing the grievance must file a grievance form (Form RP-524) with the property assessor or with the Board of Assessment Review (BAR) in the municipality where the property is located. The property owner and the assessor may agree to a reduction in the value assessment prior to Grievance Day. However, if the reduced assessment is posted on the final assessment roll, further requests for a review or reduction are not permitted.

The BAR is made up of three to five members, all of whom are appointed by the municipality's council or board, and none of whom may be the assessor or any of the assessor's staff. Although assessors are not BAR members, they are required to attend all formal BAR hearings. The complaining property owner may be heard and may present evidence to support the complaint. After this *administrative review*, the owner will receive a notice of the Board's decision and reasoning.

If not satisfied with the BAR's decision, the property owner may request a *formal judicial review* as a small claims review of a tax certiorari proceeding:

> **Small Claims Assessment Review (SCAR)** which is only available to owner-occupants of one-to-three residential dwellings or owners of vacant land too small to contain a one-to-three residential dwelling. This review requires a $30 filing fee.

> **Tax certiorari proceeding** in the New York State Supreme Court in accordance with Article 7 of the Real Property Tax Law. It is recommended that the property owner filing for this review do so with a private attorney.

Property owners filing either of these review proceedings must do so within 30 days of the final assessment roll.

Detailed information and instructions for contesting an assessment can be found in the grievance booklet found online at grievancebooklet.pdf (ny.gov).

EXEMPTIONS

StaR (School Tax Relief)
Senior citizens exemption
Veterans exemption
Exemption for persons with disabilities

While all property is assessed for value and tax purposes, not all property is actually taxed. Properties owned by religious organizations or state, federal, and local governments, such as schools, post offices, parks, fire houses, etc., are not charged property taxes. Other properties may be taxed but with a partial exemption based on the resident's age (seniors 65 and older), military status (veterans), or disability. Other properties may be eligible for a partial exemption through the School Tax Relief (STAR) program.

STaR

The School Tax Relief program no longer accepts new applications. Those previously registered continue to receive the exemption applied to school taxes but not to municipality taxes. However, New York City, Buffalo, Rochester, Yonkers, and Syracuse split the exemption between school and city taxes.

There are two STaR programs:

▸ **Basic STaR** – owner must occupy the property as the primary residence; income must be $500,000 or less; exemption is based on the first $30,000 of the home's full value

▸ **Enhanced STaR** – owner must be age 65 or older; must occupy the property as the primary residence; income must be $98,700 or less for the 2024-2025 school year; exemption is based on the first $84,000 of the home's full value

Seniors (65 years or older) who qualify for STaR may also qualify for the senior citizens exemption.

Property owners enrolled in the STaR program receive the program benefits annually either through the *STaR credit* or the *STaR exemption*.

STAR credit. Those registered for the STAR credit receive either a benefit check or direct deposit issued by the Tax Department. The recipient may then use the benefit to pay school taxes. To be eligible for the STaR credit, the recipient must own the home and use it as the primary resident. The combined income of the owner and spouse must be $500,000 or less.

STAR exemption is a reduction in school taxes. Property owners who have been receiving the STaR exemption for school taxes since 2015 may continue to receive it for the same primary residence. Their annual school tax levy will be reduced by the amount of the exemption. **Note:** The STaR exemption is no longer available to new homeowners.

Senior citizens exemption

New York allows local governments and school districts to provide exemptions in the form of reduced property taxes for seniors. The reduced taxes are calculated by lowering the home's taxable assessment up to 50%. The property owner must be 65 or older and have owned the home for at least 12 consecutive months before filing for the reduction. However, if the senior already received the reduction on the previous home's taxes, the requirement for owning the current home for 12 months is waived. The allowable income limit is set by the municipality where the home is located but must be set anywhere between $3,000 and $50,000.

For seniors with higher incomes than what is set by the local municipality, three sliding-scale exemption-per-income options exist for the municipality to adopt. Seniors can qualify for the exemption based on their income as follows:

▸ 20% exemption if income is less than $55,700, or

▸ 10% exemption if income is less than $57,500, or

▸ 5% exemption if income is less than $58,400.

To qualify for the senior citizens exemption, each of the property's owners must be at least 65 years old unless the owners are husband and wife or siblings with at least one parent in common. In either case, at least one of the owners must be at least 65.

Senior citizen exemptions also apply to the following scenarios:

Cooperative apartments. Seniors who own shares in residential cooperatives may also be eligible for the exemptions in the form of reductions in their monthly co-op maintenance fees in the amount of the exemption.

Life estates or trusts. Seniors who are life tenants and entitled to occupation of the property for the senior's lifespan and are, thus, deemed to be the owner of the property may also qualify for the exemption. The property must be in trust with all trustees or beneficiaries qualifying for the exemption.

Manufactured homes. Seniors who live in manufactured homes located on leased land may also qualify for the exemption in the form of reduced lot rent in the amount of the taxes paid.

Veterans exemption

Veterans who are eligible for property tax exemptions in New York are those who have served in the United States Army, Navy, Air Force, Marines, and Coast Guard. To apply for one of the three available exemptions, the veteran must submit the exemption application to the property assessor in the municipality where the property is located. The deadline for submission is March 1 in most communities, but veterans should contact the assessor for confirmation of the date.

The following must be attached to the application:

- ▶ Proof of honorable discharge or release (DD-214) or other acceptable military record as found online at Acceptable military records for veterans property tax exemptions

or

- ▶ A letter from the New York State Department of Veterans' Services confirming the veteran meets the character of discharge criteria for benefits per the Restoration of Honor Act as found online at Restoration of Honor Act

plus

- ▶ Proof of the times and places the veteran served while on active duty (this information may be included within the above required documentation.)

Once the above documentation is submitted, the veteran will only be eligible for one of the following three exemptions:

- ▶ Alternative veterans exemption, which is only available for a veteran who served during a designated time of war or who received an expeditionary medal.

- ▶ Cold War veterans exemption, which is only available for a veteran who served during the Cold War period (September 2, 1945 through December 26, 1991).

- ▶ Eligible funds exemption, which is available for a veteran or certain other person, either of whom must purchase the property with monies from a pension, bonus, or insurance; provides partial exemption only.

Exemption for person with disabilities

Exemptions for people with disabilities are deductions up to 50% in the assessed value of the residence. The exemption is available only in municipalities and school districts that choose to offer it and is based on the municipality's set income limit as low as $3,000 and as high as $50,000. As with senior citizens exemptions, local municipalities may use a sliding scale to provide exemptions of less than 50% to disabled persons whose income is more than $50,000. The use of this option provides a 5% exemption for qualified disabled persons whose income is below $58,400.

To qualify for this exemption, the disabled person must own the property, provide documented evidence of a disability, and meet other income and residency requirements.

Property owners who qualify for the senior citizens exemption and the disabled persons exemption may only receive one or the other. It is recommended that they select the option that is most beneficial.

TAX LIEN ENFORCEMENT

Sale of tax certificates
Tax deed
Tax sale

If taxes remain unpaid for a period of time specified by state law, the tax collecting agency may enforce the tax lien in several ways, depending on what the law prescribes.

Sale of tax certificates

Some states sell **tax certificates**. The buyer of a tax certificate agrees to pay the taxes due. After a period of time specified by law, the holder of the tax certificate on a property may then apply for a **tax deed**.

Tax deed

A tax deed is a legal instrument for conveying title when a property is sold for non-payment of taxes. The application for a tax deed causes the taxing agency to institute a **tax sale** or **tax foreclosure**.

Tax sale

A tax sale is frequently some type of auction. If the tax has not already been paid through the tax certificate process, the buyer of the property must pay the taxes due. There is usually a legally-prescribed **redemption period** during which the defaulted taxpayer has the right to buy back the property and reclaim title. If the taxpayer can redeem the property by paying the delinquent taxes and any other charges before the tax sale occurs, this right is known as an **equitable right of redemption**. If the taxpayer can redeem the property after the tax sale, this right is known as a **statutory right of redemption**. In this case, the taxpayer must pay the amount paid by the winning bidder at the tax sale, plus any charges, additional taxes, or interest that may have accumulated. If the defaulted taxpayer does not redeem the property within the allotted time, the state issues the tax deed to convey title.

Exhibit 16.1 Tax Lien Enforcement

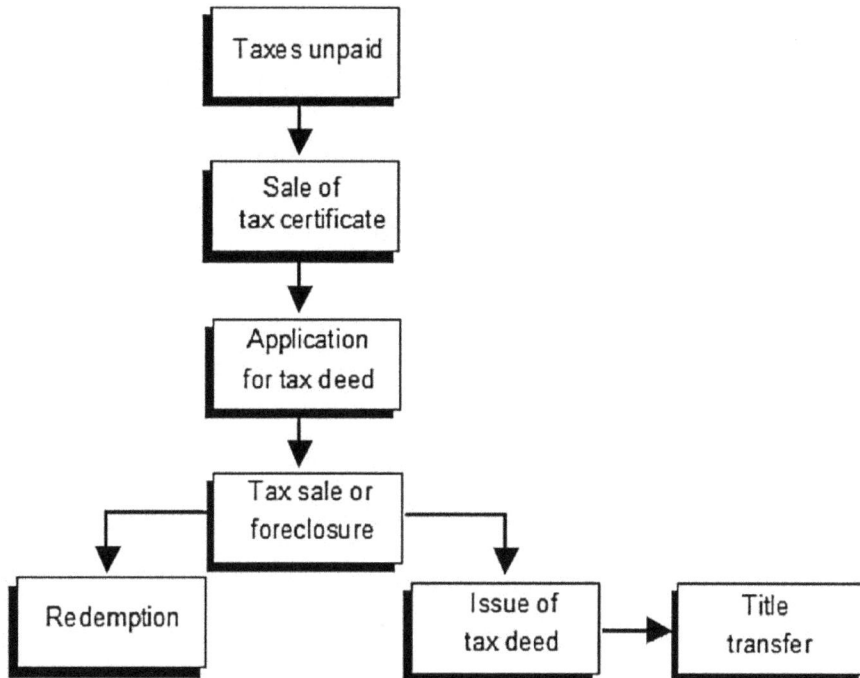

```
                    ┌─────────────────┐
                    │  Taxes unpaid   │
                    └─────────────────┘
                             │
                             ▼
                    ┌─────────────────┐
                    │     Sale of     │
                    │ tax certificate │
                    └─────────────────┘
                             │
                             ▼
                    ┌─────────────────┐
                    │   Application   │
                    │  for tax deed   │
                    └─────────────────┘
                             │
                             ▼
                    ┌─────────────────┐
             ┌──────│  Tax sale or    │──────┐
             │      │   foreclosure   │      │
             │      └─────────────────┘      │
             ▼                               ▼
     ┌──────────────┐              ┌──────────────┐      ┌──────────────┐
     │  Redemption  │              │   Issue of   │─────▶│    Title     │
     │              │              │   tax deed   │      │   transfer   │
     └──────────────┘              └──────────────┘      └──────────────┘
```

16 Tax and Assessments
Snapshot Review

GENERAL TAX AND SPECIAL ASSESSMENTS

Ad valorem tax
- property tax levied annually on the taxable value of a property in order to help fund government and public services

Special assessment
- tax levied against specific properties that will benefit from a public improvement; amount is based on a pro rata share of the cost of the improvement and the value each parcel will receive from the improvement

TAXATION PROCESS

Assessment
- based on property's market value; used to determine ad valorem taxes
- one of three methods used for value: sales approach, cost approach, income approach

How properties are assessed
assessment roll
- either at market value or a set percentage of market value; then posted o an

Equalization
- used to even out property values from one area to another; equalization rate - percentage property is assessed at compared to 100% market value; deemed necessary in NYS

Assessment roll
- online list of a municipality's properties that includes market value and tax assessment

Reassessments
- when property owner does not agree with assessed home value and requests home be assessed again

Tax levy
- amount of tax imposed on properties to secure funds needed for municipality's services

Tax rates
- (1) taxing entity determines what budget requirements must be met by ad valorem tax; (2) divide tax requirement by the tax base

Appropriation
- how tax base is to be taxed; allocation of funds obtained through taxation

Tax bill
- NY taxpayers receive two tax bills per year: school tax bill and municipality tax bill, to collect taxes levied on property owners

GRIEVANCE AND CONTESTING ASSESSMENTS
- property owner contests value assessment by requesting formal review; must be initiated with the tax assessor or the BAR by Grievance Day and only based on current tentative assessment roll
- formal judicial review: small claims assessment review or tax certiorari proceeding in NYS Supreme Court

EXEMPTIONS
- properties owned by religious organizations or state, federal, and local governments are not taxed; some other properties may receive partial exemptions

Star (School Tax Relief)
- basic STaR – owner occupies property, income below $500,000
- enhanced STaR – owner over 65, occupies property, income below $98,700

Senior citizens exemption • home value lowered 50% for seniors 65 and older; must have owned home for previous 12 months; allowable income set by municipality; varied exemptions set for seniors with higher incomes

Veterans exemption • veterans of US Army, Navy, Air Force, Marines, Coast Guard eligible for alternative veterans exemption, cold war veterans exemption, or eligible funds exemption

Exemption for persons with disabilities • deduction up to 50% of home's assessed value; income level set by municipality; varied exemptions set for persons with higher income

TAX LIEN ENFORCEMENT

Sale of tax certificates • the buyer of a tax certificate agrees to pay the taxes due and after a period of time may apply for a tax deed on the property

Tax deed • conveys title in the tax sale

Tax sale • the buyer must pay the taxes due, if still unpaid; the defaulted taxpayer may be able to redeem the property and reclaim title; if not redeemed, the state issues the tax deed to convey title to the buyer

CHAPTER SIXTEEN: TAXES AND ASSESSMENTS

Section Quiz

16.1. In New York state, excluding New York City and Nassau County, how are properties assessed for tax purposes?

    a. At a uniform percentage of market value each year
    b. At their current market value
    c. At an average of the subject property's and three comparable properties' market values
    d. At 1% more than last year's assessed value

16.2. Andrea is not satisfied with the Board of Assessment Review's decision on her property assessment grievance filing. Which of the following is open to her as a next step?

    a. Request a Small Claims Assessment Review (SCAR)
    b. File an appeal with the State Supreme Court
    c. Request a re-evaluation from the County Assessor's Office
    d. Submit a complaint to the Real Estate Ombudsman

16.3. In general, which jurisdiction imposes ad valorem property taxes?

    a. State
    b. Federal
    c. County and local
    d. National region

16.4. A taxpayer redeems his or her property by paying the delinquent taxes and any other charges before a tax sale occurs. The right to do this legally is known as a(n)

    a. statutory right of redemption.
    b. tax deed redemption.
    c. tax lien redemption.
    d. equitable right of redemption.

16.5. Why would a jurisdiction establish equalization factors for local tax assessments?

    a. To limit the percentage of increases in assessed values every year
    b. To level out the unevenness of valuations
    c. To make comparable properties more similar to the subject property in the sales comparison approach
    d. To even out the assessment roll

16.6. Real estate taxes are known as ad valorem taxes. *Ad valorem* is Latin for:

    a. in accordance with the government.
    b. according to the value.
    c. regarding property condition.
    d. for the common good.

16.7. New York allows local governments and school districts to provide exemptions in the form of reduced property taxes for

    a. first-time homebuyers.
    b. low-income property owners.
    c. senior citizens.
    d. property owners under the age of 50.

16.8. A jurisdiction's tax base is

    a. the total annual tax revenue collected by the jurisdiction.
    b. the total assessed value of all real property in the jurisdiction.
    c. the total number of taxpayers in the jurisdiction.
    d. the total income of all residents within the jurisdiction

16.9. What information do tax assessors use in an assessment to determine property taxes?

    a. The property's most recent sales price
    b. The difference between the property's sales price and its current market value
    c. The average market value of properties in the tax jurisdiction
    d. The property's market value

16.10. Which of the following parties is NOT eligible for a partial property tax exemption in New York?

    a. Marjorie, who is 65 years old
    b. Doug, who uses a wheelchair due to cerebral palsy
    c. Sylvia, a Navy veteran
    d. Michael, a first-time homebuyer in his first year of home ownership

16.11. In New York state, the most common tax districts are

    a. school districts.
    b. municipal boundaries.
    c. counties.
    d. special assessment districts.

16.12. In New York City's Business Improvement Districts, why are some properties charged a special ad valorem levy and others are not?

    a. The levy is only applied to commercial properties, not residential ones.
    b. Properties with assessed values below a certain threshold are exempt from the levy.
    c. Only those properties that will benefit from the improvement are charged this special levy.
    d. Properties that are owner-occupied are exempt from the special levy.

16.13. What is the term for the process in which jurisdictions adopt ordinances or laws that mandate how the tax base is to be taxed?

    a. Grievance
    b. Assessment
    c. Appropriation
    d. Millage

16.14. How often are tax levies imposed in New York?

    a. Every 5 years
    b. Twice per year
    c. Every 2 years
    d. Every year

16.15. The percentage of market value at which a property is assessed is called the

    a. assessment percentage.
    b. equalization rate.
    c. uniform percentage.
    d. assessment roll.

17 Condominiums and Cooperatives

Condominiums
Housing Cooperatives

CONDOMINIUMS

Definition
Condominium creation
Condominium creation issues
Governance
Airspace and common elements
Condominium acquisition
Letters of intent
Certificate of occupancy
Title issues
Closing costs
Essential legal distinctions

Definition

A condominium (condo) is a hybrid form of ownership of multi-unit residential or commercial properties. It combines ownership of a fee simple interest in the **airspace** within a unit with ownership of an undivided share, as a tenant in common, of the entire property's **common elements,** such as lobbies, swimming pools, and hallways.

A condominium **unit** is one airspace unit, together with the associated interest in the common elements.

Condominium creation

Condominiums are often created by converting other properties, such as apartment buildings, as is common in large cities such as New York City or Chicago. When the apartment building or any other shared housing is being purchased, the sale is deemed a public offering under the jurisdiction of the New York State attorney general's office. To create or convert the property to a condo, a condominium *disclosure statement* that includes the following must be filed with the attorney general's office:

> ▸ a report of the building's physical condition prepared by an architect or engineer

> ▸ a history of past expenses as well as projected expenses

> ▸ projected selling prices for each unit along with anticipated tax deductions and sample unit deeds

> ▸ an explanation of planned management

> ▸ the condominium declaration

A ***declaration and master deed*** also needs to be executed and recorded. The declaration is to include the following:

> ▸ a legal description and/or name of the property

> ▸ a survey of land, common elements, and all units

> ▸ plat maps of land and building, and floor plans with identifiers for all condominium units

> ▸ provisions for common area easements

> ▸ an identification of each unit's share of ownership in the overall property

> ▸ organization plans for creation of the condominium association, including its bylaws

> ▸ covenants and restrictions regarding use and transfer of units

After the disclosure statement, declaration, and deed are submitted and reviewed as required, the current tenants are provided an initial prospectus of the conversion details for their input and potential modifications.

After final modifications are made, it typically takes 4-6 months for a conversion and 30 days for new construction to be approved and filed with the attorney general's office. The next step in the process is to present prospective condo buyers with what is called an offering plan that covers the details of the condominium property and units for sale.

After the condominium creation is complete and the units are being sold, the condo creator will appoint the first board of directors and possibly the first managing agent to handle the business of the condo and property for the incoming new unit owners.

Condominium creation issues

If the condominiums were being created through a conversion of existing, tenant-occupied apartments, various areas within the State (e.g., New York City and Westchester county) have regulations in place that protect the rights of the tenants. One protective regulation is a ***non-eviction plan*** which prohibits the conversion unless 15% or more of the existing tenants agree to purchase their apartments as condos. Another regulation is referred to as an ***eviction plan*** which allows the condominium creator to evict existing tenants at the end of their current leases as long as 51% or more of the tenants agree to purchase their apartments as condos.

To assist in obtaining the percentages of tenant purchases as needed, the condominium creator often agrees to lower the sale price by 20 percent or more.

Exceptions to any eviction plan apply to tenants with disabilities or those over 62 years old.

In 2019, the **New York Housing Stability and Tenant Protection Act (HSTPA)** drastically altered the idea and process of converting apartment buildings into condominiums in New York City. The purpose of the Act was to provide additional protections for tenants and address the extensive conversion of rental buildings to condos.

HSTPA eliminated the eviction plan and changed the non-eviction plan to require at least 51% of current residents to agree to purchase their apartments as condos. Further, the Act gave current tenants a 90-day exclusive right to purchase and 6-month right of first refusal. HSTPA also held the eviction exemption for disabled tenants and seniors over 62 years old who do not purchase their units, unless they fail to pay rent, fail to provide reasonable access, use their premises for illegal purposes, or breach other tenant obligations. The Act also prohibited unreasonable rent increases for these tenants during their occupancy.

Governance

Condominiums have rules, regulations, and bylaws that govern the owners, tenants, and activities related to the condos. The bylaws set the covenants, conditions, and restrictions (CC&Rs) and are often referred to as the *governing documents*.

The governing documents typically provide for the creation of an **owners' association** to enforce the bylaws and manage the overall property. The association is often headed by a board of directors which organizes how the property will be managed and by whom. The documents will set how many directors will comprise the board and how they will be elected or appointed to the board, as well as what responsibilities and obligations are assigned to the board, such as overseeing the property's finances and policy administration.

Condominium properties have extensive management requirements, including maintenance, sales and leasing, accounting, owner services, sanitation, security, trash removal, etc. To obtain assistance in handling the business of the owners' association, the board may appoint or hire management agents, resident managers, supervisory committees, sales and rental agents, specialized maintenance personnel, and outside service contractors to fulfill these functions.

Airspace and common elements

The unique aspect of the condominium is its fee simple interest in the airspace contained within the outer walls, floors, and ceiling of the building unit. This airspace may include internal walls which are not essential to the structural support of the building.

Common elements are all portions of the property that are necessary for the existence, operation, and maintenance of the condominium units. Common elements include:

- ▸ the land (if not leased)

- ▸ structural components of the building, such as exterior windows, roof, and foundation

- ▸ physical operating systems supporting all units, such as plumbing, power, communications installations, and central air conditioning

- ▸ recreational facilities, such as club houses, swimming pools, tennis courts, etc.

- ▸ building and ground areas used non-exclusively, such as stairways, elevators, hallways, laundry rooms, driveways, sidewalks, landscaping, and parking areas.

Exhibit 17.1 The Condominium

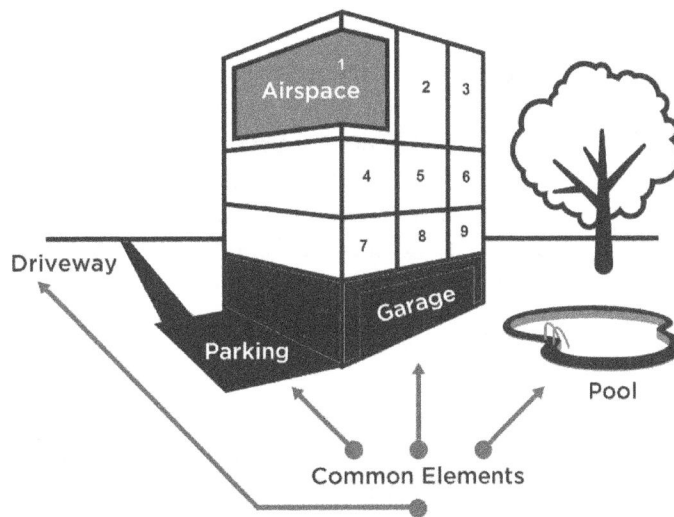

The illustration above shows a condominium building with nine units and common elements consisting of a pool, parking lot, a garage, driveway, a tree, and the building structure itself. An owner in this condo building owns an exclusive interest in the airspace inside the owner's individual condo unit and an indivisible one-ninth interest in the common elements. In other words, the owner co-owns the common elements with other unit owners.

Condominium acquisition

The New York State Attorney General's Office has enacted regulations that regulate the selling and purchasing of condominiums in the State. Selling a condo unit involves an *offering plan* which includes the terms and conditions of the sale, as well as the physical aspects of the condo building(s). Exterior physical aspects include the quality and condition of the building components such as the facade, roof, windows, etc. The interior physical aspects include such items as flooring, appliances, elevators, cooling and heating systems, electrical components, and plumbing. The offering plan must comply with applicable regulations and laws, i.e., Article 23-A of the New York General Business Law and the New York Housing Stability and Tenant Protection Act. Offering plans are reviewed by the Real Estate Finance Bureau to ensure compliance.

Buyers of condominiums should read the entire offering plan, receive and read the condo's bylaws and CC&Rs, should be provided a copy of the annual budget so they can review the finances and reserve accounts. Further, buyers should be notified of any common charge payments in arrears and impending assessments or lawsuits. The buyer should learn if the homeowners' association exercises a first right of refusal, which means the association can deny the purchase by a particular buyer as long as the association purchases the condo unit for the same price and terms as the denied buyer would have.

Upon acquisition of the condominium, the buyer will receive a deed that conveys a fee simple ownership of the unit itself and a tenancy in common interest in the buyer's pro rata share of the common elements. Condominium units are individually assessed and taxed. The assessment pertains to the value of the exclusive interest in the apartment as well as the unit's pro rata share of common elements.

Condominium units can be individually sold, mortgaged, or otherwise encumbered without interference from other unit owners. As a distinct entity, the condominium unit may also be foreclosed and liquidated. An owner may not sell interests in the apartment separately from the interest in the common elements. Each unit is individually charged a monthly condominium fee which is typically used for building and common element maintenance, insurance (property, liability, flood, etc.) for the components of the association, utilities, management, and so forth. Each unit's owner may also carry insurance to cover the interior living space of the unit.

Letters of intent

Letters of intent are similar to offers to purchase with some differences. First, they are typically used in transactions involving commercial property. They contain fewer details than purchase offers and typically simply include the purchase price, closing timeline, and contingencies. If a potential condo purchaser submits a letter of intent, the seller is being notified of the purchaser's interest. This can be done early on in the conversion or construction process to reserve a space or unit in the building. The letter of intent is not a binding contract, and no deposit is submitted with the letter. If the letter of intent includes information the seller agrees with, the seller would then request a formal offer. In a case where the condo creator needs to seek funding to complete the project, the letters of intent can be shown to lenders to show the stability of the project and convince a lender to provide funds.

Certificate of Occupancy

A Certificate of Occupancy (CO) discloses the legal use and type of occupancy that is allowed for the subject building. Every new building is required to have a CO, as are all existing buildings where any kind of construction or modification changes their use or type of occupancy.

Anyone making major alterations to an existing building or constructing a new building must submit the construction plans to the Department of Buildings. When the construction is completed, the Department issues a final CO. A Letter of Completion is issued for minor alterations. Either of these documents confirms that the construction or modifications comply with all laws, that all required documentation has been completed and submitted and that any code violations have been resolved. The final CO must be obtained prior to legal occupancy of the building.

A temporary Certificate of Occupancy (TCO) may be issued if the Department of Buildings deems the building safe to occupy prior to all outstanding issues being resolved. The issues must be resolved prior to the TCO's expiration date, which is typically 90 days from the date the TCO is issued. Once the issues are resolved, the Department will issue the final CO.

Title issues

The condominium property/building owner must hold a free and clear title to the property. Each individual condo unit owner must also obtain a free and clear title to the unit. However, there are issues that may prevent the title from being clear and, therefore, interfere with the owner's actual ownership of the property. Issues can include any of the following:

▸ a lien on the property due to unpaid taxes, contractor's fees, or other debts

▸ restrictions or encumbrances on the use of the property resulting from zoning laws or easements

▸ missing information in the deed

▸ errors in the deed

▸ fraud in the public records

Given the potential issues related to a property's title and the complications any issue may cause, it is critical for a buyer and/or developer to have the title reviewed prior to closing and obtain title insurance to protect the buyer from problems with the chain of title or its maretability.

Closing costs

Condo purchasers face closing costs similar to those related to single-family home closing costs. In New York, closing costs for both condos and single-family homes are some of the highest in the country. New York's closing cost-to-sale price before taxes is the fourth highest in the country.

Closing costs in New York are split between the buyer and the seller with the buyers paying appraisal and recording fees, title insurance, New York City mortgage tax, and miscellaneous condo fees. Buyers are also responsible for any costs related to preparation of the condo board package, i.e., applications, credit reports, contracts, financial statements, etc. Sellers, on the other hand, pay the broker commission, transfer tax and fees, and equalization fee.

Essential legal distinctions

The characteristics that distinguish condos from other types of housing include the following:

- Ownership of a condo consists of a unit of airspace and an undivided interest in common elements which is shared with other owners

- Condominiums are created by a developer's declaration

- Condos are managed by a condo owners association and management personnel

- Condos are governed by the association's bylaws

- Condo owners share in the expenses of common areas

HOUSING COOPERATIVES

Definition
Lease & shares
Interests, rights and obligations
Organization and management
Essential distinctions

Definition

A housing-cooperative, or co-op, is an organization that allows property ownership through shared resources and management. The co-op is a member-based and member-operated organization that owns real estate properties of one or more residential units. It is typically organized as a non-profit entity.

Lease & shares

In a cooperative, owners own **shares** in a non-profit corporation or *cooperative association*, which in turn acquires and owns an apartment building as its principal asset. Along with this stock, the shareholder acquires a **proprietary lease** to occupy one of the apartment units. Each resident jointly owns and governs the property and is responsible for meeting any related obligations. Ownership of a unit ties to ownership of stock in the corporation that owns the co-op structure through a fee simple interest or a leasehold interest. The shareholder will own the shares and propriety lease for the cooperative corporation's life or until the shareholder transfers those interests to someone else (a new shareholder or an existing shareholder).

The size of an owner's share is determined by the size of the apartment. The number of shares purchased reflects the value of the apartment unit in relation to the property's total value. The ratio of the unit's value to total value also establishes what portions of the property's expenses the owner must pay. Rather than paying rent, the shareholder owner pays a monthly fee to the corporation to cover the owner's share of the expenses. The cooperative is charged tax on the entire property as a whole rather than separately for each unit. Consequently, the corporation pays the tax bill. Then, shareholders each pay their proportionate share of that unit's taxes as part of the monthly maintenance fee.

Exhibit 17.2 The Cooperative

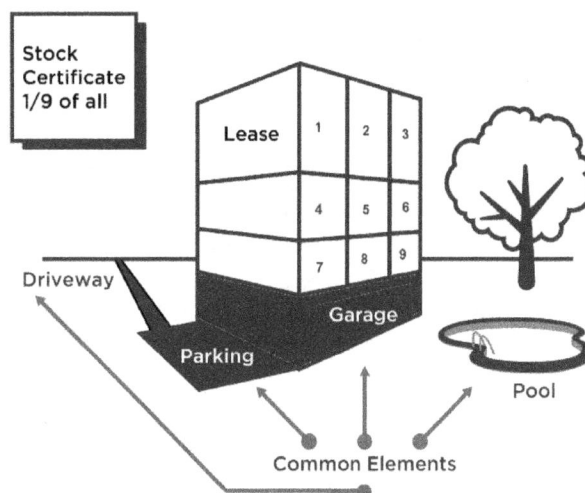

The exhibit shows a nine-unit apartment building. A cooperative corporation buys the building for $900,000. All nine units are of equal size, so the corporation decides that each apartment represents a value of $100,000, or 1/9 of the total. The co-op buyer pays the corporation $100,000 and receives 1/9 of the corporation's stock. The shareholder also receives a proprietary lease for apartment 1. The shareholder is now responsible for the apartment unit's pro rata share of the corporation's expenses, or 11.11%.

Interests, rights and obligations

Cooperative association's interest. The corporate entity of the cooperative association is the only party in the cooperative with a real property ownership interest. The association's interest is an undivided interest in the entire property. There is no ownership interest in individual units, as with a condominium.

Shareholder's interest. In owning stock and a lease, a co-op unit owner's interest is *personal property* that is subject to control by the corporation. Unlike condominium ownership, the co-op owner owns neither a unit nor an undivided interest in the common elements.

Proprietary lease. The co-op lease is called a proprietary lease because the tenant is an owner (proprietor) of the corporation that owns the property. The lease has no stated or fixed rent. Instead, the proprietor-tenant is responsible for the unit's pro rata share of the corporation's expenses in supporting the cooperative. Unit owners pay monthly assessments. The proprietary lease has no stated term and remains in effect over the owner's period of ownership. When the unit is sold, the lease is assigned to the new owner.

Expense liability. The failure of individual shareholders to pay monthly expense assessments can destroy the investment of all the other co-op owners if the co-op cannot pay the bills by other means.

Since the corporation owns an undivided interest in the property, debts and financial obligations apply to the property as a whole, not to individual units. Should the corporation fail to meet its obligations, creditors and mortgagees may foreclose *on the entire property.* A completed foreclosure would terminate the shareholders' proprietary lease and bankrupt the owning corporation. Compare this situation with that of a condominium, in which an individual's failure to pay endangers only that individual's unit, not the entire property.

Transfers. The co-op interest is transferred by assigning both the stock certificates and lease to the buyer.

Organization and management

A developer creates a cooperative by forming the cooperative association, which subsequently buys the cooperative property. The association's articles of incorporation, bylaws, and other legal documents establish operating policies, rules, and restrictions.

The shareholders elect a board of directors. The board assumes the responsibility for maintaining and operating the cooperative, much like a condominium board. Cooperative associations, however, also control the use and ownership of individual apartment units since they are the legal owners. A shareholder's voting power is proportional to the number of shares owned.

Essential distinctions

The characteristics that distinguish housing cooperatives from other types of housing include the following:

▸ Housing cooperatives are formed under the New York Business Corporations Law ("BCL"). They are subject to additional regulations mandated by the Real Property Actions and Proceedings Law ("RPAPL") and the New York General Business Law Section 352-e ("GBL"), which governs real estate syndication. There are also low-income housing cooperatives, which are generally created under the Business Corporations Law and Article XI of the Private Housing Finance Law.

▸ Under regulations implemented by the Attorney General's Office, co-op sales must adhere to the terms and conditions of an offering plan, just as condos sales do.

- In New York City, co-ops make up 75% of housing compared to condos at 25%. However, at any given time, the number of condos on the market is considerably higher than the number of co-ops.

- Closing costs for co-ops include the seller paying a flip tax, a stock transfer tax, a move-out fee, and miscellaneous co-op fees, along with several city and state fees.

- Since ownership of a co-op is owning shares and not real property, mortgage recording tax does not apply to co-ops.

Additionally, cooperative finances were drastically impacted in 2019 by the passing of the *New York Housing Stability and Tenant Protection Act* which included an unintentional error when it joined commercial landlords with cooperative boards. The Act contained provisions to protect tenants' rights in landlord-tenant relationships. However, since there is no landlord-tenant relationship in co-ops, the provisions were inadvertently applied to co-op shareholders as though co-ops were rental housing.

In doing so, co-ops could no longer ask for escrows from financially marginal applicants. The escrows were to protect the co-op in case these applicants became shareholders who could not meet their monthly maintenance payments. Without the escrows, other shareholders would need to pay escalated payments to cover the expenses. Under the Act, escrows and prepayments were limited to one month's rent, or security deposit. Consequently, co-ops were forced to reject applicants with limited financial resources.

In 2021, 2 years after the HSTPA was passed, the New York State Legislature passed A. 350-C (Braunstein) and S. 5105-C (Liu), referred to as the Braunstein/Liu Bills. These Bills corrected the error by separating co-ops out of the HSTPA, so they are no longer grouped in with landlords and rental properties. The Bills restored co-ops' authority to charge application fees, late fees, attorney fees, etc. so other shareholders are not charged for non-paying shareholders' proportionate shares of the expenses.

17 Condominiums and Cooperatives Snapshot Review

CONDOMINIUMS

Definition
- a hybrid form of ownership of multi-unit residential or commercial properties; one airspace unit together with the associated interest in the common elements

Condominium creation
- often occurs by converting apartment buildings; requires condo disclosure statement filed with the attorney general's office; declaration and master deed need to be executed; then board of directors need to be appointed

Condominium creation issues
- tenant non-eviction plans for current tenants in a conversion

Governance
- rules, regulations, bylaws, HOA govern the owners, tenants, and activities

Airspace and common elements
- airspace within outer walls, floors, ceiling of unit
- common elements include land, structure of building, operating systems supporting all units, recreational facilities, building and ground areas such as parking areas

Condominium acquisition
- involves offering plan with terms and conditions of sale to obtain a fee simple ownership

Letters of Intent
- similar to offer to purchase with fewer details; if accepted, will then need an offer

Certificate of Occupancy
- provided when construction or major modifications are complete; shows legal use and type of occupancy

Title issues
- unpaid tax lien; zoning restrictions; missing information or errors in the deed; fraud

Closing costs
- split between buyer and seller

Essential legal distinctions
- unit of airspace and undivided interest in common elements; created by a developer's declaration; managed by a condo owners association; owners share in the expenses of common areas

HOUSING COOPERATIVES

Definition
- an organization that allows property ownership through shared resources and management; member-based and member-operated organization that owns real estate properties of one or more residential units

Lease & shares
- one owns shares in a non-profit corporation or cooperative association, which in turn acquires and owns an apartment building as its principal asset; shareholder acquires a proprietary lease to occupy one of the apartment units; ownership of a unit ties to ownership of stock in the corporation

Interests, rights, obligations
- co-op association's interest; shareholder's interest; proprietary lease; expense liability; transfers

Organization and management

- association's articles of incorporation, bylaws, and other legal documents establish operating policies, rules, and restrictions; shareholders elect a board of directors; cooperative associations, control the use and ownership of individual units

Essential distinctions

- formed under business corporation laws; require offering plan for sales; unique closing costs; no mortgage recording tax; make up 75% of NYC housing

SECTION SEVENTEEN:
Real Estate Investments & Business Opportunity
Brokerage

Section Quiz

17.1. To convert a property into a condominium, a condominium disclosure statement must be filed with the attorney general's office. Which of the following is included in this statement?

  a. Survey of land, common elements, and all units
  b. Covenants and restrictions regarding use and transfer of units
  c. Identification of each unit's share of ownership in the overall property
  d. Report of the building's physical condition prepared by an architect or engineer

17.2. Common elements are defined as all portions of a property that are necessary for the existence, operation, and _____ of the condominium units.

  a. enjoyment
  b. regulation
  c. maintenance
  d. insurance

17.3. A _____ is an organization, typically a non-profit, that serves as the legal vehicle for property ownership through shared resources and management.

  a. housing-cooperative
  b. condominium
  c. residential collective
  d. multifamily enterprise

17.4. Which of the following differentiates a proprietary lease from a typical lease?

  a. A proprietary lease includes maintenance responsibilities for the entire building.
  b. A proprietary lease has no stated term.
  c. A proprietary lease allows for subletting without restrictions.
  d. A proprietary lease is only valid for commercial properties.

17.5. What kind of interest does a co-op resident have in the co-op?

  a. Real property interest
  b. Rental interest
  c. Personal property interest
  d. Leasehold interest

17.6. Which of the following is the best definition of a condominium unit?

  a. A fee simple ownership of a unit of airspace unit together with an associated interest in the common elements
  b. One living space within a condominium building
  c. A cluster of attached homes with general ownership of both the land and each individual home
  d. An entire building including all individual units and common areas, managed collectively by the homeowners' association

17.7. A cooperative shareholder obtains a _____ to occupy one of the apartment units.

  a. fee simple deed
  b. lease
  c. proprietary lease
  d. permit

17.8. What is the main purpose of a condominium's owners' association?

  a. To provide individual maintenance services to each unit owner
  b. To represent the condominium owners in municipal government meetings
  c. To appraise and assess the value of each condominium unit annually
  d. To enforce the bylaws and manage the overall property

17.9. Which act drastically altered the process of converting apartment buildings into condominiums in New York City?

    a. Emergency Tenant Protection Act
    b. New York Housing Stability and Tenant Protection Act
    c. Sherman Antitrust Act
    d. Federal Trade Commission Act

17.10. What does a co-op resident actually own?

    a. Their unit
    b. Their unit and an interest in the common areas
    c. Shares in the organization
    d. Nothing

17.11. New York City has regulations to protect tenant rights during an apartment building-to-condominium conversion. A(n) _____ prohibits the conversion unless 51% or more of the existing tenants agree to purchase their apartments as condos.

    a. eviction plan
    b. conversion threshold
    c. tenant consensus
    d. non-eviction plan

17.12. Condominium owners' associations are usually headed by a(n) _____ that organizes how the property will be managed and by whom.

    a. council
    b. executive committee
    c. board of directors
    d. advisory board

17.13. Which party or parties have a real property ownership interest in a cooperative residential building?

    a. The corporate entity of the cooperative association
    b. Each unit owner
    c. The board of directors
    d. The tenants collectively

17.14. Cooperative apartment dweller Marcus is selling to buyer Pamela because he is moving to Chicago. How will Marcus transfer his co-op interest to Pamela?

    a. By signing a purchase agreement and transferring the deed
    b. By assigning both the stock certificates and proprietary lease to Pamela
    c. By placing the property in a management trust for the corporation to handle the transfer
    d. By subletting the apartment to Pamela with management approval

17.15. In a cooperative association, which party controls the use and ownership of individual apartment units?

    a. Each owner of their own unit
    b. The board of directors
    c. The cooperative association
    d. The executive committee

18 Commercial and Investment Properties

Investment Foundations
Types of Investments
Real Estate as an Investment
Real Estate Investment Entities
Real Estate Investment Property Types
Investment Property Analysis
Commercial Property Concepts

INVESTMENT FOUNDATIONS

Characteristics
Rewards
Risks

Characteristics

The idea of investment is simple: take something of value and put it to work in some way to increase its value over time. With any investment, one wants the original investment to grow, without losing it. This idea is called **conservation of capital**. Unfortunately, no investment is truly secure. External conditions change, and the investment itself can change. Even if you do nothing with it, its value does not remain constant.

Risk versus return. The general rule in investments is that the safer the investment, the more slowly it gains in value. The more you want it to gain, and the more quickly, the more you must risk losing it. How much do you want to earn, and how much are you willing to risk to earn it? Reward in investing corresponds directly to the degree of risk.

Management. Another aspect of investment is the amount of attention you must pay to it to make it work. You can deposit cash in a passbook account and forget about it. You can use your cash to buy a business and then run the business yourself to make your asset grow and earn. How much do you want to be involved in managing your investment?

Liquidity. The issue of exchangeability is an important one in investment. How easy is it to recover your invested resource, without loss, and exchange it for another one that you want? If there is a **market** for the type of resource you have-- other people want to buy and sell it for themselves-- your investment is **liquid**. The most liquid form of financial investment is generally cash, since cash is itself a medium of exchange and people always want it. A more illiquid investment is one which takes a long time to exchange for something you prefer to own. How long are you willing to wait to recover your invested resource and its earnings?

Rewards

The basic aim of financial investment is to increase one's wealth, to add value to what you have. This can occur in several ways.

Income. An investment can generate income in some way on a periodic basis. You may consume this cash, spending it for goods and services that, when used up, have no further value. Or, you may use the cash to put into another investment.

Appreciation. Your invested asset itself may gain value over time because of an increase in market demand for it. When you sell or exchange it for something else you prefer to have, you get more than you originally put into the investment.

Leverage. You may pledge the value of your resource to borrow funds in order to make an investment that is larger than your own resource permits you to do directly. The small resource is used as a lever to make a larger investment, and thus increases your opportunity to benefit from income, appreciation, and the other rewards of investment.

Tax benefits. Some investments receive treatment under tax laws that enables the investor to reduce or defer the amount of tax owed. Tax dollars you don't have to pay are dollars you have available for some other use, such as consuming or further investing.

Risks

Investment risks come from a variety of general sources, including the market, business operations, the value of money, and changes in the interest rate.

Market risk. Changes in the demand for your invested resource may cause your investment to lose value and to become illiquid. Such changes may include job growth, population trends, and inflation.

Business risk. Changes in the operation of a business with which your investment is connected may reduce or eliminate the income- and appreciation-earning capacity of your investment. These changes can compromise the estimation of net operating income from the property's financial activities going forward.

Business risks factors include the following:

  ▶ **Static risk** – unforeseen events such as arson, theft, vandalism, damage from rain or lightning which do not change often

  ▶ **Systemic risk** – events that affect the entire real estate market, such as changes in the economy and interest rates, regulations such as zoning laws and taxes

  ▶ **Dynamic risk** – events that are difficult to predict, such as sudden changes in the economy such as pricing and income changes, environmental changes that result in physical danger, technology changes

  ▶ **Location risk** – location of the investment within a metropolitan area, crime rates, neighborhood dynamics, age of the area

> ▸ **Operator risk** – experience and track record of the individual or team that manages the property

Capital risk. Capital risk is defined as the loss of part or all of the initial investment. It can occur from market fluctuations, negative business outcomes, and speculative ventures.

Purchasing power risk. Changes in the value of money as an exchange medium, such as through inflation, may decrease the practical value of your invested resource.

Financial risk. Changes in financial markets, particularly in interest rates, may reduce the value of your investment by making it less desirable to others and by making it more expensive for you to maintain.

An investment may fail to produce any or all of the desired investment rewards listed earlier. The expected income may not be realized. The invested asset may fail to appreciate as expected. It may even decline in value. Perhaps even worse, you may be called on to **add** to the investment just to keep it in place. Your leverage may turn against you, becoming **negative leverage**. This is the situation when your cost of borrowing funds to make the investment becomes greater than the income the investment returns to you. Finally, your expectation of a tax advantage may be disappointed. Tax laws are constantly changing.

TYPES OF INVESTMENTS

Money investments
Debt investments
Equity investments
Real estate investments

Four of the most important types of investment are investments in money, equity, debt, and real estate.

Money investments
A money investment is one in which the basic form of the investment remains money. Examples are: deposit accounts, certificates of deposit, money funds, and annuities. The basic reward from a money investment comes in the form of interest. Money investments are relatively safe, with correspondingly conservative rates of return.

Debt investments
A debt investment is one in which an investor buys a debt instrument. Examples are bonds, notes, mortgages, and bond mutual funds. The basic reward comes in the form of interest. Debt investments are usually riskier than money investments and less risky than stocks or real estate.

Equity investments
An equity investment is one in which an investor buys an ownership interest in a business concern. Examples are stocks and stock mutual funds. The basic rewards

come in the form of dividends and appreciation of share value. Equity investments are generally riskier than money and debt investments.

Real estate investments

A real estate investment is one in which an investor *buys real estate for its investment benefits rather than primarily for its utility*. It may have the features of both an equity and debt investment, depending on the type of real estate involved and numerous other factors, such as the type of interest one owns. A real estate investor may invest in an income-producing property or a non-income producing property.

Income property is a property owned specifically for the investment rewards it offers. Examples are multi-family residential properties, retail stores, industrial properties, and office buildings. Rewards come in any or all of the forms mentioned earlier: income, appreciation, leverage and tax advantages.

Non-income property is a residential property used as the investor's primary residence. The basic reward, beyond the enjoyment of use, comes in the form of appreciation. There may also be tax benefits, depending on how the purchase is financed.

REAL ESTATE AS AN INVESTMENT

Risk and reward in real estate
Illiquidity of real estate
Management intensiveness

Real estate investments participate in the general risks and rewards of all investments. However, real estate investments are often complex. They are also distinguished by their lack of liquidity and by the amount of management they require. In addition, each investor has specific aims and circumstances that affect the viability of any particular real estate investment for that individual. Licensees who lack expertise in the area of real estate investment analysis should refer potential investors to a competent advisor. Nevertheless, a licensee should be familiar with the basics of real estate as an investment.

Risk and reward in real estate

Capital put into real estate is always subject to the full range of risk factors: market changes, income shortfalls, negative leverage, tax law changes, and poor overall return.

Market demand for a specific type of property can decline. For example, a business district's retailers may vacate stores in an area in order to obtain better space in a new shopping center. Market downturns leave the income property investor with an unmarketable property or one which can only be re-leased at a loss of some portion of the original investment. Thus, the expected reward from income or appreciation may never be obtained.

Another risk of the investment property is the cost of development or operation. If start-up costs or ongoing operating costs exceed rental income, the owner must dip into additional capital resources to maintain the investment until its income increases. If income does not rise, or if costs do not decline, the investor can simply run out of money.

Leverage is a constant risk in real estate investment. If the property fails to generate sufficient revenue, the costs of borrowed money can bankrupt the owner, just as development and operating costs can. Investors often overlook the fact that leverage only works when the yield on the investment exceeds the costs of borrowed funds.

Tax law is an ongoing risk in long-term real estate investment. If the investor's tax circumstances change, or if the tax laws do, the investor may end up paying more capital gains and income taxes than planned, undermining the return on the investment. An investor needs to consider carefully the value of such potential tax benefits as deductions for mortgage interest, tax losses, deferred gains, exemptions, and tax credits for certain types of real estate investment.

Another consideration is *opportunity cost*. Opportunity cost is the return that an investor could earn on capital invested with minimal risk. If the real estate investment, with all its attendant risk, cannot yield a greater return than an investment elsewhere involving less risk, then the opportunity cost is too high for the real estate investment. Despite all the risks, real estate remains a popular investment, because, historically, the rewards have outweighed the risks. Real estate has proven to be relatively resistant to adverse inflationary trends that have hurt money, debt, and stock investments. In addition, real estate has proven to be a viable investment in view of the economy's continued expansion over the last fifty years.

Illiquidity of real estate

Compared with other classes of investment; real estate is relatively illiquid. Even in the case of liquidating a single-family residence, one can expect a marketing period of at least several months in most markets. In addition, it takes time for the buyer to obtain financing and to complete all the other phases of closing the transaction. Commercial and investment properties can take much longer, depending on market conditions, leases, construction, permitting, and a host of other factors. The investor who is in a hurry to dispose of such an investment can expect to receive a lower sales price than may be ideal. Compare this with the ease of drawing money out of a bank account or selling a stock.

Management intensiveness

Real estate tends to require a high degree of investor involvement in management of the investment. Even raw land requires some degree of maintenance to preserve its value: drainage, fencing, payment of taxes, and periodic inspection, to name a few tasks. Improved properties often require extensive management, including repairs, maintenance, onsite leasing, tenant relations, security, and fiscal management.

REAL ESTATE INVESTMENT ENTITIES

Direct
Syndicates and Partnerships
Real estate investment trusts
Real estate mortgage investment conduits

Direct

Individuals, corporations or other investor entities may invest as **active investors** in a property by buying it directly and taking responsibility for managing and operating the property.

Syndicates and Partnerships

A real estate **syndicate** is a group of investors who combine resources to buy, develop, and/or operate a property.

A **general partnership** is a syndicate in which all members participate equally in managing the investment and in the profits or losses it generates. The group designates a trustee to hold title in the name of the syndicate.

A **limited partnership** is a syndicate in which a **general partner** organizes, operates and is generally responsible for the partnership's interests in the property. **Limited partners** invest money in the partnership but do not participate in operating the property. These limited partners are **passive investors**.

Real Estate Investment Trusts (REIT)

In a Real Estate Investment Trust, investors buy certificates in the trust, and the trust in turn invests in mortgages or real estate. Investors receive income according to the number of shares they own. A trust must receive at least 75% of its income from real estate to qualify as a REIT; and if certain other conditions are met, the trust does not have to pay any corporate income tax.

Office REITs invest in office properties, which are then leased as office spaces to companies. Such REITs focus on developing or acquiring large-scale commercial properties and are responsible for managing and leasing them to tenants.

Real Estate Mortgage Investment Conduits (REMIC)

In a Real Estate Investment Trust, investors buy certificates in the trust, and the trust in turn invests in mortgages or real estate. Investors receive income according to the number of shares they own. A trust must receive at least 75% of its income from real estate to qualify as a REIT; and if certain other conditions are met, the trust does not have to pay any corporate income tax.

Office REITs invest in office properties, which are then leased as office spaces to companies. Such REITs focus on developing or acquiring large-scale commercial properties and are responsible for managing and leasing them to tenants.

REAL ESTATE INVESTMENT PROPERTY TYPES

Retail properties
Offices
Residential income properties
Hotels and motels
Manufacturing properties
Unimproved land
Leasehold properties

According to use, the following classifications of real properties are commonly accepted as investment property types.

Exhibit 18.1 Classifications of Real Estate by Use

residential income	industrial
hotels and motels	mixed use
office	special purpose
retail	unimproved land

These categories are not absolute, since properties often have overlapping uses. A bank, for example, may have retail as well as office operations. An industrial distribution facility may include extensive office space. A retail center may contain offices. Residential dwellings may be income properties, such as an apartment complex.

Special purpose properties include publicly or privately owned recreational facilities, government buildings, churches and schools, and so on.

The following property types may all be utilized as investments based on the investor's plans, portfolio and expertise.

Retail properties   Retail properties, classified as commercial properties, include several types of shopping centers which all generate income from retail sales:

> ▸ Stores – Retail stores are typically free-standing and carry either one type of product, such as electronics, or a variety of products, such as food items, clothing, pharmaceuticals, and so on.

> ▸ Strip malls – These malls are rather small and contain a row of various stores and offices that are physically connected to each other. Each store typically has its own entrance directly from the parking lot. Strip malls serve their immediate community. Strip

malls may contain such businesses as an eyeglass store, one or more fast food restaurants, a hair salon, dry cleaners, a thrift store, a chiropractor's office, and so on.

▶ Big box centers – Sometimes referred to as a strip mall or shopping mall, these retail centers typically contain a big box retailer, such as Home Depot, Walmart, or Target. They may also contain a large supermarket such as Publix, Safeway, or Winn-Dixie, usually located at the opposite end of the mall from the big box store. Between the two large stores, smaller stores such as electronics stores, dollar stores, clothing stores, and/or pet stores are located. These centers have large parking lots with outside entrances to each store.

▶ Shopping malls – Although some big box centers may be referred to as shopping malls, most shopping malls are physically larger and contain a larger variety and number of retail spaces. They are also enclosed with stores and offices on both sides of a center aisle. Each business has its own entrance inside the enclosure with a few main entrances to the mall located on the exterior of the overall enclosure. Shopping malls contain anchor businesses such as department stores, movie theaters, home improvement stores, along with several other types of retail shops and offices. It is not uncommon to find an eyeglass retailer next to a pet store or craft shop.

▶ Regional malls – These shopping centers are the largest of all retail malls typically with 400,000 to 800,000 square feet of gross leasable space. Some of the super-regional malls are even larger than that. They are enclosed with main entrances from the exterior of the mall to the interior walkway. Along the interior walkway, each individual business has its own entrance. Multiple large anchor stores, such as department stores, multiscreen movie theaters, furniture stores, and home improvement stores, are located within the mall and serve to draw customers into other smaller businesses within the mall, thereby increasing sales for the smaller retailers. The malls are typically multilevel with the anchor stores having at least two levels while different smaller businesses are located on each level.

Office space

Office space is another class of commercial real estate providing consistent and predictable rental income and stability, making office spaces advantageous as long-term investments. When it comes to commercial office real estate, the variety of companies and industries that utilize the space choose it based on their particular needs. For some, location is critical while others are more concerned about cost and staying within a budget. Many are also drawn to the rentals based on building services, amenities, parking, technology, building infrastructure, and security.

Offices spaces can be constructed as one space in one building or multiple office spaces within one building, often with multiple levels. They come in a variety of sizes from a small single-tenant space to high-rise buildings with many tenants and businesses. The size and height of the building is dependent on needs and zoning restrictions. In many cities, such as New York City, building heights are restricted for a variety of reasons, such as fire or aviation dangers, view protection, character of the district, etc.

Some investors have shifted their focus from strictly location of the office space to providing return on the investment. For example, rather than the focus being on prime business locations, the focus changes to locations that are closer to suburban areas and employees' homes, thus lessening travel time and fuel costs.

Regardless of the investor's focus, from a valuation standpoint, because office space draws a diverse base of end-users that span a variety of industries, it has a long track record of delivering solid returns.

Residential properties

Residential property refers to property that is owned and used for habitation. Such properties may be further classified in terms of how many families they are designed to house, whether they are attached to other units or detached, and so forth. Return on investment in residential property is based on whether the property is purchased to be sold at a profit or to generate income as rental housing. Return on investment is also greater with multi-family housing and apartment buildings and complexes because the income is constant from month to month or year to year. The more units, the higher the income, and the greater return on investment.

When classifying residential property as an investment, owner-occupied properties are not included even though such properties are indeed an investment. Residential apartments, condominiums, cooperatives, and single-family homes may be considered as investment property if the property is owned for investment purposes and the owner does not reside on the property. These properties are also referred to as residential income properties.

Hotels and motels

Hotel and motel properties are classed as commercial hospitality properties and not residential properties. The income or return on investment of these properties is largely dependent on tourist trade in the area and the overall economy. It can also be impacted by unforeseen events like the pandemic in 2020 which resulted in record-low occupancy and profitability.

Manufacturing properties

Manufacturing properties include the following types of buildings:

▸ Heavy industrial properties – provide a place for manufacturing of raw materials into useful products

▸ Light manufacturing properties – provides a facility for assembly and distribution of products

Unimproved land

Investment in unimproved land allows the investor to choose how to develop the land and for what industry or usage. Given the location of the land, the investor may have the option of developing retail or office spaces or even residential dwellings. The investor may even choose to hold onto the land until demand leads to a particular type of development. Of course, return on investment will not be seen while the land is simply being held. However, once demand rises and the investor develops the land to meet the demand, the investor should see a lucrative return on investment. When obtaining unimproved land as an investment, the location of the land plays a critical part in the future of the investment.

Leasehold properties

With a leasehold property, the lease provides the right to occupy a property for a specific lease term, but the land itself belongs to the landowner (freeholder). The leaseholder is required to **pay land rent** and service charges to the landowner and may be restricted from making **modifications** to the property.

In contrast, a freehold property is one wherein the landowner owns the building and the land on which the building sits and has full control and responsibility of the property. Freehold owners may modify the property as they wish.

Leasehold properties can make good investments, especially in locations with high land prices. Benefits of leaseholds include the following:

- ▶ The upfront cost of obtaining the leasehold is low.

- ▶ Based on where the property is located, the rental income can be high for the investor, providing a strong return on investment.

- ▶ By carefully considering the location and property management of the leasehold, it can increase in value over time, optimizing the return on investment.

- ▶ No mortgage or insurance needs to be obtained for the leased property.

- ▶ The landowner is responsible for maintenance and repairs.

As with any investment, leaseholds also carry disadvantages or risks:

- ▶ Leaseholds do not build equity.

- ▶ The landowner's rights may supersede the leaseholder's rights.

- ▶ The value of the property decreases as the lease begins to expire, resulting in a lower sale price than purchase price and lower return on investment.

- ▶ The lease may contain a clause that allows for increases in land rent and service charge payments.

INVESTMENT PROPERTY ANALYSIS

Commercial leases
Deriving pre-tax cash flow
Identifying taxable income and tax liability
Identifying after-tax cash flow
Investment return analysis

Commercial leases   A commercial lease may be a net, gross, or percentage lease, if the tenant is a retail business. As a rule, a commercial lease is a significant and complex business proposition. It may involve hundreds of thousands of dollars for improving the property to the tenant's specifications. Since the lease terms are often long, total rent liabilities for the tenant can easily be millions of dollars.

Some important features of commercial leases are:

▶   long term, ranging up to 25 years

▶   require tenant improvements to tailor the premises to particular usage needs

▶   virtually all lease clauses are negotiable due to the financial magnitude of the transaction

▶   default can have serious financial consequences; therefore, lease clauses must express all points of agreement and be very precise

Net leases. Net leases in commercial real estate require the tenant to pay a base rent amount plus any number of the property's operating expense items. Net leases are commonly used in office and industrial leases.

A net lease for a single-tenant property makes the tenant responsible for the net rent and most or all other property expenses. A net lease for a multi-tenant property makes each tenant responsible for their own stated rent and other negotiated operating expenses that can be directly attributed to the tenant. Unallocated operating and maintenance expenses that remain are then proportionately split among all of the tenants to be paid in addition to the rent – or absorbed by the landlord.

Gross leases. In a gross lease, or a full-service lease, the tenant pays an established, fixed rent, and the landlord pays all property operating expenses, such as taxes, insurance, utilities, and other services, from the rent payments received.

Either a gross lease or net lease may include rent escalation clauses which allow the landlord to increase the rent enough to cover increased costs of property expenses. Escalation clauses are typically included in leases for more than two years.

Escalation clauses are typically used in commercial property leases with multiple units such as office buildings. Gross leases without escalation clauses are commonly used in residential leases.

Percentage leases. A percentage lease may be gross or net, but the rent is not fixed. Instead, the rent amount depends on the income generated by the tenant in the leased property. A common arrangement is to set a fixed base rent plus a percentage of the tenant's gross income or sales at the site. The percentage calculation may take effect only when the tenant's income reaches a certain level. This level is referred to as the natural breakeven point. This arrangement is commonly used in retail leases.

The formula used to determine the percentage is as follows:

Natural breakeven = annual rent + percentage of sales

The higher the annual rent, the lower the percentage that is collected due to the breakeven point needing to be higher so the tenant can earn profits. The lower the annual rent, the higher the percentage because the breakeven point would also be lower.

Loft leases. Loft leases are used for storage and warehousing where the landlord does not need to include any services in the rent.

Loft leases are also used when a former industrial building has been turned into a modern apartment and falls under the control and requirements of the New York City Loft Board. Once the loft apartment(s) are legally established, they can be leased at current market values.

Ground lease. A ground lease, or **land lease**, concerns the land portion of a real property. The owner grants the tenant a leasehold interest in the land only, in exchange for rent.

Ground leases are primarily used in three circumstances:

  ▸ an owner wishes to lease raw land to an agricultural or mining interest

  ▸ unimproved property is to be developed and either the owner wants to retain ownership of the land, or the developer or future users of the property do not want to own the land

  ▸ the owner of an improved property wishes to sell an interest in the improvements while retaining ownership of the underlying land

In the latter two instances, a ground lease offers owners, developers, and users various financing, appreciation, and tax advantages. For example, a ground lease lessor can take advantage of the increase in value of the land due to the new improvements developed on it, without incurring the risks of developing and owning the improvements. Land leases executed for the purpose of development or to segregate ownership of land from ownership of improvements are inherently long-term leases, often ranging from thirty to fifty years.

**Deriving pre-tax
cash flow**

Cash flow. Cash flow is the difference between the amount of actual cash flowing into the investment as revenue, and out of the investment for expenses, debt service, and all other items. Cash flow takes into account cash items only, and therefore excludes depreciation, which is not a cash expense.

Pre-tax cash flow, or cash flow before taxation, is calculated as follows:

Pre-tax cash flow

	potential rental income
-	**vacancy and collection loss**
=	**effective rental income**
+	**other income**
=	**gross operating income (GOI)**
-	**operating expenses**
-	**reserves**
=	**net operating income (NOI)**
-	**debt service (principal and interest)**
=	**pre-tax cash flow**

Potential rental income is the annual income amount that would be realized if the property is fully leased or rented at the scheduled rate. Vacancy and collection loss is rental income lost due to vacancies or tenants' failure to pay rent.

Effective rental income is the potential income adjusted for these losses where vacancy – or estimated vacancy – is subtracted out.

Other income is any other income the property generates, such as from laundry or parking charges. When other income is added to effective rental income, the result is the investment's maximum "top line," or **gross operating income**.

Operating expenses paid by the landlord include such items as utilities, repairs and maintenance. These outflows are deducted from gross operating income.

Reserves. Many real property investment owners set aside a cash reserve each year to build up an accrued fund for capital replacements in the future, for example, to replace a roof or a furnace.

Note that *cash reserves are not deductible for tax purposes until spent as deductible repairs or maintenance*. Note also that reserves are not necessary in deriving an investment's performance. If they are not spent, they simply amount to taxable income to the investor.

Net operating expenses (NOI). The remainder of gross operating income minus expenses and reserve allowances is **net operating income** (NOI). Generally, NOI is the *number used to derive an investment's pre-tax return* and is therefore a key figure to identify in investment analysis.

Debt service. When the annual amounts paid for debt service, *including principal and interest*, is subtracted from net operating income, the remainder is the investment's **pre-tax cash flow**. Ultimately, pre-tax cash flow is how much cash came into the investment minus how much cash went out – before accounting for taxes.

For instance, a consider that a small office building of 3,500 square feet rents at $20 per square foot per year. If fully rented, the annual rental income would be $70,000. Historically, we will assume, the property averages $4,200 in annual vacancy and collection losses. Equipment rental will provide an additional $2,000 per year in income. The owner will have to pay operating expenses amounting to ten dollars per square foot, or $35,000 per year. The owner sets aside one dollar per square foot, or $3,500 per year, for reserves. The owner financed the purchase of the building with a loan that requires annual debt service in the amount of $20,000. The pre-tax cash flow for the building is illustrated in the following exhibit.

Pre-tax Cash Flow Illustration

	potential rental income	$70,000
-	vacancy and collection loss	4,200
=	effective rental income	65,800
+	other income	2,000
=	gross operating income	67,800
-	operating expenses	35,000
-	reserves	3,500
=	net operating income (NOI)	29,300
-	debt service	20,000
=	pre-tax cash flow	$9,300

Identifying taxable income and tax liability

The owner's tax liability on income from the property is based on *taxable income rather than cash flow*. To get to taxable income from pre-tax cash flow requires accounting for reserves, depreciation, and interest paid on the loan. More specifically, reserves, which are not tax deductible, must be added back in to taxable income. Depreciation, on the other hand, is deductible, so that must be taken out of taxable income. And finally, loan interest is deductible, so that must be deducted from taxable income.

Taxable income. Taxable income and tax liability are derived from NOI as follows:

Tax Liability

	net operating income (NOI)
+	reserves (added and not spent)
-	interest expense
-	cost recovery expense
=	taxable income
x	tax rate
=	tax liability

Taxable income is net operating income minus all additional allowable deductions plus the amount allocated for reserves (since those unspent amounts are not taxable).

Depreciation, reserves and loan interest. To reiterate, **cost recovery expense, or depreciation** is allowed as a deduction from income for tax purposes, while allowances for **reserves** and payments on loan principal payback are not allowed as tax deductions. Since reserves were deducted from gross operating income to determine NOI, this amount *must be added back in.* On the loan payments, as only the interest portion of debt service is deductible, the principal amount must be removed from the debt service payments and the *interest expense deducted from NOI.* The remainder is **taxable income.** Taxable income is then *multiplied by the owner's marginal tax bracket,* to estimate the investment's **income tax liability**.

Note on tax rate: when a rental property is owned as an individual or by way of a pass-through entity (partnership, LLC treated as a partnership for tax purposes, or S corporation), its net income is taxed at the individual's personal marginal income tax rate. The next exhibit shows the tax liability for the previous example using an assumed individual rate of 24%.

Tax Liability Illustration

	net operating income (NOI)	29,300
+	reserves	3,500
-	interest expense	10,000
-	cost recovery expense	22,000
=	taxable income	800
x	tax rate (24%)	
=	tax liability	192

In the example, $3,500 in reserves must be added back to net income. Then, $10,000 interest and $22,000 depreciation (non-cash) are deducted from (net income + reserves). (Note that principal payments on the loan are not deductible.) This calculation results in $800 taxable interest. At a 24% rate, the investor's tax liability is $192.

Identifying after-tax cash flow

After-tax cash flow is simply the amount of income from the property that actually goes into the owner's pocket after income tax is paid. It is figured as pre-tax cash flow minus taxes:

After-tax cash flow

	Pre-tax cash flow
-	tax liability
=	after-tax cash flow

The after-tax cash flow for the sample property is illustrated in the following exhibit.

After-tax Cash Flow Illustration

	pre-tax cash flow	9,300
-	tax liability	192
=	after-tax cash flow	9,108

Investment return analysis

There are numerous types of investment return, each of which tells investors how well an investment has performed in a given area of its financial results. Examples include cash-on-cash, return on equity, return on investment, payback period, and internal rate of return. For the present context, we will examine the most common return ratios used in investment analysis: return on investment; return on cash; and return on equity. Each form of return uses the same three components on an investment: it's income, its value or price, and its rate of return.

Forms of investment return. There are numerous types of investment return, each of which tells investors how well an investment has performed in a given area of its financial results. Examples include cash-on-cash, return on equity, return on investment, payback period, and internal rate of return. For the present context, we will examine the most common return ratios used in investment analysis: return on investment; return on cash; and return on equity. Each form of return uses the same three components on an investment: it's income, its value or price, and its rate of return.

Income. The income component of an investment answers the question "how much money does the investment generate." This is derived by adding up total income and taking out all the relevant expenses.

More importantly, when considering whether to make an investment, a second question that must be answered is "how much money _should_ the investment generate, given its price and given the investor's required rate of return. The second question requires the investor to solve the basic return formula for income:

(Investor's required return X Value (or Price)) = Income;
or (R x V) = I

Here, to justify the investment of a given amount of money and to meet the investor's required rate of return given all the risks, the investment must generate a specific amount of income.

Take, for example, a building priced at $3 million. The investor, who must generate a 15% pre-tax return on these types of properties, completes the formula (R x V) = I and realizes the property must generate $450,000 to be worth her trouble ($3MM x 15% = $450,000). The bottom line: if this property does in fact generate $450K or more, the investment is justified.

Value or price. The value, or price, component of an investment answers the question "what is the price or value of the investment?"

In the case where an investor is considering whether to make an investment, the related question that must be answered is "how much money *should* the investment cost, given its income and given the investor's required rate of return. To answer this, we basically move the same I-R-V equation around to solve for Value:

Income ÷ Rate of return = Value or Price

Here, to justify an investment that generates a given amount of income and to meet the investor's required rate of return given all the risks, the investment must have a specific maximum price. Returning to our example, if we are considering a property that generates $300,000, and we require a minimum return of 10%, then the property must be priced at no more than $3 million. ($300,000 ÷ 10% or .10) = $3 million.)

Take, for example, a building priced at $3 million. The investor, who must generate a 15% pre-tax return on these types of properties, completes the formula (R x V) = I and realizes the property must generate $450,000 to be worth her trouble ($3MM x 15% = $450,000). The bottom line: if this property does in fact generate $450K or more, the investment is justified.

Rate of return. The third component of investment performance is the investment's rate of return, or the percent of return, or yield rate. Expressed as a percent, this number answers the question, "what is my return on the investment given its price and investment performance.

Rate of return is perhaps the most important index of an investment's performance, since it ultimately tells an investor how much money he or she can make given the amount of money the investor has to invest.

To derive rate of return, we reconfigure the same equation into its third expression:

Income ÷ Price = Rate of return

Returning to the example, we can see that the given $3,000,000 property which generates $450,000 has an investment return of 15 % ($450 K ÷ $3 million) = 15%.

Using these three equations enable investors to assess either what a property's price should be given its income and the investor's required return; what its income should be given a price and required return; and what its return is given its income and price. To review these equations, we have:

Income = Rate or return x Value or Price

Value or Price = Income ÷ Rate of return

Rate of Return = Income ÷ Value or Price

Investment performance analysis. There are three principal forms of investment returns used to evaluate investment properties. They are return on investment; cash-on-cash return, and return on equity. These are expressed in formulas as follows:

Return on investment:
net operating income ÷ price = return on investment (ROI)

Cash-on-cash return:
cash flow ÷ cash invested = cash-on-cash return (C on C)

Return on equity:
net operating income ÷ equity = return on equity (ROE)

Deriving return on investment. This is the most primary measure of an investment's performance. As discussed, it compares the investment's net income to the price paid for the investment. From our previous analysis, this would be net operating income (NOI) divided by the total price paid for the property. Reviewing our illustration, we have:

Income ÷ Price = Rate of return
$450,000 ÷ 3,000,000 = 15%

Deriving cash on cash return. If an investor wants to know his or her investment inclusive of financing, the investor must use the C on C performance measure. As shown, this is expressed as cash flow divided by cash invested. For example if our illustration example had a million dollar loan for underlying financing, and its debt service was $50,000, its C on C return would be:

($450,000 – 50,000), or $400,000 cash flow ÷ $2 million cash invested = 20%

Deriving return on equity. Many investors want to know the return on their total stake in an investment which can include not only the initial cash invested, but the accumulated depreciation, equity build-up, and appreciation of the investment as expressed by its current market value.

The formula for equity is market value (or accumulated book value) minus total current debt principal. In our example, let's assume all factors reducing the property's equity totals $800,000 (1 million loan minus some principal paydown plus nominal appreciation minus accumulated depreciation). The current market value is estimated to be $3,000,000. Thus, the investor's current equity is $2.2 million (3 million – 800,000). From the original example, net operating income is posited at $450,000.

Therefore, the property's return on equity is:

return on equity (ROE) = (net operating income ÷ equity)

$450,000 Net income ÷ **2.2 million equity = 20.4%**

Note also that some investors prefer to use cash flow to derive ROE. This would change the formula to be (cash flow ÷ equity) instead of (net income ÷ equity).

COMMERCIAL PROPERTY SPACE MEASUREMENT

Usable vs rentable area
Carpetable area

Usable vs rentable area

Usable and rentable square feet are terms commonly used in commercial leasing to describe the two principal types of office or retail space measurement and directly impact the amount of rent a tenant will pay. The most important difference to understand between usable and rentable square feet is that it is the property's rentable area, not its usable area, that will be used to calculate the annual rent.

Usable area. Usable area is the actual space within the commercial building that a tenant can occupy and use, the area to be physically occupied by offices, conference rooms, workstations, storage spaces, and other functional areas within the leased space. Usable area, measured in square feet, does not include common hallways, elevators, stairwells, building amenities, or other areas used by multiple tenants. However, there are no deductions in the usable area measurements to account for the space taken up by columns, walls, partitions, recessed entries, and other such factors. Prospective tenants need to identify how much space they need to occupy in usable terms, then *add on the additional space* taken up by non-usable areas such as elevators.

Rentable area. A rentable area is measured in square feet and includes the space that is designated for an individual tenant's use as well as a proportionate share of the building's common areas, such as hallways, elevators, lobbies, restrooms, stairwells, and any other area shared by multiple tenants. Common areas are taken into account because they contribute to the building's functionality and desirability of the building.

Rent is determined by assigning a certain dollar amount per square foot (of rentable space) then multiplying that amount by the total area of the space plus the amount for the proportionate share of the common areas. It is typical for larger areas, such as an entire floor in the building, to lease for higher per-square-foot rent than smaller areas such as a portion of a floor. Because the landlord allocates a portion of the building's common areas to each tenant in proportion to the size of their usable space, larger areas would also be assigned a higher rent for the common areas, thus adding to the total rent amount.

States may determine their own standards of calculating base rent in relation to square footage and proportionate common areas. In New York, the base rent is calculated on a dollar-per-square-foot annual amount while other areas may calculate the rent on a monthly basis. New York has no laws or regulations mandating how rentable areas are to be calculated, so it is common for landlords to use arbitrary or traditional calculations. However, members of the Real Estate Board of New York and the Building Owners and Managers Association tend to follow the guidelines provided to them by these local boards.

Loss (load) factor. The loss factor (also called the load factor) is the amount of space a tenant pays for but cannot use or does not have exclusive use of. It includes areas such as lobbies, elevators and elevator shafts, mechanical areas, interior structural components such as walls and support poles, parking garages, and so forth.

The loss factor is the ratio between the rented area and the usable area in the building. To calculate the loss factor (LF), subtract the usable square footage (USF) from the rentable square footage (RSF) and then divide that number by rentable square footage.

> **Example:**
> **7,000 square feet RSF – 5,000 square feet USF = 2,000 square feet**
> **2,000 square feet ÷ 7,000 square feet = 0.285 or 28.5% loss factor**

In the example, the tenant is paying for 7,000 square feet but is only able to use 5,000 square feet. Expressed another way, the tenant is paying for 100% of the space but only able to use 70.5% of the space. Or, the tenant is paying $X amount of rent for space with a 28.5% load factor.

Add-on factor. The add-on factor is the proportionate share of common areas that each tenant pays for as part of their rent. It is the difference between the usable area and the rentable area, is typically expressed as a percentage, and is calculated by dividing the loss factor (LF) in square footage by the usable area.

> **Example:**
> **2,000 square feet LF ÷ 5,000 square feet USF = 0.4 or 40% add-on factor**

With an add-on factor of 40%, the total rentable square footage is calculated by multiplying the usable square footage by the add-on factor.

> **Example:**
> **5,000 square feet USF x 1.4 = 7,000 square feet RSF**

In certain areas of New York State, such as New York City, commercial building owners and landlords base the rent charged on the usable square footage rather than the rentable square footage. Because rent is not applied to the non-usable square footage, the expenses related to common areas are not covered in usable area rents. Consequently, landlords determine an add-on factor for each tenant and include that factor to the rent to provide income to cover the maintenance of those common areas.

Carpetable area

As indicated earlier, the usable area of a commercial space is the actual space within the commercial building that a tenant can occupy and use. Included in that measurement are the columns, walls, partitions, recessed entries, etc. Carpetable area, however, is the actual usable area minus measurements for restrooms, columns, walls, partitions, and other structural details that would not be covered with carpet.

When considering the difference between usable and carpetable spaces, it is important to keep in mind that some usable spaces just may not be carpetable. For example, if the office space for one tenant includes a kitchen area, men and women's restrooms, and a storage closet, those areas would be included in the usable space measurement but not in the carpetable area measurement since they are not areas that typically would be carpeted. The same is true for columns and walls which are included in the usable space but cannot be carpeted.

Consequently, when evaluating the actual space needed for an office or other commercial business, the carpetable space is most advantageous as it provides a clear picture of how much furniture and walking areas the space will allow.

COMMERCIAL PROPERTY CONCEPTS
Use clause
Attornment
Lease escalation
Proportionate share
Base year
Operating and tax stop
Porters Wage escalation

Use clause

Individuals or businesses lease space for a certain reason or use. The use clause protects the landlord by limiting the property's use to what is included in this clause. The limitations may be broad or narrow, flexible or strict, and typically are based on the type of business to be conducted on the property. Landlords may limit or restrict uses that will compete with the businesses of other tenants (if the other tenants have that understanding with the landlord), uses that could potentially result in liability issues, or even uses that the landlord personally dislikes. Operating hours, business signage,

Exclusive clause. Just as the use clause protects the landlord, an exclusive clause protects the tenant by including a promise by the landlord to restrict other tenants from engaging in like businesses or selling like products. To support one tenant's exclusive clause, other tenants' use clauses would restrict them from businesses or products that would violate the one tenant's exclusive clause.

Attornment

Leases contain the amount and schedule of rent payments and to whom the rent is to be paid. Tenants are to adhere to that section of the lease. However, if the property is sold, an attornment clause mandates the tenant is to accept the new owner as the landlord and is to continue to follow the rent payments as laid out in the lease. The new owner is responsible for taking over the previous owner's rights and responsibilities. The tenant named in the lease is to be the only one paying the rent, and the owner is to accept rent only from the party named in the lease so as to avoid the possibility of occupancy and possession rights being created for the third party who paid the rent.

Lease escalation

Commercial real estate leases always include an escalation clause. The clause allows the landlord to increase the tenant's rent at specified times and for specified reasons. Escalation clauses originally replaced fixed rent to provide landlords with the funds to cover the rising cost of expenses related to the property. Over time, rents have escalated beyond merely covering costs to providing a substantial profit margin for the property owner. The clause typically raise the rent at specified times, such as annually or at lease renewal or after a set time frame. Escalation clauses can increase the rent in several ways:

Fixed bump. With this type of rent escalation, the increase is set at a specified dollar amount per square foot of the leased space.

Percentage increase. The rent increases by a pre-determined percentage at a specified time.

Inflation-based increase. The rent increases in line with inflation increases. When inflation is low, the rent increase is low. On the flip side, when inflation rises, so does the rent increase. This type of escalation is the worst for the tenant.

Proportionate share

When the portion of a building that is occupied by one tenant is expressed as a percentage of the total rental space of the building, it is known as the tenant's proportionate share, or pro rata share. The pro rata is calculated by dividing the tenant's rentable square footage by the building's total rentable square footage. So, if the tenant's rentable area is 2,000 square feet in a building with 10,000 square feet of rentable area, calculating the tenant's proportionate share goes like this:

> **Example:**
> **2,000 ÷ 10,000 = 0.20 or 20%**

This tenant's proportionate share is 20%. Consequently, when the owner's operating expenses, taxes, and other expenses increases, the tenant's rent will increase based on the tenant's proportionate share. This increase would normally take place after the first year of the lease, known as the *base year*, or at whatever time is specified in the lease clause.

Base year

Within commercial leases, the amount of rent tenants pay to property owners and the amount and timing of rent increases is included in the terms of the lease. To determine how much rent the tenant will pay, leases utilize a *base year*, which is typically the first year of the rental period. That base year sets the precedent for how much tenants will pay for building expenses for each year after the base year. After the first year, landlords determine how much operating costs were per square foot of the building.

For example, if operating costs were $10 per square foot, the tenant will be charged that amount every year of the lease. Then, if the building's operating costs rise above that $10 per square foot after the base year, the tenant's proportionate share of the increase will be added to the original $10 per square foot. As operating costs increase year to year, the tenant's rent will increase year to year in line with the tenant's proportionate share.

Operating and tax stop

Operating costs are typically determined in a dollar amount per square foot. When a specified amount of operating costs is set in the lease as the landlord's responsibility, the tenant is not charged for that expense. That set amount is known as the *stop* amount. However, if and when the operating costs exceed the stop amount, the tenant is then charged additional rent to cover the difference between the stop amount and the increased amount.

Porters Wage escalation

The term porter refers to individuals who perform certain types of labor such as cleaning, maintenance, building engineering, etc. Typically, these laborers belong to a union that negotiates with building owners for the laborers' pay rate and scheduled pay raises. Porter's wage is the minimum hourly pay the commercial property laborers are paid for a typical 40-hour workweek. Scheduled pay raises are used as an index for adjustments based on inflation. Porter's wage is a calculation formula that bases salary increases on square footage rent.

The formula is calculated on a pennies-per-penny basis wherein as operating expenses increase by a certain amount, so does the laborers' hourly wage and the tenants' per-square-foot rent. Every penny of wage increase is matched by a penny increase in per-square-foot rent. If the wage is increased by $2.00 per hour, or 200 pennies per hour, the tenant's rent is equally increased by 200 pennies ($2.00) per square foot.

The porter's wage formula is based on the assumption that the cost of labor determines the cost of cleaning and directly relates to the size of the building. Larger buildings require higher labor costs resulting in higher cleaning costs.

The pennies-per-penny formula was used mostly in New York City. Other areas of the State used simpler methods based on inflation resulting in a percentage increase each year. This formula did not account for the idea that labor costs are actually only a portion of the total cost of cleaning and maintenance. Consequently, balancing the cost of labor with the cost of cleaning was not successful.

18 Commercial and Investment Properties
Snapshot Review

INVESTMENT FOUNDATIONS

Characteristics
- the greater the risk, the higher the expected return
- some investments require more investor involvement than others
- some investments are more liquid (convertible to cash) than others

Rewards
- investors seek to increase wealth through income, appreciation, leverage and tax benefits

Risks
- risks: changes in supply and demand for the investment (market risk), changes in businesses with which the investment is connected (business risk), changes in the value of money (purchasing power risk), and changes in interest rates (financial risk)

TYPES OF INVESTMENTS

Money investments
- the real estate investor must weigh the potential risks and returns inherent in market variability, expected vs. real income, use of borrowing leverage, changes in tax treatment of capital gains and income, and the cost of capital

Money investments
- real estate is generally less liquid than other investment types: it takes time to market a property

Equity investments
- real estate tends to require more investor involvement than other investments do: maintenance, management, operation

Real estate investments
- real estate tends to require more investor involvement than other investments do: maintenance, management, operation

Exemptions from property taxes
- the real estate investor must weigh the potential risks and returns inherent in market variability, expected vs. real income, use of borrowing leverage, changes in tax treatment of capital gains and income, and the cost of capital

REAL ESTATE AS AN INVESTMENT

Risk and reward in real estate
- Risks: market downturns; cost of development or operation; reverse leverage; changing tax laws; opportunity cost

Illiquidity of real estate
- Real estate is relatively illiquid investment; not easily convertible to cash

Management intensiveness
- Real estate is relatively management intensive in terms of manpower required to sustain profitability

REAL ESTATE INVENSTMENT

ENTITIES
- Business entities employed for making real estate investments include individuals, groups of investors who form syndicates and partnerships, and REITS which allow investors to make security investments in shares of the business acquiring investment properties. REMICs are available as debt instruments for groups of passive investors

REAL ESTATE INVESTMENT PROPERTY TYPES

Retail properties
- stores, malls, retail centers – location dependent; use percentage leases; depend on mix of retail center

Offices	•	headquarters; branches; single or multi-tenant users; net or gross leases
Residential income properties	•	apartment complexes; rented dwellings; shorter leases
Hotels and motels	•	hospitality properties; quasi-retail, location dependent, tourist dependent
Manufacturing properties	•	light to heavy industrial facilities; highly use-specific
Unimproved land	•	property to be developed; highest and best use critical

INVESTMENT PROPERTY ANALYSIS

Commercial leases	•	net, gross or full service; percentage; ground lease
Investment analysis	•	pre-tax cash flow; tax liability; after-tax cash flow
Investment return analysis	•	Return on investment; cash on cash return; return on equity
Deriving ore-tax cash flow	• •	annual pre-tax cash flow is net operating income minus debt service foreign sellers subject to withholding of tax on gain by buyers
Identifying taxable income and tax liability	• •	gross income received minus allowable expenses, deductions and exclusions the seller of a principle residence owes tax on any capital gain that results from the sale unless excluded; capital gain is defined as the amount realized minus the adjusted basis
Investment return analysis	•	return on investment; return on cash; and return on equity based on its income, its value or price, and its rate of return

COMMERCIAL PROPERTY SPACE MEASUREMENT

Rentable vs usable area	•	usable area is the actual space within the commercial building that a tenant can occupy and use; the space that is designated for an individual tenant's use as well as a proportionate share of the building's common areas
Carpetable area	•	usable area that is carpetable within the confines of the demised area; e.g., excluding kitchens; bathrooms; storage areas; support columns; equipment rooms

COMMERCIAL PROPERTY CONCEPTS

Use Clause	•	limits property's use to what is included in the clause
Attornment	•	mandates the tenant is to accept the new owner as the landlord and is to continue to follow the rent payments as laid out in the lease
Lease Escalation	•	allows the landlord to increase the tenant's rent at specified times and for specified reasons

Proportionate share • portion of a building that is occupied by one tenant and expressed as a percentage of the total rental space of the building

Base year • first year of the rental period

Porters Wage escalation • minimum hourly pay the commercial property laborers are paid for a typical 40-hour workweek with scheduled pay raises used as an index for adjustments based on inflation

CHAPTER EIGHTEEN: COMMERCIAL AND INVESTMENT PROPERTIES

Section Quiz

18.1. An example of a debt investment is

    a. annuities.
    b. non-income property.
    c. bonds.
    d. stocks.

18.2. Why is real estate considered an illiquid investment?

    a. Selling a property typically takes several months and involves complex processes.
    b. Real estate always generates lower returns compared to other investments.
    c. Property values are guaranteed to decrease over time.
    d. Real estate transactions have no associated costs or delays.

18.3. What makes office space a desirable class of commercial real estate investment?

    a. High turnover rates and frequent vacancies
    b. Limited demand from companies and industries
    c. Consistent rental income and long-term stability
    d. Lack of building services and amenities

18.4. Choose the investment reward this statement describes: Your invested asset itself may gain value over time because of an increase in market demand for it.

    a. Income
    b. Leverage
    c. Appreciation
    d. Tax benefits

18.5. Gabe, Bobby, Sheila, and Al purchased an investment property together, a 10-unit apartment building. Gabe is a real estate broker, and he manages the property himself, advertising for and screening tenants, arranging for maintenance and upkeep, and the like. Bobby, Sheila, and Al invested money but do not have a direct hand in operations. Which type of investment entity does this scenario describe?

    a. Direct
    b. General partnership
    c. Limited partnership
    d. REIT

18.6. How is the owner's tax liability on income from a property calculated?

    a. Based solely on cash flow
    b. By adding depreciation and loan interest to cash flow
    c. By adjusting pre-tax cash flow for reserves, depreciation, and loan interest
    d. Based only on the amount of reserves set aside

18.7. Which of the following scenarios would most affirmatively argue for a land lease?

    a. A former warehouse building has been renovated into a modern apartment on each floor.
    b. An owner of a duplex lives in one unit, rents the other unit, but retains all rights to the back yard.
    c. A developer builds a strip mall to rent space to retail businesses.
    d. An owner wants to lease raw land to a cattle company.

18.8. One form of investment analysis used to evaluate investment properties is _____, which compares the investment's net income to the price paid for the investment.

    a. return on investment
    b. cash on cash return
    c. return on equity
    d. income

18.9. Which statement concerning commercial leases is true?

    a. Commercial leases typically have short terms and minimal tenant improvements.
    b. Commercial leases can involve high financial stakes.
    c. All commercial lease clauses are non-negotiable and standardized.
    d. Defaulting on a commercial lease usually has minor financial consequences.

18.10. When a commercial property is sold, the attornment clause in the lease

a. allows the new owner to increase the tenant's rent at specified times and for specified reasons.
b. protects the new owner by limiting the property's use to what is included in this clause.
c. protects the tenant by including a promise by the new owner to restrict other tenants from engaging in like businesses or selling like products.
d. mandates the tenant is to accept the new owner as the landlord and is to continue to follow the lease's specified rent payments.

18.11. A(n) _____ investment is one in which an investor buys real property primarily for its investment benefits rather than for its utility.

a. real estate
b. equity
c. debt
d. money

18.12. The return an investor could earn on capital invested with minimal risk is called

a. leverage.
b. cost of operation.
c. market demand.
d. opportunity cost.

18.13. What does usable area in a commercial building refer to?

a. The space leased by a tenant that includes common hallways, elevators, and building amenities
b. The area that includes space taken up by the structure's columns and walls
c. The actual space a tenant can occupy and use for offices and other functional areas
d. The total area of the building including all tenant and common areas

18.14. In a _____ lease, the tenant pays an established, fixed rent, and the landlord pays all property operating expenses.

a. net
b. ground
c. gross
d. percentage

18.15. Which of the following is a risk factor associated with investing in real estate?

a. Market changes
b. Guaranteed income
c. Positive leverage
d. Fixed returns

18.16. What factor is most important in determining the liquidity of an investment?

a. The ease in which it can be converted to cash
b. The potential for the investment to gain value quickly
c. The overall return on investment over a long period
d. The stability of the investment's value over time

18.17. Commercial real estate leases normally include an escalation clause. With a(n) _____ escalation, the increase is set at a specified dollar amount per square foot of the leased space.

a. economic outlook
b. inflation-based increase
c. percentage increase
d. fixed bump

18.18. What does cash flow in real estate investment refer to?

a. The total value of the property including depreciation
b. The difference between cash revenue and cash expenses, excluding depreciation
c. The property's appreciation over time
d. The total amount of debt service only

18.19. Investment risks come from a variety of general sources, such as dynamic risks, which are

a. the loss of part or all of the initial investment.
b. changes in financial markets, particularly in interest rates, that may reduce the value of an investment.
c. changes in the operation of a business with which an investment is connected
d. events that are difficult to predict, such as environmental changes that result in physical danger.

18.20. One measurement of commercial property area is the actual usable area minus area used for restrooms, columns, walls, partitions, and other structural details. This net amount is called

a. specific usable area
b. carpetable area
c. functional area
d. operational area

18.21. Which of the following properties would be classified as residential income property?

a. A vacation home used exclusively by the owner
b. An owner-occupied triplex with two units rented to tenants
c. A single-family home rented to tenants
d. A primary residence occupied by the owner

18.22. How is rent typically determined in a commercial building?

a. Multiplying the dollar amount per square foot by the usable space only
b. Multiplying the dollar amount per square foot by the rentable area of the space
c. Assigning a fixed amount regardless of the space size
d. Considering only the total rentable space without including common areas

18.23. How does a Real Estate Investment Trust (REIT) work?

a. Investors buy certificates in a REIT that invests in mortgages or real estate, and receive income based on rental payments, property sales, and mortgage interest.
b. Investors buy property directly from a REIT and manage it themselves, receiving income from rental payments.
c. Investors purchase individual properties and sell them to other members of a REIT for a profit.
d. Investors in a REIT invest solely in residential real estate and earn income from management fees.

18.24. How is after-tax cash flow from a property calculated?

a. Adding tax liability to pre-tax cash flow
b. Adding reserves and depreciation to pre-tax cash flow
c. Subtracting pre-tax cash flow from tax liability
d. Subtracting tax liability from pre-tax cash flow

18.25. Which type of lease is most commonly suited for storage and warehousing uses?

a. Ground
b. Percentage
c. Net
d. Loft

18.26. The main point of investing in property is for the original financial investment to grow instead of diminish. This concept is known as

a. risk versus return.
b. liquidity.
c. conservation of capital.
d. leverage of investment.

18.27. Some investments enjoy benefits under tax laws that enable the investor to

a. reduce or defer the amount of tax owed.
b. pass the tax bill along to tenants.
c. avoid paying tax altogether.
d. increase the property's market value without tax implications.

18.28. Investor Damien uses the value of his current investment property as collateral to borrow funds to invest in a more expensive property than he could buy directly using his own resources. This benefit of investment is called:

a. appreciation.
b. income.
c. leverage.
d. liquidity.

18.29. When changes in the demand for an investor's invested resource cause the investment to lose value and become illiquid, what investment risk has impacted the investor?

a. Business risk
b. Systemic risk
c. Market risk
d. Operator risk

18.30. Which of the following is a money investment?

    a. Mortgages
    b. Stock mutual funds
    c. Certificates of deposit
    d. Income property

18.31. Which type of investment requires a high degree of investor involvement?

    a. Money
    b. Equity
    c. Real estate
    d. Debt

18.32. What is the definition of a real estate syndicate?

    a. A real estate developer creates an LLC to develop multiple properties in an area
    b. A sole investor purchases multiple single-family homes in a neighborhood to rent out
    c. Investors purchase certificates in a trust that invests in real estate
    d. A group of investors combine resources to buy, develop, and/or operate a property

18.33. When an investor buys unimproved land as an investment, which criterion plays a primary part in the future of that investment?

    a. The land's location
    b. Current zoning
    c. Property taxes
    d. The land's size

18.34. _____ leases in commercial real estate require the tenant to pay a base rent amount plus any number of the property's operating expense items.

    a. Gross
    b. Net
    c. Percentage
    d. Ground

18.35. What is the component of investment performance that answers the question, "What is my return on the investment given its price and investment performance?"

    a. Cash-on-cash return
    b. Value or price
    c. Return on investment
    d. Rate of return

19 Income Tax Issues in Real Estate Transactions

Tax Reform Act of 2018
Calculating Capital Gain
Like-Kind Exchange
Low-Income Housing Tax Incentives

TAX REFORM ACT OF 2018

Standard deductions
Homeowner deductions
Points and closing costs
Active vs passive income

In December 2017, President Trump signed into law a tax reform called the Tax Cuts and Jobs Act (TCJA), known as the Tax Reform Act of 2018. The Act went into effect on January 1, 2018, as the biggest reform of the U.S. tax code since 1986.

The Act incorporated the following major changes:

▶ A reduction in business and individual tax rates, with the corporate tiered tax rate up to 35% based on taxable income changed to a flat 21%, thereby benefitting businesses through a lower federal corporate tax rate.

▶ Changes to tax brackets and individual income tax, retaining the previous seven tax brackets but lowering the rates in all but the lowest bracket and setting these changes to expire after 2025

▶ An increase in the standard deduction (almost double) and family tax credits (double)

▶ Elimination of personal exemptions

▶ A reduction in the alternative minimum tax for individuals

▶ Elimination of alternative minimum tax for corporations

▶ A doubling of the estate tax exemption

▶ A 40% estate tax for estates valued at $11.2 million and higher as opposed to the $5.6 million value prior to the Act

- Elimination of the penalty for not complying with the Affordable Care Act mandate to obtain health care coverage

- An added tax on survivors benefits for children of deceased military members, resulting in an income tax rate up to 37%

Overall, the Act lowered income tax rates for higher-income tax payers and corporations, and left the tax brackets for the lowest income filers intact.

Exhibit 19.1
Tax Brackets for Single Filers Prior to 2018 Tax Reform

Taxable Income	Marginal Rate
$0–$9,525	10%
$9,525–$38,700	15%
$38,700–$93,700	25%
$93,700–$195,450	28%
$195,450–$424,950	33%
$424,950–$426,700	35%
$426,700 and up	39.6%

As shown in the following exhibit, the Act left the number of income tax brackets at seven but changed the income ranges in several brackets, giving most brackets lower rates and, consequently, lower individual income taxes. The one exception is the lowest bracket where the rate was not changed. These marginal rates apply to income in the indicated range prior to the Act, so a higher income taxpayer will have income taxed at different rates until 2025 when these changes are set to expire.

Exhibit 19.2
Tax Brackets for Single Filers for 2018 Tax Year
(First Year of Tax Reform)

Taxable Income	Marginal Rate
$0–$9,525	10%
$9,525–$38,700	12%
$38,700–$82,500	22%
$82,500–$157,500	24%
$157,500–$200,000	32%
$200,000–$500,000	35%
$500,000 and up	37%

Exhibit 19.3
Tax Brackets for Single Filers for 2023 Tax Year

Taxable Income	Marginal Rate
$11,000 or less	10%
$11,001 to $44,725	12%
$44,726 to $95,375	22%
$95,376 to $182,100	24%
$182,101 to $231,250	32%
$231,251 to $578,125	35%
$578,126 and over	37%

Standard deductions

Under the Act, taxpayers may choose to write off either their standard deduction or itemize deductions. The standard deduction for single taxpayers in 2018 had increased from $6,350 to $12,000. For married taxpayers, filing jointly in 2018, the standard deduction had increased from $12,700 to $24,000. In 2024, The deduction for single taxpayers is $14,600 and for married couples filing jointly is $29,000. There are other standard deduction amounts for the aged, blind, and heads of households.

Homeowner deductions

When choosing between taking the standard deduction or itemizing deductions, taxpayers will want to keep in mind which is the higher amount and which real estate deductions are now restricted under this law.

The law allows for two types of deductions related to real estate: real property taxes and mortgage interest.

Property taxes. Real property taxes can be deducted for a primary home, co-op apartment, vacation home, land, cars and other vehicles, and boats. The deduction is limited to $10,000 or $5,000 if taxpayers are married and filing separately. The deduction is applied to a combination of property taxes and sales taxes or either state and local income taxes. The deduction can only be applied to the tax filing for the same year the taxes were paid.

Because of some eliminated deductions, property owners are expected to have paid and will continue to pay higher taxes under the tax reform. The eliminated deductions include interest on mortgage debt in excess of $750,000 and on home equity debt.

Mortgage interest. One of the changes under the 2018 Act restricted mortgage interest deductions to the first $750,000 of a taxpayer's primary and vacation home debt. Prior to this Act, the limit was $1 million. This change only applied to new mortgage loans taken out after December 15, 2017; so preexisting mortgage loans were not impacted.

Home equity loan interest. Another change affected home equity loan interest. Prior to the 2018 reform, a taxpayer could fully deduct the interest on a $100,000 home equity loan, regardless of how the funds were spent. Under the Act, interest on a home equity loan is only deductible if the funds were used to make substantial improvements to the property.

Mortgage insurance deduction. From year to year, Congress decides whether or not to allow a mortgage insurance deduction. If a taxpayer files without using that deduction and then learns that Congress has approved it for that year, the taxpayer may file an amended return.

Points and closing costs

Points. When purchasing a home, closing costs can be significant. Unfortunately, those costs are not tax deductible, with one exception: points that may have been paid in order to lower the interest rate on the mortgage. Each point costs 1% of the amount borrowed for the mortgage. For example, if a borrower obtains a $400,000 mortgage loan, each point would cost $4,000. When the points are applied to the loan, each one lowers the loan interest rate by ¼ of a percent, or 0.25%. Thus, if the mortgage loan's interest rate is 5%, one point would lower that rate to 4.75%; two points would lower the rate to 4.5%. The lowered rate extends throughout the life of the loan.

Borrowers purchasing points can deduct the cost of the points in full but only in the year the points were purchased and only if the following contingencies are met:

- The mortgage is for buying or building the taxpayer's primary residence at a cost not to exceed $750,000.

- Using points is a common practice in the area where the loan is obtained and the cost of the points is common for the area.

- Payments for the points is documented.

- Funds used to pay for the points are not borrowed

- The cost of the purchased points is included on the loan's closing documents.

Closing costs. A real estate purchase transaction is completed at the closing with each party to the transaction given a closing disclosure that itemizes costs and expenditures related to the transaction. These include brokers' compensation, property inspection costs, title search and insurance fees, and so on. In most cases, closing costs average between 3 and 6 percent of the mortgage loan amount. That can vary based on the amount of downpayment paid outside of borrowed funds.

Although mortgage points are deductible at tax time, other closing costs are not unless the home buyer paid real estate taxes upfront. If so, those taxes may be deductible in the same year as they were paid.

Other closing costs such as legal and recording fees, title insurance, credit checks, and so forth are not deductible. However, these costs do provide a tax benefit: they can be added to the cost basis if and when the home is later sold. By doing so, the homeowner's profit from the sale is decreased which reduces any capital gains tax due when the home is sold.

Active vs passive income

Under the Tax Reform Act of 2018, **active income** is money earned through employment to include wages, salaries, commissions, tips, self-employment, and overtime pay.

On the other hand, **passive income** does not require the recipient's involvement or employment activities. Dividends, interests, rents, royalties, stocks, and bonds are all forms of passive income. Most passive income is taxable.

Taxable income includes wages, salaries, commissions, tips, bonuses, some capital gains, self-employment income, gambling winnings, unemployment compensation, royalties, and rental income.

Non-taxable income includes child support, municipal bonds interest, proceeds from life insurance, disability benefits, gifts, inheritances, and some capital gains.

CALCULATING CAPITAL GAINS

Appreciation
Depreciation
Capital gains and recapture

Over time, a property may increase or decrease in value, based on several contributing factors, such as market changes, supply and demand, home improvements, damage or lack of repair to the structure, zoning changes, and more. The increase in value is referred to as **appreciation** while the decrease in value is referred to as **depreciation**.

Appreciation

Appreciation is the increase in value of an asset over time. A simple way to estimate appreciation on a primary residence is to subtract the price originally paid from the estimated current market value:

Current value - original price = total appreciation

For example, if a house was bought for $300,000 and its estimated market value now is $400,000, it has appreciated by $100,000.

Original price:	$300,000
Current market value:	$400,000
Total appreciation:	$100,000

Total appreciation can be stated as a percentage increase over the original price by dividing the estimated total appreciation by the original price.

The house in the above example has appreciated by 33%:

$$\frac{(Total\ appreciation)}{Original\ price} = \%\ appreciated$$

$$\frac{100,000}{300,000} = 33\%$$

To estimate the percentage of *annual appreciation*, divide the percent appreciated by the number of years the house has been owned:

$$\frac{\%\ total\ appreciation}{years\ owned} = \%\ appreciation\ per\ year$$

If the house in the previous example has been owned for three years, the annual appreciation has been 11%.

$$\frac{33\%}{3\ years} = 11\%\ appreciation\ per\ year$$

Depreciation

Depreciation is the *loss of value in an improvement over time*. Since land is assumed to retain its value indefinitely, depreciation only applies to the improved portion of real property. An important difference between income and non-income properties is that deductions for depreciation are allowed on income properties. Depreciation, also referred to as cost recovery, is not allowed for non-income properties except for that portion of a non-income property which is used to produce income. The part of a property which can be depreciated is called the **depreciable basis**.

When determining depreciation there are three factors to consider:

    ▸   Cost of the asset, i.e., the purchase price

    ▸   Salvage value, i.e., the asset's value at the end of its useful life

    ▸   Useful life, i.e., the number of years or periods of the asset's expected use

Salvage value. To determine the asset's salvage value, first, determine the number of years the asset will be useful. Then determine the amount of annual depreciation. Next, multiply the number of years by the annual depreciation amount. Finally, subtract that amount from the original purchase price.

Purchase price – (annual depreciation amount x number of years) = Salvage Value

Straight line. The straight line depreciation is the most commonly used method for determining the depreciation of a capital asset. This method reduces the value of an asset over time until the asset reaches its salvage value. The depreciated value is calculated by subtracting the salvage value from the asset cost and then dividing the result by the years or periods of useful life of the asset.

> cost of asset
> - salvage value
> ÷ years of useful life
> = annual depreciation amount

Recovery periods. Residential rental properties are depreciated over a period of 27.5 years. The basic annual deduction for such property is 3.636%, with adjustments for the month of the taxable year in which the property was placed in service. Non-residential income properties placed in service after 1994 are depreciated over a period of 39 years (basic annual percentage is 2.564%).

Depreciable basis. The depreciable basis, or depreciation base, is the original purchase cost of a fixed asset minus the salvage value (minus land value).

Annual depreciation expense. The dollar amount of depreciation each year is called the annual depreciation expense and is calculated as follows:

Depreciable basis ÷ years of useful life = annual depreciation expense

Capital gains and recapture

A property's value at time of sale along with the actual selling price will determine whether or not the seller will see a profit from the sale. If the property value has appreciated and it sells for more than what was paid for it, the amount of profit above the original purchase price is considered a profit or **capital gain**. If it has depreciated and sells for less than its original purchase price, the seller has experienced a **capital loss**.

There are two types of capital gains: short-term and long-term. When the property is purchased, held for less than a year, and then sold at a profit, that is considered a short-term gain. If the property is purchased and held onto for 1 or more years before being sold at a profit, that is deemed a long-term gain.

Under the Tax Reform Act of 2018, capital gains are taxed. Short-term gains are taxed as income and at income bracket rates. Taxes on long-term gains are restricted to a maximum 0-20% based on the taxpayer's income bracket.

Taxpayers with capital gains may qualify for an **IRS Section 121 home sales tax exclusion** of up to $250,000 of the gain if filing single or up to $500,000 of the gain if a married couple files a joint return. To qualify for the exclusion, the taxpayer must meet the following:

▸ The home must be the primary residence.

▸ The taxpayer must have owned the home for at least 2 years within the 5-year period prior to selling the home.

▸   The taxpayer must have actually lived in the home for at least 2 years within the 5-year period prior to the home's sale.

        o   However, the 2 years do not need to be consecutive; temporary absences are allowed, such as vacations, healthcare stays, military or foreign services.

▸   The taxpayer may not have claimed the exclusion on another home within 2 years of this home's sale.

▸   The house cannot have been obtained through a like-kind exchange within the past 5 years.

▸   The homeowner may not be subject to the expatriate tax, i.e., may not have given up U.S. citizenship or residency status to live abroad.

▸   The homeowner must report the sale of the home even if the capital gain from the home's sale qualifies for the exclusion.

The IRS defines gain on the sale of a home as **amount realized** from the sale minus the **adjusted basis** of the home sold.

Amount realized. The amount realized, also known as **net proceeds from sale**, is expressed by the formula:

$$sale\ price\ -\ costs\ of\ sale\ =\ amount\ realized$$

Adjusted basis. Basis is a measurement of how much is invested in the property for tax purposes. Assuming that the property was acquired through purchase, the **beginning basis** is the cost of acquiring the property. Cost includes cash and debt obligations and other settlement costs. The adjusted basis includes the cost of purchasing the property plus capital expenditures made to improve the property minus allowable depreciation.

The basic formula for **adjusted basis** is:

          beginning basis
+   capital improvements
-     exclusions, credits or other amounts received

=   adjusted basis

For example, Mary and Larry originally paid $200,000 for their home. They spent an additional $10,000 on a new central heating and cooling unit. Their adjusted basis at the time of selling it is therefore $210,000.

Exhibit 19.4 Gain on Sale

	Selling price of old home	$350,000
-	Selling costs	35,000
=	Amount realized	315,000
	Beginning basis of old home	200,000
+	Capital improvements	10,000
=	Adjusted basis of old home	210,000
	Amount realized	315,000
-	Adjusted basis	210,000
=	Gain on sale	105,000

Gain on sale is taxable unless it qualifies for an exclusion.

In the case of Mary and Larry, their capital gain was $315,000 - $210,000, or $105,000. They will owe tax on this amount in the year of the sale unless they qualify for the home sales tax exclusion.

Installment sales. Gains on sale and taxation of gains can vary if the home is sold through installment payments rather than through a mortgage loan and lump sum payment. With an installment sale, the buyer pays the purchase price in payments to the seller. The installment contract lays out the terms of the payment amounts and schedule along with the term of the contract.

The buyer does not receive the title until the contract is paid in full. Because the seller is not receiving the full price for the home all at once, taxes are paid only on the installment payments received during the particular tax year. The same pattern of installment and tax payments continues year after year until the installment contract is paid in full.

Recapture. Under the 2018 Act, depreciation claimed on earlier years' returns must be recaptured at a rate of 25%.

If the owner of an income property with a depreciable basis of $550,000 uses a 27.5-year depreciation schedule, the total depreciation taken over 5 years will be $100,000 ($550,000 ÷ 20 years = 20,000 x 5 years = $100,000). $550,000 minus the $100,000 total depreciation leaves an adjusted basis of $450,000. Consequently, this owner has $100,000 that must be recaptured at a 25% tax rates.

LIKE-KIND EXCHANGES

1031 Exchanges

Prior to the Tax Reform Act of 2018, the Internal Revenue Code Section 1031 allowed the deferment of capital gains taxes on what was called "like-kind exchanges" to include real, personal, and business property. With the signing of the Act, 1031 exchanges continued to allow exchanges of like-kind real property, but eliminated exchanges of other types of property.

1031 Exchanges   Since the changes in 2018, the U.S. Internal Revenue Code Section 1031 now only includes trade, business, and investment real property. Under 1031, investors may sell one property and reinvest the proceeds in another property, or in essence, exchange properties with another owner. By reinvesting, the tax liability from the sale of the first property is postponed.

However, there are restrictions that must be followed. First, both the sold and the purchased properties must be used for trade, business, or investment. Most importantly, the properties must be of "like kind." That is, they must both be of the same nature or character, such as both being apartment buildings. They may be different styles or even different quality, but they must be for the same type of use. Further, the properties must be located in any state within the United States or Washington, D.C. Or the U.S. Virgin Islands. Selling one property located in New York and purchasing another property in Canada does not meet the criteria of the like-kind exchange.

If one of the two properties is valued higher than the other so that a cash transfer is necessary between the buyer and seller to equalize the properties, the recipient of the cash cannot defer the tax liability on the cash. Consequently, the cash is considered capital gain (or in the exchange scenario, ***boot***) and will be taxed at income tax rates.

Originally, 1031 exchanges of ownership needed to happen simultaneously. However, the Starker family initiated a series of court cases to remove the requirement for the simultaneous timing of the exchange. The final case was won in 1979, resulting in the decision that a contract to exchange properties in the future is similar enough to a simultaneous transfer. Since this case, 1031 exchanges are now referred to as *Starker* exchanges.

To successfully and legally complete a 1031 exchange, the investor must follow these steps:

▶ Identify the investment property to be sold

▶ Hire a qualified intermediary (QI) to hold the transactional funds so the seller avoids touching the money between the sale and the new purchase

▶ List the investment property for sale with the purchase funds going directly to the QI

- Find potential replacement properties to complete the exchange; the new property must be identified within 45 days from the sale of the original property

- Purchase the replacement property within 180 days of the sale date of the original property, having the QI transfer the funds from the original property to the seller of the replacement property

- File taxes for the year of the exchange, using the appropriate tax form to notify the IRS of the exchange

Reverse exchange. A reverse 1031 exchange occurs when an investor purchases a replacement property prior to selling the original property. The rules for the reverse exchange are the same as the regular 1031 exchange with the addition of a requirement for an exchange accommodation titleholder to be used along with the qualified intermediary.

LOW-INCOME HOUSING TAX INCENTIVES

The Low-Income Housing Tax Credit is a tax credit provided to housing developers as an incentive to build, purchase, or renovate housing for low-income families and individuals. Any tax credit a developer receives can be applied fully to any federal income tax the developer may owe. The more low-income housing a developer creates, the more tax credits earned.

The federal government offers two main types of tax credits to developers to be used over a 10-year period:

- A 9% credit to be used only when the construction project does not qualify for other credits or subsidies

- A 4% credit to be used along with other tax credits

The credits are provided by the federal government to each state which then chooses developers to use the credit

19 Income Tax Issues in Real Estate Transactions
Snapshot Review

TAX REFORM ACT OF 2018

Goals of land use control
- preserve changed corporate tax rate from 35% to 21%
- changed all but one tax bracket
- increased deductions; eliminated personal exemptions

Standard deductions
- almost doubled standard deduction for single taxpayers
- taxpayers can choose standard deduction or itemize deductions

Homeowner deductions
- property tax deduction limited to $10,000
- mortgage interest deduction restricted to first $750,000 of home debt
- home equity loan interest deductible only if used for home improvements
- mortgage insurance deduction decided annually by Congress

Points and closing costs
- purchase of points at 1% of mortgage lowers mortgage rate
- deductible only in year purchased
- only mortgage points and real estate taxes paid upfront are deductible

Active vs passive income
- active income from employment; passive income from non-employment activities
- taxable income – salaries, commissions, bonuses, self employment, etc.; non-taxable income – child support, life insurance disability benefits, etc.

CALCULATING CAPITAL GAIN

Appreciation
- increase in value of asset; calculate by subtracting original price by current market value

Depreciation
- loss of value over time; land does not depreciate
- includes 3 factors: cost of asset, salvage value, useful life of asset
- straight line – method for determining depreciation

Capital gains and recapture
- profit from selling home for more than purchased is capital gain; taxable unless covered by an exclusion with restrictions
- short-term gain – held house for less than a year; long-term gain – held house for 1 or more years
- adjusted basis – how much is invested in property for tax purposes

LIKE-KIND EXCHANGE
- 1031 exchange – sell one property and buy another of like kind; tax liability postponed
- includes restrictions on type of properties and timing of purchase
- reverse exchange – investor purchases replacement property before selling original property

LOW-INCOME HOUSING TAX INCENTIVES
- developers provided tax credits as incentive to create affordable housing for low-income families

CHAPTER NINETEEN: INCOME TAX ISSUES IN REAL ESTATE TRANSACTIONS

Section Quiz

19.1. What is the flat tax rate for businesses under the Tax Reform Act of 2018?

a. 37%
b. 32%
c. 21%
d. 19%

19.2. How many tax brackets are included in the Tax Reform Act of 2018?

a. 5
b. 7
c. 9
d. 10

19.3. Under the Tax Reform Act of 2018, the standard deduction for single taxpayers

a. stayed the same.
b. increased by 5%.
c. almost doubled.
d. was eliminated.

19.4. The property tax deduction for married couples filing jointly is limited to

a. $1,500
b. $3,000
c. $5,000
d. $10,000

19.5. Taxpayers in which tax bracket benefited the least from the tax reforms in 2018?

a. Those in the highest bracket with a 37% interest rate
b. Those in the 4th and 5th brackets with interest rates of 22% and 24%
c. Those in the lowest bracket whose 10% interest rate did not change
d. Everyone benefited equally.

19.6. Should taxpayers itemize deductions or automatically take the standard deduction when filing their taxes?

a. The standard deduction because it has been increased
b. Itemize deductions to increase the amount of the deduction
c. Not itemize deductions because it is too much work
d. Whichever deduction is higher

19.7. Is a home equity loan interest deductible?

a. Only if the loan was used for substantial home improvements
b. Yes, the interest is deductible in full
c. Not unless the loan is for $100,000 or more
d. No, never

19.8. What is the cost of three points paid on a $650,000 mortgage loan?

a. $6,500
b. $65,000
c. $1,950
d. $19,500

19.9. Besides points, which closing costs are deductible?

a. Title insurance
b. Real estate taxes paid upfront
c. Broker commission
d. Legal fees paid in installments

19.10. Taxpayers may qualify for a home sales tax exclusion if they

a. owned the home for 5 years prior to selling it.
b. qualified for and used the exclusion on another home the previous year.
c. have used the home as a primary residence.
d. actually lived in the home for 2 consecutive years.

19.11. Which of the following formulas is used to calculate an adjusted basis?

   a. Beginning basis plus capital improvements minus allowable deductions equals adjusted basis
   b. Purchase price minus depreciation equals adjusted basis
   c. Sale price minus cost of sale = adjusted basis
   d. Beginning basis minus capital improvements plus amount realized equals adjusted basis

19.12. Which of the following is not a factor in determining depreciation?

   a. Purchase price
   b. Mortgage points
   c. Salvage value
   d. Useful life.

19.13. In a 1031 exchange, the replacement property must be found within how many days after selling the original property?

   a. 180 days
   b. 60 days
   c. 45 days
   d. 30 days

19.14. Which of the following parties is eligible for a low-income housing tax credit?

   a. Apartment building landlords
   b. Developers of affordable housing
   c. High rise developers
   d. Individuals selling low-income housing

19.15. What happens in a reverse exchange?

   a. The seller and buyer re-exchange the properties they bought from each other.
   b. The properties being exchanged do not need to be like-kind properties.
   c. One investor buys a replacement property before selling the original property.
   d. Both investors back out of the exchange contract.

20 Mortgage Brokerage

Mortgage Broker Defined
Mortgage Broker Responsibilities
Mortgage Broker vs Mortgage Banker
Role of Mortgage Broker in a Real Estate Transaction

MORTGAGE BROKER DEFINED

A mortgage broker is a financial professional who acts as an intermediary to bring mortgage borrowers and mortgage lenders together. In New York, they are registered by the New York State Banking Department to help individuals and businesses secure financing for real estate transactions, such as purchasing a new home, refinancing an existing mortgage, or even renovating a current home. Mortgage brokers find and negotiate mortgage loans for the borrower. They help the borrower compare rates, terms, and conditions to select and process the best loan for the individual borrower's needs.

Mortgage brokers collect a commission for their services called an origination fee. The fee is originally paid by the lender as compensation for the broker's services. However, the borrower may end up paying all or part of the fee during the closing process. The mortgage broker gets paid when the loan transaction is completed.

MORTGAGE BROKER REQUIREMENTS

To become a New York mortgage broker, one must meet the following requirements:

- ▶ Register with the New York State Banking Department

- ▶ Have 2 or more years of credit analysis experience

- ▶ Possess underwriting experience or education, unless already a licensed real estate broker or an attorney

- ▶ Provide fingerprints and credit report

MORTGAGE BROKER RESPONSIBILITIES

A mortgage broker's responsibilities include the following:

- ▶ Keeping in mind that a real estate licensee who also becomes a mortgage broker must disclose the potential dual agency to all interested clients and obtain their consent to the dual agency prior to entering into the transaction

- ▶ Educating clients about different types of mortgage loans

- ▶ Providing advice to clients on which type of mortgage works best for the client's needs

- ▶ Analyzing the client's finances (credit scores, income, employment, existing debts) to determine loan eligibility

- ▶ Evaluating and recommending appropriate lenders for the client's needs, determining interest rates, fees, and repayment terms

- ▶ Passing the client's financial information on to lenders for qualification

- ▶ Guiding clients through the loan application process by collecting related documents, completing paperwork, and ensuring all required information is provided accurately and on time

- ▶ Performing as liaison between the borrower and lenders

- ▶ Negotiating loan terms with lenders for the benefit of the client

- ▶ Following regulations and ethical guidelines, maintaining knowledge of current industry trends, legal requirements, and lender policies

- ▶ Assisting the client with concerns or issues that come up after the loan is approved

MORTGAGE BROKER VS MORTGAGE BANKER

As previously discussed, a mortgage broker is a financial professional who acts as an intermediary to bring mortgage borrowers and mortgage lenders together. In New York, they are registered by the New York State Banking Department to help clients secure mortgage loans for the purchase of a new home, refinancing an existing mortgage, or renovating a current home. A mortgage broker receives compensation for services rendered but does not use personal funds to originate mortgages.

Mortgage bankers, on the other hand, work in a loan department of a financial institution and use their own funds to originate or fund mortgages. They work with real estate licensees and mortgage brokers and have the ability to approve mortgages for a lender. The banker makes loans only from the employing institution and is typically paid a salary by that institution.

After a mortgage is originated, the mortgage banker may retain the mortgage in a portfolio, but most mortgage bankers sell the mortgage to an investor. Some larger mortgage bankers service mortgages themselves via billing, collections, keeping records, and managing escrow funds. By contrast, other mortgage bankers sell the servicing rights to specialized parties.

To become a mortgage banker in New York, one must meet the following requirements:

> Honest and trustworthy character

> Fingerprints provided and background check passed

> 5 years of verifiable experience in making or underwriting residential mortgage loans

> Licensed as New York Loan Officer

> Minimum net worth of $250,000

> $50,000 surety bond

> $1,000,000 warehouse line of credit on New York's approved Warehouse Line List with at least 3 executive officers

New York does not require special licensure education or examination and does not require a physical in-state office.

ROLE OF MORTGAGE BROKER IN A REAL ESTATE TRANSACTION

The main role of a mortgage broker is to help mortgage loan borrowers navigate the mortgage market. In doing so, the broker can save borrowers time and effort during the loan application process. The broker can also save the borrower a considerable amount of money over the life of the loan by determining the best lender and loan for the borrower's needs and individual situation.

The mortgage broker's role in such transactions is to act as an intermediary between the borrower and appropriate lenders. The broker works with everyone involved in the lending process, from the client to the real estate agent to the underwriter and closing agent to ensure the borrower gets the best loan and the loan closes on time. During the process, the broker seeks and offers the client a variety of options that would work for the client's situation. These options may include unconventional loans and loans from banks that may not work directly with the public.

The role of the mortgage broker includes the following:

- Establishing professional relationships with mortgage lenders

- Developing relationships with real estate companies

- Assessing clients' needs in relation to their situation

- Making sure the lenders have all information they need to determine the borrower's qualifications for the loan

- Negotiating with banks and credit lenders to establish the best solution for the client

- Providing the borrower with lending options from which to select the best fit

- Advising clients on their options and explaining the legal and repayment details of the loan

- Assisting clients with pre-approval on loans

- Applying for a mortgage loan on behalf of the borrower

- Ensuring loans are compliant with applicable state and federal regulations and laws

- Completing the closing paperwork with the lender, the title company, the insurance broker, and all other relevant agencies.

20 Mortgage Brokerage Snapshot Review

MORTGAGE BROKER DEFINED

- a registered financial professional who brings mortgage borrowers and lenders together

MORTGAGE BROKER REQUIREMENTS

- register with NYS Banking Department; 2 or more years of credit analysis experience; underwriting experience or education; provide fingerprints and credit report

MORTGAGE BROKER RESPONSIBILITIES

- providing information and advice to clients; analyze client's finances and inform lenders; find appropriate lender for client; assist client with loan application; negotiating loan terms and comply with regulations

MORTGAGE BROKER VS MORTGAGE BANKER

- broker acts as intermediary between borrowers and lenders

- banker works in loan department, approves mortgage loans for lender

ROLE OF MORTGAGE BROKER IN A REAL ESTATE TRANSACTION

- develop relationships with lenders and real estate companies; assess client's needs and provide information to lenders; negotiate with lenders; give borrower lending options; assist clients with pre-approval on loans; assisting client with loan paperwork

CHAPTER TWENTY: MORTGAGE BROKERAGE

Section Quiz

20.1. To become a mortgage banker in New York, one must have a minimum net worth of

a. $100,000
b. $250,000
c. $500,000
d. $1,000,000

20.2. What is the difference between a mortgage banker and a mortgage broker?

a. A mortgage banker works for a financial institution that uses its own funds to originate or fund mortgages.
b. A mortgage banker primarily focuses on appraising properties for loan purposes.
c. A mortgage broker services loans after they have been funded by the lender.
d. A mortgage broker can approve loans without needing a financial institution's backing.

20.3. To become a mortgage broker in New York, one must

a. pass a federal mortgage licensing exam.
b. hold a bachelor's degree in finance or a related field.
c. Complete an internship with a licensed mortgage broker.
d. have two or more years of credit analysis experience.

20.4. Which of the following is true about New York mortgage bankers?

a. They must take license-related education and pass an examination.
b. They service the mortgages they have funded in-house over the life of each loan.
c. They have the ability to approve mortgages for the lending institution.
d. They are required to maintain a physical office in the state.

20.5. In New York, mortgage brokers are registered by

a. the Federal Housing Administration (FHA).
b. the New York State Real Estate Board.
c. the Department of Housing and Urban Development (HUD).
d. the New York State Banking Department.

20.6. Essentially, what do mortgage brokers do?

a. Appraise the property for the lender
b. Find and negotiate mortgage loans for the borrower
c. Manage the mortgage repayment process for the borrower
d. Provide legal advice on real estate transactions

20.7. What are the experience requirements to become a mortgage banker in New York?

a. A bachelor's degree in finance and 2 years of underwriting experience
b. Completion of a state-approved mortgage banking training program
c. 5 years of experience in making or underwriting residential mortgage loans
d. 3 years of experience working as a licensed real estate agent

20.8. How are mortgage brokers compensated?

a. They earn a salary.
b. The borrower they work with pays them for services rendered.
c. The lender the borrower chooses to work with pays them a commission.
d. They receive a flat fee from the real estate agent involved in the transaction.

20.9. Which of these activities would a mortgage banker do?

a. Approve or deny mortgage loan applications based on borrower qualifications
b. Provide the borrower with lending options from which to select the best fit
c. Conduct home inspections to determine property value
d. Develop relationships with real estate companies

20.10. The mortgage broker's role is to act as an _____ between the borrower and appropriate lenders.

a. appraiser
b. underwriter
c. intermediary
d. inspector

21 Property Management

Property Manager Defined
The Management Agreement
Management Functions and Skills Required
Leasing Considerations

PROPERTY MANAGER DEFINED

Property management is a specialty within the real estate profession. A property manager is an individual who is compensated for managing the physical and financial conditions of an owner's investment property. The manager's job is to maintain the value of the property while maximizing the property's income. The manager's responsibilities include timely reporting, budgeting, handling rentals, property maintenance, and related construction. The manager may be directly employed by the property owner or may be part of a real estate agency that is contracted to handle the property owner's business related to the investment property.

Typical types of property that utilize a property manager include residential (apartments, condominiums, cooperatives, and multi-family residences), commercial (retail and office properties), industrial (manufacturing, storage, and shipping facilities), as well as PUDs (planned unit development) which include residential, recreational, and retail properties together in a single contained community. Based on the functions the manager performs, such as rent collection or maintenance, a real estate broker's license may or may not be required.

THE MANAGEMENT AGREEMENT

Components
Rights, duties, and liabilities

Components

The management agreement establishes an agency agreement between manager and owner as well as specifying such essentials as the manager's scope of authority, responsibilities, objectives, compensation, and the term of the agreement. Property managers are usually considered to be general agents empowered to perform some or all of the ongoing tasks and duties of operating the property, including the authority to enter into contracts. The agency relationship creates the fiduciary duties of obedience, care, loyalty, accounting, and disclosure. The contractual relationship ensures that the manager will strive to realize the highest return for the owner consistent with the owner's objectives and instructions. The agreement should be in writing and include at least the basics of any real estate contract, as follows.

- **Names of the parties**--owner, landlord, manager, tenant or other party to be bound by the contract

- **Property description**--street address, unit number and location, square footage, and other information that specifies the leased premises

- **Term**--time period (**months**, years) covered by the contract; termination conditions and provisions

- **Owner's purpose--maximize** net income, maximize asset value, maximize return, minimize expenditure, maintain property quality, etc.; long-term goals for the property

- **Owner's responsibilities--management** fees, plus any management expenses such as payroll, advertising and insurance that the manager will not be expected to pay

- **Manager's authority**--the **scope** of powers being conveyed to the manager: hiring and staffing, setting rents, contracting with vendors, ordering repairs, limits on expenditures without seeking owner permission

- **Manager's responsibilities--specification** of duties, such as marketing, leasing, maintenance, budgeting, reporting, collecting and handling rents; the manager should be included as an additional insured on the liability policy for the property

- **Budget**--amounts, or percentages of revenues, allotted for operations, taxes, insurance, capital expenditures, etc.

- **Allocation of costs**--who is to pay certain expenses, that is, which will be treated as expenses of the manager vs. which will be paid directly by the owner

- **Reporting**--how often and what kind of reports are to be made

- **Compensation**--the management fee or other means of compensation to the manager; there may be a flat fee based on square footage, a rental commission based on a percentage of annual rent, a combination of these, or some other arrangement; in compliance with anti-trust laws, management fees are not standardized but must be negotiated by agent and principal

- **Equal opportunity statement**--the HUD statement or equivalent concerning availability to all persons and classes protected by law, incorporated into the agreement in the case of a residential property

**Rights, duties,
and liabilities**

Both the manager and the landlord have rights, duties and liabilities under the terms of the management contract. How these are apportioned should be clearly stated in the agreement.

Landlord. The landlord has the right to receive rent according to the agreement, and to receive the premises in the specified condition at the end of the agreement term. The landlord and his or her agents may have the right to enter and inspect the premises, examine the books, hire and fire staff, and choose vendors. The landlord may retain or grant the power to enter into contracts, to set rents, and to select tenants. The landlord will have the right to terminate the management contract according to the terms of the contract. The landlord will have the duty to pay the agreed management fee, and to make other such payments as detailed in the agreement. State law will determine to what extent a principal is liable for the acts of the manager and the manager's employees. As owner, the landlord is liable for failures to comply with certain local, state, and federal laws, particularly the Environmental Protection Act and fair housing laws.

Manager. Depending on the degree of authority granted by the agreement, the manager may have the right to hire and fire, enter into contracts, and perform routine management tasks without interference from the owner. The manager has the duties described earlier: to maintain financial records and make reports; to budget; to find, retain, and collect from tenants; to maintain and secure the property; to meet the owner's objectives. The manager's liabilities include the consequences of mishandling trust funds, violating fiduciary responsibilities, and violating fair housing laws, credit laws, and employment laws.

Exhibit 21.1 Abbreviated Sample Management Agreement

MANAGEMENT AGREEMENT

Agreement made_____[date], between_____, a corporation organized under the laws of the State of _____, having its principal office at_____[address],_____[city],_____[state], here referred to as owner, and_____, a corporation organized under the laws of the State of_____, having its principal office at a*ddress]*,_____[city],_____[state], here referred to as agent.

RECITALS

1. Owner holds title to the following-described real property:_____[insert legal or other appropriate description], here referred to as the property.
2. Agent is experienced in the business of operating and managing real estate similar to the above-described property.
3. Owner desires to engage the services of agent to manage and operate the property, and agent desires to provide such services on the following terms and conditions.

In consideration of the mutual covenants contained herein, the parties agree:

EMPLOYMENT OF AGENT. Agent shall act as the exclusive agent of owner to manage, operate, and maintain the property.

BEST EFFORTS OF AGENT. On assuming the management and operation of the property, agent shall thoroughly inspect the property and submit a written report to owner concerning the present efficiency under which the property is being managed and operated, and recommended changes, if necessary.

LEASING OF PROPERTY. Agent shall make reasonable efforts to lease available space of the property, and shall be responsible for all negotiations with prospective tenants. Agent shall also have the right to execute and enter into, on behalf of owner, month-to-month tenancies of units of the property.

ADVERTISING AND PROMOTION. Agent shall advertise vacancies by all reasonable and proper means; provided, agent shall not incur expenses for advertising in excess of____Dollars ($_____) during any calendar quarter without the prior written consent of owner.

MAINTENANCE, REPAIRS, AND OPERATIONS. Agent shall use its best efforts to insure that the property is maintained in an attractive condition and in a good state of repair. Expenditures for repairs, alterations, decorations or furnishings in excess of_____Dollars ($____) shall not be made without prior written consent of owner.

EMPLOYEES. Agent shall employ, discharge, and supervise all on-site employees or contractors required for the efficient operation and maintenance of the property. All on-site personnel, except independent contractors and employees of independent contractors, shall be the employees of agent.

INSURANCE. Agent shall obtain the following insurance at the expense of owner, and such insurance shall be maintained in force during the full term of this agreement:

1. Comprehensive public liability property insurance of _____Dollars ($___) single limit for bodily injury, death, and property damage;

2. Comprehensive automobile insurance of _____ Dollars ($_____) single limit for bodily injury, death, and property damage;

3. Fire and extended coverage hazard insurance in an amount equal to the full replacement cost of the structure and other improvements situated on the property; and

4. A fidelity bond in the amount of _____ Dollars ($_____) on each employee who handles cash, and workers' compensation and employer liability insurance to cover the agents and employees of both employer and agent.

Exhibit 21.1 Abbreviated Sample Management Agreement, continued

COLLECTION OF INCOME. Agent shall use its best efforts to collect promptly all rents and other income issuing from the property when such amounts become due. It is understood that agent does not guarantee the collection of rents.

BANK ACCOUNTS. Agent shall deposit (either directly or in a depositary bank for transmittal) all revenues from the property into the general property management trust fund of agent, here referred to as the trust account. From the revenues deposited in the trust account, agent shall pay all items with respect to the property for which payment is provided in this agreement, including the compensation of agent and deposits to the reserve accounts as provided for. Agent shall remit any balance of monthly revenues to owner concurrently with the delivery of the monthly report.

RESERVE ACCOUNT. Agent shall establish a reserve account for the following items: taxes, assessments, debt service, insurance premiums, repairs (other than normal maintenance), replacement of personal property, and refundable deposits.

RECORDS AND REPORTS. Agent shall furnish owner, no later than the end of the next succeeding month, a detailed statement of all revenues and expenditures for each preceding month. Within   days after the end of each calendar year, agent shall prepare and deliver to owner a detailed statement of revenues received and expenditures incurred and paid during the calendar year that result from operations of the property.

COMPENSATION OF AGENT. Agent shall receive a management fee equal to___percent (__ %) of the gross receipts collected from the operation of the property. Any management fee due agent hereunder shall be paid to agent within _____days after the end of each month.

TERMINATION AND RENEWAL. This agreement shall be for a term commencing on_____[date], and ending on _____[date].

MODIFICATION. This agreement may not be modified unless such modification is in writing and signed by both parties to this agreement.

IN WITNESS WHEREOF, the parties have executed this agreement at [designate place of execution] the day and year first above written.

_____

_____

MANAGEMENT FUNCTIONS

Reporting
Budgeting
Renting
Property maintenance
Construction

Functions

A manager has a fiduciary relationship with the principal and, in general, is charged with producing the greatest possible net return on the owner's investment while safeguarding the value of the investment for the owner/investor. At the same time, the manager has some responsibilities to tenants, who want the best value and the best space for their money. Professional managers are therefore much more than rent collectors. They need technical expertise in marketing, accounting, finance, and construction. Property managers often specialize in one type of property - apartment, office, retail, industrial, farm, single-family-and acquire specialized knowledge of that property type. Whatever the property type and management arrangement, the manager's work involves leasing, managing, marketing, and maintaining the property. The services a manager provides thus can be seen to fall into three areas: financial, physical, and administrative. Specific functions, duties, and responsibilities are determined by the management agreement, although most agreements will include at least the following functions.

Reporting

Financial reporting to the principal is a fundamental responsibility of the property manager. Reports may be required monthly, quarterly, and annually. Required reports typically include an annual operating budget (see below); monthly cash flow reports indicating income, expenses, net operating income, and net cash flow; profit and loss statements based on the cash flow reports and showing net profit; and budget comparison statements showing how actual results match the original budget.

Budgeting

An operating budget based on expected expenses and revenues is a necessity for management. The budget will determine rental rates, amounts available for capital expenditures, required reserve funds, salaries and wages of employees, amounts to be paid for property taxes and insurance premiums and mortgage or debt service. It will indicate the expected return, based on the previous year's performance. A typical budget will contain a projection, also based on past performance and on current market information, of income from all sources, such as rents and other services, and of expenses for all purposes, such as operating expenses, maintenance services, utilities, taxes, and capital expenditures. Operating statements itemizing income and expenses are then presented to the owner on a regular basis so that the owner can evaluate the manager's performance against the budget.

Income. The total of scheduled rents plus revenues from such sources as vending services, storage charges, late fees, utilities, and contracts is the *potential gross income*. Subtracting losses caused by uncollected rents, vacancies and evictions gives *effective gross income*. Operating expenses are subtracted from this total to show *net operating income*. When debt service and reserves (which are not counted as operating expenses) are subtracted, the result is *cash flow*.

Expenses. Expenses may be fixed or variable. Fixed expenses are those that remain constant and may include operating expenses, regular maintenance costs, and administration. Variable expenses are those that may change from month to month or occur sporadically, such as specific repairs or capital expenditures.

Capital expenditures. Expected expenditures for major items such as renovation or expansion should be included as a budgeting item. Large-scale projects are typically budgeted over a period of years.

Cash reserve. A cash reserve is a fund set aside from operating revenues for variable expenses, such as supplies, redecorating, and repairs. The amount of the reserve is based on experience with variable expenses in previous years.

Renting

The property manager, whose full responsibilities include maintaining and managing the property in accordance with the owner's financial goals, include seeing that the property is properly rented and tenanted. The manager may use the services of a leasing agent, whose concern is solely to rent the space. In such a situation, some of the manager's tasks may be performed by the leasing agent. Renting the property includes the following tasks, regardless of which party is actually performing them.

Controlling vacancies. There are many possible reasons for vacancies in a building:

> ▶ rent too high or too low
>
> ▶ ineffective marketing
>
> ▶ management quality
>
> ▶ poor tenant-retention program
>
> ▶ image and appearance problems
>
> ▶ high market vacancy rate

Successful managers look for these factors and take steps to limit or counteract their effects.

Marketing. Finding and attracting the right kind of tenants for a property is the aim of a marketing program. A marketing plan based on the property's features and the relationship between supply and demand in the market area, and consonant with the money available, will determine the best mix of advertising and promotional activities. Marketing methods include:

> ▶ billboard advertising
>
> ▶ brochures and fliers
>
> ▶ meetings and presentations

- ▸ networking
- ▸ newspaper ads
- ▸ radio and television advertising
- ▸ signs
- ▸ tenant referrals
- ▸ websites and online services

The efficiency of marketing activities can be judged in terms of how many prospects per completed lease they generate. The lower the cost per prospect per lease, the more effective and efficient the program.

Setting rents. Rental income must be sufficient to cover fixed expenses, operating expenses, and desired return on investment. But rental rates must also be realistic, taking into account what is happening in the market. The manager must consider prevailing rents in comparable properties as well as vacancy rates in the market and in the property. The manager makes a detailed survey of competitive space and makes adjustments for differences between the subject property and competing properties before setting the rental rates for the property. Residential apartment rates are stated in monthly amounts per unit, while commercial rates are usually stated as an annual or monthly amount per square foot. If vacancy rates in the managed property are too high, the manager may have to lower rates or identify problems in the property or its management that are contributing to vacancy level. On the other hand, if the property's vacancy rate is significantly lower than market rates, the manager may conclude that higher rental rates are called for.

Selecting tenants. To ensure that the property produces the desired level of income from rent, it is essential to find the most suitable tenants. For commercial space, the manager must determine that:

- ▸ the space meets the tenant's needs for size, configuration, location, and quality.
- ▸ the tenant will be able to pay for the space.
- ▸ the tenant's business is compatible with that of other tenants.
- ▸ there is room for expansion if the tenant's need for space is likely to grow.

For residential space, in addition to ascertaining the tenant's creditworthiness, the manager must be careful to comply with all federal and local fair housing laws. A manager should collect the same type of information on all prospective tenants. However, even though the law prohibits discrimination on the basis of race, sex, age and other protected classes, a manager may discriminate in certain other ways. For example, a manager has the right to refuse to rent to a person who has a history paying rent late, damaging property, fighting with other tenants, or spotty employment.

Collecting rents. The lease agreement should clearly specify the terms of rental payment. The manager must establish a system of notices and records as well as a method of collecting rents on schedule. Compliance with all state laws and regulations concerning collecting and accounting for rents is a necessity to avoid unwanted legal complications. As for monies received, the manager must follow trust fund handling procedures established by law and laid out in the rental and management agreements. If authorized by the management agreement, the manager may also collect security deposits and handle them as required by law.

Maintaining tenant relations. Happy tenants remain in a rented space longer than unhappy tenants. High tenant turnover adds to increased advertising and redecorating expenses. For these reasons, it is incumbent on the manager to

> ▶ communicate regularly with tenants

> ▶ respond promptly and satisfactorily to maintenance and service requests

> ▶ enforce rules and lease terms consistently and fairly

> ▶ comply with all relevant laws, such as fair housing and ADA (Americans with Disabilities Act) regulations

Legal issues (Fair Housing, ADA, and ECOA). Fair housing laws govern landlords and tenants just as they do sellers and buyers. They ensure that persons receive fair treatment regardless of race, color, religion, national origin, sex, handicap, or familial status. Families with children must receive equal treatment with those who do not have children. Landlords cannot charge higher rents or security deposits because of the presence of children. Managers must make sure that their marketing and leasing practices are in accordance with fair housing laws.

The Americans with Disabilities Act similarly requires landlords in certain circumstances to make housing and facilities available to disabled persons without hindrance. Familiarity with this law and with the latest state, federal, and local fair housing laws is essential.

The Equal Credit Opportunity Act, which prohibits discrimination in lending, applies to how property managers evaluate potential tenants. The manager must be consistent in evaluating the creditworthiness of applicants. The same application forms and the same credit requirements should be used with all applicants.

Property maintenance

Physical maintenance of the property is one of the property manager's primary functions. The costs of services provided must always be balanced with financial objectives and the need to satisfy tenant needs. The manager will also be concerned with staffing and scheduling requirements, in accordance with maintenance objectives.

Maintenance objectives. The foremost maintenance objective is generally to preserve the value of the physical asset for the owner over the long term. Although not every property is best served by vast expenditures on top-level maintenance, it is almost always important to maintain the viability of the property as a rental. Three general types of maintenance are required to keep a property in serviceable condition: routine, preventive, and corrective.

Routine maintenance. Routine maintenance activities are those necessary for the day-to-day functioning of the property. Regular performance of these activities helps to keep tenants satisfied as well as forestall serious problems requiring repair or correction. Routine activities are such things as:

- regular inspections

- scheduled upkeep of mechanical systems-heating, air-conditioning, rest rooms, lighting, landscaping

- regular cleaning of common areas

- minor repairs

- supervision of purchasing

Preventive maintenance. Preventive maintenance goes beyond the routine in attempting to deal with situations that can become serious problems if ignored. Seasonal or scheduled replacement of appliances and equipment, regular painting of exterior and interior areas, and planned replacement of a roof are a few examples.

Corrective maintenance. When routine and preventive maintenance fail, repairs and replacements become mandatory to keep the property operational. A boiler may develop a leak, an air-conditioning unit may break down, an elevator may cease to function properly.

Maintenance contracting. Depending on building type and size, tenant needs, and budgetary constraints, a manager may decide to hire an outside firm to handle maintenance services rather than hiring on-site employees. Efficiency, competence, responsiveness, and effective cost will be major deciding factors.

Construction

Commercial and industrial property managers are regularly called upon to make alterations to existing space to accommodate a tenant's needs. They may also have to undertake or oversee construction that alters or expands common areas or the entire building itself. Again, such work may be contracted out or done by in-house employees.

Tenant improvements. Alterations made specifically for certain tenants are called build-outs or tenant improvements. The work may involve merely painting and re-carpeting a rental space, or erecting new walls and installing special electrical or other systems. In new buildings, spaces are often left incomplete so that they can be finished to an individual tenant's specifications. In such cases, it is important to clarify which improvements will be considered tenant property (trade fixtures) and which will belong to the building.

Renovations. When buildings lose functionality (become functionally obsolescent), they generally also lose tenants, drop in class, and suffer declining rental rates. Maintenance becomes more expensive because of the difficulties of servicing out-of-date building components. Renovation may solve some of these problems, but the manager will have to help the owner determine whether the costs of renovation can be recovered by increased revenues resulting from the renovation.

Environmental concerns. A variety of environmental concerns confronts a property manager, ranging from air quality to waste disposal, tenant concerns, and federal, state and local environmental regulations. The managed property may contain asbestos, radon, mold, lead, and other problematic substances. Tenants may produce hazardous waste. The manager must be aware of the issues and see that proper procedures are in place to deal with them, including providing means for proper disposal of hazardous materials, arranging for environmental audits and undertaking possible remediation. For instance, an audit may show that a building is causing tenants to become sick because of off-gassing from construction materials combined with a lack of ventilation. Remediation may consist of nothing more than replacing carpets and improving ventilation, and the manager, if empowered to do so, should take the necessary steps.

Legal concerns (ADA). The Americans with Disabilities Act requires managers to ensure that disabled employees and members of the public have the same level of access to facilities as is provided for those who are not disabled. Employers with at least fifteen employees must follow nondiscriminatory employment and hiring practices. Reasonable accommodations must be made to enable disabled employees to perform essential functions of their jobs. Modifications to the physical components of the building may be necessary to provide the required access to tenants and their customers, such as widening doorways, changing door hardware, changing how doors open, installing ramps, lowering wall-mounted telephones and keypads, supplying Braille signage, and providing auditory signals. Existing barriers must be removed when the removal is "readily achievable," that is, when cost is not prohibitive. New construction and remodeling must meet a higher standard, Managers must be aware of the laws and determine whether their buildings meet requirements. If not, the manager must determine whether restructuring or retrofitting or some other kind of accommodation is most practical.

Risk management

Many things can go wrong in a rented property, from natural disaster to personal injury to terrorism to malfeasance by employees. Huge monetary losses for the owner, in the form of civil and criminal penalties, legal costs, fines, damages, and costs of remediation can be the result. A manager must consider the possibility of such events and have a plan for dealing with them.

Risk management strategies. Depending on the nature of the risk, the size of the potential losses, the likelihood of its happening, and the costs of doing something about it, a manager and owner will generally choose one or more of the following risk management strategies:

> ▶ avoidance-removing the source of the risk, such as by closing off a dangerous area of the building

> ▸ reduction-taking action to forestall the event before it happens, such as by installing fire alarms, sprinklers, and security systems

> ▸ transference-shifting the risk to someone else by buying an insurance policy

> ▸ retention-taking the chance that the event is not likely enough to occur to justify the expense of one of the other strategies; self-insurance

Security and safety. A court may hold a manager and owner responsible for the physical safety of employees, tenants, and customers in leased premises. In addition to standard life safety and security systems such as sprinklers, fire doors, smoke alarms, fire escapes, and door locks, a manager may have to provide electronic and human monitoring systems (security cameras, security guards) and be prepared to take action against tenants who allow, conduct or contribute to dangerous criminal activities such as assault and drug use.

Insurance. Many types of insurance are available to allow for the shifting of liability away from the owner. An insurance audit by a competent insurance agent will indicate what kind of and how much coverage is advisable. Common types of insurance coverage for income and commercial properties include:

> ▸ casualty-coverage for specific risks, such as theft, vandalism, burglary, illness and accident, machinery damage

> ▸ liability-coverage for risks incurred by the owner when the public enters the building; medical expenses resulting from owner negligence or other causes

> ▸ workers' compensation-hospital and medical coverage for employees injured in the course of employment, mandated by state laws

> ▸ fire and hazard-coverage for damage to the property by fire, wind, hail, smoke, civil disturbance, and other causes

> ▸ flood-coverage for damages caused by heavy rains, snow, drainage failures, and failed public infrastructures such as dams and levies; flood insurance is not included in regular hazard policies

> ▸ contents and personal property-coverage for building contents and personal property when they are not actually on the building premises

> ▸ consequential loss, use, and occupancy-coverage for the business losses resulting from a disaster, such as loss of rent and other revenue, when the property cannot be used for business

> ▸ surety bond-coverage against losses resulting from criminal or negligent acts of an employee

The owner may opt for a multi-peril policy which combines standard types of commercial policies and may allow special coverage for floods, earthquakes, and terrorism.

The amount of coverage provided by certain types of policies may be based on whether the property is insured at depreciated value or current replacement value. Depreciated value is its original value minus the loss in value over time. Current replacement value, which is more expensive, is the amount it would cost to rebuild or replace the property at current rates.

Commercial policies include coinsurance clauses requiring the insured to bear a portion of the loss. Fire and hazard policies usually require the coverage to be in an amount equal to at least 80 percent of the replacement value.

Owner's policies do not cover what is owned by the tenant. Tenants should obtain their own renter's or tenant's insurance to cover personal belongings. Residential and commercial or business variants are available. The question of who owns tenant improvements is not only important when it is time for the tenant to leave the premises. It is also likely to determine whether the tenant's or the landlord's insurance company will be paying if the improvements are damaged or destroyed.

Handling of trust funds. Managers are responsible for proper handling of monies belonging to other parties that come into the manager's hands in the course of doing business. For property managers, such funds include rents collected from tenants, security deposits, and capital contributions from the property owner. State laws, usually incorporated into real estate commission rules and the state's real estate law, specify how a property manager is to manage trust funds. In general, the agent is to maintain a separate bank account for these funds, with special accounting, in a qualified depository institution. The rules for how long an agent may hold trust funds before depositing them, and how the funds are to be disbursed, are spelled out. The fundamental requirements are that the owners of all funds must be identified, and there must be no commingling or conversion of client funds and agent funds. Mishandling carries heavy penalties.

LEASING CONSIDERATIONS

Rent regulations
Tenant's rights

Rent regulations New York State has two types of rent regulation: *rent control and rent stabilization*, both of which are administered by the Office of Rent Administration of the New York State Division of Housing and Community Renewal (DHCR). In 1974, the Emergency Tenant Protection Act was passed for specific localities. Additionally, the Housing Stability and Tenant Protection Act of 2019 was passed to include more protections for renters.

Rent control. Rent control regulations apply to residential buildings with three or more apartments that were built before February 1947 in the municipalities of New York City and parts of Albany, Erie, Nassau, Rensselaer, Schenectady, and

Westchester counties. Rent control applies to tenants or a tenant's lawful successor who have been living in the apartment continuously since July 1, 1971 (or April 1, 1953 in some situations).

Rent control limits the rent a landlord may charge a tenant for an apartment. It also limits the landlord's right to evict tenants.

In New York City, rent controlled apartments have a maximum base rent that is adjusted to coincide with operating costs every 2 years. However, the rent must not exceed the Maximum Collectible Rent which is adjusted annually. Tenants may challenge the rent increase if the building has housing code violations, if the owner is not maintaining essential services, or if the owner's expenses do not warrant the increase.

If a tenant vacates a rent-controlled apartment, the apartment either becomes rent stabilized or ceases to be regulated, depending on the municipality where the apartment is located.

Rent stabilization. In New York City, rent stabilization applies to apartments that are not rent controlled and are in a building built before January 1, 1974 with six or more apartments. The lack of rent control on these apartments would be due to a tenant vacating without leaving a lawful successor. Rent stabilization also applies to apartments in buildings with three or more apartments that were built or extensively renovated on or after January 1, 1974. These apartments must qualify for special tax benefits.

Outside of New York City, rent stabilization applies to apartments in buildings with six or more apartments built before January 1, 1974.

Rent Guidelines Boards in New York City, Nassau, Rockland, and Westchester counties imposed maximum annual rent increases for 1- or 2-year leases.

Apartments under rent stabilization come with essential services and lease renewals with the same terms and conditions as the initial lease. These tenants may only be evicted based on grounds allowed by law.

As of June 15, 2019, other municipalities that have experienced a housing emergency may enact a rent stabilization law.

Emergency Tenant Protection Act (ETPA) of 1974. The ETPA stabilizes rents in specific municipalities that declare a state of emergency associated with available housing. The Act applies to buildings with six or more apartments that were built before 1974. In some municipalities, it applies only to buildings of specified sizes, such as at least twenty apartments. The Act regulates rent increases, entitles tenants to required services, to renewed leases, and to protection against eviction except for reasons allowed by law.

ETPA does not apply to rent controlled apartments, buildings with fewer than six apartments, motor courts, tourist homes, certain nonprofit units, certain government supervised housing, and housing build after January 1, 1974.

Housing Stability and Tenant Protection Act of 2019. This Act provides additional protections for tenants. It limits security deposits to no greater than 1 month's rent and does not allow a landlord to charge the last month's rent in advance if a security deposit has been paid. This applies to both regulated and non-regulated housing.

Additionally, late fees may not be imposed unless the payment is more than 5 days late; and the fee may only be $50 or 5% of the monthly rent, whichever is less. The landlord must send written notice by certified mail when the tenant is more than 5 days late. The tenant may not be charged more than $20 for a credit and background check and must be provided a copy of the reports. Tenants may not be denied a lease based on a previous legal conflict with a landlord.

Non-rent regulated housing. Not all housing in New York is rent regulated. For non-rent regulated apartments, rent and rent increases are not limited. However, landlords must provide written notice of any increase over 5%. The timing of the notice is based on how long the tenant has resided in the apartment.

Landlords of non-rent regulated apartments are not required to renew a lease but do need to provide the tenant with written notice of the nonrenewal. If the lease contains an automatic renewal clause, the landlord must also provide the tenant with written notice of the clause's existence between 15 and 30 days before the date the tenant is required to given the landlord notice of intention not to renew the lease.

When a tenant vacates a non-rent regulated apartment, the landlord must return the security deposit within 14 days. Landlords must also provide an itemized receipt within those 14 days for any money taken out of the security deposit for damages.

Tenant's rights

In New York State, a tenant's rights depend partially on which regulations apply to the rental property. Under New York's Real Property Law, tenants have the following rights:

- Tenants have the right not to be discriminated against because of race, creed, national origin, sex, disability, age, AIDS or HIV status, alcoholism, marital status, familial status, or lawful source of income. This right is extended in New York City to cover lawful occupation, sexual orientation, partnership status, and immigration status.

- Tenants have the right to a livable, safe, and sanitary apartment.

- If the landlord fails to maintain the apartment's habitability, the tenant has the right to sue for a rent reduction.

- Tenants have the right to be notified in advance that the landlord intends to enter the apartment to make repairs.

- If the landlord fails to make necessary repairs to the apartment, tenants have the right to make the repairs and deduct the cost from the rent.

- Tenants of buildings with multiple dwellings have the right to have automatic, self-closing and self-locking doors at all entrances.

- Buildings with eight or more dwellings must have a two-way intercom system from each apartment to the front door with tenants having the right and ability to open the entrance door from their apartments.

- Tenants have the right to safety by having mirrors in self-service elevators, by installing their own locks on the apartment door, having a peephole in the apartment's entrance door, and have locked mailboxes.

- Tenants with children under 10 years old have the right to have window guards installed.

- Tenants have the right to be notified if the apartment contains lead-based paint and what hazards the lead poses.

- Disabled tenants have the right to make alterations to the apartment at their own expense to improve accessibility.

- Disabled tenants have the right to have a service dog or companion dog regardless of the building's no pets policy.

- Tenants have the right to privacy within their apartments.

- Tenants have the right to form, join, or participate in lawful activities of an organization formed to protect tenants' rights without being harassed, punished, or penalized by the landlord.

- Tenants have the right not to be unlawfully evicted, that is, evicted without a court order.

- Tenants have the right to receive interest on their security deposit if the deposit was placed in an interest-bearing account.

- Tenants in buildings with four or more apartments have the right to sublet if the landlord consents in advance.

- Tenants have the right to share the apartment with immediate family not listed in the lease.

- Senior citizen tenants and disabled tenants have the right to terminate their lease if they are deemed unable to continue living independently.

- Tenants who are victims of domestic violence have the right to terminate their lease with appropriate notice.

- When legally evicted, a tenant has the right to be given a reasonable amount of time to remove belongings.

Manufactured and mobile homes tenants' rights include the following:

- Tenants have the same rights as tenants of other types of housing in regard to rent, rent increases, security deposits, eviction, and so forth.

- Tenants have the right to sell their homes with the mobile home park owner's consent and not pay the owner any compensation related to the sale.

Tenants and mobile home owners have the right to be provided a copy of the park's rules.

21 Property Management Snapshot Review

PROPERTY MANAGER DEFINED

- an individual who is compensated for managing the physical and financial conditions of an owner's investment property; manager's job is to maintain the value of the property while maximizing the property's income

THE MANAGEMENT AGREEMENT

Components

- names of parties; property description; lease term; owner's purpose; responsibilities; authority; budget; allocation of costs; reporting; compensation; Equal Opportunity statement

Rights, duties, and liabilities

- landlord: receive rent; receive premises in specified condition; enter and inspect; examine books; enter into contracts, hire vendors, set rents; pay management; comply with laws

- manager: hire and fire; enter into contracts; perform management tasks; maintain records, make reports, budget, collect rent, find tenants, maintain the property, meet owner goals; handle trust funds; comply with laws

MANAGEMENT FUNCTIONS

- main manager types: individual broker or firm managing for multiple owners; building manager, employed by owner or other manager to manage a single property; resident manager, employed by owner, broker, or management firm to live and manage on site.

- manager is a fiduciary of the principal; duty to act in principle's best interests; may specialize in a property type

- needed skills: marketing, accounting, finance, construction; financial, physical, administrative services; specific functions determined by management agreement

Reporting

- monthly, quarterly, or annually; annual operating budget, cash flow reports, profit and loss statements, budget comparison statements

Budgeting

- operating budget based on expected expenses and revenues; determines rental rates, capital expenditures, reserves, salaries and wages; projects income based on past performance and current market

- potential gross income: total of scheduled rents plus revenues from other sources; effective gross income: total gross minus losses from vacancies, evictions, uncollected rents; net operating income: effective gross minus operating expenses; cash flow: net operating income minus debt service and reserves

- expenses are variable and fixed; capital expenditures are outlays for major renovations and construction; cash reserves set aside for variable expenses

Renting

- manager must keep property properly rented and tenanted; vacancies managed by rent setting, marketing, tenant relations, good service

- selecting compatible tenants and collecting scheduled rents are top priorities

- legal issues concern compliance with fair housing laws, Americans with Disabilities Act, and ECOA

Property maintenance	• main consideration: balance between costs of services, owner financial objectives, and tenant needs
	• may be routine, preventive, or corrective; staffed in-house or contracted out
Construction	• tenant alterations, renovations, and expansion; also environmental remediation
	• legal concerns: Americans with Disabilities Act; applies to employers with fifteen or more employees; manager to determine feasibility of restructuring, retrofitting, new construction, or other alternatives to comply
Risk management	• risk ranges from natural disaster to personal injury, terrorism, and employee malfeasance; handled by avoiding or removing the source, installing protective systems, buying insurance, self-insuring (risk retention)
	• life safety systems include sprinklers, fire doors, smoke alarms, fire escapes, monitoring systems
	• insurance includes casualty, liability, workers' comp, fire and hazard, flood, contents, consequential loss, surety bonds, multi-peril; tenants need their own insurance
	• handling of trust funds is a major risk area; mishandling carries heavy penalties

LEASING CONSIDERATIONS

Rent regulations rights	• rent control limits amount of rent landlord may charge and the landlord's eviction
	• rent stabilization apartments provide essential services and lease renewals to match original lease with limited eviction rights
Tenant's rights	• rights depend on regulated rent; include safe and sanitary apartment; right to sue for rent reduction; notification of landlord's intention to enter apartment; right against discrimination; right to deduct the cost of repairs from rent; window guards installed when children in residence; right to privacy and safety with specific locks on all entrance doors; mirrors in elevators; right to have service dog for disability assistance

CHAPTER TWENTY-ONE: PROPERTY MANAGEMENT

Section Quiz

21.1. Property managers have a _____ relationship with the property owner.

    a. non-binding
    b. partnership
    c. fiduciary
    d. subagency

21.2. The three kinds of maintenance a property manager must oversee are

    a. constructive, deconstructive, and reconstructive.
    b. routine, preventive, and corrective.
    c. scheduled, planned, and improvised.
    d. emergency, elective, and optional.

21.3 From a property manager's perspective, what is generally the foremost objective related to property maintenance?

    a. To preserve the value of the physical asset for the owner over the long term
    b. To adhere to fair housing laws in regard to tenant disabilities
    c. To establish a system of notices and records pertaining to rent collection
    d. To save money on capital expenditures

21.4. If a property's vacancy rate is significantly lower than market rates, it may be a sign that the manager needs to:

    a. lower rental rates.
    b. find better tenants.
    c. improve management quality.
    d. raise rental rates.

21.5. Why is it important for property managers to maintain good tenant relations?

    a. To enhance the image of the property owner
    b. To ensure rent is paid on time
    c. To lower insurance costs
    d. To keep tenant turnover low

21.6. Which of the following describes the formula for deriving effective gross income?

    a. Totaling scheduled rents plus other revenue streams with cash flow
    b. Subtracting losses caused by uncollected rents, vacancies, and evictions from potential gross income
    c. Subtracting operating expenses from potential gross income
    d. Adding cash flow to net operating income

21.7. New York State has two types of rent regulation. These are

    a. rent levelling and rent protection.
    b. rent adjustment and rent balancing.
    c. rent modification and rent equalization.
    d. rent control and rent stabilization.

21.8. Which of the following statements regarding the property manager's responsibility for security and safety is true?

    a. The manager has no responsibilities for building safety beyond ensuring that fire doors and sprinklers are working.
    b. The manager's security responsibilities are limited to the common areas.
    c. A court may hold the manager responsible for the physical safety of tenants, employees, and customers in leased premises.
    d. The manager's security responsibilities are limited to tenants and their employees in their leased premises.

21.9. One of the property manager's fundamental responsibilities is

    a. obtaining construction loans for the principal.
    b. financial reporting to the principal.
    c. finding a buyer for the property.
    d. maintaining good standing in a managers' professional association.

21.10. Which of the following limits security deposits to no greater than one month's rent?

    a. Emergency Tenant Protection Act (ETPA) of 1974
    b. New York's Real Property Law
    c. Housing Stability and Tenant Protection Act of 2019
    d. Rent Guidelines Boards

21.11. The efficiency of a property manager's marketing activities can be measured in terms of:

    a. cost per tenant prospect generated per lease.
    b. number of ads produced per marketing dollar.
    c. dollars expended per square foot of vacant space.
    d. percentage of reserves expended on marketing.

21.12. Which of the following is NOT a tenant right in New York?

    a. Installing one's own locks on the apartment door
    b. Joining a tenants' rights organization
    c. Subletting the apartment without landlord consent
    d. Sharing the apartment with immediate family members not listed on the lease

21.13. Which of the following is an example of preventive maintenance?

    a. Regular cleaning of common areas
    b. Replacing a broker air conditioner
    c. Increasing the capacity of the HVAC system.
    d. Regular painting of exterior and interior areas

21.14. Which of the following is true regarding non-rent regulated housing in New York?

    a. Landlords are required to renew leases when the tenant request a renewal.
    b. Leases may not include automatic renewal clauses.
    c. Landlords must provide written notice of any rent increase over 5%.
    d. When tenants move out, landlords must return the security deposit within 7 days.

21.15. The services a manager provides typically falls into three areas: financial, physical, and:

    a. administrative.
    b. marketing.
    c. legal.
    d. promotional

22 Real Estate Mathematics

Basic Formulas and Functions
Real Estate Applications

Answer Key is on page 498

BASIC MATH

Fractions

Adding and subtracting same denominator:

Formula: $a/c + b/c = (a + b) \div c$

Example: $1/2 + 1/2 = (1 + 1)/2 = 2/2 = 1$

Adding and subtracting different denominators:

Formula: $a/c + b/d = (ad + bc)/cd$

Example: $1/2 + 1/3 = (3 + 2)/6 = 5/6$

Multiplying:

Formula: $(a/c) \times (b/d) = ab/cd$

Example: $(2/5) \times (4/6) = 8/30 = 4/15$

Decimals and Percents

Converting decimals to percentages

Formula: *Decimal number x 100 = Percentage number*

Example: $.022 \times 100 = 2.2\%$

Converting percentages to decimals

Formula: *Percent number $\div$ 100 = Decimal number*

Example: $2.2 \div 100 = .022$

Multiplying percents

Formula: 1. *Percent number ÷ 100 = Decimal number*

2. *Beginning number x Decimal number = Product*

Example: 75% of 256 (75% x 256) = ?

1.   75 ÷ 100 = .75

2.   256 x .75 = 192

Dividing by percents

Formula: 1. *Percent number ÷ 100 = Decimal number*

2. *Beginning number ÷ Decimal = Dividend*

Example: 240 ÷ 75% = ?

1. 75% ÷ 100 = .75

2. 240 ÷ .75 = 320

Decimals, Fractions, and Percentages

Converting fractions to percents

Formula: (1)   *a / b or a ÷ b = a divided by b = decimal number*

(2)   *decimal number x 100 = percent number*

Example: (1)   2 / 5 = 2 divided by 5 = 0.4

(2)   .4 x 100 = 40%

Converting a percent to fraction and reducing it

Formula: (1) $X\% = X \div 100$ or $X / 100$

          (2) $\dfrac{X \div a}{100 \div a}$ *where a is the largest number that divides evenly into both numerator and denominator*

Example: (1) $40\% = 40 \div 100$, or $40 / 100$

          (2) $\dfrac{40 \div 20}{100 \div 20} = \dfrac{2}{5}$

Converting fractions to decimals and percentages

Formula: *Decimal x 100 = Percent number*

Example: $.75 \times 100 = 75\%$

Equations

Additions and Subtractions

Formula: *if* $a = b + c$

          then $b = a - c$ *(subtracting c from both sides)*

          and $c = a - b$ *(subtracting b from both sides)*

Example: $10 = 6 + 4$

          $6 = 10 - 4$

          $4 = 10 - 6$

Multiplications and Divisions

Formula: *if* $a = b \times c$

          then $b = a / c$ *(dividing both sides by c)*

          and $c = a / b$ *(dividing both sides by b)*

Example: $10 = 2 \times 5$

          $2 = 10 \div 5$

          $5 = 10 \div 2$

Linear and Perimeter Measurement

Linear measure of rectangles

Formula: *Side A = Area ÷ Side B*

Example: A rectangular house has one side 40' side long and area of 1,200 SF. What is the length of the other side?

Side A = (1,200' ÷ 40') = 30'

Perimeter measurement

Formula: *Perimeter = Sum of all sides of an object*

Example: A five-sided lot has the following dimensions:

Side A = 50' Side B = 60'
Side C= 70' Side D = 100'
Side E = 30'

What is the perimeter of the lot?

P = 50' + 60' + 70' + 100' + 30' = 310'

Area Measurement

Square and rectangle

Formula: *Area = Width x Depth (Horizontal) or Width x Height (Vertical)*

Width= Area ÷ Depth (Height)

Depth (Height)= Area ÷ Width

Example: A house is 40' deep and 30' wide. What is its area?

Area = 40' x 30' = 1,200 SF

Triangle

Formula: *Area = (Height x Base) ÷ 2*

Note: Base is also sometimes referred to as "width"

Example: An A-frame house has a front facade measuring 30' across and 20' in height. What is the area of the facade?
Area = (30' x 20') ÷ 2 = 300 Square feet (SF)

Square foot-to-acre conversion

Formula: *Acres = Area SF ÷ 43,560 SF*

Example: How many acres is 196,020 SF?

196,020 SF ÷ 43,560 SF = 4.5 acres

Acre-to-square foot conversion

Formula: *SF = Number of acres* x *43,560 SF*

Example: How many square feet is .75 acres?

.75 acres x 43,560 SF = 32,670 SF

Linear and Area Conversion Chart

Linear measures

(cm = centimeter; m = meter; km = kilometer)

1 inch	=	1/12 foot	=	1/36 yard		
1 foot	=	12 inches	=	1/3 yard		
1 yard	=	36 inches	=	3 feet		
1 rod	=	16.5 feet	=	1/320 mile		
1 mile	=	5280 feet	=	1760 yards	=	320 rods
1 centimeter	=	1/100 m				
1 meter	=	100 cm	=	1/1000 km		
1 kilometer	=	1,000 m				

Area measures

1 square inch	=	1/144 sq. foot				
1 square foot	=	1/9 sq. yard	=	144 sq. inches		
1 square yard	=	9 sq. feet	=	1,296 sq. inches		
1 acre	=	1/640 sq. mi	=	43,560 SF	=	208.71 ft x 208.71 ft
1 square mile	=	640 acres	=	1 section	=	1/36 township
1 section	=	1 mi x 1 mi	=	640 acres	=	1/36 township
1 township	=	6 mi x 6 mi	=	36 sq. mi	=	36 sections

Metric conversions

(cm = centimeter; m = meter; km = kilometer)

1 inch	=	2.54 cm		
1 foot	=	30.48 cm	=	.3048 m
1 yard	=	91.44 cm	=	.9144 m
1 mile	=	1609.3 m	=	1.60 km
1 centimeter	=	.3937 inch		
1 meter	=	39.37 inches	=	3.28 feet	=	1.094 yards
1 kilometer	=	3,281.5 feet	=	.621 mile

Fractions of sections, acres, and linear dimensions

Fraction		# Acres
1 section	=	640 acres
1/2 section	=	320 acres
1/4 section	=	160 acres
1/8 section	=	80 acres
1/16 section	=	40 acres
1/32 section	=	20 acres
1/64 section	=	10 acres

Calculating Area from the Legal Description

Formula: (1) *First multiply all the denominators of the fractions in the legal description together.*

(2) *Then divide 640 by the resulting product.*

Examples: How many acres are in the Northern 1/2 of the Southwestern 1/4 of Section 6?

640 / (2 x 4) = 640 / 8 = 80 acres

How many acres are in the Western 1/2 of the Northwestern 1/4 of the Northeastern 1/4 of Section 8?

640 / (2 x 4 x 4) = 640 / 32 = 20 acres

Volume Measurement

Formula: *Volume = Width x Height x Depth*   *(assume objects with 90 degree angles)*

Base = Volume ÷ (Height x Depth)

Height = Volume ÷ (Base x Depth)

Depth = Volume ÷ (Base x Height)

Example: What is the volume of a 40' x 30' x 20' house?

40' x 30' x 20' = 24,000 cubic feet

LEASES

Percentage Lease Rent Calculation

Formula: *Monthly percentage rent = Sales x percent of sales charged*

Example: A store generates $50,000 per month. The lease calls for 1.5% percentage rent. Monthly rent amount?

($50,000 x .015) = $750 / month

CONTRACTS FOR THE SALE OF REAL ESTATE

Percentage of Listing Price Calculation

Formula: *Percentage of listing price = Offer ÷ Listing price*

Example: A property listed for $150,000 receives an offer for $120,000. The offer's percentage of listing price is:

$120,000 ÷ $150,000 = 80%

Earnest Money Deposit Calculation

Formula: *Deposit = Offering price x required or market-accepted percentage*

Example: A seller requires a 2% deposit on a property listed for $320,000. The required deposit (assuming a full price offer) is:

$320,000 x 2% = $6,400

Appraisal & Value

Adjusting Comparables

Rules:

1. Never adjust the subject!

2. If the comparable is superior to the subject, subtract value from the comparable.

3. If the comparable is inferior to the subject, add value to the comparable.

Example:

The subject has a $10,000 pool and no porch. A comparable that sold for $250,000 has a porch ($5,000), an extra bathroom ($6,000), and no pool.

Adjustments to comp: $250,000 (+10,000 - 5,000 - 6,000) = $249,000 indicated value of subject

Gross Rent Multiplier

Formulas:

Sales price = Monthly rental income x GRM

Monthly rental income = Sales price / Gross Rent Multiplier

Note: Gross rent multiplier is often abbreviated as GRM.

Examples:

1. What is the value of a fourplex with monthly rent of $2,800 and a GRM of 112?

   $2,800 rent x 112 GRM = $313,600

2. What is the GRM of a fourplex with monthly rent of $2,800 and a value of $313,600?

   313,600 price ÷ $2,800 rent = 112 GRM

Gross Income Multiplier

Formulas

Gross Income Multiplier = Sales price ÷ Annual income

Sales price = Annual income x Gross Income Multiplier

Annual income = Sales price ÷ Gross Income Multiplier

Note: Gross income multiplier is often abbreviated as GIM.

Examples:

1. What is the value of a commercial property with an annual income of $33,600 and a GIM of 9.3?

$33,600 income x 9.3 GIM = $312,480

2. What is the GIM of a commercial property with annual income of $33,600 and a value of $312,480?

$313,600 price ÷ $33,600 = 9.3 GIM

Cost Approach Formula

Formula: *Value = Land value + (Improvements + Capital additions - Depreciation)*

Example: Land value = $50,000; home replacement cost = $150,000; new garage added @ $30,000; total depreciation = $10,000

Value = $50,000 + (150,000 + 30,000 - 10,000) = $220,000

Depreciation

Formulas: *Annual depreciation = Beginning depreciable basis ÷ Depreciation term*

Depreciable basis = (Initial property value + Any capital improvements - Land value)

Note: The depreciation term is in number of years.

Example: Property value = $500,000; land value = $110,000; depreciation term = 39 years

Step 1: ($500,000 - $110,000) = $390,000 depreciable basis

Step 2: ($390,000 ÷ 39 years) = $10,000 annual depreciation

Income Capitalization Formula

Formulas: *Value = Annual Net Operating Income ÷ Capitalization rate*

Capitalization rate = Annual Net Operating Income ÷ Value

Annual Net Operating Income = Value x Capitalization rate

Examples: 1. A property generates $490,000 net income and sells at a 7% cap rate. What is its value?

$490,000 ÷ 7% = $7,000,000 value

2. A property has a net income of $490,000 and sells for $7,000,000. What is its cap rate?

$490,000 \div 7,000,000 = .07$, or 7%

3. A property's value is $7,000,000 and the cap rate is 7%. What is the property's net operating income?

$7,000,000 \times .07 = $490,000

Net Operating Income (NOI, Net Income)

Formula: *NOI = Potential rent - Vacancy loss + Other income - Operating expenses*

Note: NOI does not include debt payments!

Example: A building has 10 office suites generating annual potential rent of $10,000 each. Vacancy = 10% and annual expenses are $35,000. Vending machines yield $5,000. What is the NOI?

$100,000 rent - 10,000 vacancy + 5,000 other income - 35,000 expenses = $60,000 NOI

FINANCE

Points

Definition: 1 point = 1% of the loan amount or .01 x loan amount

Formulas: *Points = Fee paid ÷ Loan amount*

Fee paid = Loan amount x Points

Loan amount = Fee paid ÷ Points

Examples: 1. A borrower pays $500 for a $10,000 loan. How many points are paid?

$500 \div 10,000 = .05 = 5$ points

2. A borrower pays 5 points on a $10,000 loan. What is the fee paid?

$10,000 \times .05 = $500

3. A borrower pays $500 as 5 points on a loan. What is the loan amount?

$500 \div .05 = $10,000

Rules of Thumb: 1 point charged raises lender's yield by .125%

8 points charged raises lender's yield by 1%

Example: A lender wants to yield 7% on a 6.5% loan. How many points must he charge?

(7% - 6.5%) = .5%

.5% ÷ .125% = 4 points

Interest Rate, Principal and Payment

Caveat!

Interest rates in mortgage financing apply to the <u>annual</u> interest payment and <u>exclude</u> principal payment. Remember to convert annual payments to monthly or vice versa as the question requires, and to exclude principal payments from your calculations!

Formulas:

Payment = Principal x Rate

Principal = Payment ÷ Rate

Rate = Payment ÷ Principal

Examples:

1. A borrower has a $100,000 loan @ 6% interest. What are the annual and monthly payments?

   Annual payment = $100,000 x .06 = $6,000
   Monthly payment = $6,000 ÷ 12 = $500

2. A borrower has a $500 monthly payment on a 6% loan. What is the loan principal?

   Principal = ($500 x 12) ÷ 6% = ($6,000 ÷ .06) = $100,000

3. A borrower has a $500 monthly payment on a $100,000 loan. What is the loan rate?

   Rate = ($500 x 12) ÷ $100,000 = ($6,000 ÷ 100,000) = .06 = 6%

Total Interest, Interest Rate, and Loan Term

Formulas:

Interest-only loan: *Total interest = Loan amount x Rate x Term in years*

Amortized loan: *Total interest = (Monthly PI payment x 12 x term) - Loan amount*

Examples:

1. A borrower obtains a 10-year interest only loan of $50,000 @ 6%. How much interest will he or she pay?

   ($50,000 x .06 x 10) = $30,000

2. A borrower obtains a 10-year amortized loan of $50,000 @ 6% with monthly

payments of $555.10. How much interest will he or she pay?

($555.10 x 12 x 10) - $50,000 = $16,612

Amortization Calculation

Formulas: *Month 1:   Principal paid = Monthly payment - (Loan amount x Rate ÷ 12)*

                    Month 2:   New loan amount = (Previous month principal - Principal paid)

                                      Principal paid = Monthly payment - (New loan amount x Rate ÷ 12)

Example: A borrower obtains a 30-year $100,000 amortized loan @ 7% with a $665.31 monthly payment. What is the principal paid in the second month?

                    Month 1:   Principal paid = $665.31 - ($100,000 x 7% ÷ 12) = $665.31 - (583.33 interest paid) = $81.98

                    Month 2:   New loan amount = $100,000 previous month beginning loan amount - $81.98 principal paid = $99,918.02

                                        Principal paid = $665.31 - ($99,918.02 x 7% ÷ 12) = $665.31 - (582.86 interest paid) = $82.45

Loan Constants

Formulas: *Monthly payment = (Loan amount x Loan constant) / 1000*

                    Loan amount = (Monthly payment ÷ Loan constant) x 1000

                    Loan constant = (Monthly payment ÷ Loan amount) x 1000

Examples: 1.   A borrower obtains a loan for $100,000 with a 6.3207 constant. What is the monthly payment?

                    Monthly payment = ($100,000 ÷ 1,000) x 6.3207 = $632.07

                2.   A borrower has a monthly payment of $632.07 on a loan with a monthly constant of 6.3207. What is the loan amount?

                    Loan amount = ($632.07 ÷ 6.3207) x 1000 = $100,000

                3.   A borrower obtains a loan for $100,000 with a monthly payment of $632.07. What is the loan constant?

                    Loan constant = ($632.07 ÷ $100,000) x 1,000 = 6.3207

Loan - to - Value Ratio (LTV)

Formulas: *LTV ratio = Loan ÷ Price (Value)*

Loan = LTV ratio x Price (Value)

Price (Value) = Loan ÷ LTV ratio

Examples: 1. A borrower can get a $265,600 loan on a $332,000 home. What is her LTV ratio?

LTV Ratio = $265,600 ÷ 332,000 = 80%

2. A borrower can get an 80% loan on a $332,000 home. What is the loan amount?

Loan = $332,000 x .80 = $265,600

3. A borrower obtained an 80% loan for $265,600. What was the price of the home?

Price (value) = $265,600 ÷ .80 = $332,000

Financial Qualification

Income ratio qualification

Formula: *Monthly Principal & Interest (PI) payment = Income ratio x Monthly gross income*

Example: A lender uses a 28% income ratio for the PI payment. A borrower grosses $30,000 per year. What monthly PI payment can the borrower afford?

Monthly PI payment = ($30,000 ÷ 12) x .28 = $700

How much can the borrower borrow if the loan constant is 6.3207? (See also- loan constants)

Loan amount = ($700 ÷ 6.3207) x 1,000 = $110,747.22

Debt ratio qualification

Formulas: *Debt ratio = (Housing expense + Other debt payments) ÷ Monthly gross income*

Housing expense = (Monthly gross income x Debt ratio) - Other debt payments

Example: A lender uses a 36% debt ratio. A borrower earns $30,000 / year and has monthly non-housing debt payments of $500. What housing payment can she afford?

Housing expense = ($30,000 ÷ 12 x .36) - 500 = ($900 - 500) = $400

INVESTMENT

Appreciation Calculations

Simple appreciation

Formulas: *Total appreciation = Current value - Original price*

Total appreciation rate = Total appreciation ÷ Original price

Average annual appreciation rate = Total appreciation rate ÷ number of years

One year appreciation rate = (Annual appreciation amount) ÷ (Value at beginning of year)

Examples: 1.   A home purchased for $200,000 five years ago is now worth $300,000. What are the total appreciation amount, total appreciation rate, and average appreciation rate?

Total appreciation = ($300,000 - 200,000), or $100,000

Total appreciation rate = ($100,000 ÷ 200,000), or 50%

Average annual appreciation rate = 50% ÷ 5 years = 10%

2.   A home costing $250,000 is worth $268,000 one year later. What is the one-year appreciation rate?

One-year appreciation rate = ($18,000 ÷ 250,000) = 7.2%

Compounded appreciation

Formula: *Appreciated value = Beginning value x (1+ annual rate) x (1+ annual rate) ......
for the number of years in question*

Example: A $100,000 property is expected to appreciate 5% each year for the next 3 years.
What will be its appreciated value at the end of this period?

Appreciated value = $100,000 x 1.05 x 1.05 x 1.05 = $115,762.50

Rate of Return, Investment Value, Income

Formulas: Where Income = net operating income (NOI); Rate = rate of return, cap rate, or
percent yield; and Value = value, price or investment amount:

Rate = Income ÷ Value

Value = Income ÷ Rate

Income = Value x Rate

Examples:
1. An office building has $200,000 net income and sold for $3,200,000. What was the rate of return?

   Rate = ($200,000 NOI ÷ 3,200,000 price) = 6.25%

2. An office building has $200,000 net income and a cap rate of 6.25%. What is its value?

   Value = ($200,000 ÷ 6.25%) = $3,200,000

3. An office building sells for $3,200,000 at a cap rate of 6.25%. What is its NOI?

   Income = $3,200,000 x 6.25% = $200,000

Basis, Adjusted Basis, and Capital Gain

Formulas:
Capital gain = Amount realized - Adjusted basis, where

Amount realized = Sale price - Selling costs

Adjusted basis = Beginning basis + Capital improvements - Total depreciation

Total depreciation = (Beginning depreciable basis ÷ Depreciation term in years) x Years depreciated

Depreciable basis = Initial property value + Capital improvements - Land value

Example:
Tip: work example backwards from last formula to first formula.

An apartment building was purchased for $500,000, with the land value estimated to be $100,000. The owner added a $100,000 parking lot. The property was depreciated on a 40-year schedule (for present purposes!). Three years later the property sold for $700,000, and selling costs were $50,000. What was the capital gain?

1. depreciable basis = $500,000 purchase price + 100,000 parking lot - 100,000 land = $500,000

2. total depreciation = ($500,000 ÷ 40 years) x 3 years = $37,500

3. adjusted basis = $500,000 purchase price + 100,000 parking lot - 37,500 total depreciation = $562,500

4. amount realized = $700,000 sale price - 50,000 selling costs = $650,000

5. capital gain = $650,000 amount realized - 562,500 adjusted basis = $87,500

Depreciation

Formulas: *Annual depreciation = (Beginning depreciable basis) ÷ (Depreciation term in number of years)*

Depreciable basis = (Initial property value + Capital improvements - Land value)

Example: Property value = $500,000; land value = $110,000; depreciation term = 39 years

1. ($500,000 - 110,000) = $390,000 depreciable basis

2. ($390,000 ÷ 39 years) = $10,000 annual depreciation

Equity

Formula: *Equity = Current market value - Current loan balance(s)*

Example: A home that was purchased for $150,000 with a $100,000 loan is now worth $300,000. The current loan balance is $80,000. What is the homeowner's equity?

Equity = $300,000 value - $80,000 debt = $220,000

Net Income

Formula: *NOI = Potential rent - Vacancy loss + Other income - Operating expenses*

Note: NOI does not include debt payments!
Example: A building has 10 office suites generating annual potential rent of $10,000 each. Vacancy = 10% and annual expenses are $35,000. Vending machines yield $5,000. What is the NOI?

$100,000 rent - 10,000 vacancy + 5,000 other income - 35,000 expenses = $60,000 NOI

Cash Flow

Formula: *Cash flow = (Net Operating Income - Debt service) where debt service is PI payment*

Example: A building generates $100,000 NOI after expenses and has a debt payment of
             $40,000. What is its cash flow?

             Cash flow = $100,000 - 40,000 = $60,000

Investment Property Income Tax Liability

Formula: *Tax liability = (NOI + Reserves - Interest expense - Depreciation) x Tax bracket*

Example: An office building has NOI of $200,000, an annual reserve expense of $20,000,
             interest expense of $130,000 and annual depreciation of $50,000. Assuming a
             28% tax bracket, what is its income tax liability?

             Tax liability = ($200,000 + 20,000 - 130,000 - 50,000) x 28% = $11,200

Return on Investment

Formula: *ROI = NOI ÷ Price*

Example: An investment property generates a cash flow of $100,000 and appraises for
             $1,500,000. What is the owner's return on investment?

             ROI = $100,000 ÷ 1,500,000 = 6.67%

Return on Equity

Formula: *ROE = Cash flow ÷ Equity*

Example: An investment property generates a cash flow of $100,000. The owner has
             $500,000 equity in the property. What is the owner's return on equity?

             ROE= $100,000 ÷ 500,000 = 20%

REAL ESTATE TAXATION

Converting Mill Rates

Definition: 1 mill = $.001; a mill rate of 1 mill per $1,000 = .1%; a 1% tax rate = 10 mills

Formula: *Tax = (Taxable value ÷ 1000) x Mill rate*

Example: A tax rate on a house with a $200,000 taxable value is 7 mills per thousand dollars
             of assessed valuation. What is the tax?

             Tax = ($200,000 ÷ 1,000) x 7 mills = $1,400

Tax Base

Formula: *Tax base = Assessed valuations – Exemptions*

Example: A town has a total assessed valuation of $20,000,000 and exemptions of $4,000,000. What is the tax base?

$20,000,000 - 4,000,000 = $16,000,000

Tax Rate, Base, and Requirement

Formulas: *Tax rate = Tax requirement ÷ Tax base*

Tax base = Tax requirement ÷ Tax rate

Tax requirement = Tax base x Rate

Example: A town has a tax base of $160,000,000 and a budget of $8,000,000. What is the tax rate?

Tax rate = ($8,000,000 ÷ 160,000,000) = .05, or 5%, or 50 mills

Special Assessments

Formula: *Special assessment = Total special assessment cost x Homeowner's share*

Example: A homeowner owns 100' of an 800' seawall that must be repaired. The total assessment will be $80,000. What is the homeowner's assessment?

1. Homeowner's share = 100' ÷ 800' = .125, or 12.5%
2. Special assessment = $80,000 x 12.5% = $10,000

COMMISSIONS

Commission Splits

Formulas: *Total commission = Sale price x Commission rate*

Co-brokerage split = Total commission x Co-brokerage percent

Agent split = Co-brokerage split x Agent percent

Broker split = Co-brokerage split - Agent split

Example: A $300,000 property sells at a 7% commission with a 50-50 co-brokerage split and a 60% agent split with her broker. What are total, co-brokerage, agent's, and broker's commissions?

Total commission = $300,000 x .07 = $21,000

Co-brokerage splits = $300,000 x .07 x .50 = $10,500

Agent split = $10,500 x .60 = $6,300

Agent's broker's split = $10.500 - 6,300 = $4,200

Seller's Net

Formula: *Seller's net = Sale Price - (sale price x commission) - Other closing costs - Loan balance*

Example: A home sells for $260,000 and has a loan balance of $200,000 at closing. The commission is 7% and other closing costs are $2,000. What is the seller's net?

Seller's net = ($260,000 - (260,000 x .07) - 2,000 - 200,000) = $39,800

Price to Net an Amount

Formula: *Sale Price = (Desired net + Closing costs + Loan payoff))(1 - Commission rate)*

Example: A home seller wants to net $50,000. The commission is 7%, the loan payoff is $150,000, and closing costs are $4,000. What must the price be?

Sale price = ($50,000 + 4,000 + 150,000) ÷ .93 = $219,355

CLOSING COSTS, PRORATIONS

30-Day 12-Month Method

Formulas: *Monthly amount = Annual amount / 12*

Daily amount = Monthly amount / 30

Proration = (Monthly amount multiplied by the # months) + (Daily amount multiplied by the # days)

Example: An annual tax bill is $1,800. Closing is on April 10. What is the seller's share of the taxes?

1. Monthly amount = ($1,800 ÷ 12) = $150; no. of months = 3

2. Daily amount = ($150 ÷ 30) = $5.00; no. of days = 10

3. Proration = ($150 x 3) + ($5 x 10) = ($450 + 50) = $500 seller's share

---

365-Day Method

Formula: *Daily amount = (Annual amount ÷ 365) or (Monthly amount ÷ Length of month)*

Proration = Daily amount multiplied by the # days

Example: An annual tax bill is $1,800. Closing is on April 10. What is the seller's share of the taxes?

1. Daily amount = ($1,800 ÷ 365) = $4.93

2. Jan 1 thru April 10 = (31 + 28 + 31 + 10) days, or 100 days

3. Proration = $4.93 x 100 days = $493 seller's share

Income Received in Advance (Rent)

Logic: *Credit buyer and debit seller for buyer's share*

Example: Seller receives $1,000 rent. The month is ¾ over.

1. Buyer's share is ($1,000 x 25%) = $250

2. Credit buyer / debit seller $250.

Expenses paid in Arrears (Tax)

Logic: *Credit buyer and debit seller for seller's share*

Example: Buyer will pay $1,000 taxes. The year is ¾ over.

1. Buyer's share is ($1,000 x 25%) = $250

2. Credit buyer / debit seller $750.

INSURANCE COVERAGE

Recovery with Co-Insurance Clauses

Formula: Recovery = (Damage claim) x (Percent replacement cost covered ÷ Minimum coverage requirement)

Example: An owner insures a home for $100,000. Replacement cost is $150,000. A co-insurance clause requires coverage of 80% of replacement cost to avoid penalty. Fire destroys the house. What can the owner recover from the insurer?

Claim recovery = $150,000 x (67% cost covered ÷ 80% required) = $125,625

CHAPTER TWENTY-TWO: REAL ESTATE MATHEMATICS
QUIZ

22.1. Barrett's seller client receives an offer for $867,900. The listing price is $980,000. The offer's percentage of listing price is:

a. 88.5%.
b. 91.3%.
c. 85.4%.
d. 89.1%.

22.2. Julia is evaluating an investment property that has a net operating income (NOI) of $75,000 annually. If the property is priced at $900,000, what is the capitalization rate (cap rate) for this property?

a. 8.33%
b. 7.50%
c. 6.75%
d. 9.25%

22.3. If a mortgage loan amount is $250,000 and a borrower buys 2 points to reduce the interest rate, how much will the borrower pay for the points if each point costs 1% of the loan amount?

a. $1,250
b. $2,500
c. $7,500
d. $5,000

22.4. Calculate the total interest paid on a $250,000 mortgage loan over 20 years with an annual interest rate of 6% if the monthly payment is $1,800.

a. $143,759
b. $179,840
c. $186,872
d. $198,000

22.5. Each unit in a fourplex property has a monthly rent of $2,000. What is the property's value using a GRM of 7?

a. $56,000
b. $672,000
c. $168,000
d. $356,000

22.6. A home sells for $350,000 and has a loan balance of $250,000 at closing. The commission is 6% and other closing costs are $3,000. What is the seller's net?

a. $76,000
b. $79,000
c. $82,000
d. $84,000

22.7. Casey's potential investment property generates a gross annual rental income of $120,000 and has additional non-rental income of $15,000 from coin-operated laundry machines and vending machines. If the property is listed at $1,350,000, what is the Gross Income Multiplier (GIM)?

a. 11.25
b. 9.50
c. 10.0
d. 12.00

22.8. A borrower is purchasing a property valued at $400,000 and is securing a loan of $320,000. What is the loan-to-value (LTV) ratio?

a. 70%
b. 75%
c. 80%
d. 85%

22.9. A homeowner takes out a mortgage loan of $300,000. After the first year, the homeowner pays $15,000 in interest. What is the annual interest rate on the mortgage loan?

a. 3.5%
b. 4.5%
c. 5%
d. 6%

22.10. A borrower earns $130,000 per year and has monthly non-housing debt payments of $1,500. Using a 36% debt ratio, what maximum monthly housing payment can the borrower afford?

a. $1,900
b. $3,400
c. $2,900
d. $2,400

Section Tests Answer Key

CHAPTER ONE: LICENSE LAW AND REGULATIONS

1. c. To protect the general public (6)
2. d. Attorneys at law (8)
3. d. maintaining confidentiality of all material facts related to the property. (9)
4. b. Operate independently (11)
5. d. None of the given circumstances would enable the party to legally practice real estate in New York (11)
6. a. The office's broker or a qualified associate broker. (13)
7. b. The party must complete 77 hours of approved education (17)
8. c. the new broker must change the licensee's association prior to the licensee renewing the license. (8)
9. d. the licensee must submit a certified copy of the conviction judgment to the DOS. (9)
10. d. 22 ½ (11)
11. c. Licenses that are expired for more than 2 years require retaking and passing the examination and then reapplying for the license. (11)
12. a. Secretary of State (13)
13. c. The words Licensed Real Estate Broker (17)
14. a. The ad must identify the broker's name as the listing broker. (8)
15. b. Team names can include the word group or associate. (9)
16. c. A fee for finding a buyer after a listing agreement has been signed (11)
17. d. a $10,000 fine and up to 1 year prison. (11)
18. d. collecting rent. (13)
19. c. the seller can be held liable for the buyer's actual damages caused by the undisclosed defects. (17)
20. a. must disclose the well to the buyer prior to signing a purchase contract. (8)
21. c. Negotiate sales transactions on a licensee's behalf (9)
22. a. The principal broker must license each branch office separately. (11)
23. b. She will be required to retake and pass the state written examination. (11)
24. d. Implicit bias awareness (13)
25. d. The duly appointed administrator may use the license to complete any unfinished business within 120 days. (17)

CHAPTER TWO: LAW OF AGENCY

1. c. provide sufficient information for the agent to complete the agent's tasks. (48)
2. b. client. (38)
3. c. agent's role. (39)
4. c. universal agency. (39)
5. b. general agency. (39)
6. d. Agency coupled with an interest (40)
7. a. Listing agreement (40)
8. c. a party creates an agency relationship outside of an express agreement. (40)
9. b. an undisclosed dual agency. (53)
10. a. Confidentiality (44)
11. a. The agent has violated the duty of confidentiality. (49)
12. c. information regarding a property that might affect the buyer's decision to purchase the property. (44)
13. c. Disclosing a potential buyer's national origin to the property seller (45)
14. b. the agent has not violated fiduciary duty. (49)
15. a. fairness, care, and honesty. (43)
16. c. Previous flooding in the basement (44)
17. d. Availability (47)
18. b. The difference between the seller's asking price and the actual purchase price (48)
19. b. intentional misrepresentation (50)
20. a. Death or incapacity of the agent (50)
21. d. Dual agency (52)
22. b. When there is consent from only one party in the transaction (53)
23. c. designated agents. (53)
24. d. Transaction broker (55)
25. a. being present at a conversation where the setting of commission rates is discussed. (56)
26. a. collusion. (57)
27. c. must be an express agreement. (61)
28. a. exclusive right-to sell agreement. (60)
29. b. exclusive agency agreement (59)
30. c. open listing. (60)
31. d. net listing (60)
32. b. Exclusive right-to-sell listing (40)
33. b. the agent has a claim to a commission if the owner sells or leases to a party within a certain time following the listing's expiration. (61)
34. c. printing an explanation of exclusive right-to-sell and exclusive agency listings on the back of the listing agreement for a one- to three-family dwelling. (62)
35. c. The defaulting party may have a financial consequence. (51)
36. b. present all offers to the principal regardless of their amount. (49)
37. c. a broker who has an agency relationship with a client. (54)
38. b. One agent represents both sides in a transaction. (54)
39. a. The agent is showing the client's property to a prospective buyer. (65)
40. d. good faith, trust and confidence. (38)
41. b. exclusive right to sell. (59)
42. c. A listing that is entered in a multiple listing service to enable cooperation with member brokers. (61)
43. c. An illegal market allocation (57)
44. d. The Department of Justice (58)
45. a. Open agency listing (60)
46. a. An agency relationship disclosure (64)
47. c. at least 3 years. (65)
48. b. Prior to the buyer signing the sales contract (66)
49. a. 4-family dwelling (66)
50. b. Prior to a rental lease being signed (67)
51. c. Civil fine up to $10,000. (67)
52. d. When children under 11 years old reside in the apartment (69)
53. b. Heating and cooling bills for the past 2 years are to be provided when requested by prospective buyers of one- to two-family homes. (69)
54. c. 30 days (69)
55. d. year. (69)

CHAPTER THREE: ESTATES & INTERESTS

1. d. The Constitution (78)
2. c. Land and everything permanently attached to it. (78)
3. a. The surface of the earth and all natural things

permanently attached to the earth (79)
4. b. Immobile, indestructible, heterogeneous (129)
5. d. land does not include man-made structures. (79)
6. a. real property includes ownership of a bundle of rights. (80)
7. c. To transfer (82)
8. d. Stock. (360)
9. a. the right of others to use and enjoy their property. (83)
10. c. separable. (83)
11. d. Riparian (84)
12. b. To the middle of the waterway (84)
13. d. Homestead for a primary residence (86)
14. a. A tree growing on a parcel of land. (80)
15. b. its definition as one or the other in a sale or lease contract. (81)
16. d. A plant or crop that is considered personal property (81)
17. c. Affixing and severance (81)
18. c. The fractional part of the entire estate owned by one of the property's owners. (86)
19. c. The owner of a freehold estate (88)
20. d. Life and fee simple (90)
21. a. Conventional and legal (91)
22. b. estate for years. (94)
23. b. Tenancy in common (95)
24. c. The beneficiary controls the property. (99)
25. a. Corporation (100)

CHAPTER FOUR: LIENS AND EASEMENTS
1. b. An automatic default on the mortgage loan (109)
2. c. When the associated debt is paid in full and recorded (109)
3. a. A lien attaches to the property. (109)
4. d. equitable lien. (109)
5. a. general lien. (361)
6. b. Real estate tax lien (110)
7. a. when the lien was recorded, with exceptions. (110)
8. c. When the lien was recorded (110)
9. b. A lien placed against a property as security for annual property tax payment (111)
10. a. Mechanic's lien (112)
11. d. To prevent the debtor from selling or hiding the property. (112)
12. d. No, the subcontractors can place a mechanic's lien on Dan, causing him to pay twice for the work. (112)
13. b. Deed restrictions can take precedence over zoning ordinances if the deed restrictions are more restrictive. (113)
14. c. A lawsuit can force the new owner to forfeit ownership to the previous owner. (113)
15. a. involving the land owner and a second, non-owning party. (114)
16. d. Easement Appurtenant (114)
17. b. A shed that overlaps onto the neighbor's property (119)
18. a. Eminent domain (118)
19. d. Easement by Prescription (118)
20. d. Federal estate tax lien (112)

CHAPTER FIVE: DEEDS AND CONVEYANCES
1. d. alienation. (125)
2. c. The person who has the preponderance of evidence of ownership is the rightful owner. (109)

3. a. deed (109)
4. c. Quitclaim deed (129)
5. b. Estoppel (126)
6. a. the testator must be at least 18 years old. (132)
7. b. The property will be distributed through a court process called estate administration per New York's laws of intestacy. (131)
8. b. legal title. (124)
9. d. It is held in a land trust. (133)
10. a. Mary holds legal title to the property, and John owns equitable title. (124)
11. d. nuncupative (132)
12. c. The grantor owns the estate to be conveyed, and has the right to do so. (128)
13. b. The decedent's portion of the property will automatically be transferred to the remaining joint tenants. (97)
14. d. Constructive notice (125)
15. b. Full covenant and warranty deed (128)
16. a. voluntary alienation. (126)
17. c. title records. (125)
18. a. bargain and sale deed with covenant. (129)
19. d. habendum clause (127)
20. c. The grantee will not be disturbed by third party title disputes. (128)

CHAPTER SIX: TITLE CLOSING AND COSTS
1. b. To provide a detailed account of the final loan terms and closing costs to the borrower (143)
2. c. Title insurance (155)
3. a. buyer debits over buyer credits (154)
4. b. the third business day after receiving a loan application. (142)
5. c. lienholder (160)
6. b. RESPA (132)
7. d. 360/30-day (156)
8. b. earnest money (140)
9. d. Title passes only when the conveyance has been duly registered on the title certificate itself. (160)
10. c. title certificate (162)
11. b. free of undisclosed defects and encumbrances. (161)
12. b. the loan is intended to be sold to FNMA. (141)
13. d. $692 (146)
14. b. refinances. (144)
15. c. Taxes and mortgage interest (156)

CHAPTER SEVEN: CONTRACT OF SALES AND LEASES
1. a. Oral real estate sales contract (174)
2. b. Estate for years (167)
3. d. executory (182)
4. c. full disposition (172)
5. c. Abandonment (183)
6. a. contract for deed. (186)
7. b. nonfreehold (166)
8. b. contain a legal description of the property. (178)
9. a. Landlords are required to give 99% of interest earned on the trust account to tenants. (168)
10. b. Suit for specific performance (184)
11. b. the parties have completed an oral, executory contract. (182)
12. c. Voluntary, bilateral, and executory (182)
13. b. the optionor must perform if the optionee takes the option, but the optionee is under no obligation to do so. (188)

14. b. the vendor's rights to encumber the property may not be beneficial to the vendee. (187)
15. d. Brokers and agents may complete standard promulgated forms as long as the broker is a party to the agreement. (181)
16. a. revocation (183)
17. c. mutual consent. (179)
18. b. Estate at sufferance (167)
19. a. equitable (190)
20. b. One that is not a personal contract for services (181)
21. d. enforceable. (166)
22. a. the landlord guarantees the premises is fit for human habitation. (172)
23. d. The offeree creates a counteroffer, and the original offer is void. (180)
24. d. claim the deposit as relief for the buyer's failure to perform. (184)
25. b. It enables the renter to accumulate down payment funds while paying rent. (188)

CHAPTER EIGHT: REAL ESTATE FINANCE
1. c. deed of trust (196)
2. b. asking about an applicant's plans for child-bearing. (203)
3. a. promissory note (200)
4. b. mortgage or trust deed (195)
5. a. income ratio (204)
6. d. conforming loans. (217)
7. b. Transfer of the Property or a Beneficial Interest in Borrower (202)
8. b. Savings and loans (213)
9. c. interest. (197)
10. d. Balloon payment (204)
11. c. hypothecation. (195)
12. b. the lender can demand the mortgage balance be immediately paid in full if ownership is transferred. (202)
13. b. The trustor conveys title to a trustee to hold on behalf of the beneficiary. (196)
14. c. title-theory state. (195)
15. a. collateral (196)
16. d. civil usury (198)
17. d. evaluate a loan applicant on the basis of that applicant's own income and credit rating. (203)
18. a. Determine the borrower's total monthly debt obligations (206)
19. b. lock-in loan commitment. (208)
20. c. purchase (216)
21. b. the seller receives a junior mortgage from the buyer and uses the buyer's payments to make the payments on the original first mortgage. (224)
22. d. The loan balance increases over the term of the loan.. (222)
23. a. Purchase money mortgage (224)
24. d. dividing the monthly housing expense by monthly gross income. (206)
25. c. foreclosure. (227)
26. d. The proceeds of the sale do not cover the seller's outstanding mortgage loan balance. (230)
27. a. Return funds to primary lenders so they can make more mortgage loans. (214)
28. a. give a certificate of discharge of mortgager to the borrower. (232)
29. c. a deed in lieu of foreclosure (230)
30. a. The lender may not obtain a deficiency judgment or lien in a non-judicial foreclosure action. (229)

CHAPTER NINE: LAND USE REGULATIONS
1. c. Building codes (253)
2. a. Zoning ordinance (247)
3. b. Spot zoning (251)
4. d. Eminent domain (254)
5. a. land use plan. (244)
6. c. enforcing and administering land use regulation on an everyday basis. (246)
7. b. deed condition. (254)
8. a. Methods of growing tourism revenue (244)
9. d. cluster zoning. (249)
10. b. promoting the highest and best use of property. (243)
11. d. Ensure that improvements comply with ordinances and codes (248)
12. b. plat of subdivision. (252)
13. d. the construction complies with building codes. (253)
14. a. state legislation called enabling acts. (247)
15. a. police power. (247)
16. b. Zoning board of appeals (251)
17. d. court injunction. (257)
18. a. compliance with zoning ordinances would cause the property owner unreasonable hardship. (251)
19. a. take into account both the interests of the individual and the interests of the surrounding community. (243)
20. c. legal nonconforming use. (251)

CHAPTER TEN: CONSTRUCTION AND ENVIRONMENTAL ISSUES
1. b. Procedures for new facility construction, expansion, and rate increase acceptance (264)
2. b. Detecting, disclosing, and remediating regulated hazards (269)
3. d. individual water supply wells. (265)
4. c. Utilizing on-site environmental monitoring systems (272)
5. d. Developers, landowners, and governing bodies (260)
6. a. Commercial fire sprinkler systems (265)
7. c. They must meet the state Department of Environmental Conservation standards for installation and maintenance. (267)
8. b. New York State Department of Environmental Conservation (264)
9. c. Adding insulation to exterior walls and the ceiling below the roof (262)
10. c. Safety measures during construction (266)
11. a. Sick Building Syndrome (SBS) and Building-Related Illness (BRI) (274)
12. c. The weather, the soil, and the suction within the home (278)
13. b. Concrete slab (262)
14. b. Paints, cleaners, batteries, and pesticides (273)
15. b. Use treated wood, create a barrier between wood and the ground, and treat the soil with termiticides (273)
16. a. Asbestos (275)
17. a. Clean Air Amendment (282)
18. d. Corrosion that results in leaks (279)
19. d. environmental impact statement (EIS) detailing how the project will affect the environment. (271)
20. d. a 6-year warranty against structural defects. (265)
21. a. groundwater (265)
22. a. Formaldehyde (276)
23. b. environmental documents review, a title search, and a visual site inspection. (270)

24. d. CERCLA (281)
25. b. Balloon frame (262)

CHAPTER ELEVEN: VALUATION PROCESS AND PRICING PROPERTIES
1. b. Transferability (291)
2. b. good comparable properties. (295)
3. c. Reversionary (293)
4. d. Sales comparison (295)
5. a. Market price (294)
6. a. if two similar properties are for sale, a buyer will purchase the cheaper of the two. (291)
7. d. the highest price that a buyer would pay and the lowest price that the seller would accept for the property. (294)
8. b. The broker does not usually consider the full range of data about market conditions. (293)
9. b. replacement cost. (299)
10. b. economic obsolescence. (300)
11. c. Select comparable properties, adjust the comparables, estimate the subject's value (295)
12. b. market value is not always the same as what the property cost to build. (299)
13. a. Numerous expenses are not taken into account. (306)
14. b. effective gross income minus total operating expenses. (304)
15. d. functional obsolescence (300)
16. b. Apartment buildings (303)
17. c. Estimate net operating income and apply a capitalization rate to it (303)
18. b. Weight the comparables (296)
19. c. depreciation. (299)
20. b. every property is unique. (295)

CHAPTER TWELVE: HUMAN RIGHTS AND FAIR HOUSING
1. a. Military status (322)
2. c. "Perfect for young families" (323)
3. c. Equal housing opportunity logo (325)
4. a. Discriminatory misrepresentation (323)
5. b. Race (322)
6. c. Emotional support dogs are not considered service dogs under the ADA. (319)
7. a. She discriminated against the applicant based on national origin. (322)
8. b. New York State Human Rights Law (327)
9. b. Encouraging homeowners to sell their properties by suggesting that the entry of a particular race or ethnic group into the neighborhood will lead to a decline in property values (324)
10. c. Declining to fund loans for people who do not qualify (324)
11. a. Young at Heart Apartments requires all tenants to be 62 or older. (317)
12. d. Home Mortgage Disclosure Act (321)
13. b. Advertising may not include any substantial and intentional misrepresentation. (325)
14. b. The Sterling Society, a private club, offers dormitory-style housing to its members only. (319)
15. c. They are more robust than federal laws. (327)
16. b. Steering (324)
17. c. E-Z Lending's practice of offering a higher interest rate to Jamie may constitute unlawful source of income discrimination under New York law. (333)
18. c. Senior housing (321)
19. d. a preference or discrimination based on a protected class. (325)
20. d. Yes, the brochure might convey a preference for white tenants. (325)
21. b. prohibit discrimination in housing transactions (317)
22. a. At least 80 percent of the units are each occupied by at least one resident 55 years old or older. (318)
23. d. Although the federal Fair Housing Act allows exemptions for certain kinds of discrimination, no exemptions related to race in the private or public sale and rental of property are permitted. (321)
24. d. Providing unequal services (323)
25. a. Sex (327)
26. d. Room rentals in buildings with the owner in residence (328)
27. c. Limiting a Spanish-speaking person's unit options to a floor where other Spanish speakers live (323)
28. c. Redlining (324)
29. b. New York Civil Rights Law (328)
30. c. a couple whose 21-year-old son moved back in with them. (321)
31. c. Implicit bias is an unconscious mental process, while discrimination is an action taken based on an implicit or explicit bias (332)
32. b. Income bias (333)
33. d. It involves stereotyping based on lifestyle choices. (323)
34. b. By identifying and addressing unconscious prejudices (332)
35. d. Setting and following objective criteria for all transactions (334)
36. c. Recognizing and challenging biased assumptions (334)

SECTION THIRTEEN: TYPES OF MORTGAGES AND SOURCES OF FINANCING
1. c. File a use appeal to request a land use variance. (350)
2. a. Grievance Day (349)
3. b. Zoning (350)
4. a. Involving the municipality's designated engineer (352)
5. d. By the legislative body (348)
6. c. issuing certificates of occupancy. (352)
7. a. the final assessment roll. (349)
8. d. State Historic Preservation Office (349)
9. c. Conservation Advisory Councils (348)
10. b. Village (350)

CHAPTER FOURTEEN: PROPERTY INSURANCE
1. c. Her lender will place homeowner's insurance on the house. (357)
2. a. To cover items or situations not included in the standard policy (358)
3. d. It includes only one kind of coverage. (360)
4. c. The architectural style of the home (358)
5. d. Workers' compensation insurance (363)
6. b. To protect the property from possible loss due to damage (359)
7. b. New York Property Insurance Underwriting Association (362)
8. c. Homeowner's policies should insure the home for at least 80% of the home's replacement cost. (360)
9. b. Personal property (359)
10. a. HO-1. (361)

CHAPTER FIFTEEN: LICENSEE SAFETY
1. b. Agents should have visitors enter doorways ahead of the themselves. (370)
2. c. let the office know the agent is in trouble. (370)
3. c. To alert emergency responders (372)
4. d. Prescription medications (372)
5. a. A group of visitors near the end of the day (370)
6. d. Making sure your cell phone is fully charged before showing property (371)
7. b. requiring a buddy system after office hours. (372)

CHAPTER SIXTEEN: TAXES AND ASSESSMENTS

1. a. At a uniform percentage of market value each year (377)
2. c. Request a re-evaluation from the County Assessor's Office (382)
3. c. County and local (375)
4. d. equitable right of redemption. (386)
5. b. To level out the unevenness of valuations (378)
6. b. according to the value. (375)
7. c. senior citizens. (383)
8. b. the total assessed value of all real property in the jurisdiction. (346)
9. d. The property's market value (349)
10. d. Michael, a first-time homebuyer in his first year of home ownership. (383)
11. a. school districts. (379)
12. c. Only those properties that will benefit from the improvement are charged this special levy. (376)
13. c. Appropriation (381)
14. d. Every year. (380)
15. b. equalization rate (378)

CHAPTER SEVENTEEN: CONDOMINIUMS AND COOPERATIVES

1. b. Report of the building's physical condition prepared by an architect or engineer. (392)
2. a. maintenance (394)
3. c. housing-cooperative (398)
4. d. A proprietary lease has no stated term. (399)
5. b. Personal property interest (399)
6. d. A fee simple ownership of a unit of airspace unit together with an undivided interest in the common elements. (392)
7. c. proprietary lease (398)
8. d. To enforce the bylaws and manage the overall property (394)
9. c. New York Housing Stability and Tenant Protection Act (394)
10. b. Shares in the organization (401)
11. a. non-eviction plan (394)
12. c. board of directors (394)
13. a. The corporate entity of the cooperative association (399)
14. b. By assigning both the stock certificates and proprietary lease to Pamela (400)
15. c. The cooperative association (400)

SECTION EIGHTEEN: TAXES AFFECTING REAL ESTATE

1. c. bonds. (408)
2. a. Selling a property typically takes several months and involves complex processes. (406)
3. c. Consistent rental income and long-term stability (413)
4. c. Appreciation (409)
5. c. Limited partnership (411)
6. c. By adjusting pre-tax cash flow for reserves, depreciation, and loan interest (419)
7. d. An owner wants to lease raw land to a cattle company. (417)
8. a. return on investment (414)
9. b. Commercial leases can involve high financial stakes. (416)
10. d. mandates the tenant is to accept the new owner as the landlord and is to continue to follow the lease's specified rent payments. (427)
11. a. Real estate (409)
12. d. Opportunity cost (410)
13. c. The actual space a tenant can occupy and use for offices and other functional areas (424)
14. c. gross (416)
15. a. Market changes (409)
16. a. The ease in which it can be converted to cash (406)
17. d. fixed bump (427)
18. b. The difference between cash revenue and cash expenses, excluding depreciation (418)
19. d. events that are difficult to predict, such as environmental changes that result in physical danger (407)
20. b. carpetable area (426)
21. c. A single-family home rented to tenants (414)
22. b. Multiplying the dollar amount per square foot by the total rentable area of the space (426)
23. a. Investors buy certificates in a REIT that invests in mortgages or real estate, and receive income based on rental payments, property sales, and mortgage interest. (411)
24. d. Subtracting tax liability from pre-tax cash flow (421)
25. d. Loft (417)
26. c. conservation of capital. (406)
27. a. reduce or defer the amount of tax owed. (407)
28. c. leverage. (407)
29. c. Market risk (407)
30. c. Certificates of deposit (413)
31. c. Real estate (410)
32. d. A group of investors combine resources to buy, develop, and/or operate a property (411)
33. a. The land's location (414)
34. b. Net (416)
35. d. Rate of return (422)

SECTION NINETEEN: CHAPTER NINETEEN: INCOME TAX ISSUES IN REAL ESTATE TRANSACTIONS

1. c. 21% (436)
2. b. 7 (436)
3. c. almost doubled. (438)
4. d. $10,000. (438)
5. c. Those in the lowest bracket whose 10% interest rate did not change (437)
6. d. Whichever deduction is higher. (438)
7. a. Only if the loan was used for home improvements (439)
8. d. $19,500 (439)
9. a. Real estate taxes paid upfront 439)
10. c. have used the home as a primary residence. (442)
11. a. Beginning basis plus capital improvements minus amounts received equals adjusted basis (443)
12. b. Mortgage points (441)
13. c. 45 days (445)
14. b. Developers of affordable housing (446)
15. c. One investor buys a replacement property before selling the original property. (446)

CHAPTER TWENTY: MORTGAGE BROKERAGE

1. b. $250,000 (452)
2. a. A mortgage banker works for a financial institution that uses its own funds to originate or fund mortgages. (451)
3. d. have 2 or more years of credit analysis experience. (450)
4. c. They have the ability to approve mortgages for the lending institution. (452)
5. d. the New York State Banking Department. (451)

6. b. Find and negotiate mortgage loans for the borrower (450)
7. c. 5 years of experience in making or underwriting residential mortgage loans (452)
8. c. The lender the borrower chooses to work with pays them a commission. (450)
9. a. Approve or deny mortgage loan applications based on borrower qualifications (451)
10. c. intermediary (451)

CHAPTER TWENTY-ONE: PROPERTY MANAGEMENT

1. c. fiduciary (456)
2. b. routine, preventive, and corrective (465)
3. a. To preserve the value of the physical asset for the owner over the long term (464)
4. d. raise rental rates. (463)
5. d. To keep tenant turnover low (464)
6. b. Subtracting losses caused by uncollected rents, vacancies, and evictions from potential gross income (462)
7. d. rent control and rent stabilization. (468)
8. c. A court may hold the manager responsible for the physical safety of tenants, employees, and customers in leased premises. (467)
9. b. financial reporting to the principal (461)
10. c. Housing Stability and Tenant Protection Act of 2019 (468)
11. a. cost per tenant prospect generated per lease. (463)
12. c. subletting the apartment without landlord consent (470)
13. d. Regular painting of exterior and interior areas (465)
14. c. Landlords must provide written notice of any rent increase over 5%. (470)
15. a. administrative. (461)

CHAPTER TWENTY-TWO: REAL ESTATE MATHEMATICS

1. a. 88.5%. (483)
2. a. 8.33% (486)
3. d. $5,000 (486)
4. b. $182,000 (488)
5. b. $672,000 (484)
6. a. $76,000 (495)
7. c. 10.0 (484)
8. c. 80% (489)
9. c. 5% (487)
10. d. $2,400 (489)

New York Practice Exam

Answer key is on p. 515

1. Which of the following best describes the legal concept of "real estate"?

   a. Land and any natural things permanently attached to the earth
   b. Land itself
   c. Human-made structures
   d. Land and any natural or man-made structures attached to the land

2. Which type of deed provides the most protection for the grantee?

   a. Executor's deed
   b. General warranty deed
   c. Deed in trust
   d. Full covenant and warranty deed

3. According to the TRID rule, when must lenders provide the Closing Disclosure form to the consumer?

   a. At least 3 business days before the loan application
   b. At least 3 business days before consummation of the loan
   c. Within 3 calendar days of the loan application
   d On the day of closing the transaction

4. Which if the following is true about ECOA?

   a. ECOA permits lenders to specialize lending activity by geographical area for enhanced credit opportunities.
   b. ECOA requires lenders to offer equal credit terms to all prospective borrowers.
   c. Per ECOA, lenders must evaluate a loan applicant on the basis of that applicant's own income and credit rating.
   d. Lenders are required to consider a spouse's income when evaluating a family's creditworthiness.

5. _____ is/are illegal in New York.

   a. Zoning variances
   b. Spot zoning
   c. Nonconforming use
   d. Special exception

6. The 2020 Energy Conservation Construction Code of New York State requirements address:

   a. fire sprinklers.
   b. solar panels.
   c. smoke and carbon monoxide detectors.
   d. individual water supply wells.

7. Appraisers and brokers most commonly use the _____ valuation approach.

   a. replacement
   b. income capitalization
   c. cost
   d. sales comparison

8. What is one of a property manager's primary obligations to the property owner?

   a. Obtaining necessary loans
   b. Financial reporting
   c. Finding a buyer for the property
   d. Maintaining good standing in the community

9. The highest price a buyer would pay and the lowest price the seller would accept for the property describes:

   a. reproduction value.
   b. appraised value.
   c. market value.
   d. salvage value.

10. Allison owns a house. As part of her ownership rights, she is free to sell, bequeath, lease, donate, or assign any or all of her ownership interests. In the bundle of rights, this is known as the right to:

    a. use.
    b. transfer.
    c. encumber.
    d. exclude.

11. A borrower has a $200,000 interest-only loan at 6% interest. What are the monthly payments?

 a. $800
 b. $1,000
 c. $1,200
 d. $1,400

12. _____ are exempt from New York real estate licensure requirements.

 a. Property managers
 b. Multi-property property managers
 c. Tenant relocators
 d. Attorneys at law

13. A borrower obtains a 20-year amortized loan of $250,000 at 5% with monthly payments of $1,800. How much total interest will the borrower pay?

 a. $182,000
 b. $185,000
 c. $188,000
 d. $190,000

14. What type of insurance pays if the homeowner is sued and found to be responsible for someone being injured on the owner's property?

 a. Liability coverage
 b. Loss of use coverage
 c. Medical payment coverage
 d. Endorsements

15. Because local assessments can lead to unfairly high or low values for properties in certain areas, jurisdictions may establish _____ to level out the unevenness of valuations.

 a. uniform percentages
 b. voluntary tax liens
 c. assessment rolls
 d. equalization factors

16. Jordan lives in a residential building where he is part of a community that collectively owns the property. Jordan bought shares in the corporation that owns the building, giving him the right to live in a specific unit. Decisions about the property are made by a board elected by the residents, and each resident has a say in major decisions, such as maintenance and improvements. In what type of housing does Jordan live?

 a. Condominium
 b. Townhouse
 c. Apartment
 d. Cooperative

17. Alex failed to complete his required CE and renew his license by the expiration date. If he still wants to work in real estate, what will he need to do?

 a. Retake and pass the state written examination
 b. Retake and pass a pre-license course and reapply for a license
 c. Take the required CE and reapply for a license
 d. Request that his sponsoring broker make an appeal on his behalf

18. What type of investments are riskier than money investments but safer than stock investments?

 a. Annuities
 b. Non-income property investments
 c. Debt investments
 d. Commercial investments

19. _____ are exempt from New York State's anti-discrimination legislation.

 a. Assisted living communities of any size
 b. Homeless shelters
 c. Apartment buildings of 8 or fewer units
 d. Room rentals in owner-occupied housing with two or fewer units

20. Who handles zoning ordinance enforcement for a municipality?

 a. Mayor
 b. Zoning commission
 c. Zoning enforcement officer
 d. Zoning board

21. Which of the following holds a salesperson's license during the licensee's period of employment?

   a. Department of State
   b. The sponsoring broker
   c. The salesperson
   d. The National Association of REALTORS®

22. Which of the following would be considered real property?

   a. Above-ground pool
   b. Patio furniture
   c. Potted rosebushes
   d. Dwarf apple tree

23. A mineral fiber that was once used in buildings as insulation is:

   a. radon
   b. asbestos
   c. lead
   d. formaldehyde

24. What is the main point of a municipality's master plan?

   a. To determine an annual budget for the municipality
   b. To create a strategic vision for future development
   c. To adopt the municipality's laws and ordinances
   d. To grant authority to the planning board to review and approve land use concerns

25. Which of the following is an example of a voluntary lien?

   a. Property tax lien
   b. Mortgage lien
   c. HOA lien
   d. Mechanic's lien

26. John and Mary entered into a contract to buy a house. However, neither party followed through with their obligations under the contract. What form of contract termination has occurred in this situation?

   a. Invalidity of contract
   b. Revocation
   c. Abandonment
   d. Infeasibility

27. Seller Jim hires real estate agent Clark to sell his property. Which of the following is most likely to be the agreement they will use to create an agency relationship between themselves?

   a. Listing agreement
   b. Limited agency agreement
   c. Offer
   d. Broker agreement

28. Which of the following would be exempt from familial status discrimination?

   a. An apartment building for senior citizens when 100% of the units are occupied by people 62 or older
   b. An "active adult" housing development designed for people 50 and older
   c. A co-op where all residents take part in the rooftop garden project
   d. A neighborhood that plans events for children

29. Tom and Lisa entered into a contract for Tom to buy Lisa's condo, but Lisa failed to fulfill her obligations. Which of the following is a legal remedy that Tom as the damaged party may pursue?

   a. Sue Lisa for contract reinstatement
   b. Sue Lisa for specific performance
   c. Place a lien on Lisa's condo
   d. Require Lisa to join him in mediating the breach

30. What characteristic of a last will and testament provides that the will can be changed at any time during the maker's lifetime?

   a. Intestacy
   b. Amendatory
   c. Reciprocity
   d. Escheat

31. A peril that is typically not covered under a homeowner's insurance policy is called a(n):

   a. endorsement.
   b. condition.
   c. rider.
   d. exclusion.

32. A condominium is:

   a. A leased unit in a multifamily building
   b. A unit in a condominium building
   c. A residential building in which owners buy shares in an organization
   d. An airspace unit combined with an interest in the common elements

33. Subtracting total operating expenses from effective gross income is the calculation for:

   a. potential gross income.
   b. net operating income.
   c. income capitalization.
   d. gross rent multiplier.

34. What does equitable title to real property signify?

   a. The right to use the property but not to sell it
   b. Full legal ownership of the property
   c. The right to obtain full ownership of the property
   d. A temporary leasehold interest in the property

35. Which of the following is a feature of commercial leases?

   a. Short terms and minimal tenant improvements.
   b. Necessary tenant improvements
   c. Non-negotiable lease clauses
   d. Minor financial consequences for default.

36. Which of the following is a primary health and environmental concern of underground storage tanks?

   a. Lead contamination
   b. Asbestos disturbance
   c. Radon
   d. Corrosion resulting in leaks

37. What must lenders provide to consumers within 3 business days of a loan application under the TRID rule?

   a. Closing Disclosure
   b. Loan Estimate
   c. HUD-1 Uniform Settlement Statement
   d. Good Faith Estimate

38. Which of the following is the most effective means of ensuring fair and accurate assessments for a municipality?

   a. Equalization rates
   b. Appropriation of taxes
   c. Reassessments performed throughout the municipality
   d. Exemptions

39. A valid and enforceable contract to convey any interest in property is required to

   a. be expressed either orally or in writing.
   b. include a legal description of the property.
   c. display a notary seal and signature.
   d. contain the broker's signature.

40. Eric holds a salesperson license. Which of the following activities is he prohibited from doing?

   a. Collecting tenants' rent
   b. Working as a sole proprietor
   c. Negotiating a property sale
   d. Listing a property for sale

41. _____ is an example of preventive maintenance for which a property manager is responsible.

   a. Regular cleaning of common areas
   b. Replacing a broken air conditioner
   c. Renovating kitchen fixtures.
   d. Regular painting of exterior and interior areas

42. Under the Torrens system, when does title pass in a real estate transaction?

   a. When the court clears the title during a conveyance procedure
   b. When the conveyance has been duly registered on the title certificate
   c. After the public records are searched and the title is pronounced clear
   d. When the property deed is signed by both parties

43. What is the term for a lender's offer to lend a certain amount of money for a set period and interest rate, with a specified expiration date?

   a. Conditional loan commitment
   b. Lock-in loan commitment
   c. Firm loan commitment
   d. Take-out loan commitment

44. Which of the following zoning classifications permits residences to be immediately adjacent to or have a common boundary with another residence?

    a. Multiple use zoning
    b. Public zoning
    c. Density zoning
    d. Cluster zoning

45. Which of the following reflects or is used as a voluntary conveyance of title to real estate?

    a. Estoppel
    b. Foreclosure
    c. Deed
    d. Adverse possession

46. New York's septic system standards for houses:

    a. must adhere to the guidelines set by the local jurisdiction.
    b. fall under the regulation of the New York State Health Department.
    c. must meet the New York Department of Environmental Conservation standards.
    d. need only comply with federal EPA regulations; no state or local regulations exist.

47. Edward qualifies for an 80% loan on a home he's contracted to buy for $450,000. What is his loan amount?

    a. $320,000
    b. $340,000
    c. $360,000
    d. $380,000

48. The buyer of a property that Claudia has listed has called her several times with questions about the inspection and his options. To help move the transaction along smoothly, Claudia has assisted him with his questions. Due to implied agency, Claudia's actions could be seen to have created a(n):

    a. unlimited agency relationship.
    b. undisclosed dual agency.
    c. universal agency.
    d. broker's agreement.

49. Which of these actions would be a concern regarding agent safety?

    a. Meeting new clients at the office
    b. Parking on the street
    c. Showing properties before dark
    d. Turning your back on a client during a showing

50. What entity interprets and ensures the legitimacy of a subject property's zoning and also has discretionary powers to examine situations of hardship or inappropriate classification?

    a. Planning department
    b. Board of Assessment Review
    c. Zoning Commission
    d. Zoning Board of Appeals

51. When a property loses value over time, appraisers use the term:

    a. deflation.
    b. depreciation.
    c. deterioration.
    d. devalue.

52. Because homeowner's insurance coverage can be prohibitively expensive, the _____ is in place to assist New York property owners in obtaining coverage.

    a. Federal Emergency Management Agency
    b. New York Property Insurance Underwriting Association
    c. The National Association of REALTORS®
    d. National Association of Insurance Commissioners (NAIC)

53. Robert's will noted that his younger brother Gabe could take over the small family farm in Massachusetts and live in the farm cottage on that property. Robert's wishes also declared that when Gabe died, the farm would go to Robert's granddaughter Evie. What type of estate does Gabe hold in the farm?

    a. Life estate
    b. Fee simple estate
    c. Leasehold estate
    d. Fee simple defeasible estate

54. In New York, a conventional mortgage loan of more than 80% of the purchase price

    a. requires private mortgage insurance (PMI).
    b. is not permitted.
    c. is guaranteed by the state finance commission.
    d. must be supported by seller concessions.

55. Monica and Alex are working with a lender to see what they can afford for a home. Their combined gross income is $190,000 per year. The lender uses a 28% income ratio for the monthly principal and interest (PI) payment. What monthly PI payment can Monica and Alex afford using this ratio?

    a. $4,433.33
    b. $4,400
    c. $4,500.33
    d. $4,443.33

56. A creditor's claim against personal or real property as security for a debt of the property owner is called a(n)

    a. sufferance.
    b. easement.
    c. lien.
    d. covenant.

57. From what water source are IWS wells in New York required to draw?

    a. Perched water tables
    b. Municipal water supplies
    c. Groundwater
    d. Holding tanks

58. What discriminatory practice occurs when an agent tells a minority buyer that a seller is not considering offers with FHA or VA loans, but tells a non-minority buyer that the seller is open to all types of financing?

    a. Discriminatory misrepresentation
    b. Redlining
    c. Providing unequal services
    d. Steering

59. Prior to closing, sales contracts are

    a. unilateral.
    b. involuntary.
    c. executory.
    d. executed.

60. Stephanie bought a house in a state of disrepair in an up-and-coming neighborhood. It was structurally sound, but it needed cosmetic TLC and some plumbing and electrical repairs. With some sweat equity and some careful financial investment, the house would skyrocket in value. The house's current depreciation would be considered

    a. functional obsolescence.
    b. incurable deterioration.
    c. curable deterioration.
    d. economic obsolescence.

61. The FHA's set maximum loan amounts

    a. don't apply to New York.
    b. have higher limits for New York City and surrounding areas.
    c. depend upon the down payment amount.
    d. are only for subprime mortgages.

62. Which of the following best describes a use variance?

    a. A permit allowing a property owner to use their property in a way that differs from current zoning ordinance
    b. A temporary change in the zoning classification of a property
    c. A modification of the physical characteristics of a building to comply with zoning regulations
    d. A rezoning of a property to a different zoning district

63. Which law(s) or regulation(s) require mortgage lenders to provide an estimate of closing costs to a borrower and forbid them from paying kickbacks for referrals?

    a. Equal Credit Opportunity Act
    b. Truth-in-Lending and Reg Z
    c. Federal fair housing laws
    d. Real Estate Settlement Procedures Act

64. Per the 2018 Tax Reform Act, only points and _____ are now deductible.

    a. Title insurance
    b. Real estate taxes paid up front
    c. Broker commission
    d. Legal fees paid in installments

5. Regarding superior liens, which type of lien is first in priority?

   a. Federal income tax liens
   b. Mortgage liens
   c. Federal estate tax liens
   d. Real estate tax liens

66. The main goal of federal fair housing laws is:

   a. home ownership for all.
   b. a homebuying and leasing process free of discrimination.
   c. fair negotiations in homebuying and leasing.
   d. eliminating usury in mortgage lending.

67. Which of the following is considered non-taxable income?

   a. Gambling winnings
   b. Inheritances
   c. Royalties
   d. Unemployment compensation

68. When someone buys shares in a cooperative, what do they receive that gives them the legal right to live in one of the units?

   a. Fee simple deed
   b. Proprietary lease
   c. License
   d. Lease

69. Who do title records protect by putting the public on notice that a lien exists, and that it may be the basis for a foreclosure action?

   a. seller
   b. buyer
   c. lienholder
   d. insurance company

70. Within how many days after selling the original property does an investor have to locate a replacement property in a 1031 exchange?

   a. 180
   b. 60
   c. 45
   d. 30

71. A(n) _____ is an interest in real property that gives the holder the right to use portions of the legal owner's real property in a defined way.

   a. lien
   b. easement
   c. tenancy
   d. encroachment

72. What is one qualification taxpayers need to meet for the IRS Section 121 home sales tax exclusion?

   a. Owned the home for at least 2 years within the 5-year period prior to selling it
   b. Qualified for and claimed the exclusion on another home within 2 years of this home's sale
   c. Obtained the home via a like-kind exchange within the last 5 years
   d. Be subject to the expatriate tax

73. The property manager's primary objective related to property maintenance is to

   a. preserve the property's value for the long term.
   b. adhere to fair housing laws in regard to tenant selection.
   c. establish a system for routine and preventive maintenance.
   d. save money on capital expenditures.

74. Jeff and Lucy rent a house from Lucy's cousin. The tenancy has no specific termination date; Jeff and Lucy can rent the house as long as they want to do so, as long as they pay the rent on time. This arrangement is called an estate

   a. for years.
   b. at sufferance.
   c. from period-to-period.
   d. at will.

75. How may real property be exempted from probate?

   a. When the decedent dies testate
   b. When the decedent dies intestate
   c. When an administrator is appointed to distribute the estate
   d. When it is held in a land trust

76. Which of the following is a responsibility of local buildings departments?

a. Controlling how property can be used
b. Overseeing zoning appeals
c. Responding to structural emergencies
d. Administering zoning ordinances

77. Which type of insurance is generally triggered when a homeowner lets his or her property insurance lapse?

a. Lender-placed insurance
b. Liability insurance
c. Monoline insurance
d. An endorsement

78. Who is the principal in a real estate transaction?

a. The client
b. The customer
c. The broker
d. The agent

79. When Laurel bought her condo, she received

a. a proprietary lease to her unit and access to all common elements.
b. a deed conveying fee simple ownership of her unit and access to all amenities
c. a leasehold interest in her unit and a right to use the common areas
d. a deed conveying fee simple ownership of her unit and a tenancy in common interest in common elements.

80. New York State Legislative changes in 1982 mandated that most properties in the state were to be assessed for tax purposes at

a. a set uniform percentage of market value.
b. current market value.
c. the price at which they last sold.
d. 90% of full market value.

81. Clayton wants to hire a broker to help him market and sell his house, but he also wants the option to sell the house himself and not pay a commission. Which listing agreement meets his needs?

a. Exclusive right-to sell agreement
b. Exclusive agency agreement
c. Open listing
d. Net listing

82. What is one way that brokerage offices can help protect their agents' safety?

a. by including personal details on business cards.
b. by keeping a file on each agent's vehicle.
c. by requiring agents to carry firearms or other weapons.
d. by expecting agents to transport cash deposits alone.

83. Which of the following terms applies to a mortgage lien?

a. General
b. Involuntary
c. Specific
d. Statutory

84. Which of the following is true about the statutory right of redemption for a defaulted taxpayer who wants to buy back their property that is subject to a tax sale?

a. The taxpayer must pay the amount of the winning bid at the tax sale.
b. The taxpayer can pay the delinquent taxes and any other charges before the tax sale occurs.
c. The delinquent tax must be paid through the tax certificate process.
d. No time limit applies for a taxpayer to redeem their property after the tax sale occurs.

85. A borrower earns $80,000 per year and has monthly non-housing debt payments of $1,000. If their lender uses a 36% debt ratio, what housing payment can the borrower afford?

a. $2,400
b. $2,000
c. $1,650
d. $1,400

86. The mortgage broker's primary role is to

a. appraise properties for mortgage bankers and find appropriate buyers.
b. underwrite loans for a mortgage banker.
c. act as an intermediary between the borrower and appropriate lenders.
d. sell mortgages on the secondary market on behalf of mortgage lenders.

87. In a real estate transaction, what is the difference between a debit and a credit in the closing statement?

   a. A debit is an amount received at closing, while a credit is an amount paid at closing.
   b. A debit is an amount the seller receives, while a credit is an amount the buyer receives.
   c. A debit is an amount that must be paid by one party at closing, while a credit is an amount that must be received by one party at closing.
   d. A debit is an amount related to mortgage fees, while a credit is an amount related to property taxes.

88. Which type of investment entity involves some investors having a direct role in management while others invest money without being directly involved in operations?

   a. Direct
   b. General partnership
   c. Limited partnership
   d. REIT

89. Sarah is applying for a mortgage, and the lender calculates her debt ratio. Why does the lender use this ratio in the buyer qualification process?

   a. Determine the borrower's total monthly debt obligations
   b. Identify the maximum monthly housing expense
   c. Find the highest possible interest rate that the borrower can afford
   d. Assess an applicant's income stability

90. A co-op resident has a _____ interest in the co-op.

   a. real property
   b. rental
   c. personal property
   d. leasehold

91. Which of the following situations describes illegal dual agency in New York?

   a. A broker represents both the buyer and the seller in the transaction in any way.
   b. A buyer consents to dual agency, but the seller has not consented.
   c. Both the buyer and the seller have consented to a dual agency relationship, but the buyer won't sign a disclosure or an agreement.
   d. Any situation in which any sort of dual agency occurs.

92. Which of the following is true about the difference between a mortgage banker and a mortgage broker?

   a. A mortgage broker works for a financial institution that uses its own funds to originate or fund mortgages.
   b. A mortgage banker primarily focuses on appraising properties for loan purposes.
   c. A mortgage broker services loans after they have been funded by the lender.
   d. A mortgage banker may retain mortgages in a portfolio but will generally sell them to investors.

93. What kind of relationship do property managers have with property owners?

   a. Non-binding
   b. Statutory
   c. Fiduciary
   d. Subagency

94. If a property owner does not agree with the property's market value and/or assessment listed on the tentative assessment role, what should the owner do?

   a. Request a Small Claims Assessment Review (SCAR)
   b. Contact the county assessor for a reassessment
   c. File for a tax certiori proceeding
   d. Submit a complaint to the Real Estate Ombudsman

95. Per federal fair housing laws, it is legal to

   a. lie about the availability of housing.
   b. refuse a resident's request for a reasonable accommodation.
   c. use discriminatory language in advertisements.
   d. reject loan applications for people who do not meet the qualification requirements.

96. The issue of exchangeability, also known as _____, is an important consideration in investment analysis.

   a. income
   b. leverage
   c. appreciation
   d. liquidity

97.   When is a home equity loan interest deductible?

a. When the loan is used for substantial home improvements only
b. Always
c. When the loan is for $100,000 or more
d. Never

98.   Janice submitted a written and signed offer to purchase Brett's house. Brett signed the written offer to show his acceptance. Per contract law, their actions demonstrate one requirement for a valid contract known as:

a. competent parties.
b. legal purpose.
c. mutual consent.
d. valuable consideration.

99.   What are New York State's two types of rent regulation?

a. Rent protection and rent levelling
b. Rent adjustment and rent balancing
c. Rent modification and rent equalization
d. Rent control and rent stabilization

100. The loss of part or all of the initial investment is called_____ risk.

a. Capital
b. Purchasing power
c. Financial
d. Systemic